YALE JUDAICA SERIES

EDITOR

FRANK TALMAGE

ASSOCIATE EDITORS

JUDAH GOLDIN ISADORE TWERSKY

VOLUME XXVI

צום גדליה

איז מיין (ברית אילה) אזו זאגט מן ניט (תחנה · אך ניט שומר ישראל) · מן זאגט וואל (אבינו מלכנו)
אונ' (אל ארך אפים אונ' ואנחנו · דש מארגינש פֿר טאג זאגט מן רען (פזמון זכור ברית · אונ'
אזו דיא גאנצן (עשרת ימי תשובה ווען איין ברית אילה) ווער :

צו (מנחה היבט מן ווידר אויש אונ' ליינט ויחל) · אונ' זאגט דיא (הפטרה דרשו · קיין כהן אודר לוי
זאל דיא (הפטרה זאגן ווען איין ישראל) אין דער שולן איז · אז איך געשריבן האב בייא (שני וחמישי

ושני: דיא סליחות · דיא מן זאגט אין דער (תשובה וואוך נאך צום גדליה · פֿינט מן אין דען אחרונים)
אונ' (סליחות) · מיטליך לנד זיין (מנהג) נאך · דארום האב איך זיא ניט געשריבן :

אלי טאג אין דיא (עשרת ימי תשובה זאגט מן אבינו מלכנו נאך שמונה עשרה) · דש אובנט אונ'
מארגינש · אונ' אים (אן שבירך זאגט מן ויכתבהו בספר החיים) :

מן זאל זעהן דש מן ברוט אים הויז אכלם פֿון (ראש השנה ביז יום כפור) · אודר אויך דש מיר
וויניגשטי דען אובן (כשרן) · דען מן מאג וואול ברוט נעמן פֿון דען כותיים :

מן פֿפֿלעגט קיין (חרם צו געבן אין דען עשרת ימי תשובה) · דען מיר הענגן אם (משפט פֿון הק"בה)
מן גיבט אך קיינם קיין (שבועה) · ווען מר חייב ווער דען דיינים אך מיז מן ניט מקדש דיא (לבנה)
ביז (מוצאי יום כפור) :

שבת תשובה

שבת (תשובה איז דער שבת צווישן)
(ראש השנה אונ' יום כפור) · אם
פֿרייטג צו (מנחה זאגט מן ניט אבינו מלכנו) ·
אונ' אין (מגן אבות) זאגט מן (המלך הקדוש
שאין כמוהו) :

צו מורגן זאגט מן איין (יוצר היבט אן אור
עולם קראו · אופֿן · כי אם שם מריר-
ות · אל מוהינוטוב) (אין פולן אונ' פיהם
אערהרן · זאגט מן יוצר היבט אן · משחר ·
אופֿן · החיינו · זולת · מרעה) אונ' מן זאגט
דיא (הפֿטרה שובה ישראל) · אונ' מן זאגט
איין טייל (פסוקים אין יוצר היבט אן (תקעו
שופֿר · אונ' מן מיז מזכיר נשמות) ווייא וואול
ווען מן זונשט (יוצר אונ' אופֿן) זאגט דא מיז מן
ניט (מזכיר נשמות · אבר אם שבת תשובה)
מיז מן וואול (מזכיר נשמות : (דער מהר"יל
טרייבט מן מיז ניט (מזכיר נשמות) · אין (מי
שבירך דעם קהל זאגט מן ויכתבם בספר החיים) :

מן פֿפֿלעגט צו (דרשן פֿון תשובה :

צו (מנחה זאגט מן ניט צדקתך · דען עס שטיט דרינן משפטיך תהום רבה · אונ' מיר ביטן הקדוש
ברוך הוא) דש ער גיט זול מיט (משפט) מן אונש קומן · זונשט וואירדן מיר דש (משפט) פֿור לירן ·
דען מיר האבן געוויש אין רעכט · אבר מיר ביטן (הקדוש ברוך הוא ער זול לפנים משורת הדין) מיט אונש
גין : (דש מיז גמ... אל אונש מער טון אז מיר ווערט זיין)

Part of a page from *Sefer Minhagim,* Amsterdam, 1722, discussing the obligation to preach sermons on repentance during the Sabbath between the New Year's Day and the Day of Atonement. The woodcut, slightly modified, appears also in several seventeenth-century works. (By permission of the Houghton Library, Harvard University.)

JEWISH PREACHING
1200–1800
An Anthology

MARC SAPERSTEIN

Yale University Press

New Haven and London

The publication of this volume was made possible by a
continuing grant from the Benjamin C. Zitron Family Trust.
This first book is to honor my mother, Sarah Brodsky
Zitron, a beacon to us all, whose faith in the efficacy of
Judaism stimulated this grant.
Benjamin C. Zitron, '59

Set in Garamond No. 3 type by Brevis Press,
Bethany, Connecticut.
Printed in the United States of America by
Vail-Ballou Press, Binghamton, New York.

Library of Congress Cataloging-in-Publication Data

Jewish preaching, 1200–1800.
(Yale Judaica series ; 26)
Bibliography: p.
Includes indexes.
1. Jewish sermons, English—Translations from Hebrew.
2. Jewish sermons, Hebrew—Translations into English.
3. Preaching, Jewish—History. I. Saperstein, Marc.
II. Series.
BM735.J48 1989 496.4'2 88–28074
ISBN 0–300–04355–4 (alk. paper)

The paper in this book meets the guidelines for permanence
and durability of the Committee on Production Guidelines
for Book Longevity of the Council on Library Resources.

1 3 5 7 9 10 8 6 4 2

For
Roberta
Sara and Adina

Frank Talmage, Professor of Post-Biblical Hebrew in the Department of Near Eastern Studies at the University of Toronto and Editor of the Yale Judaica Series, died on July 10, 1988. During his short tenure as editor, Professor Talmage carefully edited two manuscripts for press, including this book, and played an important role in setting editorial policy for the series.

Frank Talmage was a man of great learning, of boundless energy, and of deep humanity. He will be sorely missed by all he touched through his teaching and writing.

David B. Ruderman
Chairman, Yale Judaica Series Administrative Committee
New Haven
September 1, 1988

Contents

Preface

This book has been written with several different audiences in mind. For academic colleagues in the various fields of Jewish studies, my work constitutes a special plea to reclaim a neglected area of Jewish creativity through further investigation. Much of the scholarly apparatus, including references to comparative material in manuscripts or in early printed books, and indications of relevant comparisons in studies of Christian preaching, is intended primarily for them.

For the many scholars devoted to research on various aspects of Christian preaching, especially the members of the Medieval Sermon Society, whose *Newsletter* and symposia have been a rich resource for me, I have attempted to render accessible a body of material in which they have evinced a keen interest. The full extent of interaction between Jewish and Christian preaching during the period I treat remains to be explored, but I believe that interaction in our respective fields of research today will yield mutually illuminating results.

For colleagues in the active rabbinate, preaching is an ongoing responsibility and challenge. The material in this book is not primarily intended to suggest model sermons or even homiletical ideas for contemporary use, but rather to foster an appreciation of the preaching tradition that contemporary rabbis represent by demonstrating how predecessors molded sacred texts to address the intellectual, social, and spiritual problems of their own time.

For college-level students of Jewish life and thought in the Middle Ages and in early modern times, this book is meant to provide an introduction to the central intellectual issues, spiritual movements, and communal centers during six critical centuries of Jewish experience. For their benefit, I have referred wherever possible to scholarly works available in English translation and to readily accessible editions, rather than to rare first editions of Hebrew primary texts.

Finally, for readers who are analogous in our own terms to the congregations for whom the sermons were originally intended, the following material can enhance an understanding of their counterparts, fostering insight into the level of education, the problems, concerns, and aspirations of the ordinary Jew. For the sermon perhaps more than for any other genre of literature, the presence of an audience is critical, and the nature of this audience must never be overlooked.

The manuscript for this book was essentially completed in June 1985, after some five years of work during my appointment at Harvard Divinity School. I am particularly grateful to John Carman, director of Harvard's Center for the Study of World Religions, for his unflagging encouragement in this project, and to the staff of the Center, who initiated me into the mysteries of word processing. My research was assisted by a fellowship grant from the American Council of Learned Societies under a program funded by the National Endowment for the Humanities, and by a grant from the Memorial Foundation for Jewish Culture. My gratitude for this support is deep and enduring.

My plan to survey a largely unplotted literature required access to a variety of texts, including manuscripts and rare editions, written in many countries over a period of six centuries. Most of the printed sermons and the material necessary to illuminate their historical contexts were available in Harvard's incomparable Widener and Houghton libraries. During the summers of 1983 and 1984, I worked at the Makon le-Taṣlume Kitbe Yad in the National and University Library of Jerusalem, where microfilms of most of the Hebrew manuscripts in the world are readily accessible in a single room. Without this unique collection and its detailed catalogues, an entire dimension of the present book would be missing. I consulted manuscripts directly in the British Library, the Bodleian Library at Oxford, and the libraries of Oxford's Christ Church College, Cambridge University, and the Jewish Theological Seminary of America. Ronald May of the Bodleian and Bernard Rabenstein of Hebrew Union College's Klau Library provided prompt and helpful responses to written queries.

Many scholars, including specialists in the homiletical literature of particular countries and periods, have helped me at all stages of my work, from general problems of conceptualization to details of interpretation and analysis. Among the most important are Rabbi Ben Zion Gold, who first planted the seed for this project more than twenty years ago, my teachers Isadore Twersky and Yosef Yerushalmi, and my friends and colleagues David Ruderman and Bernard Dov Cooperman; Louis Jacobs and Ada Rapoport-Albert in Great Britain; Joseph Dan, Moshe Idel, Meir Benayahu, Joseph Hacker, Mordechai Pachter, Robert Bonfil, Jacob Elbaum, Aviezer Ravitzky, Carmi Horowitz, and Shaul Regev in Israel.

Two editors of the Yale Judaica Series, Dr. Leon Nemoy and Prof. Frank Talmage, of blessed memory, labored to identify and rectify the stylistic quirks and technical inconsistencies that were all too plentiful in my manuscript. I am indebted to their experience and grateful for their perseverance. I also wish to express my sincere appreciation for the careful reading and astute suggestions of the Yale University Press manuscript editor, Nancy Woodington.

Temple Beth David of Canton, Massachusetts, not only gave me a sabbatical leave to work full time on this book; its members also listened to my own sermons over a period of thirteen years. I am not convinced that research into the history of Jewish preaching makes one a better preacher. But I am convinced that the experience of regularly preparing and delivering sermons made me more sensitive to the manifold problems of studying this literature.

From my father, Rabbi Harold Saperstein, I learned at an impressionable age the potential power of the sermon to educate and to inspire. His influence and his help are reflected on almost every page.

My wife, Roberta, and my daughters, Sara and Adina, bore the brunt of the time devoted to this book, including a summer of separation for my research in Israel. In some ways they are the most perceptive critics of my own preaching, and they have also given the most sustained support to this study of preaching by others. It is lovingly dedicated to them.

M.S.
Washington University, St. Louis

Introduction

The State of the Field

The importance of sermons for the various disciplines and areas of Jewish studies should require no extensive argument to demonstrate. For the historian, sermons contain reactions to significant events that are sometimes more direct and immediate than the earliest chronicles. For students of Jewish literature, the sermon is a genre with its own conventions, frequently containing illustrative stories that enrich any treatment of Jewish narrative art. For scholars concerned with the development of Jewish thought, sermons containing philosophical or kabbalistic teachings removed from their technical sources and addressed to ordinary congregations provide a crucial means for measuring the impact of ideas not merely on a small circle of original minds but also on a whole community. For those who would investigate the dynamic tensions within Jewish society, or Jewish religious practice and folk beliefs, or the institutions of Jewish leadership and the position of the rabbi, few source materials are more to the point. The burgeoning of recent research and writing on Christian preaching illustrates how central this is in an analogous context.

Yet despite significant advances in the past ten years, the history of Jewish preaching after the rabbinic period remains essentially an uncharted territory, a puzzle with gaping holes for which most of the pieces remain to be found. Joseph Dan's evaluation of the field in his Hebrew survey of Jewish ethical and homiletical literature is still apt:

> Quantitatively, homiletical literature constitutes the central literary genre in the life of the Jewish people during the Middle Ages and early modern times. . . . The homiletical literature of the past 600 years encompasses many thousands of volumes, many of them in print, and many more still in manuscript. This literature embraces all of Judaism: there is no creative Jewish community anywhere, at any period, in which homiletical literature did not hold a central place. At the same time, there is no branch in the history of Hebrew literature that has been so neglected by research.[1]

1. Dan, *Sifrut,* p. 26; cf. the more recent characterization by Hacker, "Ha-Derashah," pp. 108–11.

A brief survey of the field substantiates this claim.

The starting point in the academic study of Jewish preaching, one of the supreme achievements of the *Wissenschaft des Judentums,* was Leopold Zunz's *Die gottesdienstlichen Vorträge der Juden historisch entwickelt* (The sermons of the Jews in their historical development).[2] Zunz wrote the book in order to document the tradition of vernacular preaching as part of Jewish worship, and thereby to validate its use in the nascent Reform movement. But its value far transcends any polemical purpose, for it is still the basic bibliographical resource for printed Jewish sermons. One is hard pressed to think of another field in Jewish studies for which a book first published 150 years ago still serves this purpose.

Yet despite its initial success in defining a field and its astounding scholarly achievements, the limitations of this book for the study of Jewish preaching are obvious, even in the Hebrew edition with the supplementary notes by Ḥanokh Albeck. Its title is misleading; it might more properly have been called "An Introduction to the Literature of Aggadah." After the introduction and the first chapter, the subject of preaching all but disappears, and chapters 2 through 19 study the aggadah and the midrashic literature in which it is found. Only chapters 22 and 23 and the beginning of chapter 24 pertain to Jewish preaching from the Middle Ages through the end of the eighteenth century, and this material is primarily bibliographical. While there is some discussion of the circumstances in which sermons were delivered, Zunz's main purpose was to document the existence of Jewish preaching, not to elucidate its character. From the hundreds of names of authors and their books, few if any emerge as living personalities in a concrete historical context. There is little attempt to analyze the structure of the sermons, and even less interest in their content. The homiletical literature included in Zunz's book is described from the outside, and the reader is left with no clear idea of what the sermon was actually like.

The second major survey of the field was Israel Bettan's *Studies in Jewish Preaching.* Based on articles originally published in the *Hebrew Union College Annual* during the 1920s and 1930s, it remains to date the only full treatment of the subject available in English. Bettan selected seven individuals—Jacob Anatoli, Baḥya ben Asher, Isaac Arama, Judah Moscato, Ephraim Luntshitz, Azariah Figo, and Jonathan Eybeschuetz—for detailed investigation. Each essay follows the same pattern: a biographical sketch, a bibliographical discussion, an analysis of preaching technique (including use of Bible and rabbinic literature), and a reconstruction of the preacher's weltan-

2. On Zunz and his book, see Solomon Schechter, *Studies in Judaism,* 3 (Philadelphia, 1924), 84–142 (there is a brief summary of each chapter on pp. 118–29), and Albeck's introduction to the Hebrew edition (Zunz, pp. 11–32).

schauung. Successfully conveying enthusiasm for his subject, Bettan demonstrated a solid and careful reading of the texts. The preachers generally emerge from his pages as vital personalities with something important to say.[3]

For my own work, Bettan's essays served as an indispensable introduction. However, my book differs from his in several important respects. Even a casual glance at their respective tables of contents will reveal a first significant divergence in approach. Bettan's selection of seven major figures over a period of six hundred years was bound to leave considerable gaps. He jumped over the two hundred years between Baḥya ben Asher at the end of the thirteenth century and Isaac Arama at the end of the fifteenth, a period that witnessed some of the most important transformations in the history of Jewish preaching. By expanding the list of major figures to sixteen and by referring to several dozen other preachers in the first section of the book and in the annotation to the translated texts, I have attempted to fill in some of the gaps, providing a richer texture of continuity in the preaching tradition.

Second, my selection of major figures is not merely an expansion of Bettan's list; it also reflects different criteria. Only three of the figures to whom Bettan devoted his articles are represented by sermons below. Bettan's selection was limited to preachers whose books were printed and were readily accessible in nineteenth-century editions. My own selection includes preachers whose sermons remain in manuscript (Mattathias Yizhari, Joseph ibn Shem Ṭob, Israel of Bełżyce, Hirschel Levin, and two others whose sermons have been printed only during the past few years) and preachers whose sermons were never again published after the sixteenth century (Shem Ṭob ibn Shem Ṭob, Solomon Levi, Moses Almosnino).

Furthermore, the focus on preaching promised in the title of Bettan's book was not regularly maintained in the essays. The homiletical literature studied by Bettan includes purely literary works written in sermonic form, books drawing from oral sermons but recast in other genres, and preaching aids of various kinds, including collections of model sermons as well as records of sermons actually delivered. Bettan was not always sufficiently sensitive to these distinctions. My focus is on the written text as evidence of actual oral communication.

A final divergence is that Bettan rarely analyzed a single sermon in depth. His purview was the edited collection, or in some cases the full oeuvre of a

3. Bettan, republished in *Brown Classics in Judaica*, 1987. The chapters originally appeared in *HUCA* 6 (1929: Moscato); 7 (1930: Figo); 8–9 (1931–32: Luntshitz); 10 (1935: Eyebeschuetz); 11 (1936: Anatoli); and 12–13 (1937–38: Arama). Bettan's article "The Dubno Maggid" in *HUCA* 23 (1950–51): 267–93, was written well after the publication of the book, and it has not been republished. That same volume of *HUCA* contains Ellis Rivkin's "The Sermons of Leon da Modena" (pp. 295–317).

preacher's writings. While one can find discussions of how the preacher usually constructed his discourse or how he interpreted biblical verses or rabbinic statements, one may read Bettan's studies without ever encountering a single sermon in its totality. A major purpose of this book is to fill that lacuna by presenting the sermons themselves, making accessible one particularly important or interesting text by each preacher. Its sources are identified, its progression of thought explained, its historical context reconstructed to the fullest possible extent.

My approach is justified not only as a complement to the essays of Bettan, but as an inherent demand of the genre. Bettan's technique of reconstructing a preacher's weltanschauung by stringing together quotations culled from all of his sermons is based upon a questionable assumption about the nature of this literature. A book of sermons is not like a philosophical tract, where rigorous inner coherence and consistency is expected. Even if it deals with a philosophical issue, a sermon delivered on a particular occasion is not analogous to a chapter in Maimonides' *Guide for the Perplexed*. If the text is indeed a collection of sermons delivered at different times, for different audiences, under different circumstances, the natural unit of analysis is not the collection but the individual discourse. What is most important is not to construct a coherent system of thought from statements uttered in diverse contexts and for varying purposes, but rather to understand what the preacher chose to say on a particular occasion, and how he organized his ideas into an artistic unity.

My own research, starting with Bettan, has built upon work done during the past generation, primarily by Israeli scholars. Although none has made the subject of Jewish preaching a primary focus of research, many have begun to explore the territory pertaining to their respective fields and to mine the riches of sermonic literature. Ḥaim Hillel Ben-Sasson, Jacob Katz, and Azriel Shochat represent the older generation of historians who have drawn upon this material for their work.[4] Joseph Dan has demonstrated the organic links between homiletical and ethical literature and has broken new ground in the literary analysis of sermonic texts.

Mordechai Pachter's doctoral dissertation is an invaluable introduction to the sermonic literature of the Sephardic tradition in the late fifteenth and sixteenth centuries as well as to the problems of the genre as a whole. The work of Joseph Hacker on Salonika, Robert Bonfil on Italy, Jacob Elbaum on

4. See Jacob Katz, *Masoret u-Mashber* (Jerusalem, 1958), especially pp. 200–05 (most of the documentation is absent from the English translation), and "Qawwim la-Biyografyah shel ha-Ḥatam Sofer," *Studies in Mysticism and Religion Presented to G. G. Scholem* (Jerusalem, 1967), pp. 115–48; Ben-Sasson, *Hagut we-Hanhagah*, esp. pp. 34–54, and "ʿOsher we-ʿOni be-Mishnato shel ha-Mokiaḥ R. Efrayim Ish Luntshitz," *Zion* 19 (1954):142–66; Shochat, *ʿIm Ḥillufe ha-Tequfot*.

Poland, Mendel Piekarz on eighteenth-century Eastern Europe, and Meir Benayahu on a large range of pertinent subjects has illuminated many previously dark regions of the field. Recent American studies of individual preachers by David Ruderman, Carmi Horowitz, Hayim Perelmuter, and Henry Sosland have substantially enriched our knowledge.[5] Without the research of these men, the present book would not have been possible.

I have attempted to go beyond the investigation of individual preachers or of limited periods in specific countries to present an overview of the genre as a whole. I offer not a full history of Jewish preaching—that would be premature—but rather an introduction to the field, a survey of the major issues, and a translation of sources. My hope is to illustrate the kinds of material available, to facilitate an informed discussion of the problems, and to inspire new research with its unforeseen results.

The Nature of the Sources

The sources for the history of Jewish preaching present a special set of problems. The sermon is among the most ephemeral of literary genres, one for which there is usually no permanent written record. Contrast this with another genre of Hebrew literature: there is no way of knowing precisely what percentage of legal responsa written between the thirteenth and the eighteenth centuries is extant today, but it is safe to assume that it is fairly high. Because responsa are authoritative statements of Jewish law, they have to be consulted as possible precedents by subsequent decision makers. The need to preserve the written texts of sermons, even those of the same rabbi who wrote responsa, was far less compelling. Few of the sermons delivered are available to us today, especially from the early centuries of this period.

This is true of Christian preaching as well, but so many sermons were delivered by Christians that the preservation of even a small percentage yields a considerable number. It has been estimated, for example, that ten thousand sermons given in the single province of Westphalia between 1378 and 1517 have been published—not counting those in manuscript.[1] The number of

5. See the articles and books by these scholars listed in the bibliography. Mention should be made also of Glicksberg's *Ha-Derashah be-Yiśra'el,* which purports to be a survey of the entire field of Jewish preaching, but suffers because of the absence of any rigorous definition of the genre, so that, especially for the earlier periods, authors and texts that have only a minimal connection with sermons and preaching are discussed. The book is more useful for eighteenth-century material, although the author's approach is quite different from mine.

1. F. Landmann, *Das Predigtwesen in Westfalen in der letzten Zeit des Mittelalters* (Muenster, 1900), cited in Elmer Kiessling, *The Early Sermons of Luther* (Grand Rapids, 1935), p. 17. Cf. the estimate of the total number of sermons preached in medieval Europe in Deyermond, p. 128.

Jewish sermons in print from all of Europe during this period, even if we define the genre as broadly as possible, would not reach 5 percent of that figure.

We know of many preachers whose sermons have been lost. Some books of sermons prepared for publication disappeared before reaching the printer: such was the case with Mordecai Jaffe's *Lebush ha-Śimḥah we-ha-Śaśśon,* Nathan Hanover's *Netaʿ Shaʿashuʿim,* and Joseph ben Solomon's *Maṣmiaḥ Yeshuʿah.* Other preachers never managed to edit their written sermons in a form suitable for publication. In 1647, Manasseh ben Israel said he had 450 Portuguese sermons that had been preached in Amsterdam over a twenty-five-year period. All have apparently been lost. His colleague Saul ha-Levi Morteira was said by his disciples in 1645 to have preached 1400 sermons in his almost thirty years in Amsterdam. Of these, 500 were outlined, but only 50 were printed in the original edition of *Gibʿat Shaʾul.* Isaac Aboab de Fonseca was credited by a contemporary with 886 written sermons, but fewer than a handful were published.[2]

Solomon Levi preached on virtually every Sabbath and holiday for twenty-five years in Salonika, but less than a four-year period is represented in the 314 four-columned pages of his *Dibre Shelomoh.* Leon Modena mentions proudly the 400 sermons he had in outline at the time he wrote his autobiography. Only 21 were fleshed out for publication in his *Midbar Yehudah.* Jacob Zahalon put down the number of his written sermons as 500; while some have been preserved in manuscript, none were published.[3] None of these numbers approaches the 2300 extant sermons of Martin Luther, or the 18,000 or 40,000 estimated to have been delivered respectively by George Whitefield and John Wesley,[4] but they do represent a prodigious effort of which only minimal traces survive.

Important figures who speak about their own preaching left almost nothing written in sermon form. At the end of his introduction to *Sefer Miṣwot Gadol,*

2. Mordecai Jaffe, intro. to *Lebush Malkut* (Prague, 1623), p. 4b; Nathan Hanover, intro. to *Yewen Meṣulah,* cf. *Abyss of Despair,* trans. Abraham Mesch (New York, 1950), p. 25; Joseph ben Solomon, see Gershom Scholem, *Sabbatai Ṣevi* (Princeton, 1973), p. 596. Manasseh ben Israel, *Thesauro dos dinim* (Amsterdam, 1645), p. 150b, cited in Zunz, p. 526, n. 63; Morteira (1645), intro.; Isaac Aboab, see Johann Christoph Wolf, *Bibliotheca Hebraea,* 3 (Hamburg, 1727), 538, citing Daniel Levi de Barrios in *Vida Isaac Uciel,* p. 45. For the sermons published, see Wolf, 3:539 and Meyer Kayserling, *Biblioteca Española-Portugueza-Judaica* (1890; reprint ed., New York, 1971), pp. 26–27.

3. On Solomon Levi, see the introduction to his sermon translated below; Modena, *Ḥayye Yehudah,* cited in Nave, p. 46; and cf. Adelman, p. 327; Zahalon, pp. 116–17.

4. On Luther: Roland Bainton, *Here I Stand* (New York, 1950), p. 349; *Luther's Works,* 51: *Sermons,* 1, ed. John Doberstein (Philadelphia, 1959), p. xi. On Whitefield and Wesley: Downey, p. 156, n. 1, and p. 210. William Lichfield, a fifteenth-century English preacher, was reported to have left 3083 written sermons, none of which is extant (Owst, *Preaching,* p. 24).

Moses of Coucy informs his reader, "I preached this introduction to *the captivity of Jerusalem, that is in Sepharad* (Obad. 20) and to other Jewish communities in exile in Christendom to inspire them to the service of the God of Israel, and then I would preach to them about the commandments," but no texts of his sermons remain. The generation of the expulsion from Spain is relatively rich in the sermonic literature preserved, but such rabbis as Abraham Saba, Joseph Jabez, and Joseph Ḥayyun, known to have preached either by their own or others' testimony, left no sermons behind.[5]

In a later period, contemporary reports speak of Judah he-Ḥasid's ability to move masses of listeners by the powerful delivery of his passionate oratory. Yet he wrote down nothing of what he preached, and only a fragment of one sermon has been preserved in the work of a contemporary. Perhaps the most famous preacher of his generation, Jacob Kranz, the Maggid of Dubno, left not a single complete sermon. His written legacy comprised many bundles of scraps containing homiletical insights, "written in the most elliptical manner, as if intended only as a reminder for himself," that had to be collected, arranged, and written out in proper Hebrew by others. Like many others, he left only fragments, "like severed arms or limbs in a sculptor's studio, here a head, and there a torso," leaving us to surmise or guess what the entire sermon was like.[6]

But the problems of the source material for Jewish preaching go beyond its fragmentary nature. The authenticity of a responsum, a poem, or an ethical treatise in the handwriting of the author is ordinarily not subject to dispute. The text of a sermon written out in full by the preacher is quite

5. For Saba, see *Ṣeror ha-Mor* (1879; reprint, Tel Aviv, 1975), Gen. 50a, Exod. 29b, Deut. 6d, and cf. Dan Manor, "Le-Toledotaw shel R. Abraham Saba," *Meḥqere Yerushalayim ba-Maḥashebet Yiśra'el* 2 (1983):209; for Jabez, *Ḥasde ha-Shem* (Brooklyn, 1934), p. 10, n. 2, and pp. 22–23; and for Ḥayyun, Joseph Hacker, "R. Yosef Ḥayyun we-Dor ha-Gerush mi-Porṭugal," *Zion* 48 (1983):276, n. 17. Cf. also the references to his own sermons by Joseph Karo in *Maggid Mesharim,* p. 48a, cited in R. J. Z. Werblowsky, *Joseph Karo: Lawyer and Mystic* (Philadelphia, 1977), p. 146. A contemporary of Judah Moscato spoke of David Provençal as "the greatest of the Italian preachers in our time," but none of his sermons has been preserved (Abraham Portaleone, epilogue to *Shilṭe Gibborim* [Jerusalem, 1970], p. 185c).

6. Zalman Rubashow (Shazar), "Derashat R. Yehudah he-Ḥasid be-Sefer Ori we-Yishʿi," *Zion* 6 (1941):213–14. *Ori we-Yishʿi* also preserves quotations from the "preacher of rebuke" (*mokiaḥ*) Jacob Ratner (see "Sources," below, and the passages cited by Piekarz, p. 104, n. 27). In the second half of the eighteenth century, teachings of "Joel the Mokiaḥ" are preserved in the sermons of Zerah Eidlitz (see "Sources," below), and teachings of the mokiaḥ Leib Festiner in the sermons of Ezekiel Landau (*Derushe,* p. 29d). Most of the authentic teachings of the Baʿal Shem Ṭob were probably passages from his sermons that he did not write out himself, but that were preserved in the homiletical writings of his disciples. On the Maggid of Dubno, see *Ohel Yaʿaqob* (Pressburg, 1859), "Petaḥ ha-'Ohel," and cf. Israel Bettan, "The Dubno Maggid," *HUCA* 23 (1950–51):270–73. The quotation in the final sentence of the paragraph is from Richard Storrs, *Bernard of Clairvaux* (New York, 1893), p. 384, about the written remnants of Bernard's sermons.

different in nature. If it was written down ahead of time, what guarantee is there that he actually read it word for word? Might he not have been impelled to depart from his text by a sudden inspiration, an unanticipated response, a failure of nerve? If it was written afterward, what assurance is there that it records what he said precisely? Might he not have decided that the words originally intended for a specific time and place required editing for posterity? If there are two versions of the same sermon, one written by the preacher and another recorded by a listener, which is the more authentic?[7] Is "the sermon" what the preacher intended to say, what he claims to have said, or what those who were present remember having heard?

Even a stenographic transcript of every word would not be the whole sermon. A sermon is an act of oral communication in which the preacher is an integral part. It is composed not only of his words but also of his voice, gestures, appearance, pace, personality, conviction. Written passages that appear dry or insignificant—or even meaningless—can spring to life when charged by the energy and enthusiasm of a powerful speaker.[8] That is one reason why in so many cases the printed texts of sermons do not correspond to the preacher's reputation in his own time. Scholarship can be recorded on

7. There are numerous examples of this in Christian sources; see, for example, Bataillon, p. 22; *Luther's Works,* 51, pp. xiii–xiv; Mitchell, pp. 36–37. For a Jewish analogue, cf. Pachter, "Curiel," p. 807. Nathan of Nemirov noted that certain discourses by his master Naḥman of Bratslav had been preserved in two different versions: the notes prepared by Naḥman before he spoke, and Nathan's transcription of what Naḥman had actually said. See the introduction to *Liqquṭe MoHaRaN* (Brooklyn, 1976), p. 6b, cited by Rapoport-Albert, p. 262.

8. Cf. the following passage in a sermon by Azariah Figo: "That which is written in a book, with all its holiness, is in the final analysis nothing more than writing. The lifeless parchments make no impression and have no perceptible impact that can add to the content in inspiring the reader. But living teachers and preachers supplement the content of what they say with the power of the spoken word, whether through the sound of their voice, or their gestures, or in other ways, thereby enhancing the impact upon the listener, who is deeply affected and acts accordingly" (*Binah le-ʿIttim* 2:38b; the passage is cited by Piekarz, p. 103, but his reference in n. 26 should be corrected to sermon 46.)

Cf. Charland, chap. 9, "Le Débit [Delivery]." Charland records a story told in the *Ars praedicandi* of Thomas Waleys about a young preacher who procured a copy of a particularly effective sermon delivered by a master; when he gave the same sermon himself, there was virtually no response. He expressed his astonishment to the master and was told, "I have given you my fiddle, but you do not have the bow with which I touch the strings" (pp. 219, 332–33). While there are some examples of individuals writing sermons for others to deliver (e.g., Goitein, *Community,* p. 567, n.27; Alfalas, pp. 22a, 31b, 103b, 180b; Moses Mendelssohn, in Altmann, p. 68), and of sermons from the past being read in place of new ones (e.g., Anatoli's sermon on the lesson *Parah* in the synagogue of Montepellier [*Minḥat Qenaʾot,* p. 139]), the general principle was that the preacher must deliver something of his own, not something written for him by another or a great sermon from the literature of the past. The pressure for originality in this one area of liturgical life is itself a phenomenon that requires explanation.

paper and preserved for the scrutiny of future generations, but eloquence, magnetism, and charisma do not outlive the preacher.[9]

Ideally, then, the best evidence for a sermon would be not a written text but a videotape. Yet even this would not exhaust the sermon's dimensions. It would not tell us what in the sermon spoke to the deepest needs of the unique moment in which it was delivered, what the congregation found stirring, troubling, comforting, humorous, or dull. At its best, the sermon involves two related parties. The preacher knows his congregation, its capabilities, weaknesses, and concerns. He speaks fully aware that the people he sees before him may start to talk, sleep, interrupt, leave, absent themselves the following week, or, perhaps most exasperating, listen politely but remember nothing and emerge absolutely unchanged. Conversely, the congregation knows the preacher. They presumably feel respect for his learning and character, perhaps even awe at hearing the words of a holy man. But they may also feel suspicious of his motives, resentful of the force of his criticism, bored by his longwinded repetition of familiar points. Some of these dynamics can be reconstructed through historical investigation, but the actual impact of the sermon upon those who heard it can only be surmised.

In the absence of videotapes or stenographic transcripts, we are left with written sources that are at best several steps removed from the sermon-as-event. An obvious distinction must be made between sermons transcribed by others and those written by the preachers. Of the former, some are quite brief and general. Non-Jewish visitors sometimes provide a glimpse of the externals of Jewish preaching. Michel de Montaigne, traveling through Italy in 1580 and 1581, recorded impressions of Jewish practice in his *Diary:* "In the afternoon [of the Sabbath] their doctors, by turns, give a lesson on the passage of the day, doing it in Italian. After the lesson, some other doctor present selects some one of the hearers, or sometimes two or three in succession, to argue against the one who has just been reading, on what he has said. The one we heard seemed to [me] to have much eloquence and much wit in his argumentation."[10]

A less uplifting scene is described by the German missionary J. H. Callenberg, who reported visiting a synagogue in Berlin in which the preacher was "rebuking the people for transgressions antipathetical to brotherly love."

9. Cf. Baldwin 1: 37 (on Foulques de Neuilly); Neale, p. 222 (on Antony of Padua); Blakney, p. xxii (on Meister Eckhardt); Downey, p. 167 (on George Whitefield); and the fine essay on "Artom's Sermons" by Israel Abrahams in *By-Paths in Hebraic Bookland* (Philadelphia, 1920), pp. 297–302.

10. *The Diary of Montaigne's Journey to Italy,* ed. E. J. Trechmann (New York, 1929), p. 134; cf. p. 154, where Montaigne praises the abilities of the apostate rabbi who preached conversionist sermons to a compulsory audience of sixty Jews "on Saturday after dinner."

He then adds, "Laughter broke out, the *parnassim* [lay communal leaders] knocked loudly [to restore order], but to no avail."[11]

Jewish texts also occasionally provide an outsider's view of the local pulpit. A visitor to Safed in 1567 furnishes a unique firsthand account of Joseph Karo as preacher, describing a sermon in which the master discussed Psalm 19:8 "according to its simple meaning and its kabbalistic significance." The most extensive and significant of such reports were written by Ḥayyim Joseph David Azulai in the eighteenth century. As an emissary from the land of Israel, Azulai visited Jewish communities in Italy, France, and Holland, frequently recording information about the sermons he had heard. Even where he does not discuss their content in detail, his travel diary contains precious information about structure, rhetorical technique, language, length, and circumstances for sermons not otherwise known.[12]

Details about the content of Jewish preaching were sometimes preserved, although generally out of context and frequently distorted, in the complaints of hostile auditors about irresponsible use of philosophical doctrines, excessive flirtation with classical pagan motifs, or reference to kabbalistic teachings inappropriate for public discourse.[13] Particular insights of the preacher could also be reported objectively by an outsider. A fine example is the section of Solomon Maimon's *Autobiography* describing the court of Dov Baer, the Maggid of Mezritsh. Maimon records a homiletical interpretation he heard of 2 Kings 3:15. *We-hayah ke-naggen ha-menaggen (as the minstrel played, the spirit of God was upon him).* According to Maimon, the preacher interpreted the phrase to mean "If the minstrel [*ha-menaggen,* that is, the servant of God] becomes like the instrument [*ke-naggen*], then God's spirit is upon him." This has been shown to be a faithful report of the Maggid's quietistic ideal, requiring the human being to become passive like a musical instrument in order to be filled with God's spirit. The interpretation is confirmed by an internal, independent Hasidic source reporting the same teaching as one which the author "heard from [his] teacher . . . Dov Baer."[14]

Some reports by visitors go beyond such recording of a single point and attempt to summarize the content of an entire sermon. The most important

11. *Bericht an einige christliche Freunde von einem Versuch das arme jüdische Volk anzuleiten,* "Fortsetzung 15," p. 57, cited in Shochat, p. 110.

12. See Abraham Yaari, *Masʿot Ereṣ Yisraʾel* (Tel Aviv, 1976), p. 200. For more on Azulai, see below.

13. See "Sources," below, for writings pertaining to the conflict over the study of philosophy: the letter of Ḥayyim ibn Mūsā and the responsa of Leon Modena.

14. Joseph Weiss, "ʿAl Derush Eḥad shel ha-Maggid mi-Mezritsh," *Zion* 12 (1946–47):97 (and cf. his "ʿAl Torah Ḥasidit Aḥat le-ha-Maggid mi-Mezritsh," *Zion* 20 [1954–55]:107–08). On this conception in the circle of the maggid, see Rivka Schatz Uffenheimer, *Ha-Ḥasidut ke-Misṭiqah* (Jerusalem, 1980), esp. pp. 117–18.

example is Azulai. Here is his diary entry describing a sermon he did not particularly like, delivered on the Sabbath, the thirteenth of Iyyar, 1778:

> R. David Meza preached and cast stones, for his entire sermon was that the evil impulse is called "stone." He drew this out for an hour. In every little detail he repeated that the evil impulse was called "stone," and he made frequent comparisons with stones. He maintained that a very small sin is as heavy as a stone. His examples were Uzzah, who sinned by error as he returned with the warriors (2 Sam. 6:6–7), the person who converses between prayers [B. Soṭ 44b], and the children of Gad and Reuben, who were rebuked by Moses because they considered their herds before their own children (Num. 32:16).
>
> He interpreted the verse *He weighed the hair of his head* [*at two hundred shekels, by the king's stone* (2 Sam. 14:26)] to mean that Absalom's sin was [as thin] as a hair, but it weighed as much as a stone [weight]. The *nośe* was, *If sinners entice you, do not consent* (Prov. 1:10); the *maʾamar* was, "The evil impulse is called a stone" [Lev. Rabbah 35:5]. He preached ethical rebukes at length, but he was like a "heart of stone" throughout his sermon, repeating and repeating that the evil impulse is called a stone.

This passage, written to parody the repetition that Azulai found so tedious, tells us the basic content of the sermon: the biblical verse and the rabbinic statement quoted at the beginning, the central motif, the dominant rhetorical device, several specific interpretations, and the fact that the preacher spent considerable time criticizing the shortcomings of his congregation. Written at the end of the Sabbath (as writing is forbidden on the Sabbath), it shows what an attentive listener could recall from an hour-long sermon heard in the morning, and it reflects a critical sense that measures preaching by aesthetic standards. Other summaries recorded by Azulai are considerably more extensive and detailed even than this.[15]

There are also reports that claim to be not merely summaries but rather versions of the full sermon. Unlike their Christian neighbors, Jews did not employ professional scribes trained in rapid writing or shorthand who could transcribe what a preacher was saying while he was saying it.[16] Whether it

15. Azulai, p. 150 (on the terms *nośe* and *maʾamar,* see "Structural Options," below); cf. Azulai, pp. 135–36, 142–43, 145–46, 147–49, 152.

16. On this practice among Christians, see Deferrari, pp. 102–10; D'Avray, p. 97; Josep Sivera, ed., Quaresma de Sant Vicent Ferrer (Barcelona, 1927), p. xxv, n. 2, and fig. 2; Smith, pp. 33–34. Note also Naḥmanides' well-known explanation of the nature of aggadah: "If a bishop should stand up and deliver a sermon which someone in the audience likes and writes down" (*Kitbe RaMBaN,* ed. C. B. Chavel, 2 vols. [Jerusalem, 1963], 1:308. Notes were often taken unofficially by listeners, sometimes for purposes of rebuttal, sometimes for unauthorized publication: see MacLure, pp. 64, 144; Jones and Jones, pp. 9, 19; Mitchell, p. 36.

was because of the prohibition of writing on the Sabbath or because of the absence of an institutional structure and hierarchy that made it important to record what a major figure had said, this mode of preserving sermonic material was not available to Jews.[17] But although there was no simultaneous transcription, fairly full texts were apparently written out not long afterward by friends or disciples of the preacher.

It is not uncommon to encounter in manuscripts such introductory notices as, "This sermon I heard from the emissary Ḥayyim Modai of Safed, here in Virtsali in the year 5524 [1764]," or "What I heard from the mouth of . . . Moses Sofer, head of the rabbinical court of the community of Pressburg"; or such postscripts as, "So have I heard from the mouth of . . . Israel Curiel," or even "This have I heard from [my teacher Israel di Curiel] on the Sabbath which fell on the Ninth of Ab when he preached, and in his own copy it is written out more extensively."[18]

The best-known and most important of such sources is *Sefer MaHaRIL.* This book, a collection of Ashkenazic customs, records the teachings of the early fifteenth-century German rabbi Jacob Moellin as written down by his faithful disciple, Zalman of St. Goar. Although its content is primarily legal, it also contains many passages introduced by the phrase "our rabbi preached." These sermons were relatively infrequent, generally delivered only on the three Sabbaths preceding Passover, on New Year's Day, and on the Day of Atonement, but they remain precious examples of medieval Jewish preaching in northern Europe.

The most extensive record appears in an abbreviated translation in S. Y. Agnon's *Days of Awe.* The original begins with the words, "R. Jacob Segal preached once on the Sabbath preceding New Year's Day, on the lesson *Niṣṣabim* (Deut. 29:9–30:20): 'It is written in the lesson *Niṣṣabim, It shall come to pass* . . . Deut. 30:1).'" What follows purports to be a verbatim account of the sermon. This is interrupted near the end of the text, where the disciple reports a summary of what was said:

17. Even sermons delivered on occasions when there was no prohibition against writing were not recorded by professional scribes. The Hasidim of Bratslav did try to preserve systematically the homiletical discourses of their master Naḥman. Nathan of Nemirov reported that "this was the way I wrote from him. The Torah teachings which he delivered at a certain time—for example on the Sabbath during Hanukkah—he would later repeat for me to transcribe, phrase by phrase . . . until I completed transcribing the entire passage. Usually I would go back and read to him what I had finished writing." At a later time Naḥman no longer dictated in this manner, and Nathan wrote from memory after the end of the Sabbath on which the discourse had been delivered, usually giving his text to Naḥman to check. See Nathan ben Naphtali Herz of Nemirov, *Yeme MaHaRNaT,* 2 vols. in 1 (Bene Beraq, 1956), 1:5, 22; and the discussion by Rapoport-Albert, pp. 257–65.

18. Hebrew Union College (Cincinnati) MS 615, fol. 209; two manuscripts cited by Pachter, "Curiel," pp. 807–08.

At the end of the sermon, the rabbi, of blessed memory, returned to the intent of the scriptural lesson. He interpreted the words *And a redeemer will come to Zion* (Isa. 59:20) to mean that we should pray to God to hasten the redemption. This is the significance of the verse [in the lesson], *Things concealed belong to the Lord our God* (Deut. 29:28), meaning that messianic dates are hidden with God, for no one knows when the redemption will come. *But things revealed belong to us* (Deut. 29:28) he interpreted to mean that in another sense, messianic dates are revealed to us, insofar as we may pray about them and engage in the study of Torah and the performance of good deeds, so that God will mercifully hasten them. Thus the verse ends, *to perform all the provisions of this Torah* (Deut. 29:28).[19]

Another major category is sources that come from the preachers themselves. The fundamental question in this context is whether or not the text before us is directly related to a sermon that was really preached. "Homiletical literature" is an enormous branch of medieval Jewish writing; texts of actual sermons form a relatively small part of that literature. We can distinguish two kinds of material not directly related to sermons preached: texts written in sermon form but never intended for delivery, and texts in which material originally part of a sermon is incorporated within another genre.

A leading contemporary scholar of medieval Christian preaching has cautioned that "some of the texts presented as sermons may have been spiritual treatises cast in the form of sermons as a literary device but actually made to be read and meditated upon."[20] This applies to Jewish literature as well. It is difficult to prove that such texts are not records of real sermons, for such proof frequently depends on an argument from silence. But in the absence of external evidence and any clear internal indication of oral discourse—phrases that tie the text to a particular moment and place, references to a date, a synagogue, or an occasion, expressions of an individual's personal voice addressing people before him (all illustrated below)—we may hesitate to consider such works direct evidence of Jewish preaching.

For example, Joseph Dan has argued convincingly that Abraham bar Ḥiyya's *Hegyon ha-Nefesh,* written in the twelfth century, should be considered

19. *Sefer MaHaRIL* (Shklov, 1796), p. 42a–b; cf. S. Y. Agnon, *Days of Awe* (New York, 1965), pp. 27–30. One manuscript of *Sefer MaHaRIL* also contains capsule reports of sermons for the Sabbaths preceding Passover and the Day of Atonement delivered by Moellin's disciple Jacob Weill in the years 1431 through 1433. See Spitzer, "Derashot," and idem, "Dinim." For reports of halakic sermons by Shalom of Neustadt, a teacher of Moellin, see Spitzer, *Hilkot.* A listener or disciple apparently recorded the halakic sermons of the late thirteenth-century German rabbi Ḥayyim ben Isaac "Or Zaruᶜa": see Ḥayyim ben Isaac, intro., p. 10.

20. Bataillon, p. 21; this literary form has been termed by Michel Zink "armchair preaching" (*la prédication dans un fauteuil, Prédication,* p. 478). Cf. Bonfil, "Dato," p. 2.

"the first homiletical work [*sefer ha-derush*] in the Middle Ages written in Hebrew." His position is that *Hegyon ha-Nefesh* is a "literary-homiletical work. We must not assume that these sermons were given just as they appear in the book. But there is no doubt that R. Abraham bar Ḥiyya, in writing his book, used sermons that he was accustomed to preach, especially, it would seem, his sermons for the Days of Awe and the Ten Days of Repentance."[21] Such a connection must remain a hypothesis, given the lack of external evidence for Bar Ḥiyya's public preaching and the absence of clear internal signs of oral delivery. That he chose a sermon-like form for his treatise is noteworthy, perhaps indicating that he intended it for use by preachers. But while it may be considered the "first homiletical work" of the Jewish Middle Ages, it is not yet the first book of Jewish sermons.[22]

Active preachers often decided to recast their homiletic material in such a way that its identity as a sermon was lost. For example, a volume of biblical commentary was generally considered more prestigious than a book of sermons, and preachers often published in such commentaries interpretations originally used in the pulpit. Moses Alsheikh was known as one of the great preachers of his age, with a career in Safed that spanned four decades. The introductions to several of his commentaries refer to his preaching, stating clearly that his sermons were his source. Comments on the role and function of the preacher are scattered throughout his writings. He even states that "many who listen to me have written down my words on paper." Yet he himself wrote exclusively in the commentary form, and no single sermon of his remains, wither from his own hand or from those who heard him.[23]

Sermons contained considerably more than interpretations of biblical verses. There were also discussions of rabbinic aggadot, analyses of halakic problems, and calls to ethical and religious reform. These could all be sifted and incorporated into established genres of Hebrew literature. Discussions of rab-

21. Dan, *Sifrut,* pp. 69–70. Reference is to the ten days beginning with New Year's Day and ending with the Day of Atonement.

22. The same point may be made about *Derashot ha-RaN,* attributed to R. Nissim Gerondi in the mid-fourteenth century. That they are in a sermonic form is clear, that they influenced subsequent preachers is beyond doubt, yet they contain no indication that they were ever preached in their present form, and may well be merely literary treatises. See the introduction by Leon Feldman in *Derashot ha-RaN,* pp. 8, 13.

23. See Shimon Shalem, *Rabbi Mosheh Alsheikh* (Jerusalem, 1966); Pachter, "Sifrut," pp. 262–67, and Alsheikh's introductions to *Ḥabaṣelet Ṣiyyon, Shoshannat ha-ʿAmaqim, Maśʾat Mosheh.* References to comments about the role of the preacher are collected in Pachter, pp. 292–93. In some cases, the border between sermon and Torah commentary seems almost intentionally blurred. Baḥya ben Asher introduces his commentary on each Torah lesson with a section clearly derived from the sermonic tradition; Joseph ben David of Saragossa's *Perush ʿal ha-Torah* contains actual sermons. Cf. Hacker, "Ha-Derashah," pp. 122–23, and Dan, *Sifrut,* p. 245 (on Elijah ha-Kohen of Izmir's *Shebeṭ Musar*).

binic aggadot could be removed and collected into a separate work.[24] The same was true of legal material. Reporting the sermon that he delivered in the summer of 1780 at the engagement of his sister, Eliezer Fleckeles noted parenthetically that "the novel interpretation of halakic issues that we set forth in this sermon are written in other works—the *Seder ha-Parashiyyot* and my *Novellae* on the tractate Shabbat; in this work I am concerned not with halakic decisions but only with the ethical rebuke that we delivered on that occasion." By contrast, Ezekiel Landau's son, introducing a collection of sermons preached by his father between 1745 and 1752, warned the reader not to look for anything but halakic discussions here, for he had collected the ethical rebukes and published them in another book.[25]

The first three preachers treated in Bettan's *Studies in Medieval Jewish Preaching* give us examples of texts that have generally been considered classical collections of Jewish sermons from the Middle Ages. Yet the relationship of these texts to oral sermons needs to be carefully examined. In the introduction to his *Malmad ha-Talmidim,* Jacob Anatoli informs us that he began to preach at weddings and then accepted the responsibility of regular preaching on each Sabbath, until opposition from certain members of the congregation forced him to stop. *Malmad ha-Talmidim* is organized according to the weekly Scripture lessons, each unit is clearly in sermon form and brief enough to have been delivered as it appears without unduly burdening the listeners. But it does not at all follow, as Bettan claimed, that "many . . . if not perhaps all, had actually been delivered before congregations of Sabbath worshippers." In fact, Anatoli never asserted this.

He states rather that he wrote the work for the benefit of his sons, and characterizes it not as *derashot,* sermons, but as "words of prompting" (*dibre heʿarah*) concerning study of Torah, performance of the commandments, and knowledge of the prayers. As for the structure, "I decided to divide these words of prompting according to the division of the lessons, so that [the reader] may study one section on each Sabbath. Perhaps he may be inspired to investigate in depth [*li-derosh we-laḥqor;* possibly, "to preach in depth about"] the lesson, or a verse from it, or the meaning of one of the commandments." There is no claim that the organization of material represents

24. Jacob ben Hananel, fol. 2r, cf. fol. 16v; Pachter, "Curiel," p. 805. One wonders whether other commentaries on selected aggadot of the Talmud may have been based on material culled from sermons. For example, Joseph Garçon wrote a *Sefer Maʾamarim* that may well have included interpretations of aggadot extracted from his written sermons (see the annotation to his sermon translated below).

25. Fleckeles 1, *ʿOlat Ḥodesh,* 67b; Landau, *Doresh,* p. 2d.

sermons actually delivered. Instead, it is said to be contrived for the reader's convenience.[26]

Yet although *Malmad ha-Talmidim* does not purport to contain sermons that Anatoli had preached, it would be foolish to dismiss its relevance to the history of Jewish preaching. Remarks at the beginning of several sections indicate that the author thought the material appropriate for his or other preachers' use (for example, *Be-Haᶜaloteka* [Num. 8:1–12:16]: "This can be made appropriate for the wedding of a person of priestly descent by opening with the verse *The lips of the priest preserve knowledge* [Mal. 2:7]; it can also be made appropriate for the Sabbath during Hanukkah by adding material relevant to that holiday"). One of the discourses was actually used as a sermon in the Montpellier synagogue at a strategic juncture in the conflict over philosophical study. And a manuscript of the *Malmad* introduces the section on the lesson *Ḥayye Śarah* (Gen. 23:1–24:18) with the remark, "This is appropriate for the wedding of a distinguished groom, and I composed it for the wedding of my daughter; that is why I began with these verses (*Listen, daughter, and see* . . . [Ps. 45:11]), even though they are in the middle of the psalm." While it does not reproduce Anatoli's sermons exactly, neither is it remote from the realities of preaching.[27]

The second example is Baḥya ben Asher, author of an influential commentary on the Torah and of a collection of ethical discourses organized by subject matter in alphabetical order, called *Kad ha-Qemaḥ*. Bettan wrote, "that the sermons [in *Kad ha-Qemaḥ*] were actually preached before congregational assemblies admits of no doubt," citing as evidence three passages that appear to communicate the voice of a preacher facing a congregation. However, the fact that we know of no other Jewish preacher in this period who devoted each sermon to a different topic without any direct connection to the weekly Torah lesson makes this assumption problematic.

Here, too, the author's own introduction gives a different impression. Not a word is said about his own preaching. The audience for which the book is intended is clearly defined: Jews exhausted by the burdens of exile, too dis-

26. Bettan, p. 51; Anatoli, end of introduction. The phrase *dibre heᶜarah* is used three times in the introduction, and the book is characterized as *Sefer ha-Heᶜarot* on p. 148b (the term may have been influenced by Judah ibn Tibbon's translation of Baḥya ibn Paquda's *Ḥobot ha-Lebabot:* see *Shaᶜar ᶜAbodat ha-ʾElohim,* chap. 1).

27. Anatoli, p. 129a, cf. p. 185a; Anatoli MS, fol. 39r. On the use of his sermon in Montpellier, see above, n. 8. Anatoli MS contains many preaching suggestions not in the printed text: "This is a place to preach about the laws of leavened and unleavened bread" (fol. 83v); "to preach about the laws of nullification of vows" (fol. 118r); "about the laws of ritual immersion" (fol. 134r); "about the laws of the shofar" (fol. 144r); "about the laws of the sukkah" (fol. 152v); "about the theme of the holiday" (fols. 103v, 138r). It is not clear to me whether these remarks were original or whether they were marginalia by a later preacher, incorporated into the text by a scribe.

tracted for intensive study of Talmud, who find relief and pleasure in aggadic homiletical material. "In order that the road might be well paved, so that whoever looks may easily find what he wants, I decided to organize my work according to the alphabet. Whenever a man is inspired and asserts himself in his desire to preach, he may find each commandment and each ethical quality under the appropriate letter." According to the author, his book is designed to supply homiletical material for preachers, an undertaking analogous to the alphabetically organized collections of source material for Christian preachers that began to appear in the thirteenth century. A preacher in search of quotations praising faith, trust, or humility, or condemning pride, slanderous gossip, or groundless hatred, could turn to this book to find both the apposite passages and the homiletical interpretations of these passages ready to hand.[28]

The third example, Isaac Arama, was probably the best-known and clearly the most influential preacher in the generation of the expulsion from Spain. Like Anatoli, Arama discusses his preaching career in the introduction to *ʿAqedat Yiṣḥaq,* providing details about his responsibilities in the communities where he served. But again Bettan claimed too much in saying, "On the sermons themselves, he had been working all through his stay in Tarragona and Fraga, and not until he had removed to Calatayud . . . did he begin to revise them in preparation for their publication."

It is inconceivable that Arama did not incorporate material from his sermons into his magnum opus. But he never described the book as a record of his preaching. He says simply, "Trusting in God, I was helped to write a book [*ḥibbur*] on the Torah, consisting of two parts. The first part is an investigation [*derishah*] of particular subjects in the Torah . . . the second is a commentary [*perishah*] on its words according to their simple meaning"; "I shall not pay attention to the division of the lessons, fixed according to the weeks of the year, but rather to the various subjects," each of which is to be connected with the next in a logical manner. The two sections of each chapter are thus said to apply only to the book, not to the sermons. The literary structure of the chapters in *ʿAqedat Yiṣḥaq* tells us nothing about the

28. Bettan, pp. 95–96; Baḥya, *Kad ha-Qemaḥ,* p. 18, cf. *Encyclopedia,* pp. xi, 3, 7, 18. For contemporary Christian preaching aids, see Rouse and Rouse, "Statim," especially pp. 201–02 and 210–18, on alphabetization; idem, *Preachers;* Christine von Nolcken, "Some Alphabetical Compendia and How Preachers Used Them in Fourteenth Century England," *Viator* 12 (1981):271–88; D'Avray, pp. 64–81. If this is indeed the purpose of *Kad ha-Qemaḥ,* the passages cited by Bettan must be understood differently. Baḥya writes about the tradition of beginning a sermon with a biblical verse, concludes a discourse with a prayer that God might "forgive us on this Day of Atonement," or speaks of "a plain Israelite like myself, facing you this day" not as a record of every word he said, but as models that other preachers could use.

structure of Arama's sermons; this work, so influential among later preachers, reveals its author as preacher only indirectly.[29]

These three classics of Jewish homiletical literature are fundamentally different from texts that begin to appear in the middle of the fifteenth century and reflect a new conception of the written sermon. These texts were produced not to serve as a resource or model for other preachers to adapt, but rather to record what was said on a specific occasion. The writings of four contemporary preachers from several regions of the Mediterranean basin document this change.

The manuscript containing sermons by Michael ben Shabbetai Balbo of Candia (Crete) is filled with notes by the author describing the occasion for the sermon in a prefatory or concluding sentence. Three wedding sermons mark milestones in the preacher's life. He delivered one during the week of his own wedding (on the Sabbath preceding Purim, 1437), another at the wedding of his son Isaiah in the summer of 1463, and the third at the wedding of his son Solomon. Some of the remaining sermons are linked with other events in his life or in the life of his community, and some simply with holidays ("This sermon I delivered in Candia in the year 5231 [1471] on the last day of Passover").[30]

The dramatic circumstances of a sermon delivered in Segovia by Joseph ibn Shem Ṭob in the spring of 1452 are recounted in the introduction to the sermon.[31] The sermons of Moses ben Joab of Florence appear with similar information, whether as a marginal note ("in Florence, on Hanukkah, when a distinguished astronomer was present in the congregation"; "at the betrothal of R. Abraham da Montalcino") or as an introduction to the text ("in Florence, the discourse when the wife of R. Meir of Susa was held by the ruler, in danger").[32]

In Turkey, at about the same time, Ephraim ben Gerson identifies the occasion for several of his sermons: "This sermon I, Ephraim ben Gerson the physician, preached about R. Emanuel the physician at the time of his death in the city of Negroponte [Chalcis]"; "this sermon I preached on behalf of R. Elijah ha-Levi, on the occasion of his journey to Venice and his safe

29. Bettan, p. 137; Arama, author's intro., p. 8b. Cf. Heller-Wilensky, pp. 29–31; Dan, *Sifrut,* pp. 176–79; Pachter, "Sifrut," pp. 16–18. On Arama's *perishah* and *derishah* as technical terms, see "Structural Options," below.

30. Balbo, cf. fols. 89v, 78v, 106r, 79r, 189r, 177v (some of the dates in the catalogue are incorrect). On this figure and his family, see most recently Zevi Malakhi, "Me-Ḥibburehem shel Bene Balbo mi-Kandya ba-Me'ah ha-Ṭet-Waw," *Mika'el* 7 (1982):255–70; and Ravitsky, "Zehuto," pp. 153–54. Various sections of this manuscript have been studied, but not the sections containing Balbo's sermons.

31. See the introduction to his sermon, translated below.

32. Moses ben Joab, fols. 90v, 64r, 75v. This preacher and his sermons were described by Cassuto in "Rabbino," and in *Ha-Yehudim,* pp. 194–200.

return . . . for he went to Venice and endured great suffering, day and night, in order to ease the burden [of this community]"; "this sermon I preached when the daughter of R. Elijah ha-Levi died"; "the sermon preached about the slander against me, when they said that I placed my hands on the breasts of a young lady, being desirous of kissing her and sleeping with her against her will, and that she threw dirt in my face and hit me."[33]

Even more important than these statements is internal evidence of delivery. Preachers refer to the occasion in the course of their remarks. Moses ben Joab wrote: "Now that we have completed the interpretation of the verse in both an exoteric and an esoteric manner, it remains for us to apply it to the subject of the engagement, the reason for our gathering." He then goes on to discuss the name of the husband, Abraham.[34] They refer to themselves and to members of their family. Michael Balbo noted that he preached on that day "because my father and teacher, may God bless and preserve him, has requested me to do so, and I cannot ignore his command."[35] They mention personal circumstances, as when Israel, author of "Dober Mesharim," states that, despite the custom of preaching on the Feast of Booths (Sukkot), "because of my weakness and the dryness of my throat I would have desisted"; and again, "I am still extremely weak."[36]

They address their audience directly: "And now, my brothers and friends, look and you will see how this tragedy has come upon us"; "I ask you to follow well what I say, for I do not want any doubt about this matter to remain in the minds of the listeners."[37] They refer to the presence of particular individuals in the congregation.[38] They assume the congregation's knowledge of a specific event that would have had to be explained if intended for strangers: "Those who die in bed do not arouse as much anguish as those who die in this manner"; "an occurrence as cruel and bitter as this"—both without further elaboration.[39]

They allude to sermons preached on previous occasions: "Even though I already preached on this subject [charity] on a previous Sabbath, I have

33. Ephraim ha-Darshan, fols. 186v, 148r, 236v, 97v; cf. also 169r, 182r, 192v. (Joseph Hacker has announced his intention to publish a study of this work.)

34. Moses ben Joab, in Cassuto, "Rabbino," pp. 228–29.

35. Balbo, fol. 92r. Cf. Israel, "Dober Mesharim," fol. 233v, on the occasion of the first anniversary of his father's death.

36. Israel, "Dober Mesharim," fol. 183r; Garçon, in Benayahu, p. 160. Cf. "Dober Mesharim," fol. 126v (his first sermon after recovering from a grave illness), and fol. 16v (his first sermon in a new community). On this preacher, see "Sources," below.

37. Joseph ibn Shem Ṭob, fol. 121r (see the translation of his sermon, below); Israel, "Dober Mesharim," fol. 55r.

38. Ephraim ha-Darshan, fol. 289v; Israel, "Dober Mesharim," fols. 212v, 215r, 220r; Garçon, in Benayahu, p. 160.

39. Israel, "Dober Mesharim," fol. 19.

resumed preaching on it now"; "Although I took this verse on Sunday, when I preached . . . about the distinguished elder R. Isaac Abudraham."[40] They indicate a particular point in the calendar: "The New Year's Day, which will come this Monday."[41] They show an awareness of time constraints: "I will not speak about this poem (the Song at the Sea, Exod. 15) in all its details, for if I did my discourse would become tedious and burdensome to hear for all, but I shall discuss certain details."[42] This evidence of delivery in a specific context makes such texts considerably closer to records of actual sermons than anything extant from earlier periods.

Yet even a text that purports to be a true record of what was preached is not above suspicion. Most of the texts mentioned above were apparently written after the delivery of the sermon, and we need to assess the changes that may have occurred as they passed from oral to written form. Much depends, of course, on circumstances. Did the preacher use brief notes, a more extensive outline, or a fully written manuscript when he delivered the sermon? How much time elapsed between the delivery and the writing of the text that has been preserved?

Occasionally such information is provided by the preacher himself. Leon Modena states that he wrote the sermons incorporated into *Midbar Yehudah* "from the outline notes [*rimze rashe peraqim*] that I had written." Ephraim Luntshitz introduces *ʿAmmude Shesh* with the assertion that "all this was gathered from the various sermons I preached in that community [Prague]; I gathered from these sermons what my memory preserved." The manuscript of sermons by the seventeenth-century Polish preacher Israel of Bełżyce contains the following parenthetical remark: "The Sabbath before the Day of Atonement, 5400 [1639], in the congregation of Chęciny. This sermon was stolen from me, and this is the little I could remember." Joseph ben Ḥayyim Zarfati affirms that he wrote down what he had said "immediately" after the sermon, and that he did not change his material substantially for publication. But where an author like Shem Ṭob ibn Shem Ṭob simply states that he began "to write the things that I preached publicly," it is often difficult to know.[43]

40. Garçon, in Benayahu, pp. 189, 175; cf. p. 160.

41. Israel, "Dober Mesharim," fol. 182v; cf. anonymous, "Bibago," fol. 329: "even though we are at the end of the holiday."

42. Anonymous, "Bibago," fol. 120; cf. Bibago, col. 4, and Israel, "Dober Mesharim," fol. 198r.

43. Modena, *Midbar,* intro. p. 4b (in Nave, p. 115; cf. *Ḥayye Yehudah,* in Nave, p. 46); such preliminary notes may have been preserved in Bodleian MS Or. 5396; see Adelman, p. 324, n. 45. Luntshitz, *ʿAmmude,* p. 3b (he says [p. 2d] that he selected from his sermons that material which pertained to the conceptual framework of the current book. In the introduction to *ʿOlelot* [p. 3b], he states that he could have arranged his material according to the weekly lesson, but that he had already written *ʿIr Gibborim* in that framework and therefore

Certain changes between the spoken and the written sermon are fairly predictable. One of the most important remains somewhat controversial: the linguistic transformation from a vernacular original to a Hebrew text. A rabbi who preached in the vernacular and then decided to write out his sermons for any purpose other than personal use would want them to be intelligible not only to the relatively few Jews literate in that vernacular, but also to the Jewish community throughout the world, for which Hebrew was the universal language of literature. We know of no Jewish sermons written in a European language before the second half of the sixteenth century; all earlier texts from Europe are in Hebrew. How many of these sermons were preached in Hebrew is another question.

We may assume that preachers generally used a more highly embellished style in writing their Hebrew sermon texts than they had in speaking. Such a style, which often produced a pastiche of obscure biblical phrases that demonstrated the author's mastery of Scripture, was designed to impress the distant reader. Except in such special cases as inaugural sermons, this was usually superfluous in the preacher's own congregation, where a simpler, more direct discourse was desirable.

A lucid discussion of this process appears in the introduction to Joseph ben Ḥayyim Zarfati's *Yad Yosef:*

> It was my intention to write this book that you see in print in a rhetorical language that would be pleasant to behold, a delight to the eyes. But I changed my mind for two reasons. First, it would require considerable work to rewrite it in a style different from the original. When I first wrote it, my only purpose was to ensure that I would not forget what I had said by putting it in a more permanent form; I did not bother with rhetorical style. Now it would be burdensome to spend so much time for this purpose. Second, rhetorical language sometimes diverts attention from the actual content, and it is more demanding upon the reader. I therefore leave this to others; I shall follow the simple path.[44]

Zarfati speaks here of two stages in the writing of his sermons. The first was setting the sermon down on paper soon after the delivery, so as not to forget it. The second, which might occur many years later, was preparing the material for publication. The author's apology for his plain prose indicates that the usual practice was to elevate the style in this second stage, so that

---

chose a different structure. In other words, none of these books contains a full sermon as preached); Israel of Bełżyce, fol. 353r; Zarfati, author's intro.; Shem Ṭob ibn Shem Ṭob, author's intro. Cf. Smith, p. 32.

44. Zarfati, author's intro.

even those texts that record a sermon actually delivered do not necessarily reproduce the style of the original.

Furthermore, material included in the oral sermon was frequently eliminated from the written text. For example, topical references to specific events, issues, or problems that affected a particular congregation would no longer be relevant or even comprehensible to future readers in a different place. The rationale for eliminating such material from the final published version was articulated by Samuel Landau, who was responsible for the printing of many of his father's sermons:

> Not everything that is said is worthy of being written down and fixed in a book. There is a proper time for everything, a need for each occasion, and not all times are the same. . . . Not every sermon is relevant to all generations. . . . Whoever preaches to a congregation must arrange his message and fit his words to the taste of the listeners. . . . It is therefore absolutely necessary to be selective, to add, omit, or change the order of things so that the message will be accepted [by the readers].[45]

This impulse to filter out the ephemeral in favor of the "permanent" undoubtedly characterized the writing and publication of sermons throughout our period. Precisely the material of greatest interest to the modern historian, that which provides specific information about a concrete situation in one community at one time, is the least likely to have been thought worthy of preservation by most preachers.

The same is true of the criticism or rebuke of the congregation for ethical and religious shortcomings. Many preachers apparently felt that this was either too intimate or too stereotyped to be of much interest to outside readers. Sermon texts often contain remarks like: "Here I interrupted my discourse a bit, and I began to goad the people about the performance of the commandments," or "I spoke at length about this matter, giving ethical instruction to the people."[46] Such sentences prove that the author considered it important to give some account of the sermon as delivered, for the parenthetical remarks could have been omitted without most readers' noticing. Yet these remarks also show that certain discussions were thought to be unsuitable for formal publication.

A third type of material that is frequently lost is exegetical. The classical form of the Sephardic sermon as it began to crystallize at the end of the fifteenth century included an interpretation of a rabbinic aggadah cited im-

45. Landau, *Doresh,* p. 2d; see the discussion and examples of the process in "Sermons and History," below.

46. Katzenellenbogen, p. 44b (cited in Bonfil, *Ha-Rabbanut,* p. 194; Nigal, p. 85). *Dibre Shelomoh,* p. 13b, and cf. pp. 160a, 216a.

mediately after the biblical verse at the beginning. But details of this interpretation are often absent from the written account, as we see in the sermon by Joseph Garçon translated below. Such reticence is frequently evident in the sermons of Solomon Levi: "After that I went on to preach about the reason for the four cups [of wine] on the night of Passover, and I explained the view of Abravanel in his *Zebaḥ Pesaḥ*"; "After that I preached on the verses from the Hafṭarah [prophetic lesson] *Comfort* (Isa. 40:1–26)"; "Then I preached on the psalm *From the depths I have called* (Ps. 130) and the *ma*ʾ*amar.*" Where the interpretation could be found in another work by the author, he was even less likely to repeat it as part of his published sermon.[47]

Finally, humorous, witty, or offhand remarks were usually eliminated from written texts. But this does not imply that no humor is to be found in published sermons. The witty interpretation of a biblical verse or of a rabbinic passage was a standard homiletical tool, and the phrase *ʿal derek halaṣah* ("in the manner of jest, wit, or humor") became a technical term of Jewish preaching. Nevertheless, we can safely assume that more of such banter was present in discourse than appears in the text, for a remark appropriate between a preacher and people who knew him might convey an undesirable impression in a book to be read by strangers.

Here too, an exceptional case points to general practice. An eighteenth-century Polish maggid concluded a section of his book with the words "Because I have been overburdened, I have not reviewed some of the pages with sufficient care. Sometimes I wrote just what I said in public—including humorous or other remarks required by the occasion—although truly it is wrong to print this. I counted on being able to remove such material when it went to press, but it was printed so quickly that I had no opportunity to do so."[48]

If editing sermons involved merely elimination of material, we could properly conclude that the original sermon was longer than its written counterpart. This is, however, unlikely. In many cases it seems that the opposite is true: the written text is too long to have been preached. It is, of course, more difficult to prove that something was added than that something was omitted. But a preacher who might be content to deal with a particular intellectual problem in an abbreviated and somewhat superficial manner in front of his congregation, and excuse his lack of thoroughness by referring to time con-

47. Garçon, in Benayahu, p. 140, and cf. pp. 54 and 197; Israel, "Dober Mesharim," fols. 124v, 220r; *Dibre Shelomoh,* pp. 13b, 215d, 216a. See also Jaffe, pp. 447–48.

48. Simḥah of Zalozhtsy, cited in Piekarz, p. 11. Cf. the apology for including humorous material by Ḥayyim Aryeh Leib Fenster in the introduction to *Shaʿar Bat Rabbim* (Warsaw, 1890), 1:5b. A criticism of the amount of humor in popular sermons is cited in Dinur, p. 138.

straints, would feel compelled to explore it more fully when treating it in a book.

Joseph ben Ḥayyim Zarfati, whose defense of his simple style I quoted above, again comes to our aid: "It also occurred to me to write in a deep and complex manner, exploring all the ramifications of the various subjects. But I realized that this was not the proper way. It is a hardship when the reader is distracted from the subject of the sermon and gets entangled somewhere in the middle. Furthermore, some of these sermons are in their 'image and likeness' just what I preached publicly on various Sabbaths." The implication is that others elaborated on their material considerably.[49]

What then can be deduced about the oral sermon from a text written after delivery? As we have seen, given the uncertainty about the original language and the process of rhetorical embellishment, the text does not provide firm ground for analyzing the level of diction, the allusiveness of language, or the range of rhetorical tropes in the original. But certain elements can be safely assumed to reflect the oral sermon. All topical allusions—references to specific events or community problems, to the occasion of delivery, to individuals in the congregation, and to the preacher's situation at the moment—were undoubtedly part of what was said. There would be no reason for someone preparing his sermon for publication to introduce such material. Similarly, stories, parables, anecdotes, exempla, and other literary devices intended to illustrate or dramatize a point were probably present in the oral form, where they were used to attract or hold the attention of the audience. Perhaps most important, the basic structure of the sermon would not be likely to undergo substantial change. A lucid and logical structure facilitates both immediate comprehension and long-term retention of a sermon's content. If a preacher is going to organize his thoughts in accordance with the conventions of the genre, it is more important for him to do so when addressing an audience that must grasp and retain his message at a single exposure than it is when writing for readers who can work through the development of an idea at their own pace and return to refresh their memory when necessary. The form of the written sermon is therefore likely to be a reliable indication of what was once said.

Although most sermons that have been preserved, and certainly those in print, were given written form only after delivery, some manuscripts contain material prepared beforehand, recording what the preacher intended to say. For example, the manuscript of Joseph Garçon's sermons includes a eulogy for the author's teacher, Samuel Franco, the head of a yeshivah in Salonika. The theme verse from the Torah portion was Exodus 19:22, from the lesson

49. Zarfati, author's intro. Cf. Smith, p. 42: "A preacher preparing his sermons for the press was quite likely to lengthen them"; and Bayley, pp. 15–16.

Yitro (Exod. 18:1–20:23). On the tenth page of the text, the following statement appears: "However, I did not take this verse, because I was unable to preach during the week of this lesson [*Yitro*], for scholars preached many sermons each day of the seven days of mourning, and I was the last. I therefore preached on the following lesson, *Elleh ha-Mishpaṭim* (Exod. 21:1–24:18), taking this verse (Exod. 21:5)." What he actually preached is reported in the following manner: "I said that I am worthy to preach before this scholar, for I am his servant and his disciple. . . . Before I began the essence of my sermon, I made the following introduction. . . . I also said at the conclusion of the sermon. . . . I returned to the theme verse and said. . . . Immediately I cited the rabbinic statement with which I began, and concluded my sermon with it, helped by God."[50]

The first section was obviously a sermon he had prepared in advance, but he never had the opportunity to preach it because the verse he chose as his theme was no longer in the lesson of the current week. The second section, reporting what he said, must have been written after the fact. Was the original version, the eulogy based on Exodus 19:22, substantially revised at the time the second version was written? Apparently not, for why would a preacher revise the text of a sermon that he never delivered while leaving the account of what he actually said in apocopated form? The original version must have been written by Garçon before he was scheduled to deliver it.

Garçon even states that some of the sermons in this manuscript were never given, and he uses the word *le-ᶜayyen* as a technical term for preparing material and *li-derosh* for preaching it: "I, Joseph . . . prepared it [*ᶜiyyantihu*] to preach in Salonika on the Feast of Weeks [1500], but on that holiday the Sultan Bayezid came, and I did not preach it"; "I, Joseph . . . prepared it to preach here in Salonika at the death of Samuel Abravanel in the year 5264 [1503–04], on the eighth day of the month of Tebet, which was the seventh day after his passing, but I did not preach it because of something that occurred."[51]

"Dober Mesharim," a manuscript containing sermons contemporary with Garçon's shows similar indications of material prepared in advance. A sermon on the lesson *Ki Tiśśa* (Exod. 30:11–34:35) begins with Exodus 30:12, followed by the remark, "Because I was sick, I did not say these words at the beginning," referring to six-and-a-half lines of Spanish in Hebrew characters that gave a conventional preacher's introduction. This section, at least, was obviously written in advance.[52]

Similar hints occasionally appear even in printed works. Joel ibn Shueib introduces one of the sermons in his *ᶜOlat Shabbat* with the words, "This I

50. Garçon, in Benayahu, pp. 147–48; Hacker, "Li-Demutam," pp. 87–89.

51. Garçon, in Benayahu, pp. 143, 155.

52. Israel, "Dober Mesharim," fol. 91r.

arranged to preach about a certain bridegroom. It was the second Sabbath after his wedding, but I did not preach it." Solomon Levi notes before his Day of Atonement sermon for 1571, "I preached a little of this sermon, for there was no time to preach the whole thing."[53]

We also find indications of material added to a prepared text at the time of delivery. The manuscript of Josiah Pardo's sermons includes one for *Wa-Yesheb* (Gen. 37:1–40:23), 1649, identified in the list of sermons and subjects at the beginning with the words, "I preached it in the presence of Christian clergymen in the synagogue." The sermon itself contains the following "notice" (modaʿah): "On this Sabbath, Christian clergymen came to the synagogue, and I preached against their false doctrine and demonstrated that none of the good promises had been fulfilled up until now." But the written text of the sermon is limited to a discussion of exegetical problems at the beginning of the lesson. This text was apparently prepared ahead of time, the preacher adding his polemical remarks at the last moment in response to the surprise visitors. Only the briefest summary of these remarks was later incorporated into the manuscript.[54]

Sources for the study of Jewish preaching are extremely heterogeneous, and the problem of the relationship between written text and sermon admits of no simple solution. Some texts were written by their authors, some by others; some merely employed the literary form, others purport to record faithfully an oral address; some were highly revised, polished, and edited for publication, some were not; some were written down after delivery, some were prepared before. Each collection of sermons, indeed each individual sermon, must be carefully analyzed with such questions in mind in order to determine in which category it falls.

The Preaching Situation

The status of the sermon as an ancient and honorable tradition in Jewish life has always been beyond question. Early rabbinic literature provided ample testimony of preaching by the greatest rabbis. It was often implied, and sometimes claimed outright, that preaching continued the discourse of the ancient prophets. While homiletical excesses and abuses could diminish its reputation in particular instances, few people challenged the importance of the sermon—properly conceived.

Yet while the most minute details of Jewish liturgy, ritual, and the public

53. Joel ibn Shueib, p. 106d; cf. Pachter, "Sifrut," p. 2; *Dibre Shelomoh,* p. 63c.

54. Pardo 2, fol. 82v. The sermon was preached in Rotterdam; I have translated the word *gallaḥim* as "Christian clergymen."

reading from Scripture were thoroughly regulated, the sermon had no clear status in Jewish law. Questions relating to appropriate content, form, frequency, context, and setting within the liturgical framework, or to the preacher's status and compensation for his work, remained for the most part matters of custom, governed by popular taste and the internal conventions of the genre. They were rarely crystallized as law. That the sermon belonged somewhere in the structure of Jewish worship was generally conceded, but precisely where was anything but clear.

In many communities a sermon was expected on every Sabbath. Medieval Germany, where rabbis contrasted the ancients, who were "accustomed to sermons," with their contemporaries, who were "not accustomed to preaching," is one exception.[1] But few significant communities in southern Europe or anywhere in the Sephardic diaspora went without weekly exposure to some kind of preaching, as we can see from such various sources as the responsa literature, the texts of rabbinical contracts, and the statements and written legacies of the preachers themselves.[2] Even in Poland, where weekly preaching was not universal, many thought it should be, and some men did preach on every Sabbath.[3]

There is some evidence of preaching on weekdays as well. Manuscript sermons of Joseph ibn Shem Ṭob were delivered in the synagogue of Segovia on Monday and Thursday, the weekdays when the Torah was read as part of the morning service. According to a contemporary report, Zechariah ha-Sefaradi preached for about a quarter of an hour twice each day, following morning and afternoon prayers, in the Jerusalem academy of Obadiah Bertinoro. The Polish rabbi Judah Pukhovitser tells us, "It was our practice to preach words of ethical rebuke each day, and every Sabbath I would preach novel interpretations of the Torah." Pukhovitser even recommended that the normal terms of a rabbinical appointment should commit each rabbi "to preach words of ethical rebuke each day, or at least every Sabbath."[4]

Despite the consensus that a sermon was an integral component of the

1. MaHaRIL, *Hilkot Ḥol ha-Moʿed,* p. 25b.

2. Some preachers actually left records of sermons preached week after week (e.g., *Dibre Shelomoh;* Cantarini). Many more mention their weekly preaching in the introductions to their works (Moses Alsheikh, introduction to *Torat Mosheh;* Samuel Jaffe, introduction to *Yefeh To'ar;* Dato, fol. 2v; Zahalon, p. 109; ibn Basa, fol. 15r). Cf. Adret, *Teshubot* 2:260; Bezalel Ashkenazi, *Teshubot,* no. 24, p. 48c; ʿAqiba Frankfurter in Joseph Hahn, *Yosif Omeṣ* (Frankfurt, 1928), no. 875, p. 192; Assaf, 3:56; 4:31 and 33; Bonfil, *Ha-Rabbanut,* p. 102.

3. See Luntshitz, cited in Bettan, p. 303; *Pinqas Waʿad,* pp. 478–79; *Pinqas Liṭa,* no. 401, p. 82; *Taqqanot Mehrin,* p. 284; Pukhovitser, *Qeneh Ḥokmah,* pp. 4c, 9a (in "Sources").

4. Joseph ibn Shem Ṭob, *Derashot,* fol. 183v, 191r, 192v; Yaari, *Iggerot,* p. 157; Pukhovitser, see "Sources." Cf. also Jacob di Alba's introduction to *Toledot Yaʿaqob,* where he states he was engaged to preach every day in the Florence yeshivah (Alba, p. 2a).

communal observance of the Sabbath, no uniform custom governed its place. Some communities listened to the sermon on Friday night after the Sabbath meal, a constructive solution to the problem of how those evening hours should be spent. The peripatetic Ḥayyim Joseph Azulai reported that Israel Gedaliah Cases of Mantua delivered a full sermon, carefully prepared, every Friday night in the house of a certain Signor Sulam. Azulai himself preached a long sermon in the synagogue of Carpentras on Friday night after dinner.[5] The general pattern, however, was for the sermon to be delivered during the day, either as part of the morning service, or some time after the midday meal.

The morning sermon had to fit into the already rather lengthy service, and time constraints were pressing. However, this option guaranteed the largest audience and bestowed upon the sermon the greatest prestige as an official and integral part of the Sabbath worship. The most natural place for the sermon was after the reading of the Torah and the Hafṭarah. There it would both come as an explanation and application of what had just been read from Scripture and act as a bridge between the regular morning liturgy and the additional liturgy (Musaf) for the Sabbath.

A sixteenth-century Italian rabbi, Mordecai Dato, developed a preaching ritual with an elaborate theoretical explanation. His practice of preaching after the reading of the Torah each Sabbath was intended to ensure "that words of the Oral Law would be uttered after the recitation of the threefold Written Law [encompassing] Torah, Prophets, and Writings." Before the Torah was read, as the scroll was removed from the ark, a psalm was recited, selected to complement the subject matter of the weekly lesson. The progression thus led from the Writings (of which the Book of Psalms is a part) to the Torah, followed by the reading from the Prophets, and then the sermon ("Oral Law"), which linked the Torah reading with a passage from rabbinic literature and concluded with a recitation of Qaddish de-Rabbanan (the Scholars' Doxology). It has been recently noted that Dato clearly saw the sermon as an organic part of the public ritual that probably shared in the kabbalistic symbolism of the liturgy.[6]

However, although many sermons from Italy and elsewhere refer to "the Torah portion that was read," or to a lesser extent to "the Hafṭarah that we have heard," the custom of preaching after the reading of Scripture was not universal. In some places the sermon introduced the Torah lection. A legal query directed to Maimonides reports that "when the cantor had finished the Tefillah (Eighteen Benedictions), before the sacred Torah was taken out, the head of the congregation . . . gave a talk of religious content to the congre-

5. Azulai, pp. 79, 102.
6. Dato, fol. 2v, discussed in Jacobson, pp. 101–02.

gation, as he is accustomed to do." A mid-fifteenth-century Spanish source indicates that sermons were delivered after the Torah had been removed from the ark but before it was read, so that the preacher spoke while the Torah scroll was resting on the reading stand.[7]

Some even tried to place the sermon earlier in the service, severing completely the connection with the Torah ritual. Joseph Hahn, head of the rabbinical court in Frankfurt in the early seventeenth century, railed at the new custom of "fixing the time of the sermon on the Sabbath after the praying of Yoṣer [the first major liturgical section after the call to worship], something our ancestors never dreamed of. This causes considerable distress to the elderly and the infirm, to pregnant women and nursing mothers, for it makes them suffer [a long Sabbath morning service] until afternoon."[8] Because in traditional Jewish practice nothing was eaten before the morning prayer, the first meal on the Sabbath day could not begin until the family had returned home from the morning service. Delaying this beyond noon was considered inconsistent with the principle of observing the Sabbath as a day of joy.[9] Such thinking lies behind Hahn's argument. Citing other authorities from Poland and Russia, he established that no such custom was known in their lands. Therefore, he concluded, the preaching of long and involuted sermons that have little to do with the Sabbath and make the service last until "long after noon" was "certainly absolutely forbidden." His own preference was for an afternoon sermon, which allowed people to go home, eat a leisurely Sabbath meal, and then return to the synagogue for a sermon preceding the late afternoon service (Minḥah). This arrangement kept the morning service from being too long and allowed the preacher to speak at greater length. Its primary disadvantage was that it demoted the sermon from an integral part of the official liturgy to a supplementary exercise.

One congregation's adoption of the afternoon sermon is reflected by a communal ordinance of 1683 from Moravia. Each year three maggidim should be appointed by the community, at least two of them distinguished

7. Maimonides, *Teshubot Ha-RaMBaM,* ed. Joshua Blau, 3 vols. (Jerusalem, 1958–61), 1:189–91 (see "Sources"); Ḥayyim ibn Mūsā, p. 118 (see "Sources"). Cf. Dinur, p. 135.

8. Joseph Hahn, *Yosif Omeṣ,* no. 625, pp. 138–39. Cf. *Dibre Shelomoh,* p. 218d: a sermon preached on the Sabbath "at the time of the Tefillah."

9. See *Ṭur, Oraḥ Ḥayyim,* no. 288. Moses ben Abraham's *Maṭṭeh Mosheh* states that the preachers provide a scriptural basis for this rule: the word *ʿoneg* in *You shall call the Sabbath a delight* [ʿoneg] (Isa. 58:13) is written without the letter *waw* (whose numerical equivalent is six), and therefore only six hours of the day may elapse before eating without interfering with the delight: *Maṭṭeh Mosheh,* no. 469, p. 112. Cf. Pollack, p. 160. Note the apology by a thirteenth-century preacher on a special occasion: "If we speak somewhat at length, let it not offend you, even though the hour for dinner has already passed. Indeed it is fitting to speak at length and to postpone slightly our dining, which relates only to physical life and is ephemeral" (cited by Chazan, p. 446).

for their learning, "capable of preaching about aggadic material in such a way as to win the hearts of the people to their ethical instruction. They will preach in turn every Sabbath before the Minḥah [afternoon] prayer in the New Synagogue, that is, one hour before Minḥah."[10]

In this setting, the sermon could easily look like an optional accoutrement of the Sabbath observance. The greater interest shown by the listener who had chosen to return to the synagogue an hour early just to hear the sermon had to be weighed against the diminished size of the congregation. Not everyone agreed with the claim that it was a religious obligation to hear a sermon each Sabbath. Rabbinic authorities warned against prolonging the midday meal into the preacher's time slot, and those Italian rabbis who were inclined to permit tennis playing on the Sabbath carefully stipulated that their permission did not apply to the "hour of the sermon." Yet by the end of the seventeenth century a Jerusalem rabbi could write (undoubtedly with some exaggeration) that "it is the custom in all the communities of Israel to appoint a preacher who will preach each Sabbath in the afternoon."[11]

It was also possible to add the sermon into the Minḥah service late on Saturday afternoon. Minḥah was considerably shorter than the morning service, and a brief section from the Torah was read from the following week's lesson. Spanish preachers from the generation of the expulsion often used this time for their sermons. For example, we find the following notes in Joel ibn Shueib's *ʿOlat Shabbat:* "This sermon I preached at Minḥah in the Great Synagogue"; "This I preached on the lesson *Naśo* (Num. 4:21–7:89) at Minḥah on the Sabbath immediately preceding the Feast of Weeks"; "This I preached in the Great Synagogue in the year 5245 [1484 or 1485] on the Sabbath at Minḥah, on the lesson *Haʾazinu* (Deut. 32:1–52)." A contemporary identified his opening verse as coming "from the lesson we have read now at Minḥah."[12]

10. *Taqqanot Mehrin,* p. 284; see also Dinur, p. 134. For this practice of preaching before Minḥah in Spain, see Ṭodros ha-Levi, p. 45b, Jacob ben Hananel, fol. 1v; for southern France, see *Minḥat Qenaʾot,* p. 139; for southern Italy, see Obadiah Bertinoro, p. 243.

11. *Shene Luḥot ha-Berit* derived an obligation to hear a sermon from the Zohar, *Shelaḥ Leka;* cf. Abraham Sheftal and Isaiah Horowitz, *ʿEmeq Berakah* (Amsterdam, 1729), pp. 66b–67a. The obligation was similarly maintained by leading Palestinian rabbis but vehemently denied by Samuel de Medina (*Teshubot, Yoreh Deʿah,* no. 86), who acerbically remarked, "Would that most sermons today were . . . not in the category of that which must not be heard, but could be included in the category of what is optional." For the warning against prolonging the meal, based on B. Giṭ 38b, see *Maṭṭeh Mosheh,* no. 477, p. 115; on Sabbath ball-playing and its potential for competing with the sermon, see ibid.; Isaac Rivkind, "Teshubot ha-Rab Mosheh Provençali ʿal Miśḥaq ha-Kaddur," *Tarbiẓ* 3 (1933):374; Roth, *Renaissance,* p. 28. For the prevalence of the afternoon sermon, see Raphael Malki, in Assaf, 3:56; cf. Azulai, p. 131. But contrast *Binat Yiśśakar,* p. 12a: "Most preachers preach only during the morning or the afternoon service."

12. Joel ibn Shueib, pp. 132c, 111b, 159a; Israel, "Dober Mesharim," fol. 15r.

We even find evidence of rabbis preaching both at the morning and at the afternoon services. Isaac Aboab records a sermon on Exodus 26:6, containing the phrase *we-hayah ha-mishkan eḥad* (lit. "the Tabernacle will be one"). His account contains an interesting detail about the context of Sabbath preaching:

> Therefore I said that I have attained a considerable measure of perfection from this place, which is *mishkan eḥad,* "the Tabernacle of the One, blessed be He." I said furthermore that each and every one who prays in it is unique. In the morning I said that this would suffice, that I would leave the rest until the evening, for then the Tabernacle will be one. Now in the morning, each congregation sits in its separate synagogue, but at the time of Minḥah, the Tabernacle will truly be *eḥad,* one, for all gather together at Minḥah. I began with "*Ha-mishkan eḥad;* my sermon will investigate the question."

This passage shows that an additional advantage of preaching at Minḥah in some communities was that several congregations came together for a communal service.[13]

The Sabbaths immediately preceding and following New Year's Day and the Sabbath before Passover were of special importance in the calendar. Even communities unaccustomed to weekly preaching heard sermons then, and rabbis who generally occupied themselves with other matters were expected to preach these two or three times a year. Jacob Moellin, whose sermons were delivered primarily on these special Sabbaths, represents the Ashkenazic tradition. The largest collection of sermons by a Polish preacher, the manuscript "Tifʾeret Yiśraʾel" by Israel of Bełżyce, is dominated by sermons for these occasions, while sermons on the weekly lessons are mostly for weddings or funerals. The same is true for the manuscript of sermons delivered in London by Hirschel Levin between 1756 and 1763.[14]

The sermons on the Sabbaths surrounding New Year's Day were to be devoted to the theme of repentance. Moses ben Abraham, reflecting the Polish practice in the sixteenth century, says, "It is customary to preach on this Sabbath [between New Year's Day and the Day of Atonement] and also on the Sabbath before New Year's Day to arouse the people to repentance. I have

13. Aboab, p. 27a (on several congregations' joining to hear a preacher, cf. Goitein, *Ḥinnuk,* p. 131). For records of different sermons preached in the morning and at Minḥah of the same Sabbath, see *Dibre Shelomoh,* pp. 293d, 294d, 299a, c; and Cantarini. In seventeenth-century England, sermons on Sunday afternoon were opposed by some as "markers of Iudaizing Puritanisme," as well as "a burden intolerrable to the people" (Chandos, p. 349).

14. MaHaRIL, intro. On Israel of Bełżyce and Hirschel Levin, see the introductions to the sermons translated below. According to the document of Levin's appointment as rabbi of Berlin, he was expected to preach on the Sabbaths preceding the Day of Atonement, Passover, and the Feast of Weeks. Most of the sermons of Eybeschuetz, Eidlitz, and Landau are associated with the period of repentance culminating in the Day of Atonement, or with Passover.

found a basis for this in the Midrash on Proverbs, which says, The Holy One said, 'At the time when a scholar sits and preaches, I pardon and make atonement for the sins of Israel.' It is therefore appropriate to preach on this Sabbath, so that He will make atonement for their sins."[15]

Even those who preached every week felt that the proximity of the new year demanded a broader canvas. The publishers of Saul ha-Levi Morteira's *Gibᶜat Shaʾul* comment on the brevity and succinctness of his sermons, "except for the occasion when in all Jewish communities [preachers] become expansive: the Sabbath of Repentance [following New Year's Day]." There was a tradition in some countries that the sermon for the Sabbath of Repentance should entail prominent use of a parable (*mashal*): "On this day [the Sabbath of Repentance] each preacher uses a parable according to his ability in order to lead his contemporaries back to God." It was a time when Jews were prepared to listen to a sermon considerably more complex and extensive than usual.[16]

The tradition of preaching on the Sabbath preceding Passover, called *Shabbat ha-Gadol,* "the Great Sabbath," had even deeper roots. It was considered obligatory not only for the rabbi to preach but for the entire congregation to attend and listen. A fourteenth-century preacher affirmed that "all Jews are required to gather in synagogues and houses of study on this day called 'the Great Sabbath' . . . ; even women and small children must come." Some suggested that the Sabbath acquired its name because all rabbis, including those who did not regularly preach, delivered sermons on it. Subject matter was somewhat more diverse than on the Sabbaths surrounding the new year. Some speakers focused narrowly on the detailed laws governing the observance of the holiday. A rabbi from Saragossa was lampooned with the charge that "on the Great Sabbath he would ascend the pulpit and preach for six hours on the laws of condiments (*ḥaroset*) and parsley" (used in the seder service on the first two evenings of Passover). Others addressed the major themes of the festival with its special liturgy. These sermons remain a rich and largely untapped source for homiletical exegesis of the Haggadah.[17]

15. *Maṭṭeh Mosheh,* no. 833, p. 168.

16. Morteira, pp. 19b–20a, and cf. p. 145b, bottom. On the special nature of the sermon for this Sabbath, see Pardo 1, fols. 73r, 74v; 2, fol. 56r.

17. On the obligation to hear a sermon, see Joshua ibn Shueib, p. 38d; anonymous, "Disciple of R. Asher," fol. 92r. On the term *Shabbat ha-Gadol* and the various medieval explanations of it, see Menaḥem Kasher, *Haggadah Shelemah* (Jerusalem, 1967), pp. 50–54 (and cf. Mosheh Sharon, "'Shabbat ha-Gadol' ᶜal Ketobet Qeber mi-Ramlah min ha-Meʾah ha-ᶜAśirit," *Shalem* 1 [1934]:9–11). The explanation that it received this name because of the sermon was one of many; in addition to the sources noted by Kasher, p. 51, see Joshua ibn Shuelb, p. 38d; Joseph ben David, p. 295; *Dibre Shelomoh,* p. 125b; and cf. Baron, *Community,* 2:97. For Solomon Bonafed's lampoon, see Ḥayyim Schirman, "Ha-Pulmos shel Shelomoh Bonafed be-Nikbede Saragosah," *Qobeṣ ᶜal Yad* 4 (14) (1946):19. On the entire subject, see Saperstein, "Pesach."

Despite the longer liturgies, in many congregations sermons were given on the holidays themselves. Many thirteenth- and fourteenth-century authors refer to their own holiday sermons or cite passages from others'. Some holiday sermons, such as those for New Year's Day by Abraham ben David (RaBaD) of Posquières and Moses ben Naḥman (Naḥmanides), are among the few sermons by these authors that have been preserved. Anatoli's indication of how his discourses could be used as sermons for the first and seventh days of Passover or the beginning and end of the Feast of Booths shows that these were recognized preaching occasions.[18]

The earliest work in which actual holiday sermons are regularly interspersed in the proper place among the weekly lessons appears to be a manuscript written by a disciple of Asher ben Jehiel. It contains sermons for Purim, Passover, the Feast of Weeks (Shabuᶜot), the beginning and end of the Feast of Booths, and the Festival of Rejoicing in the Law (Simḥat Torah). Collections of holiday sermons independent of the Torah lesson come later; the earliest is apparently the manuscript of Ephraim ha-Darshan from the middle of the fifteenth century. The author had accepted the challenge of writing a sermon for each holiday based on Song of Songs 3:6, *mi zot ᶜolah min ha-midbar* (*Who is this that comes up out of the wilderness?*), and the first part of the manuscript contains the resulting sermons for Purim, the Sabbath preceding Passover, the first and second day of the Feast of Weeks, New Year's Day, the Day of Atonement, and the first day of the Feast of Booths. By the sixteenth century, books of sermons organized around the holiday cycle were not at all uncommon.[19]

The most concentrated period of preaching occurred during the month of

18. See Twersky, pp. 111–12, and Hurvitz, "Śeridim," p. 34–42, on Abraham ben David of Posquières's sermons for Passover (actually probably delivered on the preceding Sabbath) and the Day of Atonement, as well as the lost holiday sermons of other Provençal and Spanish preachers. To those noted by Hurvitz, add Shem Ṭob ibn Shapruṭ's sermon for Passover (Ravitsky, "Zehuto," p. 158), and Mattathias Yizhari's sermon for the Feast of Weeks (*Perush Alef-Bet,* ed. Dov Rappel [Tel Aviv, 1978), p. 62). Immanuel of Rome listed among his laurels that he "preached on the Day of Atonement" (*Maḥberot,* ed. Dov Jarden [Jerusalem, 1957], 1:24). For early sermons preserved, see RABaD, *R.H.* (and the review by Isadore Twersky in *Kiryat Sefer* 32 [1957]:440–43); *RaMBaN,* 1:211–52; Anatoli, pp. 56b, 94a, 185a, 189a.

19. Anonymous, "Disciple of R. Asher," fols. 71r, 91v, 104v, 146v, 153r, 155r (Jacob ben Hananel also has model sermons for the New Year's Day, the Day of Atonement, and Simḥat Torah); Ephraim ha-Darshan, fols. 2v, 3r, 6r, 15r, 29r, 45r, 53r, 60r (these sermons were not necessarily preached; the author states that he finished writing what had been agreed and showed it to his patron, who was pleased with the work [fol. 68r]). The distinction between a collection of sermons arranged according to the weekly lesson and one arranged according to the holidays would correspond roughly to the distinction in Christian works between sermons *de tempore* and sermons *de sanctis* or *de festis* (Lecoy de la Marche, p. 272; H. D. Smith, p. 30).

Tishri in the fall. Solomon Levi, a rabbi temperamentally incapable of ignoring any opportunity to preach, left records of sermons delivered on the first and second mornings of the new year as an introduction to the shofar ritual, on the Sabbath of Repentance (two different sermons in 1574), on the evening of the Day of Atonement "before the singing of [the] Kol Nidre [prayer]," during the Day of Atonement itself (again twice in 1574: early in the morning service and before the additional service [Musaf]), on the first, second, seventh, eighth, and ninth days of the Feast of Booths. Such indefatigable devotion to pulpit discourse cannot have been typical (Solomon indeed indicates that most rabbis did not preach as frequently or as regularly as he did), but even the somewhat less rigorous schedule of his colleagues must have been extremely demanding.[20]

After the conclusion of the Feast of Booths in the fall, sermons were less frequent, but in the spring another period of intense preaching began with the Sabbath preceding Passover, going on to the first and second days of Passover, the intermediate Sabbath, and the seventh and eighth days of Passover. Other documented occasions for holiday preaching include the Sabbath during Hanukkah, Purim, the Sabbath preceding the Feast of Weeks and the first and second days of that festival, the Ninth of Ab, and the first day of the month of Elul, the beginning of the forty-day period of repentance that culminates in the Day of Atonement.[21]

In addition to the ordinary holiday cycle, there were special occasions, both happy and sad, that called for preaching. The return of a community leader from an important and possibly perilous mission, the deliverance of the community from danger, the dedication of a new public building or the return of such a building to Jewish jurisdiction, appointment to a new rabbinical position, completion of a book or a unit of study, and other such occasions would often inspire celebratory preaching expressing proper gratitude to God.[22] Again, threats and tragedies resulting from either human oppression or natural forces rarely failed to produce sermons of ethical rebuke, in which the congregation was called upon to repent and ask God's forgiveness.

The frequent references to pestilence or drought scattered through the literature of Jewish preaching convey the deep distress of preacher and listener alike. In such bad times rabbinical leaders frequently ordained days of public

20. *Dibre Shelomoh,* pp. 159c, 160a (cf. 59c, 292a, 293a); 63b–c, 161c, 222a–b, 296a–b, 67c–d.

21. See the material excerpted in Eisenstein, *Derashot.*

22. Return: see Ephraim ha-Darshan, fol. 148v; Almosnino, sermon translated below. Deliverance: see *Dibre Shelomoh,* pp. 191c–92d. Dedication: see Moscato, no. 16, p. 47a; Alfalas, no. 16, p. 137a; Modena, *Midbar,* no. 11, p. 55b; Rapoport, pp. 69a–75a (75 is misnumbered 71); *Sermoẽs.* New position: see Benevento, fol. 77; Figo, no. 32, pt. 2, p. 1. Book: Alfalas, no. 5, p. 45b (*Ho'il Mosheh*); Figo, no. 33, pt. 2, p. 5b (*Gedole Terumah*).

fasting and prayer. The role of the sermon in these observances is attested to by a passing remark of Jacob ibn Ḥabib: "I have dwelt somewhat at length on this rabbinic statement because its content is beautifully appropriate for the elder who goes before the lectern to admonish the people on a public fast, especially when they go out from the synagogue to pray in the open part of the city or in the cemetery."[23]

The eighteenth century produced a new development: the day of public celebration or sorrow instituted not by the Jewish community but by the national government, and observed by the Jews as part of the larger body politic. The first Jewish sermon printed in English was delivered (in Spanish) at the Sephardic synagogue in London by Isaac Nieto on Friday, February 6, 1756, "the day appointed by Authority for a General Fast" inspired by the earthquake that had devastated Lisbon a few months before.[24]

Four of the sermons delivered by Hirschel Levin during his tenure as rabbi of the Great Synagogue of London were occasioned by national days of convocation linked with the events of the Seven Years' War. They discuss subjects such as why kings go to war for reasons that seem so trivial, and why it is appropriate to rejoice at a military victory in which thousands of human beings have perished. The sermon of public thanksgiving was becoming a recognized genre. Moses Mendelssohn's sermon after the victory of Leuthen was delivered in Berlin by David Fränkel, published in German, and then immediately translated into English and published in London. Azulai describes what happened in the synagogue on the *Bededag* (day of public prayer), that he witnessed in Holland early in 1777. Political events of various types would now inspire Jewish preaching alongside the more traditional dates in the calendar.[25]

23. Jacob ibn Ḥabib, *En Yaʿaqob* on P. Taʿan 2:3 (cited by Zunz, p. 518, n. 47). Preaching in the context of public prayer on a day of fasting was an ancient tradition, now exemplified by three recently published sermon texts from the Cairo Genizah: see Wieder, p. 21. For late medieval preaching in time of pestilence, see Moses ben Joab in Cassuto, "Rabbino," pp. 33–37; Alkabeẓ, fol. 54r; Zahalon, p. 26. For Christian preaching in time of pestilence, see Owst, *Preaching*, pp. 206–09, and cf. the two sermons of Father Paneloux in Camus's *The Plague* (New York, 1948), pp. 86–91, 200–06.

24. Isaac Nieto (for a discussion of his works, see Israel Solomons, *David Nieto* [London, 1931], app. pp. 78–83). The London *Daily Advertiser* of Saturday, Feb. 7, 1756, reported that "there were the greatest Crowds at most of the Churches, both in London and Westminster, ever known on any Occasion. The Jews Yesterday had public Worship at their several Synagogues" (p. 1, col. 1). Nieto's sermon, in the classic Sephardic form, addresses the subject of repentance in the face of God's judgment, and ends with a prayer for the king.

25. Levin, sermon translated below, and fol. 23v. On Mendelssohn's sermon, see Altmann, p. 68, and the section, "Sermons and History," below; Azulai, p. 132. For other occasional sermons, see Landau, "Hesped," and Cecil Roth, *Magna Bibliotheca Anglo-Judaica* (London, 1937), pp. 322–35, 437. On the sermon of Gershom Mendes Seixas for Thanksgiving 1789 (republished by the Jewish Historical Society of New York, 1977), see Raphael Mahler, "Ya-

The other major preaching occasions were linked with the ceremonies of the life cycle: circumcisions (*berit milah*), weddings, and funerals. The custom of preaching at a circumcision, although apparently without a halakic justification, was well established in the thirteenth century from northern Europe to southern Babylonia. Nine of the sermons recorded by Joseph Garçon at the beginning of the sixteenth century were given at circumcisions; the Polish rabbi Abraham ha-Kohen Rapaport recorded the sermon that he preached at the circumcision of his son Isaac in 1600, as well as another for a circumcision in Lvov in 1605. The setting for such sermons is not entirely clear. A short discourse may have been given at the actual ceremony or during the festive meal that followed; the longer sermons linked with the Torah lesson were perhaps preached on the Sabbath immediately following the birth, preceding the eighth day, on which the circumcision was performed.[26]

As for sermons at weddings, Abraham ben David of Posquières is said to have made a practice of preaching at the wedding feast, and Jacob Anatoli began his homiletic career with wedding sermons (as we have seen, *Malmad ha-Talmidim* contains the sermon he wrote for his daughter's wedding). Criticism of wedding sermons begins early. In the middle of the thirteenth century preachers at "feasts of religious obligation," primarily wedding celebrations, were being denounced for ranging too far afield and not limiting their material to subjects appropriate for the occasion. At the beginning of the following century, attacks against improper sermons delivered at wedding feasts were a recurring motif in the conflict over philosophy.[27]

The appropriate context for the wedding sermons was also a matter of ongoing dispute. Nissim Gerondi noted the prevalent custom of preaching at weddings, but he urged that it be done privately, in the house where the wedding was held, not in public. Two generations later, Simeon ben Ṣemaḥ Duran argued that in his time the atmosphere of the wedding feast was no longer appropriate for preaching. He therefore concluded, "It is better for the custom to be changed today, better to preach in the synagogue before the feast, so that the place of the feast will be left to the ignorant with their

---

hadut Ameriqah we-Raᶜyon Shibat Ṣiyyon bi-Tequfat ha-Mahpekah ha-Ameriqanit," *Zion* 15 (1950):106–34.

26. For thirteenth-century Europe, including the texts of three circumcision sermons, see Elbaum, "Derashot Ashkenaziyot," p. 341; for Babylonia, Isaac Śar Shalom, fols. 1v, 10r, 41r, 64r, 71r, 73r, 74v. For Garçon, see Hacker, "Li-Demutam," pp. 66–67; Rapoport, p. 53c (before 48d). On the setting in the synagogue, see Garçon, in Benayahu, p. 186. Cf. Abraham Portaleone's epilogue to *Shilṭe Gibborim* (Jerusalem, 1970), p. 185c, where he states that he kept a record of every circumcision that he performed, including not only the names and dates but also the "theme-verse of the sermon" delivered.

27. RABaD of Posquières: Hurvitz, "Śeridim," p. 36; Anatoli, introduction. For attacks, see Saperstein, *Decoding*, p. 183; *Minḥat Qenaʾot*, pp. 31, 134; En Duran, p. 147 (see "Sources").

licentious speech." At the end of the fifteenth century the wedding sermon was generally given in the synagogue on the Sabbath following the ceremony.[28]

The preacher at a wedding could be the groom, or the father of the groom or of the bride, if suitably qualified. At the beginning of the eighteenth century it was lamented that grooms were no longer capable of delivering an appropriate discourse themselves, perhaps an indication that this practice had been the norm.[29]

Unlike the circumcision and the wedding sermons, the funeral eulogy had ancient roots in Judaism. It was extensively discussed in the Talmud and had a clear halakic status. Medieval developments created new occasions for the eulogy outside the burial service. In the early sixteenth century an Italian rabbi wrote from Jerusalem, "I have preached many sermons, both in the synagogue and in the cemetery, for their custom upon the death of a scholar is to preach at the burial, on the seventh day, on the thirtieth day, and at the end of the year." If the deceased was a noted scholar, sermons might be delivered each day during the week beginning with the burial.[30]

Nor were eulogies limited to the place where the death had occurred. When news arrived that a distinguished scholar had died in a distant land, local rabbis frequently preached eulogies in his honor. This became one of the most important and widely represented genres of Jewish preaching. It developed its own literary conventions, such as the *qinah,* a lament or complaint which the preacher articulates as if it were spoken by the widow, the children, and the disciples of the deceased and eventually answers in a contrived yet sometimes dramatic dialogue. Occasionally intense emotion bursts through the conventional forms, and we sense the power of the preacher's grief. But even when this does not happen, the eulogy is a valuable resource for understanding both the contemporary image of various historical personalities and popular attitudes toward death.[31]

28. Nissim Gerondi, p. 97. Duran, *Magen Abot* on Abot 3:3 (Leipzig, 1855), p. 42a, cited in RABaD, *R.H.*, pp. 11–12; cf. Israel Bruna, *Teshubot,* no. 231 (Salonika, 1803), p. 94b. Israel, "Dober Mesharim," fol. 33 (actually delivered on the final day of the wedding week, presumably at a festive meal); cf. Garçon, in Benayahu, p. 149.

29. *Ori we-Yishᶜi, Ṣedaqah,* end of chap. 13, p. 84c.

30. On the eulogy in the talmudic period, a convenient starting point is *The Tractate "Mourning,"* ed. and trans. Dov Zlotnick (New Haven, 1966), p. 19, and index, s.v. "Eulogy"; cf. Naḥmanides' *Torat ha-ʾAdam* in *Kitbe RaMBaN* 2:80–94. On the location, see Israel of Perugia, in Yaari, *Iggerot,* p. 173; cf. Garçon, in Benayahu, p. 152 ("*be-bet ha-ḥayyim,*" and cf. p. 175, l. 1), and Azulai, p. 61 ("in the house next to the cemetery"). For Christian preaching in cemeteries, see Longère, p. 175. For daily preaching during the week following the funeral, see Garçon, in Benayahu, p. 147; Hacker, "Li-Demutam," p. 87; Azulai, p. 8. Sermons were also delivered at the end of the thirty-day mourning period and on the first anniversary of the death (Israel, "Dober Mesharim," fol. 233v; Pachter, "Demuto," p. 24, n. 10).

31. For examples of the *qinah,* see Garçon, in Benayahu, pp. 145, 154, 178; cf. the

The length of a sermon was related to its occasion and context. As noted above, a sermon preached on Saturday afternoon an hour before Minḥah could be more extensive than one given during the morning service, and congregations were generally willing to sit still longer on the Sabbath of Repentance than at other times in the year. Furthermore, tastes and tolerance changed. While a thirteenth-century Dominican praised the Jews for their ability to listen to long sermons without becoming bored, editors in the seventeenth century pointed to the brevity of Morteira's sermons as one of their great assets, "appealing to the listeners of our time, who are unable to comprehend anything too long."[32]

Preachers frequently reveal an awareness of time constraints, telling their audience that they will not be able to discuss a certain subject at length, or noting to themselves in their manuscripts, "If there is time, include the following." Solomon Levi had prepared a full sermon for the Day of Atonement in 1571 but was compelled to cut his text short, "for there was not time to preach it in its entirety, as I was obliged to pray with the large congregation all the prayers of the day." One rabbi, discussing the legal question whether it was permissible to wear a watch on the Sabbath, stated, "I have seen in a number of communities that even scholars preaching in public will take out a watch."[33]

Specific statements about the length of sermons are rare. Jonathan Eybeschuetz reveals the prevailing indifference to precise time measurements in emphasizing how important he considers "the hour or two in which I am preaching these words of ethical instruction to you." Azulai is the only listener who regularly recorded the length of sermons. Three-quarters of an hour is the most frequent length for a Sabbath sermon, although his own preaching sometimes continued for "more than an hour" or even for an hour and a half. Once, upon arriving in the synagogue of a new community, he was implored to preach without preparation. After taking fifteen minutes to collect his thoughts, he was able to preach "for about half an hour from what I could remember." When Azulai heard Jacob Saraval preach a highly rhe-

---

description of the eulogy given by the Maggid of Minsk in Zalman Shazar (S. Z. Rubashow), *Morning Stars* (Philadelphia, 1967), pp. 67–68. Bibliographical studies of later Jewish eulogies were done by Jellinek, *Bibliographie,* and Wachstein, *Bibliographie* and *Randbemerkungen.* On medieval Christian funeral sermons, see Owst, *Preaching,* pp. 265–68; D'Avray, p. 80; and the important article by Powell and Fletcher; cf. also the interesting treatment of funeral sermons and their parody by Gilman, pp. 50–60.

32. Humbert of Romans, in Tugwell, p. 280 (the basis for his statement is the biblical account in Neh. 8:3, not his observation of contemporary Jews). Morteira, intro., p. 19b.

33. *Dibre Shelomoh,* p. 63c; Meir Eisenstadt, *Panim Me'irot* (Lemberg, 1899), no. 123, 2:61b (cited by Pollack, pp. 167–68). Cf. the use of the hourglass by seventeenth-century Christian preachers (Chandos, pp. 325–26, n. 3; MacLure, pp. 3, 8).

torical weekday eulogy for "about three hours," he in no way criticized its length as excessive.[34]

The language in which the sermons were preached remains a matter of controversy. Most of the scholars who have examined the material have assumed that they were delivered in the vernacular. Leopold Zunz, who had a polemical ax to grind, says that "there is no need to say that these sermons were delivered everywhere in the language of the country understood by the preacher and the congregation." Bettan states categorically that "while these sermons have been preserved for us in the Hebrew, they were spoken in the vernacular." More recently, scholars writing about Poland and Italy have reached similar conclusions.[35]

By contrast, Joseph Dan has argued that many sermons preserved in Hebrew were preached in Hebrew. While not denying that Jews did at times preach in the vernacular, he insists that "the rules governing and guiding the structural and aesthetic forms of such sermons in other languages are totally different from the rules of the Hebrew sermon." According to Dan, the vernacular sermon is on a lower level and directed toward a congregation with minimal education. It offers information without the rhetorical and aesthetic refinements of Jewish preaching at its best. The "true" Jewish sermon requires a knowledge of the classical Jewish sources (Bible, rabbinic literature) in the original. If the congregation has such knowledge, "There is no need for a vernacular sermon."[36]

34. Eybeschuetz, 1:90d; Azulai, pp. 133, 135, 145, 131, 61, 99, 102, 8. (Cf. Reuben Brainin, *Fun Mayn Lebensbukh* [New York, 1946], p. 296, on Ḥayyim Maccoby, the Maggid of Kamenets.) The eulogy was not expected to be as long as the regular sermon; see Katzenellenbogen, no. 5, p. 15b. The ordinary Christian sermon in the seventeenth century could run an hour (see Bayley, p. 16; and George Herbert, "The Country Parson," in *The Works of George Herbert,* ed. F. E. Hutchinson [Oxford, 1964], p. 235), but this was extended to an hour and a half or two hours for special occasions (MacLure, pp. 13, 8). Vincent Ferrer was said to have preached between two and six hours (Deyermond, p. 132).

35. Zunz, p. 197; cf. pp. 200, 201, 518, n. 48. Bettan, p. 57, qualified on p. 195: Moscato "presumably [preached] in his native tongue, though some of them might well have been preached in their present Hebrew form." Ben Sasson, *Hagut,* p. 39: "When said orally, their language was Yiddish interspersed with Hebrew and Aramaic." Bonfil, *Rabbanut,* p. 192: "Except for those sermons delivered in closed circles of scholars or preached by guest sages who did not know the local language, there is no doubt that during our entire period [the fifteenth and sixteenth centuries] the sermons were delivered in the vernacular." Cecil Roth, writing about the Renaissance, affirmed that Moscato preached "in mellifluous Italian" (*Renaissance,* p. 36), but when writing about the Hebrew language he concluded that Azulai "must have spoken in Hebrew [while in Pesaro], and . . . his audience understood" (*Pesonalities and Events in Jewish History* [Philadelphia, 1953], pp. 39–40).

36. Dan, *Sifrut,* pp. 45–46; cf. Dan, "Tefillah we-Dimʿah," p. 209: "The linguistic aspect of the sermon's structure proves that it could have been delivered only in the Hebrew language"; *EJ* 12:358: "It is possible that Moscato preached both in Hebrew and in Italian. . . . However, the sermons collected in *Nefuṣot* were undoubtedly delivered in Hebrew."

Considering the importance of the question, the actual evidence is meager. The few passages in which contemporaries refer to the language of delivery have been frequently cited: Montaigne's statement that Jewish sermons in Italy were delivered in Italian, Modena's assertion that he and his colleagues preached "in the language of the country that all the congregation may understand them." Azulai is also helpful. He tells us that in Genoa, "I preached for about an hour and a half in the Spanish language." Similarly, Saraval preached "in the Gentile tongue," and David Leon "in the rhetoric of Portuguese." Nathan of Nemirov reported that Naḥman of Bratslav dictated his sermons (after they had been delivered) in Yiddish, "and I sat before him and transcribed them in Hebrew."[37]

On the other hand, Obadiah of Bertinoro reported from Jerusalem that "I preach to the congregation here twice a month in the synagogue in the holy tongue [i.e., Hebrew], for most of them understand the holy tongue." This sentence tells us three things: preaching in Hebrew was indeed possible; it was apparently unusual enough to comment on it in a letter to Italy; and not all of the congregation understood spoken Hebrew even in Jerusalem. More than a century later, in 1621, Isaiah ha-Levi Horowitz tells us that he came to Aleppo, and "Whenever I preached there, I preached in the holy tongue."[38]

A second kind of contemporary evidence comes from reports that quote the sermons. Writing in the middle of the fifteenth century in Spain, Ḥayyim ibn Mūsā described a sermon that he heard, in which the preacher maintained that the phrase *et shabbetotai tishmoru* (*You shall keep My Sabbaths,* Lev. 19:3) meant "You shall keep My insignificant things, *las mis cosas baldías,* heaven help us!" The Spanish phrase, which is in Hebrew transcription in the middle of a letter written in Hebrew, is apparently an attempt to cite what was said verbatim. The same is true of the 1598 letter of Israel Sforno, complaining

37. Montaigne, in *The Diary of Montaigne's Journey to Italy,* ed. E. J. Trechmann (New York, 1929), p. 134; Modena, *Riti,* see "Sources." At the beginning of the nineteenth century Jacob Recanati of Pesaro tells us that sermons "are said in Italian in order that the women, children, and others who do not understand Hebrew may listen and learn. However, sayings of our sages, and biblical passages cited as proof texts, are said in Hebrew and explained and clarified in good Italian, either before or after they are said in Hebrew" (*Ya'ir Natib,* cited by Alexander Guttmann, *The Struggle over Reform in Rabbinic Literature* [New York, 1977], pp. 182–83). Azulai, pp. 99, 8, 145. His explicit statement that he preached in Spanish (or Ladino) in Genoa undermines Roth's argument noted above, n. 35. To send on a fund-raising mission from the land of Israel an emissary who could communicate only in Hebrew, and whose appeal would thus not have been fully understood by many of the potential donors, would not have been much more sensible in the eighteenth century than it would be today. Nathan of Nemirov, *Yeme MaHaRNaT* (Bene Beraq, 1956), 1:5, cited in Rapoport-Albert, p. 257. Bernard Cooperman has drawn my attention to an inquisitional document from Pisa, 1600, in which a Spanish-speaking Jew explains that "in all of the Levant, our rabbis preach only in Spanish" (*Archivio Arcivescovile Pisano, Inquisizione,* 3:403a and 405a).

38. Yaari, *Iggerot,* pp. 141–42, 214.

about the use of mythology in public preaching. To illustrate the problem, he points out that a recent sermon had included the phrase *quella Santa Diana.*[39]

The most important source of evidence—the texts of the sermons—have not been systematically reviewed for clues about language. Perhaps the earliest collection of Jewish sermons identified by place and date of delivery is the manuscript called "Maṭṭeh ʿOz," by Isaac Śar Shalom. These Arabic sermons written in Hebrew letters were given in southern Babylonia between 1210 and 1232. All biblical and rabbinic quotations are in Hebrew, without translation, and the discourse passes fluidly from one language to the other. The same is true of the sermons of David ha-Nagid, Maimonides' grandson, which date from the second half of the thirteenth century.[40] There is little doubt that this linguistic pattern was characteristic of Jewish preaching in Arabic-speaking countries.

The earliest known European examples in the vernacular are Mordecai Dato's Italian sermons from the end of the sixteenth century.[41] The language is entirely macaronic. Not only are the sources quoted in the original, but phrases from a Hebrew verse are interspersed with a word or two of Italian explanation, and Hebrew and Italian elements are integrated into a single phrase. Even a quick glance at the recently published version, which uses roman letters for the Italian and Hebrew letters for the Hebrew, shows how natural the flow was. These sermons were obviously intended for an audience that spoke Italian but was sufficiently literate in Hebrew to appreciate a discussion of the intricacies of Hebrew scriptural diction, such as the explanation of the significance of adding the letter *heh* to Abram's name.[42]

The first in this collection of Dato's sermons has both a Hebrew and an expanded Italian version. The Italian text is introduced by the words, "And if someone should want to satisfy the desire of the people in the synagogue by speaking in the vernacular, I have it for you in the vernacular, except for the citations [of sacred texts], with some new interpretations." This sentence apparently indicates that at least the first sermon was originally written in

39. For Ibn Mūsā, see "Sources"; for the Israel Sforno letter, see Kaufmann, "Dispute," p. 519.

40. Isaac Śar Shalom. Cf. David ha-Nagid: a comparison of the photograph of the manuscript following the introduction with the corresponding translation on p. 29 shows the macaronic nature of the language.

41. The Ladino sermon in MS Adler 973 in the Jewish Theological Seminary Library may indeed be earlier than Dato's work. It was delivered in the "Portuguese Congregation" (of Salonika?) on the first day of Elul, but the year is not clearly legible. The macaronic nature of this text can be seen in phrases such as "*la maʿalah de la teshubah*" (fol. 2r), "*el pasuq*" (fols. 2r, 3v, 5v): "*el yeṣer ha-raʿ*" (fol. 4v), "*el yom del taʿanit*" (fol. 4v).

42. Bonfil, "Dato."

Hebrew and then rewritten in a form appropriate for preaching in an Italian synagogue.[43]

Beginning in the seventeenth century, the number of sermons preserved in the vernacular (especially Italian, Spanish, and Portuguese), both in printed editions and in manuscript, increases dramatically.[44] But from the early thirteenth century, when the first sermons written by European Jews begin, until the end of the sixteenth century, not a single known vernacular sermon text has been preserved. Assuming vernacular delivery, why is there no documentary evidence for it?

The obvious explanation is also a compelling one. Before the middle of the sixteenth century European Jews rarely wrote anything in the vernacular. While they spoke and used the vernacular in their business affairs, few read it, and Jewish scribes were not trained to copy it. With relatively few exceptions, Hebrew was the language of Jewish literary creativity in this period. Preachers who took the trouble to write a sermon in a permanent form would want it to be accessible to all Jewish people, beyond the borders of their own country and the group that was literate in a given vernacular. It is therefore fully understandable that sermons delivered in Spanish or Italian would be written down in Hebrew.[45]

But this explanation does not resolve all the outstanding questions. First, there are parts of written sermons that could not be Hebrew rewritings of a vernacular text. The sermon by Israel of Bełżyce translated below is framed by passages in rhymed Hebrew prose calling upon God to avenge the blood of those massacred by the Cossacks. The emotional energy behind these words is so dependent upon the occasion that they could hardly have been incorporated as an afterthought. Yet the literary form makes it extremely unlikely that this passage could be a translation from the vernacular. If most of the original sermon was delivered in Yiddish, these sections, at least, must have been declaimed as they appear—in Hebrew.[46]

43. Dato, fol. 3v; Jacobson, p. 106. For an example of a Christian sermon of which both a vernacular and a Latin version are extant, see Spencer.

44. Bibliography is given by Zunz, pp. 526–28, nn. 63–64, and Roth, *Magna Bibliotheca Anglo-Judaica* (London, 1937), pp. 322–25. Comparison of the Italian sermons of Dato and those of Moscato's *Nefuṣot Yehudah,* or of the Portuguese *Sermoẽs* and Morteira's *Gibᶜat Shaʾul* or Pardo would, I believe, sustain the assertion that the homiletical tradition is unified and not bifurcated on linguistic (Hebrew/vernacular) lines.

45. Medieval Christian homiletical literature also provides examples of sermons delivered in the vernacular but immediately transcribed or subsequently written in Latin; see Longère, pp. 161–64; Zink, p. 91; D'Avray, pp. 94–95. In a sermon that has been preserved only in Latin, Bonaventure apologizes for the poor French he is speaking (Longère, p. 163).

46. For Christian examples of rhymed prose in preaching, see Owst, *Preaching,* pp. 273–78; Catédra, p. 17. (The rhymed prose introductions of Ephraim ha-Darshan may have been written as literary exercises and were not necessarily delivered in the form in which they appear.)

Second, we have seen that some of the Hebrew texts were written before delivery and then not used as intended. In such cases we would have to assume either that they were written in Hebrew with the intention of being delivered in the vernacular, or that the author rewrote his vernacular in Hebrew. The first assumption is not entirely implausible. One mode of Christian homiletical preparation was to write out the full text of the sermon beforehand and then put aside the manuscript during the actual delivery so as to achieve a more spontaneous effect. But a change in language during the delivery would have been rather awkward. Assuming the existence of a vernacular text only leads back to the original question: why has none of these texts survived?[47]

Tentative conclusions are, first, that preaching in Hebrew was an option, as the letters of Bertinoro and Horowitz show, although it seems not to have been the norm. Outside the land of Israel it was probably reserved for unusual occasions. Second, the preacher was free to use Hebrew, the vernacular, or any mixture of the two. In a vernacular sermon, sources were almost always cited in the original, and whether or not they were translated depended on the preacher and his congregation.[48] Hebrew technical terms and familiar phrases could also be retained. Third, the aesthetic texture of some Jewish preaching—the plays on words from a biblical or rabbinic passage, the links between disparate statements based on a novel interpretation of a Hebrew phrase, the humorous interpretations—requires a considerable level of Hebrew education to appreciate, but it does not require that the sermon be delivered in Hebrew.[49] It does not at all follow that because many people in the congregation knew enough Hebrew to appreciate this homiletical style, preaching in Hebrew was naturally preferred. A more plausible assumption is that Hebrew was used for preaching whenever it was necessary, not whenever it was possible.

Finally, Jewish preaching is much more than just homiletical interpretations that require knowledge of Hebrew to appreciate. Many sermons pre-

47. There are reports that Innocent III once preached in Italian by extemporaneously translating a Latin homily by Gregory the Great (Humbert of Romans, in Tugwell, p. 208), but this is not the same as writing one's own text in the classical language to be preached in the vernacular.

48. One of the oldest literary works in Catalan, the *Homílies d'Organyà,* is a collection of sermons from around the year 1200 in which all biblical quotations are given in Latin and then immediately translated; see Molho. For other studies on the Christian "macaronic" sermon, see Lecoy de la Marche, pp. 253–59, and Erb. Catédra, pp. 16–17, concludes that "Preaching exclusively in Latin occurred in very special cases; for example, with an audience of High Church culture, such as a sermon to the pope." Cf. also D'Avray, p. 94.

49. Christian preachers were also capable of considerable linguistic wordplay using the Latin original in a vernacular sermon. A particularly striking example is Lancelot Andrewes' treatment of "Immanuel"; see Chandos, pp. 203–07.

served in Hebrew can be translated back into a vernacular language without destroying or even seriously damaging their aesthetic texture. Where preaching did presume a high level of traditional Jewish education, some congregants would have missed the finer points, but they would not necessarily have left the synagogue disappointed. Effective preachers could discuss problems related to Jewish belief, criticize prevalent patterns of behavior, tell parables that unexpectedly illuminated conceptual conundrums, and even explicate and apply biblical verses in such a way that listeners with little Hebrew and less Aramaic might be edified, instructed, and entertained. A few in each congregation were satisfied only by brilliant and original insights into the classical texts, and such insights often depended on mastery of the languages in which these texts were written. But dismissing everything else as alien to the true Jewish sermon imposes an arbitrary criterion of authenticity. The sources reveal many more ways of pleasing.

The Preachers and Their Congregations

It is risky to generalize about preachers in Jewish society. Just as Christian preachers in the late Middle Ages included not only priests and deacons but also "monks and Mendicants, University graduates in theology, vicars, chaplains, pardoners and recluses, even the Templar and the Hospitaller,"[1] Jewish preachers came from a wide array of different backgrounds. Even in the thirteenth century, for which the least evidence exists, we know of preaching by distinguished rabbinic scholars (Moses ben Naḥman, Moses of Coucy), by men without rabbinic credentials whose expertise had been established in other fields (Anatoli), and by relatively uneducated Jews who spoke in a semiecstatic mode or used magical techniques (a "Preaching Name") to astound rabbis with their brilliance.[2] We hear of preachers whom the rationalists denounced as intolerably ignorant and preachers whom the traditionalists attacked as dangerously heretical. Their social position ranges from the aristocracy to the marginal, the disenfranchised, and the destitute.

1. Owst, *Preaching*, p. 1.

2. See Solomon Adret (RaSHBA), *Teshubot* 1, no. 548, on "the prophet of Avila." The *Shem ha-Doresh* ("Preaching Name"), which apparently induced a kind of automatic preaching, was composed from the letters of the first three verses of Deut. 32, according to the fourteenth-century Spanish kabbalist Abraham ben Isaac of Granada (*Berit Menuḥah* [Warsaw, 1883], p. 55b–c). It was known to, and possibly used by, the seventeenth-century Polish kabbalist Samson of Ostropole (see Yehudah Liebes, "Ḥalom u-Meṣiʾut," *Tarbiẓ* 52 [1983]:92 and n. 41). According to Adret (in the same responsum), a certain Abraham of Cologne, apparently not a rabbi, who came to Spain and preached in the synagogue of Adret's father, was able to stand at one end of the synagogue and preach through a voice emanating from the Ark on the opposite side, purportedly the voice of the prophet Elijah.

After an exhaustive survey of the homiletical literature of eighteenth-century Poland, Mendel Piekarz has concluded that

> The image of the preacher of rebuke [*maggid-mokiaḥ*] is many-faceted and variegated. Sometimes . . . he began as a rabbi and ended as a preacher, sometimes the reverse; sometimes he was both a preacher and a judge or rabbi, sometimes a talmudic scholar impelled to preach by a specific need. Some were preachers for a particular community, appointed to their position by the congregation, who occasionally left their homes and traveled around preaching to other communities. Others were preachers without public appointment, wandering from town to town and uttering their rebukes at every stop, whether from a spontaneous quickening of the spirit, or because they had no other livelihood, or because a personal experience of repentance constrained them to lead others to repent.
>
> There was the talmudic scholar supported by communal funds for giving lectures to various associations of middle-class gentlemen or workers. There was the revered artist with extraordinary power to enthrall his listeners, capable of making hearts tremble and arousing the living conscience of the nation to self-scrutiny, flaying the high and the mighty with verbal chastisements while he himself retained a position of utmost respect. And there was the preacher devoid of any semblance of learning or homiletical art, an object of mockery and scorn. There was the charismatic personality, the ascetic pietist whose leadership was based on the religious and ethical demands of Lurianic Kabbalah as expressed in the literature of pietism; and there was the talmudic scholar, cautious and balanced, who viewed every departure from his way as extremism and waged battle against the tendencies toward religious radicalism in all its manifestations, against every attempt to challenge age-old patterns of living and belief.
>
> There was the preacher under indictment, in whose voice the poison of Sabbatian heresy quivered, or toward whom the accusing finger was pointed for revealing what God had concealed (though he himself was devoid of true wisdom) and there was the scholar who avoided all discussion of esoteric matters. Some spread the message of the new Hasidism, others inspired opposition to its social and ideological tendencies, and still others enthusiastically preached a wedding of external learning and Torah before the crystallization of the Haskalah in eastern Europe.[3]

Although the source material for preceding centuries is not nearly so rich as that available to Piekarz, there is no reason to assume that earlier the picture had been fundamentally different.

3. Piekarz, pp. 169–70.

The basis of the preacher's authority remained a problem that defied simple solutions. In medieval Christendom, access to the pulpit was jealously guarded. License to preach was limited to those in official positions; for a layman to preach was considered a mortal sin. Even when the privilege was extended beyond priests and deacons, the principle that only specially designated individuals had authority to preach was never successfully challenged before the Reformation, when it was challenged by a similarly unambiguous claim that the preacher was called by God to preach God's word.[4]

The position of the Jewish preacher was less clearly defined. Like his Christian colleague, he was invested with an aura of authority that other disseminators of ideas must have envied. A book carries with it only the name of the author and the power of its content, but a sermon is rooted in the sancta of the faith and surrounded by its symbols. As we have seen, the preacher frequently spoke in the synagogue as part of the worship service, immediately before or soon after the reading of the lesson from the Torah scroll. Its setting gave a sermon some of the aura of the sacred texts. The ordinary author lacked this advantage.

Yet the basis of the preacher's claim to authority was anything but clear. In the earlier period there was no "license" to preach. In theory (at least) any Jewish male who had something to say was entitled to a turn at the pulpit. The positions created in various communities, such as *marbiṣ Torah* ("teacher of Torah"), *darshan* ("teacher"), *maggid* ("teller"), entailed a contractual *responsibility* to preach without granting any special *authority.* Nor did Jewish preachers ordinarily claim that God had called them to speak.

This ambiguity created special problems both for the preacher and for the community. From the preacher's perspective it meant that there was no escaping the question "By what right does he say this?" It may not have been pressed when the preacher was a rabbi with a distinguished reputation as a talmudic scholar, although even then the authority from the decision of a rabbinic court or a legal responsum did not automatically transfer to the pulpit.[5] But when a preacher without formal credentials was appointed by the communal leadership to admonish the congregation, or when an unknown itinerant preacher came to town, his vulnerability often became painfully apparent.

Men like Jacob Anatoli and Ephraim Luntshitz describe the powerful op-

4. Owst, *Preaching,* pp. 4, 169–70; Longère, pp. 30–31, 78–86; Smith, p. 19. It was actually somewhat more complicated: see Tugwell, *Way,* pp. 117–31, app. 3: "Grace to Preach; Authority to Preach; Worthiness to Preach."

5. Particularly poignant, if perhaps somewhat naive, are the complaints in the sermons of Ezekiel Landau, perhaps the outstanding legal authority of his age, that the calls for religious regeneration in his sermons are not heeded: *Derushe,* pp. 8a, 15c. Cf. Berechiah Berak, *Zera*ᶜ *Berak Shelishi* (Frankfurt an der Oder, 1735), p. 30a, cited in Dinur, p. 135.

position of listeners who forced them to stop. When an emissary from the land of Israel was denied access to a pulpit in Constantinople, the chief rabbi, Moses Capsali, personally escorted him into the recalcitrant synagogue and defied anyone to prevent him from preaching.[6] The Hebrew slave's disdainful challenge to Moses—*Who made you chief and ruler over us?* (Exod. 2:14)—frequently cited by disgruntled congregants—signifies the tension inherent in the preacher's position.[7] Although many had the right to preach, whoever exercised it was often on the defensive, forced to justify his assumption that others should listen to what he said.

From the community's perspective the problem was one of control. As early as the beginning of the fourteenth century we hear about preachers without an official position or roots in the Jewish community, lacking mastery either of traditional Jewish texts or of philosophical writings, who preached their superficial, farfetched, possibly heretical message and then moved on. Both proponents and opponents of the ban on the study of philosophy agreed that the popular desire for such sermons should not be allowed free rein, but attempts to control the pulpit (in southern France) were stymied.[8]

In seventeenth- and eighteenth-century Poland the burgeoning number of itinerant preachers provoked a firm response. Intercommunal ordinances required that a person have authorization to preach and this *reshut* ("license"), once just a literary convention, now became an institutional reality. Authorization was to be given by the chief judge of the rabbinical court of the region's main city, with the agreement of the city elders, a procedural mechanism that both reflected and added to internal tensions. Yet despite such legislation, complaints abounded that there were "many now traveling from place to place and preaching publicly, both in the synagogue and elsewhere, without the permission and authorization of the chief rabbi of the city and the seven elders." While individuals with established reputations might be exempted from this requirement, the general ordinances provided that "if anyone has the audacity to preach without permission, without a document from the chief judge of the rabbinical court, he should be removed in derision and disgrace."[9]

6. Anatoli, intro., end; Luntshitz, *ʿAmmude,* intro., p. 2a–b; *ʿOlelot,* intro., p. 3b. On the incident involving Capsali, see Yaari, *Sheluḥe,* pp. 216–17; Baron, *SRHJ* 18:41, and 458, n. 48. Cf. also the earlier material cited by Goitein, *Community,* p. 217.

7. Menaḥem Egozi, intro. to *Gal shel Egozim,* cited in Hacker, "Ha-Peʿilut"; Luntshitz, *ʿAmmude,* intro., p. 2b (see "Sources"); Pukhovitser, *Derek Ḥokmah,* intro., l. 12; *Ori we-Yishʿi,* p. 18c (see "Sources").

8. Meiri, in En Duran, p. 167 (see "Sources").

9. *Pinqas Liṭa,* p. 17 (from 1623), and cf. pp. 33 (1628) and 144 (1667). Cf. Baron, *Community,* 2:99. Individuals could be exempted from the requirement of receiving authorization from the local rabbi and lay leadership. One example was Berechiah Berak Getsel (*Pinqas Waʿad,* pp. 478–79).

At least in theory, then, a person needed both to be certified as a qualified preacher by the rabbinic and lay authorities of his home region and to receive permission from the local rabbi. It is not always possible to tell whether the primary impetus behind such restrictions on preaching was to control the spread of radical and heretical teachings, to keep uneducated practitioners from dispensing their ignorance, or merely to retain control over local events. What is clear is that some rabbis welcomed the influence of qualified itinerant preachers, especially in communities without a permanent rabbinic presence,[10] while others were deeply concerned about the blurring of roles when a talented preacher won the people's hearts.

Eliezer Fleckeles of Prague sounded a warning in the introduction to his first collection of sermons:

> We have heard that many perversions have occurred because of experts in the realm of aggadah and enigmatic discourse who appeal to the ignorant, including women and children. They come to hear parables and rhetorical flourishes, and in their enthusiasm for such preachers they will say, "Since you know so much about aggadah, we trust you to teach us." Then they appoint him rabbi and teacher . . . saying, "Since he knows how to preach rebuke so well, let him give halakic rulings." This despite the fact that he has no expertise in talmudic study or in any of the sections of the *Shulḥan ʿAruk*!"[11]

Closely related to the problem of authority was the issue of payment. Where the remuneration for preaching was covered by the rabbi's contract, it was subsumed under the larger questions about the professionalization of the rabbinate. By the late Middle Ages these questions had been more or less resolved. But where an individual was engaged on an annual basis exclusively as a preacher, or where an itinerant preacher received a fee for each sermon, difficulties often arose.

Some opposed paying a preacher because of legal principle, arguing that the rationale for paying a rabbi—compensating him for his neglect of another trade or profession—did not apply. As an early fifteenth-century scholar put it, "One should not say, 'Give me a fee, and I shall preach for you on the Sabbath or on the holidays,' for on Sabbaths and holidays preaching does not

10. Landau, *Derushe,* pp. 24c–25a. He compared such preachers to apothecaries who traveled from town to town hawking their remedies, and thereby benefiting those who had no access to adequate medical care. Cf. Landau's *haskamah* ("approbation") to *Ereṣ Ṣebi* (Prague, 1786), according to which the author, Ṣebi Hirsch, Maggid of Wodzisław, preached in all nine synagogues when he visited Prague.

11. Fleckeles 1, unnumbered p. 3 of intro. Exactly the same fear is expressed in an earlier period in a Genizah letter published by S. D. Goitein, "Dimdume ʿEreb shel bet ha-RaMBaM," *Tarbiẓ* 54 (1984–85):98. Cf. MacLure, p. 93.

require the scholar to miss his work."[12] But the more important objection was ethical. Sensitive moralists feared that such preachers might tailor their message to please the wealthy men on whom they depended, avoiding anything that might offend those who wielded the economic power.

In the middle of the fifteenth century, Joseph ibn Shem Ṭob charged that "most of the preachers of our generation are too obsequious to the people, especially to the powerful. They tell these men that they are righteous, because they are dependent upon them for their livelihood. . . . A Gentile may preach against kings and nobles, proclaiming their sins for all to hear, but in our own nation no one will raise his tongue against any Jew whatsoever, and certainly not if the man is wealthy or a potential benefactor." According to him, the underlying problem was that the preachers were destitute, and his solution was that only those wealthy enough not to fear the consequences of adverse reaction should be allowed to preach. Complaints that economic dependence produced moral cowardice intensified through the following centuries.[13]

Even if a preacher gave proper sermons of rebuke, his motives were often suspect. The smug and the arrogant, disposed to dismiss all criticism, could readily argue that the preacher was interested only in earning a fee. Many thought of the itinerant maggidim as a nuisance and a burden; several intercommunal ordinances link the problem of itinerant preachers with that of vagabond beggars. There were also downright charlatans who claimed to be a well-known maggid in the hope that no one in the community had ever seen him. But even honest itinerant preachers were frequently treated with a condescension bordering on contempt. They might be permitted to entertain and paid the pittance they requested, but their message was not taken seriously.[14]

The itinerant preachers naturally had a very different view of themselves. Unlike their medieval Christian counterparts, they had taken no vow of poverty, and they saw nothing wrong with receiving payment for their work. They saw themselves as men of intelligence, learning, talent, and character forced to spend long periods away from their families in order to provide a

12. Anonymous, "1425," fol. 56v. The many other problems that arose when individuals contracted with a community to preach are evident from the responsa literature (e.g., Adret, *Teshubot* 2, no. 60; 5, no. 273).

13. Joseph ibn Shem Ṭob (see "Sources"); cf. Anatoli, p. 151a; Dresner, pp. 224–25; and Dinur, p. 135.

14. For itinerant preachers and beggars, see *Tosefot Liṭa,* pp. 72–73; *Pinqas Liṭa,* p. 17 (1623). For charlatans, see the stories told about the Maggid of Dubno in Heinemann, *Maggid,* pp. 257–62. For contemptuous treatment, see Aaron ben Isaiah, introduction to *Leḥem Terumah,* discussed in Piekarz, pp. 42–44; *Shibḥe ha-BESHṬ* (Tel Aviv, 1968), p. 85, and *In Praise of the Baal Shem Tov,* ed. Dan Ben Amos and Jerome Mintz (Bloomington, 1970), p. 157; Eidlitz (see n. 17, below).

meager sustenance. They had to endure the dangers of travel to isolated regions, sleep in the public house with outcasts and derelicts, hear the insults of idlers and children who mocked their appearance and mimicked their preaching manner, and suffer the humiliation of asking for payment from wealthy boors who showed little interest in their passionate appeals. It is small wonder that in some circles the itinerant preacher was romanticized as the living symbol of the divine presence in exile, the suffering servant of the Lord, driven to poverty by God precisely so that he would be forced to take to the road and preach repentance to the people.[15] Nor is it surprising that these preachers had a ready response to the charge that accepting payment automatically rendered their motives impure. The comparison between the preacher of rebuke and the physician, a commonplace in Jewish ethical literature, was applied to financial remuneration. The physician's medicine was not less efficacious because it was purchased for a price, and his fee did not depend on the success of his treatment. Even so with the preacher.[16]

A parable attributed to a "Joel Mokiaḥ" exposed the foolishness of those who dismissed the preacher's message because of uncertainty about his motives. A husband and wife occupied a loft in a village where all the houses were made of wood and the roofs were covered with straw. During a dry spell the town crier came around and bellowed out a warning that all should be careful to extinguish their candles before going to sleep, lest a disastrous fire should occur. The husband scoffed at the warning, arguing that the town crier received payment for his work and so had to be insincere. He therefore left the candle to burn and caused a fire that destroyed most of the village. Zerah Eidlitz of Prague, who reported the parable in one of his sermons, concluded that while sincerity is preferable, so long as the preacher does not temper his message because of the payment, his motivation should be of no concern to the listeners.[17]

The Jewish audience also contrasted with its medieval Christian counterpart. With the exception of sermons on important public occasions, which were addressed to all estates, the Christian preacher generally faced a fairly homogeneous audience. A sermon delivered to monks in a monastery or clergy in a university differed in language, structure, and purpose from that designed for a congregation of the laity. Christian preaching manuals often included model sermons for each of the many different groups that might be

15. See especially Mordecai ben Samuel's *Shaʿar ha-Melek* ("Sources"), analyzed by Piekarz, pp. 153–63, and compare the quotation from the introduction to *Ṭohorot ha-Qodesh* cited by Dinur, p. 133.

16. Mordecai ben Samuel, in Piekarz, p. 156. For the Christian use of this comparison, see Humbert of Romans, in Tugwell, p. 189, and MacLure, p. 121.

17. Eidlitz, p. 27a–c, in "Sources."

addressed, and classification of Christian sermons by audience is still used in contemporary scholarship.[18]

The congregation at most Jewish sermons was considerably more diverse, ranging from distinguished rabbis at least as learned as the preacher to those barely capable of mechanical Hebrew reading. Frequently children were present; in Italy attendance at sermons was part of their educational curriculum. Women tried to listen from their gallery seats. Occasionally Christian guests, with varying motivations, stopped by.[19] Moses Alfalas describes three different constituencies in the average congregation: one likes to hear parables and riddles; a second, rabbinic homilies and interpretations; a third, biblical verses and the discussion of legal points.[20] Indeed, the problem of the diversity of the audience, the difficulty of coping with such diversity, and the challenge of satisfying the variety of levels and tastes was reiterated so frequently that it became a homiletical commonplace.

Joseph ibn Shem Ṭob rehearses the various options for a preacher faced with a heterogeneous audience: it is preferable not to divide the sermon into two parts, one addressed to each level, but rather to present an integrated message that will appeal to both groups, so that "the wise will find something new and the masses will understand it." Similarly, Jacob Zahalon counsels in his *Manual for Preachers* that the ideal is to include profound material for the learned, as well as material that appeals even to the women and the young, "so that everyone present may derive some benefit from the sermon." But this was not such a simple task; what it often meant was that each group had something to be dissatisfied with. Such was the thrust of Leon Modena's half-facetious complaint as he introduced his first sermon in the synagogue of Venice: if the preacher "soars like an eagle and speaks of the great and profound mysteries of wisdom," the less educated listeners will be offended by his arrogance; if he speaks "simply and plainly, the learned who hear him will turn their backs and say, 'What does he think he is teaching us?' "[21]

18. Humbert of Romans, in Tugwell, pp. 326–39; Jacques de Vitry, in Crane, p. xxxix; Longère, pp. 145–48. On the public sermon, such as that at Paul's Cross in London, addressed to all estates, see MacLure, pp. v, 121, 144.

19. For children's attendance, see Assaf 2:157, 177, 191; for women's, Zahalon, p. 125; Stadthagen, p. 18a–b; and for Christian visitors', Baer, *HJCS* 2:251; Marx, "Glimpses," pp. 613, 617; Modena, *Ḥayye Yehudah,* in "Sources"; *Medabber Tahpukot,* p. 80; Pardo 2, fol. 82v; Baron, *Community,* 2:98. Jewish Theological Seminary MS 80 reports a speech delivered by Solomon Molcho in the presence of 'men, women, and children, Jews and Christians" (fol. 75r).

20. Alfalas, p. 2b (cf. Pachter, "Sifrut," p. 40, n. 52). On varying tastes within the congregation, cf. Luntshitz, *ʿOlelot* 2, no. 34.

21. Joseph ibn Shem Ṭob, fol. 124r, in "Sources"; cf. Zerahiah ha-Levi, p. 98; Zahalon, pp. 124–25. Modena, *Midbar,* p. 6a–b, in "Sources."

Even faced with such a challenge, though, many preachers were apparently striking successes. Sermons which most modern readers find all but impenetrable had audiences in their day. The following words, written about the preaching of John Donne, can be applied to Jewish congregations as well: "It is difficult . . . to imagine . . . a vast congregation . . . listening not only with patience but with absorbed interest, with unflagging attention, even with delight and rapture, to these interminable disquisitions, to us teeming with laboured obscurity, false and misplaced wit, fatiguing antitheses. . . . Yet there can be no doubt that this was the case."[22]

Nevertheless, an audience's receptiveness was by no means universal and never guaranteed. Listeners could make their displeasure known in various ways. It was apparently not uncommon for the beginning of a sermon to signal an exodus from the synagogue. The sixteenth-century Venetian preacher Samuel Katzenellenbogen, speaking to those who had remained, described three categories of Jews who leave the synagogue after the Tefillah and thereby miss the sermon: those who think of themselves as intellectually superior to the preacher, those who have already heard him preach and are certain that they will hear nothing new, and those who hurry to return to their business affairs. Josiah Pardo, preaching in mid-seventeenth-century Rotterdam, denounced this exit as disgracing the image of Judaism in the minds of the Gentiles.[23]

An early eighteenth-century critic from central Europe castigated those who run around all week, leaving no time for Torah, and then, when the Sabbath comes, "run some more—through the exits of the synagogue—at the time of the sermon, refusing to hear it." With bitter sarcasm he asked, "Is this the running which is the 'merit of attending a lecture?'" (B. Ber 6b). Not only this, he continues (grudgingly recognizing the outlook of those whom he attacks), but the one who gets up to leave also implores his friends to go out with him, saying, "Is it not enough that we are tied up every weekday? Must we be imprisoned on the Sabbath as well?"

22. Henry Hart Milman, cited by Logan Pearsall Smith, *Donne's Sermons* (Oxford, 1964), p. xvii. There is evidence that popular preachers in London outdrew both bearbaiting and Shakespeare (Seaver, p. 5). Cf. Ben-Sasson, *Hagut,* pp. 53–54, on the tastes of seventeenth-century Polish Christian and Jewish audiences, and Hacker, "Ha-Derashah," p. 123.

23. Katzenellenbogen, p. 16b (Cf. Nigal, pp. 82–83); Pardo 1, fol. 76r. Jacob di Alba in Florence enumerated the same three reasons for people's failing to come to hear sermons (Alba, pp. 98b–99a). An interesting rationale for absenting oneself from sermons is also given, and vigorously refuted, in the eighteenth-century text *Binat Yiśśakar,* p. 12a. Cf. Humbert of Romans (in Tugwell, p. 265): "Why People Stay Away from Sermons." One reason for leaving not mentioned by Katzenellenbogen is attested by Solomon Levi: "While I was preaching [on *Ki Tiśśa,* 1573], there was a major earthquake. I was the only one who did not notice it, so engrossed was I in the excitement of Torah discussion; most of the people got up to flee from the synagogue" (*Dibre Shelomoh,* p. 186a).

Such behavior was not always tolerated by the preacher. A German rabbi, Israel Bruna, reported that once, while he was preaching, one of the empty-headed idlers walked out, followed by many others. "I made fun of the first one, and then the others, and they complained to their relatives, who were rabbis. My response was that they were lucky I did not excommunicate them."[24]

Those who remained were not always as attentive as the preacher might wish. The synagogue had a social as well as a religious function, and the sermon provided an opportunity for conversation that could rise well above the level of whispers. The early fifteenth-century Spanish moralist Solomon Alami complained that "the preacher is dumbfounded by the talking of men and the chattering of women standing at the back of the synagogue."[25] The same eighteenth-century critic who denounced people who dashed for the exits when the preacher stood up left a colorful if somewhat repulsive description of those who remained:

"There is another group that does not budge from their places, but they clap and shout and shriek and stomp. Moreover, they inhale snuff through their nostrils, which causes them to belch, snort, sneeze, and spit during the sermon." Then there is the women's gallery, overflowing with idle chatter about the clothing and jewelry someone is wearing, or about recipes for various dishes. "Sometimes a quarrel breaks out in the women's gallery, and there is so much shouting that the men can hardly hear the maggid or the preacher." Of course, he continues, probably with thinly veiled sarcasm, "these things do not at all pertain to the large cities, but they do to the smaller towns." The women, he said, should be required to stop talking, or at least to converse in no more than an inaudible whisper, "especially since there are respected and thoughtful women who want very much to hear words of Torah and rebuke from the maggid or preacher."[26]

If the congregation was sufficiently quiet, there was the danger that the listeners might fall asleep. This was a constant complaint of Christian as well as Jewish preachers. Even St. Bernard caught his monks occasionally dozing during his homilies, and a fifteenth-century English divine was told by a parishioner that she attended sermons as a surefire cure for her insomnia. John Donne caustically noted that the Puritans delivered long sermons out of their "zealous Imagination that it is their duty to preach till their Auditory wake," and one of Jonathan Swift's few published sermons is "On Sleeping in Church."[27] Yet Jewish preachers seemed to believe that this practice was unique to the synagogue.

24. Stadthagen, pp. 17a, 18a. *She'elot u-Teshubot MaHaRI mi-Bruna* (Salonika, 1803), no. 232, p. 94b.

25. Alami, *Iggeret Musar,* in "Sources."

26. Stadthagen, p. 18a; cf. Humbert of Romans, in Tugwell, p. 279.

27. *St. Bernard's Sermons on the Canticle of Canticles* (London, 1920), 1:434–35; Hugh

Solomon Alami drew an explicit contrast: when a Jewish preacher begins to talk, "slumber weighs upon the eyes of the officers," but when a Christian addresses his people, "not one of them dozes off." In a sermon for the Feast of Weeks, Leon Modena addressed the problem with self-deprecating humor. Why did God descend to Sinai amidst thunderous sounds and the piercing blast of the shofar? Because God knew that some Jews begin to doze off as soon as they hear the words of the Torah, "as is the case to this very day among those who listen to sermons." God could make sure that no one would fall asleep while He spoke; the preacher can only implore his congregation to "cast the bonds of sleep from your eyes," so that they can hear the sermon.[28]

Other preachers, in a more serious vein, pointed to a rabbinic report about R. Judah the Prince, who resorted to an intentionally outrageous statement ("In Egypt, a woman gave birth to six hundred thousand at one time") in order to wake up a congregation that was beginning to doze off in the middle of his discourse. This was adduced as a precedent for the use of farfetched and humorous interpretations intended to capture the people's attention, so that they would be more receptive to the substance. As Mordecai Jaffe confessed, "I too have done this to arouse the congregation from their slumber."[29]

A more active form of response to the preacher was the hostile challenge to his message, which could occur at the end of the sermon or interrupt him in the middle. Decorum could not always be assured, and preachers sometimes had to struggle to complete what they had prepared. The problem was exacerbated by the similarity between the Jewish sermon and the discourse on talmudic problems, with its tradition of vigorous verbal jousting, and was compounded by the absence of recognized credentials for preaching and the presence in the congregation of individuals who were certain that they could

---

Latimer, in Chandos, p. 22 (Latimer went on to tell his congregation that he would rather have this woman attend the sermon even for this reason than absent herself completely); John Donne, *Iuvenilia, or Certaine Paradoxes and Problems,* cited in Seaver, p. 31; Swift, in *The Prose Works of Jonathan Swift, D.D.* (London, 1898), 4:222. Cf. also Bernardino of Siena (in Petry, p. 271), actually pointing to, and addressing, a woman in the audience who had fallen asleep as he talked, and the analogous incident involving George Whitefield (in Downey, p. 173).

28. Alami, *Iggeret Musar;* Modena, *Midbar,* p. 48a, both in "Sources."

29. Song of Songs Rabbah, 1:15.3; Jaffe, introduction to *Lebush Malkut,* end; cf. David Darshan, p. 127, and Zahalon, p. 127. It is reported that in the nineteenth century, Jewish preachers who noticed their congregations dozing off knew they could arouse them by citing a parable of the Maggid of Dubno (Fenster, intro. to *Shaʿar Bat Rabbim* 1: 5b). For Christian techniques of arousing somnolent listeners, see St. Augustine, *De catchizandis rudibus,* pars. 18–19 (cited in Deferrari, pp. 114–15: "We may say something of a very wonderful and amazing order"); Caesarius of Heisterbach, in Owst, *Preaching,* p. 176, n. 4 (suddenly shouting, "There was once a king called Arthur," and then rebuking the people for awakening to hear such fables); Bernardino of Siena, in Johan Huizinga, *The Waning of the Middle Ages* (1924; reprint ed., Aylesbury, Eng., 1965), p. 173 (starting to inveigh against the vices of the clergy); and cf. Smalley, pp. 41–42, and MacLure, p. 148.

preach a better sermon themselves. Such interruptions, perceived by many as a public insult to the preacher, occasionally kindled bitter controversies that higher authorities had to quell.

Various kinds of dissatisfaction inspired these attacks. Sometimes it was a general contempt for the level of discourse, a sense that the preacher was wasting everyone's time. A Genizah document tells of a visitor invited to preach in Alexandria. His first sermon, on the Sabbath preceding the Day of Atonement, caused no problems. His second, on the Day of Atonement itself, was less successful. His third was interrupted by a local judge who criticized one of his homiletical interpretations and walked out of the synagogue in protest.[30]

A similar cause célèbre is recorded in the *Responsa* of Maimonides. In the middle of a sermon delivered by a respected community officer, a scholar in the congregation rose and shouted "How long will this delirium last? All you have said is nonsense; it should not be heard, it cannot be understood." Maimonides was consulted about the proper punishment for such brazen effrontery. Several centuries later, the preachers in early sixteenth-century Constantinople were said to deliver their sermons in fear and trembling, terrified lest a member of the congregation should stand up in the middle of the sermon and say "This interpretation was written by So-and-so in his book. The preacher took it from there."[31]

At its worst, interruption could deteriorate into a narcissistic desire to show off at the preacher's expense. *Sefer Ḥasidim,* that unique compendium of medieval German-Jewish spirituality and superstition, warned students not to cause problems for someone preaching in public by raising complicated

30. Goitein, *Ḥinnuk,* pp. 130–31; idem, *Community,* pp. 217–18; idem, "Dimdume ᶜEreb shel Bet ha-RaMBaM" (see n. 11, above), pp. 97–99.

31. Maimonides, in "Sources." Abraham ibn Migash, intro. to *Kebod Elohim* (Constantinople, 1546; Jerusalem, 1977), p. 17a, cited in Joseph Hacker, "Ha-Peᶜilut," p. 572, and cf. idem, "Ha-Derashah," pp. 116–18, on "the pursuit of novelty." We might compare this passage with St. John Chrysostom's complaint, registered twelve hundred years earlier (though closer geographically), that "If a preacher introduces into his discourse anything composed by another, he is reproached more severely than if he had been guilty of stealing money. Many times when he has not really taken anything from anybody, but is only suspected, he suffers as if he had been convicted" (*The Priesthood,* 5.1 [New York, 1955, p. 81]). Cf. also Smalley, pp. 37–38.

For a legal decision that originality is absolutely necessary for proper preaching, see Jacob Reischer, *Shebut Yaᶜaqob* (Halle, 1710), *Ḥoshen Mishpaṭ,* no. 146. Eventually there was a reaction to the abuses spawned by the demand for novelty, and the argument was made, through an old rhetorical commonplace, that originality need not be an advantage: "The spider produces everything from its own body, and it is entirely dirty and revolting; the bee finds material elsewhere, collecting it from various flowers to make honey, which is sweet and beneficial. So it is with preachers" (Margolioth, p. 5a–b; cf. Ṣebi Hirsch Orliansky, *Derashot* [New York, 1922], p. 17).

legal questions—a fairly good indication that this was frequently done. S. Y. Agnon tells rather poignantly of an emissary from the land of Israel who began to discourse on Genesis 43:11 as a model for the proper way to speak about the Holy Land in the Diaspora. He was interrupted by someone in the congregation who continued to press him with problems—"for every point he finally succeeded in explaining, they asked him seven more questions"—until he was forced to descend from the pulpit in disgrace. Historical sources confirm the verisimilitude of this literary account.[32]

More important issues came up when confrontations involved not homiletical technique or legal minutiae but doctrine and belief. The literature of the controversy over the study of philosophy at the beginning of the fourteenth century bristles with accusations against preachers who incorporated philosophical interpretations into their sermons and allegorized passages from the Bible and rabbinic aggadah. While many allegations are based on hearsay, there are also firsthand reports. En Duran describes in detail a philosophical sermon delivered at a wedding. After it was over, he claims that he waxed angry and publicly chastised the preacher. When during a synagogue service Abba Mari of Lunel, leader of those who sought to restrict philosophical study, interpreted a phrase in Numbers 22:7 as referring to "instruments of divination, such as the astrolabe," he was immediately challenged by a communal worthy who insisted that the astrolabe had been used by the sages in talmudic times.[33]

Even those who used philosophical doctrines to buttress the faith were not immune from attack. In the early fifteenth century a Spanish preacher discussed the oneness of God using philosophical dialectic: "If God is not One, such and such would follow," leading to a reductio ad absurdum. According to the eyewitness report of Ḥayyim ibn Mūsā,

> One of the leaders of the synagogue, a deeply religious man, rose and said, "They seized all of my property in the massacres of Seville [in 1391]; they beat me and covered me with wounds until they left me for dead. All this I endured through my faith in *Hear O Israel, the Lord our God, the Lord is One* (Deut. 6:4). Now you come upon the tradition of our ancestors with your philosophical investigation, saying, 'If God

32. *Sefer Ḥasidim* (Bologna MS) no. 963. Agnon, "Maʿaśeh ha-Meshullaḥ me-ʾEreṣ ha-Qedushah," in *Kol Sippuraw* (Jerusalem, 1964), 2:399–400, trans. Harold Saperstein, *Brandeis Avukah Annual of 1932*, pp. 718–19. For confirmation, see Azulai, p. 61 ("The sermon is a difficult task, for they preach about a technical matter, and everyone raises questions for the preacher, who must respond to them, and embarrassment often occurs"), and Yaari, *Sheluḥe*, p. 48. Cf. the story told about the first sermon delivered by the Ḥakam Ṣebi as rabbi of Amsterdam, in Levin, pp. 170–71.

33. En Duran, p. 147; *Minḥat Qenaʾot*, p. 106 (both in "Sources").

is not One, such and such must follow.' I believe more in the tradition of our ancestors, and I have no desire to hear this sermon."

With that, the author reports, he walked out of the synagogue, followed by most of the congregation.[34]

The preacher could never be quite sure what effect his words would have. Even if there were no immediate objections to a sermon, repercussions from the message could occur later, as listeners or those who had heard about the sermon from listeners lodged complaints with the powerful. Or a patently uncontroversial message could be misconstrued and perverted. The story of the simple man who misunderstands a sermon and acts in a ludicrous manner thinking that he is doing what the preacher wants, a familiar motif in folklore, is represented in Jewish literature by the tale of a *converso* who left Portugal to return to Judaism in Safed. Upon hearing a sermon in which the rabbi lamented the absence of the showbread (Lev. 24:5–9) since the destruction of the Temple, the *converso* has his wife bake two loaves of bread each Friday and leaves them in the synagogue as an offering to God. The preacher, who berates the *converso* for his anthropomorphic conception of God, is in turn rebuked and punished, dying at precisely the moment when his next sermon was to be delivered.[35]

Doctrinal issues could arouse powerful feelings, but the preacher who addressed concrete social and religious problems was treading on equally perilous ground. The more vehement and specific his condemnation of patterns of behavior, the greater the chance that he would be publicly challenged by those who felt that their way of life was being threatened.

Abraham ben Eliezer ha-Kohen, author of the homiletical tract *Ori we-Yish*ᶜ*i,* reported that once, as he was castigating the people for their shortcomings, he noticed certain scoffers in the congregation who refused to hear the message of rebuke. His clever reply contains a graphic reconstruction of what a preacher might expect: "Occasionally . . . an evil scoundrel will stand up in the midst of the congregation, face the preacher of rebuke, open his mouth, and say, '*Who made you chief and ruler over us?* (Exod. 2:14). Do you

34. Ibn Mūsā, p. 117 (in "Sources"); cf. Baer, *HJCS* 2:251. Cf. the "reincarnation" of this account as a story about Ḥasidim, told by Hillel Halkin, *Letters to an American Jewish Friend* (Philadelphia, 1977), p. 109.

35. *Mishnat Ḥakamim,* quoted in Simḥah Assaf, "Anuse Sefarad u-Fortugal be-Sifrut ha-Teshubot," *Zion* 5 (1933):25–26; M. J. Bin Gorion, *Mimekor Yisrael,* 3 vols. (Bloomington, 1976), 2:524–26. See my discussion of this story in "The Simpleton's Prayer," *Judaism* 29 (1980):297–99. An interesting detail is that the rabbi comes to the synagogue on Friday to practice from the pulpit the sermon he is to deliver the following day; cf. Zahalon, p. 145. For a current Jewish folkloristic variant, see Dov Noy, ed., *The Golden Feather* (Haifa, 1976), pp. 39–42. Cf. also Mark Twain's *The Adventures of Huckleberry Finn,* end of chap. 8. The Thompson Motif is X 434.4: "sermon misinterpreted."

want to kill me with your words? Who asked you to trample on my turf, my own private business? Insult yourself in your preaching—don't insult me. Let a true priest perform the divine service, not a puny pauper like you. Have you ever seen such a man? You're a phony and a fraud! My walking stick will communicate with you if you don't shut up!' " The allusive rhetoric expresses the tension inherent in the preacher's lack of recognized credentials and of social status, and the anger at an outsider's telling people how to live their lives.[36]

Similarly, Elijah ha-Kohen of Izmir reported in a sermon that he was once castigating the wealthy for their stinginess. A wealthy member of the congregation apparently waited until he had finished and then launched into a diatribe against Torah scholars, whom he accused of exploiting the pulpit to express whatever they felt like saying without even knowing the rudiments of proper speech. Elijah, who heard of this from reliable witnesses, tells his audience that had he been present, he would have beaten the man to death out of zeal for the honor of Torah—a pointed message to anyone who might have been considering a similar response.[37]

The most vulnerable to attack, as we have noted, were the itinerant maggidim. Their authority could be challenged, their motives maligned, their integrity besmirched. They were denounced for pandering to the powerful if they suppressed their criticisms, and for slandering the people if they uttered them.[38] This was a problem that someone coming without credentials and expecting a fee for insulting those whom he addressed could scarcely escape. But even when the preacher was the rabbi of the community, the preaching of rebuke held special challenges that were not easily overcome.

Every preacher knew that no matter how sincere his appeal and how eloquent his message, the obstacles he faced were formidable. Those most in need of rebuke were the self-centered, the hardhearted, the callous and smug—those who were least likely to heed what was being said. While it

36. *Ori we-Yishᶜi,* p. 18b–d, in "Sources." Cf. the purported challenge to preachers of rebuke in Luntshitz, *ᶜOlelot,* intro., p. 2a (cited by Elbaum, "Aspects," p. 163, n. 26), and in Berechiah Berak, cited in Ben Sasson, *Hagut,* p. 194. For interruption of Christian preachers, see Lecoy de la Marche, pp. 216–17; MacLure, p. 49 (on a dagger thrown from a tree) and p. 51 (on a shot fired from a house). Stephen Langton, archbishop of Canterbury, once began a sermon with the biblical verse "My heart hopes in the Lord," at which point someone in the congregation got up and shouted, "You are a liar; your heart does not hope in the Lord." The source reports that after a moment of silence the troublemaker was thrown out of the cathedral (Roberts, p. 51).

37. Elijah ha-Kohen of Izmir, *Midrash Eliyyahu,* sermon 3 (translated below). Cf. also the passage in *Ḥemdat Yamim* discussed by Isaiah Tishby, *Netibe,* pp. 124–25.

38. For this charge of slandering, see *Shibḥe ha-BESHṬ,* p. 145, *In Praise of the Baal Shem Tov,* pp. 182–83; cf. S. Y. Agnon, *Haknasat Kallah,* in *Kol Sippuraw* (Jerusalem, 1964), 1:43–44, *The Bridal Canopy,* trans. I. M. Lask (Garden City, N.Y., 1937), pp. 43–44.

was always possible for a preacher's words to bring about genuine repentance, anger and hostility were certainly more likely products, especially if what the preacher demanded had adverse economic consequences. Even a famous rabbi was dependent on the support of powerful laymen and vulnerable to their efforts to dismiss anyone who hurt their interests. Criticism of improper behavior might make the preacher appear to be setting himself above the rest of the congregation. If he was not clearly superior in spiritual stature to the others, this would look like arrogance and effrontery; if he was, he could be accused of setting up unreasonable standards.

The task of the preacher was fraught with paradox. If he admonished the people for their behavior and they ignored his warning, he would actually increase their sinfulness by making them conscious transgressors instead of ignorant ones. The effect of his striving would be the opposite of what he had intended. And if some responded to his words and, for example, closed their shops on the Sabbath, the more recalcitrant might even benefit from having ignored him. Denouncing a sin too graphically always runs the risk of arousing interest and exciting temptation.

Finally, if people did not mend their ways, what was the preacher to do next? Those who came to a sermon wanted to hear something original, not just the same old litany of complaints. Preachers were expected to base their rebukes on novel interpretations of biblical verses or rabbinic statements. But this constant demand for ingenuity and originality risked alienating people who realized that the simple meaning of a passage had nothing to do with the preacher's point. The choice between being implausible and boring was not a happy one.[39]

This bewildering array of problems produced a variety of rhetorical strategies. The easiest option—simply to exclude ethical and religious criticism from the sermon and to focus on novel interpretations of traditional texts or on edifying parables and stories—was certainly elected by some, for it was excoriated by moralists who viewed it as a blatant dereliction of the preacher's primary duty.[40] It was, however, acceptable for the preacher to indulge in ingenious interpretations before his ethical rebuke. This satisfied the tastes of some in the congregation, and more important, it established the preacher's credentials as a scholar. Zerah Eidlitz of Prague gave this idea a mordant twist, suggesting that the custom of incorporating novel interpretations into the sermon of rebuke had been developed so that the preacher could dem-

39. These problematics are discussed in the passages by MaHaRaL of Prague, Luntshitz, Pukhovitser, Abraham ben Eliezer ha-Kohen, Eidlitz, and Landau, translated in "Sources." Cf. also Bettan, pp. 286–88.

40. Pukhovitser, *Derek Ḥokmah,* in "Sources," at end; Eybeschuetz, 2:14c, cited by Bettan, pp. 328–29.

onstrate that he had not gone crazy, for those who publicly rebuke a congregation would not otherwise be above that suspicion.[41]

Effective criticism required a combination of artistic flair, intellectual agility, psychological insight, and plain common sense. One technique was to keep the criticism general, so that no one in the congregation would know at whom it was directed, while the guilty parties could silently apply the message to themselves. This method was recommended by some as a way of allowing both the preacher and the listener to cover themselves by pretending that the criticism was really meant for someone else. Others, however, scorned it as cowardly.[42]

Citation of classical texts could also be used as a form of indirect criticism. The listeners would think they were hearing mere exegesis; only gradually would they come to realize that the message applied to them. But since it came from familiar and sacred writings, it could not easily be repudiated. Here is how one Polish moralist explained it:

> What does the truly wise rabbi do? He bases his rebuke on the simple meaning of biblical verses. It is as if the verses themselves were uttering the rebuke. Then, as the simple meaning enters the ears of the listeners and pleases them, the rebuke emerging from the sermon automatically enters their ears as well. Afterwards, when the sermon is over, the people say, "This was the new Torah interpretation given by the scholar, and this is the rebuke that flows from it." Thus they become aware of their own failings, and learn how to correct them and return to God.[43]

Use of parables could be similarly effective. Here the preacher goes further, for the meaning of the parable is made explicit and not left for the listeners to interpret. But the path to the message is indirect: first the entertaining and apparently harmless story that wins the listeners' assent, then the application that they cannot deny.[44]

As for the preacher's own position, it was crucial that he include himself in the group being criticized by speaking not of "you" but of "we." Azariah Figo articulated the question that occurred to congregants and preachers alike: "How can I presume to criticize your conduct, when I myself am lacking in worth, short on good deeds, possessed of but little knowledge and understanding?" He suggested an answer: "I am my own best audience. I preach mostly to myself. If I address myself to others, it is because I deem it the

41. Pukhovitser, *Derek Ḥokmah,* in "Sources"; Eidlitz, p. 80d; cf. *Binat Yiśśakar,* p. 3a.

42. *Ori we-Yishᶜi,* in "Sources"; contrast the criticism by Eidlitz, p. 20c: "Even distinguished preachers do not rebuke specific sins; they preach publicly in a general manner, and who knows whether any individual feels that the words apply to him?"

43. *Zeraᶜ Berak,* in Ben Sasson, *Hagut,* pp. 50–51.

44. Margolioth, p. 5a.

best way of impressing the truth of the lesson upon my own soul."[45] The preacher scrutinizes his own behavior and allows others to look on. If they take the message to their own hearts as well, so much the better.

Emerging from this complex of problems in the relationship between the preacher of rebuke and his congregation is a new theory of preaching, found in the circles of the Maggid of Mezritsh. Rivka Schatz Uffenheimer has shown how the principle of quietism, emphasizing the total passivity of the human being, whose individuality all but disappears as he becomes a vessel of God, was transformed into the social activism of a preacher capable of criticizing the conduct of even the most powerful without fear for his own popularity or well-being. The preacher is like the shofar: God's words enter at one end and come out the other, and it is not really the preacher who speaks, but God. In this way the preacher can disclaim responsibility for what he says and protect himself from the wrath of the powerful, while his words continue to challenge without compromise the imperfections of Jewish life.[46]

Did such preaching really make a difference? This question was perhaps the most troubling of all. For the true preacher, it was not enough to establish a reputation for preaching ability. He wanted to change people in a lasting way. The important thing, as one put it, was not the impression made during the sermon but what was left afterward.[47] Not a few confessed their doubts about the efficacy of their labors.

Obadiah of Bertinoro wrote back to Italy that in Jerusalem "they praise and extol my sermons, they listen to what I say, but they do not do it," a sentiment that many preachers must have shared. One of the greatest of them, Ephraim Luntshitz, admitted sorrowfully that "most of what the preachers say is not accepted," that despite their best efforts during the High Holy Days, "at the end of that period, all is forgotten, and the people return to their accustomed ways." Even a rabbi with the prestige of Ezekiel Landau, halakic authority beyond compare and chief rabbi of Bohemia, confessed his discouragement in a sermon for the Sabbath preceding the Day of Atonement: "My words have not been successful, nor borne fruit, for you have not accepted my ethical instruction. Worse than this: the more I continue to chastise, the more the dissoluteness grows."[48]

45. Figo, pt. 2, no. 66, cited by Bettan, p. 235. Cf. also Zahalon, p. 147, and Landau, *Derushe,* p. 32d.

46. Rivka Schatz Uffenheimer, *Ha-Ḥasidut ke-Misṭiqah* (Jerusalem, 1980), pp. 117–18 (and see Joseph Weiss's article as noted there, p. 117 at n. 35). Note Piekarz's stricture, pp. 117–18. However, the passage in question is adumbrated in the context of social criticism by Eybeschuetz, 1:80d.

47. Aboab, p. 38a.

48. Yaari, *Iggerot,* p. 14; Luntshitz, *ʿAmmude,* "Torah," end of chap. 3, p. 11a, *ʿOlelot* 2:34, par. 239; Landau, *Derushe,* p. 8a. Cf. Solomon Bonafed: "My rebukes in my sermons

Indications of truly efficacious preaching are not entirely absent. The scenario in Shem Ṭob Falaquera's "Iggeret ha-Musar," in which a preacher comes to town, delivers a stereotyped sermon of rebuke, and sees the congregation transform its behavior in sincere repentance, is of course fantasy, if not satire. But according to contemporary sources, the sermon of rebuke preached in 1281 by Ṭodros ha-Levi Abulafia in Toledo, cataloguing the shortcomings of the people and advocating specific institutional changes, did apparently play a significant role in that city's reform movement. And when Jonathan Eybeschuetz, in his inaugural sermon as rabbi of the "Three Communities," forbade his congregation to keep statues and figurines in their homes, "even those of porcelain that come from India and are kept on pedestals as objects of beauty," his archenemy Jacob Emden had to concede that "they carried out his instruction immediately, smashing the beautiful figurines into small pieces."[49]

For the most part, however, success was on a more modest scale. The novel interpretation, the clear and unanswerable argument, the humorous story with a serious message, or the parable that hit the mark, might long be remembered by some who had heard it.[50] And individuals, at least, were occasionally inspired to change their ways. Elijah ha-Kohen of Izmir, widely known for his fire-and-brimstone preaching, recounts that one Saturday night a man came to him and thanked him for the sermon he had delivered earlier that day. The man had planned an illicit rendezvous that very evening with another man's wife, but the power of the sermon had broken his will to sin, and he abandoned the plan.[51]

Most preachers did not expect to change the world overnight. A late fifteenth-century Spaniard defined his conception of his role with a familiar metaphor: "I am like the owner of a field who sows kernels of his wheat. At

---

have not led sinners to repent," *Qobeṣ ʿal Yad* 4 (14) (1946):16. And note the wry comment on the efficacy of preaching in "Des Antonius von Padua Fischpredigt" of *Des Knaben Wunderhorn*: "The pike remain thieves / The eels pursue pleasure; / The sermon enjoyed / They remain just the same."

49. "Iggeret ha-Musar," ed. A. Habermann, *Qobeṣ ʿal Yad* 1 (11):76–78. For Ṭodros ha-Levi, see Baer, *HJCS* 1:257–60 (the source of the quotation about the sermons' impact, on p. 259, is not identified), and cf. Michal Oron, "Derashato shel R. Ṭodros ben Yosef ha-Levi Abulafia le-Tiqqun ha-Middot we-ha-Musar," *Daʿat* 11 (1983):47–51. Jacob Emden, *Sefer Hitʾabbequt* (Lvov, 1877), p. 4a–b.

50. See, for example, the report in a letter of a sermon preached by the writer's father on the Sabbath preceding Passover forty years previously, when the writer was only seven years old (Levin, pp. 26–27). Jonathan Swift may well have been correct when he counseled a young clergyman: "A plain convincing reason may possibly operate upon the mind both of a learned and ignorant hearer as long as they live, and will edify a thousand times more than the art of wetting the handkerchiefs of a whole congregation" (*The Prose Works of Jonathan Swift, D.D.* [London, 1898], 3:206).

51. Elijah, *Shebeṭ Musar*, chap. 27, p. 50.

first glance, it may appear that he is throwing them away to rot or to be wasted. But when one sees the great benefit that results, that waste is considered fine."[52]

Two centuries later an East European colleague propounded the parable of a king who spends the entire day hunting and galloping through the woods but in the evening comes home with only a single hare. Yet he rejoices in his meager catch, thinking that next time he will succeed in bagging a splendid buck. So with the preacher: "The first time he may help one person, the second time another, until eventually his power will increase to the point where he will help many, including some more important than these."[53] At a time when social forces undermining traditional Jewish behavior were gathering strength, the long-term approach was one for which many preachers were satisfied to settle.

Structural Options

The proper beginning for a Jewish sermon was a verse from the Bible; in this respect Jewish and Christian homiletics were alike. Jewish preachers thought of this as an ancient tradition that could not be casually ignored, even if the sermon itself was largely independent of the verse. Around the time of the expulsion from Spain (1492), Isaac Aboab explained the function of this practice to his listeners. Beginning with Genesis 33:10, his discourse continued:

> It is an ancient custom of our people for those who preach in public to begin their sermons with a verse or a few words from the Torah. There are two reasons for this: first, to inform the congregation that if the sermon contains condemnation and rebuke, the preacher's criticism of the people is based not upon his own opinions but upon the Torah; second, to demonstrate the greatness of the Torah, by showing that ideas seemingly new are already present in it by allusion. The Torah, written by God, encompasses everything. That is why preachers try to teach something about the content of their sermon at the very beginning. Therefore I say that these words [the Torah verse] with which I

52. Israel, "Dober Mesharim," fol. 55r. For the metaphor of the preacher as sower of seeds in Christian sources (based on Matt. 13:4–9, 18–23), see Humbert of Romans, in Tugwell, pp. 269–71; Jacques de Vitry, in Petry, p. 186.

53. *Ori we-Yishᶜi,* p. 19d, attributed to the "rebuker" (*mokiaḥ*) Jacob Ratner. See "Sources." Cf. Landau, *Derushe,* p. 8a: "If I find a single person upon whom I have the effect of helping to purify the heart, even this is a great accomplishment."

began inform you of the reason for my speaking now, and the purpose of my discourse.[1]

While the analysis of the function of a scriptural beginning is quite cogent, Aboab was not historically accurate in asserting that choosing a verse from the Torah was an ancient custom. This was not done consistently before the second half of the fifteenth century, and it represents a significant change, with implications for the entire structure of the Jewish sermon.

The sermon models preserved from the thirteenth and early fourteenth centuries generally begin with a verse from the Writings, the Book of Proverbs being by far the most popular choice. Perhaps the best example of consistent structure in this period is a recently published manuscript of sermons attributed by its editor to Jonah Gerondi. Of the fifty-one complete sermons in this collection, all but one begin with a verse or verses from Proverbs. This verse is usually given several different interpretations and then about midway through the sermon is applied to the Torah lesson, which is discussed in the second half. The structure seems to be in direct continuity with the homiletical method of classical midrash, and many of the proems preserved in the various midrashim look as if they might be outlines for this kind of sermon.[2]

Proverbs is also the source most frequently used by Jacob Anatoli and Joshua ibn Shueib, as well as by Baḥya ben Asher (in the introduction to each lesson of his Torah commentary). The choice of verse might be suggested by a verbal link, as in Proverbs 9:10, containing the word *qedoshim,* and used by Anatoli, "Anonymous," and ibn Shueib at the beginning of their sermons on the lesson *Qedoshim* (Lev. 19:1–20:27). There may be an obvious thematic connection, as in Proverbs 13:25 on eating, used by Anatoli and ibn Shueib for their sermons on *Shemini* (Lev. 9:1–11:47), which contains a detailed

1. Aboab, p. 38a. Cf. Baḥya, *Kad ha-Qemaḥ,* beginning of "Gezel," p. 96 (cited in Bettan, p. 96); Ruderman, "Exemplary Sermon," p. 31. On "the reason for my speaking," see below, nn. 32 and 33.

2. See *Derashot.* For a discussion of the authorship of this manuscript and a representative example see the sermon translated below. There is a large literature on the midrashic proem; a convenient starting point is Joseph Heinemann, "The Proem in the Aggadic Midrashim: A Form Critical Study," *Studies in Aggadah and Folk-Literature,* Scripta Hierosolymitana 22 (Jerusalem, 1971), pp. 100–22. The assumption of formal continuity between the sermon of the talmudic period and the thirteenth-century sermon would raise problems for Heinemann's thesis that the proem was not an introductory section of a larger sermon, but the full sermon, used as an introduction to the Torah reading. The "Midrash" of David ha-Nagid contains sermons in a similar form, beginning mostly with verses from Proverbs. Similarly, the sermons of the thirteenth-century German rabbi Ḥayyim ben Isaac "Or Zaruʿa" begin with a verse from Psalms or Proverbs, although their content is primarily practical halakah. This shows that the convention was almost universal among Jews. For the aesthetics of this technique, see Dan, *Sifrut,* pp. 41–44.

exposition of the dietary laws (Lev. 11). Or there might be a larger conceptual relevance, as in Proverbs 19:21, on the relationship between human initiative and divine Providence. That text was used by Anatoli, "Anonymous," ibn Shueib, and an unknown early fourteenth-century Spanish author for the beginning of their sermons on *Wa-Yesheb* (Gen. 37:1–40:23), which begins the Joseph story. While some connections are more ingenious than others, there must have been a fairly well established homiletical tradition relating particular Proverbs verses to lessons.

At the beginning of the fourteenth century other options were available. The sermons of Joshua ibn Shueib are conservative in form, but an unknown contemporary of his, the author of a collection of sermons organized according to the scriptural lessons, felt free to begin his discourses in a variety of ways. Many start with a verse from the Writings (Proverbs, Psalms, Ecclesiastes), but others begin with a verse from the Prophets, a passage of midrash or aggadah, or a one-sentence statement of an important commandment (to love God, to walk in God's ways, not to covet a neighbor's property). Occasionally the preacher begins immediately with a verse from the Torah lessons. This particular work is characterized by the absence of a clear and consistent sermon structure. Its fluidity of form indicates that while old conventions were being abandoned, new ones had not yet crystallized.[3]

A similar fluidity can be seen in the sermons of Jacob ben Hananel of Sicily near the beginning of the fourteenth century and of Mattathias Yizhari at its end. They may begin with a verse from the Prophets or with a verse from the Writings; Yizhari occasionally opens with a passage of aggadah. These initial quotations are always related to the Torah lesson, as can be seen in Yizhari's sermon translated below, in which a familiar prophetic passage is first discussed in historical context and then explored in a different light by relating it to the story of Jacob.[4]

We might have expected a clear statement of how the sermon was to be constructed from Joseph ibn Shem Ṭob in the middle of the fifteenth century. He was the author of the earliest surviving Jewish treatise on preaching, and

3. Anonymous, "Disciple of R. Asher," Proverbs: fols. 5v, 25r, 132r; Psalms: 42v, 80v, 89v; Ecclesiastes: 46v: Prophets: 2r; rabbinic aggadah: 29r, 34r, 37r, 50r, 53v, 58v; commandment: 11r, 14v, 118r, 121v; verse from the lesson: 123r, 136r.

4. Jacob ben Hananel of Sicily's *Torat ha-Minḥah* is a collection of model sermons, including several on each Torah lesson, intended to aid other preachers, and based on the author's own preaching on Sabbath afternoons. He states that the three major topics of his sermons were the existence of God, the problem of theodicy, and the perfection of the soul and its mysteries. Much of the midrashic material used in his preaching is not included in this text, the reader being referred for this to another book entitled "Talmud Torah." After the opening verse, the sermon generally begins with "This verse was said by King Solomon," or ". . . by Isaiah," etc. For the traditional proem form, see fols. 19v, 54r. For Yizhari, see the introduction to his sermon translated below.

his sermons are among the first in Christian Europe to describe circumstances of their delivery. Yet this expectation is soon disappointed. "ʿEn ha-Qore" discusses many aspects of preaching, but except for urging preachers not to abandon the Torah lesson it says nothing about proper sermonic structure.

Joseph ibn Shem Ṭob's sermons show that new conventions for sermon structure were not yet fixed. When he preached in Segovia during the weeks following Passover, he began his sermons with a passage from the chapter of the tractate Abot read in the synagogue on that Sabbath, hardly touching upon the scriptural lesson at all. On other occasions he began with a verse from the Hafṭarah or from Psalms. Finally, there were times when he began directly with a verse from the Torah lesson. His sermon on *Qoraḥ* (Num. 16:1–18:32), starting with Numbers 16:28, is devoted entirely to the "enormous benefits" that we derive from the story of Korah's rebellion.[5]

Various considerations influenced the preacher's choice of an opening citation. Joseph ben David of Saragossa gives a humorous reason for his selection of Proverbs 6:23 as the lead verse of a sermon for the Sabbath preceding Passover. A lamp must be used in performing the commandment of removing the remnants of leaven from one's house before the festival, "and because the lamp is essential to the fulfillment of the commandment, it may fittingly be said, '*Ki ner miṣwah,* the commandment entails a lamp.'" Ephraim ha-Darshan accepted a challenge to write an entire series of holiday sermons on whatever verse his patron should choose; they agreed on Song of Songs 3:6. The selection of verses from the prophetic literature frequently shows that the preacher was trying to address the historical situation or the psychological needs of his contemporaries.[6]

This variety in sermon form lasted through the middle of the fifteenth century. Then, in a process that cannot yet be fully documented or explained, new ideas took over. The sermon structure of preachers from the generation of the expulsion, such as Shem Ṭob ibn Shem Ṭob, Isaac Arama, Joel ibn Sheuib, Joseph Garçon, Isaac Aboab, and Israel, author of "Dober Mesharim," is governed by established norms and conventions. Changes from the earlier sermons are substantial.

First, as Aboab noted in the passage cited at the beginning of this section, the sermon regularly commences with a verse from the Torah lesson. It was rare to start with a verse from the Writings or the Prophets; the flexibility of previous generations seems to have disappeared.

5. Joseph ibn Shem Ṭob (Montefiore MS), fols. 112r, 122v, 133r; *Derashot,* fols. 180r, 186v. On Korah, see Montefiore MS, fol. 102r (on *benefits* as a homiletical term, see below, n. 27). Ibn Shem Ṭob's sermon for Simḥat Torah begins with Deuteronomy 33:29, from the Torah lesson read that day (Montefiore MS, fol. 139v).

6. Joseph ben David, p. 295; Ephraim ha-Darshan, fols. 2v, 68r; Yizhari, fol. 1r and sermon translated below.

Second, this verse from the Torah lesson has now acquired a name, *nośe.* This term, used widely in the homiletical writing of Spanish Jews at the end of the century,[7] translates the Latin *thema,* a technical term for the biblical verse cited at the beginning of the medieval Christian sermon. On occasion the word *thema* is actually used in Hebrew texts in place of *nośe.* However, the foreign origin of the Hebrew technical term was quickly forgotten, as we see in one preacher's explanation of its etymology: "since the *nośe* is like *hyle,* the primal matter, which can receive any form, it is called *nośe,* 'that which bears,' for all parts of the sermon should be borne aloft by it." This technical term may be contrasted with the circumlocutions of earlier preachers: "the verse that is the pillar of the sermon," "the verse with which we opened," "the verse that the discourse is based upon."[8]

After the *nośe* from the Torah lesson most preachers immediately cited a passage of rabbinic aggadah, called the *ma'amar.* Some tended to use a midrashic comment on the verse, others an aggadic statement not obviously relevant to it. Although the *ma'amar* was cited at the beginning of the sermon, its explication generally came near the end, after the Torah verse and the conceptual problems about which the preacher was concerned had been addressed. While this was not an invariable practice, it was common enough that sixteenth-century preachers felt compelled to justify departures from it: "Even though it is the custom to speak first about the verses and then about the *ma'amar,* nevertheless, because I intend to discuss the entire section, I shall explain the *ma'amar* first"; "Although it is my pattern always to explain the *ma'amar* with which I began at the end of the sermon, I shall depart from this order."[9]

The choice of the *nośe* from within the Torah lesson was determined not by the need to connect it with another verse, but by what the preacher wanted

7. A few representative passages establishing the use of *nośe* as a technical term are Aboab, pp. 8a, 38a; Abraham Saba, *Ṣeror ha-Mor* (1879; reprint ed., Tel Aviv, 1975), Deuteronomy, p. 3a; Garçon, in Benayahu, pp. 147, 148, 154.

8. The first to suggest the connection between *nośe* and *thema* was apparently Pachter, "Sifrut," p. 31, no. 19; I was unaware of this when I made the same suggestion in "Art Form," p. 260, n. 9. For the use of *thema* in Hebrew sources (to mean not "question" but *nośe*), see Garçon, in Benayahu, pp. 161, 175, and Israel, "Dober Mesharim, fol. 139r. The Hebrew etymology of *nośe* is given by Israel, "Dober Mesharim," fol. 91v. His explanation may be compared with that of John of Wales: "thema, quod est tocius operis fundamentum . . . in quo omnia dicenda virtute contineantur," cited by Etienne Gilson, "Michel Menot et la technique du sermon médiéval," *Les idées et les lettres* (Paris, 1932), p. 101. For circumlocutions, see Zerahiah ha-Levi, p. 100; Moses ben Joab in Cassuto, "Rabbino," p. 229; Abraham Farissol in Ruderman, "Exemplary Sermon," p. 31. I have not found the term *nośe* used by Shem Ṭob ibn Shem Ṭob or by Arama.

9. Alkabeẓ, fol. 50r; Alfalas, p. 95b (cited by Pachter, "Sifrut," p. 41, n. 54). The actual interpretation of the *ma'amar* is sometimes omitted from the written sermon, as in the Garçon sermon translated below. Cf. Garçon, in Benayahu, p. 186.

to say. A century later Saul Morteira, one of the greatest preachers in the classical Sephardic tradition, imposed upon himself a demanding discipline. He used the first verse of each lesson during the first year of his tenure in Amsterdam, the second verse during the second year, and so on in an orderly progression.[10] But we know of no preachers in the generation of the expulsion who restricted their choice in this manner. The preacher was free to select any verse from the lesson that would fit his homiletical needs.

Occasionally we get a glimpse of the thinking behind the selection. Israel, author of "Dober Mesharim," articulated his own deliberations in a eulogy at the end of the week of mourning for a man named Abraham who had been killed. The lesson was *Lek Leka* (Gen. 12:1–17:27), and the *nośe* that he selected was Genesis 15:1. But this was not his original choice. He states that the disaster was so great that at first he intended to use a different *nośe* from the same lesson, *a great dark dread descends* (Gen. 15:12), "but since I found in this *nośe* no comfort for him and for those who mourn him, I did not want to use it, and I chose this other verse, for it both tells of his calamity and comforts him and his mourners, speaking to their hearts." The original verse was more effective in communicating the calamity that had occurred, but the eulogy had to be more than this, and a different verse was chosen through which the preacher could express both sorrow and comfort.[11]

Sometimes circumstances beyond the preacher's control compelled him to change the *nośe* that he had planned to use. We have already seen how Joseph Garçon prepared a eulogy for the eminent scholar Samuel Franco, using the verse Exodus 19:22 from the lesson *Yitro* (Exod. 18–20), but did not get a chance to preach it until the end of the memorial week, by which time the lesson had changed to *Mishpaṭim* (Exod. 21–24); he therefore recast his sermon on the basis of a new *nośe,* Exodus 21:5. Good preachers were able to adapt the same sermon to various Torah lessons or occasions, and thus to different theme-verses. Verses from several lessons are occasionally found at the beginning of a sermon, with instructions how to use the sermon in a different setting.[12]

In the older sermon (beginning with a verse from the Writings or from the Prophets), the verse was generally discussed alone before being connected to the Torah lesson. This tradition was still frequently observed after the shift

10. See Saperstein, "Art Form," p. 246.

11. Israel, "Dober Mesharim," fol. 8r.

12. Garçon, in Benayahu, p. 147; cf. Israel, "Dober Mesharim," fols. 33r–34r. Israel's sermon on fol. 212r has two alternative theme-verses at the beginning, only one of which is used in the sermon as written. The interchangeability of theme-verses can be seen in the fact that Leon Modena, editing the sermons of Samuel Ashkenazi, actually changed one himself so there would be a sermon with a *nośe* from the lesson *Bere'shit* (Gen. 1:1–6:8) (see Pachter, "Sifrut," p. 35, n. 29).

to the sermon beginning with a verse from the lesson. Many preachers insisted that the simple meaning of the *nośe* should first be explained in context and only afterward be employed for homiletical purposes. Like those who explicated the *ma'amar* before the *nośe,* those who departed from this tradition often felt the need for self-justification: "Even though the custom of preachers is not to play with the words of the *nośe* without explaining to some extent its simple meaning, nevertheless I will be daring and not continue with further explication, so as not to burden you"; "Even though the pattern of preachers is to explicate the verses from which the *nośe* is taken, I shall depart from this pattern, because the verses and the subject of my discourse are all the same."[13]

Perhaps the most interesting innovation of the later fifteenth century is a technique of using the *nośe* that would dominate Sephardic preaching for more than a century. The origin of this technique remains one of the great enigmas in the history of Jewish homiletics. Instead of merely reading the theme-verse as it appears in the Torah, the preacher breaks it into fragments, sometimes only two words in length, usually ending with the verse in its entirety. During the course of the sermon, each short phrase is given separate interpretation.[14]

At least four varieties of this approach to the theme-verse can be discerned. The most common can be called *incremental,* for each phrase adds to what precedes it. There could be only two parts, a fragment of the verse followed by the verse in full, but more frequently there were three: *The king of Salem. The king of Salem brought out bread and wine. The king of Salem brought out bread and wine; he was a priest of God Most High* (Gen. 14:18). Nor was it necessarily limited to three parts, as we see in the following example: *Arba, which is Hebron. In Kiryat Arba, which is Hebron. Sarah in Kiryat Arba, which is Hebron in the land of Canaan. Sarah in Kiryat Arba, which is Hebron in the land of Canaan, and Abraham came to mourn. Then died Sarah in Kiryat Arba, which is Hebron in the land of Canaan, and Abraham came to mourn her and to bewail her* (Gen. 23:2).[15]

The second approach is a variation of the first with a different rhetorical

13. Israel, "Dober Mesharim," fol. 220v; Alfalas, p. 164a (cited by Pachter, "Sifrut," p. 38, n. 47); *Dibre Shelomoh,* pp. 4b, 125a. Cf. Garçon, in Benayahu, pp. 143, 149 (twice), 153, and anonymous, "Bibago," fol. 328; the word *kawwanati* is frequently used in these passages as a technical term referring to the preacher's homiletical use of the verse.

14. This technique, exemplified in the sermons of Garçon and Almosnino translated below, has been mentioned by Pachter, "Demuto," p. 24, n. 8, and "Sifrut," pp. 31–32, and by Benayahu, "Yaffeh," p. 437 (and cf. Benayahu, p. 56). But I know of no attempt to explore its origins, the extent of its use, or its rhetorical implications.

15. Garçon, in Hacker, "Li-Demutam," p. 92. Examples of a two-part *nośe* are Garçon, in Benayahu, pp. 161, 174. For the division of Gen. 23:2, see Israel, "Dober Mesharim," fol. 239r.

function. By adding the negative (usually *lo*) the preacher transforms a positive assertion into the negative one that appears in the Bible. This mode can be called *antithetical.* For example: *It is good* [ṭob] *for man to be alone; It is not good* [lo ṭob] *for man to be alone* (Gen. 2:18). *The Lord will be willing* [yobeh] *to forgive him; The Lord will not be willing* [lo yobeh] *to forgive him* (Deut. 29:19). *Let there be* [tehi] *strife between you and me; Let there be no strife* [al na tehi] *between you and me* (Gen. 13:8). *By bread alone does man live; Not by bread alone does man live* (Deut. 8:3).[16]

Less common is an approach that can be called *progressive,* using different parts of the theme-verse or even parts of two adjacent verses. For example: *Stretched his hand against the work of his neighbor. For every manner of offense, against ox and against ass* (end of Exod. 22:7 and beginning of 22:8).[17]

The fourth approach is the *repetitive,* in which the same phrase recurs several times without change. The repetition is only apparent, however, for the preacher eventually gives a different meaning to each recurrence of the phrase. Any one translation is therefore misleading; one example is the fourfold repetition of *Rab lakem shebet ba-har ha-zeh* (Deut. 1:6; NJV: You have stayed long enough in this mountain) used by Samuel Uceda at the beginning of his eulogy for Isaac Luria of Safed.[18] There were also increasingly complex schemas, combining several of the techniques above, interspersing long and short phrases from the theme-verse without any apparent pattern. The Almosnino sermon translated below provides an example.

The rhetorical functions of this homiletical technique were varied. Many preachers used the fragments of their theme-verse for an original treatment of conventional introductory material, particularly to state their reasons for preaching. For example, in another sermon Joseph Garçon claims to have hesitated because a serious illness had left him weak; the first part of his theme-verse, *God is with you* (Gen. 21:22), showed him his obligation to preach because God had been with him and had restored his health, and the second part, *God is with you in all that you do,* indicated that God would help him in his present task.[19]

16. Israel, "Dober Mesharim," fol. 85r and fol. 175r (in "Sources"); Alfalas, no. 19, pp. 150b, 157a; Garmizan, *Debarim,* fol. 54r.

17. Israel, "Dober Mesharim," fol. 238r.

18. Pachter, "Demuto," p. 34.

19. Garçon, in Benayahu, p. 160. There does not seem to be a single term used to refer to the various fragments of the theme-verse. In this passage, Garçon uses *ḥeleq* ("part," cf. also p. 150). Elsewhere we find the form *ḥaluqah* ("division": Garçon, in Benayahu, p. 143; Israel, "Dober Mesharim," fols. 133r, 182r); *kawwanah* ("meaning": Israel, "Dober Mesharim," fols. 2r, 231v); *pan* ("facet" or "aspect": Israel, "Dober Mesharim," fol. 8r, and cf. Ephraim ha-Darshan, fol. 343v); *shittuf* ("homonymous or amphibolous meaning": Garçon, in Benayahu, pp. 56, 180); and *sebibah* (literally, "encircling": Uceda, in Pachter, "Demuto," p. 35). The term *ḥaluqah* might suggest a connection with the Christian technical term *divisio,*

When the verse fragments were used to raise and answer questions, the initial reading became the outline of an internal dialogue. Israel, author of "Dober Mesharim," used the end of Exodus 22:7 in a eulogy for one of his pupils who had died young: "This is the question in my *nośe*: *shalaḥ yado bi-mele'ket reʿehu?* (lit., "laid his hand on his neighbor's work") meaning, 'How could God have stretched His hand?' referring to His mortal blow (as in Exod. 9:3) and caused the death of this youth, who is 'the work' of his parents?" The answer comes from a homiletical interpretation of the second part of the theme verse, the beginning of Exodus 22:8. The antithetical mode described above was used to establish the premises of a disputed question. Each position is sustained by arguments before a resolution is reached.[20]

Solomon Alkabeẓ used the parts of his theme-verse to construct a model halakic dispute (in which the preacher uses the verse to argue both sides) about the propriety of his preaching a *Shabbat ha-Gadol* sermon on the preceding Sabbath: "My *nośe* asks in amazement. . . ? To answer this question, I went back and said again . . . But my *nośe* responded and said that this was no justification . . . I replied that this too is incorrect . . . Then I went back and said. . . ."[21]

A very different rhetorical function is illustrated in Judah Moscato's use of this technique. Beginning a sermon for the Day of Atonement with the obvious choice of Leviticus 16:30, he breaks it up into a combination of the incremental and the repetitive approaches: *You shall be pure before the Lord. From all your sins you shall be pure before the Lord. From all your sins you shall be pure before the Lord.* The theme-verse is then temporarily neglected as the preacher discusses the problematics of repentance and the status of the penitent. After all the exegetical and conceptual problems have been resolved, Moscato returns to the starting point:

> And this is the teaching that my *nośe* has placed before the children of Israel [a striking play upon Deut. 4:44]. When it says *You shall be pure before the Lord,* it calls upon future generations to purify themselves through the pure and perfect repentance of love: "Be pure before God." When it says *From all your sins you shall be pure before the Lord,* it predicts that your soul will indeed be pure from *all* your sins, even inadvertent sins, unlike those who repent out of fear, whose intentional sins are considered to be like inadvertent ones, leaving a stain of transgression, as discussed above. Even more than this, your transgressions will be

but the division of the theme in the medieval Christian sermon never entailed the kind of repetition of elements we find in this technique. The rhetorical function was thus quite different. For an example close to the Christian *divisio* see Aboab, p. 52d.

20. Israel, "Dober Mesharim," fol. 238r; also fol. 175r, in "Sources."

21. Alkabeẓ, fol. 3r.

> transformed into merits, becoming a source of light for you, as we have explained. This is indicated by the repetition of *From all your sins you shall be pure before the Lord,* meaning "*because of* all your sins you shall ascend to the level of the pure."

As always with this technique, the theme-verse is shown to have different possible meanings: the verb serving as an imperative and as a prophecy, the preposition meaning "be pure from your sins" and, paradoxically, "be pure because of your sins." But more important, it serves as a summary of the preacher's points, drawing the entire sermon together at its conclusion.[22]

The most common rhetorical function is simply to entertain and edify the congregation through the preacher's ingenuity in teasing multiple meanings from the biblical language. This is especially true with the repetitive mode, in which each repeated phrase is eventually given a different significance.[23]

Several preliminary conclusions may be drawn about this new homiletical technique of fragmenting the theme-verse. First, it is clearly a product of the oral sermon rather than of a written form. The verse fragments or phrases were obviously read with different emphases, intonations, and rhetorical effects, hints of how they would ultimately be interpreted, none of which can be indicated in the written text. The recitation of the theme-verse at the beginning of the sermon was no mechanical exercise, but a miniature piece of theater.

Second, this particular homiletical style presumes a congregation that understands Hebrew. The entire sermon need not be delivered in Hebrew, but the level of linguistic knowledge demanded of the audience is relatively high. Phrases are taken out of their context and invested with new meanings, words are interpreted in ways that could not possibly have fitted the original verse, syntactical units meaningless in isolation are reinterpreted to serve the author's purpose in a manner that would not have worked in translation.[24] While it is impossible to know how many in the congregation appreciated the subtleties of such preaching, the preacher's expectations were clearly considerable.

Finally, the fragmented theme-verse introduces a new kind of aesthetic

22. Moscato, sermon 38 (end), p. 106c. Moscato uses this technique in only two other sermons (12 and 29) of his *Nefuṣot Yehudah.* On the whole, it seems to have been more common among preachers of Spanish origin than among Italians, although it was used in the early sixteenth century by Joseph ben Ḥayyim of Benevento, fol. 103r.

23. E.g., the explication of four different meanings of *qiryat arba*ᶜ (Gen. 23:2) by Israel, "Dober Mesharim," fol. 233v, and Samuel Uceda's fourfold interpretation of *rab lakem shebet ba-har ha-zeh* (Deut. 1:7), in Pachter, "Demuto," p. 34.

24. E.g., *ha-laylah* ᶜ*ad* (Lev. 6:2, lit., "the night until"): Garçon, in Benayahu, p. 188; *ha-*ᶜ*edut asher* (Exod. 38:21, lit., "the testimony that"): Almosnino, p. 3a, sermon translated below.

tension between preacher and audience. In the earlier sermons, which began with a verse from the Writings, the listener was puzzled about the relevance of that verse to the Torah lesson. The challenge of the form was to show an unsuspected connection in a way that cast new light on both the verse and the Torah passage. The sermon beginning with a verse from the Torah lesson gave preachers an opportunity to pose a different kind of question. Attentive listeners, hearing the disconnected phrases from a familiar verse, would wonder what sense they could possibly make; or, hearing the same phrase repeated three or four times, they would wonder why such repetition was necessary. The challenge was not to demonstrate the unanticipated connection between different parts of the Bible but to show that the possibilities of meaning in a single Torah verse were unlimited, that apparently nonsensical combinations of words have significance, that even in the subsyntactical units of its verses, the Torah has the power to address the specific occasion or the needs of the time.

We have traced some significant changes in the structure of the sermon by focusing on the treatment of the biblical verse with which the preacher began. Of course, the problem of sermon structure goes far beyond the use of a single verse. What models for organizing an entire sermon were available to medieval and early modern Jewish preachers? This question must be approached inductively, beginning with a detailed literary analysis of individual sermons, moving to conclusions about the complete oeuvre of particular preachers, then generalizing about the options in any generation, and finally extrapolating about tradition and innovation in the period as a whole.

The first model is the *homily.* This was a technical term used by Christian theoreticians to characterize preaching that treated a section from the Bible verse by verse. The dominant mode during the patristic period, it continued into the high Middle Ages, when it was overshadowed by the new Scholastic sermon based on the division of a single verse.[25] Although the corresponding Hebrew technical term, *perishah,* was not widely used before the end of the fifteenth century, the homily model is preeminent until the last generation in Spain.

Most extant sermons from the thirteenth through the mid-fifteenth centuries, which begin by discussing a verse from a biblical book outside the Torah and then apply it to the Torah lesson, continue in the homily form. The link between the external verse and the Torah lesson is soon forgotten, and the preacher moves through a part (or even all) of the lesson, discussing various exegetical problems and drawing freely from the rabbinic literature pertaining to the verses treated. Such sermons generally lack conceptual unity.

25. On the Christian homily, see Kennedy, pp. 182–83; Owst, *Preaching,* pp. 309–13; Smyth, p. 43; Chamberlain, pp. 44–45, 109–10.

They tend to become diffuse, their cohesiveness provided not by the idea developed but by their framework, a series of successive verses. Among the sermons translated, the anonymous thirteenth-century text and those of ibn Shueib, Mattathias Yizhari, and Solomon Levi exemplify this form. Jacob Anatoli's sermon is a homily on a series of verses from Proverbs in which the Torah lesson is used only tangentially.[26]

Two important refinements of the homily model should be noted. The first specifies the lessons or "benefits" to be derived from the section of verses under discussion. Best known in medieval Hebrew literature from the Torah commentary of Levi ben Gershom (Gersonides), this form may well have been introduced as a preaching technique that found its way into biblical commentary by way of the sermon. Anonymous thirteenth-century sermons frequently summarize what "we have learned from the Torah lesson," usually principles regulating conduct. Although Gersonides' term *toᶜelet* (benefit) does not regularly appear in this context, we find it in one passage: "Even though the story of Balak does not contain an additional commandment, nevertheless it bestows great benefit upon us [*hoᶜilanu toᶜelet gedolah*], as we explained there; similarly, the recounting of the travels [in the lesson *Masᶜe,* Num. 33:1–36:13) entails great benefit." By the fifteenth century this technique, with the technical term *toᶜelet,* was quite common.[27]

The second refinement had an even greater influence on the history of Jewish preaching and biblical exegesis. This was detailing a series of difficulties (*she'elot* or *sefeqot*) arising from the passage under discussion and then resolving them in the course of a commentary on that passage. Popularized by Abravanel's Torah commentary and Arama's *ᶜAqedat Yiṣḥaq,* this refinement was widely used in the generation of the expulsion. Its earlier history cannot yet be traced, but it may well have moved from Scholastic literature into Jewish preaching and Bible commentary. This technique is used with an

26. Many of the other chapters in Anatoli's *Malmad ha-Talmidim* do include homilies on sections of the Torah lesson. Where almost all of the lesson appears to be discussed by the preacher, it is quite likely that the text was not preached in its present form, but rather was composed as a model joining together material from several sermons. In some cases the boundary line between a collection of sermons and a Torah commentary seems somewhat blurred. Baḥya ben Asher's commentary, in which each Torah lesson is introduced with a discussion of a verse from Proverbs, is actually quite close formally to *Midrash David ha-Nagid* and the sermons of Joshua ibn Sheuib; Joseph ben David of Saragossa's commentary on the Torah, which frequently begins and ends each lesson with sermonic material, is similar to some of the "sermons" of Mattathias Yizhari.

27. *Derashot,* pp. 38, 43–44, 65–67, and the sermon translated below. *Toᶜelet* is used on p. 249. Cf. also David ha-Nagid, pp. 73–75: "We have learned from this lesson [*Wa-Yera*] a number of important and beneficial ideas. . . ." In the fifteenth century, Zerahiah ha-Levi, p. 100; Joseph ibn Shem Ṭob, fols. 102r–12r and *Derashot,* fol. 185r; Shem Ṭob, pp. 13a, 18d.

aggadic passage in the sermons by Shem Ṭob ibn Shem Ṭob and Moses Almosnino translated below.[28]

The second major type of sermon, increasingly popular during the fifteenth century, focused on one central conceptual problem, which the preacher undertook to investigate. This problem was called in Hebrew *derush.* The actual subject matter might be an abstract theological conundrum (for example, whether or not a miracle creates faith in the human soul without the concurrence of the will) or one of the perennial problems of medieval Jewish thought (examples are the status of the penitent, God's hardening of Pharaoh's heart, fear and love of God, Jewish suffering in exile). As we shall see, it could be addressed as a formal disputed question, with arguments marshaled on opposing sides, through interpretation of rabbinic passages and discussion of previous Jewish thinkers, or in an organized exposition patterned on the theme-verse.[29]

Purely exegetical sections, such as the interpretation of a lengthy passage from a psalm, were frequently incorporated into the *derush* by sixteenth-century preachers like Moscato and Almosnino. The critical point is that the sermon's structure was determined not by the succession of biblical verses but by the subject matter. The sermons of Shem Ṭob ibn Shem Ṭob, Judah Moscato, and Saul Morteira (translated below) exemplify this model: their subject can be defined in a single phrase, and their structure is immediately apparent.[30]

Late fifteenth- and sixteenth-century preachers were careful to distinguish

28. From the late fifteenth century, Shem Ṭob, pp. 6c–d, 8b, 9c, 39c ("one who does not raise doubts will not know"); Joel ibn Shueib, pp. 123a, 126a; Karo, fol. 178v; Garçon, in Benayahu, p. 156. Earlier than the late fifteenth century, Joseph ben David of Saragossa, pp. 18–21; *Derashot ha-RaN,* pp. 136–40. Yizhari (fol. 14r) stated that "R. Ḥayyim ben David, a disciple of the RaSHBA, wrote that in this [tenth] plague there are several questions [*she᾿elot*], etc., as you can find in his 'Book of Sermons.'" This might indicate the existence of the technique in sermons of the early fourteenth century. (MS Ḥayyim ben David, beginning with fol. 62r, contains a series of selections from a larger work by this author, organized according to the Torah lessons. This larger work, apparently lost, could be the "Book of Sermons" mentioned by Yizhari, but there is no way to prove it.) The synonymous use of *she᾿elot* and *sefeqot* in this context may reflect the equivalence in Scholastic usage of *quaestiones* and *dubitationes*: see F.-A. Blanche, "Le Vocabulaire de l'argumentation et la structure de l'article dans les ouvrages de Saint Thomas," *Revue des sciences philosophiques et théologiques* 14 (1925):168–69.

29. On the term *derush,* see Ben Yehudah, *Millon* 2:995–96, indicating the relatively late evidence for the word (the earliest source cited is Gersonides, then Crescas; all the others are from the fifteenth century). Ravitsky, "Zehuto," p. 158, n. 41, links this term with the Latin *quaestio.* Cf. Joseph Sermonetta, "Ha-Sifrut ha-Pilosofit be-Sefer Porat Yosef le-Rabbi Yosef Ṭaiṭaṣaq," *Sefunot* 11 (1) (1971–78):139, n. 4; 140, n. 5; 155, n. 1.

30. The *kelal ha-derush,* which appears in the written text of Moscato's sermons before the biblical theme-verse, was almost certainly not part of the oral sermon, as there is abundant evidence that the verse was the first thing that the preacher spoke.

between these two modes of preaching; the verbs *peresh* and *darash* were carefully used by men like Joseph Garçon, so that no confusion would arise. The more formal sermon began with a *nośe* and a rabbinic *maʾamar.* The homily, which merely commented on a section from the Torah lesson, required less preparation and was used for less important occasions. Moses Alfalas began several of his sermons with a disclaimer ensuring that no one would be misled: "Although I have taken a *nośe* and a *maʾamar* like one who wants to preach (*il-derosh*), my intention is only to explain (*le-faresh*) the verses according to the rabbinic midrashim," ". . . only to explain the *nośe,*" ". . . only to fulfill my obligation." His listeners must not expect the full formal sermon his opening implies. Isaac Arama welded these two models together to compose each chapter of his *ʿAqedat Yiṣḥaq,* including an exegetical section (*perishah*) after each substantive investigation (*derishah*), but this hybrid form was probably unusual in the actual preaching of the time.[31]

Sermons with unified subjects often included stylized introductory sections. Fifteenth- and sixteenth-century introductions had two common components. First came a justification of the sermon itself, with reasons for the preacher to remain silent and then the stronger reasons for preaching. This section was rife with conventional material—professions of modesty and unworthiness, praises for the virtue of silence, complaints about insufficient time to prepare, the burdens of travel, or the confusion engendered by recent events—and not every preacher was capable of transforming these commonplaces with an original touch. While there is occasionally important biographical information or evidence of true homiletical ingenuity, many of these introductions are stereotyped, predictable, tedious, and long.[32]

At least one preacher (at the beginning of the sixteenth century) questioned the entire convention:

> I am amazed at those preachers who use their sermons to give reasons for their preaching. This seems to me to be a great mistake. If someone were to ask his neighbor why he put on phylacteries or a fringed garment, his very question would show him to be a fool. . . . Now the study of Torah is not only an obligation like the other commandments, it is equivalent to all the others together. Therefore, no preacher need give a reason for preaching on the Torah, for he is merely doing what he is obligated to do.

31. Alfalas, pp. 193a, 77a; cf. 128a, 142b, 173b. Cf. also the introduction to Albelda, where the reader of this book of *derushim* is directed to a different book for the *perishah,* or exposition of the Torah lessons. This author seems to be repudiating the hybrid form made famous by Arama. For a statement of the custom that some treatment of the lesson was supposed to accompany the *derush,* however, see Israel, "Dober Mesharim," fol. 198r.

32. See the introduction to Garçon's sermon translated below. Examples of stereotyped "reasons" are obvious in the work of Balbo and Alfalas.

Yet the man who said these words, Joseph Garçon, failed to follow his own advice, more than once paying obeisance to the convention in the sermons he delivered.[33]

The "reasons" for preaching were generally followed by a formal statement that the sermon was being delivered by permission (*reshut*). This was actually an older convention rooted in the halakic requirement that one must receive permission to teach Torah in the presence of his masters. The simplest form was to say, "With the permission of God, of the Torah, and of the learned scholars and of the entire congregation, I shall begin," but an elaborate introductory form had already developed by the end of the thirteenth century, as the models provided by Baḥya ben Asher attest. The fifteenth century reveals such new attempts to breathe novelty into a stylized form as Ephraim ha-Darshan's rhymed prose introductions and Michael Balbo's interminable disquisitions on God and the Torah. Neglect of this convention required an explanation, as we see in one preacher's introduction to a eulogy for his wife: "Because I am overwhelmed by grief, I do not have the wit to take permission [in a formal manner]; do not blame me, for sorrow excuses." Once again, Joseph Garçon maintained that the convention was superfluous and should be abandoned, but he conceded its power by following it himself.[34]

A different kind of introduction to the *derush,* intended to capture the listeners' attention, generate interest, and eventually to articulate the central subject that the preacher would address, developed alongside this wholly conventional material. In Saul Morteira and in other masters of this form, the sermon's introductory paragraphs are miniature essays with their own structure, and they prepared the listeners for what was to follow without anticipating the major points. Morteira's introductions always end with a succinct formulation of the sermon's topic, followed by the words, "That will be our *derush* today, which we begin with the help of God," a cue to the listeners that the body of the sermon was about to begin.[35]

33. Garçon, in Benayahu, pp. 196–97, as contrasted with pp. 144, 157, and the sermon translated below.

34. On the *reshut,* see Goitein, *Community,* p. 164; the sources listed by Hacker, "Li-Demutam," p. 83, n. 140; and the discussion by Sosland in Zahalon, p. 136, n. 79. Michael Balbo could extend a *reshut* for many pages (e.g., fols. 79v–82r, 98r–100v). The excuse in the eulogy appears in Israel, "Dober Mesharim," fol. 19v (cf. fol. 241r: "I shall take that permission [*reshut*] that all are accustomed to take"). Garçon, in Benayahu, pp. 144, 150. The claim made by Toviah Preschel in "Reshut li-Derashah," *Sinai* 89 (1981):93–94, that there is no evidence of the *reshut* in sermonic literature before the second half of the eighteenth century, was retracted in *Sinai* 92 (1982–83):95–96.

35. See Saperstein, "Art Form," p. 247; cf. Zahalon, pp. 135–38. In the sermons of Josiah Pardo, a disciple of Morteira, the section immediately following the *ma'amar* is formally entitled *haqdamah* ("introduction"); after the appeal for God's help come the term *derush* and the body of the sermon. This fulfills the requirements of the exordium in Cicero's *De partitione*

The third model appeared later. At the beginning of the eighteenth century, Moses Ḥayyim Luzzatto wrote a brief analysis of homiletical conventions and styles, distinguishing between two kinds of sermons in his time. In the first, the classical Sephardic *derush,* which Luzzatto associated with a Ciceronian model, "the preacher chooses one subject, and makes his entire discourse focus on explaining what needs to be explained and proving his point in various ways." In the second, "the discourse meanders over various different subjects, but they are linked together in one way or another. For example, they may all be pertinent to the weekly lesson from the Torah, or one point may lead to another."[36]

The two subtypes of Luzzatto's second category are actually quite different. The first is, of course, the homily, which had reached its peak of influence many centuries before. The second, a more recent development, was widely prevalent when Luzzatto wrote. Closely linked with the learned halakic discourse of the academy, it consists of a chain of exegetical insights: the interpretation of one biblical or rabbinic passage leads to an association with another, which is then interpreted and associated with a third, and so forth. The sermons of Israel of Belżyce and Jonathan Eybeschuetz, translated below, exemplify this *catenary* style.[37]

Much of the most important preaching of the eighteenth century followed this form. Sermons on this model were not necessarily limited to exegesis. Social criticism, ethical instruction, or illustrative parables could be interspersed among the interpretations or added in a separate section. Nor was the form inherently barren and pedantic. The literature shows that it could accommodate brilliant insights and striking creativity. But the catenary model does tend to produce amorphous sermons. The listener rarely has much sense of where the preacher is leading or what he is going to talk about. It is even hard to tell if the sermon is almost over or still near the beginning. What may be remembered is a single innovative interpretation or a particular parable, but not a summary of the sermon as a whole. Those who have talked about the decadence of Jewish preaching in the eighteenth century generally had in mind the less inspired uses of this form.

The three structural models, homily, *derush,* and catenary, can be linked with different eras of our period. The homily form, introduced by a verse

---

oratoriae, a text known to Jewish peachers like Moscato (see Altmann, "Ars Rhetorica," pp. 12, 16). It may also have been connected with the medieval Christian protheme, which, like Morteira's introductions, concludes with an appeal to God for help.

36. Moses Ḥayyim Luzzatto, "Maʾamar ʿal ha-Derashah," ed. Abraham Habermann, with *Sefer ha-Meliṣah* (Jerusalem, 1950).

37. This term is used to describe a type of sixteenth-century French Christian preaching, characterized by a "profusion of disparate elements and entire lack of continuous argument," in Bayley, p. 85.

from the Writings or the Prophets, predominated during the thirteenth and fourteenth centuries. The *derush,* an investigation of a single subject, introduced by a theme-verse from the Torah lesson and a rabbinic statement and accompanied by new conventions, emerged in the fifteenth century and was widely used by Sephardic preachers for several centuries thereafter. The catenary style came into its own in the seventeenth century and predominated in the eighteenth.

Yet while this picture is correct in its broad outlines, it is also misleading. Styles of preaching are not born suddenly, nor do they disappear overnight. The homily and the *derush* were both vigorous in the sixteenth century. Indeed, the practice of raising questions about a passage from the Torah lesson gave new strength to the homily, and Arama tried (at least in his written work) to create a new form by joining them. Saul Morteira's eulogy for the martyr Isaac de Castro Tartas (unfortunately no longer extant) was preached in Amsterdam only half a year before Israel of Bełżyce delivered his response to the Chmielnicki massacres in Poland, but if Morteira's other preaching is any guide, their two sermons were worlds apart formally. The classical Sephardic *derush* retained vitality at least through the nineteenth century, and Morteira's sermons are closer in form to most modern Jewish preaching than are those of Jonathan Eybeschuetz.

Nor can use of the same sermon form be assumed even for a single generation in the same city. Comparison of the sermons by Moses Almosnino and Solomon Levi, translated below, which were preached in Salonika five years apart, reveals that they are entirely different in form. Solomon Levi's sermon harks back to the old homily tradition, and Almosnino's pushed the *derush,* with its divided theme-verse, to new levels of complexity and sophistication. Even the same preachers could use different models for different occasions. And in those who, like Morteira, were consistent in their choice of structure, there was still room for considerable variety of form. The best preaching always bursts through the conventional structures and adapts the inherited forms to the needs of the subject and the time.

Sermons and History

The value of sermons as a source for the study of history is hardly a matter of debate among historians of medieval and early modern Christian Europe. In many regions and periods the pulpit served as one of the finest mirrors of contemporary events. Few issues of significance escaped the scrutiny and judgment of the clergy. Furthermore, the preacher was frequently in the forefront of historical movements, whether as a mouthpiece of the established church against heretical challenges, as a trumpet of dissent, or as a sounding board for the antagonists in social conflict.[1]

Unfortunately, expectations that Jewish sermonic literature might serve as a vast untapped repository of historical information are not likely to be realized. Most extant Jewish sermons from our period are long on exegesis of traditional texts and on exploration of abstract intellectual problems and short on responses to concrete historical situations.[2] There are at least two explanations for this fact.

The first is the nature of the selection process. In general, sermons were not preserved unless the preacher first proceeded to write what he had said in a more permanent form and then decided to incorporate this text into a book. But no matter whether the preacher's purpose in writing was to preserve material for his own future consultation, to make it accessible to other preachers who might use it as a model, or to benefit distant readers with the fruits of his learning, it was precisely the timely, topical sermon that was least likely to be considered of value. What was immediate, vital, and pressing in the hour of delivery would not be usable by the same preacher twenty years later, nor would it be of interest to another preacher in search of homiletical insights, nor yet would it be comprehensible to future readers in different countries. Timely content was the most likely to be eliminated during the transformation from oral to written text. The more general, theoretical, and "timeless" content would be expanded.

This process is clearly illustrated in a passage from Solomon Levi's *Dibre Shelomoh*:

> The day of the Sabbath preceding Passover, 10 Nisan, 5333 [1573]. I did not preach, nor did the other sages of the city [Salonika] preach in their congregations, for we were in emergency session [*maʿamad*] all day long, discussing the crisis attendant upon the building of the walls, brought upon us by that enemy and adversary, that evil Haman, the regional judge Musliḥ al-Dīn, may his name and memory be blotted

1. In addition to the abundant material on the historical significance of the thirteenth-century mendicant orders, there are many studies of the English sermon that would bear out these generalizations. See Chandos; MacLure, pp. 20–115; Seaver; and essays like E. W. Kemp's "History and Action in the Sermons of a Medieval Archbishop," in *The Writing of History in the Middle Ages,* ed. R. H. C. Davis and J. M. Wallace-Hadrill (Oxford, 1981), pp. 349–65.

2. Of course, many Christian sermons are also of a theoretical nature with little direct response to historical events. But the enormous number of extant Christian sermons makes even a relatively small percentage dealing with historical issues yield a considerable harvest. Furthermore, the institutional position of certain Christian preachers as adversaries or allies of the government made it necessary for them to respond from their pulpits to contemporary events. This was a kind of pressure that Jewish preachers seldom faced.

out! Members of the various congregations had been thrown into prison. But praise be to God, a great miracle was performed for Israel, and on the first night of Passover, at midnight, God smote him dead, and *there was light and joy for the Jews* (Esther 8:16).

The text then continues, "The first day of Passover, 5333 [1573], I preached on *It is the Passover sacrifice to the Lord*" (Exod. 12:27). A conceptual question relating to the festival is introduced and discussed: ordinarily, deeds are more important than words in the fulfillment of the commandments, yet one cannot fulfill the commandment to observe the Passover without talking about the Exodus. Then the account of the sermon concludes as follows: "And I explained the *nośe* as applying to the miracle performed for us in the death of the adversary." There is no way of knowing how long or detailed this section of the sermon was, but it is reasonable to assume that it contained additional information about the episode not known from other sources.[3] Yet the preacher considered this less worthy of transcription than the homiletical portion, which he assumed would be of interest to readers far away.

A second reason why sermons are often disappointing as historical sources lies in the nature of the medium. Because the sermon is an act of communication between a particular preacher and a particular congregation, there is usually no need for the preacher to provide the kind of information that a chronicler, writing for an unknown distant or future audience, would have to include in his work. A general statement or a passing reference is sufficient to make everyone present understand, and details and explicit applications are often superfluous.

This was certainly true when the preacher was called upon to deliver a eulogy in a case of unnatural death. Even where the names are given, the circumstances of death, already known to the listeners, are usually not made explicit. The texts of these sermons furnish frightening glimpses of murders and martyrdoms, of sinister forms of violence unmentionable from the pulpit except by euphemism.[4] Such details do give a general picture of the uncer-

3. This account of the episode, in *Dibre Shelomoh,* pp. 191c and 192a, is the only one we have. See Salomon Rosanes, *Qorot ha-Yehudim be-Turqyah we-ʾArṣot ha-Qedem,* 5 vols. (Husiatyn-Sofia, 1930–45), 2:119; I. S. Emmanuel, *Histoire des Israélites de Salonique* (Paris, 1936), p. 231. No confirmation from Ottoman archives has yet been discovered.

4. Cf. e.g., "In this context I spoke about the killing of Abraham ha-Kohen. . . ; since this is so, how could he have been killed in such a manner?" (Israel, "Dober Mesharim," fol. 151v). "The sermon that I, Isaac Karo, preached in Magnesia in the year 5269 [1508] at the slaying of Don Solomon ben Isaac ha-Kohen of Botargo" (Karo, fol. 1v): "This I preached when the scholar . . . R. Tobias Zarfati was slain, when that ugly thing happened to this pious man. . . . If this event had entailed a matter of martyrdom, we certainly know that he would have given up his life" (Ashkenazi, pp. 154a, 159a): "The sermon that I preached upon the slaying of R. Solomon Narboni . . . and six others (not to mention the injured and maimed), because of our sins. . . . We saw with our own eyes God's wrath, something not done to Israel from the earliest years" (Sassoon MS 692, fol. 1).

tainties of Jewish life, but they can seldom be expanded into a recognizable historical event.

Where the stage is broadened and the events are of larger significance, frustration at the allusive style of the preacher often increases. For example, although the number of Spanish Jewish preachers from the generation of 1492 who left written legacies is considerable, not a single extant sermon can be viewed as a direct and immediate response to the upheavals of Iberian Jewry's final decades: the unification of Aragon and Castile, the establishment of the Inquisition, the trial of the "murderers" of the "child of La Guardia," and the Edict of Expulsion.

Certainly there are allusions to the events of the day, both on the local and on the national levels. Preaching on the subject of creation, Abraham Bibago noted, "On the previous Sabbath, in the middle of the holiday [the Feast of Booths], I began to preach to this distinguished company, but when the alarming tumult [*ha-behalah we-ha-mehumah*] that you saw arrived, I was forced to stop, and we were all left dismayed, bereaved, and deeply concerned about that tragedy." Few in the congregation could have had any uncertainty about the event to which the preacher was referring. For readers like us, the actual circumstances remain a tantalizing riddle.[5]

Shem Ṭob ibn Shem Ṭob expresses a weary skepticism about the political foundations of Jewish life in Spain. Just like Jacob, he noted in a sermon on *Wa-Yishlaḥ* (Gen. 32:4–36:43), "We send to [the Gentiles] to say that everything we own is theirs, yet we still do not find favor in their sight. We have emissaries in the royal courts and palaces, but they are not received. . . . Kings and nobles say that we are their servants, but they do not protect us. When they accept large gifts, they appear as if they love us in order to obtain even more." This might have been interpreted as a bitter response to the failure of Jewish courtiers to prevent the promulgation or implementation of the Edict of Expulsion, but the book was completed before that, in 1489. While the passage expresses an important critical stance, questioning the value of the royal alliance, it is impossible to determine precisely what evoked it.[6]

Joel ibn Shueib incorporated the following comment into a sermon on *Be-Ḥuqqotai* (Lev. 26:3–27:34): "Every day, new calamities arise resulting from that calamity [the destruction of the Temple]. They recall it to mind, never

5. The year and the city where Bibago delivered the sermon entitled "Zeh Yenaḥamenu" ("This will console us") are not specified. Zinberg states without hesitation that there was an anti-Jewish riot (*History of Jewish Literature,* trans. Bernard Martin [Cleveland, 1973], 3:256). This may be true, but the language is too general to serve as historical evidence.

6. Shem Ṭob ibn Shem Ṭob, p. 17b–c. On the "royal alliance," see Y. H. Yerushalmi, *The Lisbon Massacre of 1506 and the Royal Image in the Shebet Yehudah* (Cincinnati, 1976), pp. 37–66.

allowing it to be forgotten. Thus it is today throughout the kingdom of Castile and Aragon." These words would undoubtedly have resonated in the minds of listeners who associated them with particular events. For the modern reader, they remain little more than an intriguing hint. Further in the same sermon, he remarked, "When Jews are in the lands of many kings, it is well for them however fortune turns, for if one king should decide to destroy them, they can go to a different land. But when they are under one king, as we are today in Spain, there is no escape except to God alone." For anyone seated in the audience, the message would have been abundantly clear. Today, not knowing whether these words were spoken in the 1470s after the unification of the realms, or in June of 1492 between the promulgation of the Edict of Expulsion and its deadline, their precise significance is an enigma.[7]

The following passage appears in a sermon on the binding of Isaac found in manuscripts of two different late fifteenth-century preachers:

> Rabbi Ḥasdai [Crescas] said that Abraham's act had this significance: in preparing to sacrifice Isaac upon the altar, he prepared to sacrifice all the generations of his descendants, for it was already promised that *through Isaac offspring will be referred to as yours* (Gen. 21:12). It was therefore tantamount to his having sacrificed all future Jews. Through his actions he also taught us, as it were, that all those who want to be among the descendants of Abraham must be prepared to offer their lives for the sanctification of God's Name when the proper time comes. Otherwise they are not from the seed of Abraham. That is why all of the righteous and virtuous Jews gave their lives as martyrs: in order to demonstrate that they were descendants of Abraham and Isaac. Every Jew should think that, being from the seed of Abraham, a father should be prepared to kill his child . . . as Abraham did, in order to fulfill the will of his heavenly Father.

Was this a message to *conversos* facing the possibility of death at the hands of the Inquisition, or merely a theoretical disquisition on the traditional theme of martyrdom? To an audience faced with the actual choice, the poignancy and power of this passage would have been considerable. Without knowledge of the actual circumstances under which it was delivered, the sermon's resonance can only be guessed at.[8]

7. Joel ibn Shueib, pp. 105c, 106a. Cf. Baer, *HJCS* 2:507, n. 2.

8. The sermon is found, with some variations, both in MS Cambridge Dd. 10.46/6 of the sermons of Shem Ṭob ibn Shem Ṭob (although not in the printed editions) and in Israel's "Dober Mesharim." The passage cited is on fols. 35v and 211r, respectively. It is not clear exactly where the quotation from Crescas ends, but given the death of his own son in the pogroms of 1391 (Baer, *HJCS* 2:104–05), the model of the ʿ*aqedah* would have been especially poignant for him. I intend to publish and analyze this sermon in a separate study.

Finally, a parable in Isaac Aboab's *Nehar Pishon* has been identified by modern historians as a messianic message of comfort to the exiles from Spain: "A father and son were walking on a road. The son, tired and weak, asked the father if they were far from the city [their destination] or near it. The father said, 'Remember this sign: when you see a cemetery, that will indicate that we are near the city. . . .' Thus when we see calamities draw near, it is a sign of the coming of the Messiah."[9] But none of those who have cited this passage noted that the parable comes from the Midrash, and that it was probably a commonplace not only of Jewish but also of Christian response to tragedy.[10] It was not necessarily a reaction to the expulsion; it is so general that without specific knowledge of when and where it was said, its historical value is minimal. More such allusions, immediately comprehensible to the listener but frustratingly ambiguous to the historian, are all too common.[11]

Many sermons delivered at crucial moments in Jewish history have apparently been lost. In the aftermath of the traumatic 1391 pogroms in Spain, Ḥasdai Crescas is said to have "preached publicly in the synagogues that the Messiah was born in Cisneros, in the kingdom of Castile." Zerahiah ha-Levi is reported to have preached in the synagogue of Tortosa in 1413 immediately before the infamous disputation began. According to inquisitional records, a rabbi named Levi ben Shem Ṭob of Saragossa delivered three sermons on successive Saturdays in 1490, exhorting his people to obey the edict compelling Jews under pain of the ban to testify about Judaizing *conversos*; he used the biblical account of Achan (Judg. 7) as a model.

Yom Ṭob Lipmann Heller, subjected to imprisonment and a ruinous fine

9. Aboab, p. 9a; cf. Midrash Tehillim, 20 (YJS 13:290). The passage was first cited by H. H. Ben-Sasson, "Galut u-Geʾulah be-ʿEynaw shel Dor Gole Sefarad," *Sefer Yobel le-Yiṣḥaq Baer* (Jerusalem, 1961), pp. 217–18, n. 10, and subsequently by Baron, *SRHJ* 13:145; in *EJ* 13:1000, it is presented as an "immediate, live reaction to the expulsion."

10. Cf. the following passage in a sermon of John Donne: "As he that travails weary and late towards a great City is glad when he comes to a place of execution, because he knows that he is near the town; so when thou comest to the gate of death (be) glad of that, for it is but one step from that to thy Jerusalem." (*XXVI Sermons,* no. 20, cited by Evelyn M. Simpson, "The Literary Value of Donne's Sermons," in *John Donne,* ed. Helen Gardner [Englewood Cliffs, N.J., 1962], p. 145). Donne apparently used "place of execution" rather than "cemetery" because Christian cemeteries were usually inside the church or in the churchyard in the middle of the city.

11. Cf. Albelda, p. 92a: "We ourselves will see divine judgment against us because of our sins, for the hand of the Lord has gone out against all the Gentiles around us." A manuscript of seventeenth-century sermons by a Maghribi preacher contains a long reference to persecutions that afflicted the Jewish community of a foreign country, but the passage is so general that David Sassoon, describing the manuscript in his catalogue, could not decide whether it referred to persecutions in Palestine in 1625 or to the Chmielnicki persecutions in Poland of 1648–49 (*Ohel Dawid: Hebrew and Samaritan Manuscripts in the Sassoon Library,* 2 vols. [London, 1932], 2:676–77).

by imperial officials, delivered a farewell sermon in the Meisels Synagogue of his beloved Prague on the second day of Tammuz, 5391 [1631], before departing for Polish territory. When a report reached Amsterdam early in 1648 that the Marrano Isaac de Castro Tartas had been burned at the stake as a martyr in Lisbon, he was eulogized by the master preacher Saul ha-Levi Morteira. At the height of the Sabbatian movement, in 1665–66, a Polish preacher in Posen delivered a series of messianic sermons, while an opponent of the movement insisted in a sermon preached in Jerusalem that "a man may not allow himself to be made into a god, and he may certainly not make himself into a god."[12] Any one of these sermons would have illuminated an individual and a community situation at a turning point. As far as is known, none has survived.

Yet the importance of sermons for Jewish history should not be minimized. Sermons frequently include biographical details that are otherwise unattested. Manuscripts that identify the place and date of delivery for each sermon, such as those of Joseph Garçon and Israel of Bełżyce, facilitate a reconstruction of a preacher's career by placing him in particular communities on specific occasions. Sermons preached at milestones in a preacher's life can contain noteworthy evidence of his mental outlook and intellectual development.[13] Eulogies are among the most important sources for verifying the date on which a significant figure died. Eulogies for members of the preacher's own family frequently allow us rare glimpses of personality and expressions of genuine emotion.[14]

Sometimes sermons are the primary source of information about historical events. The sermon by Joseph ibn Shem Ṭob following an Easter Week pogrom against the Jews of Segovia in 1452 (translated below) is a good example. Its reference to Prince Henry fits both the chronological framework and what is known about the prince's special relationship with Segovia, and

12. For Crescas, see Baer, *HJCS* 2:160, 476, n. 46; for Zerahiah, Solomon ibn Verga, *Shebeṭ Yehudah* (Jerusalem, 1947), p. 97; for Levi, (Yitzhak) Fritz Baer, *Die Juden im christlichen Spanien,* 2 vols. (1929–36; reprint ed., Farnborough, England, 1970), 2:450–51, cf. *HJCS* 2:372 and Baron, *SRHJ* 13:37–38; for Heller, see *Megillat Ebah* (Jerusalem, 1971), p. 12; for Morteira, Isaac Cardoso, cited in Y. H. Yerushalmi, *From Spanish Court to Italian Ghetto* (New York, 1971), p. 398; for a Polish preacher, Gershom Scholem, *Sabbatai Ṣevi* (Princeton, 1973), p. 596; for an opponent, Garmizan, fol. 274 (Maftehot: Ḥayye Sarah, Derush 1). Cf. Meir Benayahu's introduction to Garmizan's Mishpeṭe Ṣedeq (Jerusalem, 1945), pp. 20–21. The first part of *Imre No^cam,* in which the sermon would have been found, is apparently lost, and Scholem's reference to this sermon in *Sabbatai Ṣevi,* p. 361, is misleading.

13. E.g., Naḥmanides' New Year's Day sermon delivered not long after his arrival in the land of Israel (*Kitbe RaMBaN* 1:214–52, esp. p. 251); Joseph Garçon's first sermon in Salonika after he escaped from forced apostasy in Portugal (translated below); Solomon Alkabeẓ's announcement that he was leaving Turkey to live in the Holy Land (Alkabeẓ, fol. 37v).

14. E.g., Israel, "Dober Mesharim," fol. 233v; Jaffe, pp. 441–42.

the outbreak of anti-Jewish violence during Easter Week was certainly no infrequent occurrence. But there does not appear to be any other Jewish or Christian source that speaks about this incident. Although the sermon provides few details about the violence, leaving us ignorant as to how many were killed, how much damage was done, and who was responsible, the information it does give is an important addition to the history of fifteenth-century Castilian Jewry.[15]

For events that are documented by other sources, the retrospective analysis of the preacher can provide interpretation and context. No extant sermon is known to have been delivered during the actual period of the Black Plague, but a passage in the *Derashot* of Nissim Gerondi written thirteen years later (around 1451) still conveys some of the anxiety, confusion, and terror that must have overwhelmed those who had lived through it.[16]

Azariah Figo conveys a similar sense of emotion recollected in tranquility in a sermon for the Sabbath preceding the Day of Atonement, delivered in Venice:

> How terrified we were during those days by the awesome portent of the bolts of lightning that descended into the courtyard of our dwellings—and fire entered some of the houses and began to burn . . . making a fearful impression! But through God's mercy only one Jew was killed. This after God's hand was against us and our children because of our sins in previous years, and you know what happened [*yaṣeʾu mah she-yaṣeʾu,* a euphemism, born of intimacy with an audience], for then we saw a number of our Jewish youths killed, fallen by the sword."[17]

The following retrospective passage, delivered by Zerah Eidlitz at the High Synagogue of Prague in 1766, powerfully recapitulates the traumas of a tumultuous generation:

> No community, large or small, has suffered as many blows in a short time as we have suffered since the year 1740. Tragedies came upon us in pairs, in each case the second tragedy more painful than the first. First, the many tributes to the king of France, which, however, could be paid separately, month by month. When [the French] left, then Her

15. Cf. Angus MacKay, "Popular Movements and Pogroms in Fifteenth-Century Castile," *Past and Present* 55 (1972):33–67. The same is true of the apocopated text of the sermon preached by Solomon Levi, mentioned above. See also Alfalas, p. 95b, and the sermon delivered by Abraham Rapoport in 1609 upon the recovery of the synagogue in Lvov that had been seized and used by the Jesuits: Rapoport, pp. 69a–75a (p. 75 is misnumbered 71); cf. Jecheskiel Caro, *Geschichte der Juden in Lemberg* (Cracow, 1894), pp. 41–43.

16. *Derashot ha-RaN,* pp. 173–74.

17. Figo, p. 45a; cf. 32c.

> Majesty the empress [Maria Theresa] commanded us to give her what had been given to him all at once, and an additional tribute as well.
>
> Second, when the king of France occupied our city and the soldiers of Her Majesty the empress besieged it, we were in great distress and suffered from hunger, yet we were not in mortal danger. Afterward, when we were besieged by the Prussian king, we feared for our lives night and day, and they plundered and ravaged us. Third, when the Prussian king and his army first came, three Jews were killed. The second time, when he left here, many times that number were killed, and more than a hundred were permanently injured.
>
> We were expelled twice. The first time it was not even for a full year, the second time it lasted three years and was more severe than the first, in that we were not permitted to lodge for the night even in the proximity of our city. Similarly with the fires: the first time Her Majesty the empress compensated us for the damages incurred, but the second time the Tandelmarkt was burned, and many respectable men became paupers.[18]

In a passage like this the preacher himself becomes something of a historian, not only reviewing events for his audience but imposing order upon them to make them more comprehensible.

No less important than such a putting in order is the way the sermon can take the historian back to a unique historical moment in all its ambiguity. In many ways the sermon reflects a particular event almost directly, while a book, produced over a period of months or years, refracts and diffuses the experience. Few other sources have the potential of capturing the historical moment so effectively.

The sermon that responds to an event is the product of the preacher's best judgment about the meaning of what has occurred, the message his people need to hear, and what it is permissible to say, all crystallized under the pressure of time. A chronicler recording events that have shaken his community has the leisure of waiting until he is ready to commit himself in writing. He can gather information from various sources, attempt different ways of putting it together, and wait until vexing ambiguities are clarified and ramifications become known. Preachers frequently do not have this luxury. They must face their congregations immediately and attempt to make sense out of what has happened, often without knowing all they would like, and certainly without knowing where events are leading. Whether it is Israel of Bełżyce trying to explain the Cossack massacres of 1648 on the basis of a

18. Eidlitz, p. 72c–d. The Tandelmarkt was a large market in the Old Town of Prague where many Jewish merchants sold secondhand wares. I am grateful to Wilma A. Iggers of Canisius College for this information.

new kabbalistic worldview, or Perez ben Moses, a Polish maggid, responding in the land of Israel to news of the Frankist apostasy, or Ezekiel Landau defending the Edict of Toleration while warning against its potential dangers, the sermon preached under pressure and drawing on the limited evidence available reveals an event as perceived by those who still felt the aftershocks.[19]

As a public utterance the sermon reveals not only the preacher's mind but also the constraints of his position. Joseph ibn Shem Ṭob, sent as an emissary of Prince Henry to Segovia and therefore addressing his congregation in a semiofficial capacity, apparently felt no compunction about publicly affirming that Jesus deserved to be put to death by the Jews in ancient times. Ezekiel Landau's position as chief rabbi of Prague at the end of the eighteenth century was quite different. No matter what he felt about the anti-Jewish policies of Maria Theresa, he was limited in what he could say in her eulogy. And no matter how ambivalent he may have been about the Edict of Toleration of her successor, Joseph II, he could not openly criticize it from the pulpit. Determining the limits on a preacher's freedom of expression is an important historical task.[20]

Finally, there is the audience. Although generally mute, the audience had its own interests, expectations, and response, which are as much a part of the preaching event as is the preacher. One who reads the sermon delivered by Moses Almosnino upon his return to Salonika from Constantinople (translated below) can sense the presence in the congregation of some who were antagonistic toward the preacher, suspicious of his behavior and perhaps even of his motives, ready to argue that his achievement was less than the total triumph he claimed. The confrontation with a group of potentially hostile listeners makes that sermon into a rhetorical tour de force. Whether his hearers were convinced by his eloquence or perhaps more just overwhelmed by his perseverance, we cannot know.[21]

Nor are we better informed about how the audience received sermons in times of crisis and tragedy. We can analyze the literary form and the thought pattern in the sermon by Israel of Bełżyce and appreciate its value as an immediate response to the Cossacks' havoc. But the reaction of the listeners

19. For Bełżyce, see the sermon translated below; for Perez, Abraham Yaari, *Meḥqere Sefer* (Jerusalem, 1958), pp. 455–57; for Landau, the sermon translated below.

20. See the annotation to the sermons by Joseph ibn Shem Ṭob and Ezekiel Landau translated below. Landau's eulogy for Maria Theresa (Prague, 1780) was one of two sermons published during the preacher's lifetime. It was not included in any of the posthumous collections of Landau's sermons, and it has hardly ever been discussed among his works. Because the published version was small in size and ephemeral in nature, it is extremely rare today. I was able to consult copies in the British Library and the National Library in Jerusalem. I hope to republish this fascinating text in the near future; meanwhile, see Saperstein, "Empress."

21. See the annotation to the Almosnino sermon.

is also a historical question. Whether they found comfort, inspiration, and strength from his words, or whether he appeared to them like the pathetic preacher conjured by Bialik—

> He whispers empty verses over their open wounds
> But not a single mighty word comes forth from his mouth,
> Not a single tiny spark is kindled in their hearts.
> God's flock is standing, old and young,
> Some hear and yawn, the heads of others nod—[22]

will perhaps never be known. Some of the historical dimensions of the sermon as response-to-event and as event itself will continue to elude even the most thorough attempt at reconstruction.[23]

Sermons and Literature

The importance of the Christian sermon in the study of European literature is attested by an impressive body of scholarly work. Students in many countries have followed the path outlined two generations ago by G. P. Owst in his magisterial investigation of the influence of preaching on all branches of English literature. Examination of the exemplum or illustrative story and its relationship to narrative collections in English, French, Spanish, German, and Italian has been an ongoing task. S. L. Gilman's recent *The Parodic Sermon in European Perspective* demonstrates that the parody of the sermon was a pervasive and influential literary genre.

Due emphasis has been given to the sermon's function in such works as *The Canterbury Tales,* in which Chaucer explores the full possibilities of the sermon as a performance integrating the personality of the preacher, the message and delivery, and the reaction of the audience. The significance of the sermon in the novel, from *Tristram Shandy* through *Moby Dick* and *Portrait of the Artist as a Young Man* to Camus's *The Plague* and Updike's *Month of Sundays* has been noted. At the same time, the literary study of the sermon proper has proceeded apace. The prose of John Donne and Jacques Bossuet

22. H. N. Bialik, "Be-ʿIr ha-Haregah," ll. 226–30.

23. For example, Abraham Neuman's assertion (*The Jews in Spain* [Philadelphia, 1942], 2:267) that Joseph ibn Shem Ṭob came to Segovia and "stirred the worshipping congregation with a fervent sermon [the one translated here] which fired their hearts with renewed courage" may well be true, but it is mere speculation.

is a standard object of literary analysis, and recent literary theoretical principles have been applied to the work of other celebrated preachers as well.[1]

The task of documenting the relationships between the Jewish sermon and Hebrew literature is considerably more difficult. There is little overlap between the most important periods of Jewish preaching and the great ages of Hebrew literary creativity. By the time the first medieval collections of Jewish sermons appear in the thirteenth century, the "Golden Age" of Hebrew poetry has already ended. The renewal of Hebrew literature in the nineteenth century coincides with a displacement of the sermon from its central position in Jewish life. Nevertheless, the material justifies a quick review, touching both on the sermon in literature and on literature in the sermon.

At the very beginning of our period, one of the seminal works of Hebrew belles lettres uses a sermon in a position no reader could miss. The second chapter of Judah Alḥarizi's *Sefer Taḥkemoni* (written between 1215 and 1235) purports to record the words of a "learned preacher in the isles of the sea," a renowned mokiaḥ (preacher of rebuke). This sermon is a successful literary exercise, for the power and eloquence of the preacher's denunciation of temporal vanities and his call to repentance genuinely impress both narrator and reader. However, as evidence for the history of Jewish preaching, its value is problematic. None of the (admittedly few) extant thirteenth-century Hebrew sermons is anything like this one. Every known Jewish sermon begins with a biblical verse; this one does not. More important, this sermon does not contain a single homiletical exegesis of a biblical verse or of a rabbinic statement. While the theme *de contemptu mundi* is not unfamiliar, the approach to this theme is totally different from that of actual Jewish preaching. The dominant motifs—the world as a mere inn for the night, the grave as the great leveler, the putrefaction of the body in the ground, *Ubi Sunt, Dies Irae*—are all motifs from general literature. They are familiar not from thirteenth-century Jewish sermons but from Samuel ha-Nagid's *Ben Qohelet* and from certain pessimistic poems of Moses ibn Ezra, both written under the influence of Islam.

What is reflected in this chapter of *Taḥkemoni* is probably a tradition of ascetic Muslim preaching. Alḥarizi appears to have recast this tradition in Hebrew, just as he did with the *maqāmah* ("session") genre itself. It is an ironic comment on the state of early thirteenth-century Jewish homiletics that the one significant sermon incorporated into a central work of medieval He-

1. The literature is enormous. Among the most important relevant works, in addition to Owst, *Literature,* are the studies of the exemplum by Crane, Welter, Tubach, and Brémond; Francisco Rico, *Predicación y literatura en la España medieval* (Cadiz, 1977); Deyermond (Spanish narrative); Moser-Rath (German narrative); Gilman (parody); Susan Gallick, "A Look at Chaucer and His Preachers," *Speculum* 50 (1975):456–76; Stanley Fish, "Structuralist Homiletics," in *Is There a Text in This Class?* (Cambridge, Mass., 1980), pp. 181–96.

brew literature was probably intended to be read as the sermon of a Muslim preacher.[2]

Nor is the sermon in Shem Ṭob Falaquera's "Iggeret ha-Musar" from the second half of the thirteenth century more helpful. The preacher, an itinerant sage who identifies his country of origin as India, enters the house of prayer and, "seated above the people," delivers a rebuke and a call to repentance. As in Alḥarizi, the style is the pastiche of biblical and rabbinic phrases one expects in Hebrew rhymed prose. But this text is a pale shadow of the powerful Alḥarizi sermon. Its content is such a stereotyped and conventional treatment of the *de contemptu mundi* theme that the sudden and profound transformation of the congregation at its conclusion seems unjustified, bringing the entire episode suspiciously close to parody. Here, too, there is no connection with any attested thirteenth-century model of Jewish preaching.[3]

Medieval Hebrew literature may show surprisingly little evidence of the impact of Jewish preachers, but modern Hebrew literature is by no means a barren source. Although the literature is outside our period, the point is worth making. Several leading figures of the eastern *Haśkalah,* including Abraham Lebensohn, published model sermons at the instigation of the Russian authorities. Memoirs written by literary figures raised in the traditional society of Eastern Europe also testify to the power of the maggidim and the impact they could have. Satires and parodies of famous maggidim begin to appear in various late nineteenth-century fictional works. Agnon's short story "The Messenger from the Holy Land" pivots upon the dramatic confrontation between a visiting preacher and an unreceptive audience.[4]

A preacher and his sermons are critical to the plot and the thematic texture in two central works of modern Hebrew literature. Rabbi Grunam Yequm Purqan sporadically reappears in Agnon's *Temol Shilshom* as a fiery and popular

2. Judah Alḥarizi, *Sefer Taḥkemoni* (Hanover, 1924), "shaʿar" 2, pp. 15–19 (trans. Victor Reichert, *The Taḥkemoni of Judah Alḥarizi,* 2 vols. [Jerusalem, 1965], 1:59–68). For Islamic preaching on these themes see Johannes Pedersen, "The Islamic Preacher," *Ignaz Goldziher Memorial Volume* (Budapest, 1948), esp. pp. 238–41, and Yosef Sadan, "ʿAl 'Torah' bat Yeme ha-Benayim," *Meḥqere Yerushalayim be-Maḥashebet Yiśraʾel* 3 (1983):414–45. Cf. also Norman Roth, "The 'Ubi Sunt' Theme in Medieval Hebrew Poetry," *Hebrew Studies* 19 (1978):56–62.

3. Shem Ṭob Falaquera, "Iggeret ha-Musar," ed. Abraham Habermann, *Qobeṣ ʿal Yad* 1 (11) (1936):75–78.

4. *Haśkalah* sermons: *Safah le-Neʾemanim* (Vilna, 1963), cf. Glicksberg, pp. 422–23. Memoirs: S. Z. Rubashow (Zalman Shazar), *Morning Stars,* pp. 61–73; Reuben Brainin, *Fun Mayn Lebensbukh,* pp. 293–98 (I am indebted to Rabbi Ben-Zion Gold for this reference); Gershon Schoffmann, *Kol Kitbe,* 5 vols. (Tel Aviv, 1960), 5:151, cited in Piekarz, p. 151. Parodies: Eleazar Shulman, "ʿIqqesh u-Fetaltol," *Ha-Shaḥar* 4, no. 5 (1873):284, cf. Israel Davidson, *Parody in Jewish Literature* (New York, 1907), index, s.v. "Homilies." Maggidim: Moshe Leib Lillenblum, *Qehal Refaʾim* (Odessa, 1870), pp. 53–60, Agnon, *Haknasat Kallah* and "Ha-Meshullaḥ me-ʾEreṣ ha-Qedushah" (see "The Preachers and Their Congregations," above, nn. 38 and 32).

preacher drawing upon the rhetorical traditions of the Eastern European maggid. When first introduced, he is using a typical "preacher's *mashal*" (analogy): the impulse to evil plays with us as a sadistic child plays with a dog, holding a piece of meat above its reach until the dog jumps for it and then lifting the meat still higher, until the tantalized animal becomes frantic with its frustrated desire. Near the end of the book we find both a description of Yequm Purqan preaching and a record of "part of his sermon" delivered from a Jerusalem yeshivah. Unlike the sermon in Alḥarizi, this is clearly related to actual preaching both in form and in content, although Agnon's characteristically ironic undercutting is apparent.[5]

In Yehudah Amichai's *Lo Me-ʿAkshaw, Lo Mi-Kaʾn* the cultural background is not Eastern Europe but Germany, the preacher not a maggid but Rabbi Dr. Mannheim, the sermons delivered not the traditional *derashot* but "orations" (*neʾumim*). The narrator, Joel, visits the elderly Dr. Mannheim in a Jerusalem pension and hears the old man deliver the German speech that had been prepared for his bar mitzvah in Weinburg. Upon hearing that the narrator plans to visit Weinburg, Mannheim asks a favor: "Look for my collected sermons. They were hidden in a trunk. When they came to arrest me, I locked them up. . . . Maybe my friend the bishop saved them." Later the narrator accidentally breaks the wooden box containing the manuscripts, and most of the pages fall into puddles or are scattered by the wind. They end up in a heap of rubble or floating in the river, are used as wrapping for a bunch of cherries or a bottle of wine—a powerful image for the disintegration of the religious discipline of the narrator's childhood.[6]

For this book the literature in the sermon is more important than the sermon in literature. Our literary concern, however, is not primarily with ornamentation and embellishment in the language of discourse. While the writings of such preachers as Judah Moscato and Leon Modena contain passages of subtle allusiveness and pungent wit as sophisticated as any in premodern Hebrew prose, there is no reliable way to tell whether or how much these qualities were present in the address. But there are literary elements unlikely to undergo a fundamental change in the transition from oral communication to written text (see the discussion in "The Nature of the Sources"). The structure of the sermon, the artistic form into which the preacher casts his thoughts, has already been treated. Here I shall concentrate

5. *Temol Shilshom,* in *Kol Sippuraw,* 7 vols. (Tel Aviv, 1964), 5:221, 257, 584–87. See the discussion by Arnold Band, *Nostalgia and Nightmare* (Berkeley, 1968), pp. 414–47.

6. Yehudah Amichai, *Lo me-ʿAkshaw, Lo mi-Kaʾn* (Jerusalem, 1963), pp. 44–46, 398–99, 407, 417–19, trans. Shlomo Katz, *Not of This Time, Not of This Place* (London, 1973), pp. 28–31, 236–38, 243, 246–67. Cf. Glenda Abramson, "Amichai's God," *Prooftexts* 4 (1984):119.

upon the use of the *mashal,* revealing the capacity of the sermon to serve as a vehicle for the cultivation of a Jewish narrative art.

As in most medieval Hebrew writing, the word *mashal* was used promiscuously to characterize quite different literary devices. Its various meanings include analogy, parable, exemplum, and allegory.[7] Its simplest meaning was close to "analogy." (In a characteristic piece of linguistic imperialism, Judah Moscato argued that the word *simile* was taken from the Hebrew *mashal* with a simple transposition of letters.)[8] In this sense, the *mashal* is used by preachers for clear and vivid expression of theological concepts otherwise difficult to comprehend.

For example, an anonymous thirteenth-century preacher used an analogy to illustrate his point that it is unnecessary for the Jew to understand the precise reason for every commandment.

> There is a *mashal* of a man who had never before seen a mill. When he brought wheat to be ground, they told him to place the wheat in the hopper above the millstones. However, the wheel that turns the millstones was obstructed and did not move. They told the man to go down beneath the millstones to the place where the wheel was obstructed and to strike the pin with a hammer to keep it from blocking the wheel. He went and did what he was told, not knowing that by doing this he would free the millstones to grind his wheat above them. Upon ascending, he found it fully ground. So it is with one who performs a commandment in this world: when he reaches the world to come, he will find his reward ready for him because of the actions he has previously performed."[9]

Leon Modena testifies to the value of the analogy in dismissing the theological crux of an unchanging God responding to prayer.

> Why, the least distinguished of the preachers can explain this in a manner comprehensible to all by means of a simple *mashal.* It is like someone in a boat on the river, who casts a rope around a post on the land and pulls the boat closer to shore. An observer might say that the shore is being pulled to the boat, and that this is how they draw near to each other. But it is not so, for the boat is approaching the land

7. Contrast the distinction in medieval Christian preaching theory between the *similitudo* and the *exemplum* (Bremond, pp. 155–58), or in Spanish preaching between the *comparación* and the *exemplum* (Smith, pp. 69–78).

8. Moscato, sermon 31, p. 76c.

9. *Derashot,* p. 283. Cf. Fleckeles 2:32b: just as a child can learn to wind a clock and tell time without understanding the inner mechanism of the clock, so can we perform the commandments according to tradition without knowing the esoteric mysteries of how they affect the Godhead.

> because of the pulling, while the land remains in place. So it is with prayer. Prayer is the rope attached on high to God's will, which does not change, but the one who prays, once far away from it, draws closer through his prayer to God.[10]

And Modena's protégé, Saul ha-Levi Morteira, suggested a startling analogy to resolve the perennial problem of the sustained power and success of nations who were not as close to God's heart as the Jews.

> My *mashal*: think of a woman who nurses her infant, playing with him and speaking to him with joy. If that baby should die, or become gravely ill, or be kidnapped, the woman might take her servant's baby in order to ease the pressure of the milk that naturally wells up in her breasts each day that she does not nurse. Thus the milk intended for her own child would be given to the child of her servant. But her playfulness in facial expression and speech, the delightful words with which she frolicked with her child . . . these would be totally absent, for the woman would sit in silent anguish over the loss of her son.

So it is with the Gentiles during the period of Jewish exile. They triumph and prosper because God's beneficent effluence, like the milk of the nursing mother, must be released to flow into the world. But the joy once felt when this was directed toward God's own people has been lost, to be restored only when the Jewish people is once again its recipient.[11]

Such analogies possess various degrees of originality and sophistication. None of them, however, could be considered an actual story, and therefore the term *parable* is inappropriate. They have no inner tension or development; they could not be told for their entertainment value independently of the preaching context in which they appear. While the same word, *mashal,* is used for parables and exempla, such stories are quite different from the analogies cited above. Drawn from various sources—written works of medieval Hebrew literature, folklore, non-Jewish sources, and the imagination of the preacher—the *mashal* constitutes one of the most important manifestations of literary content in the sermons.

That the Bible and the rabbinic texts were inexhaustible repositories of narrative material for Jewish preaching is obvious. What remains to be seen is how much various Jewish preachers drew upon medieval Hebrew belles lettres for homiletical purposes. The extensive narrative taken by Mattathias

10. Modena, *Ari Nohem,* in Nave, p. 217. Moshe Idel has discussed the background of this analogy in "Differing Conceptions of Kabbalah in the Early Seventeenth Century," in *Jewish Thought in the Seventeenth Century,* ed. Isadore Twersky and Bernard Septimus (Cambridge, Mass., 1987), pp. 176–77.

11. Morteira (1645), p. 87d.

Yizhari from Nissim of Kairuwan's anthology of exempla (called by the preacher *Sefer ha-Maʿasiyyot*) is discussed in the annotation to the sermon translated below. A story from *Midrash ʿAśeret ha-Dibberot,* another of the most important medieval Jewish narrative collections, appears in an anonymous collection of sermons completed in 1425. Illustrating the danger of slanderous talk, the preacher tells of three daughters, one lazy, another prone to stealing, the third a malicious liar. All three are married, and the first two are able to overcome their problems. The third, however, is not, and this leads to tragedy for all, in a literal illustration of the rabbinic statement, "Slanderous talk kills three: the one who speaks, the one who hears it, and the one about whom it is said."[12]

Stories for sermons were also found in translations or adaptations of non-Jewish sources. The tales in the Oriental collection *Kalilah wa-Dimnah* were praised by Hai Gaon as an important repository of religious truths. A late fifteenth-century manuscript of sermons takes from the Hebrew translation of this work an exemplum about a scholar who found an ancient medical text, which said that certain herbs grown in the mountains of Greece were capable of restoring life to the dead. He convinced the king to furnish an expedition to Greece but found that the herbs did not work as he had been led to expect. Puzzled, he consulted the Greek sages, who told him that he had erred by reading his text too literally. The "mountains" were the sages, the "herbs" alluded to the good doctrines they discovered, and "restoring life to the dead" referred to eternal life in the spiritual realm. The preacher then concludes, "True wisdom bestows life upon its possessor, for true wisdom is the Torah; thus 'the more Torah, the more life.'"[13] Here a secular story in praise of philosophical wisdom has been altered at the last moment to fit the Jewish context by the substitution of the Torah for the wisdom of ancient Greece.

Even more intriguing is Isaac Arama's transformation of a story "that appears in the works of earlier writers; although they used it for a different

12. Anonymous, "1425," fol. 136v: the rabbinic statement is from Deut. Rabbah 5:10. The text in the sermon should be carefully compared with other versions of the story. It is considerably more developed than the version in Parma MS 2269 (473) of *Midrash ʿAśeret ha-Dibberot,* and closer to the version in Jellinek's *Bet ha-Midrash,* 4:145 (cf. Gaster, *Maʿaśeh Buch,* pp. 537–39). On the significance of *Midrash ʿAśeret ha-Dibberot* for medieval Hebrew narrative art, see Dov Noy, "Ṭippusim Ben-Leʾumiyyim wi-Yhudiyyim be-Midrash ʿAśeret ha-Dibberot," *Proceedings of the Fourth World Congress of Jewish Studies* (Jerusalem, 1968), 2:353–55, and Joseph Dan, *Ha-Sippur ha-ʿIbri bi-Yme ha-Benayim* (Jerusalem, 1974), pp. 79–85.

13. Anonymous, "Bibago," fol. 244; cf. David Sassoon, *Ohel Dawid: Hebrew and Samaritan Manuscripts in the Sassoon Library* 2:674. The same story was used by Arama in *ʿAqedat Yiṣḥaq,* chap. 62, p. 41a–b. For the source, cf. Joseph Derenbourg, *Deux versions hébraïques du livre de Kalilah et Dimnah* (Paris, 1881), pp. 319–20 (the version of Jacob ben Eleazar), where it is the mountains of India, not Greece. For the statement of Hai Gaon on the value of such fables, see B. M. Lewin, *Oṣar ha-Geʾonim,* 6:2, Sukkah (1934), pp. 31–32.

purpose, I will expand it and make it into a fine *mashal* for the subject we are discussing." A king engaged two artists to paint the walls of his palace. One immediately set about his work and completed an admirable painting by the deadline; the second, a lazy man, wasted his time until it was no longer possible to perform his task. He therefore covered his wall with a mirror that reflected the work of his colleague. The king, delighted with the ingenuity of the second artist, rewarded him even more generously than the first.

The story, which appears in several medieval Jewish sources, was probably taken by Arama from Abraham ibn Ḥasdai's *Moʾzne Ṣedeq,* a translation of al-Ghazālī's *Mīzān al-ʿAmal.* In the original it is used to explain an epistemological doctrine by comparing the paths to truth followed by the philosophers and the Sufis. Arama used the same story for an entirely different purpose: to express the relationship between the person of consistent righteous behavior and the sinner who returns to God in repentance.[14]

More folkloristic is the following, used by an unknown Jewish preacher at the beginning of the fifteenth century to illustrate the dangers of calumny and the rabbinic statement, "A wrong inflicted by words is worse than wrongful taking of money" (B. BM 58b). A poor elderly woodcutter with three daughters was pitied by a thief, who helped him earn a decent living for the first time. When the father described his benefactor to the daughters, he qualified his praise with the statement that "the only bad thing about him is that he has foul breath." The thief eventually heard of this insult. He summoned the man, handed him an ax, and ordered him, "Strike me as hard as you can on my head." Some time later he summoned the man again and demonstrated that "the wound caused by the axe has healed, but the wound caused by your words has not healed." Whereupon he killed him. This is an early and somewhat anomalous version of a well-known Near Eastern folktale, an important piece of evidence for the relationship of literature, homiletics, and folklore.[15]

14. Arama, chap. 100, p. 84b; cf. Abraham ibn Ḥasdai, *Moʾzne Ṣedeq* (Leipzig and Paris, 1939), pp. 52–54. On the parable of the mirror in Islamic thought, see Annemarie Schimmel, *Mystical Dimensions of Islam* (Chapel Hill, 1975), pp. 190, 295; and Hava Lazarus-Yafeh, *Studies in al-Ghazzālī* (Jerusalem, 1975), pp. 312–15. Arama's use of this parable was praised in sermons by both Moscato (sermon 38, p. 102d) and Katzenellenbogen (beginning of sermon 3). For the various versions of the story in Jewish literature, see Bin Gorion, *Mimekor Yisrael,* 3:1340–43.

15. Anonymous, "1425," fol. 135v. Cf. Dov Noy, *Sippure Baʿale Ḥayyim be-ʿEdot Yiśraʾel* (Haifa, 1976), pp. 198–99; Haim Schwartzbaum, *The Mishle Shuʿalim (Fox Fables) of Rabbi Berechiah ha-Nakdan* (Kiron, 1979), p. 127, p. 135, n. 30; Thompson Motif W 185.6: "Wound is healed but not the ache." The story has been recently documented by folklorists both in a Neo-Aramaic and a Judeo-Spanish version (Iddo Avinery, "A Folktale in the Neo-Aramaic Dialect of the Jews of Zakho," *JAOS* 98 [1978]: 92–96; Samuel Armistead and

Other tales were apparently taken by Jewish preachers directly from non-Jewish works and incorporated into their sermons for idiosyncratic purposes. The Christian origin of the following exemplum, told by the same early fifteenth-century preacher, is obvious:

> It once occurred long ago that the pope died, and they wanted to appoint a successor. They found no worthy candidate except for one man in another city. They sent emissaries to him. When they arrived, they found him mixing bran and feeding it to the fowl: such was his humility. Seeing this, the emissaries were astonished and dumbfounded. He asked, "What are you doing here?" They told him, "The pope has died in our city, and they have sent for you to be pope in his place." He replied, "I am an insignificant man; who am I to be pope? However, I shall fix a date on which I shall be there, in order to satisfy those who sent you." With that he bade them farewell, and they left.
>
> Arriving back home, they related what had happened. Upon hearing this report, those who had sent the emissaries appointed another pope from their own city. On the day that the humble man had fixed, he arrived and discovered that the pope they had chosen was already sitting on the throne and preaching. The man entered and sat at the new pope's feet. Before the pope finished preaching, the lowly man began to rise little by little, and the pope they had chosen began to descend little by little, until he was at the feet of the humble man. When they saw this, they realized that he was worthy and the other was not, and they appointed the worthy man pope. This is the meaning of the verse *Before honor, humility* (Prov. 15:33). And so with Pharaoh, who arrogantly believed himself to be God: see how his pride led to his fall!

This is an astonishing performance. A Christian story, in which the model of humility becomes pope through an act of miraculous divine intervention, is used without any self-consciousness or apology to illustrate the contrast between the humility of Moses and the arrogance of Pharaoh. Then the lesson is applied to the experience of Jewish life in exile, past and future: "What is written about Israel, submissive as strangers [in Egypt]? *I made you walk erect* (Lev. 26:13), and *The children of Israel were departing boldly* (Exod. 14:8). Just as we went forth from humiliation under the power of Pharaoh in Egypt to exaltation, so shall we go forth from under the power of Edom [= Rome] in this exile; just as God brought plagues upon Pharaoh, so shall He bring

---

others, "Words Worse than Wounds: A Judeo-Spanish Version of a Near Eastern Folktale," *Fabula* 23 [1982]: 95–98).

them upon Edom." It would be hard to find a more striking transformation of non-Jewish material for a Jewish purpose.[16]

Similarly, Isaac Karo, in the generation of the expulsion, uses a *mashal* which he identifies rather cryptically with the Spanish phrase *la primera piedra* ("the first stone"). The story is about a prince whose bizarre behavior baffled his parents and the entire court, for despite his other fine qualities, he would frequently throw himself into the mud and roll around with the pigs. Finally a physician discovered that a nurse had secretly given him pig's milk. A lengthy regimen of purification was followed.[17] Although this story is used to solve an exegetical problem in Deuteronomy 8:3, it draws from contemporary Spanish ideas about the power of lineage and early nurture, and it may conceivably express the preacher's attitude toward *conversos* who had returned to Judaism yet retained behavioral patterns that still showed the influence of their Christian upbringing.[18]

Leon Modena's allegory of Good and Evil and their exchange of garments, resulting in the universal spurning of Good and the honoring of Evil, was a story that he had heard—apparently from Christians—although this may not have been obvious to Jonathan Eybeschuetz when he used it (unattributed) in the sermon translated below.[19] Modena incorporated into another sermon,

16. Anonymous, "1425," fols. 171v–172r. This story would seem to be linked with the medieval legend about the selection of Pope Gregory I; see *Gesta Romanorum,* trans. Charles Swan (New York, 1871), 2:22–24, and Hartmann von Aue, *Gregorius: A Medieval Oedipus Legend* (Chapel Hill, 1955), chap. 9. Here too there is a search far from Rome for a humble man (indeed, a penitent sinner) who is God's choice for pope. However,, there is no competitor chosen in Rome, and the motif of one man rising as the other is lowered does not appear. Cf. also the Irish folktale in which a boy accompanying a priest to Rome is selected as pope when the papal chair moves toward him as they enter the room: Sean O'Suilleabhain, *Scealta Craibhtheaca* (Bealoideas, 21) (Dublin, 1952), story 27b, English summary, p. 309, and variants in idem, *A Handbook of Irish Folklore* (Detroit, 1970), p. 633.

17. Karo, fol. 169r; the significance of *la primera piedra* is unclear in this context. The story is obviously linked with the first story for the second night in *Le piacevoli notti* (*The Facetious Nights*) of the sixteenth-century Italian writer Giovan Francesco Straparola. Indeed, Straparola's sentence, "Whenever [the prince] came near to any mud or dirt, he would always wallow therein, after the manner of pigs, and return all covered with filth," is almost identical with the earlier Hebrew text. However, in the Italian tale the prince was born in the shape of a pig, the reason had nothing to do with milk drunk as a baby, and the cure is marital love. The original source is the *Panchatantra,* where the son is born as a serpent; this story, however, was not incorporated into any of the renderings of the Indian text that circulated in medieval Europe, and no direct source for Straparola's tale of "King Pig" is known. See A. L. Deslongchamps, *Essai sur les fables indiennes* (Paris, 1838), pp. 40–41, n. 2.

18. On the concept of character affected by the milk drunk as an infant, Francisco Márquez has directed my attention to an apparently apocryphal story told about the sixteenth-century Spanish mystic Fray Diego de Estella, O.F.M.: after suffering temptations in his faith, he was told by his mother that he had been nursed by a woman who turned out to be of Jewish stock (*Archivo ibero-americano* 11 [1924]:26–27).

19. Modena, p. 15a. This story would appear to be linked with a fairly well-known

a eulogy for a noted rabbinic scholar, a story that he introduced, "I read it in a non-Jewish book. I shall tell it in a shortened form, adding something of my own in showing how it agrees with rabbinic statements."

The story is about a young man who was told that he did not know whether he was alive or dead, and who decided to travel from country to country in search of the solution to his quandary. Wherever he went, people laughed at him. The sages of Egypt said, "Since death is the cessation of activity, you are alive by day and dead at night." The sages of Persia suggested that on the basis of this assumption, he was alive while he was active, but dead when he was idle. The sages of Greece could not agree on any solution. In Italy they proposed that whatever position he took, they would argue the opposite.

He met a warrior, who said, "If you like, I will kill you, and then you will know what is death, and what is life." Then he met a monk (*nazir*) sitting in the field, who responded to his query by saying, "I am alive because I consider myself dead."

> But the youth did not understand these words. Still despondent, he came upon a cemetery, where he decided to stay the night. He thought, "As I have asked the living whether they are alive, I shall now ask the dead whether they are dead."
>
> He opened a coffin and removed a corpse. Eventually he heard a spirit speaking. It said, "You who ask, what you do think: are you alive or dead?"
>
> The youth replied, "Alive."
>
> "How do you know?"
>
> "Because I see, hear, eat, and walk."
>
> "That is proof that you are dead."
>
> "How?"
>
> "Because the living do not need senses or movement. . . ."
>
> The youth then asked, "If so, who is alive?"
>
> "The one who does not see or hear, speak or walk. . . ."
>
> "How then can I live?"
>
> "By dying. . . ."
>
> "And you, are you alive or dead?"
>
> "Dead, so long as I am talking with you."
>
> The youth replied, "If so, go to life," and closed the coffin. He understood what the monk had said. The next morning, he returned home. His reply to all who asked was, "I am dead so that I may live."

Renaissance emblem in which Death and Love (Mors and Amor, la Mort and l'Amour) exchanged garments and roles, so that the young die and the old fall in love. See A. Alciati, *Omnia emblemata* (Paris, 1618), no. 154.

This, the preacher concludes, is the essence of the story, "although I have greatly abbreviated it."[20]

As a rhetorical instrument, this passage must have been a tour de force. One can imagine an effective preacher squeezing every ounce of drama from the climactic graveyard dialogue. But it is also revealing as an expression of culture. A Christian story, in which the principle of renouncing the world is articulated by a monk, is incorporated into a Jewish eulogy. Every view expressed is shown to be consistent with a statement of the Bible or of the rabbis, and the entire story is made to illustrate the aphorism, "The righteous are called alive in their death" (B. Ber. 18a–b). The foreign material is not clumsily stitched, but artistically woven into the sermon's fabric. There is a homiletical boldness here, a vigorous self-confidence that cannot but impress.

Many stories came from the preacher's own imagination. Eighteenth-century Jewish preaching in particular cultivated the ideal of spontaneity and improvisation in the creation of the *mashal.* Some viewed the supreme gift of the preacher to be the capacity to create, on the spur of the moment, the perfect *mashal* for the context. The talents of the Maggid of Dubno were legendary in this respect; when impostors impersonated him, this was the acid test by which the true Maggid was able to prove his identity. According to one report a verse from the Torah and a sentence from the liturgy were chosen at random, and the preacher had to create a *mashal* that explained their connection. Such a combination of intellectual acumen and artistic creativity could make the performance of the greatest preachers a source of both edification and entertainment.[21]

Of course, the value and the propriety of the *mashal* were not beyond dispute. That many important preachers refrained from using it, or used it but rarely, indicates that it was not universally recognized as an essential component of Jewish preaching. The opposition was mustered on several fronts. Some argued against the mixing of realms, the illustrative story being viewed as an indecorous intrusion of the secular into the sacred domain of God's word. This appears to be Moses Almosnino's point when he says, "It is not my way, nor do I find it congenial, to tell profane stories in my sermons. God forbid that this be done in the presence of this sacred and awesome

20. Modena, pp. 76b–77a. I have eliminated in my summary the Jewish material with which he reinforces the statements of the sages from Egypt and Persia, of the monk, and of the dead man in the cemetery. While the central theme of mortification as the path to true life is not alien to classical Jewish sources (see, e.g., B. Tam 32a and ARN B, 32), the story itself would seem to be of Christian origin. Cf. Straparola, *Le piacevoli notti,* fourth night, fifth fable, in which a young man sets out in search of Death and asks various people for help, including a hermit. While there is a certain similarity, this could not have been Modena's source.

21. For the ideal of improvisation see *Toledot Yosef,* in "Sources." On the Maggid of Dubno, see Heinemann, *Maggid,* pp. 260–68.

people! I shall therefore interpret three or four verses from the first section of the Scroll of Lamentations, and from these verses every aspect of our position on this matter will become clear."[22] Certain material simply does not belong in the context of preaching, and the need to clarify and explain can be fulfilled just as effectively, and with greater piety, through the explication of biblical verses.

More substantive is the complaint that a captivating tale distracts from the preacher's real purpose. Listeners may well remember the story but not the message, the *mashal* but not the *nimshal* ("moral"). The frequent republication of the *meshalim* of the Maggid of Dubno—like the exempla of Jacques de Vitry—removed from their homiletical context and presented as if they were the essence of his preaching, illustrates the point. Not only would the story alone be remembered; it might even be all that was heard. Already in the thirteenth century we find a warning about those whose only purpose in listening to sermons is to hear "a fine phrase or a beautiful *mashal,* and who never intend to take the warnings to heart." In such cases, the author says, it is better not to preach at all, and better if the listener heard nothing.[23] That maggidim in later centuries pandered to such low-level popular desires is abundantly attested.

The most serious claim is that the *mashal* may be not only a diversion but a perversion. *Derashot ha-RaN* contains the following interpretation of Proverbs 26:9: "*As a thorn that comes into the hand of a drunkard, so is a* mashal *in the mouth of a fool.* Just as a drunkard standing among rosebushes sometimes thinks he is plucking a rose but ends up with a thorn in his hand, so the fool thinks that he is inventing *meshalim* which are helpful, for he intends to use them to provide guidance for the soul, but instead of a helpful *mashal* he ends up with a thorn in his hand, a *mashal* which is harmful." Not only could listeners be seduced into regarding the preaching *aid* as the *essence.* They might actually be misled by an appealing story into erroneous or even dangerous conclusions.[24]

The preachers who employed the *mashal* in their sermons were able to mount a strong defense. They had a powerful argument from tradition: the Bible and the rabbinic literature contain innumerable models of the *mashal* used for various purposes. Thus we hear Josiah Pardo in mid-seventeenth-

22. Almosnino, sermon 13, p. 120b.

23. *Derashot,* p. 183; cf. Fleckeles 2:6a–7a, on contemporaries interested only in hearing stories. For Christian criticism of such listeners and the preachers who pandered to them, see Dante's *Paradiso,* 29:103–20, and Erasmus, *The Praise of Folly* (Ann Arbor, 1958), pp. 105–09. The exempla of Jacques de Vitry were copied as early as in the thirteenth century, independently of the sermons in which they appeared (Welter, pp. 123–24).

24. *Derashot ha-RaN,* sermon 6, p. 105. Cf. the use of this passage in Judah Leib Eidel, *Afique Yehudah* (Lemberg, 1828), p. 7a.

century Rotterdam saying, "Beginning with Solomon, sages of early and more recent times learned to use the *mashal* in their sermons and tracts, especially in ethical rebukes, which bestow life. Especially on this day [the Sabbath preceding the Day of Atonement], each preacher uses a *mashal* according to his ability, in order to lead his contemporaries back to God."

A similar appeal to tradition is voiced by a Polish preacher: "R. ʿAqiba is proof. He was sitting and preaching and the congregation was dozing off, so he roused them cunningly by telling a story about Esther. Similarly, the prophets saw visions through parables: *Utter a* mashal *to the rebellious house* (Ezek. 24:3). . . . Therefore, let not the *mashal* be alien to you." A literary tool employed by prophets and sages was certainly not to be excluded from the repertoire of contemporary preachers.[25]

Other justifications for the use of the *mashal* were themselves dependent upon the analogy or image. One major function of the *mashal* was pedagogical. By putting an abstract, complex truth into concrete terms, the preacher helped the listener comprehend it: "One of the things that greatly facilitates a person's learning is the *mashal*; without it, we would not attain full and deep knowledge and understanding."[26]

Rabbinic literature already provided an image for this: the *mashal* was like an inexpensive lamp that could be used to provide the light to find a lost gem.[27] Somewhat more original was Judah Moscato: the *mashal* is like the mirror that enables us to see things that would hurt our eyes if we gazed upon them directly. "Just as glass mirrors are extremely valuable in impressing the image of that which is to be perceived upon the sense of sight, so the *mashal* is extremely valuable in envisioning that which is to be intellectually conceived, for through it an idea becomes more accessible to the intellect."[28]

The second major function of the parable, the ethical, was used especially in the sermon of religious rebuke. The most frequent image for this function rested on the trope of the preacher as physician for the soul: the *mashal* was like the sweet coating frequently placed on a tablet of bitter medicine. The danger that someone might suck off the sweet coating and spit out the bitter medicine was recognized, but there was considerably less chance that the medicine would be taken at all without a coating.[29]

25. Pardo, 1, fol. 74v; *Ori we-Yishʿi,* intro.; cf. ibid., pp. 10a, 19c.

26. Pardo, 1, fol. 74v; cf. Morteira (1645), p. 86a.

27. Song Rabbah, intro., cf. Morteira (1645), p. 86a.

28. Moscato, sermon 31, p. 76c.

29. Fleckeles 2, beginning of sermon 1; *Toledot Yosef,* in "Sources." Earlier, this image had been used to justify the discussion of aggadah in sermons: see Katzenellenbogen, sermon 3, p. 19a (cited by Bettan, p. 226, and Bonfil, pp. 197–98). This was actually a commonplace in classical and Christian literature: see the end of the introduction to Juan Manuel's *El Conde Lucanor,* and the sources (Tasso, Lucretius, Horatio) listed in the edition of Hermann Knust (Leipzig, 1900), p. 298.

One late eighteenth-century preacher, Judah Leib Margolioth, used yet another image: "Just as the locksmith has many kinds of implements that he may use in addition to his keys to open various kinds of lock, so the preacher must retain in his mind many kinds of *mashal,* whether of his own creation or of others." The *mashal* is "a great key, with which the closed heart of the listener can be opened."

Margolioth's insight into the psychological effect of the parable in the sermon of rebuke is quite perceptive. While the preacher is depicting a particular sin in a *mashal,* the listeners, not yet knowing how it will apply, will give their assent, agreeing with the preacher that a particular action is reprehensible. Then, when the *mashal* is explained and the listeners realize that it applies to their own conduct, they will be much more likely to accept the rebuke and alter their behavior than they would be if they had been faced with a direct attack.[30] The *mashal* disarms the natural defense mechanisms of the sinner. Here the literary device is justified by the theory that the listener's response leads to an ethical and religious goal.

A Hasidic justification for the use of stories in preaching had important repercussions. The Lurianic doctrine of the divine sparks imprisoned in the realm of the shells meant that holiness could be encountered everywhere, even, according to some, in stories told by Gentiles. There was no story so secular or mundane that it did not contain a sacred spark. All that was needed was the knowledge possessed by the *ṣaddiq* (the Hasidic master) of how to tell it properly.[31] Within the context of traditional Jewish society, it would be difficult to imagine a more powerful ideological justification for the function of literature in sacred discourse.

The Sermons: Selection and Translation

Even to the reader fully competent in medieval Hebrew, the texts of sermons delivered by Jewish preachers from the thirteenth century through the eighteenth are not readily accessible. Some are preserved only in manuscripts, many of which have never been studied. Others, published in fine sixteenth- or early-seventeenth-century editions, were never reprinted; they can be found only in major libraries with significant collections of rare Hebrew books. And the many hundreds of volumes of Hebrew homiletical literature published during the past two hundred years present by their sheer bulk a formidable challenge to the nonspecialist. The present selection of sermons, which has been culled from the legacy of six centuries, translated, and extensively an-

30. Margolioth, p. 5a.

31. On this doctrine see Yosef Dan, *Ha-Sippur ha-Ḥasidi* (Jerusalem, 1975), pp. 40–52.

notated, attempts to sketch the contours of the field, illustrate its value and importance, and define a body of material as the starting point for further discussion.

The absence of an informed scholarly consensus about a canon of "great Jewish preachers" has made the choice of texts a particularly difficult task. Perhaps the most important criterion is that a text convince me, for the reasons discussed above in "The Nature of the Sources," that it reflects fairly accurately a sermon actually delivered. I have avoided texts that claim no direct relationship to an oral sermon or that appear to have been recast to the point where their form has been altered. This is the reason why Baḥya ben Asher, Isaac Arama, Ephraim Luntshitz, and the Maggid of Dubno, all subjects of essays by Israel Bettan, are not represented in the examples below. The examples from the thirteenth and fourteenth centuries do not fully meet this standard, as relatively few texts from this period purport to record a sermon actually delivered. In the absence of explicit indications of oral delivery, the inclusion of the first four sermons is justified by the considerably weaker claim that the written text *could* have been delivered without substantial change.

Second, I have favored preachers who left a significant corpus of homiletical writings, in most cases at least twenty different sermons (and often many more), that allow selectivity, comparison, and responsible generalization about the author's preaching technique. Such major figures as Naḥmanides and MaHaRaL of Prague, who left only a few sermon texts each, are not represented for this reason.

Third, I have tried to avoid leaving inordinately long periods unrepresented. A fuller exemplification of some of the richest periods of Jewish preaching has been sacrificed in order to demonstrate the continuity of the tradition. I have also attempted to incorporate models from a variety of places, including Spain, Italy, Turkey, Holland, Poland, France, England, and Bohemia, and to illustrate different homiletical styles, although in this regard the lacunae are perhaps more significant, as will be noted below.

As for the selection within the corpus of each preacher's writings, I have preferred sermons that fit a specific historical context and react to an identifiable event or a particularly pressing intellectual problem instead of sermons that could have been written two hundred years before or after the author's lifetime. Furthermore, I have tried to choose sermons with at least a minimal level of literary art, clarity and directness of expression, and consciousness of the requirements of structure and form. Needless to say, the two standards of historical significance and aesthetic appeal are not frequently met in a single text.

I have eliminated many sermons because of their length. While other scholars have focused on brief excerpts of particular interest, my approach has been to present the sermons in full, both to facilitate discussion of sermon structure and to replicate the experience of listening to a sermon. Of my sixteen sermons, twelve are complete. In four cases (Joseph ibn Shem Ṭob, Moses Almosnino, Elijah of Izmir, Jonathan Eybeschuetz), I felt that the intrinsic merit of the material warranted inclusion despite its excessive length and made deletions (primarily of exegetical or digressive material) that did not affect the sermon's structure. Each deletion has been noted, with a brief characterization of the material omitted.

Finally, any anthology must reflect to some extent the taste of the anthologizer. Certain preachers, or particular sermons, may unexpectedly strike a responsive chord in a reader, standing out from dozens of similar texts for reasons that cannot always be fully articulated. I see no reason either to overstress or to deny the impact of such subjective considerations.

Experts in various periods and arenas of Jewish history and culture may be disappointed or even outraged to find one of their favorite preachers absent. It would be no exaggeration to say that a similar anthology, not only with sixteen different sermons but with sixteen different preachers, could be as defensible as mine. Some broad areas in the history of Jewish preaching are not represented here at all, and these should be noted at the outset.

Karaite preaching is a subject that awaits its first scholarly redeemer. The same is true of preaching in Judeo-Arabic. The multitude of sermon texts from Arabic-speaking Jewish communities, both in the Genizah archive and in other manuscripts, represents a virgin field for investigation. Nor have I included any examples of the vernacular sermons—especially in Italian, Spanish, and Portuguese (and, at the end of our period, in English)—that became common in the seventeenth and eighteenth centuries. These sermons, some published almost immediately after delivery and many more remaining in manuscript, deserve a study of their own.

The most common type of preaching in many lands was the halakic sermon, intended to teach the congregation the laws relating to various holidays or life-cycle events or to explore the problematics of a legal passage from the Talmud. No purely halakic sermon appears below (although halakic material occasionally finds its way into a nonhalakic sermon), partly because the difficulty of the subject matter requires extensive technical annotation, partly because such content is generally impossible to associate with a particular historical context. Ashkenazic Jewry is not represented until the year 1648, and Sephardic Jewry is not represented after the year 1683. The paucity of appropriate Ashkenazic sources in the earlier period that meet the criteria outlined and the shift in the center of cultural gravity away from the Sephardic Diaspora in the eighteenth century are the primary explanations for these lacunae.

Whatever the selection, for the first time it will be possible for the English reader interested in what Jews were preaching and how the homiletical tradition developed and changed over six hundred years to turn to the sources and study representative examples.

In rendering the Hebrew texts into English, I have opted for a smooth and lucid expression of the idea rather than a slavishly literal translation of each word and phrase. These sermons are not like technical philosophical texts where each word is often crucial and no nuance of expression may be casually overlooked. For the most part, the texts translated below are Hebrew reworkings of sermons originally delivered in a vernacular language. Many of the Hebrew rhetorical embellishments that resist translation were probably not present in the sermon when it was spoken. Furthermore, in the absence of critical editions for any of the sermons, textual problems abound, and an effort to render exactly every detail of the Hebrew original seems unwarranted. Translations based on questionable readings and those entailing special problems have been explained in the notes.

I have used the new Jewish Publication Society translation of the Bible (NJV) and the Soncino translation of the Talmud as starting points for rendering the quotations used in the sermons, but my divergence from these standard English versions is frequent. Wherever a preacher understood a verse or a talmudic statement in an unusual manner, my translation attempts to reflect the way the text is actually used. I have also modified the translation of biblical and talmudic material (for example, by recasting third-person masculine singular pronouns into plural forms) where gender-inclusive language could be used without changing the meaning or sacrificing the style of the original.

However, while I have tried to be sensitive to this issue, gender-specific language is not completely absent from my introduction or my translations. Jewish preaching during the period of my study was an exclusively masculine domain;[1] to use expressions like "he or she" and "his or her" with regard to the preachers would convey an impression that conflicts with historical reality. Second, the Hebrew language, which has no neuter gender, is dependent upon masculine terminology for God. It is possible to speak or write about God in English using only inclusive language, but the attempt to eliminate all gender-specific language from a translation of Hebrew texts is fraught with problems. It seemed justified in many cases, but not in all. Faithfulness

1. Although Glicksberg lists in his detailed table of contents the rubric "female preachers" (*nashim darshaniyyot*), a perusal of the discussion on p. 257 of his book confirms this generalization. The Christian context was rather different, as can be seen in a recent study limited to the seventeenth century in England: Antonia Fraser, *The Weaker Vessel* (New York, 1984), pp. 244–64. Cf. also Bonnie Anderson and Judith Zinsser, *A History of Their Own*, vol. 1 (New York, 1988), pp. 234–38.

to the original text and felicity of expression frequently mandated use of language about God that some readers may find outmoded.

It may not be superfluous to reiterate the point made above in "The Nature of the Sources" about the relationship of the written text to the sermon. Removed from their setting and context, divorced from the personality and voice of the preacher, written sermons are no more than a shadow of the event they represent, and they invariably seem flat and lifeless when read. Those who have ever been moved by a fine preacher and later read the same sermon in print will attest to the inadequacy of the written word to capture the fullness of what they heard.

Even assuming the most accurate texts and the most faithful translations, these texts are to the actual sermon what a script is to a dramatic performance or a score to the sound of a symphony. While the technically trained reader can use the script to envision the play or the score to "hear" the music, the notations remain a sign of something beyond themselves. Ideally, the following texts will stimulate a similar act of the imagination, an attempt by the reader to recreate the historical moment in which preacher faced congregation with the message before us. The annotation is intended not merely to identify sources, but to recapture insofar as possible the resonances and associations the preacher's words would have had for the listeners who first heard them.

Following the sixteen sermons, there is a section entitled "Sources on the History and Theory of Jewish Preaching." This contains a collection of *pièces justificatives* for the introductory survey above. Some of these briefer passages are drawn from sermons and homiletical works of preachers not otherwise represented. Others illustrate the importance of literary genres such as rabbinic responsa, polemical epistles, ethical treatises, biblical commentaries, and autobiographical statements for reconstructing the situation in which the preacher worked. These sources are only a sample. I hope that they will encourage the search for other such texts that will eventually make a full history of Jewish preaching a realizable goal.

Sermons

Jacob Anatoli

Jacob ben Abba Mari Anatoli was a product of the cultural upheavals that transformed Jewish intellectual life in southern France during the late twelfth and early thirteenth centuries.[1] He married a daughter of Samuel ben Judah ibn Tibbon, a noted scholar and translator of Maimonides' *Guide for the Perplexed,* who became his mentor in philosophical studies. Apparently acquiring some of the Tibbonide zeal for translation, he recast several Arabic works of technical logic and astronomy into Hebrew. Chief among these were the first five books from the medieval corpus of Aristotle's *Organon.* According to his introduction, he was impelled to translate this material because "without knowledge of [Aristotelian] logic, we Jews are unable to stand up against the clever scholars of the other nations who polemicize against us."[2] The work of translation, begun in southern France, was completed in Naples under the patronage of the emperor Frederick II, for whose support the author expresses deep gratitude.[3]

Anatoli's major contribution to medieval Hebrew literature was a book called *Malmad ha-Talmidim* (Goad for students).[4] The introduction to this work states that after studying Greek philosophy and Maimonides' *Guide,* the author began to use his newly acquired tools to investigate the deeper meaning of various biblical passages. He would communicate his insights through informal homilies at weddings, but business commitments prevented him from writing these down in literary form.

Eventually he undertook to preach regularly each Sabbath. Before long, however, opposition from members of the congregation forced him to stop. Anatoli never claims that *Malmad ha-Talmidim* is a record of the sermons he

1. On these transformations, see Isadore Twersky, "Aspects of the Social and Cultural History of Provençal Jewry," in H. H. Ben-Sasson and Shmuel Ettinger, *Jewish Society through the Ages* (New York, 1969), 185–207, esp. sect. 4.

2. *Averrois Cordubensis Commentarium Medium in Porphyrii Isagogen et Aristotelis Categorias,* ed. Herbert Davidson (Cambridge, Mass., 1969), p. 1.

3. Anatoli MS cites several of Frederick's own interpretations in the name of "our lord the great king, the emperor Frederick, may he live many years" (fol. 68v, 111r); cf. also *Literaturblatt des Orients* (1848):195–96. On the intellectual life of this court, see Ernst Kantorowicz, *Frederick the Second* (New York, 1957), chap. 5, pt. 3, esp. pp. 343–45.

4. Published by Meqiṣe Nirdamim (Lyck, 1866). Cf. Bettan, pp. 49–88; Dan, *Sifrut,* pp. 82–91.

delivered, although one is identified in a manuscript as having been composed for the wedding of his daughter.[5] He refers to his work as "words of prompting" (*dibre heʿarah*), divided according to the Torah lessons for the convenience of those who would study the book on the Sabbath. It is clear, however, that he also intended the book to be used as model sermons for other preachers. It was widely read and quoted in the Middle Ages, and there is at least one case in which a section from the book was read publicly at an important synagogue gathering.[6]

Most of the sermons in the book begin with a verse from the Writings, primarily Proverbs or Psalms, and eventually relate this verse to the Torah lesson. The organizing principle of the sermon on *Wa-ʾEra,* however, is not the lesson itself but a group of verses from the Book of Proverbs (22:28–23:12). The homiletical exposition of these verses is interspersed with interpretations of other verses from Proverbs, Psalms, and Hosea, and of passages from rabbinic literature.

The Torah lesson is introduced through the rabbinic interpretation of Proverbs 22:29 as applying to Moses, and Anatoli explores this nexus fully in the first section. But the major portion of the sermon is devoted to an analysis of the relationship between teacher and student, and this is linked with the verses from Proverbs. The whole is both a fine example of the homily form and an important expression of attitudes toward education and the transmission of culture.

What was there in a text like this that might have provoked the opposition to which Anatoli refers in his introduction and elsewhere in the book? What he actually preached in the synagogue may have been more radical than what appears in the book; a preacher who was pressured to discontinue his efforts might well have articulated his thoughts in a more guarded and moderate form when he wrote them for public dissemination. In the present text, Anatoli takes pains to dissociate himself from extremist philosophical positions, warning the philosophers not to rely exclusively on their own wisdom to the point of spurning the teachings of the Torah. He maintains that it is better not to use the logical method at all than to abuse it by building upon false premises, and he chastens those who seem to show disrespect for the Bible because of its difficult and puzzling style.

At the same time, he insists that Jews can and should learn from Gentiles, that the highest form of knowledge, vouchsafed to the select few at Sinai, is

5. See my discussion in "The Nature of the Sources," above.

6. There were reportedly a hundred manuscript copies of *Malmad ha-Talmidim* circulating in Yemen alone in the late Middle Ages; see Joseph Kafiḥ, "Ketab Haganah mi-Teman," *Qobeṣ ʿal Yad* 5 (15) (1959):48. Three weeks before a ban on the study of philosophy was promulgated by R. Solomon ben Adret, one of Anatoli's sermons was read in the synagogue of Montpellier by a group opposed to such a ban; see *Minḥat Qenaʾot,* p. 139.

knowledge derived from logical proof, and that metaphysics, as the culmination of the educational curriculum, is what bestows perpetual life in God's presence. These doctrines might indeed have rankled with those opposed to legitimating philosophical study, especially when the preacher was able to present them so artistically as the message of Solomon and the prophets.[7]

Sermon on *Wa-ʾEra:* A Homily on Education (First half of thirteenth century)

See a man skilled at his work—he shall stand before kings, he shall not stand before obscure men (Prov. 22:29).

Solomon's subject in this verse, and in the verses preceding and following it, is the supreme vocation: study of the Torah, philosophical wisdom, and the pursuit of prophecy. We already know that *skilled scribe* (Ps. 45:2, Ezra 7:6) refers to the master scholar, whose philosophical task is similar to that of a scribe diligently engaged in writing.[1] That is why this verse was interpreted homiletically to refer to Moses our teacher.[2] Since he was the supreme prophet, it is appropriate to call him a *man skilled at his work,* for he attained the perfection of prophecy more than anyone else because of his diligence in learning from everyone.

This is the definition of a wise man, according to the rabbis: "Who is wise? He who learns from everyone, as the Bible says, *From all my teachers I have gained insight, for Your decrees are my study* (Ps. 119:99).[3] Their proof from this verse shows that they understood it to mean not that the speaker

7. The ideological ambiguity reflected even in common Hebrew words like *ḥokmah* and *ḥakam* presents a serious challenge to the translator. *Ḥokmah* has the general meaning "wisdom," but in medieval Hebrew it takes on the specific meaning "discipline"—such as logic, arithmetic, or physics—and the word is often used to mean "philosophy" in the broad sense, covering all the subjects of Aristotle's curriculum. *Ḥakam* can mean "a wise man," one of the rabbinic sages, or a person who has mastered the philosophical curriculum. Obviously, the entire thrust of the sermon can be affected by the choice of "wisdom" or "philosophy" as the translation for *ḥokmah*. I have tried to choose according to context, but this occasionally involves trying to read the author's mind.

1. Cf. Ps. 45:2 and Rashi's comment on this verse. Anatoli discusses this comparison at length in *Ḥayye Śarah* (*Malmad,* pp. 19b–20a). Just as the expert scribe is able to produce beautiful letters in a short time, so the philosopher expresses much content in few words. Both make each letter count.

2. Tanḥuma, ed. Solomon Buber (Vilna, 1885), *Wa-ʾEra,* sect. 17.

3. Abot 4:1; the verse is translated here as the rabbis understand it in this context.

was praising himself for having greater wisdom and insight than his teachers,[4] but that he learned and acquired wisdom from everyone he found capable of teaching him, even if that person was not of his faith, which can be a cause of hatred. But since he relies upon the Torah and applies himself to know it fully, learning from an adherent of a different religion can bring nothing but great benefit. This is the meaning of *for Your decrees are my study.*

This same idea is the subject of the preceding verse, which says, *Your commandment enables me to gain wisdom from my enemies, for it always stands by me* (Ps. 119:98). Because he relies and depends upon the Torah, because the commandments are an enduring support, it will benefit him to learn from everyone. This is the desired diligence with regard to wisdom: to seek it from everyone, whether esteemed or scorned, whether a believer or a heretic. An intelligent person who finds a nut breaks it open, eats the kernel, and throws away the shell.[5] That is what Moses our teacher did when he was raised as a son by the king's daughter. Many sages were there, as was common in the courts of ancient kings, and Moses learned as a youth from every sage he encountered, both those from his own people and those from other nations.[6] Because he excelled all others in his diligence, he achieved a status attained by no one else, either before or since.

The verse from Proverbs indicates that we should not scorn prophecy or philosophy because we see the prophet or the philosopher surrounded by inferior, unenlightened neighbors.[7] This shows not that he lacks stature, but rather that they lack discernment. Let us recall that Moses our teacher arose powerfully against Pharaoh in response to God's instruction to lead the multitudes of the slaves out of the land. Earlier he had killed the Egyptian

4. The Hebrew of the verse is ambiguous. It can also be translated, "I have more understanding than all my teachers."

5. Based on B. Hag 15b: "R. Meir found a pomegranate; he ate [the fruit] within it and threw away the peel." This metaphoric expression of R. Meir's relationship with the heretic Elisha ben Abuya was frequently quoted by the defenders of philosophy in the controversies over the legitimacy of philosophical study in Judaism.

6. Anatoli may be alluding here to his own experience in the court of Frederick II. He includes in his sermons many interpretations attributed to the Christian scholar Michael Scotus (see *Malmad*, pp. 2b, 5b, 28a, 38a, 45b, 53b, 54b, 65a), referring to Scotus as "my learned colleague" (*he-ḥakam she-hitḥabbarti itto;* Anatoli MS cites "the Christian scholar," fol. 54r, 68v). Toward the end of his introduction, he insists that one must not dismiss such interpretations because they come from someone of a different faith, but rather evaluate them on their own merit. For other expressions of this idea, see Moses ibn Ezra, *Sefer ha-ʿIyyunim we-ha-Diyyunim,* ed. A. S. Halkin (Jerusalem, 1975), p. 227; Maimonides, intro. to "Eight Chapters," in *A Maimonides Reader,* ed. Isadore Twersky (New York, 1972), p. 363; and Joseph ibn Aknin, *Hitgallut ha-Sodot we-Hofaʿat ha-Meʾorot,* ed. A. S. Halkin (Jerusalem, 1964), p. 491. Cf. also *Al-Kindi's Metaphysics,* trans. Alfred Ivry (Albany, 1974), p. 58 (I am indebted to Jeffrey Macy for this reference).

7. The "obscure men" of the verse.

because he [Moses] could not endure injustice, even though the Egyptian was one of the nobles and Moses himself had an honored position in the royal palace, having been raised by the king's daughter, who loved him like a son. He was undoubtedly also wise, as his later life proves, for prophecy belongs only to one who is wise, strong, and wealthy.[8]

Yet despite all this honor, one inferior Israelite, whom Moses tried to prevent from committing a crime, spoke to him in an insulting and threatening manner, saying *Who made you chief and ruler over us? Do you mean to kill me as you killed the Egyptian?* (Exod. 2:14). Moses could not stand up to him, and because of this criminal he fled from his own people. But eventually, he *stood before kings* (Prov. 22:29): before a king of flesh and blood, and before the King of kings of kings, the Holy One, blessed be He.

The same verse (Prov. 22:29) can be interpreted in a different way. This is that the *ḥashukim* ("obscure men") refers to a people walking in *ḥoshek* ("darkness")—the ignorant—and *kings* refers to the philosophers, who understand the secrets of the Torah and therefore have diadems and crowns, as Solomon said, *She will crown you with a glorious diadem* (Prov. 4:9), and *Through me kings reign and rulers decree just laws* (Prov. 8:15).

Because the Torah is perfect, making the ignorant wise, and because it is necessary for everyone, since human wisdom cannot endure without religious awe and ethical discipline, Solomon warned all philosophers not to rely so much on their own wisdom that they make light of the Torah's teachings. That is why he said, *Do not remove the ancient boundary stone that your ancestors set up* (Prov. 22:28). He called the Torah an *ancient boundary stone* because it is the primal and eternal set of limits. And he said *your ancestors,* in the plural, because Aaron was also God's prophet. God did not transmit everything exclusively to Moses. Rather, Moses was in the position of God and Aaron of a prophet, as the Bible says, *[I set you in God's place to Pharaoh;] and your brother Aaron shall be your prophet* (Exod. 7:1).[9]

This was because Moses our teacher was slow of speech and tongue (Exod. 4:10). Even though God worked many great and wondrous deeds through Moses, it was not God's will to remove his speech impediment by a miracle. Because of Moses' superiority over other great men, God wanted to make him somewhat lower than the angels, so that, remembering his affliction, he would recognize his human nature. This was His purpose in saying, *Who gives a person speech? Who makes a person dumb?* (Exod. 4:11). In other words, it was God's will that Moses was slow of speech. If this were not the meaning of the verse, it would not have been a sufficient answer to Moses.[10]

8. B. Shab 92a.

9. Cf. Exod. Rabbah 11:1. With this verse, the preacher has arrived at the Torah lesson for which the sermon is intended.

10. Moses protested, *I am not a man of words . . . for I am slow of speech and slow of tongue*

Another reason was so that Moses' perfection would not be diminished and his reception of divine inspiration interrupted. A person who causes divine inspiration to flow over others has no opportunity to draw it to himself, as the rabbis said with regard to physical matters: "While it is involved in discharging, it does not absorb."[11] Therefore it was God's will that Aaron be his prophet, and that both of them be *ancestors*. It is possible that *your ancestors* refers to Abraham, Isaac, Jacob, Moses, and Aaron, and that *a man skilled* refers to Moses alone, for he was the most skilled, the one who *stood before kings,* not the others, as the Bible says, *But by My name YHWH I did not make Myself known to them* (Exod. 6:2). The meaning of this has already been explained.[12]

After mentioning diligence in the mastery of philosophical wisdom, Solomon indicated to the student the proper method of study, saying, *When you sit down to dine with a ruler, consider well who is before you; thrust a knife into your gullet if you have a large appetite* (Prov. 23:1–2). The rabbis interpreted these verses as applying to a student sitting before his master, saying, "If you know that your master is capable of answering the question sensibly, you may ask it; if not, try to understand on your own; if not, *thrust a knife into your gullet; if you have a large appetite,* leave."[13] They meant by this statement that students must not accept anything from their teacher unless the teacher explains the reason for it. This is good, appropriate advice for the student who has already worked hard and achieved something in a particular discipline, but for the beginner in that discipline it is not so.

Since the verse says *When you sit down to eat,* it seems to apply to beginners in their studies, warning them about what is necessary and appropriate. They

---

(Exod. 4:10). God's response—*Who gives man speech? Who makes him dumb?* (Exod. 4:11)—might seem to strengthen Moses' argument: "Since You, God, are responsible for my speech impediment, it should be obvious to you that I am not the one for the mission." Cf. Abravanel's commentary on this passage, question 25. Anatoli's interpretation is that God is implying by this answer the potential perfection of Moses in every realm except this one.

11. Cf. B. Ḥul 8b. The context is a discussion of laws relating to ritual slaughter: while the organs of the throat keep on discharging blood, they will not absorb any fat from the knife.

12. This is the opening verse of the lesson, which is shown to explain the opening verse from Proverbs (for Anatoli's discussion of the tetragrammaton, see *Malmad,* p. 47a). The sermon to this point is in the form of a traditional proem, and the preacher might have proceeded to a discussion of the lesson (see the three sermons that follow and the discussion in "Structural Options"). Instead, he returns to Proverbs and continues to interpret later verses in accordance with his subject.

13. B. Ḥul 6a, somewhat paraphrased. This is declared by the rabbis to be the simple meaning of the biblical verse. Note that Anatoli explains the rabbinic interpretation but then goes on to reject it and suggest his own. Common to both is the reading of biblical language about eating as a metaphor for learning, for which cf. Ernst Curtius, *European Literature and the Latin Middle Ages* (Princeton, 1973), pp. 134–36, "Alimentary Metaphors."

should concentrate solely on what they hear from their teacher, thinking about it and attempting to grasp it fully. They should not allow their minds to become agitated, and they should not ask about other things, even if related to the matter at hand. This will spoil their learning; they will be so engrossed in questioning that they will not grasp properly what they have heard, and they will force their teacher to explain things out of place. The teacher must simplify for his students at the beginning, and the students must take in the material little by little, in the proper order, whether learning from a teacher or reading from a book. In this way they will master the discipline they study.

They will not do so if they act like a glutton invited to dinner. When the host cuts a slice from one side [of the roast], the glutton says, "Cut me a piece from the other side," or "Cut me a different slice." This is not good manners for one who is invited to dine. A person of refinement[14] should graciously accept what is served. This is what Solomon meant when he said, *Thrust a* sakkin (lit., "knife") *into your gullet.* I believe that the word *sakkin* here refers not to the implement that cuts, but rather to the piece of food cut by it, which is called by the name of the implement, just as this implement is also called *ma᾿akelet,* because of the *okel,* or food, that it cuts. This is not so strange in our language. We find *This is the finger of God* (Exod. 8:15) referring to that which was done by means of His "finger." We also have the word *hand* used for that which is done by means of the hand. Just as a person of refinement who is invited to dine should control his appetite and eat the portion given to him, so the discerning student should accept information from his teacher in the proper order.

This applies if the teacher is known to be a true philosopher, and expert in the various disciplines of logic, which lead to truth. Referring to the student of such a teacher, Solomon said, *One who is sparing with words becomes knowledgeable, one who is reticent gains discernment. Even a fool who keeps silent is deemed wise; intelligent, if he seals his lips* (Prov. 17:27–28). This is a great and beneficial rule for all students: that they make their ear a hopper,[15] never departing either in word or thought from concentrating on what the teacher says, in the precise order of presentation.

To warn against the opposite of this quality, Solomon said, *He who isolates himself seeks his own desires, and disdains all sound wisdom* (Prov. 18:1). This refers to the seeker, that is, the student, for both in our language and in

14. The phrase *ba῾al nefesh* is understood by Anatoli to mean someone who masters his desires and impulses; cf. the introduction to Abraham ben David's *Sefer Ba῾ale ha-Nefesh.* This is the opposite of the common interpretation of the phrase in Prov. 23:2, for which see Rashi.

15. B. Ḥag 3b. The hopper is the container that receives grain being ground on the millstone.

Arabic the student is also called *seeker.*[16] Solomon said that when the seeker isolates himself by moving from one subject to another, and *disdains all sound wisdom,* that is to say, when he mixes into everything and gets entangled there, his seeking is motivated by naked desire, not by good intentions. His purpose is to show off his knowledge of many subjects by speaking a little about one after another. Therefore Solomon said in the following verse, *A fool does not desire understanding, but only to air his thoughts* (Prov. 18:2).

After this, he went on to warn students not to choose as their teacher someone who speaks at great length and argues with sophistries that are false and deceiving,[17] namely, by stating premises constructed in a sophistical way. Wisdom cannot be attained in this manner. This is what he meant when he said, *Do not crave for his dainties* (Prov. 23:3), for that food will not satiate those who eat it. Whoever stuffs his belly with it will starve his soul, for they are words filled with vanity and emptiness, *counterfeit food* (Prov. 23:3).

He may have based this metaphor on the playful prank of young boys, who sometimes put coarse bran or sand inside fine, white dough, completely concealing it. Someone who sees how beautiful it looks may want very much to taste it, but when he chews it his mouth will be filled with gravel. This is like the verse, *Bread gained by fraud may be tasty to a man, but later his mouth will be filled with gravel* (Prov. 20:17). He also spoke elsewhere about such teachers, who boast about their wisdom by setting up extensive premises at the beginning of their lecture, in the manner of the Mutakallimūn, who are mentioned in Maimonides' *Guide.*[18]

Concerning this kind of teacher, Solomon said, *Like clouds, wind—but no rain—is one who boasts of gifts not given* (Prov. 25:14). He raises clouds in the proper manner as if to reveal true secrets, and creates much wind by discussing the many false premises presented to the students. But in the end his words do not help in the attainment of truth, which is called *rain,* the goal that is sought. They are no more than clouds and wind.

This is a most corrupt method of teaching, for it leads to an unfortunate result. When the premises from which syllogisms are constructed to produce true conclusions are discovered to be false, the truth derived from these premises will be suspect. It would have been better not to have investigated such matters rationally at all. Solomon alluded to this when he said, *Those*

16. This connotation of the word probably underlies the title of a well-known book by Shem Ṭob Falaquera. See *Falaquera's Book of the Seeker,* trans. M. H. Levine (New York, 1976), p. 9: "Inasmuch as he devoted himself completely to his search for knowledge, all those who knew him in those days of the past called him *Mebaqqesh* (Seeker)."

17. For the technical meaning of *haṭaʿah* in logic, see Maimonides, *Millot ha-Higgayon,* chap. 8, sect. 3; Israel Efros, ed., *Maimonides' Treatise on Logic* (New York, 1938), pp. 48–49.

18. *Guide for the Perplexed* 1:71–76.

who spurn gifts will live long (Prov. 15:27), for it is better not to accept premises established in an illogical way, but rather to rely upon tradition concerning what is found in the Torah and the other books of prophecy, even though this is not knowledge derived by logical demonstration.

Such knowledge[19] is without doubt like rain, as is seen in the statement of the prophet Hosea, *Let us pursue knowledge of the Lord and we shall attain it. His appearance is as sure as the daybreak; He will come to us like rain, like latter rain that refreshes the earth* (Hos. 6:3). Moses, the supreme prophet, alluded to this same matter when he said, *My speech shall distill as the dew* (Deut. 32:2), teaching that his speech was not obviously and notably beneficial like the rain. That is why there is no explicit mention of rain during the revelation at Sinai, only darkness, cloud, and thick fog (Deut. 4:11).

In fact, there *was* a little rain in the cloud and the fog, proportionate to the capacity of those who received the revelation. Little could be apprehended by all, and few could apprehend very much. Consequently, there was no general rainfall. This is what Deborah said: *O Lord, when You came forth from Seir, advanced from the country of Edom, the earth trembled, the heavens dripped, yes, the clouds dripped water* (Judg. 5:4). This verse teaches that no more than a few drops of rain were there.[20]

Similarly, the psalmist said, *The earth trembled, the sky dripped, because of God, even Sinai,* and then, *With bountiful rain You quenched our thirst* (Ps. 68:9, 10).[21] Maimonides alluded to this in the ninth chapter of part 3 of the *Guide:* "It was misty, cloudy, and a little rainy." It is better to live by means of that little rain than to toil after vanity, surrounded by wind and clouds that have no rain at all. Solomon referred to this when he said *clouds and wind* (Prov. 25:14). An intelligent person should strive to acquire knowledge of God, as the prophet said, *Let us pursue knowledge of the Lord and we shall attain it {His appearance is as sure as daybreak, and He will come to us like rain}* (Hos. 6:3). The three things mentioned in this verse should be carefully examined, namely, *pursue,* which implies movement, then *daybreak,* which is the first rays of light, and then *rain.*

It makes most sense to me that *pursue* alludes to the propaedeutic disciplines, which provide the path for the pursuit of wisdom; the first rays of light allude to the natural sciences, and *rain* to the metaphysical sciences, which truly quench the thirst.[22] It may be that the prophet hinted at this in

19. That is, knowledge derivable by logical demonstration. According to Anatoli and other philosophically oriented Jews, this type of knowledge has the highest degree of certainty. On the allegorical interpretation of rain, cf. Saperstein, *Decoding,* pp. 74, 114, 175–76.

20. The verb *naṭefu* is interpreted to mean only a few drops (*ṭippot*).

21. I have tried in my translation of the verse to convey the meaning understood by the preacher. For "quenched our thirst," see Abraham ibn Ezra.

22. The propaedeutic disciplines (*ḥokmot limmudiyyot*) include arithmetic, geometry, as-

the previous verse, *In two days He will make us whole again, on the third day He will raise us up, and we shall live in His presence* (Hos. 6:2). These are diverse paths, mastered one after the other. All of them together bring life from God, but the third brings perpetual life in God's presence.[23] This is like the rain that comes from Him after proper searching, not superficial reading or inferior searching, of the Torah. Solomon warned against this when he said, *Do not crave for his dainties* (Prov. 23:3).

He then warned students not to disregard the precise formulation of what they learn from their teacher. This applies even to students who are extremely bright and think that they need not worry if they forget something the teacher says, since their own sharp minds will enable them to learn the subject by reviewing it themselves. Such an approach makes students too weary to attain true wealth and leads to a waste of time. Had they concerned themselves properly with the formulation of what they learned, they would not have needed to make such an effort [to review], and they would have had free time to study whatever they wanted. Solomon hinted at this when he said, *Do not toil to gain wealth, have the sense to desist. You see it, then it is gone; it grows wings and flies away, like an eagle, heavenward* (Prov. 23:4–5).

He went on to warn students further that they should not sit before a teacher, even one with a reputation for wisdom, if that teacher, jealous of his own disciples, withholds food and imagines that he will lose what he teaches to others. One who is stingy in this way makes his students idle and wastes their time with trivial tasks, causing them to flit from one subject to another without attaining wisdom. His own wisdom will progressively diminish, just as he imagined it would if he had taught his students properly. That would have been good for him, for his wisdom would have increased day by day. The rabbis compared this to small trees that kindle large trees.[24] But this is not what he imagines. He thinks of it as students snatching his daily bread from him, leaving him to die of hunger. He therefore guards his wisdom as a miser guards his money, keeping what is good from those entitled to it—and thereby robbing it. One should not take up lodging with a miser,

---

tronomy, and music, the quadrivium of the Scholastic curriculum. On the threefold classification of the theoretical sciences into propaedeutic, physical, and metaphysical, which goes back to Aristotle, see Harry A. Wolfson, "The Classification of the Sciences in Mediaeval Jewish Philosophy," *Studies in the History of Philosophy and Religion,* ed. George Williams and Isadore Twersky (Cambridge, Mass., 1973) 1:493–545.

23. That is, one must go through the entire curriculum of the disciplines in their proper order, but it is the knowledge of metaphysics that brings about the immortality of the soul through its intellectual apprehension of God. Cf. Maimonides' parable of the castle, in *Guide* 3:51.

24. B. Taʿan 7a.

for the lodger will be dissatisfied. At the same time, the miser will act as if he is sorely aggrieved at the loss of his food, or he will die as Nabal died when the servants of David came to him.[25] Similarly, no student should sit before such a teacher.

With this in mind, Solomon said, *Do not eat of a stingy man's food, do not crave for his dainties. He is like one keeping accounts; "Eat and drink" he says to you, but he does not really mean it* (Prov. 23:6–7). This shows that you will derive no benefit from a relationship with such a person. You will harm him just as he imagines you will. By pointing this out to the student, Solomon has affirmed that the teacher should not guard his wisdom as a miser would.

He then proceeds to assert that the teacher should rather guard his wisdom like a benefactor,[26] who dispenses wealth justly, giving to those who deserve the gift and withholding from those who do not. Such benefactors do not give equally to all. Those who give generously to evil people, frequenters of prostitutes, drunkards, and idlers are not called benefactors but squanderers and wasters of money. Their influence upon the drunkard or the lecher is actually detrimental. A benefactor should therefore withhold money from such people.[27]

Similarly, a teacher should not teach a student of unfit character, for that violates wisdom and gives it a bad reputation. The results are bad for the student, who rises to a level where he does not belong and then plummets downward. Concerning this matter, Solomon said, *The morsel you eat you will vomit; you will waste your courteous words. Do not speak to a dullard, for he will disdain your sensible words* (Prov. 23:8–9). One of the philosophers once said on this subject, "Do not transmit wisdom to one who is unworthy, lest you violate wisdom, and do not withhold wisdom from those who are deserving, lest you violate them."[28]

Similarly, all philosophers who attain some philosophical insight that is not written should write it down, lest they rob those of their generation or any posterity who are worthy of it. That is why the ancients took the trouble to write books. At the same time, they should write in such a way that not everyone will apprehend what is meant in their book, lest the ignorant pervert the author's fine thoughts and show contempt for the reasoning in his words.

25. See 1 Sam. 25 on Nabal's refusal to provide supplies for David's band and his (Nabal's) subsequent death.

26. The printed text (p. 51a) omits 9 words between ll. 24 and 25 because of a haplography. My translation is based on the correct text in Anatoli MS: ". . . *shemirat kilai. We-aḥar zeh ba le-haʿir ha-rab she-yishmor ḥokmato shemirat nadib. . . .*"

27. On this idea, see Abraham Cronbach, "Social Thinking in the *Sefer Hasidim*," *HUCA* 22 (1949):37–43.

28. *Mibḥar ha-Peninim* (London, 1859), 1:54; cf. Davidson, *Oṣar*, p. 103.

Deep truths are not fitted to the whole people. If a matter is made explicit in a book, many people will be led to discuss what they do not understand, and they will speak rebelliously about God. The prophet or sage who has written so explicitly awakens the "sleeping dog."

Solomon alluded to this when he said, *A passerby who gets embroiled in someone else's quarrel is like one who seizes a dog by the ears* (Prov. 26:17). Explicit explanation of esoteric matters is *someone else's quarrel.* Silence is preferable, for the masses are troubled by ontological problems.[29] This is as he said in subsequent verses, *For lack of wood a fire goes out; without a querulous person, contention is stilled* (Prov. 26:20). Regarding those who speak at length explicitly about profound matters, he said, *Charcoal for embers and wood for a fire and a contentious person for kindling strife* (Prov. 26:21).

Truly, this is the reason why the content of the Bible is so difficult. This is why they wrote elliptically and enigmatically, so that great scholars disagree about the meaning. Even conflicting interpretations are the words of the living God.[30] Let no one who has aspired to perfection through philosophy fail to show respect for a single one of their words that are known by tradition, or draw heretical conclusions,[31] or mock them, for their authors are not alive to inform us of the true meaning of what they said. This is a great sin; one who does so perverts the Torah and rebels against God.

The rabbis warned against criticizing a leading scholar in any generation, saying, "You must not argue against the lion after his death."[32] It is all the more necessary to be careful with regard to the words of the Prophets and the Writings, and even more so with regard to the Torah. This is what Solomon warned at the conclusion of the section when he said, *Do not remove ancient boundary stones; do not encroach upon the fields of orphans, for they have a mighty kinsman, who will surely take up their cause with you* (Prov. 23:10–11).[33]

He called the sacred writings *fields of orphans* because the authors, who are the "parents," have died. As these authors are known for their wisdom or prophecy, every intelligent person should judge the content of their books favorably. All their words should be accepted as an enduring tradition, just

29. The translation of this phrase is based on the text in Anatoli MS: "*we-ṭobah ha-shetiqah mimennu, le-fi she-yaqsheh lahem. . . .*" Cf. Abraham ben David's caustic comment on Maimonides' discussion of freedom of the will in *Code,* I,v (*Teshubah*) 5:5: "It would have been better for him to have left the matter for the simple faith of the naive, and not to have agitated their minds and left them in doubt."

30. B. ʿErub 13b.

31. Literally, "cut the shoots," as in B. Ḥag 14b and 15a; cf. Rashi on B. Ḥag 15a, s.v. "aḥer."

32. B. Giṭ 83a.

33. The occurrence of the phrase "ancient boundary stone" in this verse, as in 22:28, serves to delineate the section from Proverbs used for the homily.

as Solomon said: *Apply your mind to discipline, and your ears to wise sayings* (Prov. 23:12). May God in His mercy enable our minds to understand and to discern, to heed and to perform in love all the words of instruction in His Torah.[34]

34. The sermon concludes with a quotation from the Ahabah Rabbah benediction of the morning liturgy. Many of Anatoli's sermons end with an expression of hope for enlightenment rather than with the more traditional messianic sentiments.

Anonymous

The following sermon is a bibliographical puzzle. It is taken from a collection of sermons in British Library MS Add. 27,292 (fols. 157r–325r). The first part of this manuscript contains a series of sermons from the first half of the fourteenth century that I have called "Anonymous, Disciple of R. Asher."[1] The scribe finished copying the first section in the year 1384, and the second part appears to have been completed at about the same time. No author is given for either series. The manuscript belonged to the Gerondi family of Italy for many generations.

As far as I can discover, the manuscript had never been studied until the sermons of the second part were published in 1980 by Samuel Yerushalmi under the title *Derashot u-Ferushe Rabbenu Yonah Gerondi ʿal ha-Torah.* In his introduction to this edition, Yerushalmi attempted to document his contention that the sermons were indeed written by Jonah Gerondi, the well-known thirteenth-century Spanish ethical writer and halakist. As the attribution has not yet been questioned in any review of this book, my unwillingness to accept Yerushalmi's attribution requires some justification.

The basis for Yerushalmi's attribution of an anonymous text to a famous author is the similarities he detects between these sermons and Gerondi's known works, especially his commentaries on Proverbs and Abot and *Shaʿare Teshubah.* The methodological underpinning is summarized in the following statement: "Since comparisons can be made on virtually every page between the content [of the sermons] and the writings of Rabbenu [Jonah], it is to be concluded that this is the work of Rabbenu [Jonah]" (introduction, p. 6). A number of such comparisons are then given (pp. 6–14). The interested reader should study them carefully. In my view, more than a few fail to establish any direct connection between the works in question.

The more important point, however, is that even if we grant such a connection, these comparisons can at best demonstrate only the dependence of one work upon the other or upon a third work from which both drew—not the identity of the author. In the absence of any reference in the sermons to the other works, or any reference in the other works to the sermons, it is not

1. See George Margoliouth, *Catalogue of the Hebrew and Samaritan Manuscripts in the British Museum,* 4 pts. (London, 1899–1935), 2:6–7.

enough to list points of convergence. We must also ask whether there is material in the sermons inconsistent with what is otherwise known about Jonah Gerondi. I believe that there is.

Jonah Gerondi is known in Jewish history as one of the protagonists of the campaign undertaken in 1232 to ban the philosophical writings of Maimonides. The late thirteenth-century report of his eventual penitent obeisance to Maimonides is viewed by most contemporary scholars as a fabrication of the rationalists. His writings represent a school termed *rabbinical ethical literature,* one of whose primary characteristics is its opposition to philosophical thought. His warning against the study of "empty and evil external disciplines" is well known.[2]

Many of the sermons in this manuscript, by contrast, contain views that would have to be characterized as those of a moderate philosopher. This judgment is not based simply on the use of such philosophical terms as "Prime Mover" (p. 240), "separate intellects" (p. 240), "rational soul" (p. 295 and passim), "world of generation and corruption" (p. 133), for by the second half of the thirteenth century such phrases had spread beyond the philosophical camp. But the influence of the philosophical weltanschauung on the author of this text is far deeper. On the major issues of the controversy of 1232, he stands with the philosophers.

First, the preacher considers the external disciplines an integral part of the Jewish curriculum. He speaks of an orderly progression of these disciplines, with a subject like astronomy serving as a prerequisite for metaphysics, "just as the student of Talmud must first have acquired a knowledge of Bible and Mishnah" (p. 283; cf. pp. 27, 102, 178). And he celebrates the power of the human intellect to apprehend the heavenly spheres and their movements, the separate intellects, and the Prime Mover, through "true rational proofs" (p. 240; cf. pp. 180, 200).

Second, the commandments are not to be observed merely as part of a tradition or as God's arbitrary edict. Certainly, in one sermon the preacher criticizes both contemporaries who were more interested in the reason for a commandment than in the proper way to observe it and those who used the reasons for the commandments to justify their failure to observe them at all (pp. 149, 151). Yet in other sermons, he himself employs well-known rational reasons (alluding cryptically to more exalted [kabbalistic?] ones), whether for forbidden foods (pp. 176, 196), the shofar (p. 306, citing Maimonides), or the entire group given to inculcate good ethical qualities (p. 173). Perhaps the most striking example of borrowing in the entire text is a passage taken

2. On Jonah, see Abraham Shrock, *R. Jonah b. Abraham of Gerona* (London, 1948); Baer, *HJCS* 1:250–57; Daniel J. Silver, *Maimonidean Criticism and the Maimonidean Controversy, 1180–1240* (Leiden, 1965); Dan, *Sifrut,* pp. 147, 155–57. The quotation about external disciplines is taken from Jonah's commentary on Prov. 1:8.

not from Jonah Gerondi but from Jacob Anatoli's *Malmad ha-Talmidim,* where the preacher reiterates Anatoli's extreme statement that it is better not to put on phylacteries or fringes at all than to observe the commandments mechanically, without consciousness of their inner meaning (pp. 239–40; *Malmad,* pp. 148b–49a).

Third, these sermons frequently resort to allegorical interpretations of biblical material in the rationalistic mode. Maimonides' interpretation of Proverbs 25:11, strategically placed in the introduction to the *Guide,* is used by the preacher to explain his own approach (p. 80). The esoteric content of Proverbs is understood to be the scientific and philosophical disciplines that bequeath eternal life (p. 276; cf. pp. 122, 323), and many of the actual interpretations are clearly in the tradition of philosophical allegory (e.g., pp. 282–83, 310).

Finally, the influence of Maimonides is noticeable throughout, not only on relatively minor matters found in Maimonides' *Commentary on Abot,* but on central issues such as the rational reason for dietary laws and shofar (above), the nature of biblical allegory (above), the explanation of *our image* in Genesis 1:26 as intellect (p. 21), the solution of a problem about freedom of the will (p. 99, where he reproduces Maimonides' solution without mentioning Naḥmanides' critique of this position), and the thesis that love and fear of God are to be attained through the study of creation (pp. 93, 112).

All of this hardly seems like the work of a man who wanted the *Guide for the Perplexed* and the *Book of Knowledge* banned. If these sermons were written by Jonah Gerondi, we would have to revise almost all that is known about him from contemporary sources and his established works. The more conservative view that the author of these sermons was someone else (whose identity we do not know) is preferable.

What then can be said about this text? It contains a series of sermons organized according to the Torah lessons, with lacunae in Leviticus and Numbers, written by a Spanish or Provençal preacher some time after the year 1240 (p. 21). There is no evidence that he was competent in technical philosophy, but he was deeply influenced by the philosophical weltanschaaung. He also appears to have been close to the movement of communal reform associated with the figure of Gerondi, and he may well have known Gerondi's writings. He was certainly familiar with the growing literature of ethical writings available in Hebrew in the mid-thirteenth century.

Although the sermons themselves give no date or place, they show some signs of oral delivery. For example, the sermon for the first day of Passover contains the statement, "Even though we spoke about the laws of leavened and unleavened bread last Sabbath, we must now tell of the miracles performed for our ancestors at their Exodus from Egypt. (Here we said some of the things that appear previously in the lessons *Wa-ʾEra* [Exod. 6:2–9:35] and *Bo el Parʿoh* [Exod. 10:1–13:16])" (p. 190). There is a summary of a Purim sermon delivered but not recorded in full (p. 161; cf. p. 177).

The sermons are particularly important because of their structure. Most of them begin with a verse from Proverbs, which is given several different interpretations, each developed for a paragraph or two. The verse is then applied to the Torah lesson, and there follows a discussion of a section from the lesson in homily form. There are obvious similarities between this and other thirteenth-century models (Anatoli, David ha-Nagid), but these are perhaps the most consistent examples of a structure that may well have been preserved in direct continuity from the period of the classical homiletical midrash.

The sermon translated below exemplifies this pattern. The Proverbs verses cited at the beginning (Prov. 19:21–22, but actually including v. 20) are given three different interpretations, applied to the need to accept advice from those who know more while continuing to trust in God, the conflict between the Torah and worldly impulses, and the relationship between God's plan and human freedom to do good or evil. The fourth interpretation applies these verses to the first verse of the Torah lesson.

The sermon then proceeds as a homily through the first four verses of the lesson, addressing a number of exegetical and conceptual problems and drawing freely from midrashic literature. As this section ends, the precepts and doctrines to be learned from the beginning of the Joseph story are expounded. Three separate subjects in the sermon allow the preacher to empty his commonplace book for the listeners' edification: the evils of lying, the nature of dreams, and the dangers of unwarranted hatred. A return to the motif of God's plan serves as a bridge from the patriarchal narrative to a messianic conclusion.

Sermon on *Wa-Yesheb*
(Second half of thirteenth century)

Many designs are in the human heart, but it is the Lord's plan that is accomplished. Lust (taʾawat) *is a reproach* (ḥasdo) *to a person; better be poor than a liar* (Prov. 19:21–22).[1]

1. Prov. 19:21 was also used as the opening verse for a sermon on *Wa-Yesheb* by Anatoli (p. 33a), Joshua ibn Shueib (p. 15c), and anonymous, "Disciple of R. Asher" (fol. 26r). While the thematic link with the Joseph story is obvious, the frequency of use in this context may indicate that preachers were aware of a tradition governing the homiletical use of verses from Proverbs.

Solomon's general pattern in the book of Proverbs was to provide admonition concerning our everyday conduct.[2] He followed this pattern in these verses and the preceding one, namely, *Heed advice* (ʿeṣah) *and accept ethical discipline, in order that you may be wise in the end* (Prov. 19:20). His admonition was for people to accept the advice of those who know better, for this is how they may improve their ways. It is as he said elsewhere, *Plans based on sound advice will succeed* (Prov. 20:18). This means that even a wise person may be impelled by desire to select an improper course of behavior, but an advisor can look at the choices objectively, evaluating their advantages and disadvantages, and know how to choose what is good and spurn what is evil.[3] Similarly, he said elsewhere, *{Ointment and perfume gladden the heart;} so does the sweetness of one's friend through advice for the soul* (Prov. 27:9).

He further admonished people to accept the ethical discipline of those who rebuke them, for this is how they acquire the character traits that earn them universal respect. He went on to give the reason—*in order that you may be wise in the end*—for in addition to the improvement in one's conduct that comes from accepting advice, by continually probing the various implications of each act and learning what is good and bad about it, the person will become *wise in the end.* This is like the verse, *One whose ear heeds the discipline of life abides among the wise* (Prov. 15:31).

Then he went on to say, *Many designs are in the human heart . . .* (Prov. 19:21). In other words, although I have admonished you to seek advice in your affairs and to accept the counsel of advisors, there must be trust that God will sustain that counsel. For although advisors may engender many designs in the human heart, *it is God's plan that is accomplished.* Next, he turned to explain the reason for the admonition about accepting advice. One usually seeks advice only from someone who is knowledgeable and intelligent. Such a person is called *adam,* human, as in the verse, *And you, My flock, the flock that I tend, you are* adam, *human* (Ezek. 34:31), for this is the essential difference between the human being and the beast. Thus he said not to worry about following advice.[4]

2. Compare the beginning of Anatoli's sermon on *Wa-Yesheb* on the twofold nature of Proverbs (*Malmad,* p. 33a). Our author states at the beginning of his sermon on *Mishpaṭim* that the purpose of Proverbs is "to make known the importance of wisdom and its benefit to the human soul, and even to the body" (p. 122); elsewhere he maintains, like Anatoli, that the "disciplines of knowledge (*ḥokmot*) that bestow life in the world to come are the esoteric content of Proverbs" (p. 276). Contrast Jonah Gerondi's interpretation of *ḥokmah* in his comment on Prov. 1:2.

3. Precisely the same point is made (although in different words) in Shem Ṭob Falaquera's "Iggeret ha-Musar," ed. Abraham Habermann, *Qobeṣ ʿal Yad* 1 (11) (1936):79. There would appear to be a common source for both passages.

4. *Taʾawat adam ḥasdo* is understood to mean "the {seeker's} desire for a true human being {to give advice} is God's lovingkindness," or perhaps, "what a true human being desires is to advise with lovingkindness."

Finally, he went back and warned the person seeking advice not to distort what he says or to lie in his request for counsel, for the advisor will not be able to give the counsel truly needed for the situation. On the contrary, the advice that fits the lie may actually harm the one who receives it when applied to the real circumstances. It is better then to remain *poor,* without any advice, than to accept advice based on a lie.

Another interpretation. *Heed counsel* (ʿeṣah): this is Torah, as in the verse, *Li ʿeṣah, Mine is counsel and resourcefulness* (Prov. 8:14). It is another term for the positive commandments. *And accept ethical discipline* refers to the negative commandments. *In order that you may be wise in the end,* for one who studies these commandments and thinks about them constantly will indeed become wise in the end. All wisdom is contained in the Torah, as David once said, *Open my eyes that I may perceive the wonders of Your Torah* (Ps. 119:18).[5]

Then he went back to say that he had admonished you about this because something permanent is at stake. *Many designs are in the human heart* pertaining to worldly affairs—the effort to fulfill one's lusts and desires, the pursuit of power and conquest, and all the other things that depend upon the body, which cannot endure after the body is reduced to nothingness—*but the Lord's counsel,* which is the Torah and the commandments, *shall endure* as the soul endures, bestowing upon that soul life in the world to come.

Next he said, *A person's beauty* (taʾawat) *is his kindness* (ḥasdo): see that the beauty of a human being and the good memory left behind are not the result of wealth or bravery or the capacity to instill fear in the hearts of others or to take vengeance upon enemies. It is rather the result of *ḥesed,* kindness, toward other people. The word *taʾawah* can mean "beauty," as in the phrase *holiness is beautiful* (naʾawah) *for Your house* (Ps. 93:5).[6] He went on to say, look at wealth, considered by most people the most valuable thing in this world. A wealthy man who fails to perform acts of kindness proportionate to his wealth—for example, saying "I really don't have so much" in order to give less—is worse than a pauper. This is all the more true for someone who makes a vow but does not pay.

Another interpretation. *Heed the plan* (ʿeṣah) *and accept ethical discipline.* Since "all is in the power of Heaven except the fear of Heaven,"[7] Solomon admonished the people to heed the plan that God provides for each individual. All that occurs to a person is preordained by God, and no one is able to change

5. Cf. Zohar 1:132a.

6. This interpretation assumes that *naʾawah* is a *nifʿal* form of the root *ʾwh*: that which is beautiful is desired. The same interpretation, citing Song 1:10 instead of Ps. 93:5, was used by Jonah Gerondi in his commentary on Prov. 19:22.

7. B. Ber 33b; this is discussed by Anatoli near the beginning of his sermon on *Wa-Yesheb* (*Malmad,* p. 33a).

a thing that divine wisdom has decreed in judgment. The sages said, "One does not lift a finger on earth unless it was so decreed in Heaven."[8] This is consistent with the verse, *Whose eyes observe all the ways of human beings, so as to repay every one according to his ways* (Jer. 32:19). Concerning this, Solomon said *shemaᶜ ᶜeṣah,* which can mean "heed the plan."

Then he said, *accept ethical discipline,* namely, that of the Torah. For although what happens to us is decreed by God, our own actions and voluntary movements are within our power to control, and we have freedom of will. It is as Rabbi ʿAqiba said, "All is foreseen, yet free will is given."[9] And it is written in the Torah, *See I have set before you today life and good, {death and evil} . . . ; choose life* (Deut. 30:15–19). He said, *in order that you may be wise in the end,* by investigating these two principles.

Next Solomon went back to explain the meaning of the *ᶜeṣah* or plan mentioned: *Many designs are in the human heart, {but it is the Lord's plan that is accomplished},* and then to support the *ethical discipline,* saying *Lust is a reproach to a person.* This means that the lust for food and drink and sexual pleasure is a disgrace to human beings, for because of such lust they become publicly known by their most repugnant qualities.[10]

Intelligent people are embarrassed and ashamed when they see themselves being overpowered by lust. The intellect is repelled by acts of lust and holds them in contempt, especially when thought is preoccupied by them. That is the meaning of the rabbinic statement "Thoughts of sin are worse than sin."[11] Intelligent people are repelled because they know that human beings have free will, and that they have chosen something contemptible. In order to show the intellect's contempt for those who choose the evil way, Solomon went on to say that the pauper, though hated by all his brothers and spurned by his friends, is better than one who is wealthy but a liar.

We might also say that Solomon intended to express what one scholar did in the statement, "The company of a thief is better than the company of a liar, for the thief steals your money, while the liar steals your mind"[12] and your intellect, by asserting as true something that never was. This is the meaning of *better be poor {than a liar}.* It is as he said elsewhere, ". . . *lest, being impoverished, I take to theft* (Prov. 30:9).[13]

8. B. Ḥul 7b.

9. Abot 3:15.

10. In this interpretation, *ḥasdo* is understood in a negative sense (see Lev. 20:17), as "something shameful."

11. B. Yoma 29b.

12. Cf. Abraham ibn Ḥasdai, *Ben ha-Melek we-ha-Nazir,* ed. Abraham Habermann (Tel Aviv, 1951), p. 44, and Falaquera's "Iggeret ha-Musar," p. 81.

13. The preacher's proof seems to be based on the prior verses: *Two things I ask of You; do not deny them to me before I die: keep lies and false words far from me; give me neither poverty nor*

Lying is indeed a despicable quality. Virtually all the fundamentals of the Torah depend upon [truth]. The sages said, "Amos [sic] came and set the commandments upon one affirmation: *And the righteous will live by his trustworthiness* (Hab. 2:4)."[14] They also said, "The seal of the Holy One is Truth."[15] If you think about it, you will realize that if you commit yourself never to say anything but the truth, you will be wary of all the transgressions of the Torah. For if you were to go to commit a sin, you would calculate that someone might meet you and ask where you were going or coming from, and then you would have to tell the truth and be humiliated, unless you were to break faith and lie.[16] Furthermore, liars are one of the four groups that do not receive the Divine Presence.[17] The Bible says, *The remnant of Israel shall do no wrong, and speak no falsehood* (Zeph. 3:13).

We can further interpret these verses as applying to this lesson. We might say, *Many designs are in the human heart*: this is Jacob, who is described as *a simple man* (Gen. 25:27).[18] The sages said, after all the sorrow Jacob had experienced, when he saw what happened to his father, Isaac, and saw that Esau went away to another land, he thought he would settle down and rest, as the Torah says, *Jacob settled* (Gen. 37:1). But this was not what God had in mind.[19] Solomon indicated that God's plan would prevail; He brought it about that Jacob went down to Egypt. That is why it was said, *Many designs are in the human heart, but it is the Lord's plan that is accomplished.*

Another interpretation. Since it was said in the previous lesson that *Esau settled in the hill country of Seir* (Gen. 36:8), as one gravitates to his own kind, it was written similarly that Jacob chose to live with his father in the chosen land. The phrase *where his father sojourned* (Gen. 37:1) is like the expression

---

riches, but provide me with my daily bread, lest being sated, I renounce, saying "Who is the Lord?" lest being impoverished, I take to theft (Prov. 30:7–9). Since the first wish was to avoid lies, this is more important than to avoid poverty.

14. B. Mak 24a; the correct reading should, of course, be Habakkuk.

15. B. Shab 55a.

16. This idea, sometimes accompanied by an exemplum, is a commonplace in medieval Jewish ethical and homiletical literature. See *Sefer Ḥasidim,* ed. Jehuda Wistinetzki (Frankfurt, 1927), no. 113; Judah b. Asher in Israel Abrahams, *Hebrew Ethical Wills,* 2 vols. (Philadelphia, 1926), 2:176; Joseph Albo, *Sefer ha-ʿIqqarim,* ed. Isaac Husik, 5 vols. (Philadelphia, 1930), 3:289–90; *Maʿaseh Book,* ed. Moses Gaster (Philadelphia, 1934), pp. 638–40; Vega, p. 25a; Eybeschuetz, 1:85c. The entire passage seems to be based on a collection of source materials pertaining to various subjects addressed by preachers, analogous to the numerous Christian commonplace books, or Baḥya ben Asher's *Kad ha-Qemaḥ*. Such a collection would have provided the various quotations on lying and truthfulness. Cf. the sections on dreams and on groundless hatred below.

17. B. Sanh 103a.

18. The link is provided by the word *ish* in both verses: *be-leb ish,* literally, "in the heart of a man" (Prov. 19:21), and *ish tam, "a simple man" (Gen. 25:27).*

19. Cf. Gen. Rabbah 84:3.

elsewhere, *the land in which they lived as sojourners* (Exod. 6:4). For it was said to Abraham, *Your offspring shall be sojourners* (Gen. 15:13).

Another interpretation. The righteous know that they are as strangers sojourning upon the earth, for they follow their intellect. Now the rational soul[20] is hewn from the supernal Rock; hence, this world cannot be its world. This is what David expressed: *I am an alien, resident with You* (Ps. 39:13). But the wicked say, *The earth was given to us as a possession* (Ezek. 11:15). So it was said of Esau, *These are the clans of Edom, in their settlements in the land that they possess* (Gen. 36:43).

The Torah then began to tell how the matter developed. It said, *These are the* toledot *of Jacob* (NJV: *This is the line of Jacob*) (Gen. 37:2), meaning "the events that occurred," as in the phrase *mah yeled yom, what a day brings forth* (Prov. 27:1).[21] The sages interpreted this on the basis of *toledot Shem* (Gen. 11:10) and *toledot Pereṣ* (Ruth 4:18), teaching homiletically, "Why does it say 'Joseph' without mentioning the other sons? Because Joseph was his principal offspring." This was because Rachel was the woman Jacob loved, the one for whom he worked all those years. That is why the Bible calls her alone *Jacob's wife* (Gen. 46:19).

Similarly, we find that only when Joseph was born did Jacob think of returning to his father's house and making a home of his own, for it was only then that he considered himself truly to have offspring. Furthermore, Joseph brought the others down to Egypt and supported them there, and it was through his merit that they were liberated from Egypt. We see this in the verse, *By Your arm You redeemed Your people, the children of Jacob and Joseph, selah* (Ps. 76:16). Finally, he enabled them to inherit the land, for Joshua was his descendant.[22]

In addition, the sages interpreted the phrase *elleh toledot Yaᶜaqob Yosef* (NJV: *This is the line of Jacob: Joseph*) (Gen. 37:2) to mean, "all that occurred to Jacob occurred to Joseph." Just as Jacob's mother bore two children, so did Joseph's. Both were hated by their brothers. Both were shepherds. Both married women and had children outside the land of Canaan. Both of them rose to greatness as a result of a dream. Both of them died in Egypt and

20. The author regularly uses the philosophical terminology for the different souls in the human being: the rational soul (*ha-nefesh ha-maśkelet*), as here, the appetitive soul (*ha-mitᵓawwah*), and the vital soul (*ha-ḥiyyunit*). For the philosophical doctrine of the three souls, see Abraham ibn Ezra's comment on Exod. 23:25 and Naḥmanides' comment on Gen. 2:7.

21. This interpretation, with the proof text, is in both ibn Ezra's and David Kimḥi's comments on this verse, and it is quoted disapprovingly by Naḥmanides. Any of these could have been our author's source.

22. For this and the second half of the preceding paragraph, cf. Gen. Rabbah 84:5. In Gen. 11:10, *toledot Shem* is followed by mention of only one son, although he had five, according to Gen. 10:22; similarly, only one son of Perez is mentioned in Ruth 4:18, although he had two, according to Num. 26:21.

were embalmed, and their bones were brought up [for burial in the land of Canaan]. And so it is with several other characteristics.[23]

They also interpreted the phrase *elleh toledot Ya*ʿ*aqob Yosef* in comparison with the verse in the previous lesson, *We-*ʾ*elleh toledot* ʿ*Eśaw, These are the* toledot *of Esau, the ancestor of Edom* (Gen. 36:9). The sages said that when Jacob saw Esau and his chieftains, he was afraid. The Holy One said to him, ["Of these you are afraid? One spark from you and one spark from your son, and you burn them all"].[24] That is to say, the Torah mentioned that Jacob had Joseph over against all of Esau's descendants, as the Bible says, *the House of Jacob shall be fire [and the House of Joseph flame, and the House of Esau straw; and they shall burn it on them and consume it]* (Obad. 18).

It says that he was *seventeen years old* (Gen. 37:2) in order to indicate how much time he was unable to see his father.[25] Furthermore, to indicate that the seventeen years he supported his father corresponded to the seventeen years his father supported him: we see this in the verse *Jacob lived [in the land of Egypt seventeen years* (Gen. 47:28).[26] They interpreted *he was still a lad* (Gen. 37:2) to mean that he did a childish thing.[27] And so it was, as he *brought bad reports of them to their father* (Gen. 37:2). Even though he told the truth—far be it from him to lie![28]—and his intention was to correct their fault, it was not right for him to do this, since he was younger than they were. That is why they hated him.

The reason he brought these reports was that his father loved him for his wisdom. The Torah says that Joseph was Jacob's *ben zequnim* (NJV: *child of his old age*) (Gen. 37:3), which the Targum translates as "a wise child." Benjamin was, of course, younger than he was.[29] When Joseph realized that he was wiser than the others and that his father loved him, he decided to *bring bad reports of them to their father* and also to tell them his dreams, which showed that he thought of himself as above them.

23. Cf. Gen. Rabbah 84:6. Our author omits the fanciful comparisons based on midrashic wordplays (e.g., both were born circumcised, both were stolen twice) and lists only those characteristics apparent from the simple meaning of the respective narratives.

24. Cf. Gen. Rabbah 84:5.

25. *Joseph was thirty years old when he stood before Pharaoh* (Gen. 41:46); thus thirteen years had elapsed. Adding to this seven years of plenty and two of famine (Gen. 45:6), the result is twenty-two years of separation from his father (cf. B. Ber 55b).

26. Zohar 1:180a.

27. Gen. Rabbah 84:7; the childish behavior specified in that statement, however, is not linked with his "bringing bad reports."

28. Here the preacher picks up the motif of lying and truthfulness that he had developed in the first part of the sermon. He will return to it once more near the end in speaking of Judah and Tamar.

29. Since Joseph's younger brother, Benjamin, had been born by this time, Benjamin should have called the "child of Jacob's old age." The Targum's rendering *bar-ḥakkim* is apparently based on the rabbinic identification of the *zaqen* with the *ḥakam* (B. Qid 32b).

That is why it says, *they hated him all the more for his dreams* (Gen. 37:8). According to the simple meaning, they did him an injustice by hating him for his dreams, for what difference did they make? But the dreams revealed his inner thoughts, as we see in the verse, *the thoughts that entered your mind in bed* (Dan. 2:29). Furthermore, as he told them his dreams, it became clear that he himself believed in their validity, and that he looked forward to the time when they would come true. The phrase *and for his talk* (Gen. 37:8) refers to his bringing bad reports.[30] Before this it said, *his brothers saw that their father loved him* (Gen. 37:4). Thus there were three reasons for their hatred.[31]

Now the sages were critical of Joseph because of his immature behavior, but they also said, "A person should never single out one child from the rest, for because of the coat of many colors that Jacob made for Joseph alone of all the brothers, they hated him," and the result was eventually that our ancestors went down to Egypt.[32] In a purely homiletical manner, they said that those who sold him and bought him corresponded to the letters of the word *passim,* "many-colored": *peh,* Potiphar; *samek, soḥarim,* merchants; *yod,* Ishmaelites; *mem,* Midianites.[33]

From something negative said about the brothers we learn something positive: that they openly expressed their hatred for him, as the verse says, *they could not speak well of him* (Gen. 37:4). Whatever they thought, they said. But of Absalom, the Bible tells us, *Absalom did not utter a word to Amnon, good or bad* (2 Sam. 13:22). He kept what he thought suppressed. Of such it is said, *A person who conceals hatred has lying lips* (Prov. 10:18).

Furthermore, we have learned from this lesson that there are dreams to which careful attention should be paid and whose outcome should be attentively awaited. The sages said, "A dream is one-sixtieth of prophecy."[34] Dreams may be divided into three categories. Some are actual prophecy, like the dream of the ladder, and so the Torah says, *If there is a prophet among you . . . I shall speak to him in a dream* (Num. 12:6). Then there are dreams that signify nothing; indeed, most are of this kind. Of these it is said, *and the dreams speak lies* (Zech. 10:2). Finally, there is the dream that is one-sixtieth of prophecy. It is worth paying special attention to this, as we said. Such a dream occurs when the dreamer sees that the image is composed of things known through the senses, although the specific image has never been perceived.[35]

30. Rashi on Gen. 37:8.
31. I.e., his bringing bad reports, their father's favoritism, and his telling of his dreams.
32. Gen. Rabbah 84.8.
33. Ibid. 84:9.
34. B. Ber 57b.
35. Compare with this Maimonides' discussion of the imagination in *Guide* 1:73, proposition 10, and contrast the discussion of dreams in the Zohar, 1:183a.

For example, sheaves do not have the power to move, but the imagination may show them moving about in the dream and bowing down. Similarly, although the sun and the moon do actually move, no one has ever seen them bowing down to a human being. That is why Joseph expected this to happen. When he saw what befell him, he knew that ultimately the dreams would be fulfilled. He did not want to send word to inform his father about his station, because he was waiting for the fulfillment of those dreams, knowing that this was God's will.[36] And God, by whom actions are measured, brought it about that our ancestor Jacob went down to Egypt in honor. For he should have gone down in iron chains, as the sages said.[37]

What does all this teach us? As we see that none of their plans came to fruition—not those of Jacob, nor of any one of the brothers, nor of all together—we learn that *a person's way is not his own* (Jer. 10:23). This is the meaning of the verse, *Many designs are in the human heart, {but it is the Lord's plan that is accomplished}*.[38]

This verse is also exemplified by the incident concerning Judah. He arranged for Tamar to marry two of his sons, but ultimately it was God's plan that was fulfilled when she gave birth for him to Perez and Zerah (Gen. 38:29–30). This same incident exemplifies the following verse: *A person's lust is a source of shame; {better be poor than a liar}*, according to the last interpretation we gave. When *she sent to her father-in-law* (Gen. 38:25), he admitted all without shame; far be it from him to be a liar! *Judah acknowledged . . .* (Gen. 38:26).

We have also learned how necessary it is to avoid groundless hatred, for this was the reason that our ancestors went down to Egypt. The sages said, "The Second Temple was destroyed only because of groundless hatred."[39] See how the Torah repudiates it, saying, *Do not hate your brother in your heart* (Lev. 19:17). In other words, even if you see a person committing trangression, and you are able to rebuke him, you must not hate him (although the Bible says, *Do I not hate those who hate You, O Lord?* [Ps. 139:21]). Rather, *You shall surely rebuke your neighbor, but incur no guilt because of him* (Lev. 19:17) by hating him. All this is to repudiate that evil quality. But that was not enough. The Torah went on to command, *Love your neighbor as yourself* (Lev.

36. This is similar to Naḥmanides' approach to the narrative in his comment on Gen. 42.9.

37. B. Shab 89b.

38. The return to the opening verses from Proverbs at this point gives a unity to the sermon despite the midrashic material that has led away from the central subject. The following paragraph, applying the same verses to the narrative in Gen. 38, could either be omitted or expanded, depending on time constraints.

39. B. Yoma 9b.

19:18). Hillel said to that man, "The entire Torah is, What is hateful to you do not do to your neighbor. The rest is commentary; go, study."[40]

Come and see how painful the divine providence seemed to our ancestors, while God was actually looking out for their welfare.[41] Even though He decreed from the days of Abraham that they would be subjugated in Egypt, He brought them there with great honor, and they lived in honor during the lifetimes of Jacob's sons. Later, when He liberated them, though He had not promised to send a messenger in advance, He mercifully began to reveal Himself to Moses in the bush and requested Moses to go on His mission and liberate them from Pharaoh. The first thing He said to Moses was, *I have marked well the plight of My people* (Exod. 3:7).

How much more will this be so for those of us here in our servitude, who have gone into this exile in captivity and humiliation. God has promised to send us a messenger in advance, as we see in the verse, *How beautiful upon the mountains are the feet of the herald bringing good news* (Isa. 52:7), and the verse, *Behold I send you Elijah the Prophet* (Mal. 3:23). Just as He sent signs and portents in the heavens and on earth when He brought them out of Egypt with a high hand, so will He lead us out, liberated, from this exile, as the Bible says: *For you shall leave in joy, and be led home secure; before you mountains and hills shall shout aloud, and all the trees of the field shall clap their hands* (Isa. 55:12). And just as God went before them day and night in the pillar of cloud, so will it be in the future—may it come speedily and in our days! *For you will not depart in haste, nor will you leave in flight; the Lord will march before you, the God of Israel will be your rearguard* (Isa. 52:12).

40. B. Shab 31a. This paragraph weakens the structure of the sermon. It does not fit what came before, where the preacher carefully explained the reasons for the brothers' hatred, faulting both Joseph and Jacob for their conduct. It would seem that the preacher simply could not resist inserting either into the oral form or the written text some standard ethical sentiments based on well-known quotations, despite their tenuous connection with his previous material.

41. This statement, fitting the contrast between human designs and God's plan in the opening verse from Proverbs, provides the transition to an uplifting coda of messianic hope.

Joshua ibn Shueib

Little is known about the life and career of Joshua ibn Shueib.[1] He was a disciple of Solomon ibn Adret, the distinguished leader of Aragonese Jewry who died in 1310. He consistently refers to Adret as "my teacher," either as a living contemporary or with the epithet "of blessed memory." This has led to the conclusion that some of his sermons were delivered before 1310, so that ibn Shueib would have been born no later than about 1290. Menaḥem ben Zerah wrote in the introduction to his *Ṣedah la-Derek* that he had studied under ibn Shueib for about two years in Navarre around the year 1328 before moving to Castile in 1331. In a passage discussing the observance of the Feast of Booths (Sukkot), ibn Shueib contrasts the custom in Catalonia with "our practice" (*Derashot,* p. 94d, bottom). Thus he flourished in the first half of the fourteenth century in Navarre, probably in Tudela.

Whether or not he was the author of an "Explanation of the 'Secrets' of RaMBaN," explaining the kabbalistic interpretations alluded to in the great Torah commentary of Moses Naḥmanides, remains an issue of scholarly dispute.[2] What is clear, however, is that his circle, consisting of Adret's disciples, was involved in the popularization and diffusion of Kabbalah, and that ibn Shueib's major work, the *Sermons (Derashot) on the Torah,* is an important expression of this trend. After circulating in many manuscripts, it was published twice in the sixteenth century (Constantinople, 1523; Cracow, 1573), and cited frequently thereafter.[3]

The *Derashot* contains a sermon for each Torah lesson of the year, interspersed with sermons for the first and last days of Passover (40c–44a), the Feast of Weeks (58d–61c), the New Year's Day (89b–90d), the Day of Atonement, the first day of the Feast of Booths, and the Eighth Day of Assembly (92a–96d). A second sermon on the lesson *Teṣawweh* (Exod. 27:20–30:10), not included in either printed text, has recently been published from a manu-

1. On the few details of ibn Shueib's life, see Horowitz, "Shuᶜeib," pp. 1–4.

2. On this problem, see the references in Horowitz, "Unpublished Sermon," p. 264, n. 4, and his discussion in "Shuᶜeib," pp. 9–10.

3. The Cracow edition was republished in Jerusalem in 1969 with an extensive introduction by Shraga Abramson. This analyzes ibn Shueib's use of sources (other than kabbalistic ones) and discusses how later writers cited him.

script, indicating that for some lessons more than one sermon may have existed.[4]

In form these sermons are quite similar to the thirteenth-century models. Almost all begin with a biblical verse, mostly from Proverbs and Psalms, although more than a few are from the Prophets. This verse is then discussed, sometimes on different levels (simple meaning, allegorical, midrashic), until it is eventually applied to the Torah lesson. Frequently, as in the sermon translated below, a particular thesis is established in this opening section and carried over into the lesson.[5]

Once the lesson is reached, however, the preacher generally does not restrict his discussion to the original thesis. Ibn Shueib uses the homily form to move through the verses of either part or all of the lesson, discussing whatever exegetical or conceptual problems arise, bringing whatever good midrashic material he has at hand. Many of the sermons therefore seem to digress and lose their focus in the middle.

Whether this diffuseness is characteristic of the oral sermon or merely of the written work is difficult to determine. On the one hand, there are few clear indications of oral delivery in the work. The collection was extensively edited as a written text, with cross-references to sermons coming earlier and later in the cycle. It is unlikely that someone who expected to preach regularly in a community would exhaust all his best material in one sermon (as he does, for example, in the sermon translated). The homily section that we have may have been expanded with material from more than one treatment of the lesson.

On the other hand, there are occasional indications of a particular setting. The sermon for the Sabbath preceding Passover refers to the occasion of delivery: "Since it is a commandment on this day to discuss matters pertaining to Passover and its laws, I will discuss some laws briefly. . . . It is customary to preach in clear language to men and women, for indeed some commandments are given over to women" (p. 38d).[6] And the sermon for *Wa-ʾEtḥannan* (Deut. 3:23–7:11) has an unusual beginning, a citation from the talmudic tractate Taʿanit concerning the Fifteenth of Ab. At the end we learn that "now in this year" the Fifteenth of Ab fell on the Sabbath when the sermon was delivered (pp. 78b, 80a).[7]

Although somewhat disappointing in their lack of obvious links with an oral sermon and their avoidance of explicit reference to historical conditions,

4. Horowitz, "Unpublished Sermon."

5. On the "form and style" of the sermons, see the discussion by Horowitz, "Shuʿeib," pp. 41–53.

6. Cf. Horowitz, "Shuʿeib," p. 48, on this quotation as a possible implication that the sermon was delivered in the vernacular.

7. Cf. Abramson in *Joshua ibn Shueib*, intro. p. 43, n. 2.

these homilies remain important texts in the history of Jewish preaching. Few preachers drew so extensively from the resources of midrashic literature as did ibn Shueib. In fact, one of the purposes of the book (and perhaps one of the functions of his preaching) may have been to bring less familiar traditional material to the attention of (listener and) reader.[8] This implies an audience for which originality was not paramount, an audience that enjoyed traditional material brought together in an artistic way.

Second, this is an important text for the popularization of Kabbalah. It is not always possible to know how many of the kabbalistic references in the text were really included in the discourse.[9] And we still have too few examples of fourteenth-century Jewish preaching to conclude that ibn Shueib was unique in his use of Kabbalah. The absence of protests against using kabbalistic material in sermons at this time (when philosophical allegories in sermons aroused bitter controversy) could mean any of the following: (1) ibn Shueib was not known as a preacher beyond his immediate community during his lifetime, (2) he did not include Kabbalah in his oral delivery; or (3) kabbalistic interpretations were not particularly unusual in sermons.[10] In any case, this text provides an important example of the sermon as a vehicle for the diffusion of ideas.

The sermon I have translated is clearly divisible into sections. The first, heavily dependent on Proverbs, establishes the theme of stratagems and cunning, applied immediately to Jacob as an individual and to the Jewish people as a whole. The second, focusing on the suffering of Jacob, contains a quick review of the Torah lesson from a particular point of view, summarizing earlier material, treating the problematics of the Dinah episode in Genesis 34, and highlighting the death of Jacob's mother and of Rachel.

After the appropriate lesson is drawn, the third section begins, a homily proceeding almost verse by verse from Genesis 32:5 through Genesis 33:15. The homily is heavily dependent on midrashic material and devoid of thematic unity. Its last section introduces a messianic coda. Throughout much of the sermon, the biblical narrative is applied to the situation of the Jewish people in exile through the mode of typological interpretation made famous by Naḥmanides. While the listeners might have found that this resembled their

8. Cf. Abramson, p. 6.

9. Horowitz, "Shuʿeib," p. 45, n. 27, and "Unpublished Sermon," p. 262, argued that the kabbalistic material was frequently an integral part of the sermon and was therefore not added in the written text. The sermon translated, however, is one in which the kabbalistic references are quite incidental, and could have been added. There is not yet a complete study of ibn Shueib's kabbalistic sources.

10. For example, the "Book of Sermons" of Ḥayyim ben David, another disciple of Adret (see n. 28 to "Structural Options") may well have included kabbalistic material. I have not found such material in other early fourteenth-century manuscript collections of sermons, for example, anonymous, "Disciple of R. Asher," or Jacob ben Hananel.

own circumstances, it lacks historical specificity. In content (although not in form), it is a sermon that could have been delivered 250 years later without substantial change.

Sermon on *Wa-Yishlaḥ*
(First half of fourteenth century)

For with clever stratagems you shall wage your war; in the multitude of your counselors there is victory (Prov. 24:6).[1]

In this verse, Solomon has informed us that clever stratagems are absolutely necessary in worldly affairs. Elsewhere he said, *Every purpose is established through counsel; with clever stratagems wage war* (Prov. 20:18), and *Without clever stratagems, a people fall* (Prov. 11:14). In other words, only through such stratagems can human beings survive in this world. Those who do not devise a scheme to prepare for their needs will be defeated and left without hope of recovery.

Look at Jacob. Even though God was with him, having promised, *Behold, I am with you* (Gen. 28:15), Jacob spared no effort in providing for his own needs and in accumulating wealth, so that he would not be dependent upon others. Day and night he suffered physical distress. Never assuming he could rely upon a miracle,[2] he resorted to clever stratagems like the wooden rods.[3] He shows that each person must be attentive about the necessities of life. One must not be lazy, as we see in the verses, *How long will you lie there, lazy one?* (Prov. 6:9) and *Yet a little sleep, a little slumber . . . so shall your impoverishment come like a runner* (Prov. 6:10–11). The meaning of these verses is clear.

Similarly, a situation may arise where one person must be wary of another who wants to harm him. We know that the natural dispositions of different people vary, and this results in hatred, envy, lust, competitiveness, even widespread war. Therefore, in the verse with which we began, Solomon warned that a wise man who goes to battle should seek clever stratagems and cunning devices to save himself from his enemies, whether by seeking peace, by expending his wealth, by desisting submissively, or by demonstrating to

1. Prov. 20:18 was chosen by Anatoli as his opening verse for the sermon on this same lesson. Ibn Shueib's treatment of this subject may have been influenced by Anatoli's *Malmad* (see below, nn. 4 and 6).

2. Cf. B. Taʿan 20b.

3. Gen. 30:37–43.

his enemies that he is extremely powerful, as he said in the preceding verse, *A person of knowledge increases strength* (Prov. 24:5).[4] In short, he must actively seek his own safety and not assume that he can rely on a miracle.

On this subject, Solomon said elsewhere, *Happy is the one who is always fearful* (Prov. 28:14). He meant that a person should be fearful of the dangers that may beset him rather than rely upon his own merits. But then he should do everything possible to keep himself from trembling and looking weak, for this would be a source of strength to his opponent. Solomon's statement, *A person's fear lays a snare* (Prov. 29:25) applies to this.[5]

That is what our ancestor Jacob did. Once he realized that his brother was strong enough to harm him, he did not rely on his righteousness. Even though God had made him a promise, he feared that his own sin might have nullified it.[6] This entire episode was written in order to teach later generations that they should always follow his example.[7] The prophet said, *The Lord sent something to Jacob, and it has fallen upon Israel* (Isa. 9:7), his offspring, which is under the power of Esau's offspring. We should therefore act as Jacob did.

Furthermore, *He sent something to Jacob, and it has fallen upon Israel* means that its prohibition has spread throughout all Israel,[8] namely, that what happened to Jacob as he wrestled with Esau's guardian angel, indeed everything that occurred to him in that episode, has all fallen upon Israel in our current exile. We should follow his example, for he endured many instances of sorrow and distress. His entire life was filled with pain, his days were *few and evil* (Gen. 47:9), yet he endured it all cheerfully. We have already asserted on previous lessons that whatever happened to the patriarchs was a sign for their descendants.[9]

The sages had a tradition that Jacob erred by sending emissaries to his brother and stirring him up, for Esau was not thinking about what had

4. Cf. Anatoli, *Malmad,* p. 31a, ll. 4–6.

5. The preacher thus resolves the apparent contradiction between Prov. 28:14 and 29:25. Cf. the commentaries of Menaḥem Meiri and Joseph ibn Naḥmias.

6. Cf. Anatoli, p. 31a, ll. 7–9.

7. Cf. Moses Naḥmanides' introduction to *Wa-Yishlaḥ* (*Commentary on the Torah: Genesis,* trans. C. B. Chavel [New York, 1971], p. 394).

8. B. Ḥul 91a, interpreted by the preacher in a different manner (cf. below, at n. 58).

9. Tanḥuma, *Lek Leka,* 9; Naḥmanides on Gen. 12:6 (trans. Chavel, p. 169). On this mode of typological interpretation, see Funkenstein, "Parshanuto," and "Symbolical Reading." Funkenstein's assertion that this mode of interpretation was neglected before and after Naḥmanides (Hebrew version, p. 45; cf. English version, pp. 141–42) needs to be qualified on the basis of the sermonic literature, which reveals that Jewish preachers were very much influenced by it. See, for example, David ha-Nagid, *Wa-Yishlaḥ,* p. 142, at n. 92; Shem Ṭob ibn Shem Ṭob, pp. 7b and 17b; and the sermon of Solomon Levi, below. Cf. Frank Talmage, "Apples of Gold: The Inner Meaning of Sacred Texts in Medieval Judaism," in Arthur Green, ed., *Jewish Spirituality,* 1 (New York, 1986):314.

happened long ago.[10] It is not a good stratagem to stir up old problems; this is like seizing the ears of a dog to incite a conflict. It comes under the category *A person's fear lays a snare* (Prov. 29:25). The rabbis therefore said that Jacob acted like *one who seizes a dog by the ears, passing by and meddling in a quarrel not his own* (Prov. 26:17). They meant that this mission was what aroused Esau and made him come to cause trouble, as we said. He was heading toward his own territory when Jacob incited him to turn around, and it was then that he set out toward Jacob's camp.

The same thing happened to us, causing our exile. The kings of the Second Commonwealth, seized by fear, sent messengers to the Romans asking to enter into an alliance, and they fell into Roman hands.[11] That is what Jacob did. His premature approach to his brother, who did not even remember what had happened, served as a reminder. This exemplifies *A person's fear lays a snare.* Furthermore, because of the sin of calling Esau "lord" eight times, eight kings reigned in Edom before the first king ruled over Israel.[12]

However, once Esau had been incited and intended harm, all that Jacob did from there on—the clever devices to save himself, such as dividing his camp, and sending gifts, and demonstrating courage by saying, *for I have seen your face as one sees the face of God* (Gen. 33:10), meaning, your face resembles that of your guardian angel,[13]—these are examples of good stratagems. Of this it was said, *Happy is the one who is always fearful* (Prov. 28:14), for fortune smiles upon him. This episode was written as instruction for future generations, who would read it and act likewise, not relying upon their own merits or upon a miracle. This was how Moses acted in his wars, and Joshua, and David. The entire episode was written so that we might learn a lesson and act after the manner of the patriarch.[14]

Indeed, it contains several good lessons. First, we see that Jacob endured many afflictions after the divine promises. As a man of absolute piety, he accepted all cheerfully. How much pain we find him enduring! At the very beginning of the story, he is hounded in his mother's womb: *The children*

10. Cf. Gen. Rabbah 75:3.

11. Cf. B. AZ 8b, and Naḥmanides on Gen. 32:4 (trans. Chavel, p. 395).

12. Gen. Rabbah 75:11; the eight times occur between Gen. 32:5 and 33:15, and the eight Edomite kings are named in Gen. 36:31–39. Cf. David ha-Nagid, pp. 139 and 141.

13. Cf. Rashi on Gen. 33:10. The meaning is that Jacob is informing Esau that he has already met and struggled with Esau's guardian angel, thereby indicating his courage.

14. This concludes the first part of the sermon, focusing on the motif of stratagems, in which the verse from Proverbs has been applied to the Torah lesson. It also provides a transition to a new section by identifying Jacob as a model worthy of emulation and indicating that there are other lessons to be learned from his adventures. The next section deals primarily with the travails endured by Jacob. The analysis of the principles of guidance for behavior (*musarim*) taught by the Torah lesson is similar to Gersonides' listing of "benefits" (*toʿaliyyot*) pertaining to conduct. See the discussion of this form in "Structural Options."

struggled within her (Gen. 25:22). Then comes the conflict with his brother, and Esau's hatred, and his flight from his father's house. Then his experience in the house of Laban, who changed his wages ten times (Gen. 31:41): *by day the drought consumed him, and the frost by night, and his sleep fled* (Gen. 31:39). He was pained by the upbringing of his children; as we read, "*Who rescued Abraham* (Isa. 29:22): rescued him [i.e., Abraham, but not Jacob] from pain in the upbringing of children."[15]

Then, after his return, Esau set out toward him, *and Jacob was extremely afraid and distressed* (Gen. 32:8). The rabbis interpreted, *He was afraid of Esau and he was distressed* because of our exile,[16] for he envisioned his descendants under his brother's power. As soon as he escaped from this distress, there was the distress of his daughter. Scripture teaches us incidentally that a woman should be modest, not a gadabout, for it says, *Then Dinah the daughter of Leah went out* (Gen. 34:1), indicating that her going about outside the home caused what happened (the rabbis said, "like mother, like daughter: *Then Leah went out*" [Gen. 30:16]).[17]

The defiling of his daughter by an uncircumcised man distressed Jacob greatly, and this was compounded by the anguish he felt over the actions of Simeon and Levi. He called them *troublemakers* (Gen. 34:30), and near the end of his life he said, *Weapons of violence are their kinship* (Gen. 49:5), for it seemed like profound treachery that they commanded Shechem and Hamor to be circumcised—and then attacked and killed them.

According to the Midrash, the men were in pain and they regretted that they had been circumcised; that is why Simeon and Levi killed them.[18] The significance of *on the third day* (Gen. 34:25) is that they had finished circumcising everyone, otherwise why would they feel more agony on the third day than on the first? Furthermore, the taking of captives and plunder appeared to Jacob to be sinful, even though they acted legally and properly, because of the terrible act of violence and robbery committed, in violation of all law, as if Dinah were a piece of abandoned property. See Rashi's interpretation of *ha-ke-zonah,* "abandoned property" (Gen. 34:31).

Rabbi Moses ben Maimon wrote in the "Book of Judges" about the reason why Jacob's sons did this to the men of Shechem, and Naḥmanides replied

15. B. Sanh 19b.

16. I have not found this interpretation. Cf. the common interpretation in Gen. Rabbah 76:2 and the discussion of its problematics by Elijah Mizraḥi, supercommentary on Rashi's comment on this verse.

17. Tanḥuma, *Wa-Yishlaḥ,* 7; cf. Gersonides' fourth *toʿelet* on this section.

18. Menaḥem Kasher's *Torah Shelemah* on Gen. 34:25 gives this statement by ibn Shueib as the only source for this midrash (Hebrew [Jerusalem, 1934], p. 1328, n. 52; English [New York, 1959], 4:182, n. 36). However, the same interpretation appears in *Daʿat Zeqenim* on this verse ([Leghorn, 1783], p. 18a).

to this in his commentary.[19] The Torah does not tell what happened to Dinah. Most probably Simeon took her, and she remained as a widow in his house, and went down to Egypt and died there. Simeon, having compassion for her, brought back her bones, just as all the bones of Jacob's children were brought back, and buried them in the land of Israel. Her grave is known in the city of Arbel, together with the grave of Nittai the Arbelite.[20]

To return to our subject, Jacob was angry about what Simeon and Levi had done, even though they acted legally. The men of the city, having been forewarned, were liable to the death penalty, and since they were guilty of a capital offense, the property in the city was considered abandoned and ownerless. Nevertheless, Jacob was angry because his sons had acted and spoken deceitfully, as it says, *Jacob's sons answered {Shechem and Hamor his father with guile}* (Gen. 34:13). Now we might well ask, if Jacob was present at the time, why did he later find this so difficult to bear?

In my opinion, Jacob thought that the deceit was merely that the men, by being circumcised, would suffer excruciating pain for having taken Dinah, but that nothing else would be done to them. Or if someone was to be killed, his plan was that only the perpetrators of the crime should be punished. Thus Jacob was duped by his sons' deceit. Certainly Jacob never considered giving his daughter to Shechem, even if they were circumcised. The entire episode was painful to the old man.

Now the sages said that these misfortunes befell Jacob because he delayed fulfilling the vow he made when he left the land of Israel: *If God remains with me . . . {then this stone, which I have set up as a pillar, shall be God's abode}* (Gen. 28:20–21). He had not fulfilled his vow, and he was still unaware of this. The sages said, "In three situations a man's account book is open: when he goes on a journey alone, when he sits in a precariously standing house, and when he has made a vow but not yet fulfilled it."[21] Finally God said to him, *Go up promptly to Bethel* (Gen. 35:1), and he put away the strange gods that were among his entourage, as it says, *Jacob buried them* (Gen. 35:4). There is a reference to this in the talmudic statement, "[The Samaritans] found a figure of a dove on the top of Mt. Gerizim and they worshiped it."[22]

The Torah narrative does not always follow chronological order.[23] Rachel's

19. See Maimonides, *Code,* XIV,v (*Melakim*) 9:14; Naḥmanides on Gen. 34:13 (trans. Chavel, pp. 417–20). The preacher mentions these sources but does not discuss them.

20. Louis Ginzberg cites this passage as the source for the medieval tradition about Dinah's grave: *Legends,* 5:336, n. 96. However, twelfth- and thirteenth-century travelers already report visiting Dinah's grave in Arbel; see Elkan Adler, ed., *Jewish Travellers* (New York, 1931), pp. 95, 106, 125.

21. For this and the previous rabbinic statement, see Tanḥuma, *Wa-Yishlaḥ,* 8.

22. B. Ḥul 6a; the Samaritans were proscribed because they worshiped one of the false gods hidden by Jacob. Cf. *Daʿat Zeqenim,* p. 18a.

23. B. Pes 6b; this exegetical principle is discussed by A. J. Heschel, *Torah min ha-Shamayim,* 2 vols. (London, 1962), 1:199–202.

death occurred before the instruction to go to Bethel, as the Bible indicates: *If you have nothing to pay, why should He take away your bed from under you?* (Prov. 22:27). From this we learn that the death of a person's wife may result from the sin of failing to fulfill a vow.[24] *It is a snare for a person rashly to say, "Holy"* (Prov. 20:25).

After this Jacob heard of the death of his righteous and beloved mother. She died in sorrow and grief before he had seen her, and he mourned and wept for her, calling the place *Allon-Bakut,* (*the oak of weeping*)" (Gen. 35:8).[25] It is improbable that he would have mourned over the death of an elderly wet nurse [as it appears from the verse]. Rather, the wet nurse died on the road, for Rebekah had sent her to help rear Jacob's children, and she died on the way back. Rebekah died around the same time, and when the news came to Jacob, he mourned for her. Thus the rabbinic interpretation of the verse *God appeared to Jacob and blessed him* (Gen. 35:9), for why is this blessing mentioned here? The rabbis said, "It was a blessing for the mourner, bringing comfort."[26]

It has already been asked why Scripture concealed the death of Rebekah. One suggestion is that unlike the death of Sarah, her death lacked honor. Isaac was blind and confined to his home, Jacob was not in the vicinity, and Esau was not sufficiently reconciled with her to come to her burial, nor did Isaac want to wait for him lest people say, "Cursed be the one who gave birth to this man." He therefore ordered that she be buried at night. All of this brought great pain to Jacob, the righteous.[27]

Then, Rachel died in an unusual manner. This was the greatest agony of all, as he later said, *Rachel died because of me* (Gen. 48:7).[28] Her burial by the roadside also caused him pain, for burying the body in a special place is extremely important. God, for Whom all eventualities are possible, brought it about that Leah would be buried in the cave of Machpelah, for she, being of the "left side," needed to be joined with the righteous one in her grave. But Rachel's soul could encompass Jacob wherever she was buried, for she was his true partner.[29]

24. Tanḥuma, *Wa-Yishlaḥ*, 8.

25. See Naḥmanides on Gen. 35:8 (trans. Chavel, pp. 422–23).

26. Gen. Rabbah 81:5, 82:3.

27. This paragraph is based on Naḥmanides (trans. Chavel, pp. 423–24).

28. This translation follows the preacher's interpretation of the reason for Rachel's death and is linked with Tanḥuma, *Wa-Yishlaḥ,* 8.

29. This appears to be a kabbalistic answer to the exegetical question, although it shows independence from the standard solution of the Zoharic tradition, which held that Leah symbolized the concealed realm (*Binah*) and was therefore concealed in the cave, while Rachel symbolized the revealed realm (*Malkut*) and was therefore buried along a major thoroughfare. See Isaiah Tishby, "She'elot u-Teshubot le-Rabbi Mosheh de Leon be-ʿInyene Qabbalah," *Qobeṣ*

The rabbis also gave another explanation for her burial by the roadside. When the exiles [to Babylonia] would pass by that road, she would seek mercy on their behalf, for she was the true mother, the foundation of the household. Thus it is written, *A voice is heard on high . . . [Rachel weeping for her children]* (Jer. 31:15).[30] Then came the sorrow caused by the plight of his beloved Joseph, the child of his old age. Referring to all this he said, *Few and hard have been the years of my sojourns* (cf. Gen. 47:9).

All these experiences were a great trial and test for our ancestor Jacob. All of the patriarchs were tested, but their trials were not like these. The rabbis said in the Midrash, *A refining pot for silver* refers to Abraham, who was silver, *a furnace for gold* refers to Isaac, who was gold, *but the Lord tries the hearts* (Prov. 17:3) refers to Jacob." *Hearts* was said in relation to Jacob because he was our true father, the foundation of the world, from whom the hearts of all human beings are derived.[31]

All his experiences allude to our own; his trials hint of our trials. We must follow his example and withstand these trials as he did, acting as he did toward his brother when he realized that he was in danger.[32] Just as he behaved submissively toward Esau, calling him "lord" through his emissaries, and commanding them to say, *This is a message from your servant Jacob* (Gen. 32:5), so do we learn that we must act humbly toward his descendants in our exile, and call them lords. We are indeed servants to them, as Ezra indicated: *For we are servants* (Ezra 9:9). The rabbis said in the Midrash, "R. Judah [ha-Nasi] sent a message to Antoninus 'from your servant Judah.' Antoninus was displeased with this and said, 'Would you have me be your servant in the world to come?' R. Judah replied, 'I am not greater than my ancestors, nor are you greater than yours.' "[33]

ʿal Yad 5 (15):19–20, and Zohar 1:158a, 1:223a.

Ibn Shueib's sermons are among the earliest examples of the use of Kabbalah in this genre. See Horowitz, "Shuʿeib," p. 45, arguing that the sermons are "a bold attempt to popularize Kabbalah by integrating it into the very fabric of the sermon." The present example does not fit this generalization; it is neither bold (limited to the single word *śemaʾlit* with regard to Leah), nor is Kabbalah integrated into the sermon's fabric. Cf. below, nn. 31, 59, 62.

30. Gen. Rabbah 82:10.

31. This too seems to be a kabbalistic reference, used to interpret the midrashic comment on Prov. 17:3 (I have not found the source). Again it is independent of the standard Zoharic identifications of Jacob with the *sefirah Ḥokmah* or *Tifʾeret* (Tishby, "Sheʾelot," pp. 20, 27). For the kabbalistic doctrine of Jacob as supreme among the patriarchs, see the sources listed by Reuben Margaliot, *Shaʿare Zohar* (Jerusalem, 1978), p. 282, on Gen. Rabbah 76:1.

32. Here begins a new section of the sermon, moving verse by verse through the lesson in homily form.

33. Cf. Gen. Rabbah 75:5 and Joseph ben David, p. 43. There may be an allusion in this paragraph to the legal status of the Jews as *servi camerae*. Note the contrast between this positive evaluation of Jacob's behavior and the negative evaluation in the midrash cited by the preacher above, at n. 12.

Jacob also humbled himself by saying, *I stayed with Laban* (Gen. 32:5), implying that he had not become a prince or a ruler. The Midrash interprets *garti* ("I stayed") as "I have observed *taryag miṣwot,* 613 commandments."[34] *I have an ox and an ass* (Gen. 32:6) means: my father's blessing, *of the dew of the heaven and the fat of the earth* (Gen. 27:28) has not been fulfilled in me, for these are neither of the heaven nor of the earth.[35] He mentioned these animals to minimize his wealth. All this was an exercise in humility.

The Midrash also gives an esoteric interpretation: *ox* refers to Joseph, the adversary of Esau, as it says, *his firstborn ox* (Deut. 33:17). *And ass* refers to Issachar, as in the verse, *Issachar is a strong-boned ass* (Gen. 49:14).[36] Issachar, like Joseph, was a tent dweller: *And Issachar in your tents* (Deut. 33:18). From this point on, he was not afraid. Another interpretation is that *ox* refers to Messiah son of Joseph and *ass* to Messiah son of David, of whom it is written, *humble, riding upon an ass* (Zech. 9:9). *Flock* [refers to the people of Israel], as in the verse, *You are My flock* (Ezek. 34:31). [*Male and female slaves* are] in accordance with the verse *As the eyes of slaves {follow their master's hand}, as the eyes of a slave girl {follows the hand of her mistress, so our eyes are toward the Lord our God}* (Ps. 123:2).[37]

It would appear from the simple meaning of the passage that Esau did not want to see the emissaries, and that they therefore sent him the gifts, for the Bible does not tell how he received them, saying only *the messengers returned* (Gen. 32:7). However, they heard in Esau's camp that he intended to set out toward Jacob with a large entourage, bursting with anger. Then *Jacob was afraid* of Esau, *and distressed* because of the death of his father. Esau had said, *Let but the mourning period of my father come, {and I will kill Jacob}* (Gen. 27:41), and now he was coming to kill him. Jacob therefore concluded, My father must indeed be dead. That is why he said in his prayer, *God of my father Isaac* (Gen. 32:10), for this formula was not used while the person was alive.[38]

There is another interpretation in the Midrash. "Why was he afraid? Because of Isaac's great trembling [when he discovered that Jacob had deceived him, Gen. 28:33]. He said to himself, 'Esau honored [our] father, while I

34. Cf. Rashi on Gen. 32:5 for the two interpretations. The letters of *garti* rearranged form *taryag;* both are numerically equivalent to 613, the traditional number of the commandments.

35. Rashi on Gen. 32:6.

36. Gen. Rabbah 75:12.

37. Gen. Rabbah 75:6; the text in ibn Shueib is incomplete, and I have reconstructed it in accordance with the midrashic source.

38. The idea that Esau's apparent preparation for war led Jacob to conclude that his father was dead, used to interpret the apparently superfluous word "distressed" in Gen. 32:8, appears in *Daᶜat Zeqenim,* p. 17d. Cf. also Luntshitz, *Keli Yaqar,* citing *Sefer Toledot Yiṣḥaq.* Contrast the midrash cited above, at n. 16.

caused him pain.' "[39] According to another midrash, "R. Simeon ben Gamaliel said, I have ministered to my father throughout my life, yet I have not done for him one one-hundredth of what Esau did for his father. I would minister to his needs in soiled house clothes, and then dress up to go out, while Esau wore everyday clothing when he went out but put on his finest garments to attend to his father's needs."[40] That is why Jacob was greatly afraid. And God promised to save him—*fear not, My servant Jacob* (Isa. 44:2)—from that which made him tremble.

Jacob prepared himself for three things: for gifts, for prayer, and for war. He armed his people underneath, and clothed them in white on the outside, and divided them into two camps, saying, *If Esau comes to one camp {and attacks it, then the other will escape}* (Gen. 32:9).[41] The sages of blessed memory said, "against his will," meaning that Jacob knew all his seed would not fall into Esau's hands. This informs us that Esau's descendants will not pass a decree to obliterate our name entirely. They will harm only some of us.

One of their kings may pass a decree in his country against our wealth or our persons, while another king will show compassion and save the refugees. So the rabbis said in Genesis Rabbah (76:3), "*If Esau comes to the one camp*: these are our brothers in the south; *then the other camp will escape*: these are our brothers in the Diaspora." The sages realized that the entire chapter alludes to future generations. They also said, "The Torah has taught that a person should not put all his wealth in one corner."

After preparing himself for war, he prayed, *O God of my father Abraham* (Gen. 32:10). He added *and God of my father Isaac* in order to include this divine attribute as well, as God had done at the ladder (Gen. 28:13). . . .[42] Rabbenu Hananel of blessed memory wrote that Jacob incorporated all thirteen divine attributes {found by the rabbis in Exod. 34:6–7} into his prayer. . . .[43] Some interpret the phrase *the mother with the children* (Gen.

39. Cf. Gen. Rabbah 76:2. This midrash and the following about R. Simeon ben Gamaliel are cited by Joseph ben David, p. 43.

40. Gen. Rabbah 65:16.

41. Naḥmanides on Gen. 32:9 (trans. Chavel, p. 398), citing Rashi and Midrash. The phrase "against his will," in the following sentence, was used by Rashi and debated by ibn Ezra and the major commentators on Rashi. The rest of the paragraph, except for the last sentence quoting Gen. Rabbah 76:3, is taken without attribution from Naḥmanides (trans. Chavel, p. 398).

42. I.e., this is the form used by God in Gen. 28:13. The sense of the following seven Hebrew words in the printed text is not clear to me. The manuscripts contain different readings, and the textual tradition needs clarification.

43. There follows a long passage attributed to R. Hananel, linking the divine attributes of Exod. 34:6–7 with Jacob's prayer in Gen. 32:10–13. This passage is known only from the present source; see Abraham Berliner, *Migdal Ḥananel* (Berlin, 1976), p. 27. The Hebrew is not completely clear, and the textual tradition of the passage is rather corrupt. An English rendering at this stage would be futile.

32:12) to imply that Jacob was not afraid for himself, as God had already promised, *Remember, I am with you* (Gen. 28:15).[44] *Qaṭonti*: "*I am too small* (Gen. 32:10) to endure all this." The translation of Onkelos is well known.[45] R. Moses [ben Naḥman] explained, "I am too small to be worthy of all these mercies."

After this he prepared himself for gifts, as we see in the verse, *{He selected} from what was at hand {these presents for Esau}* (Gen. 32:14). The sages said, "gems that a man carries on his hand."[46] But Rabbenu Tam suggested that this refers to a falcon, which a man may bring on his hand, for Esau was a hunter. *Two hundred she-goats* (Gen. 32:15): the quantity has significance. The sages said that this is the basis in the Torah for the principle of a husband's marital duty toward his wife. The she-goats were mentioned first for a purpose.[47] *Keep a distance* (Gen. 32:17) hints that if troubles come upon his children, there will be an interval between them.[48] The threefold occurrence of the word *gam* ("also") [in v. 20] refers to the three exiles of Egypt, Babylonia, and Edom, hinting to all who subjugate his descendants that they must behave peacefully toward us in this subjugation.

We might well ask, having instructed them first to say *He himself is right behind us* (Gen. 32:19), what purpose was there in repeating, *Your servant Jacob himself is right behind us* (Gen. 32:21)? The Tosafists explained this as follows: "Tell him the reason why I come last: that this does not imply arrogance, like that of kings and nobles whose retinues precede them. It is rather so that *I may propitiate him with the present {that precedes me}* (Gen. 32:21)." It says, *So the gift passed before him* (Gen. 32:22) in the same sense as, *then the Lord passed before him, and proclaimed* (Exod. 34:6). This is what they hinted in the midrash comparing this prayer with Moses' prayer of the thirteen attributes.[49]

The word for wrestling, *hitʾabbequt,* is linked with the word *ḥibbuq* ("clasping"). The rabbis said that they raised *abaq,* or dust, with their feet up to the Throne of Glory,[50] meaning that this matter had implications on high,

44. This interpretation is found in *Daʿat Zeqenim,* p. 17d, and ibn Ezra's comment on 32:9 (rebutted by Naḥmanides on Gen. 32:13, trans. Chavel, pp. 400–01). It assumes that the word *we-hikkani* in v. 12 means "smite what is mine" (see Saadia Gaon's comment on this verse).

45. The Targum, as understood by Rashi: "My merits have diminished as a consequence of the kindness You have done." This is the way the verse is used in the Talmud (B. Taʿan 20b).

46. Tanḥuma, ed. Buber, *Wa-Yishlaḥ,* 11, cited by Rashi. For the translation "falcon" in R. Tam's interpretation, see Baḥya ben Asher.

47. Gen. Rabbah 76:7.

48. Gen. Rabbah 75:13, cited by Naḥmanides (trans. Chavel, p. 401).

49. See above, at n. 43.

50. B. Ḥul 91a.

reflecting strife in the celestial realm. The "man" was the guardian angel of Esau, who came to hurt Jacob and to exterminate his line. That it happened at night alludes to the exile; *until the breaking of dawn* alludes to the redemption. All this actually occurred, it was not merely a vision [in Jacob's mind]. That is why he was left limping.[51] It teaches us that the righteous are higher than angels, as the Midrash says, "*Indeed, My servant shall prosper, {be exalted and raised to great heights}* (Isa. 52:13): exalted above Abraham, raised above Moses, high above the ministering angels."[52]

When he saw that he had not prevailed against him, he wrenched Jacob's hip at its socket (Gen. 32:26). This means that he hurt the righteous who would some day emerge from his loins during a generation of persecution, such as that of R. Judah ben Baba.[53] It is as the rabbis said, "'Why are you being led out to be burned?' 'Because I have taken a palm branch.' 'To be stoned?' 'Because of phylacteries.' 'To be strangled?' 'Because of the sukkah.' This is what the prophet meant in the verse, *And if he is asked, 'What are those sores on your back?' he will reply, 'From being beaten in the house of those who make me beloved {by God}'* (Zech. 13:6)."[54]

Realizing the true stature of Jacob, whose form was engraved on the Throne of Glory,[55] he implored him [to be released]. Finally, he conceded the validity of Isaac's blessings. Although Jacob did not really need the blessing of his adversary, there was an act of confirmation, similar to that in the rabbinic statement, "A document of divorce is confirmed only by those who sign it."[56] Thus God wanted His children to be blessed even by their enemies like Balaam.

In the Hafṭarah for this lesson, we find Obadiah prophesying about the redemption. Obadiah was an Edomite proselyte, the same Obadiah who was *the steward of the palace* and summoned by Ahab (1 Kings 18:3). The rabbis said, "From the very forest itself comes the [handle of the] axe [that fells it]. The Holy One, blessed be He, said, Let Obadiah, who has lived with two wicked persons yet did not learn from their deeds, come [and prophesy against the wicked Esau, who lived with two righteous persons yet did not learn from their deeds]."[57]

51. The preacher is referring to a dispute between Maimonides and Naḥmanides about the nature of prophetic vision in the Bible. Maimonides argued that the vision of the men who appeared to Abraham and the man who wrestled with Jacob occurred entirely in the mind of the prophet (*Guide* 2:42). Naḥmanides caustically replied, "But if this be the case, I do not know why Jacob limped on his thigh when he awoke" (on Gen. 18:1, trans. Chavel, p. 227).

52. Tanḥuma, *Toledot,* 14.

53. Cf. Gen. Rabbah 77:3 and Naḥmanides on Gen. 32:26 (trans. Chavel, pp. 405–06).

54. Cf. Lev, Rabbah 32:1.

55. Tanḥuma, *Be-Midbar,* 19. See the final paragraph of the sermon.

56. Gen. Rabbah 78:11.

57. B. Sanh 39b. The use of the Hafṭarah from Obadiah follows the Sephardic practice that would have been expected in ibn Shueib's synagogue.

The commandment relating to the sciatic nerve was given through Jacob. The rabbis interpreted the verse, *The Lord sent something upon Jacob {and it fell upon Israel}* (Isa. 9:7) as applying to the sciatic nerve. The fact that this prohibition was not reiterated by Moses has great significance. Our digging after the sciatic nerve [to this day] shows the power of Jacob. Some [authorities] are so strict as to prohibit any benefit at all derived from it, even throwing it to a cat.[58] All these are matters of great import to which allusion is made in this section.

Jacob prostrated himself seven times (Gen. 33:3), in accordance with the verse, *A righteous man falls seven times and rises* (Prov. 24:16). This alludes to the seven-year cycles.[59] According to Genesis Rabbah [78:8], he kept on stretching himself out until he caused the quality of strict justice to be engulfed by the quality of mercy, just as that wise man did to the serpent in the house of study.[60] The simple meaning is that he prostrated himself in order to show that Isaac's blessing, *Your mother's sons shall bow to you; I have made you master over your brothers* (Gen. 27:29), had not been fulfilled. That was the seventh blessing. The sons of the servant women acted arrogantly in not bowing down before Esau (Gen. 33:6). Even though they saw their mothers bowing, they said to themselves, "We are greater than our mothers." But the sons of Leah and Rachel, seeing their mothers prostate themselves, did the same (Gen. 33:7). R. Abraham wrote, "The contemptible are always more arrogant than the esteemed."[61]

There is significance in the contrast between Esau's statement, *Yesh li rab* [lit. "I have much"] (Gen. 33:9) and Jacob's statement, *Yesh li kol* ("I have all"] (Gen. 33:11), for Esau was similar to his guardian angel, who struggled, *rab,* on his behalf, and Jacob was similar to the divine attribute [called *kol*].[62]

From this section, we can learn that although Jacob was aware of his own stature in the supernal realm and understood its significance, he did not excite his mind to engage in matters too great or wondrous for him. He

58. The interpretation of Isa. 9:7 is in B. Ḥul 91a. On the law relating to the sciatic nerve, see B. Pes 22a, Maimonides, *Code* V,ii (*Maʾakalot Asurot*) 8:14 and commentaries, and *Sefer ha-Ḥinnuk* (Jerusalem, 1961), p. 57.

59. Gen. Rabbah 78:8; cf. the discussion by Joseph ben David, p. 47. The final phrase is the preacher's addition. This may be an allusion to the kabbalistic doctrine of the *shemiṭot,* on which see Gershom Scholem, *Les Origines de la Kabbale* (Paris, 1966), pp. 485–99.

60. The reference is apparently to the story about Ḥanina ben Dosa, who carried a serpent into the house of study in order to demonstrate that "it is not the serpent that kills, but sin that kills" (B. Ber 33a). The connection between the story about a snake and this passage may have been suggested by Zohar 1:166b–167a.

61. On the behavior of the servantwomen's sons, cf. *Daʿat Zeqenim,* p. 17d. Compare the proverb cited by Moses ibn Ezra; "Arrogance is found only among the lowly" (Davidson, *Oṣar,* p. 139).

62. On the kabbalistic significance of the divine attribute called *kol,* see Naḥmanides on Gen. 24:1 (trans. Chavel, pp. 291–92).

remained constantly apprehensive and fearful, sending gifts as mentioned in Genesis Rabbah [cf. 78:16]: "During the period when Jacob was in Sukkoth, he honored Esau with a gift each month." All of this pertains to us in our exile.

Esau's statement, *Let me assign to you [some of the men who are with me]* and Jacob's response, *Oh no, my lord is too kind to me!* (Gen. 33:15) also contains a hint that we should accept no favors from them. For they draw near a person only for their own benefit. The rabbis of blessed memory said that "when our rabbi [Judah] had to travel to the government, he would look at this text and would not take Romans with him. On one occasion he did not look at it and took Romans with him, and before he reached Acre, he had already sold his horse."[63] They knew that this section hints of the future exile.

Furthermore, Jacob's statement *until I come to my lord in Seir* (Gen. 33:14), in which he exaggerates his intended journey, is a fine stratagem, the kind to which Solomon referred when he said, *With clever stratagems you shall wage your war* (Prov. 24:6). Our sages said that he hinted to Esau of messianic times, when he would indeed come to Seir, as it says, *For victors shall march up [on Mt. Zion to wreak judgment on Mt. Esau]* (Obad. 21).[64] The last letters of the Hebrew words *abo el adoni śeᶜirah* (*until I come to my lord in Seir*) spell "Elijah," the prophet.

They also interpreted *Let my lord go on ahead* (Gen. 33:14) as a hint to him that he, Jacob, would serve him first, with Esau as master and Jacob as servant.[65] *While I travel slowly* in exile hints that we shall go in exile under his dominance; therefore *slowly,* that tragedies may not come upon us without end. *Le-regel ha-melaʾkah* (NJV: *At the pace of the cattle*) refers to those who engage in the study of Torah, as we see in Abot [2:16]: "It is not incumbent upon you to finish the task" (*melaʾkah,* understood as the task of Torah study). *U-le-regel ha-yeladim* (NJV: *and at the pace of the children*) refers to the pupils, as in the prophet, *Here stand I and the* yeladim (lit. "children," understood to mean "disciples") *whom the Lord has given me [as signs and portents in Israel]* (Isa. 8:18). *Until I come to my lord* (Gen. 33:14), for we shall seize sovereignty after them. When the Roman lady asked R. Joshua ben Levi "Who shall

63. Gen. Rabbah 78:15.

64. Gen. Rabbah 78:14. The following sentence is taken from Baḥya ben Asher. The preacher links the midrashic passage both with the "stratagems" he has discussed at the beginning and with the messianic motif with which he will conclude his sermon.

65. *Midrash Abkir,* cited in *Yalquṭ Shimᶜoni* ad loc. The rest of the verse is interpreted as applying to the Jewish experience in exile: Israel makes slow "progress" in worldly affairs because of its commitment to Torah learning. Cf. Joseph ben David, p. 45.

seize sovereignty after us?" he showed her the verse, *His hand was holding on to the heel of Esau* (Gen. 25:26).[66]

When Esau asked Jacob, "Shall we divide the two worlds?" Jacob responded, *You know that the children are frail* (Gen. 33:13) and are unable to endure Gehinnom. *And the flock* refers to Israel; if they are driven into Gehinnom even for a single day, the entire flock will perish.[67] *Let my lord go on* (Gen. 33:14) first and take possession of this world, and I shall endure the exiles. This is also the meaning of the verse, *Then we moved on, away from our kinsmen, the descendants of Esau who live in Seir, . . . from Elath and from Ezion-Geber* (Deut. 2:8). *Then we moved on* corresponds to *Let my lord go on. From Elath*: [proceeding] from the *alah,* or oath, of the Holy One. *And from Ezion-Geber*: from the *ʿeṣah,* or counsel, of Abraham, who foresaw the exile. *We marched on in the direction of the wilderness of Moab* (ibid.) refers to Ruth the Moabite, an allusion to the Messiah.[68] All of these verses hint of the future, as does *Jacob came* shalem, *safe* (Gen. 33:18).

I will assemble the lame (Mic. 4:6) refers to Jacob, who limped because of his thigh. We shall attain exalted grandeur, wisdom, and prophecy, a great reward, in return for being humble and scorned and meek, just as Jacob received exalted grandeur. By accepting all his afflictions cheerfully he acquired his share in the world. So we, the house of Israel, are assured of receiving sovereignty and true stature.[69] That is what King Solomon meant when he said, *For he can emerge from a dungeon to become king* (Eccles. 4:14).

Right before this, he said, *Better is a poor but wise child,* referring to Israel, as we see in Isaiah, *When he—that is his children—behold what My hands have wrought in his midst, they will hallow My Name* (Isa. 29:23). *Poor* refers to their being impoverished and degraded in exile, gravely afflicted. *Wise* because in the beginning they accepted the yoke of divine kingship. *Than an old but foolish king*: *king* refers to Esau, whose sovereignty preceded ours, for his kingship predated the reign of the first Israelite king; it was before Moses, as we see in the verse, *There was a king in Jeshurun* (Deut. 33:5). *But foolish,* because he did not know enough to be wary, and by accepting kingship first

66. Cf. Gen. Rabbah 63:9.

67. Cf. David ha-Nagid, p. 142 and n. 92; Baḥya ben Asher; Joseph ben David, n. 45.

68. The translation of this passage is made from Paris MS 237; the Cracow edition omits about twenty words through haplography. Cf. Deut. Rabbah and Baḥya ben Asher on Deut. 2:8; ibn Shueib's source, however, is different. For the connection between Gen. 33:14 and Deut. 2:8, see *Yalquṭ Shimʿoni* on the Deuteronomy verse. With the citation of Gen. 33:18, ibn Shueib completes the homiletical-exegetical section of the sermon. This paragraph, giving historical interpretations of Torah verses, provides a transition to the brief concluding section, which is suffused with messianic motifs and addressed to the experience of the audience.

69. This recapitulates the point made at the beginning of the second section of the sermon: Jacob's cheerful acceptance of affliction is a model for our own behavior, and his ultimate victory prefigures our own redemption.

he inherited Gehinnom. *For he can emerge from a dungeon to become king* refers to Israel, which will go forth from the exile in which it is imprisoned and become king in the messianic age, when the Messiah reigns. *Although in his kingship he was born poor,* for when Moses reigned at first, he was impoverished and poor in the Egyptian exile.[70]

He further said, *Happy are you, O land whose king is a master,* referring to the land of Israel; *and whose ministers dine at the proper time,* meaning that they will ultimately receive sovereignty; this is *with strength, and not with guzzling* (Eccles. 10:17), with the strength that comes from having engaged in Torah during the exile, not from eating and drinking. *Alas for you, O land whose king is a boy* refers to Esau, who was spiritually immature, unprepared for the commandments; *whose ministers dine in the morning* (Eccles. 10:16), for they received sovereignty first, in the morning, losing the world to come. (All this is in the Midrash.)[71]

And all applies to us, referring to the relationship between Jacob and his brother in this lesson. He went forth from his tribulations to peace, returning peacefully to his home, unblemished, *shalem,* in body, wealth, birthright, and learning. He attained such stature that God called him "Israel." Moreover, we read in tractate Megillah [18a], "Where do we find that the Holy One called Jacob 'God'? From the verse, *He called him 'God'*" (Gen. 33:20). In Genesis Rabbah they formulated this same idea somewhat differently: "He said to Him, 'I am God in the lower realm and You are God in the supernal realm.'"

R. Moses [ben Naḥman] said that the sages were alluding to their frequent assertion that Jacob's likeness is engraved on the Throne of Glory, and also to the statement, "The patriarchs are the Divine Chariot."[72] We too are assured in the name of God that we will be worthy of ascending to an exalted position because we have been humiliated and scorned and have suffered in exile for our love of God. The enemy will suffer greatly, while we shall have total reconciliation.[73] May the redeemer come speedily and in our days, in

70. This typological historical interpretation of Eccles. 4:13–14 is strikingly different from the ethical interpretation of the rabbinic literature (e.g., Eccles. Rabbah), which became standard in medieval Jewish ethical literature. Contrast also the mystical interpretation in Zohar 1:95b.

71. The sentence "all this is in the Midrash" does not appear in Paris MS 237, nor have I found a midrashic source for this interpretation. It appears to be the preacher's own interpretation.

72. See Naḥmanides on Gen. 33:20 (trans. Chavel, p. 413); Gen. Rabbah 79:8; Zohar 1:138a. Paris MS 237 has the intriguing (though chronologically implausible) reading, "R. Moses ben Naḥman of blessed memory told me. . . ."

73. The phrase about the suffering of the enemy, taken from Paris MS 237, is not in the Cracow edition; internal censorship may account for its excision.

accordance with the verse, *For victors shall march up on Mt. Zion to wreak judgment on Mt. Esau, and dominion shall be the Lord's* (Obad. 21), as it is said, *The Lord shall be King over all the earth; on that day there shall be one Lord with one Name* (Zech. 14:9).[74]

74. The messianic hope is expressed through the verse from the Hafṭarah, cited in the sermon in connection with Jacob's promise to Esau in Gen. 33:19 (see above, at n. 64). The final verse from Zechariah, not in the Cracow edition, is taken from the Paris MS.

Mattathias Yizhari

Not much is known about the life of Mattathias Yizhari.[1] According to one autobiographical passage in his work, his family originally lived in Narbonne until they were expelled from France, probably in 1306. From there they went to Catalonia and Aragon, where they experienced additional upheavals.[2] Mattathias was born in the middle of the fourteenth century. He was apparently a student of the distinguished theologian Ḥasdai Crescas. If he is indeed the same person as the "Rabbi Mathatias Caesaraugustanus" mentioned in a Christian source, he lived in Saragossa. He participated with other leaders of Spanish Jewry in the disputation held at Tortosa in 1413–14, but his role, at least as recorded in the sources, was not outstanding.[3]

Yizhari was the author of an extensive commentary on Psalm 119, which has been published in its entirety;[4] a commentary on Abot, of which a selection has been published;[5] and a book of model sermons arranged according to the weekly lessons of the Torah, part of which has been preserved in a unique manuscript, Parma MS 2365 (De Rossi 1417). In this work he also refers to his commentary on the Ten Commandments, apparently no longer extant (fol. 2r).

While no introduction to his sermon collection has been preserved, the purpose of the work can be readily perceived in occasional remarks clearly intended for the benefit of future preachers. For example, "On this subject [the dangers of wealth] you may add what seems appropriate to you from the Gemara and the Midrash" (fol. 3v); or, "On this subject [the creation of man] you may move from passage to passage, as God supplies you, from the Midrash and Rashi and [Baḥya ibn Paquda's] *Ḥobot ha-Lebabot* (Duties of the heart), until you return and conclude with the verse with which I began. In [the talmudic tractate] Sanhedrin, chapter 4, you will find material relating

1. For the relevant material, see Michael A. Schmidman, "An Excerpt from the Abot Commentary of R. Mattathias ha-Yizhari," in Isadore Twersky, ed., *Studies in Medieval Jewish History and Literature* (Cambridge, Mass., 1979), p. 316, n. 1.

2. See the introduction to his commentary on the tractate Abot, published by Isadore Loeb, "R. Mattatya ha-Yichari," *REJ* 7 (1883):153–55.

3. See Baer, *HJCS* 2:173–229.

4. *Perush Alef-Bet,* ed. Dov Rappel (Tel Aviv, 1978).

5. By Schmidman (see n. 1, above). Cf. also Schmidman's doctoral dissertation, "R. Joseph ibn Shoshan and Medieval Commentaries on Abot" (Harvard Univ., 1980), passim.

to the creation of man; in the book *Ḥakmoni,* written by the learned R. Shabbetai {Donnolo}, you will also find such material; and in my explication of the Ten Commandments you will find material about the sleeping of the man, who did not yet awaken for the commandment *You shall not commit adultery* (Exod. 20:13)" (fol. 2r). And again, on "R. Jose says, Whoever honors the Torah is himself honored by all" (Abot 4:6):

> There are many aspects of honor for the Torah, as {I have shown} in my {commentary on} Pirqe Abot. When you arrive at the phrase "is honored by all," you can discuss Hezekiah, who honored the Torah and taught it to Israel. . . . And here you can mention the statement in the first chapter of {the talmudic tractate} Soṭah {9b, 13a} that Joseph was worthy of burying his father, and he was rewarded {when his bones were taken up by Moses at the time of the Exodus}. In this context you can bring in some of the blessings that Jacob used to bless his sons, following either the Midrash or Rashi. Select what you think is appropriate. Then come back and say, "How great is the reward of one who honors the Torah," and return to Jacob . . . (fol. 60r–v).

The manuscript contains sermons for all the lessons in Genesis, although *Lek Leka* (Gen. 12:1–17:27) and *Ḥayye Śarah* (Gen. 23:1–25:18) are incomplete, and for the lessons in Exodus through part of the sermon on *Teṣawweh* (Exod. 27:20–30:10). The whole work may have provided sermons for all the lessons of the Pentateuch. Yizhari refers in his commentary on Psalm 119 to his sermon for the Feast of Weeks (Shabuᶜot), so it is possible that there were model sermons for the holidays as well.

In form these sermons are similar to our thirteenth- and fourteenth-century exemplars. They begin by discussing a quotation from outside the Pentateuch and eventually apply it to the Torah lesson. As has been shown above (see "Structural Options"), the range of source material available for the opening text is significantly wider than in the sermons of thirteenth-century preachers or for ibn Shueib, including not only Proverbs and Psalms but also Job, Ecclesiastes, the Prophets, and even rabbinic literature.

While Yizhari occasionally resorts to philosophical material in allegorical interpretations of traditional passages (examples are fols. 23v, 26v), he is clearly a moderate in his use of such material. On the whole, he is more interested in ethical and religious instruction than in philosophical doctrine (see fols. 40r–v, 62r–65r). He draws extensively from ethical literature like *Mibḥar ha-Peninim* (see fol. 64r), and he is extremely fond of illustrative stories and parables (fols. 41r–42v).

The sermon on *Toledot* (Gen. 25:19–28:9) is clearly divided into two parts. The first section discusses the verses from Isaiah 40 according to their simple meaning. This includes an extensive citation from Nissim ben Jacob's *Ḥibbur*

Yafeh me-ha-Yeshuᶜah (called here *Sefer ha-Maᶜaśiyyot*). While there is little explicit reference to contemporary events—the sermons were after all models for future preachers—the allusion to martyrdom at the beginning of this text would certainly have been resonant for a Spanish audience after the riots of 1391.[6] Unlike other moralists of the period following that traumatic year, Yizhari does not emphasize the theme of punishment for sin, and there is no call for repentance. He insists, however, that there is a purpose in Jewish suffering, and he tries to convince his listeners to remain faithful and to trust in God even when the divine ways are not readily understood.

The second part of the sermon applies the verses from Isaiah to the Torah lesson, "following the method of the Midrash." According to the midrashic reading of the Torah narrative, Jacob was a fully righteous man and Esau a total sinner; therefore, the preacher asserts, Jacob in his naiveté may have questioned why his wicked brother enjoyed greater success than he did. A discussion in homily form of various problems in the Genesis narrative draws on the aggadic tradition for their solution. Although this section becomes somewhat less focused than the preceding one, the problem of theodicy provides an overall unity that the sermons of ibn Shueib, with their wide-ranging homilies on the Torah lesson, rarely have. The conclusion is not explicitly messianic. Jacob is a model for any Jew, demonstrating that all can find strength to transcend afflictions through faith in God.

Sermon on *Toledot*
(Ca. 1400, Spain)

Do you not know, have you not heard: The Lord is God from of old, Creator of the earth from end to end. He never grows faint or weary, His wisdom cannot be fathomed. He gives strength to the weary, fresh vigor to the spent. Youths will grow faint and weary, and young men stumble and fall, but those who trust in the Lord shall renew their strength as eagles grow new plumes. They shall run and not grow weary, they shall march and not grow faint (Isa. 40:28–31).[1]

These verses were spoken by the prophet Isaiah following his initial words of comfort.[2] His purpose was to console the people of Israel, so that they

6. See Baer, *HJCS* 2:95–134.

1. These verses are the beginning of the Hafṭarah for *Lek Leka*, and they would have been read in the synagogue three weeks earlier. The quotation of these verses at the beginning of a sermon on *Toledot* would probably have caused momentary disorientation and surprise among many listeners.

2. Isa. 40:1–27.

might endure the sorrows that would befall them in the future. The basic meaning of the passage is this: we must understand that all power and authority belong to God, for this knowledge will strengthen those who trust in God while afflicted because of their belief in His unity, namely, those who suffer in this distant exile.[3]

That is why he said, *Do you not know?* . . . In other words, you must know and understand that the blessed Creator, who created the ends of the earth, is, when He so desires, certainly capable of rewarding those who do His will and of punishing those who transgress it. This is what David said, *Yours, O Lord, is greatness* . . . , concluding with *yes, all that is in heaven and earth* (1 Chron. 29:11). Similar is the verse, *I, the Lord, have abased the lofty tree and exalted the lowly tree, I have dried up the green tree and made the withered tree bud* (Ezek. 17:24). Therefore, *He never grows faint or weary,* and the rest of the passage with which we began.

Now according to the simple meaning of this passage, we might say that the prophet Isaiah was responding to many of his contemporaries who could not comprehend God's plan. Human intellect and knowledge led them to conclude that God had turned His eyes away from human affairs. Seeing so many examples of God's apparent reluctance to act in the world, they murmured contentiously, "Perhaps God has abandoned the earth." Some of them even said openly, "Who watches us, who is aware of us?"

To this Isaiah responded as one who admonishes and rebukes, *Why do you say, O Jacob, why declare, O Israel?* (Isa. 40:27): how could it even have occurred to you to speak so improperly? Know that His thoughts are not the same as yours. This is as he said elsewhere, *plans from a distance, steadfast faithfulness* (Isa. 25:1), meaning that God's plan and His thoughts are by no means fully comprehensible to us. Therefore, if you do not want to go astray, you must have faith in Him, believing firmly that all is revealed before His throne of glory.

Indeed, it is not only *God's* work that baffles those who would comprehend it. Even the sages used to do things that were incomprehensible to their disciples until the reason for them was explained. This is what is told of R. Eliezer, whose disciples came to comfort him when his servant died. When he saw them, he climbed to the upper floor of his house. They followed. He went into a room. They followed. He went out to an anteroom. They followed. Finally he said to them, "I thought you would be scalded by warm water, but you are not scalded even by boiling water. Did I not teach you, We do not accept condolences for servants, nor is a row of comforters formed? Rather

3. *Sobele ha-galut ha-raḥoq ha-zeh*; this would appear to refer to the preacher's own Jewish community in the Iberian peninsula. The reference to those "afflicted because of their belief in His unity" (*meyussarim ʿal yiḥudo*) may well allude to the martyrdoms of 1391 (on which see Baer, *HJCS* 2:95–134).

we say, 'May God replenish their loss.' "[4] Thus, even though he hinted several times by his meanderings that he did not wish to accept condolences, they did not understand what he was doing until he reminded them of this rule. If this is so, how can one expect to comprehend God's awesome work, which we cannot even see?

Similarly, it is told that R. Joshua ben Levi fasted repeatedly in order to cause Elijah the prophet to appear to him. God heard his prayer. Elijah appeared and said to R. Joshua, "Why do you want to accompany me in my travels? Know that you will be unable to bear what I do, for it will seem to you to be the opposite of what you think is right. You will not be able to refrain from asking about everything you see me do, and it will be a burden for me to explain it." R. Joshua replied, "My lord, I will not ask or test you, I will not burden you with a single question." Elijah then stipulated that if R. Joshua should, in spite of his promise, ask him to explain the mystery of his behavior, he would do so, but then he would depart, and R. Joshua would no longer be able to accompany him.

All day the two of them traveled together. Finally they reached the house of an unfortunate pauper. All the man had was a single cow that stood in the yard. The man and his wife were sitting near the gate. Seeing strangers approach, they joyfully went out to greet them. They had them sit on the good bed, served them what there was to eat and drink, and invited them to stay the night.

The next morning, as they prepared to continue on their way, Elijah prayed that the cow should die, and immediately it died. Then the two of them departed. R. Joshua was astonished at this. Dumbfounded at what Elijah had done, he asked, "Was this the reward for this poor man who honored us: to kill his only cow? Why did you kill this poor man's cow?" Elijah replied, "Remember our agreement that you would remain silent. Do you want to leave me?" R. Joshua did not speak another word.

All day the two of them traveled together. At evening they came to the house of a wealthy man, who did not greet them graciously. That man had a wall to build. Elijah prayed over it, and the wall was immediately built. [They went on until they came to a certain community. Entering the synagogue, they found seats of gold and silver, each person sitting in his own seat.] But they were not given lodging, food, or drink. Elijah then prayed that these men should become leaders. Later they came to another community, where the people honored them to the best of their ability. Elijah then prayed that here there should be but a single leader.

At this point R. Joshua could no longer endure Elijah's behavior and finally asked him to explain his actions, which appeared to be so unjust. Elijah then

4. B. Ber 16b, with slight variations in the text.

explained it all, as set forth in the *Book of Tales* written by Rabbi Nissim.[5] Thus we see that R. Joshua could not control his curiosity in dealing with a human being like himself. As for the deeds of the Creator, it is enough for us to understand that He knows what He is doing, and that no one can fathom His wisdom. This is the meaning of the verses with which we began.

Now following the method of Midrash, we might apply these verses to this Torah lesson. Isaiah saw how the righteous feel dismayed at the wicked who continually prosper. Sometimes the righteous gnash their teeth and murmur contentiously that God is unfair. This may result from the excessive naiveté of these people. We find that Jacob is called *ish tam, a simple, naive man* (Gen. 25:27), and Job is called *tam we-yashar, simple and straightforward* (Job 1:1). Because of their naiveté, they did not appreciate the subtlety of God's work. This is why we find in both cases that their friends quarreled with them.

Of Job it is said that *because he justified himself* (Job 32:2), his friends attacked him. Zophar asked him, Why do you insist upon complaining and arguing to the point where you think you have made an irrefutable case? *Is a multitude of words unanswerable; must a man full of talk be right?* (Job 11:2). Just because you speak so many falsehoods, do you think you will silence all replies? Is this why you say, *My doctrine is pure?* (Job 11:4). And he went on to say, *Your prattle may silence people; you may mock without being rebuked* (Job 11:3), but why do you insist, *My doctrine is pure* (Job 11:4)?

If only God would speak and talk to you Himself (Job 11:5), for, if it were His will to speak with you, He would have revealed why He is contending against you. If you knew His work, you would realize that you are still in His debt. This is the meaning of *He would tell you the secrets of wisdom . . . ; know that God has overlooked for you some of your iniquity* (Job 11:6). In other

5. Cf. Nissim ben Jacob ibn Shāhīn, *An Elegant Composition Concerning Relief after Adversity,* trans. William M. Brinner (New Haven, 1977), pp. 13–23. The preacher's refusal to complete the story and cite the explanation for Elijah's actions is effective and appropriate. His point about the suffering experienced by his contemporaries is that there are an explanation and a purpose, but it is not his intention to speculate about the details of God's plan.

For discussions of the story from various perspectives, see Julian Obermann, "Two Elijah Stories in Judeo-Arabic Transmission," *HUCA* 23/1 (1950–51):387–404, Haim Schwarzbaum, "The Jewish and Moslem Versions of Some Theodicy Legends," *Fabula* 3 (1959):119–69, and "Eliyahu ha-Nabi we-Rabbi Yehoshuᶜa ben Lewi," *Yedaᶜ ᶜAm* 25 (1962):22–31. The use of the story in this sermon is an important piece of evidence for the history of the Hebrew text of Nissim's work, as it indicates the existence of a Hebrew version, entitled *Sefer ha-Maᶜaśiyyot,* that would have been readily accessible to Spanish readers in 1400. Note also the allusion to the story without identification of its source by Joseph Albo, *Sefer ha-ᶜIqqarim* 4:13 (ed. Isaac Husik, 5 vols., Philadelphia, 1930, 4:106–07). For a review of the complex textual problems relating to the Arabic and Hebrew versions, see Shraga Abramson, *Rabbenu Nissim Gaʾon: Ḥamishah Sefarim* (Jerusalem, 1965), pp. 363–94, and Brinner's intro. to *An Elegant Composition,* pp. xvii–xx.

words, God's insight is so abundant that no creature can comprehend it. If He told you of His wisdom, you would appreciate His forbearance and realize that despite the great losses you have suffered He exacts payment for only some of your sins. This was also the point made by Elihu, until finally Job conceded. We have discussed this on a different occasion.

Similarly, Isaiah was speaking about Jacob, who murmured contentiously that the wicked Esau had shortened Abraham's life. The sages said that Abraham should have lived 180 years as Isaac did. Why was he deprived of five years? God said, I have promised that he would be buried *be-śebah ṭobah,* which means literally *a good old age* (Gen. 15:15). If he sees his grandson falling into bad ways, where is the "good old age"? Therefore, when Esau went out to the field, Abraham died.[6]

The sages said that Esau committed three transgressions on that day: he had sexual intercourse with a married woman, he committed murder, and he denied the existence of God. They derived all of this from the following verses. *Esau came in from the field, and he was weary* (Gen. 25:29) was interpreted to imply sexual intercourse and murder, and *Esau spurned his birthright* (Gen. 25:34) was understood to imply denial of God.[7] Therefore God caused the premature death of Abraham, lest he suffer the anguish of seeing his grandson's wickedness. This is the significance of the verse, *That is why I have hewn down the prophets, I have slain them with the words of My mouth* (Hos. 6:5)—not because of their own deeds, but *with the words of My mouth.*[8]

Furthermore, Abraham died prematurely so that he should not suffer the anguish of seeing his son Isaac blind and confined to his house. Isaac had to become blind because he had gazed at the divine presence while he was bound upon the altar.[9] The Holy One said, "Shall I punish Isaac? That would cause pain to Abraham. Shall Abraham die? It is not yet his time. Shall Abraham not die and Isaac not be punished? Then Isaac will bless Esau, while Jacob deserves the blessings." What did He do? He shortened Abraham's life and took away Isaac's sight, so that Jacob received the blessings. (There is a similar passage in the talmudic tractate *Taʿanit* about Samuel of

6. Gen. Rabbah 63:12.

7. Cf. B. BB 16b, which speaks of five sins. "Murder" is derived from the comparison with the word "weary" in Jer. 4:31; "rape" from the comparison with the world "field" in Deut. 22:25. That this exegesis is not explained probably indicates that the preacher assumed that his listeners were familiar with it. In this source, the sin of atheism is derived from *Why this to me?* (Gen. 25:32), compared with *This is my God* (Exod. 15:2). The selling of the birthright is considered a separate sin. Cf. Gen. Rabbah 63:12 and 63:13. In the sources where three sins are mentioned (e.g., Tanḥuma, ed. Buber, *Toledot,* 3), the third sin is not atheism but theft.

8. Cf. B. Taʿan 5b and Rashi. The idea is that Abraham died not because of any sinful action of his own but because of a divine decree to save him from anguish.

9. Gen. Rabbah 65:10.

Ramah.)[10] Esau caused his father to lose his sight in many ways, according to the Midrash—for Isaac used to look favorably at that wicked man who trapped and deceived him with what he said—by asking his father to teach him how one takes a tithe of salt and of stubble.[11] Isaac loved him and kissed him, and was punished for it in his eyes.

Moreover, he caused the departure of the divine presence from his father's house because of the women whom he brought there, who would burn incense to idols. Each day Isaac agonized over the departure of the divine presence, until God said, "How long will this suffering continue? I will remove his sight."[12] The passage about Esau (Gen. 26:34–35) immediately precedes the statement about Isaac's vision (Gen. 27:1), indicating that Esau was responsible for everything: Abraham's death and Isaac's inability to see. This is the implication of the verse *Yizzaker awon abotaw el Adonai* (Ps. 109:14) (NJV: *May God be ever mindful of his fathers' iniquity*), which means 'may the sin affecting his fathers' relationship with God be remembered," *we-ḥaṭṭaʾt immo ʿal timmaḥ* (NJV): *and may the sin of his mother not be blotted out*), "and may the sin affecting his mother at the time of his birth not be blotted out," for he tore out her womb so that she could never again conceive.[13] That is why Isaac's sight became dim.

Now Jacob thought to himself: this wicked man lives in tranquility and prosperity, surrounded by his children and grandchildren. Everything turns out well for him. But I, *a simple man who sits in tents* (Gen. 25:27), I, who am always on the move from the academy of Shem to the academy of Eber and from there to the academy of my father,[14] suffer every day, and God does not protect me. Perhaps, heaven forbid, *my way is hidden from the Lord.* God responded: *Why do you say, O Jacob, why declare, O Israel, "My way is hidden from the Lord . . . ?" Do you not know . . . ?* (Isa. 40:27–28). This means, you should know that My entire plan is for your benefit, enabling you to receive the blessings of physical well-being.

10. The parenthetical remark made by the preacher refers to B. Taʿan 5b: "The Holy One, blessed be He, said, 'How shall I act? Shall Saul die? Of this Samuel will not approve. Shall Samuel die young? People will speak ill of him. Shall neither Saul nor Samuel die? The time has come for David to reign. . . .' Thereupon the Holy One, blessed be He, said, 'I will make him prematurely old.' "

11. Cf. Rashi on Gen. 25:27, based on Tanḥuma, *Toledot,* 8; *Midrash Aggadah,* ed. Solomon Buber (Vienna, 1894), p. 64; David ha-Nagid, p. 103. The point is that salt and stubble were exempt from tithing even according to rabbinic law, and Esau "trapped and deceived his father with words" by making Isaac think he was zealously scrupulous in observing the law.

12. Tanḥuma, *Toledot,* 8.

13. Tanḥuma, *Ki Teṣe,* 4.

14. Cf. Gen. Rabbah 63:10.

Even though God would bless Jacob, He wanted him to be blessed by his father. Once Esau was passing by the door of the academy and overheard the laws relating to the priesthood: "These are the ones punished by death: those who are intoxicated, those whose hair is unkempt."[15] When Jacob came out, Esau asked him what they had been saying. He replied that any priest who offers a sacrifice or enters the sanctuary intoxicated or with unkempt hair is liable to be put to death by God. There were also other injunctions concerning the profaning of sacred things with improper intentions, eating of the heave-offering in a state of ritual uncleanness, and so forth.[16] Esau asked, "To whom do these things apply?" He was told, "To the firstborn." "All of this is bound up with the priesthood? As firstborn, I shall become the priest, and I shall be punished for it! Buy the status of firstborn from me if you want it." But Jacob in his naiveté paid no attention to this.

Returning to his teacher's home, Jacob told him about the entire episode. His teacher asked, "Why did you not acquire the birthright and become a priest who serves God with the sacrifices? You could have become His first-born, the one whom God has chosen." From that day on, it was like a poison eating away at Jacob's heart. Then, when he saw the opportunity—Esau asking for the pottage—he said, *Sell me today (ka-yom,* lit. "as the day") *your birthright* (Gen. 25:31), meaning, "Sell it to me just as you would have sold it to me on that day when we discussed it." Esau replied, *Look, I am going to die* (Gen. 25:32), meaning, "Since there are so many injunctions that I will not be able to observe, I will die because of it; that is why I do not want it."[17]

Some maintain that this was the first day when Esau went out into the field, and as we already said, he committed those sins. In the field he was spotted by the wicked Nimrod, a *mighty hunter* (Gen. 10:9) who plundered everyone. Seeing Esau, he said, "Do you not know that no one in the world can match me in valor? How dare you enter this forest? I will do battle with you; you will be either defeated or victorious." Esau replied. "It is not appropriate to do so now, for I have not brought my weapons. Tomorrow we shall face each other in combat." They gave each other their hand and made a solemn agreement to do battle on the next day.

Now Esau was only fifteen years old, and he was worried about slaying or being slain. Therefore, when Jacob said, *Sell me today {your birthright},* he replied, *I am going to die.* "What value or benefit will the birthright be to

15. B. Sheb 36b, B. Sanh 22b.

16. *Mefaggel ba-qodashim. Piggul* refers to the flesh of a sacrifice which the officiating priest had formed the intention of eating at an improper time.

17. The passage in these two paragraphs is an expansion of Rashi's comment on Gen. 25:32. Cf. David ha-Nagid, pp. 105–06.

me? Take it for nothing." Nevertheless, Jacob said, "Swear to me," and he did so, thereby spurning the birthright of service to God.[18]

When Esau complained about Jacob, saying, *He has supplanted me twice* (Gen. 27:36), Isaac asked, "When was the other time?" Esau replied, *He took my birthright.* "And why did you sell it?" asked Isaac. Then Esau recounted the entire episode. "Up until now," Isaac said, "I was troubled that I might have blessed him improperly. Now that I know you were so evil as to sell your birthright, I know that he took the blessings rightfully, *and he will indeed be blessed* (Gen. 27:33)."[19]

The Midrash suggests another novel interpretation. Jacob was actually the elder because he was conceived from the first drop of sperm, so that even though Esau was the first to be born, Jacob had legitimately acquired the birthright.[20] But if this is so, why did God cause the blessings to be given to Jacob unintentionally, with Isaac thinking he was blessing Esau? The answer is that it was in order to allow for the exiles [of Jacob's descendants], which God had decreed. Had the blessings been given to Jacob intentionally, he would have merited even the blessings of freedom from exile, and the original decree would have been nullified. But this was impossible, since Abraham had chosen exile over Gehenna.[21]

As for the birthright, with twins there is the firstborn in God's sight, the one conceived from the drop that enters first, and there is also the physical firstborn, the one that first leaves the womb. Esau was allowed to be the firstborn in this latter sense, yet still he sold and spurned his birthright. By showing that he did not want it, he forfeited all claim to that status. Think of a king who gives to each of two brothers a precious stone to keep. The first one guards it properly, the second shows that he holds it in contempt. The king will then draw close to the former and distance himself from the latter, who did not guard it properly.

So it was with Jacob and Esau and their respective birthrights. Jacob, conceived from the first drop, was the firstborn in God's sight. He served God with his birthright by *dwelling in tents* (Gen. 25:27). Esau, the first to leave the womb, should have served God by offering the sacrifices, but he spurned this. Therefore God drew close to Jacob, making him His special treasure, as the Bible says, *For the Lord has chosen Jacob for Himself, Israel as*

18. Esau's fear of Nimrod is noted in Gen. Rabbah 63:13; cf. the "midrash" cited in *Perush ha-Tosafot* and *Daᶜat Zeqenim,* on Gen. 25:32. The closest version to that of Yizhari that I have found is in the Yemenite manuscript *Or ha-ʾAfelah,* quoted by Menaḥem Kasher, *Torah Shelemah* 4 (Jerusalem, 1934):1035, no. 204. However, Yizhari's version contains an element of the medieval chivalric tradition that is absent from the other sources.

19. Rashi, on Gen. 27:36; cf. Tanḥuma, ed. Buber, *Toledot,* 23.

20. Cf. Gen. Rabbah 63:8 and Rashi, on Gen. 25:26.

21. Gen. Rabbah 44:21.

His treasured possession (Ps. 135:4). But He distanced Himself from Esau, as the Bible says, *Behold, I make you least among the nations, most despised* (Jer. 49:15) and also, *Esau I hated* (Mal. 1:3). Isaac wanted to draw him near and at least bestow material blessings upon him, but God did not allow this.

Yet because of his naiveté, Jacob was still unaware of all this favor. The suffering that Esau had caused his father and grandfather made him wonder and say, *My way is hidden {from the Lord}* (Isa. 40:27). Then God responded, "It is all for your own good. *Do you not know . . . ? His wisdom cannot be fathomed. He gives strength to the weary* (Isa. 40:28–29) and the fatigued by Torah, *fresh vigor* to those whom Torah study has worn out. Those devoid of Torah and commandments may boast of their youthfulness and their power, but they will eventually experience overwhelming fatigue: *Youths will grow faint and weary . . .* (Isa. 40:30). But as for those who wait for Him with self-discipline, who bear their sorrows with patient endurance, I will give them strength renewed like that of the eagle, as we find in the verse, *So your youth is renewed like the eagle's* (Ps. 103:5)." This is the meaning of *Those who trust in the Lord shall renew their strength as eagles grow new plumes. They shall run and not grow weary, they shall march and not grow faint* (Isa. 40:31).

Joseph ibn Shem Ṭob

The ibn Shem Ṭob family played a leading role in the intellectual life of fifteenth-century Spanish Jewry. Joseph's father, Shem Ṭob ibn Shem Ṭob, was the author of the controversial *Sefer ha-ʾEmunot,* a powerful critique of the entire tradition of medieval Jewish rationalism, including its most revered exemplar, Moses Maimonides. Joseph and his brother, Isaac, apparently rejected their father's position. Isaac wrote technical supercommentaries on several of Averroës' reworkings of Aristotle and a commentary on Maimonides' *Guide,* as well as some sermons, which are mentioned in his extant work but have been lost.[1] Joseph's son, Shem Ṭob ben Joseph, is discussed in the following chapter.

In addition to his own writings, Joseph had a distinguished and important political career. Like the far better known Don Isaac Abravanel, who referred to him as his mentor,[2] Joseph held positions on a cabinet level under kings John II and Henry IV of Castile. He was superintendent of accounts for the king as well as court physician. As trusted royal advisor, he was sent on delicate diplomatic missions, including one to negotiate a marriage with the princess of Portugal.[3] He apparently suffered a severe reversal of fortune, however, as he describes himself at one point as an impoverished vagrant with poor eyes.[4] According to a later tradition, he died a violent death as a martyr.

S. W. Baron has written, "Surely a comprehensive biographical study of this physician, scholar, apologist, and statesman would shed some interesting new light also on the equivocal status of Castilian Jewry in the crucial years before the reign of Isabella."[5] The themes of such a biography might include

1. See Harry A. Wolfson, "Isaac ibn Shem-Ṭob's Unknown Commentaries on the *Physics* and His Other Unknown Works," *Studies in the History of Philosophy and Religion,* 2 (Cambridge, 1977): 479–90.

2. Abravanel, *Commentary on the Torah,* Exod. 30:8. He did not hesitate to incorporate entire sections from Joseph's work into his commentaries (for example, much of the comment on Isa. 58:1 is taken from *ʿEn ha-Qore*).

3. See Baer, *HJCS* 2:250–51, 270, 485, n. 7; Baron, *SRHJ* 10:193–94.

4. Introduction to *ʿEn ha-Qore,* published by Adolf Jellinek, *Quntres ha-Mafteaḥ* (Vienna, 1881), pp. 30–32.

5. Baron, *SRHJ* 10:386, n. 33. Such a study would need to integrate knowledge of the Castilian monarchy, including archival sources, with information in Joseph's own works.

the balancing of responsibilities in the Christian world and the Jewish community, the competing claims of political position and cultural aspirations, and the drama of intellectual revolt against a father whom he continued to revere.

Even without the distractions of these other roles, his literary productivity would be judged impressive, although very little of his work has been published. His competence in technical philosophy is revealed by commentaries on works by Aristotle (*Ethics, De anima*) and by Averroës (*Epistle on the Possibility of Conjunction*). He wrote a brief commentary on Lamentations, and polemical tracts against the claims of Christianity. His major theological work, *Kebod Elohim,* a comparison of the Aristotelian and Jewish conceptions of the summum bonum, repudiates the work of his father by defending the value of philosophical reasoning and at the same time defends the Jewish tradition against an extreme rationalist stance. Another theological work, "Daᶜat ᶜElyon," on the problem of divine knowledge and freedom of the will, has not survived.[6]

Most important for our purposes is "ᶜEn ha-Qore," the earliest known Jewish treatise on preaching, selections from which are included in "Sources," below. This work emerged from Joseph's own experience as a preacher apparently much in demand. It is not known if he collected his sermons into a full book; what remain in several manuscripts are isolated sermons delivered on various occasions. Fifteen sermons have been preserved in this manner.[7]

The sermon translated here is the most dramatic in its context, which is explained in the preacher's introduction. It is one of the earliest Jewish sermons to be placed by its author in such a specific setting, with date, place, and circumstances of delivery. Given on the third Sabbath after Passover, when the third chapter of Abot was read in the synagogue, it is based on a long statement by R. ᶜAqiba from that chapter. The first half of the sermon has been omitted. The poor condition of the manuscript makes many readings in this part questionable, and much of the material in this half is of a rather technical philosophical nature. The second half is an independent unit with organic cohesiveness.

The section translated is readily divisible into three parts. The first is a detailed exegesis of R. ᶜAqiba's metaphor of the store in Abot 3:16, which

Despite the biographical material at the beginning of Shaul Regev's Ph.D. dissertation on Shem Ṭob's thought (Regev, pp. 6–14), this remains to be done comprehensively.

6. The full corpus of theological works has been studied by Regev. An example of his technical philosophical writing can be seen in Regev, "Ha-Perush ha-Qaṣar shel R. Yosef ibn Shem Ṭob le-ʾIggeret Efsharut ha-Debequt le- ʾibn Rushd," *Meḥqere Yerushalayim be-Maḥashebet Yiśraʾel* 2 (1982):38–93.

7. There is a full list of the extant sermons in Regev, pp. 34–36. Three of the sermons in Montefiore MS 61/2 are from successive weeks in the spring of 1452; several in Houghton MS 61 form a series delivered successively during the following summer.

develops the thesis of accountability for one's actions before God. The statement that the collectors "are paid by those who are aware and by those who are not aware" forms the bridge to the second part, based on the story of Joseph's brothers in Genesis 42. The central point is the distinction between divine justice and human justice. The fate of Joseph's brothers exemplifies the truth that although the accused may be innocent of the particular crime with which they are charged, their suffering is nevertheless deserved, their punishment nevertheless just. At the end of this section we return to R. ʿAqiba, and his statement, discussed earlier, is now made to reflect the insight he attained through his martyrdom.

The final section, introduced by a dramatic appeal to the audience ("And now, my brothers and friends . . ."), contains the "application" of these principles to the Holy Week anti-Jewish riot of 1452 that is the sermon's context. The crime of which the Jews are accused—the crucifixion of Jesus—is not the reason for their persecution at the hands of the Christians. Yet divine justice is still at work, for other sins are being punished. Joseph's brothers, who realize the true reason for the calamity that has befallen them and appreciate the wondrous justice of God's ways, provide a model for the Jews of Segovia.

The message is traditional: suffering is an effect of divine displeasure, and it should cause a reformation of conduct. Yet the technique with which it is presented, the manner in which it is made to emerge from the rabbinic and biblical sources, and the way the preacher mixes consolation with rebuke, are all evidences of a sophisticated homiletical art.

Sermon on Abot 3:15–16
(Third Sabbath after Passover, 1452; Segovia)

In the year 5212 [1452] of the world's creation, when the principe Don Enrique,[1] may God bless him, had come to the cities of Andalusia, the community of Segovia sent to him two distinguished Jews. Their mission concerned those who had risen against them and spread evil libels on the day

1. Principe Don Enrique, here transcribed in Hebrew letters, is the formal title used for Prince Henry in Spanish sources. For his unique relationship with Segovia, the city of his birth and his favorite home as a youth, see Townsend Miller, *Henry IV of Castile* (Philadelphia, 1972), pp. 54–57. Even after acceding to the throne in 1474, Henry IV was accused by nobles of favoritism to Jews and *conversos* (Baer, HJCS 2:282).

of the hanging of their messiah in order to plunder and despoil. He commanded me to go to the people giving me letters to the governor and leaders of the city and a document of good faith for the Jewish community, bringing them solace and reassurance.

I arrived in the city on Friday, exhausted from the long journey. I was also emotionally wrought up. I stood trembling and berated the nobles and city notables for not having intervened against their enemies.[2] Early the next morning, the entire [community] gathered in the Great Synagogue.[3] After the reading of the Torah, I stood up and began to speak. This is what I said: "All is foreseen, and free will is given" (Abot 3:15). . . .[4]

[R. ʿAqiba] compares the status of rebels and sinners, or indeed of society as a whole, to a pharmacy and its owner.[5] There in his pharmacy, he mixes from various kinds of powder the simple and complex drugs, including poisons and antidotes.[6] All can be cured through his work. The pharmacist is a good and generous man, concerned about the welfare of his city. When people want something, he gives them whatever they request, whether it be food or medicines or drugs, but it goes on their account, and they must pay him the true value.

This pharmacist has considerable power in the city. His net is spread over its inhabitants so that no one can flee owing him money for what has been taken. The store is open day and night, and the inhabitants of the city can easily obtain whatever they need from it, but the pharmacist watches carefully to see what everyone decides to take. As a wise man who tries to ensure that he will be paid what is owed him, he writes down in his record book all

2. My translation reflects a reading of the passage quite different from that of Regev, who wrote (p. 11) that the preacher claims to have criticized the Jews for not rising to defend themselves against their attackers. I understand the point to be rather that, according to ibn Shem Ṭob, the anti-Jewish rioters were enemies of the established city leadership, who should have opposed them more actively.

3. The former "Great Synagogue" had been seized and transformed into a church in the wake of accusations concerning the desecration of the host in 1410. See Oscar d'Araujo, "La Grande Synagogue de Ségovie," *REJ* 39 (1899):209–16.

4. The first part of the sermon discusses four brief statements of R. ʿAqiba from the third chapter of Abot. It lays the theological groundwork for a doctrine of God's omniscience not inconsistent with human free will.

5. The full text under discussion is, "All is given on account, and the net is spread over all the living. The store is open, the storekeeper circulates, the account book is open, the hand writes, whoever wants to borrow may come and borrow, the collectors make their rounds frequently every day and collect payment from those who are aware and from those who are unaware, and they have a basis of support, the verdict is a true one, and all is prepared for the banquet."

6. The Hebrew text reads *atriacano;* compare the old Spanish word *atriaca* (derived from Arabic), meaning antidote (*Diccionario historico de la lengua española,* 1-A [Madrid, 1933], p. 977).

that he gives out. "The account book is open, and the hand of the scribe is writing."

His collectors are always going around the city to collect the payments owed. Some people are aware of what they owe and pay it. Others are requested to pay although they are unaware of the debt, having forgotten what they took from the shop. They pay unwillingly, complaining bitterly about the collectors, maintaining that they owe nothing. This, however, is not true, for the collectors have a valid receipt recording the merchandise given and fixing the payment due. They receive the customer's payment fairly; they are truthful in their judgment.

Now although this shop contains some dangerous things—including poisons—the drugs are actually extremely beneficial. However, an ignorant person who does not know their beneficial properties may be harmed by them. For example, syrup of anacardium[7] can be fatal, yet if properly prepared and administered it can help with weakness of mind and forgetfulness. Someone who takes it for pleasure may hallucinate, but there is no problem when it is used properly. "All is prepared for the banquet."

This marvelous image refers to important issues concerning the equity of God's actions. The *Judge of the entire world* (Gen. 18:25) has given human beings free will and empowered them to eat *from all the trees in the garden* (Gen. 2:16), to make use of all things placed in this world as they choose. These things are good when they are used in the proper place and in proper measure. One might say that even the impulse toward evil is good, for without it we would not be able to have children. This is what R. Meir said in Genesis Rabbah: *Ṭob meʾod—ṭob mot*" [*ṭob meʾod,* "very good" in Gen. 1:31 implies *ṭob mot,* "dying is good"]. [The same passage contains the interpretations] "*ṭob meʾod*—this is Hell," and "*ṭob meʾod*—this is the impulse toward evil."[8]

This passage explains that things thought to be fundamentally evil are actually fundamentally good when properly used. Some are good because of their effect. An example would be punishments that cleanse the soul and turn it in the proper direction. That is what was meant in the statement "This is Hell." And some are good because of what necessarily follows them. An example would be death, which is necessarily followed by a different mode of being.

7. In Hebrew, *debash ha-baladur*; see Eliezer ben Yehudah, *Millon* 1:545, with references to Avicenna's *Canon*. *Balādur* is the Arabic-Persian name for the nut of the Indian tree *semecarpus anacardium,* the oriental cashew. On the medicinal uses of this nut, including the popular belief that it sharpens the intellect and strengthens the memory, see *Moses Maimonides' Glossary of Drug Names,* ed. Fred Rosner (Philadelphia, 1979), p. 50.

8. Gen. Rabbah 9:5, 7, 9. The final source contains the assertion that without the evil impulse, we would not have children.

The saintly ʿAqiba said "All is given on account," meaning that whoever wishes to enjoy the pleasures of the world is free to do so, but "a person's legs are surety": he will pay what he owes.[9] "The net is spread over all the living" in such a way that it is impossible for anyone to flee and escape from paying what is owed for these pleasures. "The store is open" refers to the ease with which these worldly things, potential stumbling blocks, can be found.

"The store owner circulates"[10] refers to the Creator's knowledge. God sees everything a fool, imagining that pitch darkness conceals his improprieties, may steal from the store. "The account book is open, and the hand writes" refers to what is meant by the statement "There is no forgetfulness before the Throne of Glory, and nothing is hidden from Your eyes," and the statement "Know that above you are a seeing eye and a hearing ear, and all your deeds are written in a book."[11]

"The collectors make rounds every day" refers to the continuous chain of cause and effect that brings about suffering. "And are paid by those who are aware," for to some people calamity and misfortune occur measure for measure, and they accept the justice of the verdict. But some are compelled to pay unaware of the evil they have done that leads inexorably to their present misfortune. They may be blamed for a particular misdeed of which they are really innocent, while they are caught because of different sins.[12]

That is what happened to Joseph's brothers. Falsely accused with the charge *You are spies* (Gen. 42:9), they knew that they were innocent. Yet seeing this danger and the impending disaster, they were amazed at God's justice, amazed at how punishment was reaching them despite their innocence of the crime with which they were charged. For they understood that the demands of divine equity are different from those of political equity. By human standards they were innocent of the crime of espionage. But divine equity brought about a false and groundless accusation in order to exact recompense for another sin.

That is why they said, *Abal ashemim anaḥnu: Rather, we are guilty* (Gen. 42:21). Now the word *abal* does not ordinarily come at the beginning of a statement in our language. It shows that they were in the midst of a debate over this judgment. That is the meaning of "are paid by those who are aware and those who are not aware": payment was exacted from these fine men until

9. See B. Suk 53a; in this context, a person walks unknowingly to the place of his death.

10. This translation of *ha-ḥenwani maqqif* is indicated by the preacher's explanation. The phrases from Abot were probably cited in Hebrew, the interpretations following in the vernacular.

11. From the New Year's Day liturgy of Zikronot and Abot 2:1.

12. Here the preacher introduces the motif that will become the focal point of the sermon and is applied at the end to the experience of his congregation.

they found the answer that enabled them to vindicate God's verdict. They therefore said, *This is why this distress has come upon us* (Gen. 42:21).

That statement refers to another important matter. Since the misfortune encompassed all of them together, it must have been for a sin that encompassed them all. For if it had been caused by each person's individual sins, how could the punishment be the same and equal for all? Searching their own behavior, each of them found sins and transgressions, but none would have justified this all-encompassing disaster. Then they searched for a sin that would include them all, as the misfortune included them all, and said, "*Rather,* all of us *are guilty on account of our brother . . . ; this is why this* general *distress has come upon us.*"

Then Reuben answered that they deserved to be killed because of the evil they had done after ignoring his warning and his plea that Joseph was but a child who did not deserve to be punished because of his dreams and the things he had said. Reuben emphasized the magnitude of their sin, the evil and cruelty of their actions in not heeding Joseph when he pleaded with them as they looked upon his anguish (cf. Gen. 42:22). Now *also his blood* which was shed—for they did not know what had become of him—must be avenged (cf. Gen. 42:22). He said *and also his blood,* meaning that not only their cruelty, but also Joseph's death, was being avenged in the false charge laid against them.

God's equitable judgments have ways to exact payment from those who are aware and those who are unaware. "The verdict is true," but we are ignorant of the ways of that verdict, ignorant of how natural forces work upon us. It is said that we "govern" and that God "governs," but the word means two different things.[13] Similarly, divine equity is very different from political equity.

Those righteous brothers, possessing the powerful belief they received from their fathers that "there is no death without sin and no suffering without transgression,"[14] discovered in their behavior the cause of their present misfortune. Otherwise, they would have complained bitterly about the ways of divine equity, accusing God of having brought calamity upon them when they were not guilty of espionage as charged. They might have denied God's providence or knowledge or cast aspersions upon the way God governs the world. This always happens with those who are weak in their faith.

It happened to Job. When he suffered calamities, he said, "There is no justice and no judge."[15] Some of his friends said, *You know that your wickedness*

13. This idea, which is developed in detail, is based on the Maimonidean doctrine of homologous terms, which underlies much of the first part of the *Guide.*

14. B. Shab 55a.

15. Cf. the discussion of Job's "blasphemy" in B. BB 16a. The specific phrase *let din we-let dayyan* is not used in that context, but the preacher probably associated it with Job 9:24.

is great, and that your iniquities have no limit (Job 22:5). They meant that while the misfortune that had befallen him was indeed great, his sins must have been even greater, indeed boundless, to cause all that had happened. Others said that even though Job was unaware of any transgressions, if only God would speak He would reveal the cause of Job's suffering (cf. Job 11:5–6).

But those righteous brothers, knowing the natural order of the world and the equity of God's rule, rejoiced in their afflictions, aware that these afflictions were justly ordained, and that if they accepted them cheerfully, God would forgive them their sin and once again comfort them graciously. I imagine that our righteous ancestors had thought until that moment that they bore no guilt for what they had done to Joseph, so irksome had been his disposition and his behavior. But when calamity befell them, they said *Rather, we are guilty,* for he was *our brother,* and he deserved to be forgiven *when we looked on at his anguish and he pleaded with us* (Gen. 42:21). They found themselves guilty of a lesser crime: their failure to forgive and their cruelty. But Reuben understood that they were guilty of Joseph's death, and he said, *Also his blood is being avenged* (Gen. 42:22).[16]

In short, R. ʿAqiba's entire statement deals with the mystery of God's rule and the ways of an equity that is essentially different from ours, although the same words *rule* and *equity,* are used in referring to human affairs. His simple language points to the exalted wisdom for which he was well known. For example, "The collectors make rounds every day and exact payment from those who are aware and from those who are unaware, and they have a basis of support, and the verdict is true." He did not say "The verdict is correct" because he wanted to distinguish it from a political verdict.

A political verdict may be correct but not true, as in the case of a judge before whom false testimony is given, which leads to the conviction of the defendant. This is correct in a political sense, not in a divine sense. There can also be a verdict that is true but not correct, as in the case of a judge who saw a man kill his brother after being warned not to do so. No other witnesses were present at the act. If he is convicted on this basis, the verdict will be true, but not correct.[17] God's judgments are always true, and this is

16. Compare the reworking of this material by the preacher's son, Shem Ṭob ben Joseph ibn Shem Ṭob, in his sermon on *Mi-Qeṣ* (*Derashot,* p. 20a). Our preacher indicates that the brothers had not referred to Joseph as *our brother* before this time; he was *the dreamer* (Gen. 37:19) and *your son* (Gen. 37:32). (Only Judah had referred to him as *our brother* in attempting to save his life [Gen. 37:26].) Now, facing calamity, all of them think of Joseph for the first time as *our brother,* for whom they should have had some empathy. For a modern literary discussion, see Robert Alter, *The Art of Biblical Narrative* (New York, 1981), pp. 161, 166–67.

17. Jewish law requires two eyewitnesses, in addition to a warning before the act, for conviction in a murder trial.

their equity. *The judgments of the Lord are true, they are altogether just* (Ps. 19:10) means that correctness and truth are fully compatible in God's judgments.

That is why God commanded us to say the benediction "Blessed is the True Judge" when something bad occurs.[18] For God observes not equity in a political sense, but truth, which is equity in a divine sense. Most of the complaints over the problem of the righteous suffering from evil and the wicked enjoying good[19] arise from the assumption that these two kinds of equity are equivalent and of the same type. When the righteous are found innocent and the wicked guilty according to political equity, people who do not know all of the circumstances complain bitterly. But this only reveals their ignorance and their simplistic understanding of how the world is governed.

This is explained in the marvelous Book of Job, which Moses our teacher wrote on this subject.[20] He had already alluded to it when he said, *As parents discipline their children, so does the Lord your God discipline you* (Deut. 8:5). Think of the conduct of a parent and the way domestic decisions are made regarding the discipline of a beloved child. This does not conform to political standards of equity. It is equity of a totally different kind. The way a home is run is not the same as the way a state is run, even though the home is part of the state. No, the way a father manages his household, and his standards of fairness in punishing and rewarding, do not conform to the standards of fairness appropriate in managing a state, even though the same word is used for both kinds of authority.

This is all the more true for God's governing of the world. Just as human actions are different from natural ones, so the two types of governing are different from each other. Maimonides dealt with this in that marvelous twenty-third chapter of part 3 [of the *Guide*]. There he indicated that the governing of a state and the standards of equity involved, and indeed all the various kinds of human management, are products of human artifice, performed through deliberation and intelligence, through reason and thought. But as for works of nature, whether we comprehend them completely or in part, the natural force that directs them is different in kind from that which governs a state. How much more is the divine rule, that governs everything, different from all other kinds of rule! No comparison can be made between the one and the other.

[R. ʿAqiba] was correct in saying "they have a basis of support," for "there is no death without sin and no suffering without transgression." Though the person is innocent of a charge falsely leveled against him, payment is being

18. B. Ber 60b.
19. B. Ber 7a; cf. Abot 4:15.
20. B. BB 15a.

exacted from him now for other things he may no longer remember. It does not matter whether he is aware of them or not. The verdict is true, and the Judge is true. There are no grounds for complaining that God furnished the cause of one's downfall, for "All is prepared for the banquet." God made everything fit for its proper time, even the impulse toward evil. The fool perverts himself by untimely and intemperate indulgence. In his failure to use things properly, he is like one who swallows syrup of anacardium because he is hungry and enjoys the taste. Whatever happens to him is now his own fault.

Look what was revealed by this great master, R. ʿAqiba. Even Moses envied him when, in prophetic vision, he saw ʿAqiba in full stature and strength, discussing a halakic matter, analyzing logical arguments, reducing them to their underlying premises.[21] It was not until Moses finally heard ʿAqiba say, "It is a halakah of Moses from Sinai" that his spirit was restored. For all knowledge is ultimately derived from Moses. From his splendid wisdom and true comprehension the faithful draw wisdom and enlightenment.

After witnessing ʿAqiba's knowledge of Torah, Moses was shown ʿAqiba's reward: how iron combs pierced his flesh. Then Moses recoiled, aghast. At first, assuming that there was only one way of governing, he asked, "Such learning, and this is his reward?!" But eventually he understood that this was God's plan, that God's mode of governing is different from ours, and that the verdict was a true one even though we are ignorant of how it was reached, just as we are ignorant of the complete chain of causes that operate in the natural realm.

When Job complained and denied [divine justice], perplexed because he did not see the world being governed in the manner he thought proper, these same insights were revealed to him by the godly Elihu, scion of a great family.[22] And in these mishnaic passages another great master [ʿAqiba] revealed in simple language the profound truths about the creation and greatness of the human being, the greatness of a portion of humanity, Israel, and the greatness of its Torah. He resolved the doubts that would arise when an unexpected fate befell him, demonstrating that everything resulted from a verdict which, by God's standards of governing, was just.[23] These are all profound mysteries, which God, through ʿAqiba, one of His greatest treasures, has revealed to those who revere Him and to those who direct their thought to Him.

21. B. Men 29b; this is the preacher's interpretation of the assertion that Moses "did not know what they were saying."

22. The preacher apparently understood *mi-mishpaḥat ram* (Job 32:2) to mean "from a great family." According to one rabbinic view, Elihu was none other than Isaac (P. Soṭ 20d); according to the Zohar (2:166a), he was a descendant of Ezekiel.

23. Note the link between the statements of the Mishnah and ʿAqiba's own experience as a martyr.

And now, my brothers and friends, look, and you will see how this tragedy has come upon us. You know, of course, that our hands did not shed the blood of that man in whose name our enemies in every generation have risen against us to destroy us.[24] Rather, our righteous ancestors, basing themselves upon the Torah and justice, hanged him on a tree.[25] A court of seventy-one came to an understanding of his case. This is the legal rule: "The false prophet is not put to death except at the order of the Great Court."[26] Even though it is a principle of our law that capital cases are tried in a court of twenty-three—the Small Sanhedrin[27]—the case of the false prophet is different and more serious.

In this case [of a false prophet] it is necessary to judge the truth of a prophecy and to know the criteria of prophetic status. The chief of these is that the person must possess intellectual perfection in the various branches of knowledge, ethical perfection in his conduct, and perfection in the creative power of his imagination.[28] This determination is extremely difficult. The intellectual powers of the self-proclaimed prophet may well be inadequate.

Such was the case with this man and his disciples. They made errors in biblical verses that even schoolchildren understand.[29] Their words reveal many serious and momentous mistakes. They were masters of the imagination, and because of this they had dreams and delusions that made them think they had acquired true knowledge without study. Maimonides alludes to this in chapter 41 of part 2 [of the *Guide*]. It is a marvelous passage: look it up.[30]

24. This probably indicates that the anti-Jewish uprising on Good Friday had been linked with the charge that the Jews were Christ killers.

25. Unwillingness to deny Jewish responsibility for the crucifixion was a characteristic Jewish stance in premodern times. Of the many versions of *Toledot Yeshu,* none tries to exculpate the Jews (Ernst Bammel, "Christian Origins in Jewish Tradition," *New Testament Studies* 13 [1967]:328). Cf. also Ḥayyim ibn Mūsā, *Magen wa-Romaḥ,* ed. Adolf Posnanski (Jewish National and University Library MS 8vo 787 [Jerusalem: Hebrew University, 1970]), p. 47; the sources cited by Yehudah Liebes, "Hashpaʿot Noṣriyyot ʿal Sefer ha-Zohar," *Meḥqere Yerushalayim be-Maḥashebet Yiśraʾel* 2 (1938):67; Yosef Kaplan, *Mi-Naṣrut le-Yahadut* (Jerusalem, 1983), p. 222. For the charge in Christian writings that Jews defend their ancestors' crucifixion of Jesus, see Martin Luther, in *Luther's Works,* vol. 47, ed. Franklin Sherman (Philadelphia, 1971), pp. 262–63; Todd Endelman, *The Jews of Georgian England, 1714–1830* (Philadelphia, 1979), p. 88.

26. Cf. Sanh 1:5.

27. Sanh 1:4.

28. This discussion is based on Maimonides' treatment of prophecy. For the perfection of intellect and imagination, see *Guide* 2:37; for actions and character, *Guide* 2:40, end. A detailed discussion of the author's doctrine of prophecy, based on all his works, is in Regev, pp. 139–54.

29. Cf. Profiaṭ Duran, *Kelimmat ha-Goyim,* in *Kitbe Pulmos le-Profiaṭ Duran,* ed. Frank Talmage (Jerusalem, 1981), p. 59. The accusation that the apostles were uneducated and ignorant was originally made by pagan polemicists like Porphyry; see Timothy Barnes, *Constantine and Eusebius* (Cambridge, Mass., 1981), p. 177.

30. The reference should be to *Guide* 2:37. Commenting on Maimonides' treatment of the

They also did amazing things through magical tricks, just as the Egyptian magicians did before Moses. Nature can be changed either through natural causes or through divine intervention. Therefore, a miraculous act proves nothing, for it can be done through enchantment and sorcery.[31] Even in our own time we can see masters of illusion performing amazing tricks. That is why our Torah and tradition insist that the claim to prophecy not be based on miraculous evidence. The Master of the Prophets commanded, *{If there appears among you a prophet or a dream-diviner,} and he gives you a sign or a portent . . . and the sign or portent comes true {on the basis of which he said to you "Let us follow and worship another god"}*, the conclusion is that you should not heed him or revere him, for that prophet has spoken maliciously. It is commanded that he be put to death (Deut. 13:2–6).

I once heard from my father, the distinguished rabbi (may the memory of the righteous be for blessing),[32] a fine interpretation of the verse, *Our ancestors in Egypt did not perceive Your wonders, they did not remember Your abundant love, but rebelled at the sea, at the Sea of Reeds* (Ps. 106:7). He said that when our ancestors in Egypt saw that the magicians, like Moses, were capable of changing natural phenomena, despite their preference for Moses they paid no attention to God's wonders. They did not understand the difference between the two kinds of changes, that of the magicians, performed through the natural properties of things, and that of Moses, performed through the power of God alone. The wicked magicians themselves admitted that what Moses did was truly supernatural, saying *This is the finger of God* (Exod. 8:15). But our ancestors thought it was all the same. That is why they rebelled at the Sea of Reeds, saying *Was it for want of graves in Egypt that you brought us to die in the wilderness?* (Exod. 14:11).

Eventually, however, they saw what happened to the sea: a miracle no one could doubt was the work of God. *When Israel saw the wondrous power which the Lord had wielded against the Egyptians, the people feared the Lord; they had faith in the Lord and in His servant Moses* (Exod. 14:31). They had seen supernatural acts, performed by divine power with no natural mediation or trick. This was the true reality.

---

group whose imaginative faculty has been perfected but whose rational faculty is inadequate, the preacher's son Shem Ṭob wrote, "You will understand to whom he alludes. He hints that you should not think that the one alluded to made himself out to be a prophet knowing full well that he was not. Rather, he thought that he was a prophet, and he worked wonders, but they were done through strange and obscure tricks. This was also the case with the disciples" (cf. Narboni). The two passages illuminate each other.

31. This passage reverses the charge that the Jews were gullible and credulous in their readiness to accept false messiahs who could produce apparently miraculous signs. This charge in an exemplum of the famous Spanish Christian preacher Vincent Ferrer is cited in Welter, p. 412, n. 5.

32. Shem Ṭob ibn Shem Ṭob, author of *Sefer ha-ʾEmunot*.

Similarly, the accursed magicians thought at first that Moses was doing the same sort of thing they did. The sages in the talmudic tractate Menaḥot report that the leading magicians said to Moses, "Are you bringing straw to ʿAfarayim?!"[33] Only later did the truth of the matter become clear to them. Thus we see why the investigation of prophecy and wondrous acts, and the identification of true and false prophets, requires men of stature like those who sat in the Great Court. They alone can judge.

There is no guilt either upon us or upon them. This is not why evil befalls us, just as the misfortune that befell Joseph's brothers was not because they were spies. *Rather, we are guilty* of other things, and "The collectors make their rounds each day and exact payment" from us, whether or not we are aware of the reason. All is in accordance with a true verdict.

He is a fool who says that had it not been for that incident [the crucifixion], those murders and conflagrations and forced apostasies would never have befallen our sacred communities. Nothing prevents God from fabricating new causes and different libels to be directed against us as justification for the collection of His debt. "He has a basis of support." Look at the Jewish communities in Islamic lands. Murders and forced apostasies have befallen them without any libels relating to the death of that man.[34]

Instead, we should look into our behavior, as individuals and as a community. This is why these tragedies occur. They are brought by the collectors who make their rounds each day to collect the debts. The situation can be remedied only by removing the cause. It is a foolish physician who concentrates exclusively on treating the illness and its symptoms without removing the underlying cause. Treating the immediate cause does not necessarily cure the disease. Only removing the underlying cause will accomplish this.

Now making requests of kings and entreating the great nobles, all of whom are direct and immediate causes of events, is an appropriate human endeavor. But it is not a fundamental remedy.[35] The essential, underlying cause is our transgressions. This will lead to the cure of the disease itself. Once this is remedied, all else will be, for *The mind of the king is in the hand of God* (Prov. 21:1). In particular, what must be remedied is the abuse of bans of excommunication, acts of informing to the authorities, the eating of forbidden foods, and the drinking of Gentile wine, in which matters very many have stumbled. *Great is the Lord and full of power* (Ps. 147:5). He has already seen that our people have done evil, and He has permitted them [Christians] to chastise us for our sins. "All is foreseen, and free will is given."

33. B. Men 85a, equivalent to the English expression "bringing coals to Newcastle."

34. Cf. Solomon ibn Verga, *Shebeṭ Yehudah* (Jerusalem, 1947), p. 154.

35. In this way, the preacher justifies the political activism of the courtier without undermining the traditional religious call for reformation of conduct. The shortcomings specified in the following sentences are standard in Spanish ethical literature, and would have been appropriate even for a preacher who did not have firsthand knowledge of the community.

Shem Ṭob ibn Shem Ṭob

A scion of a distinguished family of Spanish Jews, Shem Ṭob ibn Shem Ṭob followed the model of his father Joseph by combining a commitment to philosophy with a vigorous interest in homiletics. He was the author of several works of technical philosophy as well as a commentary on Abot. He is most famous, however, for his commentary on Maimonides' *Guide for the Perplexed,* which appears in the standard traditional Hebrew text of *Moreh Nebukim,* and for his book of sermons entitled *Derashot ha-Torah.* The three separate sixteenth-century editions of this homiletical work (Salonika, 1525; Venice, 1547; Padua, 1567) are a clear indication of its popularity.

In a brief introduction, Shem Ṭob reports that he decided to write down some of the material he had been preaching lest he should forget it because of the passage of time and the afflictions of old age. At the end he expresses a hope that the material he has written will be of use to those who themselves intend to preach and to inspire the people to penitence. The date of completion was 1489.

The book contains a sermon for each lesson of the Torah, interspersed with a few occasional sermons (for example, "For a Wedding," pp. 5c, 9d), and culminating in a series of sermons for the Ten Days of Penitence dealing with the theme of repentance. The sermons ordinarily begin with a verse from the Torah lesson and a passage of rabbinic aggadah. Many of them treat a particular intellectual problem that is clearly defined and thoroughly explored. For example, one wedding sermon linked with the lesson *Bereʾshit* (Gen. 1:1–6:8) begins with the verse *It is not good for man to be alone* (Gen. 2:18) and poses the question whether human perfection is ideally to be attained in isolation from other human beings or as part of a society. This is analyzed through the structure of the scholastic disputed question: first the arguments in favor of isolation, then the arguments for the Torah's view that isolation is not good and that individuals need the society of others, and finally a refutation of each argument on behalf of isolation (pp. 5c–6c).

In general the sermons are not restricted to a single verse. In addition to a particular issue, they often discuss the lesson as a whole, using the older homily form. Several literary techniques familiar from Jewish biblical exegesis appear in Shem Ṭob's preaching. He will sometimes list beneficial lessons (*toʿalot*) to be learned from a passage, in the manner of Gersonides' commentaries (pp. 13a, 18d, 59d–60a; compare p. 65c–d). In the stories of Genesis especially, he works with the midrashic assumption popularized by Naḥmanides that what happened to the patriarchs would occur to their descendants, who should learn from their example (pp. 7b, 17b). He frequently lists a series of problems (*sefeqot*) relating to a section of the Torah even if they are not intrinsically connected to the issue under discussion, and then resolves all of these problems, in the manner of Abravanel and Arama (see pp. 6c–d, 8b–9a, 9b–c).

The structure of the sermon on *Wa-Yeḥi* (Gen. 47:28–50:26) is outlined in the opening sentence. It is a three-part sermon discussing three modes of salvation. What makes it a sermon rather than merely a treatise is that each mode is connected—if somewhat tenuously—with the Torah lesson recounting the end of Jacob's life. The discussion is presented through an analysis of three rabbinic aggadot, each linked with Jacob's deathbed.

The statement that Jacob intended to reveal to his sons the "end of days" (B. Pes 56a) leads to a discussion of the Messiah, as well as to several other important themes in medieval Jewish thought. The statement that God shows the righteous their reward before their death, exemplified by the case of R. Abbahu (Tanḥuma, *Wa-Yeḥi*), is related to the spiritual salvation of the soul in the world to come. The statement about the patriarch's longing to be buried in the land of Israel (Gen. Rabbah 96:5) points to the theme of resurrection. This last rabbinic passage provides the preacher with an opportunity for vigorous criticism of what he considers to be an erroneous assumption held by some of his contemporaries: that observance of the commandments during one's life is not as important as the accoutrements or location of one's burial. The traditional messianic hope expressed at the end of the sermon is especially appropriate here in light of its content.

In the earliest printed edition of the *Derashot* (Salonika, 1525), substantial passages from the end of the first and second parts of this sermon were omitted, apparently to save space, without any indication of their excision. These passages have been translated from the Cambridge University manuscript (see notes 15 and 27 below), restoring the symmetrical conclusions of the sermon's three parts.

Sermon on *Wa-Yeḥi*
(1480s, Spain)

For your salvation I wait, O Lord (Gen. 49:18).

"Jacob said, *Gather together that I may tell you {what will befall you in the end of days}* (Gen. 49:1). He wished to reveal to them the secret of the messianic advent, but the divine presence departed from him. He said, 'Perhaps, God forbid, there is one unfit among my children, [and I am] like our father Abraham, from whom there issued Ishmael, or like Isaac, from whom there issued Esau.' His sons replied, '*Hear, O Israel, the Lord our God, the Lord is One* (Deut. 6:4); just as there is only One in your heart, so is there only One in our heart.'[1] At that moment, the old man opened [his mouth] and said, 'Blessed is the name of His sovereign glory forever and ever.'

"The rabbis said, How shall we act? Shall we recite it? But Moses our teacher did not say it. Shall we not recite it? But Jacob said it! They ordained that it should be recited quietly.[2] R. Isaac said, This is like a king's daughter who smelled a spicy pudding. If she reveals [her desire], she suffers disgrace; if she does not reveal it, she suffers pain. So her servants began bringing it to her in secret" (B. Pes 56a).

There are three modes of salvation that we anticipate; they are the foundation of our faith and the esential meaning of our Torah. The first is physical: the coming of our Messiah. The second is spiritual: the life of the world to come. The third is a composite of both: the time of the resurrection. As these three are fundamental principles of our Torah, we shall discuss them at length. This lesson [Gen. 47:28–50:26] makes reference to each of these modes of salvation.

The coming of the Messiah is alluded to in Jacob's statement, *that I may tell you {what shall befall you in the end of days}* (Gen. 49:1). The rabbinic passage with which we began raises many problems.[3] First, why did the power of prophecy disappear from Jacob as he was about to reveal the secret of the messianic advent? Second, why did he say, "Perhaps, God forbid, there is one unfit among my children"? Third, why did he say, "Blessed is the name of His sovereign glory forever and ever"?

Fourth, how did the rabbis say, "Shall we recite it? But Moses our teacher did not say it. Shall we not recite it? But Jacob said it." If the law is that we should say it, what difference does it make whether Moses did not say it or Jacob did? An even stronger argument is that we should do what Moses taught us and refrain from saying what Moses did not say. But if so, and we should not recite it, why should it be said quietly? According to the sages,

1. According to the aggadah, the sons are addressing their father, Israel.

2. I.e., the sentence "Blessed is the name of His sovereign glory for ever and ever." Although uttered by Jacob in response to "Hear, O Israel," it was not said by Moses (Deut. 6:4–5). The rabbinic compromise is that it be said by Jews quietly, between Deut. 6:4 and 6:5 in the morning and evening liturgies.

3. *Sefeqot.* For this technique of addressing a rabbinic statement, see "Structural Options," at n. 28, and cf. Almosnino's sermon below, et n. 46.

an action forbidden for the sake of appearances is forbidden even in one's innermost chamber.[4] Finally, what do we learn from the parable of a king's daughter who smelled [a spicy pudding]?

The meaning of this important passage is as follows. Although we believe that the redeemer, our Messiah, will indeed come, it was clear that his arrival would be in the distant future. However, if the ignorant masses knew that the Messiah would not come during their lifetime, few of them would remain Jews. They would instead become assimilated to the Gentiles.[5] The ignorant, to whom the salvation of the soul is very remote, serve God only for the hope of living in peace and security. Therefore, if Jacob had revealed this secret about the coming of our Messiah in the distant future, great harm would have ensued. That is why the divine presence departed from him.

When Jacob realized that the divine presence had departed, he said, "Perhaps, God forbid, there is one unfit among my children." This means, there may be one among my children who serves God only because of the Messiah's coming. If he knew that the Messiah would not come during his lifetime, he would become assimilated to the Gentiles. (If you ask, how can one who is accursed issue from the loins of one who is blessed, the answer is that this had already occurred: Ishmael came from Abraham, Esau from Isaac. A righteous man may indeed father a wicked child.)

His sons replied that they served God because of His unity, power, and grandeur, not because of the coming of the Messiah. This was what they meant when they said, "*Hear, O Israel, {the Lord our God, the Lord is One}*; just as there is only One in your heart, so is there only One in our heart." As Jacob accepted alien status for himself and his offspring, foretold in the verse *your descendant will be an alien* (Gen. 15:13), so did they accept God's divinity, unity, and decrees. Whether the Messiah comes or not, *the Lord our God, the Lord is One.*

Hearing this, the old man said, "Blessed is the name of His sovereign glory forever and ever," for it is a source of great glory for a father to have so many sons who are righteous and good. His grandfather and his father each had two sons, one righteous and one wicked, while Jacob had twelve

4. B. Shab 64b.

5. Other fifteenth-century sources provide a context for this striking assertion. See Joseph Hacker, "Ha-Ye'ush," esp. p. 195, n. 2, and Isaiah Tishby, *Meshiḥiyyut be-Dor Gerush Sefarad u-Fortugal* (Jerusalem, 1985), p. 70. Shem Ṭob's statement about the critical importance of messianic faith for Jewish identity stands in dramatic contrast with the tendency to minimize its importance in such other texts as Naḥmanides' "Disputation" (see Frank Talmage, *Disputation and Dialogue* [New York, 1975], p. 85), and Leon Modena's *Magen we-Ḥereb* (Jerusalem, 1970), p. 64: "Even if the Messiah should delay in coming twice ten thousand years, the Jew will not depart one iota from his Torah and his faith because of such delay." Both of the above are polemical works, in which the emphasis may be quite different from that in a sermon.

sons, all devoted to the Most High. He therefore gave thanks and praise for this glorious honor bestowed upon him but not upon his fathers. Moses did not say, "Blessed is the name of His sovereign glory forever and ever," because his sons were unworthy, while Jacob's sons were righteous. Moses was glorified not through his sons but through Joshua. It was therefore inappropriate for him to say this, while it was appropriate for Jacob, who was glorified through his sons.[6]

Now each person should imitate the models of perfection insofar as possible. On the one hand, the sentence should be recited to inform us of the glorious honor that came to Jacob; on the other, it should not be recited, since Moses did not enjoy such glory, but only the glory of a worthy disciple. So that we might imitate both of these exemplars, the sages ordained that we say it quietly. Each of us will either be glorified through our children, like Jacob, or not, like Moses. You must examine carefully the parable of the king's daughter, for it will become clear after this explanation of the rest.

Some commentators have maintained that the questions, Shall we recite it? But Moses did not, and so forth, allude to the fact that Jacob made extensive use of imaginary honors and temporal triumphs. Possessing flocks and servants, having four wives and many children, he derived considerable pleasure from this material world. Having all he could want of worldly glory, he said, "Blessed is the name of His sovereign glory forever and ever."

But Moses did not make use of the glories of this world. You will not find in the Torah any mention of his eating or drinking, or of his drawing near to a woman. He must indeed have had relations with Zipporah in order to father children by her, but the Torah does not say, "She conceived and gave birth for him." And although they invited him to eat bread (Exod. 18:12), it does not say, "He ate bread." Rather, we find the opposite: *He did not eat bread [nor drink water]* (Exod. 34:28). His sons are hardly mentioned in the Torah; it is as if he had none. He owned no flocks or herds or wealth. All his concerns were circumscribed by the mountain and the people. In short, he had no use for the pleasures of this world. When he ate, he was not aware of eating; when he drank, he was not aware of drinking. The same is true of other physical activities. He performed them, but he derived no pleasure from them. That is why Moses did not say, "Blessed is the name of His sovereign glory forever and ever."[7]

6. The linguistic basis for linking *kebod malkuto* with the blessing derived specifically from children is not clear in the text. It may be Num. Rabbah 3:8: "The glory (*kebod*) of the Holy One, blessed be He, is derived from males, and about them David said, *Sons are a heritage of the Lord* (Ps. 127:3)."

7. In this interpretation, *kebod malkuto* is taken to signify things that pertain to this terrestrial world. Moses becomes the model of asceticism and Jacob of this-worldliness. Cf. Israel, "Dober Mesharim," fols. 60v–61r: "There are those who interpret this [aggadah] as

When the rabbis asked, "Shall we recite it?" they meant, "Shall we make use of imaginary honors and temporal triumphs as Jacob did?" This is not appropriate for one who strives toward perfection, for it will undermine one's intellectual achievement. "Shall we avoid all use of material wealth and glory, like Moses?" But these are necessary to attain a higher standard of ethical achievement. Since many things, including some of the commandments, are fulfilled through use of physical implements, wealth and glory are essential.

Therefore one is obliged to take what is necessary to satisfy the Torah and its commandments, and to leave the rest.[8] Such is the meaning of "We should recite it quietly": take what is needed, and leave what is superfluous, for it is the superfluous that causes harm, as the philosopher said in the seventh book of his *Ethics*.[9] Similarly, Solomon said (peace be upon him), *{Give me} neither poverty nor wealth* (Prov. 30:8), but rather the proper amount, for both extremes lead to undesirable results, as he continued, *Lest, being sated, I renounce, {saying, "Who is the Lord?" or, being impoverished, I take to theft and profane the name of My God}* (Prov. 30:9).

This is the interpretation of the passage according to its manifest, public meaning. But truly, it has a secret, hidden meaning, which I shall now explain to you. You know that the prophecy of our ancestor Jacob and of the other prophets came through the mediation of an angel.[10] Jacob invoked *the angel {who redeemed me from all evil}* (Gen. 48:16), on which Rashi commented, "the angel accustomed to come to me in all my sorrows." Moses, however, used God's great Name exclusively. All the miraculous deeds he performed were through the tetragrammaton, the name YHWH, *I will be what I will be* (Exod. 3:14).

---

applying to worldly things," and Aboab, p. 17a. I have not found such an interpretation of the aggadah in another commentator, but it is in the style of Isaac ben Yedaiah (see Saperstein, *Decoding*) whose commentary on the tractate Pesaḥim is no longer extant.

8. The recommendation to aim for the mean between total asceticism and inordinate worldliness by avoiding superfluous things is almost a commonplace in Jewish philosophical ethical literature. See, for example, Baḥya's *Ḥobot ha-Lebabot, Shaᶜar ha-Perishut,* 3 ("individuals who walk in the middle of the road in regard to abstinence, completely rejecting the superfluities of this world"); Maimonides, *Code* I,ii (*Deᶜot*) 3:1; Anatoli, *Malmad,* pp. 24b, 97b; Baḥya ben Asher, *Shulḥan shel Arbaᶜ*, in *Kitbe Rabbenu Baḥya,* ed. C. B. Chavel (Jerusalem, 1970), p. 495.

9. It is not clear to me which passage in the seventh book of Aristotle's *Nicomachean Ethics* Shem Ṭob could have in mind. Compare the passage cited by the preacher's father, Joseph ibn Shem Ṭob, in "ᶜEn ha-Qore" ("Sources," at n. 15). Joseph wrote a commentary on the Hebrew translation of the *Ethics* (see Moritz Steinschneider, *Die hebräischen Übersetzungen des Mittelalters* [Berlin, 1893], pp. 212–14, and Regev, esp. p. 137). Shem Ṭob quotes his father's commentary in his sermon on *Wa-Yiqra,* p. 41a.

10. Cf. Maimonides, *Guide* 2:34: "All prophets except Moses receive the prophecy through an angel." Shem Ṭob's comment on this phrase is that "angel" here means "the imaginative faculty." Cf. also *Code* I,i (*Yesode ha-Torah*) 7:6.

Now it is improper for us Jews to call upon an angel or a seraph. We must, like Moses, pray only to God Himself, who did wondrous things for us.[11] But Jacob, who resorted to an angel for every purpose—these angels being the *kabod,* or glory, of God, in Aramaic *yeqara*—blessed the angel who frequented him, saying, "Blessed is the name of His sovereign glory forever and ever."[12]

Inasmuch as we must acknowledge that angels of the Most High do exist, that prophecy comes to human beings through them and from them, and that through their instrumentality divine decrees affecting the world are carried out, it is fitting that we make mention of them, as did Jacob. But inasmuch as Moses uttered only the great Name, we should refrain from reciting this statement. Therefore, in order that we might pattern ourselves insofar as possible after both models of perfection—the true patriarch, and our king and deliverer—we fulfill our obligation to both of them by reciting it quietly.

Now for the parable of the princess who smelled a spicy pudding. As angels are discerned in the world, failure to mention them would bring trouble upon us; it would be as if we did not recognize their existence. Yet to speak of them openly and publicly is a disgrace to God's people, for it is unseemly to mention names of angels or seraphim. The sages therefore ordained that we say it quietly, since the existence of angels is perceived, but is not publicly manifest.

The glory of God fills the world, and God is the universal Mover, as we see from the verse, *Who rides upon the heaven as your help* (Deut. 33:26).[13] The angels cause motion in particular things. They are vastly different from God, for the movements caused by the separate intellects are subject to the diurnal motion, and they all move from east to west, while at the same time they have particular movements.[14] Understand all that I have said concerning this

11. For opposition, especially among the Jewish philosophers, to the practice of invoking angels in prayer, see Saperstein, *Decoding,* pp. 191–93.

12. The new, esoteric interpretation suggested is that the phrase *kebod malkuto* refers to the angel through whom God manifests Himself in the world. The idea of the *kabod* as a special being has a long and complex history in medieval Jewish thought: see Saadia Gaon, *Emunot we-Deʿot,* 2:10; Joseph Dan, *Torat ha-Sod shel Ḥasidut Ashkenaz* (Jerusalem, 1968), pp. 104–68; Colette Sirat, *Les théories des visions surnaturelles dans la pensée juive du Moyen Âge* (Leiden, 1969); Harry A. Wolfson, *Crescas' Critique of Aristotle* (Cambridge, 1929), pp. 461–62.

13. This interpretation of Deut. 33:26 as referring to God's role as Prime Mover is taken from Maimonides' *Guide* 1:70 (near end). Cf. Shem Ṭob's commentary on this passage: "Of [the all-encompassing sphere] it is said, *Who rides upon the heaven as your help,* for there can be found the First Mover of everything." For another contemporary interpretation of this aggadah dealing with God's providence, see Aboab, p. 17a.

14. The passage reflects several assumptions of medieval cosmology. The all-encompassing

aggadic passage, for it is marvelous, but the true meaning of the aggadah is what I said last, as God knows.

The redeemer whom we await has many identifying signs, for he will stand out as an ensign to the peoples. These signs have been stated by the prophet Isaiah (peace be upon him), who said that the Messiah would be a fruitful offshoot from the root of Jesse: *There shall come forth a shoot out of the stock of Jesse* (Isa. 11:1).

He also said, *There will rest upon him the spirit of the Lord,*[15] [*wisdom and insight, a spirit of counsel and valor, a spirit of knowledge and reverence for the Lord* (Isa. 11:2). This verse states that the spirit of the Lord will rest upon the expected Messiah, who will be a prophet. You already know that prophecy is to be found only in one who is "wise, valorous, rich."[16] Now the philosopher has explained that it is difficult or even impossible for a person to cultivate all of the virtues. Yet we see that Israel's deliverer will combine all of the intellectual virtues, the virtues of practical reasoning, and the moral virtues. Moreover, he will surpass even these by being a great prophet.

Thus the *spirit of wisdom and insight* will rest upon him. *Insight* and *counsel* are among the virtues of practical reason. *Valor* is one of the moral virtues. The *spirit of knowledge and reverence for the Lord* encompass the intellectual [and moral] virtues, for the spirit of knowledge is an intellectual virtue, while *reverence for the Lord* is the fear of sin, namely, the virtue of temperance, to be found in a person devoid of carnal desires.

After recording the qualities that distinguish the Messiah from all other human beings, the prophet went on to make another distinction. Whoever must judge between two adversaries should listen to the arguments of both parties. The law is that after having heard the arguments of the adversaries, the judge should summarize and say, "This one claims so, the other so."[17] But the expected Messiah *will not judge by what he sees, nor decide by what he*

---

sphere revolves each day from east to west, causing motion in everything else. The lower bodies may also have particular motions, as a person does while walking upon a moving boat. These movements of the part are caused by the separate intellects or "angels." See Maimonides, *Code* I.i (*Yesode ha-Torah*) 3:1, and *Guide* 1:72.

15. The first section of the sermon in the printed edition ends here. The following section in square brackets, discussing the "identifying signs of the Messiah" through an exegesis of Isa. 11, has been restored from Cambridge University MS Dd.10.46/6, fols. 53v–54r. This and a subsequent passage from the sermon were apparently omitted by the editors of the first printed edition of the *Derashot* (Salonika, 1525, only a generation after they were first written) with no sign that they had been deleted. The entire section should be compared with Abravanel's commentary on Isa. 11, in which he too discusses attributes of the Messiah. I see no hint of direct dependence.

16. Cf. B. Ned 38a and Shab 92a, which speak not of "prophecy" but of the *shekinah*. The formulation here is that of Maimonides in *Code* I,i (*Yesode ha-Torah*) 7:1, and *Guide* 2:32.

17. See Maimonides, *Code* XIV,i (*Sanhedrin*) 21:9, and talmudic references, based on 1 Kings 3:23.

hears (Isa. 11:3). As a great prophet, he will not have to hear the arguments of the adversaries.

An alternative meaning is that even though he will be the greatest of the prophets, he will not judge by what he sees or by what he hears, but he will follow Moses, our teacher. The Messiah will not come to add to or subtract from what is written in the Torah of Moses and in the Talmud concerning what is forbidden or permitted, who is innocent or guilty, what is pure or impure.[18]

Then he said that this Messiah will be distinguishable in a third way. He will have no need for sword or ax or cudgel to avenge those who hate him. Rather, he will kill them with the ineffable Name, as the prophet wrote, *He will strike down a land with the rod of his mouth, and slay the wicked with the breath of his lips* (Isa. 11:4).

Fourth, this Messiah will be unique because his recognizable signs, justice and faith, will be like clothing (Isa. 11:5). Justice is the greatest of the [moral] virtues, as the philosopher wrote in the fifth book of the *Ethics,* and faith is the supreme intellectual virtue.[19] Because of faith, Abraham inherited the land: *He had faith in the Lord* (Gen. 15:6). Because of faith, Israel went out of Egypt: *The people had faith . . . they bowed low in homage* (Exod. 4:31). Because of faith, they crossed the sea: *They had faith in the Lord* (Exod. 14:31). Because of faith, they defeated Amalek: *His hands were* emunah, *steadfast as faith* (Exod. 17:12). Because of faith, the Messiah will come: *I will betroth you by faith* (Hos. 2:22).[20] His distinguishing signs were thus faith and justice, precious virtues that encompass much.

As we have fully explained this passage elsewhere, here we shall be brief. A fifth distinguishable sign is that he brings together opposites. It is beyond the power of description. The wolf and the lamb will be dwelling together, the leopard will lie down with the kid (Isa. 11:6), and the other animals of opposing natures will live together in harmony. A small child will lead these wild animals, and a *yoneq,* an even smaller child, will play on the viper's hole (Isa. 11:6, 8). None of these animals will do any harm (Isa. 11:9).

18. This was a constant theme in Jewish polemic against Christianity. There were two medieval Jewish views about Jesus in this regard: (1) Jesus departed from the commandments of the Torah, and therefore could not have been the Messiah (see Maimonides, *Code* XIV,v [*Melakim*] 11:4 in the uncensored version translated in Twersky, *A Maimonides Reader,* p. 226: Jesus "was instrumental in changing the Torah"), and (2) Jesus observed the Torah fully, and the Christian religion subsequently perverted his teachings by abandoning it (see, e.g., *Kitbe Pulmos le-Profiaṭ Duran,* ed. Frank Talmage [Jerusalem, 1981], pp. 24–26).

19. Aristotle, *Nicomachean Ethics,* 1129b. For the sense in which "faith" could be considered the supreme intellectual virtue, see the discussion by Shalom Rosenberg, "The Concept of *Emunah* in Post-Maimonidean Jewish Philosophy," *Studies in Medieval Jewish History and Literature,* 2, ed. Isadore Twersky (Cambridge, Mass., 1984):273–307.

20. This passage is based on Mekilta, *Be-Shallaḥ,* on Exod. 14:31 (ed. Lauterbach, 1:252–54). Cf. Joshua ibn Shueib, p. 26a–b.

This is a metaphor for evil men who prey upon others: they will live with the poor and the needy, without the power to harm them.[21] A small boy, wise despite his youth, will lead them. These arrogant men will do no destructive evil. Maimonides has explained how all evil that comes to the world, whether from one nation to another or from one person to another, is the result of ignorance.[22] That is the danger. When the redeemer has come, all will know the Lord, from the least to the greatest (Jer. 31:34). Consequently, they will do nothing destructive or bad. We see this in the verse, *All your children shall be taught about the Lord, and great will be the peace of your children* (Isa. 54:13). In the messianic age there will be peace in the world between opposing forces. This is the fifth distinction. *The earth will be filled with knowledge of the Lord* (Isa. 11:9). This is the sixth.

There is also a seventh distinction. All peoples will seek him out, and he will be as a standard for the nations (Isa. 11:10). The eighth distinction is that under all past leaders and judges of Israel, there were wars and conflicts, but in the days of the Messiah *all the earth will be at rest, tranquil* (Isa. 14:7). And as tranquility does not appear to flatter the mighty warrior, the prophet said that this tranquility will be a mark of honor for them (Isa. 11:10).

At this time *the everlasting doors will be raised high, and the King of glory will enter* (Ps. 24:7). It will not be said that God is *mighty and valiant* (Ps. 24:8), as was said in the past, but rather, *Who is this King of glory? {The Lord of Hosts, He is the King of glory,} selah.* In the time of Solomon's temple and the Second Temple, God was mighty and valiant, but in the time of the Third Temple, may it be built quickly and in our days, He will be a King of glory. We, the entire community of Israel, all await this salvation. That is why it is said, *For Your salvation we wait, O Lord* (cf. Gen. 49:18), in the sense that is rendered by the Aramaic Targum, "For Your salvation: [not for a temporary salvation,] but for the salvation brought by Messiah, the son of David."][23]

We also anticipate a salvation even greater than this: the life of the world to come. We find allusion to this in the verse, *For Your salvation I wait* (Gen. 49:18). For from the tribe of Dan would issue Samson, who *bit the horse's heels* (Gen. 49:17). He was the one who leaned and rested upon the two pillars, one on each hand, and then with his great might pulled them down, so that all the people in the temple were killed.

You may ask, how could Samson kill himself in order to bring death to

21. The metaphorical interpretation of these verses reflects the influence of Maimonides, *Code* XIV,v (*Melakim*) 12:1.

22. *Guide* 3:11: Maimonides uses these verses from Isa. 11 as support for his position.

23. This is the reading in one version of the Palestinian Targum. The citation of the theme-verse signals the end of the first section of the sermon.

his enemies? The answer is that this death was a source of great salvation for him, enabling his intellect and soul to cleave to the separate intellect. As he brought death to his body, he brought life to his soul.[24] Similarly, the three righteous men threw their bodies into the fire in order to save their souls (Dan. 3:23), trusting in God's saving power. This is strong proof that these righteous men believed in the existence of another world beyond this perceptible one, believed that the soul does not die, but lives on forever.

The rabbis of blessed memory said, "When R. Abbahu was dying, the Holy One, blessed be He, showed him thirteen streams of balsam. Amazed, he said, 'All these are for Abbahu?' He applied to himself the verse, *Yet I had thought, I have labored for nothing* (Isa. 49:4)."[25] There is a major problem in this passage. Could it be that Abbahu did not believe in a reward for the righteous in the world of souls until God showed him this reward? Whoever does not believe that there is another world beyond this is a heretic! How could he have said, "*I have labored for nothing*"? Why did the Holy One show him thirteen streams, and why were they all of balsam?

The answer is that R. Abbahu did believe in the world of souls more than anyone else. The meaning of the passage is this. After he saw the full glory hidden away for him, he said that all his labor other than for the sake of wisdom and understanding was in vain. He had wanted all his effort and enterprise to be for this purpose. Yet even though he did not achieve this goal, God rewarded him as if he had.

Or it might be held that R. Abbahu served God not in order to receive a reward, but because of His unique preeminence. This indeed is why we must serve God: because of His unique preeminence, or because of the favors we have received from Him, not in order to receive any benefit. The Torah says, *You must surely give to him* (Deut. 15:14), and right next to it, *for you were a slave . . .* (Deut. 15:15), showing that it should not be in order to receive a reward, but to repay our debts. And this is what R. Abbahu said: that he served God *for nothing*—not in order to receive a reward, but because of His unique preeminence, or because of the favors he had already received from Him.

Or it might be maintained that R. Abbahu belittled himself. Although he believed in an expansive world prepared for the righteous, he nevertheless thought himself unworthy of such a place and such a sign of distinction. That is why he said, "*I have labored for nothing.*" God showed him thirteen rivers because the attributes of God are thirteen. They were of balsam because

24. The link between Gen. 49:18 and Samson was made by the Midrash (see Gen. Rabbah 99:11), although not in the same way we see here. Shem Ṭob's "proof" from the story of Samson of the soul's immortality and reward in the next world is interesting, because it contradicts the literal statement of Samson: *Let my soul die with the Philistines* (Judg. 16:30).

25. P. AZ 42a; Gen. Rabbah 62:3; Tanḥuma, *Wa-Yeḥi,* 4.

the aroma of balsam fortifies the soul. The sages said, "*Let every soul praise God, Hallelujah* (Ps. 150:6). What is it that fortifies the soul? It is fragrant aroma."[26] They are all of one kind because all of the attributes are reduced to one simple essence, with no plurality or composite nature.

They were rivers to show the abundant flowing, as we see in the verse, *How precious is Your lovingkindness, O Lord; human beings find shelter in the shadow of Your wings;*[27] [*they feast on the rich fare of Your house; You let them drink at Your refreshing stream* (Ps. 36:8–9). This verse teaches that the most valuable and important things are as nothing unless human beings use them. If no one were to use silver and gold, what value would they have? Likewise, those who do not use their intellect for the apprehension of the intelligibles are considered like beasts: *One who does not understand value {is like the beasts that perish}* (Ps. 49:21).

So it says here that those undeserving of God's lovingkindness act as if it had no value at all. If, however, these people would devote themselves to the service of God, His lovingkindness would be supremely precious. This is the meaning of *How precious is Your lovingkindness, O Lord.* If all human beings were devoted to the acquisition of metaphysical knowledge and virtue and the performance of the commandments, then God's lovingkindness would be supremely precious. The more good spreads, the more it is good, as the philosopher explained in the eighth book of the *Ethics*.

The sages said that even if all human beings were to become righteous and morally upright, all would attain the measure of God's goodness and

26. Cf. B. Ber 43b.

27. Compare the comment of Yedaiah Bedersi on Tanḥuma, *Wa-Yeḥi* (*Perush ha-Midrashim*, Paris Hebrew MS 738.3, fol. 296v; Escorial Hebrew MS G-III-8, fols. 88v–89r). Yedaiah explains that the rivers of balsam indicate the abundance of the reward pertaining to the soul alone, and the verse cited by Abbahu means that he had striven to serve God not out of hope for a reward, but purely for love of the Creator ("I have labored for nothing," i.e., for no extrinsic purpose). This is the second explanation suggested by Shem Ṭob. The interpretation of the thirteen rivers as pertaining to the attributes of God, all ultimately reducible to one pure essence, is cited in the name of Shem Ṭob by Samuel Jaffe in *Yefeh To'ar* on Gen. Rabbah 62:3 (Venice, 1597, p. 368c).

The entire passage on this aggadah seems to have been used by Joseph Garçon in a sermon delivered in Damascus in 1514 (see Garçon, in Benayahu, pp. 177–78). In particular, the explanation of the balsam, based on B. Ber 43b, looks like a direct quotation. Since the first edition of Shem Ṭob's sermons was published at Salonika in 1525, we may conclude one of three things: (1) Garçon heard Shem Ṭob preach in Spain and recalled his interpretation; (2) Garçon had access to a manuscript of Shem Ṭob's *Derashot*; or (3) there is a third source, either prior to both Shem Ṭob and Garçon from which both drew, or between the two, that provided the connection.

The second section of the sermon in the printed edition ends here. The continuation in square brackets has been restored from Cambridge University MS Dd.10.46/6, folios 54v–55r (cf. n. 15, above).

love that they deserved.[28] All would be able to partake to their satisfaction, having enough not only for themselves but also to enable them to benefit others. This is the meaning of *They feast on the rich fare of Your house.* Wealth and honor, though deemed good, never satisfy. Those who love money can never have enough of it. But the reward that comes to those who engage in Torah and commandments will fully satisfy them, for this goodness spreads like the water of a brook. No matter how many draw from it, it is not diminished. Just as a spring of fresh water never fails, so does God's beneficence never fail, satisfying all. Just as the light [of the sun] can illuminate the entire world without diminishing, so the goodness of the world to come will not diminish, no matter how many share in it through their intellectual attainments (cf. Ps. 36:10). This is unlike external goods, which diminish when there are many owners.

The psalmist said that failure to attain the divine goodness is not the fault of God, who is in no sense a miser. It is rather that person's own fault, or the fault of those evil people who appear to befriend him. That is why David prayed that even if not all were to attain this level of perfection, God's lovingkindness would not be denied him because of his own inadequacy or because of evil neighbors. Thus he said, *Bestow Your lovingkindness upon those who know You, Your beneficence upon the upright; Let not the foot of the arrogant tread on me, or the hand of the wicked drive me away* (Ps. 36:11–12).

We cannot know the essence of the world to come, which is the world that comes to the human being after death,[29] for it is totally remote from our experience. The psalmist says, *How abundant is the good that You have stored away for those who fear You, that You do for those who take refuge in You* neged bene adam (NJV: *in the full view of men*) (Ps. 31:20). This means: that which benefits the soul is extremely good, beyond the capacity of the human being to measure, for it transcends human experience. Alternatively, the verse might mean that God rewards the righteous in the world to come, although they are also rewarded in this world. This could also be the meaning of *neged bene adam*.

When David realized how much was prepared for the righteous in the time to come, he asked God to show him the way to reach it, requesting divine help in attaining this goal. He said, *You say to the Lord: You are my Lord, my welfare depends entirely on You* (Ps. 16:2).[30] This means that the soul

28. This is apparently a paraphrase and expansion of the aphorism. "The righteous of all peoples have a part in the world to come" (cf. Jacob Katz, *Exclusiveness and Tolerance* [New York, 1962], p. 174, incl. n. 4).

29. Shem Ṭob follows here the Maimonidean understanding of the "world to come": cf. *Code* I,v (*Teshubah*) 8:8.

30. The remainder of this section is constructed as a homily on Ps. 16. The incorporation of such homiletical-exegetical passages into sermons became increasingly common in sixteenth-century preaching. Cf. the sermon by Almosnino below.

is praying to God, saying that it is unworthy of any reward, for the good already bestowed upon it by God was undeserved. It is similar to R. Abbahu's statement, "*I said, I have labored for nothing,*" as we already explained.

However, God must do good for *the holy ones that are in the land* (Ps. 16:3a). Those who are strong and mighty (Ps. 16:3b) deserve to be beneficently rewarded. Indeed, *my only wish* (Ps. 16:3b) and desire is that these righteous ones be rewarded and that the evil ones who oppose them be punished with *many sorrows* (Ps. 16:4) and misfortunes. Those who take a stand away from God must pay the price, as we see in the verse, *Whoever sacrifices to a god shall be proscribed* (Exod. 22:19). Such people were so repugnant to David that he did not want to mention their names or to receive their offerings or their libations of revolting blood (cf. Ps. 16:4).

After this, he said that human beings have various desires and different goals, each following a unique path, and that he alone was fully devoted to God, who helped him in this, for "God helps those who want to become pure."[31] So the verse says, *The Lord is my allotted share and portion, You sustain my destiny* (Ps. 16:5). Now the lot of most human beings is to search without attaining knowledge or understanding, because of a weak constitution. He therefore said that he was fortunate in the intellectual powers that had befallen him, a good allotment that enabled him to apprehend a greater measure of wisdom and Torah than others had. That is why his *estate,* referring to God's Torah, was *lovely indeed* (Ps. 16:6).

Then he said that this restful estate came to him from God, who counselled and guided him in the attainment of this goal: *I bless the Lord who has guided me* (Ps. 16:7a). He was also helped in that *Even while I am lying on my bed, my conscience admonishes me* to apprehend God, for there is no other ultimate goal (cf. Ps. 16:7b). Now the goal and the fruit of all branches of knowledge is to apprehend the one intelligible, which is also the one intellect and the one source of intellectual activity, namely, God.[32] Just as the unique vision of the eye is the color white, so the unique object of intellectual perception is God.

Therefore he said, *I am ever mindful of the Lord; He is at my right hand, I shall not be shaken* (Ps. 16:8). Just as a person will never forget his right hand even for an instant because it is used so much, this is the reason why *I shall not be shaken,* either in this world or after the soul has separated from the body.[33] For when the soul departs, it rejoices in its apprehension of God. The verse says, *My heart rejoices, my whole being exults* (Ps. 16:9). The *being* and the *heart* refer to the intellect, which endures after death. Indeed, even when

31. B. Shab 104a. Menaḥem Meiri quoted the same rabbinic aphorism in his comment on this verse.

32. Cf. Maimonides, *Guide* 1:68.

33. Cf. ibid. 3:51 on this verse.

it is with the body, the flesh shall rest secure, for God watches providentially over those who fear Him.

After that he said that God would save his soul from Sheol because of His justice and fairness, for no pious person could bear being cut off from eternal life like a beast. Thus the verse says, *You will not let Your faithful one see the Pit* (Ps. 16:10). As there are many paths leading to this goal, David prayed that God would instruct him: *Teach me the path of life.* Now he said that the ultimate goal is apprehension of God, that many pleasures are to be found in this, as in the aggadic statement about thirteen streams of balsam, and that they are given abundantly, as is implied by the word *streams.* He further said that they endure eternally.

To summarize. The good rewards of the world to come are manifold. Second, they satisfy all human desires. Third, they are all to be found in the apprehension of God. Fourth, they are pleasures of the most exalted nature. Fifth, they endure eternally. All this is included in the verse, *Teach me the path of life. In Your presence is perfect joy; delights are ever in Your right hand* (Ps. 16:11). Thus it is the goal of every aspiration to attain this salvation, and we therefore say, *For Your salvation I wait, O Lord* (Gen. 49:18).][34]

There is yet another mode of salvation, both physical and spiritual.[35] This too is hinted at in the lesson, as we see in the following rabbinic statement, "Why were the patriarchs so demanding of burial in the land [of Israel]? R. Eleazar said, There is a hidden reason for this. What did he mean by There is a hidden reason for this? Said R. Joshua ben Levi, *I shall walk before the Lord in the lands of the living* (Ps. 116:9)."[36] The question here is why the patriarchs set their hearts so fervently on being buried in the land of Israel, so that if they were outside the land, they made their children swear to carry them there despite the undeniable hardship involved. We should seek to discover a reason and purpose for this. For if it were only for the preservation of the body, which is an "accessory of holiness," burial could be performed anywhere.[37]

However, they had a tradition that the land of Israel is the "land of the living," that the dead will come to life in it, and that all who die outside the land will roll [through underground caves] until they reach it.[38] The toil

34. Here too (as above, at n. 23), the citation of the theme-verse signals the end of a major division in the sermon.

35. The Hebrew text of both the Salonika and the Venice editions, as well as the Cambridge University MS, reads *nafshit we-ruḥanit,* "pertaining to the soul and spiritual." My translation, which assumes that *nafshit* is an error for *gashmit,* is consistent with the very beginning of this sermon.

36. Gen. Rabbah 96:5; P. Kil, chap. 9, 32c.

37. Cf. B. Meg 26b, "Accessories of holiness are to be stored away."

38. See B. Ket 111a.

and effort to be buried in this land was to teach us this secret. That is why Jacob made Joseph swear, and Joseph made his brothers swear, and the same with other fathers and their children. This tradition informs us that the land of Israel alone is "the land of the living." Just as all Jews yearn to live in it, as the Talmud says, "Whoever lives outside the land is like one who has no God,"[39] so even the dead desire to be buried in this land, as we see in the verse, *I shall walk {before the Lord in the lands of the living}*.

You might argue that this contradicts the continuation of the passage, about the two sages who saw the coffin of a corpse coming from outside the land to be buried in the land of Israel. Rabbi [Judah] said to R. Eleazar, "What has this man availed by coming to be buried in the land when he expired outside the land? I apply to him the verse, *You made My heritage an abomination*—during your lifetime you did not immigrate here—and in your death, *you defile My land* (Jer. 2:7)." It seems clear from this that being buried in the land brings no benefit to one who died outside the land. On the contrary, it is a grave sin, defiling the land. This would seem to refute what I have said.

The answer is as follows. There are many people, about whom it is said, "they are not for the Lord," who throughout their lives engage in the vanities of the world, promoting their own destruction. They seek wealth and riches and the pleasures of mortals. Even their concern with the commandments is rebellious, for they perform them by rote. Yet when the time of their death draws near, they command their children to give money to charity, money they no longer can use, which should go by inheritance to their children. Yet they transfer their estate from a good son so they can be a benefactor to someone they do not know or understand.[40]

Others are worse than these. They do not bequeath their money to be given away, but they command their children to bury them in a prayer shawl and a four-cornered garment with fringes.[41] Even though everything they

39. B. Ket 110b. On the complex history of interpretation of this statement, see my article "The Land of Israel in Pre-Modern Jewish Though: A History of Two Rabbinic Statements," in *Land of Israel: Jewish Perspectives,* ed. Lawrence Hoffman (South Bend, Ind., 1986), pp. 195–203.

40. Cf. B. Ket 53a: "Keep away from transfers of inheritance even from a bad son to a good son." This entire paragraph and the following one were incorporated by Abravanel into the end of his commentary on Genesis, completed sometime in 1505. Cf. the second paragraph of n. 27, above. The practice of deathbed philanthropy as a means of compensating for a self-centered and materialistically oriented life bears comparison with contemporary Christian attitudes toward the disposition of assets after death, on which see Philippe Ariès, *The Hour of Our Death* (New York, 1982), pp. 191, 194. Ariès's thesis that only in the eighteenth century did the conception of an obligation to heirs take precedence over the obligation to charities (pp. 196–97, 471) is challenged by the present source.

41. The use of *ṭallit* and *ṣiṣit* in burial was a subject of some controversy among halakic

wore while alive was made of both wool and linen,[42] in the hour of their death they become righteous. As if the commandments could be performed by the dead! The sages of blessed memory said, "What is the meaning of the verse, *and a slave free from his master* (Job 3:19)? Once a person dies, he becomes free from the commandments."[43]

Now since the dead can do nothing, no commandment performed on behalf of the dead can benefit them in any way. On the contrary, it is a source of shame, defiling the commandments. Of such people it is said, "In your lifetime you did not acquire merit; in your death . . . ." It is with reference to them that the Scripture said, *You come and defile My land* (Jer. 2:7). These are people who have sinned throughout their lives, who have not performed actions proper for the living. Concerning them the Torah says, *{the commandments} that a person shall do while alive* (Lev. 18:5).[44] Yet later, as death approaches, they want to rectify what cannot be rectified.

With reference to this, the sages said that it is forbidden for a person to make even a saddlecloth for his ass out of material containing both wool and linen, but that he may use such material to make shrouds for the dead, thereby teaching that *a living dog is better than a dead lion* (Eccles. 9:4).[45] The means through which we may perform the commandments no longer exist in the dead. It is as Solomon said, *Whatever it is in your power to do, do with all your might, for there is no action, no reasoning, no learning, no wisdom in the grave, where you are going* (Eccles. 9:10). If so, the good done after a person's life—for example, dressing him in fringes and placing phylacteries upon him[46] for his burial—does not avail, and it is done in vain. This is the meaning of the statement, "In your lifetime you did not immigrate here; [in your death *you come and defile My land.*]"

---

scholars. See B. Men 41a with Rashi; Rabbenu Tam in Tosafot Ber 18a, *Le-maher*; Tosafot Nid 61b, *Abal*; Naḥmanides, *Torat ha-Adam,* in *Kitbe RaMBaN,* 2:98–100; *Ṭur Yoreh Deʿah,* no. 351. See also the summary in Leopold Greenwald, *Kol Bo ʿal Abelut* (New York, 1965), pp. 93–95. The problem was especially delicate in the case of one who was not careful in observing the commandment of fringes during his life: see the responsa of Jacob Emden (*Teshubot Yabeṣ,* 1:124) and of MaHaRaM Schick, *Yoreh Deʿah,* no. 350.

42. This is, of course, a forbidden combination (Deut. 22:11).

43. B. Shab 30a, 151b; there the conclusion is based on Ps. 88:6, *Among the dead {I am} free.* Job 3:19 is used in B. BM 85b to teach that "Whoever makes himself like a slave to the Torah in this world becomes free in the next." The sermon gives what appears to be a conflation of the two passages.

44. The translation reflects what would appear to be the preacher's new homiletical interpretation of the word *wa-ḥai* in Lev. 18:5.

45. B. Pes 40b: "A garment in which *kilʾayim* is lost must not be sold to a Gentile nor made into a saddlecloth for an ass, but it may be made into shrouds for a corpse."

46. Burial in phylacteries raises an additional halakic problem: the destruction of sacred writings. Greenwald (*Kol Bo ʿal Abelut,* p. 92) refers to a responsum of RaDBAZ in pt. 4 of his *Teshubot* on this issue.

However, those worthy of observing the Torah and going during their lifetime to the "land of the living," that is, the land of Israel, will in their death be worthy of great exaltation. Such was the case of the patriarchs. They were worthy of going to the land of the living while alive, and they were worthy of being buried in it, so that they would attain the expected goal, namely, the era of resurrection, which will occur in the land of Israel without pain or subterranean rolling. But concerning those unworthy of fulfilling the Torah in their lives, who command that they be buried in the land of Israel, Scripture says, *You come and defile My land.*[47] Thus it is clear that the patriarchs wanted to be buried in the land of Israel for a marvelous reason, namely, the resurrection of the dead, as we see in the verse *I shall walk before the Lord {in the lands of the living}*.

The resurrection of the dead is one of the fundamental principles of the Torah.[48] It is not something that occurs naturally to the perfected soul, as is the reward in the world to come, for the spirit by its nature returns to God who gave it, just as dust returns to the earth as it was. It is therefore said that the resurrection of the dead is only for the righteous, as God will not perform a miracle for the wicked.[49] They are called "dead" even while they are alive.[50] How can they possibly live after their death, and why should there be a supernatural occurrence for them?

Just as we believe in all the miracles and wondrous acts, so should we believe in the resurrection. It is beyond our human power to understand or to perform miracles, but it is within God's power, as the psalmist said, *Who alone works great wonders* (Ps. 136:4). He alone can do them, and He alone knows how they are done. Ours is but to marvel at them and to prostrate ourselves upon the ground, as we are told, *When they saw it, all the people flung themselves {on their faces and cried out, "The Lord alone is God"}* (1 Kings 18:39).

When the God of spirits showed Ezekiel the dry bones, He asked, *Can*

47. For other medieval expressions of opposition to the practice of bringing bodies for burial in the land of Israel (based on this passage in the Midrash and the Jerusalem Talmud), see Yedaiah Bedersi, *Perush ha-Midrashim,* on Gen. Rabbah 96:5, published in my "Selected Passages from Yedaiah Bedersi's Commentary on the Midrashim," *Studies in Medieval Jewish History and Literature* 2:428–29, and Zohar 2:141b. Samuel Jaffe may have had this passage in mind when he wrote, "There are those who say that burial in the land of Israel is of no benefit except to one who goes there while alive" (*Yefeh Marʾeh* on P. Kil [Amsterdam, 1727], p. 46a).

48. *Yesod mi-yesode ha-Torah.* The identification of the "fundamental principles of the Torah" was one of the most controversial topics in fifteenth-century Spanish Jewish intellectual history. Shem Ṭob follows Maimonides in including the physical resurrection of the dead in this category.

49. See Maimonides, *Commentary on the Mishnah,* intro. to chap. *Ḥeleq* of Sanhedrin (in Twersky, *A Maimonides Reader* [New York, 1972], p. 414).

50. B. Ber 18b.

these bones live?" Ezekiel replied, *O Lord God, {only You know}* (Ezek. 37:3). God then showed Ezekiel, whether as an optical illusion or a prophetic vision, how the dead will come to life. First He said that He will make similar parts of the body piece by piece, namely, the sinews and the flesh. Second, that He will bring them near each other, and make from them a corporeal receptacle.[51]

[Then He will join them together into a single unit and mold upon them the skin. Third, after this, the soul will come to them from afar. As the flesh and bones were made of earth and the other elements, to which they returned at their death, and the soul returned to God who gave it, the resurrection must entail a return of the soul from God. Thus the soul will come to the corporeal receptacle] and make it a complete body, just as it was at first.

It will be able to do important things that it did not accomplish while in this world, and afterward it will receive a great reward, while the soul is still joined to the body. This is in accordance with the view of the rabbi who said, "The dead that the Holy One will resurrect will not return to their dust again."[52] Or they will live in order to receive a great reward after the body separates from the soul for a second time, a reward they did not merit in this world.

This salvation is only for Israel. The Bible says, *These bones {are the whole house of Israel}* (Ezek. 37:11), and *I will place My breath in you and you shall live again* (Ezek. 37:14). This is the salvation we await, as we see in the verse with which we began: *For Your salvation I wait, O Lord.* May the Lord God in His steadfast love make us worthy and sustain us in life for all these salvations, and may He make speed and hasten His purpose (Isa. 5:19), that we may rejoice and exult in His deliverance.

51. Ezek. 37:6 and 8 are taken to indicate that the sinews, flesh, and skin will be formed separately, and then joined together to make a complete body. Cf. Gen. Rabbah 14:5. The following sentences, in square brackets, were apparently omitted from the printed text through haplography with the phrase "corporeal receptacle" (*geshem keliyyi*). They have been restored from Cambridge University MS Dd.10.46/6, fol. 55v.

52. B. Sanh 92a. The question is whether a reward will be given to the righteous while they live in their resurrected bodies, or whether the purpose of the resurrection is to allow the righteous to attain even greater merit—and consequently a greater spiritual reward—for their souls after a second death.

Joseph Garçon

Joseph ben Meir Garçon is a newly discovered star in the galaxy of Jewish preachers. Although the manuscript containing his sermons (British Library Or. 10726) has been known for some time, it has been read only during the past generation, carefully studied and fully described only during the past ten years. H. H. Ben-Sasson first drew attention to its value as a source for the self-conception of those who had lived through the expulsion from Spain. From a totally different point of view, Mordechai Pachter succinctly analyzed its significance for the form and structure of the late Spanish sermon.

During the past few years, two major independent studies of the manuscript by Meir Benayahu and Joseph Hacker have appeared. These are concerned less with the art of preaching than with historical and bibliographical questions.[1] The importance of Garçon now seems established, not as a giant in the tradition of Jewish preaching, but as one whose work exemplifies the most influential homiletical style of his time.

The only source of information about Garçon's life is his sermons. As far as is known, he is not mentioned in any other contemporary document.[2] A few details about his early life can be established with certainty. Various evidence indicates that his family originated in Castile,[3] and Garçon probably studied in the talmudic academy of Fromista under Samuel Franco. No doubt his preaching career began in Spain.

At the time of the 1492 expulsion, he was among the thousands of Spanish Jews who sought refuge in Portugal. According to the most plausible reconstruction,[4] he was in Portugal during the forced conversion of 1497, and, together with all other Jews in that country, he lived for a while as a *converso*. For about three years, as he states in the sermon below, he was cut off from the wellsprings of his faith. Eventually he was able to leave Portugal and reach Salonika, where his former teacher, Franco, and many other Spanish

1. H. H. Ben-Sasson, "Dor Gole Sefarad ʿal ʿAṣmo," *Zion* 29 (1961):27, 41, 44–45; Pachter, "Sifrut," pp. 28–34; Benayahu; Hacker, "Li-Demutam." Hacker has promised a second study, on the worldview of Garçon.

2. Benayahu, p. 46; Hacker, "Li-Demutam," p. 24, cf. p. 29.

3. See Hacker, pp. 25–29.

4. That of Hacker, pp. 29–36; see my annotation to the sermon, below.

exiles had settled. The sermon translated below, delivered in the late winter of 1500, was his first in the new land.

None of the other works he mentions has survived. These include a tract on the expulsion, a commentary on parallelisms in the prophetic literature called "Meʿarat ha-Makpelah," a commentary on the liturgy, and "Sefer Maʾamarim," a collection of aggadot from rabbinic literature, perhaps with interpretations, and quite possibly intended for the use of preachers.[5]

The autograph manuscript of his sermons, called "Ben Porat Yosef," contains sermons for various occasions delivered in Salonika from 1500 to 1504, in Amasia of Asia Minor in 1504–05, and in Damascus from 1506 through 1523. His intention had been only to visit Damascus on his way to the land of Israel, but he apparently stayed there until the year of his death. The introduction to the collection is a poignant personal statement. After many years without children, he had been blessed with a daughter, who died at the age of nine. Now he has gathered his sermons not only to prevent himself from forgetting them, but also "so that from them, some memory of me may remain for future generations."[6] Meanwhile, other preachers are invited to use the material in their own sermons, provided that his name is mentioned.

Each sermon is identified by a precise statement of date, place, and occasion. Many are eulogies, some for such well known personalities as Jacob ibn Ḥabib, Abraham Zacut, Samuel Abravanel, Samuel Franco, and Joseph Hamon, others for less well known figures. The many names mentioned in the sermons, placed in their context, are of value to the historian of Jewish life in the Near East at this time.[7]

In form, the sermons represent the classical structure of the Spanish sermon crystallized at the end of the fifteenth century (described above).[8] They begin with a verse from the Torah lesson (the *nośe* or *thema*) and a passage of aggadah from the Talmud, Midrashim, or Zohar (the *maʾamar*). The verse is generally divided into fragments of increasing length, each of which is given a particular significance during the sermon. The conventions of fifteenth-century homiletics are well represented, including the introduction in which the preacher justifies his enterprise after rehearsing the reasons he should have remained silent, and the request for *reshut,* or permission to preach. The *maʾamar* is usually explicated near the end of the sermon, but this discussion is not always included in the written text.

The sermon I have chosen is dramatic in its setting: the first sermon of

5. On these other works, see Benayahu, pp. 51–52; Hacker, pp. 68–69.

6. Garçon, in Benayahu, p. 133; Hacker, p. 72.

7. See the full list of those eulogized in Hacker, p. 69, and the extensive discussion of all figures mentioned in the sermons by Benayahu, pp. 81–132.

8. See "Structural Options."

an exile in a new land, quite likely of a forced apostate returning to Judaism. The preacher's account of his own experience and his impassioned call not to forget the plight of brothers who remain in Portugal infuse the conventional motifs with pulsating vitality. One can only surmise the emotions generated in listeners who were both grateful for their own decision to choose Salonika over Portugal and, at the same time, concerned about the fate of former neighbors and friends who had not been so fortunate.

Once the introductory section has ended, however, the sermon becomes disappointingly routine. The central subject, concerning the relationship between chance and providence, was standard fare. The discussion of the verses from the lessons *Bere᾽shit* (Gen. 1:1–6:8), *Noaḥ* (Gen. 6:9–11:32), and *Be-Ḥuqqotai* (Lev. 26:3–27:34) is quite commonplace. The treatment of the lesson *Pequde* (Exod. 38:21–40:38) is drawn almost entirely from Baḥya ben Asher.

It is not until the final section of the sermon, when the preacher discusses the conditions of human perfection and links them with the biblical verses used as proof texts in the midrash on *Pequde* and with an allegorical interpretation of Genesis 2:1–3, that some homiletical ingenuity reappears. Much of the middle of the sermon might be used to illustrate the kind of offering that sophisticated Ottoman audiences were known to dismiss impatiently as trivial and commonplace. By this combination of the dramatic and the humdrum, the text represents both the potentials and the pitfalls of Jewish preaching in the generation of the expulsion.

Sermon on *Elleh Fequde*
(1500, Salonika)

1. *The records of the tabernacle, the tabernacle of the testimony, which were recounted at the bidding of Moses.*

2. *The* pequde *of the tabernacle, the tabernacle of the testimony,* asher *recounted* ᶜal pi.

3. *These are the records of the tabernacle, the tabernacle of the testimony, which were recounted at the bidding of Moses* (Exod. 38:21).[1]

"Rabbi Nehorai began and said, *Hear, O Israel, the Lord our God, the Lord*

1. In this form of sermon, the preacher repeats either the entire theme-verse or sections of it several times at the beginning. Each repetition indicates a different use of the verse to come in the body of the sermon. See the discussion in "Structural Options," above; for a fuller example, see the sermon by Almosnino.

is One (Deut. 6:4). This verse makes sense when Jacob's sons said it to their father,[2] or when Moses said it to Israel. But when all Israel says, *Hear, O Israel, the Lord our God, the Lord is One,* to whom are they speaking? This is what we were taught: Our father Jacob did not die (B. Taᶜan 5b). The Holy One sequestered and concealed him in His Throne of Glory, so that he might be a constant witness that his descendants affirm the unity of God's Name. When they do so, Jacob is taken upon four wings outstretched in all four directions, and is raised [to the presence of the Holy One] on High who says, 'Blessed is the father who has such descendants on earth, blessed are the children who provide such a crown for their father.' At that moment, all the hosts of heaven begin to say, 'Blessed is the name of His sovereign glory forever and ever.' "[3]

O men of learning and wisdom, let it be known to your excellencies that I see myself as unworthy of speaking even about everyday matters in your presence. How much less, then, am I worthy of addressing you with a discourse on Torah!

There are two reasons for my unworthiness.[4] First, my wisdom is inadequate for a serious Torah discourse, and therefore it would be better for me to remain silent. Second, regarding whatever wisdom I may possess, it would be better for me not to speak now, but [to wait] until my mental composure has returned. I have suffered greatly from the upheavals of our time. For three years I have been unable to study.[5] More than this, the curse of Cain has been fulfilled in me and in all my contemporaries of this wretched and bitter generation: *You shall be a ceaseless wanderer upon the earth* (Gen. 4:12).

Your excellencies are aware that when Ahasuerus summoned the sages of Israel to judge Vashti, they replied that they lacked the wisdom to judge because they had been constantly on the move, and the uprooted wanderer

2. See B. Pes 56a and the beginning of Shem Ṭob ibn Shem Ṭob's sermon.

3. This Aramaic passage, identified by the author as coming from "Midrash ha-Zohar," is actually from *Zohar Ḥadash, Ruth* (ed. Reuben Margaliot, Jerusalem, 1978), p. 78c.

4. The preacher is using a familiar rhetorical convention: though it would be better for him to remain silent, he is compelled to speak. See below, n. 15. For a formal introduction based on this motif and encompassing almost one-third of the sermon see Moscato, *Nefuṣot Yehudah,* beginning of sermon 12.

5. Joseph Hacker, in his article on Garçon (p. 31), understands this as referring to the period 1497–1500, from the time of the forced conversion in Portugal to the time he was able to escape to Salonika (pp. 31–36; cf. nn. 8 and 10, below). Tishby, "Genizah," p. 86, notes other indications in Garçon's work that he lived for a period in Portugal as a forced convert. If, as reported by Abraham Saba, Jews in Portugal had been forbidden to preach publicly at this time (*Ṣeror ha-Mor,* Deut., p. 8b), the present sermon would have been even more poignant. On the verse quoted in the following sentence, and the Cain motif in general applied to the generation of the expulsion, see H. H. Ben-Sasson, "Galut u-Geʾulah be-ᶜEnaw shel Dor Gole Sefarad," *Sefer Yobel le-Yiṣḥaq Baer* (Jerusalem, 1961), pp. 216–17.

has no leisure to devote to the study of Torah and wisdom. They therefore recommended that he turn to Moab, which had remained peaceful and tranquil in its home, as the Bible tells us: *Moab has been secure from his youth on, he is settled on his lees, and has not been poured from vessel to vessel* (Jer. 48:11). Thus Moab could render the decision.

(Now actually the Great Sanhedrin said this to Ahasuerus not because they were ignorant of the law, but because they wanted an excuse to avoid fulfilling the king's request. They thought, "If we decide that she should be put to death, then tomorrow, when the effects of the wine wear off, he will feel remorse and accuse us of decreeing the death penalty illegally. We will then be in danger. But if we acquit her, people will say that we fail to respect the prestige of the monarchy." That is why they sought this excuse.)[6]

It all proves that one who is uprooted and forced to travel lacks sufficient mental composure to engage in serious Torah discussion.[7] And I have been traveling for some time—since the day I left Spain because of the expulsion—to seek the word of the Lord. "God helps those who want to become pure."[8]

There is yet another consideration that should prevent me from performing this act. Prophecy is not to be found in the midst of sadness but only in the midst of joy.[9] We see this in the verse, *As the musician played, God's spirit was upon him* (cf. 2 Kings 3:15), and in the verse, *the spirit of Jacob their father revived* (Gen. 45:27). But as for me and all my contemporaries, our lot should be sorrow, anguish, and grief throughout our lives, because of our land, because of our brothers who remain in the great devastation in Spain, because of those who want to come and serve the Lord but are not permitted to leave and must worship other gods against their will.[10] Can any God-fearing person feel joy while our brothers and our loved ones remain victims of that devastation?[11] All the curses proclaimed in the Torah have been fulfilled upon us!

6. See Esther Rabbah 4:1 and B. Meg 12b. The defense of the Sanhedrin actually undermines the preacher's point, for it makes the reference to the negative impact of traveling upon intellectual activity an empty excuse.

7. Cf. Almosnino's sermon, at n. 49. This appears to be another topos, developed in different ways.

8. B. Yoma 38b. According to the reconstructions of both Hacker (pp. 31–32) and Tishby (p. 86, n. 104) this is an acknowledgment by the preacher of divine help in his quest to return to Judaism by leaving Portugal for Turkey.

9. Benayahu and Hacker both note that the talmudic text (B. Shab 30b) speaks of the divine presence (*shekinah*), not prophecy, and refer to a passage in *Midrash ha-Gadol, Wa-Yiggash*. Garçon's source, however, may well have been Maimonides' *Code*, I.i (*Yesode ha-Torah*) 7:4. The Genesis verse in the following sentence indicates that when Jacob learned that his son Joseph was alive, the 'spirit' of prophecy returned to him.

10. On this passage, see Hacker, pp. 32–33, and Tishby, pp. 85–86. It is probably a reference to the forced conversion of 1497 in Portugal. *Sefarad* would then have to be a general term for the Iberian peninsula. Tishby argues that the preacher's reluctance to utter the name "Portugal" expresses a deep antagonism.

11. Speaking to a congregation which either came to Salonika directly from Spain in 1492

I have often been asked how God can acquiesce in our being forced to worship idolatrously,[12] acquiesce in our crying out to Him from the very depths of our hearts and souls and receiving no response. My answer is in accordance with my theme-verse: *These are the records of the tabernacle, the tabernacle of the testimony, which were recounted at the bidding of Moses,* meaning, all these accounts that we settle in this "tabernacle," which is the world we live in, all these matters have been destined and foretold in our sacred Torah by Moses.[13] Nothing he has said has fallen by the wayside.

If we worship idolatrously, it was foretold by Moses: *There you shall serve other gods. . . . If you search there for the Lord your God, you shall find Him, but only if you seek Him . . .* (Deut. 4:28–29). This is to be understood according to its simple meaning, for it is what we have seen with our own eyes. It is not as Onkelos translated [into Aramaic], "You shall serve those who serve false gods." He rendered it this way because he could not comprehend how becoming idolaters could be part of God's curse, given God's jealous zeal against idolatry. He therefore translated the verse as if it meant that we would serve idolaters. But if Onkelos had lived in this wretched generation, he would have seen with his own eyes that the verse is to be understood according to its simple meaning.[14]

Similarly, you will find that Jeremiah also spoke of this: *And when you announce all these things to that people, and they ask you, "Why has the Lord decreed upon us all this fearful evil? What is the iniquity and what the sin that we have committed against the Lord our God?" say to them, "Because your forebears deserted Me—declares the Lord—and followed other gods and served them and worshiped them; they deserted Me and did not keep My instruction. And you have acted worse than your forebears, every one of you following the willfullness of your evil heart and paying no heed to Me. Therefore I will hurl you out of this land to a land which neither you nor your forebears have known, and there you will serve other gods, day and night; for I will show you no mercy"* (Jer. 16:10–13).

Jeremiah said, in short: You have continued clinging to the evil your forebears did. If so, he was apparently referring in the final sentence to the

---

or managed to leave Portugal before 1497, the preacher is urging them not to forget that they might have been back there as well.

12. Note the assumption that Christian worship is idolatry (*ʿabodah zarah*). While many rabbinic authorities disputed this, there was a strong Sephardic tradition that concurred. Cf. Yosef Kaplan, *Mi-Naṣrut le-Yahadut* (Jerusalem, 1983), pp. 226–27.

13. This is the first use of the theme-verse: the *tabernacle* is this world, *records* are the events of history, *at the bidding of Moses* means that they were prophesied in the Torah.

14. Cf. Abravanel's fourteenth question on this section from *Wa-ʾEtḥanan,* and Isaac Arama's *ʿAqedat Yiṣḥaq,* chap. 98. On the significance of this entire passage in Garçon, see H. H. Ben-Sasson, "Dor Gole Sefarad ʿal ʿAṣmo," pp. 44–45, and Tishby, p. 88; it should probably be seen as an expression of the *converso* ideology of self-justification for choosing idolatry over martyrdom.

actual worship of false gods, not what Onkelos translated. It is a case of the punishment's fitting the crime. If God has not answered us, this too was foretold by Moses: *I will keep My countenance hidden from them* (Deut. 31:18). To summarize, God has brought about what was decreed against us because of our sins. There is no cause for surprise about this. But with all that we have experienced, none of us should be able to feel the joy necessary to speak words of Torah.[15]

However, what impels me to perform this act is my trust in God, my trust that He will inspire me with His abundant goodness, and that I shall feel the inspiration that flows from the great sages who stand before me on this sacred occasion, especially the inspiration from the consummate scholar. . . .[16] This is the second meaning of my theme-verse, *the* pequde *of the tabernacle, the tabernacle of the testimony,* asher *recounted* ʿal pi. I interpret this to mean, let the princely notables sitting in this sacred tabernacle, and the "tabernacle of the testimony," who is the consummate scholar . . . , a tabernacle and dwelling place for Torah (which is called "testimony"), bestow felicity (*osher*) upon that which will be rendered by my mouth (*ʿal pi*) in this sermon.[17] I interpret *pequde* to mean "notables," as in the verse *let the king appoint notables* [peqidim] (Esther 2:3).

We find that the seventy elders received from Moses the inspiration that made them prophets (cf. Num. 11:25). We further find that when Saul prophesied, he did so only because of the inspiration he received from the other prophets, not because of his own powers. This the Bible tells us, recounting how Samuel told Saul that he would find donkeys and a band of prophets in Gibeah, and that he would prophesy in their midst. It then says,

15. Here the preacher concludes the reasons he should remain silent. He now turns to justify his preaching. One of the clearest and most consistent exponents of this convention was Michael ben Shabbetai Balbo, whose sermons are preserved in Vatican MS Ebr. 105. See, e.g., fol. 78v: "There is no doubt that silence is an extremely fine quality, even for the wise . . . and therefore I should cover my mouth and refrain from speaking. . . . However, the reasons that have impelled me to break the bounds of silence are two. . . ." Cf. also fols. 70v, 92r, 108r, 177v–178r. Garçon himself expressed opposition to the convention he uses here: "I am very surprised at those preachers who, when they preach, want to give reasons for their sermons, as this would seem to be a misguided practice. . . . No preacher need give a reason for preaching on the Torah, for he is simply doing what he is obliged to do (fol. 24r; Benayahu, p. 196; he again ignores his own counsel by giving a reason on fol. 39v; Benayahu, p. 157).

16. Hebrew: *he-ḥakam ha-shalem we-kulleh.* Benayahu and Hacker suggest that the reference was to R. Samuel Franco. In such sermons notables present in the congregation were frequently singled out for praise, but the details were usually not recorded in the written text. For example, see Ephraim ha-Darshan, fol. 30v, and Joseph of Benevento, fol. 104v.

17. In this second interpretation of the theme-verse, *pequde* refers to "great men" (see the end of the paragraph), *tabernacle* to the synagogue, *tabernacle of the Testimony* to one special scholar, *asher* ("which") to felicity (*osher*), *puqqad ʿal pi* ("rendered by my mouth") to the sermon.

And when they came there, to Gibeah, he saw a band of prophets coming toward him. Thereupon the spirit of God gripped him, and he spoke in ecstasy among them. When all who knew him previously saw him speaking in ecstasy together with the prophets, the people said to one another, "What's happened to the son of Kish? Is Saul too among the prophets?" But another person there spoke up and said, "And who are their forebears?" Thus the proverb arose: "Is Saul too among the prophets?" (1 Sam. 10:10–12). The meaning of these verses is known to apply to me.

And now, with the permission, etc. . . :[18] *These are the records of the tabernacle, the tabernacle of the testimony, which were recounted at the bidding of Moses.*

Many have thought that all occurrences in this universe are the result of chance. Because God saw that so many would err in this doctrine, the Torah begins with the creation of heaven and earth, saying, *Be-reʾshit bara Elohim et ha-shamayim we-ʾet ha-ʾareṣ* (Gen. 1:1). Rashi said that the word *be-reʾshit* here is in the construct form, and its meaning is as if the verse said, "In the beginning of the creation of heaven and earth." This is consistent with every other occurrence of *be-reʾshit* in the Bible. All that was created on the first day was light and dark. The sense of these verses is, in the beginning of the creation of heaven and earth, when the earth was unformed and void, God said, *Let there be light* (Gen. 1:3).[19] Rashi's view was that if the Bible had intended to assert that heaven and earth were created on the first day, it would have said *ba-riʾshonah,* "at first."

Baḥya [ben Asher] interpreted this word as if it were *ba-riʾshonah.* His evidence for this was the accent mark, for the accent mark in the word *be-reʾshit* indicates that it is not in the construct.[20] Alternatively, we might say that the word implies the following: "as a true and primary axiom, you must believe that God created heaven and earth, creating the world from nothing," for this is meant by the word *beriʾah.*[21] From this it follows that all occurrences result from God.

Rashi also said that the Torah could have begun with *This month* (Exod. 12:2), for the essential function of the Torah is to inform us of God's com-

18. The full form of the *reshut* asks for permission from God, from the Torah, from the notables present, and from the congregation, concluding, "I shall now speak on the lesson. . . ." On this form, see Hacker, p. 83, n. 140, and the discussion in "Structural Options," above.

19. This is the interpretation incorporated into the NJV.

20. I.e., *be-reʾshit* is written with a *ṭipḥa,* one of the disjunctive accents. Baḥya ben Asher wrote his commentary on the Torah at the end of the thirteenth century. Much of the present sermon shows the influence of that commentary, not all of which is acknowledged (as is noted below).

21. I.e., the word *be-reʾshit* refers not to chronological time but to the logical priority of an axiom. For the interpretation of *bara* to mean creation ex nihilo, see Abraham ibn Ezra (who rejects it), David Kimḥi, and Naḥmanides (trans. Chavel, p. 23) on Gen. 1:1.

mandments, which we are required to perform. Why then did it begin with the creation of the world? The answer is that God began with the account of creation, *revealing to His people His powerful works* (Ps. 111:6), so that as a result of His actions in creating this universe from nothing, all might know of His sovereignty.

We might also say that God followed here the path He would use at the revelation of the Torah. Before giving the Torah to Israel, He reiterated for them the favors He had done for them, as the Bible says, *You have seen what I did to the Egyptians, how I bore you on eagles' wings and brought you to Me. Now then, if you will heed My voice and keep My covenant, you shall be My treasured possession among all the peoples, for all the earth is Mine* (Exod. 19:4–5). In other words, because of all these favors I have done for you, you should take upon yourselves whatever I might decree upon you. But all I want is for you to *heed My voice . . . and be My own treasure.*

Here too, He followed this path. He would give the first man commandments—*Of every tree in the garden you are free to eat; {as for the tree of the knowledge of good and evil, you must not eat of it}* (Gen. 2:16–17), the commandment to be fertile and increase (Gen. 1:28), and others. The purpose was to inform the man that he had a Master whose decree he was obliged to observe. Otherwise, seeing himself alone in the world, he might conclude that he himself was the master of everything.

But before God made His decree and required the man to perform these commandments, He began with the creation of heaven and earth. This informed the man that God had done him a great favor by the creation of this world, as God Himself did not need it, *enthroned at the flood* (Ps. 29:10).[22] Furthermore, *I have said, "the world is built as an act of lovingkindness"* (Ps. 89:3), meaning, in order to perform an act of lovingkindness for its creatures. Therefore, since He created the world as a favor for human beings, they are obliged to do all that He commands them. That is why He began with the account of creation.

Let us return to our main point, that God began with the creation account in order to inform us that we must hold it as a true axiom that He created heaven and earth, and that all occurrences in this world result from Him, not from accident or chance. Were this not the case, He would not have commanded the first man or watched over him so as to punish him when he transgressed.

Noah recognized that all occurrrences in this world result from God, not from chance. Therefore, the Torah said, *These are the* toledot *of Noah: Noah was a righteous and blameless man in his age; Noah walked with God* (Gen. 6:9).

22. I.e., God did not create our world for His own benefit, since He was already sovereign over the angels.

Baḥya interpreted *toledot* to mean "occurrences," as in the verse, *mah yeled yom,* what a day brings forth (Prov. 27:1), for after this the Bible goes on to say, *Noah was the father of . . .* (Gen. 6:10), mentioning his offspring.[23] Or we can say that *toledot* is to be understood in its more common meaning, for the true offspring of a righteous person are his good deeds, as Rashi maintained.

The verse mentions three praiseworthy qualities that distinguished Noah from his contemporaries. First, he was *ṣaddiq,* righteous in his behavior, not a violent man like his contemporaries, of whom it was said, *The earth was filled with violence* (Gen. 6:13). Second, he was *tamim,* or perfect in all character traits.[24]. The beast that is physically perfect and without blemish is called by the Bible *temimah;* this word is used to characterize the red heifer (Num. 19:2) and the paschal lamb (Exod. 12:5). Now the blemishes of a human being are repugnant character traits. That is why it was said that Noah was *tamim,* without any such ethical blemishes. The Bible also says *ashre temime darek (NJV: Happy are they whose way is blameless*) (Ps. 119:1), referring to those perfect in their character traits. This too was the opposite of his contemporaries, whose character traits were reprehensible, as the Bible says: *all flesh had corrupted its way* (Gen. 6:12).

Third, *Noah walked with God.* This quality of "walking" applies only to a select few in each generation.[25] It means that he was always cognizant that God created the world and that everything resulted from Him. That is why it says *et ha-ʾElohim, with* the *God,* known by His creation of the world. This too was the opposite of his contemporaries, as the Bible says: *the earth was corrupt before God* (Gen. 6:11). They thought that all occurrences in this universe were the result of accident or chance, and that there was no reward or punishment. Therefore they did not believe Noah when he told them day after day that God would bring a flood to the world. Thus they robbed each other, as the Bible says: *The earth was filled with violence.*

Know that this is true, for the Bible says, *On the seventh day, the waters of the flood came upon the earth* (Gen. 7:10). The sages maintained that these were the seven days of Methusaleh. God waited before bringing the flood because of the seven days of mourning for Methusaleh, so that proper respect could be shown and a eulogy made for that righteous man.[26] But it seems to me that it was a punishment fitting the crime. They denied that the world was

23. Therefore, *toledot* in the previous verse must mean something other than "offspring."

24. The distinction between *maʿaśaw* ("behavior") and *middotaw* ("character traits") is that the former refers to externally observable behavior and the latter to inner dispositions.

25. This sentence and the entire preceding paragraph are taken almost verbatim from Baḥya ben Asher. At this point, the preacher interprets the significance of "walking" somewhat differently from Baḥya, in accordance with his own thesis.

26. Cf. B. Sanh 108b and parallels.

created in six days, and therefore their punishment came on the seventh day. For the seventh day, the Sabbath, teaches about the creation of the world, as we see in the verse, *In six days the Lord made heaven and earth, and on the seventh day He ceased from work and was refreshed* (Exod. 31:17).

We also find that the inhabitants of Sodom sinned in this matter. The verse, *the men of Sodom were wicked sinners against the Lord, exceedingly so* (Gen. 13:13), means that they denied the existence of a God who had created the world and sustained its existence, believing instead that the world follows its established pattern and that everything occurs by chance. This is the significance of the phrase *against the Lord, exceedingly.* It means that they denied the essence of God, which is why their sin was so great. The punishment they received fitted this sin. They sinned against the Name that teaches about God as the sustainer of existence,[27] and they were judged and punished through that very Name, as the Bible says, YHWH *caused {sulfurous fire} to rain upon {Sodom and upon Gomorrah}* (Gen. 19:24).

Pharaoh also sinned in this matter. Moses said to him, *Thus says the Lord, "Let My people go that they may serve Me"* (cf. Exod. 5:1). and he replied, *Who is the Lord, that I should heed His voice? I do not know the Lord . . .* (Exod. 5:2). Finally, because of the plagues, he himself conceded and said, *The Lord is in the right, while I and my people are in the wrong* (Exod. 9:27). This means that he believed God was rewarding and punishing justly, watching over the behavior of human beings so as to repay them according to their ways, and that he and his people were wrong in believing that there was no judge and no justice.

In the lesson *Be-Ḥuqqotai* (Lev. 26:3–27:34) we read: *They shall confess their iniquity and the iniquity of their forebears, in that they trespassed against Me* [be-maʿalam asher maʿalu bi], *yea, were even hostile to Me* [we-ʾaf asher haleku ʿimmi be-qeri]. *I, in turn, shall be hostile to them and remove them into the land of their enemies. Then* [o az] *at last shall their obdurate heart humble itself, and they shall atone for their iniquity. Then will I remember My covenant with Jacob; I will even remember My covenant with Isaac, and even My covenant with Abraham; and I will remember the land. For the land shall be forsaken of them . . .* (Lev. 26:40–43).

Now you might ask, How can God say, after they have confessed, *I, in turn, shall be hostile to them?*[28] We should also look into the phrase *we-ʾaf asher*

27. There were many who interpreted the divine names differently, with *El Shaddai* expressing God as sustaining the ordinary existence of the universe, and the tetragrammaton expressing God as worker of supernatural miracles. See the sources cited by Warren Zev Harvey, "Yesodot Qabbaliyyim be-Sefer Or ha-Shem le-R. Ḥasdai Crescas," *Meḥqere Yerushalayim be-Maḥashebet Yiśraʾel* 2 (1983):83, 86. Garçon's explanation of the tetragrammaton is also given in the sermon of Abraham ha-Kohen of Bologna printed in Bonfil, *Rabbanut,* p. 289.

28. The same question was raised by several contemporaries: cf. Abravanel's tenth question

haleku, (were even hostile), and also the phrase *o az,* which literally means *or then {shall their obdurate heart . . .}*, for the word *o* ("or") in the Bible always follows a prior alternative.

I would say that the confession they made was not accepted by God because their offense remained with them and was never abandoned.[29] This is the meaning of *be-maᶜalam asher maᶜalu bi,* which can be understood to mean that they confessed while their offense remained with them. This is like a person who immerses himself to become ritually pure while holding a reptile in his hand.[30] If you say that *maᶜal* is a relatively minor sin, it is not true. It is the greatest sin possible.[31]

The phrase *we-ʾaf asher haleku ᶜimmi be-qeri* means they believed that God does not watch over this world. That is a criminal offense. Therefore, *af ani elek ᶜimmam be-qeri,* meaning, "I will leave them to *miqreh,* chance."[32] In the land of Israel, there is always divine providence, as we see from the verse, *the eyes of the Lord your God are always upon it* (Deut. 11:12). God therefore said, *I will remove them into the land of their enemies,* which is outside the land of Israel, given over to the heavenly constellations, so that they will remain governed by the chance configurations of the stars.

O az, or then, at that time when they are outside the land, they will return in repentance and subdue the evil impulse in their obdurate heart. As a result of the afflictions they experienced while in exile, they will atone for their iniquity, and *then I will remember my covenant with Jacob, and even My covenant with Isaac, and even my covenant with Abraham, and I will remember the land, for the land will lie forsaken without them.*

But we still need to explore the following problem: after the words of comfort—the remembering of the patriarchs—why did God utter yet another curse, *the land will lie forsaken*? Furthermore, why did He mention the patriarchs in reverse order?[33] And why was the word *af, even,* used with Isaac and Abraham, but not with Jacob? The answer is that *I will remember* is not

---

on *Be-Ḥuqqotai*; Shem Ṭob ibn Shem Ṭob, *Derashot,* p. 51b; Abraham Saba, *Ṣeror ha-Mor* (1879; reprint ed., Jerusalem, 1975), p. 17d. On the technique of raising a series of questions about a passage and then resolving them—frequently associated with Abravanel's commentary on the Torah but actually a popular homiletical device from the end of the fifteenth century, if not earlier—see the discussion in "Structural Options," above.

29. This is the solution given by Abravanel and Shem Ṭob (see preceding note). Abraham Saba cites it with "Some say," but gives a different answer. Cf. also Arama's *ᶜAqedat Yiṣḥaq,* chap. 70, on these verses.

30. See Maimonides, *Code,* I,v (*Teshubah*) 2:3.

31. *Maᶜal* is understood as the treachery of an empty and hypocritical confession. Cf. Shem Ṭob ibn Shem Ṭob, p. 51b.

32. The interpretation of *qeri* as a form of *miqreh,* "chance," became common in Jewish exegesis of this passage, following Maimonides in *Code,* III,ix (*Taᶜaniyot*) 1:3, and *Guide* 3:36.

33. These are Abravanel's eleventh and twelfth questions on the passage.

an expression of comfort. God was saying: children should be like their forebears, and I remember that they come from the seed of Jacob, who was entirely perfect. We see this from the prophet's statement, *I planted you with noble vines, all with choicest seed* (Jer. 2:21), using the word *śoreq,* a kind of vine which produces grapes without pips, to indicate that Jacob contained nothing inferior. That is why the word *even* was not used of him. But the Israelites were not like Jacob in their behavior.

Not only will I compare them with Jacob, I will even compare them with Isaac, who was not quite so perfect, for he was the father of Esau. That is why the word *even* was used of him. Yet the Israelites were not like Isaac. And I will compare them with Abraham, who was not quite so perfect as Isaac, for Isaac had the merit of his father, while Abraham came from Terah and thus had a bad root. Yet the Israelites were not like Abraham. The word *even* was used of Abraham because of Ishmael.[34] In short, they are not like their ancestors. I shall also remember for the land of Israel the sins that they committed in it, failing to observe the sabbatical and jubilee years. That is why the *land will lie forsaken without them.*[35]

This was God's purpose in making the tabernacle. He wanted His presence to dwell among us so that His providence would be manifest, and we would recognize that all things result from Him. He therefore commanded that every aspect of the work of creation be found in the tabernacle, thereby providing a link between this world and the supernal realm.

The sages said in the Midrash:[36]

> *These are the records of the tabernacle, the tabernacle of the testimony:* why the repetition, *the tabernacle, the tabernacle?* To teach that the temple below is intended to correspond to the temple above, as the Bible says, *The place You made Your abode, O Lord* (Exod. 15:17). The tabernacle is balanced against the creation of the world. Of the creation it is written, *Who spread out the skies like fine gauze, and stretched them out like a tent to dwell in* (Isa. 40:22), while of the tabernacle, *You shall make cloths of goats' hair for a tent* (Exod. 26:7). A clear link is established in the verse, *Who spread the heavens like a tent cloth* (Ps. 104:2).
>
> Of the creation it is written, *It shall divide water from water* (Gen. 1:6), while of the tabernacle, *The curtain shall divide for you {the Holy from the Holy of Holies}* (Exod. 26:33). Of the creation, *Let the waters be*

34. For rabbinic views on the superiority of Jacob to Abraham, see Ginzberg, *Legends* 5:275, n. 35.

35. Up to this point, this could have been a sermon on *Be-Ḥuqqotai* using units on *Bere'shit* and *Noaḥ*. Here begins the discussion of the week's lesson.

36. Cf. Tanḥuma, *Pequde,* 2. The quotation continues for the next three paragraphs and may well have been taken from Baḥya.

gathered (Gen. 1:9); of the tabernacle, *Make a laver of copper for washing* (Exod. 30:18). Of the creation, *Let birds fly* (Gen. 1:20); of the tabernacle, *The cherubim shall have their wings spread above, shielding with their wings* (Exod. 25:20). Of the creation, *God created the human* (Gen. 1:27); of the tabernacle, *Advance Aaron your brother near you* (Exod. 28:1).

Of the creation, *The heaven and earth were finished* (Gen. 2:1); of the tabernacle, *All the work of the tabernacle was finished* (Exod. 39:32). Of the creation, *God blessed the seventh day {and sanctified it}* (Gen. 2:3); of the tabernacle, *Moses blessed them* (Exod. 39:43), and then, *He sanctified it and all its furnishings* (Num. 7:1). Of the creation, *For on it He rested* (Gen. 2:3); of the tabernacle, *Six days shall work be done, but on the seventh day {you shall have a sacred sabbath of complete rest}* (Exod. 35:2), followed immediately by *Take from among you gifts.* This shows that the work of the tabernacle is balanced against the creation of heaven and earth.

Furthermore, the furnishings of the tabernacle bind this world with the supernal realm, each appurtenance serving like a fork to seize the corresponding one above and to bring divine effluence down upon it, so that this effluence can radiate upon our world. Then, when the divine effluence is in this world, we can be absolved of all our sins. For God makes His effluence radiate only upon the good.[37]

This is the meaning of the rabbinic statement, "They sinned with *these,* and they became reconciled with *these.* They sinned with *these* as we see in the verse, *These are your gods, O Israel* (Exod. 32:4); they became reconciled with *these* as we see in the verse, *These are the accounts of the tabernacle* (Exod. 38:21)."[38] According to the simple meaning, this verse refers to what was mentioned above it, asserting that the tabernacle and its appurtenances, including the structure and the courtyard and all that was done to them, were accounts of the work of the Levites, commanded by Moses through Ithamar. But the sacred furnishings, including the ark, the table, the lamp, and the altars, are not in the category of *the tabernacle.* They are the responsibility of Eleazar.[39]

The Midrash gives another explanation for the repetition, *the tabernacle, the tabernacle {ha-mishkan mishkan}.* It is because the temple was destined to be

37. The idea of a corresponding tabernacle in the supernal realm was widely cultivated in kabbalistic thought; cf. Zohar 1:35a, 2:143a. The "fork" seems to have been a popular image of the preacher.

38. Cf. Exod. Rabbah 51:8.

39. The interpretation according to the simple meaning is taken from Baḥya, who is citing an interpretation attributed to others by Naḥmanides. For Eleazar's responsibility over the sacred furnishings, see Num. 4:16.

mortgaged (*le-hitmashken*), twice. This is also the significance of *ḥabol ḥabalnu lak, We have certainly offended You* (Neh. 1:7).[40]

Now if you understand the numerical significance of the phrase *ha-mishkan mishkan ha-ᶜedut,* you will find that it alludes to the number of years that the First and Second Temples stood, and the number of years from the Exodus to Solomon's building of the temple. The numerical significance of the letters in *ha-mishkan* [415] alludes to the Second Temple, of *mishkan* [410] to the First Temple; and *ha-ᶜedut* [479], spelled without a *waw,* is equivalent to the 480 years from the Exodus until Solomon's building of the temple. The reason why the numerical equivalent of *ha-ᶜedut* is actually one less than 480 is that the tabernacle was not built until the second year after the Exodus. All these calculations were seen by Moses through the holy spirit. This is the meaning of *elleh fequde ha-mishkan,* which can be translated, *These are the calculations of the tabernacle.*[41]

All I have said clearly establishes our obligation to believe that God watches providentially over this universe, and that what occurs in it is not accidental, but essentially and originally from God. We should therefore proclaim His unity each day. That is why we find in the recitation of the *Shemaᶜ* the doctrines of both the unity of God and reward and punishment. I will now explain the rabbinic passage that I read at the beginning.[42]

According to my limited understanding, the statement about the tabernacle that I quoted before is intended to teach us how a human being may attain perfection of soul in this realm of darkness, murky fog, and gloom, so that the soul may be bound up in the bundle of life.[43] It asserts that there are four requirements for this goal. The fulfillment of these requirements is the purpose of one's creation. Upon seeing that a person has reached perfection in this realm, God leads him into the world to come, where he is rewarded by God for all his good deeds.[44]

40. Cf. Exod. Rabbah 51:3. The passage is taken from Baḥya.

41. This entire paragraph is taken from Baḥya. According to rabbinic chronology (see B. Yoma 9b), the Second Temple was in existence 420 years. This would require adding 5 (the number of letters in the word *ha-mishkan*) to 415 (the sum of the numerical equivalents of each letter). The 410 years for the First Temple is given in the same source. For the 480 years from the Exodus to the building of Solomon's temple, see 1 Kings 6:1.

42. Having moved from the subject of divine providence to the recitation of the Shemaᶜ, Garçon introduces the rabbinic *maʾamar,* which speaks of Deut. 6:4. It is clear that he actually explained the passage in the oral sermon, but that he did not think it necessary to include this in his written text. This may be because he incorporated these interpretations into a separate work called "Sefer Maʾamarim" (see introduction on Garçon, at n. 5).

43. The "statement" is the one quoted at n. 36. After extensive (and unattributed) use of material from Baḥya, the preacher is now about to give his own homiletical interpretation of the midrash. On "darkness, murky fog, and gloom" as code words for the corporeal element of the human being, see Saperstein, *Decoding,* pp. 63, 65.

44. The critical question for the interpretation of the following passage is whether it is

The four requirements are as follows. First, one must make a sustained effort in matters of the mind, continuing to the point where precise mastery is attained and one's own intellect becomes *daq,* refined and sharpened.[45] This is signified by the verse, *Who spread out the skies* ka-doq, *like fine gauze* (Isa. 40:22), for it is well known that "heavens" alludes to the intellect.

Second, after intellectual probing, including analysis of contradictory assertions about each matter,[46] the investigation must lead to the ability to distinguish between true and false interpretations, for this is necessary if the soul's apprehension is to be true.[47] This is signified by the verse, *It shall divide water from water* (Gen. 1:6), for it is well known that Torah is represented allegorically by water, as we see from the verse, *Whoever is thirsty, come for water* (Isa. 55:1).[48]

Third, after distinguishing between true and false interpretations, the true ones must be collected together and internalized, for they are what endure for a person after death. This is signified by the verse, *Let the waters be gathered into one place, and let the dry land appear* (Gen. 1:9), meaning, let the true interpretation be gathered into one special place, and let there appear *dry land,* referring to false interpretations that contain no moisture at all, but are like a desiccated and lifeless tree.

Fourth, after all this effort has been made in the intellectual realm, the final effort is for the soul to cleave to God who created it and provides it with strength to perform its task.[49] This is signified by the verse *Let birds fly* (Gen. 1:20), meaning, let him soar with his soul and his intellect to cleave to his Creator, as the bird does when it soars upward.

---

speaking about study of philosophy or study of Talmud. Which of these led to perfection of the soul was an issue that continued to divide Spanish Jewry at the time of the expulsion, as it had for centuries before (see, e.g., Profiaṭ Duran, *Maʿaśeh Efod,* intro., pp. 4, 9). The terminology in the following two paragraphs could be used for either discipline. Indeed, it almost seems as if the passage is intentionally ambiguous, so that listeners could understand the preacher in either way.

45. For the "sharpening of the mind" in a philosophical context, see Maimonides, "Eight Chapters," chap. 5; in a talmudic context, see Duran's *Maʿaśeh Efod,* p. 4, and the talmudic passages listed in the sermon by Moscato, at n. 43.

46. The phrase *ḥelqe ha-soter* is a technical term in logic referring to two contradictory propositions (see Joseph Albo, *Sefer ha-ʿIqqarim,* 1:8, 24; Joseph ben David, p. 298, cf. Ravitsky, "Ketab," p. 706; Aboab, pp. 57d, 58a). It was employed in a discussion of talmudic methodology by Isaac Canpanton, *Darke ha-Gemara* (Vilna, 1901), p. 14.

47. For the distinction between true and false as the goal of the intellect in philosophy, see Maimonides' *Guide* 1:2. In talmudic study, see Ḥaim Bentov, "Shiṭat Limmud ha-Talmud bi-Yshivot Saloniqah we-Turqyah," *Sefunot* 13 (1977–78):49–52, and Daniel Boyarin, "Meḥqarim be-Farshanut ha-Talmud shel Megorshe Sefarad," *Sefunot* 17 (1983):169.

48. For the allegorical use of "water" as philosophical knowledge, see Saperstein, *Decoding,* pp. 73–75.

49. This statement would be appropriate both for the philosopher (see *Guide* 3:51) and the talmudist.

This fulfills the ultimate purpose of creation. Human beings were created in order to devote themselves to the service of God and to the Torah. So we find that Solomon wrote, *The end of the matter, all having been heard: {fear God, and keep His commandments, for this is the whole of the human being}* (Eccles. 12:13). The entire world was created only so that human beings could receive God's commandment.[50] Similarly, the verse *God created man* (Gen. 1:27) indicates that this fulfilled the purpose of the world's creation.

When God sees that a person has perfected his soul and fulfilled the purpose of his coming into this realm of being, He takes him into His intimate presence, removing that soul from this realm. Such is the meaning of *the heavens were finished* (Gen. 2:1): the person has completed his intellectual task[51] and done all that is necessary, and now he should be taken before he returns to sin. "It is better that he die innocent. . . ."[52] Joḥanan served as high priest for eighty years, yet at the end of his life he became a Sadducee.[53] The sages said, "Do not believe in yourself [until the day of your death]."[54]

After God has gathered the person to Himself, He makes His goodness radiate into the world to come, bestowing pleasure and reward. This is signified by the verse *God blessed the seventh day* (Gen. 2:3). As you know, the seventh day, Sabbath, alludes to the Garden of Eden, for the sages referred to "a world that is entirely Sabbath," and they said, "One who toils on the day preceding the Sabbath will eat on the Sabbath."[55] After God bestows this reward, the soul remains in a condition of restful bliss in the world to come. This is signified by *for on it He rested* (Gen. 2:3), meaning that the soul will rest and remain tranquil. Such is the significance of the rabbinic statement, as I understand it, to the best of my limited ability.[56]

As an act of lovingkindness toward us, God commanded us to make a tabernacle in which there would be hints of all these things, so that we might perceive them with our senses and ponder their meaning. The tabernacle thereby impels us to take this luminous path leading to perfection of our souls and fulfillment of the purpose of our creation. All this is for our own good.

In order to achieve this perfection at present, when we have no tabernacle, we must wholeheartedly affirm the unity of the Lord our God each day. If

50. Cf. B. Ber 6b.

51. This allegorical interpretation of Gen. 2:1 is based on the assumption, explained three paragraphs back, that "heavens" is a code word for the human intellect.

52. Cf. Midrash Tehillim 27:2; B. Ber 29a.

53. B. Ber 29a.

54. Abot 2:4.

55. B. Sanh 97a; B. AZ 3a.

56. This entire passage interpreting the midrash as referring to four stages in the quest for perfection of the soul was used by the preacher in a different sermon, recorded in the manuscript on fol. 100. See Hacker, p. 80, n. 100; Benayahu, pp. 66–67.

we affirm His unity wholeheartedly, we will be worthy of all that I said at the beginning, in the opening dictum from the Midrash Zohar.[57] May God in His abundant mercy and love have compassion upon us and make atonement for our sins and gather our people, scattered and dispersed. May He rebuild our sacred and glorious temple and bring our triumphant Messiah, speedily and in our days. Amen.

(I, Joseph son of Rabbi Meir Garçon, of blessed memory, prepared this sermon and preached it in Salonika, in the kingdom of Turkey. It is the first sermon I preached after the expulsion from Spain, which came upon us in the kingdom of Portugal. I preached it in the year 5260 of the creation [1500]. May God in His mercies find me worthy of preaching many sermons expounding his Torah. Amen.)

57. This characterization shows that the preacher thought of the Zohar not primarily as a kabbalistic text but as a work of rabbinic midrash. Benayahu's assertion that "a similar use of statements from the Zohar in the manner of rabbinic midrashim, and in such quantity . . . is apparently not to be found again until about 80 years after the expulsion" (p. 57) needs to be modified. The sermons of the Italian rabbi Joseph ben Ḥayyim of Benevento (Parma Heb. MS 2627, [De' Rossi 1398]) from the years 1515–30 regularly use passages from "Midrash ha-Zohar" as the rabbinic statement following the theme-verse from the Torah lesson.

Moses Almosnino

Moses Almosnino was born ca. 1515 to an important family of Aragonese origin that had suffered greatly during the tumultuous years of the Inquisition and the expulsion from Spain. The family tradition, articulated by Moses in a eulogy for his mother in 1570, was that among his immediate ancestors were some who had been burned at the stake and died the death of martyrs.[1] Like many others from the aristocracy of Spanish Jewry, the Almosninos found refuge in Salonika. Moses' father, Baruch, was apparently successful enough in business affairs to become an important patron of Jewish learning. Moses' older brother seems to have taken over the primary responsibility for the family's financial affairs, leaving Moses to cultivate his wide-ranging intellectual interests.

The full bibliography of his writings is an astonishing testament to a mind of great versatility and power.[2] Some would be expected of a rabbi: responsa to legal queries (never collected, but cited by contemporaries), sermons (see below), commentaries on biblical books (*Yede Mosheh* [Salonika, 1572], on the Five Scrolls, as well as commentaries on Proverbs and Job [lost but mentioned in his other works]), supercommentaries on the classical Torah commentaries of Rashi and Abraham ibn Ezra (in manuscript).[3] He wrote a commentary on Abot (*Pirqe Mosheh*), and a book investigating particular subjects in the Torah and the liturgy (*Tefillah le-Mosheh* [both Salonika, 1563]). Other writings of an ethical nature—a commentary on Aristotle's *Ethics,* a commentary on al-Ghazālī's *Intentions of the Philosophers* (both in manuscript), and a Ladino tract accompanied by a treatise on dreams (*Regimiento de la Vida* [Salonika, 1564])—were somewhat more eccentric in his time.

What might not have been predicted at all, however, were his other works. He wrote a commentary, now lost, on part of Aristotle's *Physics.* As a young

1. See *Me'ammeṣ Koaḥ* (Venice, 1588), p. 97; Isaac Molho, "Rabbi Mosheh Almosnino Mebi ha-Ḥerut li-Qehillat Saloniqah ba-Me'ah ha-Shesh-ʿEśreh," *Sinai* 4 (1940–41):246.

2. A complete bibliography is provided by Naphtali Ben-Menachem, "Kitbe Rabbi Mosheh Almosnino," *Sinai* 10 (1946–47): 268–85; much of the following discussion is based on this article.

3. See Naphtali Ben-Menachem, "Tosefet Be'ur ʿal Dibre ha-Rab Abraham ibn ʿEzra ʿal ha-Torah le-Rabbi Mosheh Almosnino," *Sinai* 10 (1946–47): 138–71.

man he wrote two works on astronomy, the first a commentary on *Sphaera mundi* by the thirteenth-century English astronomer John Sacrobosco, and the second a translation of and commentary on *Theorica novae planetarum* by the fifteenth-century German astronomer Georg Peuerbach (both in manuscript). Perhaps most unusual and important as a historical document was a Ladino account, part travelogue, part history, of his political mission to Constantinople, on which he reported in the sermon translated below (*Extremos y Grandezas de Constantinopla* [Madrid, 1638]).[4]

Unlike Solomon Levi, his colleague in Salonika, Almosnino does not seem to have preached every Sabbath. The sermons preserved, like those in Judah Moscato's *Nefuṣot Yehudah,* were delivered on holidays or special Sabbaths (preceding Purim, Passover, the Day of Atonement), on special occasions in the life of the community or the preacher, or as eulogies for members of his family and various notables.[5] His popularity as a preacher is demonstrated by the fact that sermons in his *Me'ammeṣ Koaḥ* (Constantinople, 1582; Venice, 1588) were delivered in seven different synagogues of Salonika, in addition to the great Talmud Torah building, which was supported by the community as a whole.

What remains is clearly only a selection of what Almosnino preached. In one of his extant sermons, he refers to a collection of "sermons on women," all of which have apparently been lost, including one delivered at the end of the thirty-day period of mourning for Doña Gracia Nasi.[6] Yet the combination of a book published during the preacher's lifetime and manuscripts containing both sermons included in the book and others not included provides an unusual resource for understanding the process by which an oral message eventually finds its way into print.[7]

In one case, Almosnino prepared a eulogy for the wife of Meir Arama, to be delivered on a particular occasion, and then abandoned his text entirely, writing an entirely new sermon on the same theme-verse (Exod. 17:16), which he did deliver. The text of the sermon he did not preach is preserved in Moscow Ginzburg MS 1053; the other is in *Me'ammeṣ Koaḥ.* Although several of the sermons in this manuscript purport to be the same as sermons in *Me'ammeṣ Koaḥ,* significant differences can be found. In general, the texts in the manuscript lack the literary polish of their printed counterparts.

4. On this work, see the annotation to the sermon below.

5. For a full list of the sermons in *Me'ammeṣ Koaḥ* and the occasions on which they were delivered, see Ben-Menachem, "Kitbe . . . Almosnino," pp. 273–75.

6. *Me'ammeṣ Koaḥ,* p. 134a; cf. Baron, *SRHJ* 18:83.

7. A preliminary study comparing Moscow Ginzburg MS 1053 with *Me'ammeṣ Koaḥ* has been done by Mordechai Pachter, "Sifrut," app. 3, pp. 510–12; the conclusions that follow are based on these pages. Sermons apparently by Almosnino are also found in Moscow Ginzburg MS 158, fols. 1–71.

Though the sermons in *Me'ammeṣ Koaḥ* preserve many indications of oral delivery, comparison shows that they were reworked by the preacher into a more finished artistic form.

Structurally, Almosnino's sermons develop the formal conventions of the late fifteenth-century Spanish sermon with unprecedented sophistication.[8] This development can be readily seen by comparing Garçon's sermon with Almosnino's. Both are on the same Torah lesson and use the same *nośe,* the first verse of the lesson. Both use the technique of fragmenting the *nośe* and establishing the significance of each fragment in the course of the sermon. But in Garçon's sermon, this technique is applied only to the introductory section, which contains both the conventional hesitation and reasons for preaching and the personal, autobiographical material. After the introduction, Garçon's material becomes quite stereotypical and could even have been taken from a sermon for a totally different occasion.

Almosnino divides the theme-verse in many more ways, and his use of the fragments and repetitions helps to unify the entire discourse. Personal material is not limited to its conventional place in an introduction; it is integrated with exegetical insights throughout the sermon. The interpretation of the rabbinic *ma'amar* cited at the beginning is not a superficial, almost superfluous exercise (frequently omitted from the written text, as in Garçon's sermon), but a complex form, developing content particularly appropriate for the occasion.

One other change is to a length that would undoubtedly seem excessive to most modern readers, and certainly to modern listeners. Of course the occasion for the sermon translated—Almosnino's triumphant return from Constantinople in 1568 with a newly ratified charter of liberty for the Salonika Jewish community, his mission accomplished despite the obstacles and setbacks—invited a leisurely and detailed account.[9] Having endured much hardship for the sake of his people, the preacher could be forgiven for basking in the glory of his accomplishment, even as he argued that all the credit and the gratitude belonged to God.

However, it is not so much the historian's impulse to record the whole story that makes the sermon so long as it is the incorporation of long exegetical passages, especially from Psalms. These are often independent units more appropriate for a commentary than a sermon, and they can be removed without any significant interruption of the sermon's flow. In my translation I have

8. See the discussion by Pachter, "Sifrut," pp. 35–38. Pachter's conclusions are well exemplified by a comparison of the sermons by Garçon and Almosnino, as indicated below.

9. This mission has been discussed frequently by Jewish historians, although I know of no attempt to find confirming evidence in the Ottoman archives. For details of the mission, see the sermon and its annotation below.

made such deletions and indicated each in a note. The sermon as it appears below is approximately half the length of the text in *Me'ammeṣ Koaḥ*.

Sermon on *Elleh Fequde* (1568, Salonika)

1. *The testimony* asher.

2. *Which was recounted by Moses.*

3. *Which was recounted by Moses: the service of the* lewiyyim.

4. *The tabernacle* [is] *the tabernacle of testimony.*

5. *The tabernacle* [is] *the tabernacle of the testimony* asher.

6. *These are the records of the tabernacle, the tabernacle of the testimony, which were recounted by Moses* (Exod. 38:21)[1].

Berakot, chapter 9: "Rab Judah said in the name of Rab, Four need to offer thanksgiving: those who have crossed the sea, those who have gone through the wilderness, one who has been sick and recovered, and one who has been imprisoned and set free.

"Whence do we know this of those who cross the sea? From the biblical verses, *They that go down to the sea in ships . . . these saw the works of the Lord. . . . He raised the stormy wind . . . they rose to the heaven, they went down to the deeps. . . . They reeled to and fro and staggered like a drunkard. . . . They cried to the Lord in their trouble, and He brought them out of their distresses. . . . He made the storm a calm. . . . Then they rejoiced because they were tranquil. . . . Let them give thanks to the Lord for His mercy and for His wonderful works toward human beings* (Ps. 107:23–31).

"Whence for those who go through the wilderness? From the biblical verses, *They wandered in the wilderness in a desert way; they found no city of habitation. . . . Then they cried to the Lord, and He guided them in a direct path. . . . Let them give thanks to the Lord for His mercy* (Ps. 107:4–8).

"One who was sick and recovered? From the verses, *Crazed because of their transgressing way, afflicted because of their iniquities, they abhorred any kind of food. . . . They cried to the Lord in their trouble, and He saved them from their distresses; He sent His word and He cured them. . . . Let them give thanks to the Lord for His mercy and for His wonderful works toward human beings* (Ps. 107:17–21).

"One who was imprisoned and set free? From the verses, *Those who sit in*

1. On this technique of dividing and repeating the theme-verse, see "Structural Options," above.

darkness and gloom . . . for they rebelled against the words of God. . . . He humbled their heart with travail. . . . They cried to the Lord in their trouble. . . . He made them emerge from darkness and gloom. . . . Let them give thanks to the Lord for His mercy (Ps. 107:10–15).

"What blessing should he say? Rab Judah said, 'Blessed is He who bestows lovingkindnesses.' Abbaye said, He needs to offer his thanksgiving in the presence of ten, as it is written, *Let them exalt him in the assembly of the people* (Ps. 107:32). Mar Zuṭra said, Two of them must be rabbis, as it is said, *And in the seat of elders, praise Him* (ibid.)."[2]

I will recount God's acts of love and His great praises, according to all He has done for us, the great goodness for the House of Israel (Isa. 63:7). Through His marvelous providence and compassion for His people, His flock, a charter of liberty called *Musselemlik*[3] has established freedom for all the inhabitants of the land, protecting us against every oppressor, enemy, and antagonist, so that we may be led in the way of the Source of life. I stand here before the august congregation of Israel[4] in this great and holy place to testify to you today about all the hardships that befell us on the way, to proclaim in the heights of your sanctuary the specific manifestations of God's wonderful providence and beneficent mercy.

This is why I said at the beginning, *the testimony* asher, *which was recounted by Moses,* meaning that this testimony, which will be arranged by Moses, is true and enduring. This is *the testimony* asher, the word *asher* in the language of the Talmud means lasting, enduring, as in the phrase *asharta de-dayane,* "the attestation of the judges" (B. Ket 21b). And it is the testimony given in detail by this Moses, your servant.[5]

Truly this testimony I give today will inform you of the service rendered by my dear brothers and friends, who accompanied me on this journey and died in the service of the Almighty. They rest in their graves at peace with God, but they were the source of our glorious and life-giving freedom.

2. The rabbinic statement is from B. Ber 54b.

3. This word apparently refers to a "self-governing political entity independent of the city in which it was situated" (Cecil Roth, *The House of Nasi, the Duke of Naxos* [Philadelphia, 1948], p. 168). On this special status of the Salonika Jewish community, see Mark A. Epstein, "Leadership of the Ottoman Jews," in *Christians and Jews in the Ottoman Empire,* ed. Benjamin Braude and Bernard Lewis, 2 vols. (New York and London, 1982), 1:109.

4. The various congregations of Salonika had gathered for a community-wide event. On the different congregations, see Joseph Hacker, "Ha-Ḥebrah ha-Yehudit be-Saloniqah wa-ʾAgapeha ba-Meʾot ha-Ḥamesh-ʿEśreh we-ha-Shesh-ʿEśreh" (Ph.D. diss., Hebrew University, 1978), pp. 224–25, listing twenty-seven in all; S. W. Baron, *SRHJ* 18:38, 55–56, 62, 70.

5. The word *asher* in the first phrase is read not as a relative pronoun ("that") but as a predicate adjective, based on the talmudic meaning of *le-ʾasher,* "to confirm." The "Moses" in the phrase is, of course, the preacher.

Therefore I say as a third meaning, *which was recounted by Moses: the service of the* lewiyyim—this testimony, given in detail by your servant Moses, recounts the service of those who have drawn near to the Lord, those who accompanied me. I was the least of them, may their memory be for blessing. This is the *service of the* lewiyyim, "those who accompanied. . . ."[6]

At the very beginning, as I tell of my deeds in honor of the King of kings, I say that on my journey I saw the concrete evidence of His providence over each and every step. God arranged it all. I discovered that what seemed to us to be chance events opposing our purpose turned out to be for our good, helping us to accomplish our vital task.[7] We should therefore give thanks and praise to God for the individual providence He bestows upon us. It may therefore be truly said that the tabernacle of our city testifies to glory and splendor: that His presence dwells among us. This is the fourth meaning I gave at the beginning: *the tabernacle* [is] *the tabernacle of testimony*—from this day on, our dwelling place is a tabernacle of testimony and of instruction that God makes His name and His presence reside among us now.[8]

Therefore I can truly say what Deborah did in her beautiful song: *Hear me, you kings, give ear, o princes: I am the Lord's, I shall sing, I shall raise a psalm to the Lord, the God of Israel* (Judg. 5:3). *Hear me, you kings* refers to the rabbis, who are called "kings";[9] *give ear, o princes,* nurtured in the purple of perfection, and learn from me a marvelous lesson, proclaiming His wonderful providence. What I shall sing is not the victory itself, but the emanation of that victory from God. This is what shows that *I am the Lord's,* for He watches over me. The words *I am the Lord's, I shall sing* mean, the subject of my song is my belonging to God, cleaving to Him because He watches over me. And truly, *I shall raise a psalm to the Lord,* in addition to that which pertains to me individually, because of His encompassing providence for all Israel. This is the meaning of *to the Lord, the God of Israel:* I shall raise a psalm to the Lord because He is the God of Israel, watching over each Jew individually with great power, unlike the other nations that deny him. . . .[10]

6. *Lewiyyim* is read not as "Levites" but as "the ones who accompanied," from the root *lwh*. Omitted is a brief repetitive passage.

7. This is the central thesis of the sermon. Theologically, it affirms the doctrine that God's providence extends to everything that occurs. Politically, the preacher is beginning to lay the foundations for a case in his own defense against those who accused him of bungling. The following sentence, an exhortative conclusion, is clearly linked with the rabbinic statement cited at the beginning, to which the preacher will later return.

8. In this interpretation, "tabernacle" is understood to refer to the city of Salonika.

9. Cf. B. Giṭ 62a.

10. I.e., the Jews enjoy individual providence, while the fate of the nations is guided by a general providence effected through the stars. This was a commonplace of medieval Jewish thought. Omitted is a long section (p. 3b bottom to p. 5b middle) interpreting all of Deut. 32 and Isa. 55:6–10.

Now I have experienced this. For God has guided me on the path to a success resulting not from my own decisions and choice but from His wonderful providence. Five times our endeavor was stymied, and we wept and moaned, for despite what we judged to be all the preparation possible, the result was not what we wanted. But God had set obstacles in our path to frustrate our efforts. Our hearts choked and our eyes grew dim as we concluded that our sins had upset our plans. Later, as we returned on the sixth attempt, we realized that if the project had succeeded on any of the five previous occasions, everything could easily have been ruined. I have discussed this at length, recounting in order all that occurred to us from our departure to my return, in my Ladino report.[11]

On the night of the twenty-fifth of Shebat of this year, the year of the verse *Yeᶜerab ᶜalaw śiḥi* (Ps. 104:32), 5328 [1568],[12] my daughter gave birth in Adrianople to a baby boy. That night I could not sleep. Toward morning, I dozed off briefly; dreaming, I uttered a complete verse out loud: *O happy Israel! Who is like you, a people delivered by the Lord, the shield your help, the sword your triumph. Your enemies shall come cringing before you, and you shall tread on their backs* (Deut. 33:29). Those who were standing around heard me and awakened me saying, "Get up, give thanks to God, for it is a day of good tidings. You yourself can accomplish them, with God's help."

On that very day we went before the sultan's gate, and the content of the document containing our request was read before the sultan; on that day he commanded that the entire charter be confirmed. We returned home with hearts singing for joy. It was a time of favor, the hour when all our desires were fulfilled through the life-preserving charter of liberty. Then we realized that if the matter had been concluded earlier, on one of the previous five attempts, and if the decrees had not been postponed through God's providence, we would have all been lost. All our efforts would have been fruitless, and our good intentions to no avail.

Thus I understood correctly the verse I had called out that night in my dream. I realized that through a true dream it was proclaimed that the entire

11. Almosnino is referring to a tract that he wrote during his stay in Constantinople, 1566–68; his own mission is described on pp. 199–239. The original Ladino tract exists in manuscript; see *Fontes Ambrosiani* 45, *Hebraica Ambrosiana* (Milan, 1972), no. 45; it was described by Moses Lattes, whose father owned it, in "Della cronaca turca di M. Almosnino secondo l'originaria sua forma ed il testo manoscritto," *Mosè* 1 (1878):378–84. It was published in Spanish, in a partially revised form that omitted most of the material about his own mission, as *Extremas y Grandezas de Constantinopla* (Madrid, 1638).

12. The numerical equivalent of the letters in the word *śiḥi* add up to 328, referring to the year 5328 (1568). This technique of citing a year by means of a word or phrase from the Bible was common, especially on title pages. The personal, autobiographical material is intended to strengthen the argument that every aspect of Almosnino's mission was part of God's plan.

community of Jews in Salonika is truly blessed and worthy, peerless in the exile of this people, liberated not by their own efforts but by the Lord. This is the meaning of *a people delivered by the Lord.*[13] I would say that *the shield your help* refers to the obstacles, which are like a shield that prevents something from passing and fulfilling its purpose (all this is implied by the word *magen,* "shield"), diverting and interrupting something on the way. All of this became helpful and beneficial, as we have explained.[14]

Furthermore, that which was harmful to us—the *avariz* of 50,000 aspers per year asked of us on the fifth time, and also the sum of 300,000 aspers demanded on the sixth time as an advance payment,[15] which seemed to be an avenging sword threatening our covenant of hope—turned out to be for our benefit, raising us up exalted above all other inhabitants of the city, ensuring that our freedom would be more enduring than theirs. This is the meaning of *the sword your triumph:* the sword standing against us became a life-preserving source of exaltation, as occurred on that day. And it said that our enemies, who thought that we would achieve nothing now, would come cringing to us, and we would actually exceed them in our freedom. This is the meaning of *you shall tread on their backs.*

Now in this manner I interpret Psalm 14. . . .[16]

Based on what I have said, you can see how the details of our activities on this journey reveal God's individual providence, for everything resulted from Him. Furthermore, after careful reflection, we discovered that the numbers pertaining to all the participants in this venture, from beginning to end, were all connected with the letters *alef, heh, waw, yod,* the letters of the Divine Name. R. Abraham ibn Ezra dwelt at length on the properties of

13. I.e., the phrase *ʿam noshaʿ ba-ʾadonai* ("a people liberated by the Lord") refers to the Jewish community of Salonika.

14. That which appeared to be an obstacle (*magen,* lit. "shield," but something that deflects from its purpose) turned out to help us.

15. Although the passage is not as clear as it might be, it seems that Almosnino was able to avoid the obligation of an annual payment of 50,000 aspers and attain a confirmation of the charter for a one-time outright payment of 300,000 aspers. For the purchasing power of these amounts, see Morris Goodblatt, *Jewish Life in Turkey in the XVIth Century* (New York, 1952), pp. 58–60, 64, 68: Ḥaim Gerber, *Yehude ha-Imperyah ha-Otomanit* (Jerusalem, 1983), pp. 28, 41, 90–92, 150; Suraiya Faroqhi, "Taxation and Urban Activities in Sixteenth-Century Anatolia," *International Journal of Turkish Studies* 1 (1979–80):30–35. The Hebrew text contains the word *firiś(h)*; compare the term *azfiriś(h)* in *Teshubot ha-MaBIṬ* 2:79, cited in Gerber, p. 147. According to Bernard Lewis, this is a corruption of the Turkish *avariz,* a special levy or tax ("The Privilege Granted by Meḥmed II, to His Physician," *Bulletin of the School of Oriental and African Studies* 14 [1952]:552. I am grateful to Benjamin Braude for his help on this Turkish term.)

16. Omitted is a section (p. 6a middle to p. 7a top) of exegetical material on Ps. 14. Almosnino's extensive use of such psalm exegesis in his sermons has been noted and discussed by Pachter, "Sifrut," pp. 37–38, n. 44. See also below, at n. 37.

these numbers in his commentary on Exodus 3:15 and the end of Exodus 33, as I have discussed in detail in my supercommentary on those passages.[17] All this teaches us that what happened was not accident or chance, but resulted from God through His wonderful providence.

The number *one* is God Himself, for He is one and His Name is one. He carefully ordained our entire journey, guiding us in our path from beginning to end in order to bring deliverance to this His people. *And their king goes before them* (Mic. 2:13): this is our lord, His Majesty the sultan. God arranged providentially that he would be king from beginning to end. Even when his father was alive, he was the one with authority over all that pertained to the beginning of our renowned victory, as can be seen from the first decree he gave us. And God brought it about that the son would reign in place of his father before the completion of our task, so that our entire venture would be under one king.[18] This is the power of *alef,* one.

Those who acted as intermediaries were five, from beginning to end, not more nor fewer. First was the noble duke Don Joseph Nasi. We first approached him while the sultan's father was still alive, as I said. He showed wondrous kindness to us, helping us from beginning to end.[19] Second was the wise physician, R. Judah de Segura, who helped us with the imperial treasurer[20] at the beginning and at the end.

The third was the clever and influential R. Abraham Salama; in his great kindness he interceded for us with the grand mufti,[21] through whom the matter was brought to a conclusion. They were our spokesmen before His Excellency the grand vizier. The fourth was the wise R. Meir ibn Sanche; he planned our strategy with wisdom and kindness; through his advice and his

17. With these passages in ibn Ezra's *Torah Commentary,* compare his *Sefer ha-Shem* (Fuerth, 1834), pp. 6b–7a. One of the properties of the numbers 1, 5, 6, and 10 (equivalent to *alef, heh, waw, yod*) is that they alone always appear at the end of any exponential power of themselves. Almosnino's supercommentary on ibn Ezra is extant only through Gen. 29:27 (Oxford Bodleian MS 234). See Naphtali Ben-Menachem, "Tosefet Be'ur . . . le-Rabbi Mosheh Almosnino," *Sinai* 10 (1946–47):137.

18. Almosnino arrived in Constantinople and began his negotiations in the spring of 1566, shortly before Suleiman left the city on his Hungarian campaign. The sultan died on the night of September 5, 1566, outside of Szigetvár. Thus he was never directly involved in the negotiations, and Almosnino could argue that only Selim II had been responsible. See Roger Merriman, *Suleiman the Magnificent* (Cambridge, 1944), pp. 286–89.

19. On Joseph Nasi, see, most recently, Baron, *SRHJ* 18:84–118, and the bibliography in the relevant notes. The appointment of Joseph as duke of Naxos was one of the first acts of the new sultan, Selim II, and this appointment was described by Almosnino in his Ladino tract.

20. The Hebrew text contains the Turkish word *defterdar*; on this position, see Albert Lybyer, *The Government of the Ottoman Empire in the Time of Suleiman the Magnificent* (Cambridge, 1913), pp. 167–68.

21. The Hebrew text contains the Turkish word *nazir*; see Lybyer, p. 201.

effort his lamp shone over our heads, may God reward him fully. The last is most precious: the blessed noble and physician R. Joseph Hamon,[22] who kept the matter secret and sealed it, praise be to God. This is the power of *heh,* five.

The viziers in the royal court, through whose intercession the matter was concluded, were *six,* as is known. The first is His Excellency the grand vizier Meḥmed [Sokolli] Pasha, son-in-law of the sultan.[23] The second was Pertev Meḥmed Pasha. The third was Ferhad Pasha, the fourth Aḥmed Pasha, the fifth Piale Pasha, son-in-law of His Majesty the sultan. The sixth was Maḥmud Pasha, called Zulficar Pasha, another son-in-law of the sultan.[24]

Five times we were ready to conclude the matter with the sultan and his viziers, but it was not concluded until the sixth time. Then we realized that had it been concluded previously, it would not have been sustained as it was this last time, with a commitment of 300,000 aspers as a [one-time] advance payment, for all was arranged by God. He commanded the blessing of eternal life through this number, six, that is perfect by being equal in its parts, as R. Abraham ibn Ezra explained in his commentary on Exodus.[25] This is the power of *waw,* six.

After careful review of all the intermediaries, the number ten is also to be found. For those in the royal court were ten when counted in a different way: the six viziers and the four royal scribes who signed our charter of liberty. Similarly, ten Jewish leaders were involved in this project. At first there were seven elected officers here, and we were three, making ten. After the death of the great scholars R. Jacob and R. Moses Baruk, may their souls rest in Eden, the elected officials added two more, making nine. And God arranged that R. Shem Ṭob Surnag, chosen by his people for glory, be sent to join me when I remained alone.[26] Thus we were ten; this is the power of *yod,* ten.

From all this you see God's marvelous providence over all the intricacies of our venture, see that we are a people delivered through His providence,

22. Joseph Hamon was the son of Moses, one of the most important court physicians of Suleiman. See Baron, *SRHJ* 18:72–77, and the bibliography in n. 32 on p. 470 of that volume. Judah de Segura was appointed with Joseph Hamon as royal physician after the death of Moses. On the ibn Sanche family, see Jacob Siegal in *Sinai* 47 (1983):183–85. Cf. Roth, *House of Nasi,* p. 167.

23. Meḥmed Sokolli, grand vizier from 1565 to 1579, was one of the most effective and powerful men to hold this position. On him, see Moritz Brosch, *Geschichte aus dem Leben dreier Grosswesire* (Gotha, 1899), pp. 1–69; Merriman, *Suleiman the Magnificent,* p. 290; Baron, *SRHJ* 18:47, 87, 101, 128.

24. Cf. Almosnino's fuller characterization of Ferhad, Pertev, Aḥmed, and Maḥmud in *Extremas y Grandezas de Constantinopla,* pp. 134–35, 168. Piale was the well-known admiral of the Turkish fleet.

25. I.e., the sum of its factors is equal to the product of its factors ($1 \times 2 \times 3 = 1 + 2 + 3 = 6$).

26. See the characterizations in Roth, *House of Nasi,* p. 166. He identifies "R. Jacob" as ibn Naḥmias; on the latter, cf. Naphtali Ben-Menachem, "Kitbe," *Sinai* 10 (1946–47):283.

and that all the participants fit the numbers corresponding to the letters of His name. It is absolutely correct that we were delivered through His name, as I saw in my dream.[27] We must therefore praise the One who created us for His glory, Who has shown us such great favor. From this day forth we need not fear our many constant enemies. And the recalcitrant among our own people, who to this very day refuse to heed [communal] discipline, will submit and pay homage to the glory of our people and the synagogue, all accepting the yoke of rabbinical rule—"For who are kings? The rabbis"[28]—following their wise and beneficial decisions.[29]

When influential Jews join together, they are strong enough to provide the leadership needed in this city. They have not previously had this strength, fearing those who, without grounds and in violation of Jewish law, informed about their money to the authorities.[30] But when many are joined and united, they are far stronger than when they are separate and scattered. You can see this in the power of many voices: the more there are, the greater the power [when raised in unison], and they can be heard far away. This is analogous to the power in many congregations.

A concise expression of this idea is the rabbinic statement, "When the righteous gather together, it is good for them and good for the world."[31] So it is in the nature of all things to become stronger and more difficult to break when they are bound together. A single piece of wood may be easily broken by one man, but if you take ten such pieces and put them together, even ten men exerting all their strength at once may be unable to break them. The same is true of other things. Interpreting the verse *A king's glory lies in the multitude of his people* (Prov. 14:28) with the comment "a king with many subjects is more praiseworthy than a king with few," the rabbis referred to the power of unity when there are many separate parts.[32]

That is why we find in the account of creation that after each separate creative act it says, *it was good,* but at the completion of the entire task it says, *God saw all He had done, and behold, it was very good* (Gen. 1:31). This shows that when God saw the totality of all created things, arranged in the proper order, interacting with each other, He saw a special goodness in the

27. I.e., *ʿam noshaʿ ba-ʾadonai* (Deut. 33:29) in the dream means, "the people delivered by the numbers [1, 5, 6, 10] signified by the letters of the Divine Name."

28. B. Giṭ 62a.

29. This may be a reference to the problem of Salonikan Jews' ignoring rabbinic jurisdiction and turning to Muslim courts; see Goodblatt, pp. 87–88, 122.

30. Although such informing was a perennial problem for medieval Jewish communities, according to Goodblatt, very few instances of Jewish informers are mentioned in the responsa of Samuel de Medina (p. 104).

31. B. Sanh 71b (the Hebrew quotation is a paraphrase of the original).

32. I have not succeeded in finding this exact interpretation of Prov. 14:28 in the rabbinic literature.

totality that transcended the value of each separate entity. This seems to me a fine interpretation of the nuance in the verse. The rabbis alluded to this in the statement that God was called complete when the world was complete.[33] Although God was in essence perfectly complete already, He described Himself with a complete name when He was exalted and praised by the beautifully ordered interaction of all created things, the foundation of the perfection of the world which, in its entirety, gives glory to God.

I believe this is also the explanation of a very profound and perplexing statement from a rabbinic Midrash discussed briefly and allusively by R. Abraham ibn Ezra in his book *Yesod Mora*: "Said R. Ishmael, 'Whosoever knows the dimension of the Creator is assured of belonging to the world to come, and ʿAqiba and I guarantee this.' "[34] He said this as an explanation of *Shiʿur Qomah.* But the true meaning becomes clear from what we said. "The dimension of the Creator" refers to the order and unity and relatedness of all things, from the beginning, the First Cause, to the lowliest beings. He said that one who knows this cleaves to God and reflects upon Him properly, and that through this communion he becomes assured beyond doubt of belonging to the world to come. R. Ishmael meditated upon this in seclusion with R. ʿAqiba his colleague, and thus the two of them envisioned the spiritual realm during their lives. That is why he said that he and ʿAqiba would guarantee the supreme pleasure they had envisioned.

I too am assured that these, God's people, who have seen all these signs and marvels through His wonderful providence over them, will all cleave perpetually to the Lord their God. They will come together to serve Him in unity, ultimately beholding the spiritual realm during their lives and deriving pleasure from the splendor of the divine presence. Then their tabernacle will be . . . ,[35] the special place for His Torah. That is why I said at the beginning for the fifth meaning of the verse, *the tabernacle, the tabernacle of the testimony* asher, namely, this tabernacle, the dwelling place of these God's people—whether referring to the entire city or to this great and holy house of the *Ḥebrat Talmud Torah,* the glory of our city—is the tabernacle of Torah, a blessed tabernacle. This is *the tabernacle of the testimony* asher, from *osher,* "blessedness."[36]

33. Gen. Rabbah 13:3.

34. Abraham ibn Ezra, *Yesod Mora* (Prague, 1833), end of chap. 12, p. 43. For a convenient summary of medieval attitudes toward this work, see Alexander Altmann, "Moses Narboni's 'Epistle on *Shiʿur Qoma,*' " *Jewish Medieval and Renaissance Studies* (Cambridge, Mass., 1967), pp. 226–38. Almosnino follows the philosophical tradition that *Shiʿur Qomah,* the "dimension of the Creator" cannot refer to God's body, as would appear to be the simple meaning of the text.

35. About five words of the printed text are blotted so as to be illegible, possibly in an act of censorship.

36. On the *Ḥebrat Talmud Torah,* see Goodblatt, pp. 20–21 and Baron, *SRHJ* 18:552,

All of us together could say Psalm 27, composed by David, beginning, *The Lord is my light and my victory; whom shall I fear?* Our explanation of this psalm reveals the praises of God's precious congregation that dwells in this city. . . .[37]

Now each of us living in this city could say this psalm about ourselves, collectively and individually. I certainly apply it to myself. *The Lord is my light and my victory; whom shall I fear?* (Ps. 27:1a), for He illumined a path for me and guided me as I traveled, bringing me total victory. I will therefore not fear the masses. *He is the strength of my life; whom shall I dread?* (Ps. 27:1b). From this day forth, *when evildoers close in on me to devour me* (Ps. 27:2a) as they have done until now, rising to destroy us through slanderous informing,[38] it will redound to my own benefit, for I shall take vengeance upon them, and we will be recompensed even for past troubles already forgotten. In this way *my enemies, my assailants will stumble and fall* (Ps. 27:2b).

I can therefore say that from this day on, *if an enemy should encamp against me, my heart will feel no fear; if a battle arises against me, I shall be secure* (Ps. 27:3) in this triumph, by which God's cause prospers in our hands. From now on *there is one thing I ask of God* in my prayer as I praise Him: *that I may dwell in this House of God* whatever time remains in my life, devoted to the study of Jewish law in all its array, faithfully kept, a source of clarity and illumination for me. I have had enough of traveling. I yearn to dwell in God's House, *to gaze upon His beauty, to seek Him in His temple* (Ps. 27:4) which is all to His glory.

As for material goods, if He should graciously lavish them upon me, *I shall sing to Him and praise Him with psalms* (Ps. 27:6c), but this is not the essence of my request. It is rather that I dwell in God's House: in my Torah academy, the source of my glory, which raises my head high in personal triumph. I understand the two following verses (Ps. 27:5–6) to mean, when God does me all these favors, hiding me in His pavilion [the academy] at a time of misfortune to come, *my head will be raised high above my enemies around me, and I shall offer jubilant sacrifices in his tent,* rejoicing for the many material benefits mentioned. For all this, *I shall sing songs of praise to God,* who has graciously lavished upon me all I could want.

Yet my prayer is only for essential inner good, and therefore I say, *O Lord, hear my voice beseeching, respond favorably and answer me* (Ps. 27:7). What I ask is to dwell in God's House. For the other favors I sing songs of praise, but

---

n. 113. This is the fifth interpretation given for a section of the theme-verse, based on yet another meaning of the root *ʾshr.*

37. The interpretation of Ps. 27, here omitted, goes from p. 8b top through p. 11b bottom.

38. *Mesirut u-malshinut*; cf. above, n. 30. The motif of opposition to the preacher, underlined by his choice of a psalm for explication, here becomes more explicit.

my true prayer is for the fulfillment of my request to dwell in God's house. This will be fulfilled when You hear my voice as I implore, and respond in the fullness of Your favor and answer me.

On Your behalf, my heart and my inner spirit said, *seek My face*; I shall indeed seek Your Presence (Ps. 27:8) throughout my life. I pray to You, O God, *Do not hide Your face from me, never turn away in wrath from Your servant, for you have been my help* on this journey. *Do not leave or abandon me, O God my deliverance* (Ps. 27:9). Although *my father and mother* (the source of my physical being) *have left me and drawn away, God will gather me up* (Ps. 27:10) for the world to come, for He has given me my soul, upon which the ultimate and true perfection depends. This is the meaning of *God will gather me up*: He will gather me up to Him, for He gathers my spirit and soul to Himself. I shall therefore strive throughout my life toward spiritual perfection.

That is why I pray further to God, *Teach me Your ways, O Lord,* namely, the way of spiritual perfection, the true intellectual contemplation called "God's way," and also perfection in actions: *guide me in a level path because of those who observe me* (Ps. 27:11). This means, my request that I not stumble in my actions, that You *guide me in a level path,* is *because of those who observe me.* I am not at all interested in those who observe me with regard to my intellectual activity, for this is something between myself and God. But as for publicly known actions affecting other human beings, I ask for guidance *because of those who observe me.*

Furthermore, I pray that God will not give me over to the greed of my foes, who maliciously sin against me, plotting ill. *For false witnesses have risen against me, breathing malice* (Ps. 27:12), charging that I lingered there [in Constantinople] not in order to attain our charter of liberty, but rather to profit in my business affairs! Their "proof" was that the charter of liberty was not forthcoming, as they wrote to me there each day.[39] *If I had not believed that I would see the goodness of the Lord in the land of the living* (Ps. 27:13) as a reward for my effort and toil, and therefore remained with this task until the very end, their claims and "testimony" might have been almost credible.

That is why, wherever I have seen weakness and drunkenness and corruption in our time, I have always said to myself *Wait for the Lord, be strong, take courage* (Ps. 27:14). Even when this affair was so prolonged and delayed, I still said to myself, *Wait for the Lord.* And my living God fulfilled my hope—all praise to Him—gagging the mouths of the liars, and rewarding me for my honesty and integrity throughout this entire journey. He has repaid me

39. The Hebrew syntax is not entirely clear, but it is apparent that Almosnino was the object of considerable criticism during the time he spent in Constantinople, so one function of his sermon was to quell opposition in his own community. It is unclear whether the letters mentioned came from opponents or friends.

fairly, and He will requite the evildoers for their wickedness. May the Lord of Israel reduce them to silence!

Now I turn to you who draw near to the Lord, lest one of the listeners before whom I have recounted the tale of my toil on this journey suspect me of having spoken for my own benefit and aggrandizement, out of hope or desire for financial reward, God forbid! I lift my hands to heaven and say that whatever material benefit may accrue to me because of my toil and travail on this journey from the day I left this city of these holy congregations shall be offered in sacrifice to God, from this time forth.[40] I have enough to sustain myself, praise to my living God!

This is my request of you, our congregations, glory of Israel: fulfill these three wishes as my reward. First, for the future welfare of the city, make assessments in each of the sacred congregations.[41] I know full well that without this there will be strife rather than peace based upon equity. It is a terrible offense, oppressing the poor, perverting right and justice in this land.

Second, for the welfare and purity of the soul, appoint men as guardians of moral standards to remove the thorns from the vineyard of the Lord, the house of Israel.[42] Third, let me remain in my academy, never again burdened to join my dedicated colleagues in their public responsibilities. I can no longer bear that burden; old age has taken its toll.[43] Though my place will be empty in the council of sages nurtured in the purple of truth and justice to repair the breaches of our glorious city, nothing will be lost. May the One who takes the clouds for His chariot enable you to ride on heights of true success. May you dwell in prosperity amid praise, for God has bestowed His wondrous providence upon you, favoring the remnant, preserving your lives on this day.

The traditional text of the Bible may contain a hint of this. I have discovered that the word *moshabeka* [lit. "dwelling place"] occurs three times in the Bible. The first is etan moshabeka, *your refuge, secure* (Num. 24:21); the second is yippaqed moshabeka, *your place is empty* (1 Sam. 20:18); the third is mi-shemane ha-ʾareṣ yihyeh moshabeka, *Your dwelling shall be from the richness*

40. This would appear to indicate that Almosnino did engage in business ventures while in Constantinople.

41. The reference is apparently to the problem of assessing the amount of liability for taxation to meet the community's obligations. Each congregation had its own board of assessors (Goodblatt, pp. 78–79). On the problem in general, see Baron, *The Jewish Community,* 3 vols. (Philadelphia, 1942), 2:279–89.

42. *Memunne ʿaberot.* The idea of this institution goes back at least to thirteenth-century Spain; see Baer, *HJCS* 1:252, 258; Baron, *The Jewish Community,* 2:313.

43. Almosnino was only fifty years old at the time. However, in a sermon delivered about two years later, he said, "I have grown old and gray, and from this point on, I and my contemporaries over fifty must devote ourselves to study" (in preparation for death) (*Meʾammeṣ Koaḥ,* p. 109, quoted by Isaac Molho, in *Sinai* 4 [1940–41]:247).

of the land (Gen. 27:39).[44] I have written and preached on a different occasion that this textual tradition can be applied to human perfection. When a person strives in this world to perfect his *moshab* or essential condition by perfecting his soul, then even when he dies and his *moshab* is empty in this world, his *moshab* will be from the richness of the land—the land of eternal life—for the word *ha-ʾareṣ* may refer to the land of eternal life.

But this tradition may also contain a hint of my request. I have striven in this burdensome endeavor with all my strength and ability, and God's compassion upon us has made our *moshab* in this city permanently secure. Thus even if my *moshab* will be empty of the leadership I exerted in my prime, because of my infirmity at this time, your *moshab* will be from the richness of the land. With God's help, nothing will be lacking. This is the sixth meaning I said at the beginning: *These are the records of the tabernacle, the tabernacle of the testimony, which were recounted by Moses.* I have pondered the specific manifestations of God's providence on this journey and examined the help given by noble intermediaries (for many worked with me beneficially, as I described), and I have found no shortcoming except that it has been *recounted by Moses,* your servant, when there was truly need for a tongue capable of doing justice to the grandeur of these events and filling the world with their praise.[45]

I come now to explain the rabbinic statement with which I began. In order to understand fully the meaning of the rabbis, I will indicate some problems readily discernible by all who examine this statement.[46] The first is an enormous problem for me: why did they not say, "Four *must* offer thanksgiving"? After all, it is an obligation to give thanks, as we learn from the psalm which is the basis for the entire passage: *Let them give thanks to the Lord for His mercy* (Ps. 107:8, 15, 21, 31).

44. See the *Masorah Magna* on Gen. 27:39. The use of the Masorah for homiletical purposes is noteworthy; the technique requires that each biblical occurrence of a particular word be integrated into a coherent assertion. Early evidence of this technique is provided in the work "Ṭaʿame Masoret ha-Miqra" by Meir of Rothenburg; see *MaHaRaM mi-Rotenburg: Teshubot, Pesaqim, u-Minhagim,* ed. Isaac Kahana, 3 vols. (Jerusalem, 1957), 1:5–41 (a particularly good example is on p. 39). This collection of homiletical interpretations may have been used by preachers. For examples of use in actual sermons, see Alkabeẓ, fol. 5v; Modena, *Midbar,* p. 77b; Rapoport, p. 52d; *Binat Yiśśakar,* frequently throughout. In this case, the preacher gives two different possibilities, one that he has used before, the other new for this occasion.

45. In the sixth interpretation of the theme-verse, the word *puqqad* is understood to imply a failing or lack, suggested by *yippaqed moshabeka* ("your place is empty"), just discussed.

46. This technique of addressing a rabbinic statement by raising difficulties and then solving them was a favorite homiletical and exegetical practice from the late fifteenth century (if not earlier) on. See "Structural Options," above, and Shem Ṭob ibn Shem Ṭob's sermon, at n. 3.

The second problem: why did they not retain the order of the biblical verses? The psalm says first, *they wandered in the wilderness,* then it speaks of the prisoner, then of the person who is sick, and then of those who go to sea. The Tosafot on this chapter recognized this problem and suggested the solution that the psalm placed the most dangerous condition first, while the Talmud placed the most common condition first.[47] Yet we must still ask why the Talmud did not put the most dangerous condition first, as the psalm did. The problem with the Tosafot is even greater, since it truly seems that going to sea is the most dangerous condition of all. Indeed, in my view, the Tosafot would have been more correct had they said precisely the opposite: that the Talmud placed the most dangerous condition first, and the psalm the most common.

The third problem: why did they not say, "those who go to sea *and come to shore,* and those who travel through the wilderness *and reach their destination,*" which would give the reason for their thanksgiving, parallel to "one who has been sick and recovered, and one who was imprisoned and set free," in the past tense? From their failure to say "and come to shore" or "and reached their destination" it would seem that they have to offer thanks while they are still at sea or in the wilderness, while this is not true for one who is sick or in prison. Fourth, why did they mention "those who go to sea and those who travel in the wilderness," plural, while "one who is sick" and "one who is imprisoned" are singular?

The fifth problem: why did they quote from the psalm more extensively for those who go to sea than they did for the others? Sixth, why did Rab Judah say, "Blessed is He who bestows lovingkindnesses," a general blessing? He should say as an individual, "Blessed is He who has bestowed this lovingkindness upon me." Why should he be concerned [in this context] with the favors God has done to others so as to include them in his blessing?

Seventh, Abbaye's statement, which follows ["He must utter his thanksgiving in the presence of ten"], may seem to apply to what Rab Judah said, but the two statements are not at all similar. Rab Judah never referred to the question before whom the blessing must be said, only to the formulation of the blessing, so they are talking about totally different things. Furthermore, the thought that underlies the statements of Abbaye and Mar Zuṭra should be explained: why do they hold that one must offer thanks in the presence of ten? Should it not fulfill one's obligation to say the blessing in God's presence alone?

We shall solve these problems one by one, as I am fond of doing. As for the first problem, I refer to the basic thesis I explored at the beginning of this sermon: that recognizing and publicizing the specific manifestations of

47. Tosafot B. Ber 54b, s.v. "Arbaʿah."

God's great and loving providence is extremely beneficial. Of course there is the obligation of thanking God and uttering a blessing with the divine Name for everything good received from Him, whenever it may be, so that all may recognize that God watches providentially over individuals and communities. But in addition, such thanksgiving will guide and direct the speaker in straight paths leading to true felicity. For those who recognize that all is arranged by God's providence will themselves strive to be moral in God's sight, and God will then direct them properly.

That is why Rab said that these four categories have not only an obligation to give thanks, which is clear from the biblical verses and need not even be mentioned, but also a great need to give thanks, so that such benefits might occur to them again. He therefore said, "Four *need* to offer thanksgiving." If he had said, "Four are required to offer thanksgiving," it might have implied that there was no inner need, only the fulfillment of an obligation derived from what had happened to them. By saying "need," he taught that in addition to the obligation there is a need for thanksgiving, which benefits the person involved, helping him to understand and acknowledge that all is arranged by God. Uttering the blessing and giving thanks for God's individual providence that bestows lovingkindness will benefit both him and others in the future, leading to the acquisition of firm, true faith, based on experience, in God's marvelous providence over particular human actions.

This basic principle and thesis are explained in the psalm itself, for after speaking of thanksgiving in each of the four cases, it says, *Whoso is wise, let him preserve these things, they will consider the mercies of the Lord* (Ps. 107:43). This means that the wise man will preserve these miracles in his memory, for it will benefit him when similar things occur to him on another occasion, as he recalls how he learned that all is arranged by God through wondrous individual providence. This is then explained: *they will consider the mercies of the Lord.* It means, when the wise man remembers these things after they have occurred to him, in thinking of them he will be mindful of the acts of love which God performs for those of His creatures who serve Him and do His will. This is the meaning of *they will consider the mercies of the Lord.* In this way the first problem is solved.

In addition to the person's individual need, he should speak publicly because of the benefit accruing to others when God's marvelous providence is made known. This is indicated by the verse, *The upright see it and rejoice* (Ps. 107:42). It means that the upright will see the wondrous miracles and rejoice profoundly at the evidence of the goodness of the divine order, expressed through His individual providence over all the paths of the perfect. *And iniquity,* which stands for "the person of iniquity" as R. David Kimḥi explained, will no longer have any basis for speaking against providence, as he used to do. When the true order of God's providence is seen, such a person will not rejoice like the upright but grow sad, and then he will *stop up his mouth,* having no basis for refutation or dispute.

Because of all these benefits to be derived from public statements—the sanctification of God's Name, the resulting benefit to the inner lives of the upright, and the confounding of the wicked who are compelled to concede God's providence—the sages ordained that the blessing be phrased in general terms. The public recounting of thanks will benefit many over and above the benefit already resulting in the experience of the individual who gives thanks. This is the solution to the sixth problem: since this private good leads to a public acknowledgment of all the good done by God, the blessing is formulated in general terms.

That is why Abbaye's statement, that "he needs to offer thanks in the presence of ten," fits well with the text of the benediction explained by Rab Judah, and this is the solution to the seventh problem. Abbaye understood Rab Judah's purpose in the general formulation: to acknowledge that the blessing experienced by the individual is part of the general order derived from God's all-encompassing individual providence. He therefore said that one must offer thanks in the presence of ten, so that the incident would be made public and the benefit of this dissemination accrue to many.

Mar Zuṭra said that two of these must be scholars, who would understand the specific manifestations of divine providence from the account. If all were ignorant, they might not recognize and understand God's mercies. This is why the psalmist said, *Whoso is wise, let him preserve these things,* as we explained. Mar Zuṭra said there must be two scholars so that they can discuss and debate all that happened, thereby reaching an understanding of God's mercies.

This may be the reason why *those who go to sea* are mentioned first in the Talmud. They are the last group in the psalm, and immediately after come the verses *The upright will see and rejoice* and *Whoso is wise, let him preserve these things.* Now since the purpose of the talmudic statement was to emphasize the *need* to give thanks in addition to the *obligation,* the speaker indicated that these last verses apply not only to "those who go to sea," the category that immediately precedes them, but to all four. By mentioning the last first, he made it clear that the need implied by the last two verses applies to all four categories. This is the significance of the change. Up to this point, the first two problems and the last two have been solved.

One might also give another reason for the order used by Rab Judah in the name of Rab, which departs from the order in the psalm. This is that the psalmist placed them in order of frequency. Most common are those who travel by land on business matters. Then come those confined in prison. This too results from business affairs among both creditors and debtors; it is quite common. Then those who are sick: a physical weakness strikes them down, and they fall into bed. Finally, the seafarers who endanger themselves to earn a livelihood by transporting goods from afar.

But Rab used a different order, which fitted his purpose, namely to implant in us the thesis we have discussed, the fundamental principle of God's individual providence over His people and His flock in every detail of their actions. That is why he wanted the matter to be told publicly before a large congregation, and why the blessing is in a general form, and why he said "need to offer thanksgiving" rather than "are required," as we said.

Therefore he mentioned first those who have crossed the sea, for with this group more than any other God's marvelous providence may be widely manifest. Of them the psalmist said, *They saw the works of the Lord and His wonders,* because they encounter the greatest dangers, and the various kinds of miracles and marvels performed for them number in the thousands. So many verses from the psalm are quoted as proof in order to teach about the multitude of miracles, more than for any other group. They were mentioned first because they constitute the greatest public evidence of God's providence. In this manner, the fifth problem is resolved.

He then mentioned those who traverse the desert, as they are in the same category as those who cross the sea: both endanger themselves by traveling from one place to another to earn money through trade, both go in groups, both go out of choice. Even though they see the danger, they choose to go out of desire for profit. This is not true of the prisoner and the diseased; their condition is not a matter of choice, nor are there others in a group with them. Thus those who cross the sea and those who traverse the desert are linked together at first—because their danger is greater (as we said), because they travel in groups (which is why the plural is used) and because their actions are freely chosen. In this way, the fourth problem is resolved.

The diseased and the prisoner are linked together and mentioned in the singular because they are equivalent in suffering their ordeals individually. These ordeals are not freely chosen, like the first two. Furthermore, with regard to the first two, the miracle for which one must render thanks may occur in various forms throughout the entire journey, while for the diseased and the prisoner, the miracle occurs only at the end of their ordeal, involving either a cure from the disease or release from prison. Therefore, in the case of the first two the present tense is used, rather than "those who have returned from the sea," for the miracle occurs while they are still at sea or in the desert, unlike the case of the prisoner or the diseased. This answers the third problem. The meaning of the sages has been properly explained, and all the problems resolved.[48]

48. After the solution of all textual and conceptual problems, the preacher now applies the rabbinic passage to his own situation.

My primary purpose in discussing this rabbinic statement, in addition to its fitting in every way what I have said, is that I realized I had discovered the specific manifestations of God's wondrous providence on my own journey, and for all the reasons explained this should be divulged before a large congregation. To my misfortune and dismay, all these things occurred to me on this journey. I went to sea when we traveled to Bursa; I traveled dangerous paths by land from there to Kara Hisar [Karamursel?]; I fell sick on several occasions; I was frequently imprisoned, though not in an actual jailhouse, in chains of poverty.

Furthermore, all will admit that whoever goes to sea in a ship is a kind of prisoner, for he cannot move freely, and he truly becomes sick because of the motion. This happened to me, as it says in the verse, *They reeled to and fro, staggering like a drunkard* (Ps. 107:27). It is therefore truly proper that I offer thanksgiving, because of all four reasons at the same time. Any one of them requires an expression of gratitude; now that all of them together have occurred to me, it is obviously impossible to remain silent.

This is why I say, Behold I have come to offer thanksgiving and to give praise to the One who has done all these marvels for us. My only purpose in this is to tell the whole truth about the experiences I have mentioned, in order to publicize God's providence. It is not to preach about a Torah verse or abstract wisdom. Having been traveling for several years, I no longer have the capacity for such a task. One who is always on the move is unable to think systematically or philosophically, as David said, *They reeled to and fro, staggering like a drunkard, and all their wisdom was swallowed.* This means, because of their constant traveling, not only were they unable to come up with new and original ideas, but even that which they once knew was lost.[49]

We might say that the verse *the people saw; then they moved and stood at a distance* (Exod. 20:15) fits this idea. The Bible tells us that the people at Sinai attained full intellectual comprehension so long as they stood still and engaged in tranquil contemplation. This idea is contained in the phrase *the people saw,* for the "seeing" mentioned here is a term for intellectual contemplation. Then it says that when they began to move, they stood far away from this comprehension and communion. Thus *when they moved, they stood at a distance. . . .*[50]

Thus I say that having been for a long time on the move, I am unable to settle down and preach words of true wisdom properly to this distinguished congregation of God's holy people. I have come only to recount all that has happened, the minor as well as the major events, as described in my sermon.

49. The idea that traveling and uprootedness make it difficult to conceive profound or original thoughts was something of a commonplace; cf. the sermon of Garçon, above, at n. 7. The interpretation of Exod. 20:15 in this context, however, appears to be original.

50. Omitted is about half a page (15a) discussing another rabbinic statement.

This was my intention at the outset in the seventh meaning of the verse *These are records of the tabernacle*: the totality of what has been told by your servant is the story of this *tabernacle,* namely, that which God made happen to us regarding the charter of liberty for this city, the *tabernacle of the testimony.* I have come only as a spokesman and interpreter, to recount them. This is what was meant when I cited, *as it was recounted by Moses.*[51]

I hope in the Lord and implore him to guide and direct us in paths of righteousness for His Name's sake, and in His love to help us always. So long as there is peace among us, nothing good can be missing. The prophet said, *How beautiful upon the mountains are the feet of the messenger who announces peace, who brings good tidings* (Isa. 52:7).[52] This means, when the messenger announces to Israel that true peace will prevail among them, this in itself brings them news of absolute good, for peace is the beginning of the ultimate good in any group whatsoever. Therefore the prophet said that the feet of the messenger upon the mountain are beautiful and pleasant when he announces peace, for upon this depends the welfare of the entire group, and it is as if he had said explicitly, *Your God reigns* (Isa. 52:7).

When peace prevails in a region, it may be known that God rules and keeps providential watch over a particular people, as He does for His people in this land of ours. Peace points to God's individual providence over a people. Therefore the prophet said that when the messenger announces peace, he brings good tidings and thereby says to Zion, *Your God reigns.* He did not say "*and* brings good tidings *and* says to Zion"; the absence of the conjunction indicates that the announcement of peace is itself the good tidings and the assertion that *Your God reigns.*

To your entire community (may God increase your like a thousand times) I say that you must strive to make peace prevail among you. Each person must recognize his own status, and the lesser people must obey the greater ones, for the well-being of any people depends upon this. It is what David meant when he said, *Alufenu mesubbalim* (JPS: *(our) cattle are well laden*), *with no breach, and no outbreak and no wailing in our streets* (Ps. 144:14). This means, when our *alufim*—the great men of the community—are *mesubbalim,* borne and carried aloft over the lesser ones, who pay them proper respect, then there is no breach and no outbreak and no wailing in the streets of the town. It is then appropriate to say, *Happy is the people like this, happy is the people whose God is the Lord* (Ps. 144:15). For when a people has such internal peace, then truly the Lord is their God, and He watches over them individually.

51. This seventh use of the theme-verse indicates that it was cited at the beginning of the sermon yet another time, although this is not recorded in the written text.

52. The introduction of a messianic verse would indicate to the listeners that the final section of the sermon is about to begin.

At the same time, the great men, the wealthy, must be *mesubbalim,* laden down by bearing the burdens of the impoverished and the destitute, namely, the taxes and levies which they are unable to pay. In this way there will be no breach or wailing resulting from the plundering of the poor or the crushing of the destitute. *Alufenu mesubbalim* means, they are laden down with the poor whom they carry in all their misery upon their shoulders. Then there will be no breach, no outbreak, no wailing, and it may be justly said, *Happy is the people who have it so.*[53]

As a reward for this, God will be quick to redeem us, now that we have seen with our own eyes the local redemption from an enemy which He brought about through our charter of liberty, through His great mercy upon us and our children, and by removing robbery and violence from our midst. In this way I understand the prophetic verse, *Behold God is my victory, I will trust and not be afraid, for the Lord is my strength and song and He has become my victory* (Isa. 12:2). This means, *Behold God is my* complete, future *victory*; *I will trust and not be afraid* that it will be incomplete in any way, for I have seen that *the Lord has been my strength and song* and has already been to me the source of victory on a local level. How much more will the comprehensive victory for all Israel be complete in every way.[54] May it come speedily and soon. Amen.

53. The phrase *alufenu mesubbalim* is doubly ambiguous, and the preacher exploits the ambiguity, in fine homiletical style, to express his social doctrine. *Aluf* can refer either to an ox or to a chieftain, an aristocrat, or a wealthy man. *Mesubbalim* can refer either to that which is carried aloft or to that which is laden down with a burden. Thus the wealthy and powerful must be in a position of preeminence over the poor (cf. Rashi) and must bear the financial burdens of the poor.

54. Local redemption (*ge'ulah peraṭit*) becomes a type of the ultimate redemption for all.

Solomon ben Isaac Levi

Solomon Levi (Shelomoh le-Bet ha-Lewi) was born in Salonika in 1532 to a distinguished family of Portuguese exiles.[1] His wealthy father (also born in Salonika) allowed him to spend much of his life acquiring a broad education. He excelled at talmudic studies in the academy of Joseph ibn Leb, mastered the classics of Jewish philosophical and kabbalistic literature, and even studied some of the "Gentile languages" in order to gain access to non-Jewish literature.[2] In his early thirties, he published a commentary on Abot (*Leb Abot* [Salonika, 1565]). Other writings, not published, also come from this period.

Not long after the publication of *Leb Abot,* his father died. Solomon's life changed dramatically as he began to assume the burdens of communal responsibility. In 1568 he became rabbi of the community in Üsküb, Yugoslavia (his first sermon is recorded in *Dibre Shelomoh,* pp. 139–41). From this time on, as he wrote twenty-five years later, he preached virtually every Sabbath and holiday. In 1571 he returned to Salonika, where he served as rabbi of the Provençal congregation. In the spring of 1573, he was chosen rabbi of the influential Evora congregation (*Dibre Shelomoh,* p. 197d). He continued to hold both these positions until his death in 1600.

The demands of his positions prevented him from finding the time to prepare another book for publication until the final decade of his life, when he published his book of sermons (*Dibre Shelomoh* [Venice, 1596]), a commentary on selected aggadot from the Talmud and Midrashim (*Leḥem Shelomoh* [Venice, 1597]), and a commentary on Isaiah (*Ḥesheq Shelomoh* [Salonika, 1600]). A book of his responsa to legal questions, which he originally intended to publish before his sermons, never went to press. Some of these responsa, as well as other writings of various kinds, survive in manuscript.[3]

Dibre Shelomoh is one of the most extensive and complete records of preach-

1. Solomon is mentioned in the various histories of the Jews in Salonika and Turkey, but the most extensive study is that of Joseph Hacker. For the outlines of his biography, see Hacker, "Yiśraʾel ba-Goyim," pp. 43–44, which promises a biographical study of the family and a full monograph on Solomon's life, work, and thought.

2. *Leḥem Shelomoh,* p. 2a; in this work, he cites Ovid, Democritus, and Empedocles (pp. 11a, 14b).

3. He also refers to a work called *Shemaʿ Shelomoh* (*Dibre Shelomoh,* p. 78d).

ing preserved in Jewish literature.[4] Beginning in March of 1571 with a sermon on *Wa-Yiqra* (Lev. 1:1–5:26) and ending in late December of 1574 with a sermon on *Wa-Yeḥi* (Gen. 47:28–50:26), the book proceeds week by week (with an interruption only during the summer of 1572, when he was traveling outside Salonika). Hardly an occasion when it would have been possible to preach is missed, and sometimes there are two different sermons for the same day. The book contains 314 folio pages, each with four columns of fifty-three lines. The sermon translated below encompasses four such columns, or three-tenths of a percent of the entire book—which itself represents less than four years of a thirty-year preaching career.

These are of course not stenographic transcriptions of the sermons delivered. Some of the texts are incomplete versions of what was said, and the reader is informed that "I spoke at great length providing guidance and direction for the people, and here I have written it briefly" (p. 160a), or "I spoke at length, for I have written here only the main points" (p. 164d). Occasionally there is more than what was actually delivered: "I preached a little of this sermon, for there was no time to preach it in its entirety" (p. 63c). The material was obviously reworked for publication. Yet it remains an extraordinary document, revealing how much of a rabbi's time and energy must have been devoted to his preaching tasks, as well as the expectations and educational level of the congregation that heard him. It also contains a hint of the energy that went into the delivery of the words. In the introduction to one sermon, the author reports that he was so engrossed in the excitement of his preaching that he was totally unaware of a strong earthquake that made most of his congregation scurry for safety (p. 186a).

The sermon translated was delivered in Salonika only a few years after the sermon of Moses Almosnino, but it is different in many ways. Intended for an ordinary sabbath rather than a spectacular occasion, it is considerably shorter, and it uses the simple theme-verse rather than the elaborate technique of a fragmented *nośe*. In form it combines elements from the thematic sermon (a verse from the Torah lesson, a conceptual problem defined at the beginning), and the older homily style of proceeding through consecutive verses of the lesson. It is thus somewhat similar to the form of the "chapters" (*sheʿarim*) in Arama's *ʿAqedat Yiṣḥaq,* though on a much smaller scale.

The *nośe* and the *maʾamar* are both clearly relevant to the lesson, although their relationship to one another is not apparent at the beginning, for the verse speaks of Abraham, while the aggadah focuses on the birth of Jacob and Esau. Immediately following the *maʾamar,* a conceptual problem is defined in a manner typical of the sermons in *Dibre Shelomoh.* In this case, it is the

4. The significance of this work for the history of Jewish preaching is discussed briefly and incisively by Pachter, "Sifrut," pp. 42–44.

problem of theodicy: why did the patriarchs, all outstandingly good men, suffer so much in their lives? The simplest solution, that suffering in this world is necessarily linked with reward in the next, is dismissed. Instead, the answer is drawn from a long tradition of Jewish typological exegesis, associated paradigmatically with Naḥmanides: the actions of the patriarchs provide a model for their descendants. Their behavior is intended to teach Jews what is ultimately important in this life and to illustrate persistent survival despite all hardships. The application to contemporary Jewish experience is made explicit.

The second section of the sermon provides a bridge from the conceptual problem to the verses from the lesson to be discussed. The treatment of Isaac's journey to the "Philistine" city of Gerar (Gen. 26:1) is triggered by an interpretation of the patriarchal travels as prefiguring the exiles of the Jewish people. Isaac's uniqueness as the only patriarch never to leave the borders of the land of Israel leads to an exploration of the interrelationship of circumcision, sexual purity, and the land, a discussion drawing freely from kabbalistic motifs. The third section follows, a homily on Genesis 26:1–5, culminating with the theme-verse.

The final section, as expected, treats the *ma'amar*, accomplishing two tasks. First, it establishes a connection between this aggadah and the theme-verse. Jacob was holding his brother's heel (*ʿeqeb*), and his name should have been *ʿEqeb,* but God bestowed upon him a *yod* from the Divine Name to form *Yaʿaqob*. *ʿEqeb* remains, however, as the first word of the *nośe* (Gen. 26:5), where it has just been shown by the preacher to provide important information about Abraham's career. A common thread is thus drawn from Abraham (in the theme-verse) through Isaac (the subject of Gen. 26) to Jacob (in the rabbinic *ma'amar*). More important, the aggadah returns to the problem of Jewish life in exile addressed near the beginning of the sermon, and the "suffering of the righteous" reappears as an integral part of God's plan, a prelude to ultimate triumph.

The sermon is significant not as an example of a peak moment in the history of Jewish preaching, but as a representative sample of the rather high-level fare a distinguished preacher might serve to his congregation week after week.

Sermon on *Toledot*

(Late autumn 1573; Evora Synagogue, Salonika)

{*Inasmuch as* (ʿeqeb)} *Abraham obeyed Me* (be-qoli) {*and followed My mandate: My commandments, My laws, and My teachings*} (Gen. 26:5)

In the Midrash Rabbah (Gen. Rabbah 63:9), "A certain bishop[1] asked Rabban Gamaliel, 'Who will hold power after us?' He brought a blank piece of paper, took a quill, and wrote on it, *Then his brother emerged, holding on to the heel of Esau* (Gen. 25:26). See how ancient words become new in the mouth of a sage! This teaches how much suffering was endured by that righteous man."

It is well known that the foundations upon which the entire people of Israel rests are the patriarchs. Even Moses, the master of the prophets, based his request on their merit.[2] Most of what has been promised to us was for their sake. Indeed, Maimonides even said that all good comes to us as a result of their merit (see his chapter on *debequt*).[3]

Now you will agree that it is possible to enjoy "two tables"—namely, this world and the world to come—for the Tosafists wrote that the correct reading of the talmudic text is not "No one enjoys two tables," but rather, "Not everyone enjoys two tables."[4] David, Solomon, the saintly Rabbi Judah [the Prince], and many other important people have actually enjoyed both. But if this is so, who would be more deserving of reward in both worlds than the three patriarchs? Yet we find that all three were persecuted!

Our father Abraham was persecuted by Nimrod.[5] Later he was forced to go down to Egypt, where they seized his wife. Then he went to Abimelech, and he was compelled to purchase a field as a burial plot to bury his wife.[6] We will not speak about Jacob, who never knew a moment's serenity or tranquility or rest.[7] Look at Isaac, an unblemished offering, who uncovered

1. The word *hegmon* in the rabbinic text means "general." I have translated it in accordance with its medieval meaning, "bishop," for this is how the preacher understood it (see his discussion of the aggadah at the end of the sermon, where the *hegmon* is clearly a representative of Christianity). The reading "asked Rabban Gamaliel," attested in the *Yalquṭ Shimʿoni* of Venice, 1566, is a corrupt one: see *Bereʾshit Rabbah,* Theodor-Albeck ed. (Berlin, 1903), p. 692.

2. See Exod. 32:13, where Moses implores God not to destroy the people of Israel.

3. See *Guide* 3:51: the patriarchs were able to fill their minds with the love of God even when engaged in worldly affairs, and God therefore extended His providence to them "and their descendants." The term *debequt* ("communion with God") is not used by Maimonides in this context; this characterization for the chapter was probably influenced by Naḥmanides' commentary on Deut. 11:22.

4. Tosafot Ber 5b, *lo.*

5. For Abraham's persecution by Nimrod, see Ginzberg, *Legends,* 1:186–217, and accompanying notes in vol. 5.

6. In a different sermon Solomon explained that Abraham wanted only a cave, and that Ephron insisted that he buy the entire field, thereby demanding a much higher price than Abraham wanted to pay (*Dibre Shelomoh,* p. 305b).

7. Cf. Job 3:26. The Zohar applies this verse to Jacob (1:179b; cf. Zohar 1:180a: "Jacob passed all his life in fear and anxiety").

his neck on the altar. He suffered from famine and was compelled to go to Abimelech, for his statement to Abimelech implies that he had gone to prostrate himself and implore that the king provide him sustenance, out of love for his father.[8] You know R. Abraham ibn Ezra's lengthy comment on this section, attempting to prove that Isaac became impoverished toward the end of his life.[9]

It seems to me that you will find the answer in the commentary of Naḥmanides. He astutely explained how everything that happened to the patriarchs was a sign for their descendants. All the narrative episodes indicate just what would occur to future generations. Look it up, for everything is precisely as he said.[10] God foresaw that our people would suffer throughout most of their history from degradation and exile, migrating and wandering from one calamity to another, from one kingdom to the next.[11] He knew that despair might sprout in their hearts, and that they might have doubts about His judgments.[12] For in reviewing our history, we might well conclude that the only good period for Israel was the forty-year reign of King Solomon.[13]

Therefore, in His great wisdom, He decreed exactly what He wanted to show us: that those who aspire to perfection desire only communion with Him, the opportunity of serving Him with devotion, the well-being of the spirit. All temporal goods are vanity and delusion; there must come a time when they are taken away and lost. Yet the achievement of the supreme goal does not require a person to suffer terrible afflictions and absolute want, going hungry, thirsty, and naked.[14] We must simply be satisfied with the necessities,

8. I do not understand how any statement of Isaac to Abimelech reported in the Bible implies this; the Hebrew text of the passage is elliptic and possibly somewhat corrupt. Cf. David Kimḥi on Gen. 26:1.

9. See Abraham ibn Ezra on Gen. 25:34 (and the lengthy refutation by Naḥmanides).

10. Naḥmanides, introduction to *Wa-Yishlaḥ* (tyrans. Chavel, *Genesis,* p. 394). On this typological approach to the patriarchal narratives, see Joshua ibn Shueib's sermon, above, at n. 9.

11. On the preacher's characterization of the experience of *galut,* see Joseph Hacker, "Yiśra'el ba-Goyim be-Te'uro shel R. Shelomoh le-Bet ha-Lewi mi-Saloniqah," *Zion* 34 (1969):50–52.

12. Concerning the despair of redemption among fifteenth- and sixteenth-century Jews, see Shem Ṭob ibn Shem Ṭob's sermon, above, at n. 5. Cf. the statement by the preacher's Italian contemporary, Samuel Judah Katzenellenbogen: there are Jews who "despair of redemption, saying 'Will God make windows in the heavens to overthrow the constellations that are arrayed against us?'" (Katzenellenbogen, p. 42a).

13. Cf. Abraham Bibago, *Derek Emunah* (Constantinople, 1522), p. 22d (in the edition of selections edited by Hava Fraenkel-Goldschmidt, p. 143): "I would almost say that this nation has never known full prosperity except during the era of King Solomon."

14. I.e., wealth and economic status are not in themselves evil, so long as they are acquired honestly and not made into ultimate ends. See Hacker, "Yiśra'el ba-Goyim," p. 82.

and rejoice in our spiritual lot more than in worldly honor and wealth. This is the model provided by our saintly patriarchs.

We should also pay careful attention to another aspect of their experience: their continued survival. Even though Nimrod and the four kings tried to destroy Abraham, God did not abandon him to their power. Though he and his wife were barren, God sustained his line. Similarly with Isaac and Jacob: God made them fertile and numerous, promising them that their offspring would survive, and that those who sought to harm them would be destroyed.

Similarly, you find that this has always been true of us. All the sovereign nations that flourished in antiquity have come to a calamitous end; they are hardly remembered today. All of them tried to wipe us out, but God never abandoned us to their power. Those who complain about the triumphs of the Gentile nations fail to understand this. Look at the answer to Habakkuk, who complained about Nebuchadnezzer, his kingdom and his country; what God said is indeed what happened.[15]

Look at the answer to Asaph, *Until I entered {the sanctuary of God and considered their latter end}* (Ps. 73:17). This the meaning of the Hafṭarah that we read today: *I have loved you, says the Lord* (Mal. 1:2). You can see what I have written about this elsewhere.[16] The prophet proves that God will not punish or afflict Israel for their sins against Him by total destruction of the people and eradication of their name, as He will do with Esau. Read it yourselves.

Therefore, as Naḥmanides has explained at length, the patriarchs had to go from one calamity to another as a sign for their descendants: so that future generations would see the promise that destruction would never overtake them in any age; so that they could be shown the true, spiritual well-being bound up with devoted service to God; so that they would know that God watches over those who serve Him as parents delight in their child. How valuable is Naḥmanides' comment that Abraham's descent to Egypt prefigures the exile of his offspring in Egypt, Isaac's descent to Gerar prefigures the Babylonian exile, and Jacob's departure and all that happened to him prefigures this exile in which we now live.[17] You should review the passage.

Now it is well known that all Jews are called *ṣaddiqim,* "righteous," be-

15. See Hab. 2:2–8, on the impending downfall of Babylonia.

16. The preacher discussed the Hafṭarah in his sermon on *Toledot* two years before this one: "*I have loved you, said the Lord* (Mal. 1:2). The commentators have found this passage problematic. In my opinion the meaning of the verses is, this is the way God's love for us is known: when Israel sins, God will afflict them, but He will not destroy them. He will reproach them as a father does a son. However, He does indeed hate Esau because of his sins; He will send him irrevocably from His presence and totally devastate his cities . . ." (*Dibre Shelomoh,* p. 79b).

17. Naḥmanides on Gen. 26:1, intro. to *Wa-Yishlaḥ,* Gen. 32:9 (trans. Chavel, pp. 325–26, 394, 398).

cause of the sign of the sacred covenant upon them, which alludes to *ṣaddiq yesod ha-ʿolam, the righteous, the foundation of the world* (Prov. 10:25).[18] It is further known that this is why they are worthy of the land of Israel. For the land of Israel alludes to the uncovering of the corona, an integral part of circumcision: "Whoever circumcises without uncovering the corona does not perform a valid circumcision."[19] Finally, it is known that the essential significance of this commandment depends upon never defiling the sign of the sacred covenant in any impure place, never straying beyond the boundary line with a menstruous woman, a Gentile, a servant woman, a prostitute, or the like.[20] Because of such abominations, the land spewed forth the Gentiles who were in it, as Naḥmanides has explained at length in his comment on *Aḥare Mot* and elsewhere.[21]

That is why the Bible says, *{So long as} your people are all righteous, they shall possess the land for all time* (Isa. 60:21). This means that if, God forbid, they should defile this sign [of the covenant through sexual immorality], they will be expelled from the land. They will then lose both the terrestrial and the celestial land of Israel, for both are called "the lands of the living." The world to come is the land of the living because it is devoid of death,

18. Kabbalistic doctrine associates circumcision with the *sefirah Yesod* ("Foundation"), which represents the genital organ in the supernal Man. See Zohar 1:93a; Joseph ibn Gikatilla, *Shaʿare Orah,* ed. Joseph Ben-Shelomoh, 2 vols. (Jerusalem, 1970) 1:114. The "sign of the sacred covenant" is the letter *yod,* which, imprinted on the male body through circumcision, transforms the *shin* and *dalet* already imprinted there from *shed* ("demon") to *Shaddai* ("Almighty"). See Zohar 1:95a–b.

19. The quotation is from B. Shab 137b. Ibn Gikatilla (ibid.) explains the statement as follows: "*Periʿah* ["uncovering"] refers esoterically to "Adonai" [the *sefirah Malkut*]. When one does not uncover [the corona], the *sefirah* through which it is possible to first enter into the Godhead is absent." *Ereṣ* ("land, earth"), *ereṣ Yiśraʾel,* and *ereṣ ha-ḥayyim* ("the land of the living") are also understood by the kabbalists as alluding to *Malkut.* See ibn Gikatilla, pp. 82, 174–75; the discussion of Isa. 60:21 in Zohar 1:93a, 2:23a; and *Dibre Shelomoh,* p. 73a: "*Ereṣ Yiśraʾel* alludes to the supernal 'land' from which the divine effluence comes to the heavens and their hosts." Perhaps the clearest association in kabbalistic sources between circumcision and the land of Israel is a frequently cited passage from Moses Cordovero's *Or Yaqar*: "Therefore one who dwells in the land must circumcise his flesh, for otherwise he pollutes the land. Thus you learn that the acceptance of God's divinity depends upon dwelling in the land, and dwelling in the land depends on circumcision, and accepting the divinity depends upon circumcision" (*Or Yaqar* [Jerusalem, 1967] 4:213b).

20. The Zohar regularly characterizes sexual immorality by a Jewish male as "profaning the sacred sign of the covenant," or "letting the mark of holiness enter alien precincts" (2:3b, 7a, 87b; 3:142b). Cf. Baer, *HJCS* 1:262.

21. Naḥmanides on Lev. 18:25 (trans. Chavel, pp. 274–75); cf. *Dibre Shelomoh* on *Lek Leka,* pp. 72d–73a. In this sentence and the previous one, the printed text reads "Egyptian" where I have translated "Gentile." The context in both instances makes it clear that the original reading was *goyah* and *goyim.* This was apparently changed to *miṣrit* and *miṣrim* by the printer or proofreader in Venice. For a discussion of such substitutions as a form of self-censorship, see Hacker, "Yiśraʾel ba-Goyim," pp. 66–67, n. 137.

and the terrestrial land of Israel is "the land in which the dead live first."[22] This also means that those who die in it and suffer afflictions are paradigmatically "the living." You may recall what is written in *Libnat ha-Sappir* on the verse, *My people, remember what Balak king of Moab plotted . . . from Shittim to Gilgal* (Mic. 6:5).[23] It is a text worth consulting.

We all know that our father Isaac was the first to be perfected through the sign of the covenant of circumcision on the eighth day. Circumcision essentially applies to the eighth day; this is the subject of *For the leader on the eighth* (Ps. 12:1), for it is the eighth from Supernal Wisdom, the beginning of God's self-revelation.[24] Furthermore, the sign of Isaac's circumcision never strayed beyond the sacred boundary. Even our father Jacob married two sisters, which was a tiny blemish in him; this was why he did not want to take the cup of blessing.[25] Moreover, each man can have only one true mate in marriage.[26] Such was the case with Isaac, but not with Abraham or Jacob, who had concubines. Although the Zohar indicates that both Abraham and Isaac had four wives, this is a mystical teaching [not to be taken literally].[27] Look it up yourselves.

This, then, is why our father Isaac was worthy of cleaving to the land of Israel to such an extent that he never left it at all. He was an *ʿolat tamim,* an unblemished offering, and it is known that one who is circumcised is called *tamim,* whole, as in the verse, *Walk in My ways, and be* tamim, *whole* (Gen. 17:1). This is the opposite of having a blemish. While it might seem that the removal of the foreskin would create a blemish in a man, it, on the contrary, removes the blemish and makes him whole.[28] In Genesis Rabbah

22. See Gen. Rabbah 96:5 and parallels.

23. Cf. the preacher's own explication of this verse (in an earlier sermon): "*Remember now what Balak king of Moab devised,* for even though he was king, he did not want to fight against you, and he devised to contend with you by means of supernal forces. *And what Balaam the son of Beor answered him*: when you were near to entering the land of Israel, that wise son of a wise father said that evil befalling you at that juncture could not be repaired, and that no power could prevail over you unless you lost your state of perfection. That is why he counseled that the daughters of Moab should be set loose for you" (*Dibre Shelomoh,* p. 145a).

24. Reference is to the second *sefirah, Ḥokmah.* As the first *sefirah* was often identified with the totally transcendent, unknowable God (*En Sof*), *Ḥokmah* was the "beginning" of God's self-manifestation. The eighth *sefirah* from *Ḥokmah* is *Yesod* (see above, n. 18). For the link of Ps. 12:1 with circumcision, see B. Men 43b. For a somewhat different kabbalistic explanation of the choice of the eighth day in relation to the *sefirot,* see Moses Cordovero, *Or Yaqar* 4:216a.

25. B. Pes 119b; cf. Naḥmanides on Lev. 18:25 (trans. Chavel, p. 251), explaining that Jacob could not live with two sisters within the Holy Land, and Zohar 1:168a.

26. Zoharic doctrine recognizes only monogamous marriage. See Baer, *HJCS* 1:437, n. 19, and the sources cited there.

27. Zohar 1:133b.

28. This is a commonplace in Jewish exegesis, linking Gen. 17:1 and its assertion of wholeness (*tamim*) with the commandment of circumcision in the following verses.

on this chapter (Gen. Rabbah 64:1), the sages said, "*The Lord knows the days of those who are whole* (Ps. 37:18): this is Isaac," for Isaac and Rebecca were whole in this sense. Therefore, *their inheritance,* the land of Israel, uniquely appropriate to be associated with them in this respect, was *forever* (Ps. 37:18), unlike the case of the other patriarchs, who departed from it.

Therefore God said to Isaac, *Reside in this land* (Gen. 26:3), do not depart from it, for you are an unblemished offering, and you must not go beyond the Temple enclosure, as the sages said (Gen. Rabbah 64:3). Circumcision itself alludes to the offering. We have explained on the basis of circumcision the statement in the Mishnah, "The burnt offering belongs to the most holy things."[29] Just as the offering is disqualified if it goes beyond the boundary [of the Temple], so Isaac was warned not to depart from the land of Israel.

We have thus explained that all the wanderings endured by the patriarchs occurred so that their descendants might find refuge in a fortress of simple perfection, realizing that the only goal worthy to be sought is communion with God and perfection of the soul and nothing else. Furthermore, just as the patriarchs were promised that they would endure and survive and that no temporal destruction would prevail over them, so it is with their descendants.

That is why Solomon said, *So follow the way of the good, and keep to the paths of the righteous* (Prov. 2:20). The saintly patriarchs were both *good* in their character traits, and *righteous,* clinging to the divine righteousness symbolized by the sign of the sacred covenant, because of which they were called *ṣaddiqim,* "righteous." Concerning the *good,* he said *way* [singular], for a character trait encompasses a broad general pattern of behavior, not specific details.[30] This first category, *the way of the good,* also refers to the positive commandments. Since observing these is not so difficult, it is called *way.* But when referring to the avoidance of transgressions, which are crooked paths, he said, *and keep to the paths* [plural] *of the righteous.*

The upright in their character traits *will inhabit the land* of Israel, which is suitable for them. *And the* temimim, *the unblemished* (namely, the *ṣaddiqim* mentioned in the previous verse, those who are sanctified by the sign of the sacred covenant and are called both unblemished and righteous) *will remain in it* (Prov. 2:21).[31] This means that the land of Israel will not spew them out as it did the Canaanites; they will remain there permanently. By contrast,

29. Zeb. 5:4; B. Zeb 53b. The next sentence is taken from Gen. Rabbah 64:3.

30. For example, "generosity" would be such a general ethical quality, but the ethical theorist would not necessarily specify precisely how much one has to give and in what manner. Transgressions, by contrast, are defined in detail, and that is why the plural "paths" is appropriate. Cf. Judah Moscato's sermon, at n. 34.

31. This is the verse that is particularly significant within the context of the sermon, reinforcing points the preacher has made before.

the wicked in their behavior *will vanish from the land,* and vanishing from the terrestrial land of Israel implies that the soul will vanish from the *land of the living. And the treacherous* in their beliefs *will be rooted out of it* (Prov. 2:22).

The sages also interpreted the verse *They shall not come to grief in bad times; in famine they shall eat their fill* (Ps. 37:19) as pertaining to Isaac and the "evil" of Abimelech (Gen. Rabbah 64:1). The verse was understood to mean that Isaac's household would not be ashamed of having to go to Abimelech for sustenance, since in a time of famine they are satisfied and content, without having excessive desires. The reason they did not come to grief in bad times is that they endured patiently and contentedly, without nurturing the physical desires of most human beings. This is in accordance with the verse *A sated person disdains honey, but to a hungry man anything bitter seems sweet* (Prov. 27:7).

The verse [in this section of the lesson] states, *There was a famine in the land—aside from* [mi-lebad] *the previous famine that had occurred in the days of Abraham* (Gen. 26:1). From Naḥmanides' commentary we know that Abraham's first descent, to Egypt, was intended to allude to the exile [of the Israelites] in Egypt, for he was compelled to go there because of the famine. But Abraham's journey to Abimelech did not refer to a future exile.[32]

Isaac's journey prefigures the Babylonian exile, and the Torah mentions *the previous famine that had occurred in the days of Abraham* to indicate that the two are to be interpreted in the same way. It also teaches us that the two famines were similar in all respects. God thought, perhaps Isaac will think of following Abraham and going to Egypt, for this famine is exactly the same as the one that occurred during his father's life: the same places were blighted as in the first famine, and so forth. All this is implied by the expression *mi-lebad,* "aside from."

Therefore God had to tell him, *Do not go down to Egypt* (Gen. 26:2). Isaac had almost decided to go, even though he thought that Abimelech might favor him because of his father. Hence God's instruction, *Do not go down to Egypt, stay in the land which I point out to you.* This means, even though your father was not permitted to remain in this land permanently, I will permit you to stay in this land where I commune with you and speak to you. Similarly, the sages said, *Stay in this land* means: be a sower, be a planter" (Gen. Rabbah 64:3). From this time forth Isaac was permitted to sow seed in the land, something Abraham had never done. The reason is as I said: permanence in the land was more appropriate for Isaac.

Lest this result in the loss of the ethical perfection attained by his father and the other forefathers who considered themselves as resident aliens in the land (as David said, *For we are sojourners with You, were transients like our*

32. See Naḥmanides' comment on Gen. 26:1 (trans. Chavel, p. 325).

forefathers, 1 Chron. 29:15),[33] God said immediately afterward, *Reside in this land.* But do not put your trust in Abimelech, for *I will be with you* as your soul cleaves to Me, and from this it follows that *I will bless you.* The reason for this is that *to you and your offspring I will give all these lands* (Gen. 26:3). The sages said, "these hard lands" (Gen. Rabbah 64:3), meaning, lands that tolerate only righteous inhabitants.[34] This is why I must be with you, bound together.

So long as your offspring cling to this bond, they will remain in these lands, but if they do not, the lands will spew them out. In this way, *I will fulfill the oath I swore to your father Abraham* (Gen. 26:3). There will also come a time when I will *arbeh* (Gen. 26:4), which means to make something great (this is the sense of *arbeh et zarᶜaka, I will make your offspring great {like the stars of heaven},* Gen. 22:17). This will take place in the messianic age. The oath He swore to Abraham has already been fulfilled, but this one will be fulfilled in the messianic age, when we believe that "all the nations of the earth shall bless themselves by our offspring" (cf. Gen. 26:4).[35]

Inasmuch as Abraham listened obediently to My voice (Gen. 26:5).[36] This means that as soon as he heard My voice for the first time, he immediately began to observe the negative commandments (*he followed My mandate*), as well as *My commandments* (the positive ones), *My laws* (beliefs beyond reason), *and My teachings* (beliefs that are verified by reason).[37] The rabbinic statement, "our father Abraham came to know his Creator when he was forty-eight years old" (Gen. Rabbah 64:4), may be based on the numerical equivalent of the word *ᶜeqeb,* "inasmuch," for the letter *ᶜayin* in its *mispar qaṭan* is 7, *qof* is 100, and *bet* in *mispar gadol* is 20, giving a total of 127. Adding 48, you get 175 [the total number of years in Abraham's life].[38]

33. Cf. the preacher's sermon on *Ki Tabo* (*Dibre Shelomoh,* p. 55a–56d), which develops the theme that all should consider themselves alien sojourners on earth.

34. The midrash interprets the word *ha-ᵓel* in Gen. 26:3 in connection with *el,* meaning "great, mighty, hard" (cf. Ezek. 17:13); the preacher explains the rabbinic "hard lands" in connection with the Naḥmanidean doctrine that the land of Israel is uniquely intolerant of sinfulness (above, n. 21).

35. I.e., the promise of giving the land to Abraham's offspring was fulfilled in the time of Joshua, but the promise concerning the greatness of his offspring remains to be fulfilled in the messianic age. Note the interpretation that the Jews will be as *great* as the stars, not as *numerous*; the more usual rendering must have seemed increasingly unrealistic to Jewish thinkers. With the final sentence, compare *Dibre Shelomoh,* p. 73d, on Gen. 12:3: "*all the families of the earth* that enter under your wings and the wings of your offspring *will be blessed like you.*"

36. This is the theme-verse of the sermon.

37. On the question of Abraham's observance of the commandments, see Rashi on this verse, and Naḥmanides' extensive critique of his interpretation.

38. *Mispar qaṭan* ("small number") eliminates the zeros in the numerical equivalent of a letter. *Mispar gadol* ("large number") ordinarily applies only to letters with a special final form; here it seems to mean the numerical equivalent multiplied by ten. The gematria is obviously

It is also possible that *be-qoli,* "to My voice," although written here without a *waw,* is interpreted as if written *plene,* with a *waw,* for every *ḥolam* has a potential *waw.* (We see this in *be-yom kallot Mosheh, On the day Moses finished* (Num. 7:1); *kallot* is interpreted as if it were *plene,* for the *waw* is there potentially.)[39] Thus the word *be-qoli* may be interpreted as follows: the letter *qof* stands for the word *qol,* "voice," and the other letters, *bet, waw, lamed, yod,* equal forty-eight. Thus Abraham listened to "voice: forty-eight," meaning, when he was forty-eight years old. But the more convincing interpretation is that he was three years old, according to the number of *ʿeqeb,* 172 [subtracted from the 175 years of his life].[40] This is much simpler. Look into it.

The aggadah cited at the beginning states that the bishop thought of our Torah and called it an "Old Testament," whose time has already passed, as the Christians claim.[41] He therefore said, "Who will hold power after us?" In other words, he maintains that "there is no doubt that your time has passed and you have no more portion in the world, and there is no doubt that we are extremely strong. Who will be able to wrest power from our hands?" He also maintained that "we shall endure so long that there will be no time left for any kingdom to hold power after us."

Rabban Gamaliel brought out a blank piece of paper, indicating that the Torah is new each day in the hearts of the forefathers, for "each day God makes new law in the Heavenly Court" (Gen. Rabbah 64:4).[42] It is not dependent on time, nor is it swept away by time. This is the meaning of the verse *which I command you* today (Deut. 6:6); look into it yourselves.[43]

He continued, *Then his brother emerged* (Gen. 25:26), implying that it was God who made Jacob emerge last. Proof of this is *He called his name Jacob* (Gen. 25:26): it was the Holy One who gave him this name,[44] for He took the *yod* from the Divine Name and gave it to him to protect him during

---

forced; indeed, there is no satisfactory link of age forty-eight with this verse (see *Bereʾshit Rabbah,* Theodor-Albeck ed., pp. 703, 274).

39. Although our text of the Bible has *kallot* written *plene* in Num. 7:1, many midrashim and medieval commentaries assume a reading without the *waw.* See *Minḥat Shai.*

40. On the question of Abraham's age when he discovered God, see Ginzberg, *Legends,* 5:209–10.

41. The printed text reads *koferim* ("unbelievers"); this was probably changed from the original "Christians" by the Venetian proofreaders of the book. See above, n. 21. On the aggadah, cf. Arama, chap. 23 (p. 136a).

42. The printed text says, "for each day a heavenly voice goes forth, etc." It is probable that the preacher or the printer misquoted the statement appearing in the translation, which is taken from the chapter of Genesis Rabbah under discussion and is fully appropriate to the idea being developed.

43. Cf. Sifre and Rashi on this verse: "Do not let them seem to you like an antiquated ordinance to which no one pays any heed, but rather like a new one which all run to see."

44. Cf. Gen. Rabbah 63:8; Zohar 1:138a.

that entire period of time. His name should have been ʿEqeb,[45] but the Holy One gave him the *yod* from His own name to protect him and preserve him. It is therefore not of his own doing that he will eventually reign; rather, it is God who brings this all about. When he finally does reign, it will be God's will.

We see this in the verse, *It will surely come, without delay* (Hab. 2:3), meaning that there is no delay regarding its arrival, it comes at the proper time.[46] That is why the bishop said that the ancient words, while indeed ancient, become new, teaching that the so-called "old" testament becomes new every day, as I said. And he concluded, "How much suffering was endured by that righteous man" in serving as a sign to his descendants. All is part of God's plan. Nothing happens by chance.[47]

45. Note how the aggadah about Jacob is here linked by association with the theme-verse about Abraham, as the central idea of the sermon—God's providential ordering of the lives of the patriarchs and the history of the Jews—is reinforced.

46. For the preacher's attitude toward the calculation of the messianic date, see Hacker, "Ha-Yeʾush," pp. 208–12.

47. The final sentences recapitulate three important motifs: (a) the *ṣaddiq* (previously associated with Isaac, here with Jacob), (b) the patriarchal experience as a sign to their descendants, and (c) divine providence.

Judah Moscato

Judah ben Joseph Moscato was one of the leading lights in that florescence of sixteenth-century Italian Jewish culture which is frequently associated with the Renaissance. It has been claimed, though perhaps with some exaggeration, that he "comes closer than any other Jewish scholar of the period to the ideal of the *uomo universale* of Renaissance days."[1]

He was born in a small community in the Papal Sates in about 1530.[2] As a young man, forced to leave his home by the upheavals of the Counterreformation, he found refuge with relatives in Mantua, where he remained until his death in 1590. During this period Mantua was the center of vigorous Jewish culture, the home of distinguished rabbinic scholars like Moses Provençal, whom Moscato later eulogized as master and teacher, the brilliant and controversial historian Azariah de' Rossi, and a host of lesser figures who led in the cultivation of a dynamic Jewish theater, music, belles lettres, and dance alongside the more traditional disciplines of Jewish learning.[3]

Moscato found this environment quite congenial. He was deeply interested in music, and he wrote poetry. His two major extant works, a massive commentary on Judah Halevi's *Kuzari* (*Qol Yehudah* [Venice, 1594]) and his collection of sermons (*Nefuṣot Yehudah* [Venice, 1589]), reveal a scholarship that is widely eclectic yet not without depth. Moscato is at home with classical and Arab as well as Jewish philosophers. In addition to Aristotle, he cites Plato,[4] Cicero, Quintilian, Seneca, and Ovid. He incorporates material from Maimonides, but by no means does he overlook the Zohar and the kabbalists. Alongside Jewish luminaries of the previous generation he refers to such Christians as Pico della Mirandola.[5] Perhaps most important for our purposes, he expresses a commitment not only to the quest for truth, wherever it may be found, but also to the art of communicating that truth to others.

1. Isaac Barzilay, *Between Faith and Reason* (The Hague and Paris, 1967), p. 167.

2. The most complete biographical study is by Abraham Apfelbaum, *Toledot Rabbi Yehudah Moscato* (Drohobycz, 1900). I have not followed this work on all points.

3. See Shlomo Simonsohn, *History of the Jews in the Duchy of Mantua* (Jerusalem, 1977), chaps. 7 and 8, pp. 600–741.

4. On Moscato's Platonism, see Barzilay, pp. 172–76.

5. On his citation of Pico in sermon 8, see Dan, "ʿIyyun," pp. 107–08.

Unfortunately, Moscato left little information about the course of his preaching career. Unlike other introductions to collections of sermons, his introduction reveals little about his position in Mantua, his preaching responsibilities, or the process of preparing material for publication. It is not known whether or not Moscato was accustomed to preach every Sabbath, as were many of his Italian and Sephardic colleagues. *Nefuṣot Yehudah* contains fifty-two sermons, but they are not based on the weekly Torah lesson. Most of them are connected with holidays, special Sabbaths, life-cycle events (circumcision, wedding, funeral), or special occasions in the life of the community. The basis for the selection, or the order of arrangement within the book, is anything but clear.

Few Jewish preachers have enjoyed as much attention as has Moscato,[6] yet fundamental questions about the significance of his homiletical oeuvre are matters of continued debate. Especially important questions concern the extent and the precise nature of the influence of "external" (classical, Italian) rhetorical theory upon his preaching, and the language in which the sermons of *Nefuṣot Yehudah* were delivered. The links between Moscato's sermons and the homiletical tradition that crystallized at the end of the fifteenth century in Spain now seem beyond doubt: the basic building blocks of Torah verse (*nośe*) and rabbinic statement (*maʾamar*) (although these are not invariable),[7] the occasional use of the fragmented *nośe,*[8] the conventional introductory self-justification and asking for permission to preach (*reshut*), the conception of the sermon as an exploration of a conceptual problem (*derush*). At the same time, there are new elements: the use of a title for each sermon, the development of the introduction beyond stereotyped motifs into a supple rhetorical tool that could serve various functions, and the elevation of the sermon to a high level of artistic self-consciousness, undoubtedly expressed not only in the published text but in the oral delivery.

The structure of the sermon translated below is readily apparent; indeed, the preacher is careful to give the listener explicit signals about it. The sermon, which was delivered on the second day of the Feast of Weeks (Shabuʿot), is thematically linked with the sermon for the previous day, although it can stand independently as well. The subject, appropriate for the occasion, is the Torah, or more precisely, the value of the Torah, as compared with external sources of knowledge, in leading to the fulfillment of the highest human potential.

Such potential is of two kinds, one pertaining to the intellect, the other

6. In addition to Apfelbaum and Barzilay, see Bettan, pp. 192–226; Dan, "ʿIyyun," and "Tefillah we-Dimʿah," in *Sifrut,* pp. 191–97; Israel Zinberg, *History of Jewish Literature,* 12 vols. (Cincinnati and New York, 1972–78), 4:100–05; Altmann, "Ars Rhetorica," p. 16.

7. See Bettan, p. 196.

8. See the example in "Structural Options," above.

to conduct, and this distinction divides the sermon into its two major sections. The subdivision of the first section is announced in the opening paragraph following the rabbinic *maʾamar*: the preacher will investigate the value of Torah for the intellect in three ways—by arguments from reason, by interpretations of rabbinic statements, and by interpretations of verses from the Torah itself. This is then accomplished; the philosophical argument against philosophy is followed by an explication of the lead aggadah, and the case is clinched with Obadiah Sforno's allegorical interpretation of the sanctuary in the wilderness.

The second section of the sermon addresses the question whether human knowledge unaided by Torah is sufficient to establish proper ethical conduct. Moscato's negative answer is established through an elaborately prepared explication of one of the perennially intriguing talmudic stories of Rabba bar bar Ḥana. An extremely important general statement defending the preacher's technique of deriving recondite teachings from allegorical interpretations of aggadah leads to a succinct summary and recapitulation of the sermon's message. As a whole, the sermon testifies not only to the art of the preacher, but also to what must have been the rather high intellectual level of the audience.

The Power of Those Who Toil in Torah
Sermon for the Second Day of the Feast of Weeks
(Ca. 1585, Mantua)

[We read] in the Midrash [cf. Ruth Rabbah 5:4]: "R. Abin said, There are wings to the earth, wings to the dawn, wings to the sun, wings to the cherubim, wings to the seraphim. Wings to the earth: *Have you seized the wings of the earth?* (Job 38:18); wings to the dawn: *If I take the wings of the dawn* (Ps. 139:9); wings to the sun: *the sun of righteousness, with healing in its wings* (Mal. 3:20); wings to the cherubim: *the sound of the wings of the cherubim* (Ezek. 10:5); wings to the seraphim: *each one had six wings* (Isa. 6:2). Great is the power of those who toil in Torah and those who perform acts of kindness, for they find shelter not in the shadow of the wings of the earth, or of the dawn, or of the sun, or of the cherubim or seraphim. In whose shadow do they find shelter? In the shadow of the One at whose word the world was created, as it is said, *How precious is Your lovingkindness, O God! Human beings find shelter in the shadow of Your wings* (Ps. 36:8)."

Yesterday we began to reveal the great and powerful benefit attainable in no other way than through devotion to the Torah.[1] Let us now pass to a theoretical investigation of this matter, to be taken as far as the subject allows, and then supplement it with hidden content of mighty statements from the rabbis and the Bible.[2]

Reason and logic make it clear to all that nourishment must befit the nature of that which is to be nourished. Now just as this is true for the body and its physical nourishment, so is it true for the rational soul: it is nourished and sustained by that which characteristically pertains to the intellect alone. But the rational soul is derived from the realm of the supernal and eternal beings. Just as they are nourished and sustained in life with nourishment befitting their nature by the rational apprehension of their Creator, so the rational soul must receive its nourishment and life-giving sustenance from this same source. None other will do.[3]

As we now search through the various philosophical disciplines, the correctness of my premise will be established. Do you not see that the propaedeutic disciplines cannot possibly serve as nourishment befitting the vital sustenance of the rational soul? Their subject matter depends entirely upon things conceived by the intellect that have no reality outside the mind, things that are intellectually abstracted from matter, both ontologically and categorically. In this sense they do not really exist. Nor can the natural sciences, for their subject matter is constantly changing.[4]

Nor can that which is called in philosophy "the divine science," that is, metaphysics, for theoretical investigation in this realm is merely wild speculation and surmise fraught with doubt, as its practitioners themselves concede. Further proof of this is the variety of incompatible views on basic questions.[5] And even that which they are able to apprehend through their

1. This reference to the sermon on the previous day, the first day of the Feast of Weeks, points to a concrete setting for the present address. It is the kind of detail that indicates a fairly close relationship between the text before us and what was actually spoken.

2. This sentence reveals the structure for the first half of the sermon, dealing with the theoretical content of the Torah. The thesis that no external disciplines can take the place of the Torah is sustained in three ways: by independent reasoning, by an esoteric interpretation of a rabbinic statement (the *ma'amar* quoted by the preacher at the beginning), and by an esoteric interpretation of a passage from the Torah. Compare the mode of argumentation in Moscato, sermon 18, where each position is established by an argument from reason and then by arguments from the rabbis and from biblical verses.

3. This argument is cast in the form of a syllogism. For the underlying metaphor of knowledge as nourishment, cf. the commonplace expressed by Abraham ibn Ezra in his comment on Isa. 55:1; "Wisdom is to the soul as food is to the body"; the sermon of Jacob Anatoli, above at n. 12; and *Derashot,* p. 282.

4. On the threefold division of the sciences underlying this passage, see n. 22 to Anatoli's sermon, above. For Moscato's characterization of the propaedeutic or mathematical sciences, cf. the article by Wolfson cited in the aforementioned note, p. 495, n. 8, and p. 529.

5. On the inadequacy of metaphysics, cf. Judah Halevi's *Kuzari* (Warsaw, 1880), 4:25,

rational investigation is but *base silver laid over earthenware* (Prov. 26:23), for although they acknowledge the existence of a First Cause, they have *ardent lips with an evil mind* (ibid.) in associating the Name of God with something totally different, from which, as they assert, everything results by necessity.[6] In short, all of the disciplines of human learning are inadequate as sources of vital sustenance for the rational soul.

This is not true of the divine Torah. Its subject matter is the creation of the world, the wondrous works of the One who is perfect in knowledge: pure intelligible ideas, capable of fully satisfying the rational soul with appropriate nourishment. Thus the benefit to be derived from the Torah, great and powerful, is unattainable from any other source.[7] This is the meaning of the verse, *For man does not live by bread alone, but by all that issues from the mouth of the Lord* (Deut. 8:3). As the human being is composed of body and soul, there must be a special kind of nourishment for each part. Bread, composed of the [physical] elements, befits the body, which is also composed of them. But *that which issues from the mouth of the Lord* befits the rational part, for God has made one correspond to the other for our perpetual good.

As for the way in which this important doctrine is taught by the sages, consider the statement with which I began as an introduction to my message.[8] Even though many have perused it, all reflecting their own concerns, there is still room left for me to express my view, although its value may be no greater in relation to the others than a single point is to the circumference.

You recall the various levels of being: inanimate, vegetative, animal, rational. All are natural. The intellect acquired by apprehending the disciplines of learning is left within the realm of human choice: human beings may make it fully actual. The people of Israel have yet another soul, from the soul of God on high, whose light shines over their heads.[9]

Let us note further that when one of the senses encounters and perceives something, it cannot reach the level of intellection until its image and immaterial form have been conveyed to the common sense, from which it is

---

end (p. 129) and 5:14 (pp. 71–72), both of which speak of the lack of consensus. Compare also Abravanel on 1 Kings 3 (*Nebi'im Ri'shonim* [Jerusalem, 1955], pp. 474b–76a).

6. Compare Halevi's contrast between the god of the philosophers and the God of Jewish faith: *Kuzari* 1:1, 4:13.

7. Here the preacher might have said: *quod erat demonstrandum*. After the argument based on the actual tools of philosophy, the section closes with a homiletic interpretation of Deut. 8:3 to clinch the case.

8. The reference to the *ma'amar*, which had been cited by the preacher at the start of the sermon, begins the second section of part 1, sustaining the thesis from an esoteric interpretation of a rabbinic aggadah.

9. This sentence would seem to combine a concept from the *Kuzari* (e.g., 1:95) with the terminology (*nefesh yeterah*) of the Zohar (e.g., 2:204b).

conveyed, refined to the utmost, to the imaginative faculty. There that imaginative form is transmuted into an object ready for intellectual action.[10]

The eye may be prepared in every respect to see, yet it will not succeed in doing so unless the light of the sun or some other luminous body illuminates the air surrounding the object to be seen. Similarly, some active intellect must illuminate the imaginative forms as they are being abstracted by corporeal perceivers and transmuted into intelligible forms, so that they may be impressed upon the material intellect and become the object of actual intellectual knowledge.[11] It makes little difference that there is a dispute about the essence of this active intellect: whether it is separate [from the human being], as is the view of Avicenna, or an essential part of the human intellect, which would then contain two faculties, an active intellect and a material receptive intellect, as, according to the foremost scholars, was the view of Aristotle.[12]

This being so, our rabbinic statement maintains that the dark earth, which stands for foul matter, will take on wings to ascend by receiving the form of inanimate, vegetative, and sensate things, all three being "earth" because of their lowly and turbid nature. (In this category are also the "wings of the wind," which the author of the statement did not need to mention to express his message; thus *the wind passes by it and it is no more* [Ps. 103:16].) The "wings of the dawn" represent the imaginative faculty, from which intellectual illumination emerges as surely as the dawn breaks forth at the beginning of the day. The verse *Who is this that shines through like the dawn?* (Song 6:10) refers to this.[13]

10. Cf. Harry A. Wolfson, "The Internal Senses in Latin, Arabic, and Hebrew Philosophical Texts," *Studies in the History of Philosophy and Religion,* 1 (Cambridge, Mass., 1973):250–314. The "common sense," is "the center at which all the senses converge; it distinguishes between the qualities of the different senses; it adds the element of consciousness to sensation; but while it *receives* all the impressions of the senses, it does not *retain* them" (p. 277). See also Moscato's extensive discussion of these internal senses in his *Qol Yehudah* on *Kuzari* 5:12 (Warsaw, 1880), pp. 38–42.

11. The analogy between the active intellect and the sun was apparently first suggested by Themistius (based on Aristotle's analogy between the function of the active intellect and light), and taken up by al-Fārābī and Avicenna. See Herbert Davidson, "Alfarabi and Avicenna on the Active Intellect," *Viator* 3 (1972):109, 112, 138, 163. Moscato uses the analogy with the sun in *Qol Yehudah* on *Kuzari* 5:4 (p. 15) and 5:12 (p. 59).

12. According to Davidson (p. 109), the debate about whether Aristotle understood the active intellect as part of the human being or as a transcendent entity is still alive today. Cf. *Qol Yehudah* on *Kuzari* 5:12 (p. 60). The preacher takes a position against Avicenna's later in this sermon.

13. This interpretation is in the tradition of Jewish philosophical exegesis of the Song of Songs, which read that book as an allegory of the interrelationship among the various faculties of the soul and the active intellect in the quest for full intellectual apprehension. The classic example is that of Gersonides, although Moscato's interpretation of this verse shows no dependence on him. On the Jewish commentators in this tradition, see Siegmund Salfield, *Das Hohelied Salomos bei den jüdischen Erklärern des Mittelalters* (Berlin, 1879), pp. 81–100.

"Wings to the sun" refers to the rational faculty, part of which is active and generates intelligibles, and part of which is passive and receives them. This is then made explicit by the phrase "wings to the cherubim," as will soon be explained. *And the sound of the wings of the creatures* [ḥayyot] (Ezek. 3:13) is explained in relation to these two faculties which are *ḥayyot,* "alive"; the level of anything in the chain of life depends upon its level of intellectual apprehension. The continuation of the verse, *beautiful as the moon, radiant as the sun* (Song 6:10), pertains to this, for the moon receives light from the sun.

"Wings to the seraphim" alludes to the intellect acquired through apprehension of intelligibles, which are themselves actually acquired by it, as it "burns away" (*śaraf*) all the masks of ignorance, removes all obstacles, and illumines the darkness until it brings the hidden into the light, clothing itself as in silk with the ornaments of wisdom, as we have explained in the rabbinic statement used on the first day. In this regard the verse concludes, *awesome as bannered hosts* (Song 6:10), for this acquired intellect is the supreme banner of human enlightenment. But truly this is not the banner of love that bestows life to our souls. For all disciplines of human learning, although considered a kind of perfection for a person, are essentially *much study and wearying of the flesh, which is much futility* (cf. Eccles. 12:12, 6:11).[14]

"Great is the power of those who toil in Torah and those who perform acts of kindness, for they do not find shelter in any one of these." This means that they do not hide themselves in the shadow of any of the wings mentioned, by using them to fly above the earth and soar to great heights. For they understand that these float upward in thick clouds of smoke, leaving nothing behind that can restore the soul, unless they rectify their thought and their conduct[15] according to God's will by means of the divine Torah, which bestows life upon all who master it. These are the wings, and no others, by which one may soar to the heavens like an eagle, to enjoy the splendor of the divine presence and find shelter under God's wings.

Thus the proof brought from the verse, *How precious is Your lovingkindness, O God! Human beings find shelter in the shadow of Your wings* (Ps. 36:8).[16] That is to say, how precious is Your friendship, O God, in extending Your lovingkindness to those who share in Your covenant through the light of Torah and commandments. Now human beings may find shelter under Your wings, which will lift and raise them high by the supreme power made available to

14. After using philosophical doctrine for the interpretation of the aggadah, the preacher uses it to reject the significance of all disciplines of human learning external to the Torah as a means for the attainment of ultimate perfection and felicity.

15. "Thought" and "conduct" allude to the two major sections of the sermon; cf. also the final sentence in the following paragraph.

16. This is the conclusion of the *maʾamar* under discussion.

them by the divine revelation, not by the power of their natural wings, which are raised by themselves. Those who fly with these natural wings will not succeed in ascending to the heavenly pinnacle of intellectual knowledge and exalted ethical traits that bring bliss to those who possess them.

Now may the strength and power of this people blessed by God increase, that they may ascend the mountain of the Lord and find shelter under His wings, a goal otherwise extremely difficult to attain. In this regard it was correct to say, *awesome as bannered hosts* (Song 6:10), for this is certainly a banner of exaltation and love, *a standard to be displayed because of its truth* (Ps. 60:6). Let us remain under the banner of the One about whom it is said, *My beloved is white and ruddy, preeminent above ten thousand* (Song 5:10). Let us *set up our standards in the name of our God* (Ps. 20:6).

We must therefore conclude that eternal bliss cannot be attained through the disciplines of human learning, which exhaust their masters to no avail. It is like the passage in the first chapter of the tractate Bekorot [9a], where the emperor says to R. Joshua that he may do with the sages of Athens as he wishes.[17] Fetching the water that the Athenians had taken from the straits (*mayya da-ʾato mi-be beliʿe*), he poured it into a jug; he then told them to fill it, and left. They tried to fill it by pouring in more water, but all the water they poured in was absorbed. They continued until their shoulders were wrenched, and they perished. (Rashi explained *mayya da-ʾato mi-be beliʿe* as the water of the ocean, which absorbs all other water that falls into it and carries such water into the depths, from which it is discharged, as the verse indicates, *yet the sea is not filled* [Eccles. 1:7]. He interpreted *tinara* as a vessel, or jug.)

Now this was truly an appropriate punishment for them, fitting their crime. He gave them an unending task, just as they had wasted their time to no avail in the pursuit of these disciplines which do not provide a destination through which one may reach the goal of immortal life.[18] This statement reminds me that the poets have included among the punishments of hell the sentence of Sisyphus, who must roll a stone from the bottom of the mountain to the top and then return to do it again in an unending and purposeless cycle. Similarly, the daughters of Danaus were sentenced to work perpetually at an empty task, filling sieves with water.[19] Such was the sentence of these others, too, in my judgment.

17. The account of the debate between R. Joshua ben Hananiah and the "sages of Athens" (B. Bek 8b–9b) was frequently interpreted by Jewish commentators and preachers; see, e.g., Samuel Edels (MaHarSHA), *Ḥiddushe Aggadot.* The emperor gives R. Joshua permission to do with the sages as he wishes, because Joshua succeeded in defeating them in disputation and bringing them to the emperor.

18. Thus the preacher provides the philological material (from Rashi) necessary to understand the simple meaning of the passage, and applies it to his general theme.

19. For Sisyphus, see *Odyssey* 11.593; cf. Marsilio Ficino, "Five Questions Concerning

As for us, who share in the covenant of Abraham, let us offer in His tabernacle jubilant songs, raising our voices loudly and majestically: *How precious is Your lovingkindness, O God!* For we shall now take the wings of the dawn and ascend to the heavens.

If you want evidence from the Torah itself, consider the cherubim, the curtain, and the ark. According to the learned [Obadiah] Sforno, the ark covered with gold *inside and outside* (Exod. 25:11) alludes to the rabbinic scholar who must not appear different from his inner character, and the curtain made entirely of gold (Exod. 25:17) teaches about the "image of God." And he was right. Indeed we know that gold does not itself become oxidized or tarnished unless it is mixed with other metals that can become like this; such is the meaning of *How has the gold become dim* (Lam. 4:1). So the intellect is in itself an essence pure and clean, derived from a pure source, and naturally producing purity and clarity. The curtain was not to be affixed to the ark, indicating that this intellect is not mingled with the body that bears it.[20]

The cherubim were made of matter taken from the curtain itself, as the Torah says, *from the cover shall you make the cherubim at its two ends* (Exod. 25:19). This indicates that the two components of the intellect mentioned are both of its essence. The active intellect is not separate, as Avicenna and his followers believed.[21] The cherubim facing each other indicate the act of engendering and receiving the intelligible. The sages have said in the tractate Yoma [54b] that the cherubim are male and female, in order to reinforce this doctrine of action and reception.

All of this [intellectual activity] should occur while looking to the Torah, for no thought or action can be perfected unless it is defined in a manner based on Scripture. Thus, *the faces of the cherubim shall be turned toward the cover* (Exod. 25:20), for that was where the Torah was placed. They spread their wings upward, for *the path of life leads upward for the wise* (Prov. 15:24). These wings have the power to raise us to the heavenly peak of felicity, where we may find shelter under the wings of the divine presence.[22]

---

the Mind," in *The Renaissance Philosophy of Man,* ed. Ernst Cassirer et al. (Chicago, 1948), pp. 208–09. For the punishment of the daughters of Danaus, see Plato, *Republic* 2.363d, and *Collected Works of Erasmus,* vol. 31, *Adages* (Toronto, 1982), pp. 360–61: "To draw water in a sieve."

20. Obadiah Sforno's interpretation of Exod. 25:11 merely cites the talmudic interpretation in B. Yoma 72b. His interpretation of the curtain fuses two motifs separated by Moscato. The pure gold alludes to the intellect, the "image of God" in Maimonidean thought, and the absence of physical contact between curtain and ark alludes to the fully incorporeal nature of the intellect. See Sforno, *Beʾur ʿal ha-Torah,* ed. Wolf (Zeʾev) Gottlieb (Jerusalem, 1980), p. 189, and *Torah Shelemah,* ed. Menaḥem Kasher, 20, no. 40, n. 142.

21. Cf. n. 12, above.

22. The motif of the wings provides a link between this section and the preceding one interpreting the rabbinic *maʾamar.*

The cherubim were in the form of children in order to show that we should become accustomed to the ways of the Torah from childhood, from the moment when the spirit of God begins to make itself felt.[23] Aristotle has said in the first book of his *Ethics* that it makes a great difference if the person is accustomed to do good or evil from youth, for throughout our lives we feel the effects of the habits developed in that period. This is why David has said, *Whose children are like saplings well tended in their youth* (Ps. 144:12), and Solomon has said, *Train a child in the way he ought to go, {he will not swerve from it in old age}* (Prov. 22:6).

The sages frequently used the term "wings" to refer to the components of the rational soul. I am reminded that Plato used to call the theoretical and practical reason "the wings of the soul."[24] God referred to these wings when He said, *I bore you above eagles' wings and brought you to Me* (Exod. 19:4). This means that He lifted them to soar above the heavens, revealing what is known by the astronomers—that there is a star by the name of "Eagle."[25] In the scroll of Ruth, which we are accustomed to read today, there is also a hint of this when Ruth says to Boaz, *Spread your wings over your servant woman* (Ruth 3:9). She meant by this that he should spread upon her some of his sacred splendor and enable her, through his wisdom, to soar like a hawk to the heavens.

Similarly, as the learned Sforno wrote, the lamp indicates that one cannot succeed either in theoretical or in practical endeavors unless they are defined and directed toward the divine will. One light comes from the individual branches, as the verse says, *to throw light over against it* (Exod. 25:37), meaning that the light from the right and the left was directed toward the middle. This indicates that the light of reason, both theoretical and practical, should

23. Cf. Abravanel, *Perush ʿal ha-Torah: Shemot* (Jerusalem, 1964), p. 252a–b. The Aristotelian reference in the following sentence is to the *Nicomachean Ethics* 2.1, end: "Accordingly, the difference between one training of the habits and another from early days is not a light matter, but is serious, or rather all-important."

24. Moscato is probably referring to the famous allegory of the winged horses and charioteer in Plato's *Phaedrus* (246–56). Indeed, this passage, in which the metaphors of nourishment for the soul and wings of the soul recur frequently, may underlie much of the first part of the sermon. Compare Pico della Mirandola, "Oration on the Dignity of Man," in *The Renaissance Philosophy of Man,* pp. 234, 236.

Note the assumption of consistency in code language between the philosophers and the sages. Cf. Maimonides' *Guide* 1:17: "Plato called matter 'female' and form 'male' "; this was used by Maimonides in the interpretation of biblical passages and by his followers in the interpretation of aggadah (see Saperstein, *Decoding,* pp. 60–61).

25. Exod. 19:4 is the theme-verse for sermon 18, also for the Feast of Weeks. There the preacher says that *nesher* ("eagle") "alludes to the theoretical and the practical," "the wings for flying allude to the theoretical, the legs for walking to the practical" (pp. 50c, 47a). The following reference to the Book of Ruth "customarily read today" is another detail placing the sermon on a specific occasion; see n. 1, above.

be directed toward the supernal light and toward the light of the divine Torah, for *the commandment is a lamp and the Torah a light* (Prov. 6:23). This is how we shall indeed see light, shining from light's great source.[26]

I shall not refrain from discussing the inability of the disciplines of human learning to define suitable moderate actions through which human beings may live in accordance with God's will. This message emerges from a remarkable statement recorded by the sages in the tractate Baba Batra, chapter 5 (74a–b): "R. Joḥanan related, Once we were traveling in a ship, and we saw a chest set with precious stones and pearls, surrounded by a species of fish called *birśa*. A diver went down to retrieve the chest, but a fish noticed him and tried to wrench his thigh. He poured out a bottle of vinegar and the fish fled. A heavenly voice was heard saying, 'What business do you have with the chest of the wife of R. Ḥanina ben Dosa, who is to store blue (*tekelet*) in it for the righteous in the world to come?' "[27]

Now this great sea is the entire tempestuous world, as the poet said, "The world is a raging sea, and time a precarious bridge over it."[28] The ships traveling upon it are human beings, who move ahead through the world, impelled by their vital natures. They all share a common desire for a haven where they will find blessed safety; this is the goal of all, but they differ in their ways of reaching it. For some He has ordained the right path, while others journey by a different route. This is what the philosopher explained in the first book of the *Ethics*; the thrust of his words is that human felicity is dependent upon the level attained by the activity of the soul.[29]

This is also what [Isaac] Arama was referring to in chapter 77 of the *ʿAqedah*:[30] "The vital nature generally lets the faculties, affects, and acquired traits loose, without discerning between good and evil, or selecting among

26. Cf. Abravanel, *Perush ʿal ha-Torah: Shemot,* p. 253a. The final sentence is taken from Sforno's comment at the end of Exod. 25. This concludes the first major division of the sermon; the next paragraph begins the second division, which deals with the necessity of the Torah for proper conduct.

27. The Hebrew text has the Aramaic source interspersed with Hebrew explanations of the difficult words. These explanations may well have been given in Italian when the sermon was delivered. The name of the fish, given as "*birśa*" twice in the text of this sermon, is slightly different from that given in the standard texts of the Talmud.

28. Yedaiah ha-Penini, *Beḥinat ʿOlam,* beginning of sect. 8. For ships as an allegorical representation of human beings in this world, cf. Saperstein, *Decoding,* p. 53. The sea as a figure for the world was a commonplace in medieval Christian preaching as well; see the sermon of Innocent III in Petry, pp. 177–80.

29. See Aristotle, *Nichomachean Ethics* 1.6.

30. Isaac Arama's *ʿAqedat Yiṣḥaq* was one of the most influential and frequently cited of all Jewish homiletic works (cf. Bonfil, "Dato," p. 6). The following paragraphs contain a mixture of summary, paraphrase, and direct quotation of the passage near the beginning of chap. 77.

the various ways in which something can be pleasant or beneficial, so that the human being is not above the animals in his actions. Thus the Psalmist said, *Man does not understand honor; he is like the beasts that perish* (Ps. 49:21). But the rational faculty defines and measures these actions, selecting from them that which is suitable and good for a life lived within boundaries, and rejecting that which is excessive or insufficient."

Now as for the definition of human actions and the acquisition of stable, moderate traits which the wise person would choose, as explained there, it is of no use: human reason is incapable of defining and measuring those actions suitable for human felicity. We see this in the statement of the Jew in the *Kuzari,* who said, "Even the social and rational practices can be known only by their main feature, not by how much is required. [We know that charity and chastening of the spirit by means of fasting and meekness are incumbent on us; that deceit, immoderate intercourse with women, and incest are abominable, that honoring one's parents is a duty, and so forth], but the definition and measurement of these duties so as to serve the common welfare is God's" [3:7].

This is what Arama wrote: the Torah's definition of human actions is not the same as Aristotle's, namely, that the acquired traits are stable and moderate. They may instead be traits that are excellent in God's perspective.[31] In this manner he explained the passage about fringes. He said that the fringes, *ṣiṣit,* are connected with *haṣaṣah,* gazing or peering, as in the verse *meṣiṣ min ha-ḥarakkim, he peers through the lattice* (Song 2:9). God commanded that the people make a sign by which they would look and gaze in both a sensory and an intellectual way. This is the meaning of *instruct them to make for themselves fringes . . . and attach a cord of blue to the fringe at each corner* (Num. 15:38).

What is observed is a perfect allusion to both subjects. First, the rational is hinted at by the color blue, *tekelet,* which alludes to the Supreme Being, the *taklit,* or ultimate cause, of all existing things, for which all eyes strain. The sages have said, "*U-re*ʾ*item oto* [*You shall see it* (i.e., the blue fringe)] (Num. 15:39): this indicates that whoever performs the commandment of fringes is as one who encounters the divine presence, for the blue is like the sea, and the sea is like the firmament, and this is like the throne of glory, as the verse says, *Above the firmament . . . [the semblance of a throne]* (Ezek. 1:26)."[32] They meant by this that the phrase *u-re*ʾ*item oto* refers to God—

31. The idea, to be developed more fully in the paragraphs to come, is that the Torah ethic transcends the Aristotelian ethic of moderation. Actions that appear to be extreme from a human perspective may be desirable in God's sight, and only the Torah can inform us of this.

32. B. Men 43b; the rabbinic statement is explained by the preacher as alluding to the process of rational investigation.

"You shall see Him," that is to say, the divine presence. The reason they gave is that the blue thread is like the sea, and so forth; but this is really the process of rational investigation, ascending the ladder step by step from the lower beings to the upper ones, until this rational ascent leads to the Highest Cause.

This thread also alludes marvelously in two ways to the proper order of action and its rectification. The first is the doctrine of moderation in all ethical qualities, averting extremes, for excess and insufficiency are shortcomings, while the mean is good. So the sage has declared, *Do not swerve to the right or the left, keep your foot from evil* (Prov. 4:27). Now blue is by its nature intermediate between the appearance of white, which disperses color, and black, which concentrates it. Blue is the combination of both, and it facilitates seeing, for it is appealing to the eyes. This is the reason for *that shall be your fringe; you shall see it* (Num. 15:39), meaning, when you place a blue thread among the white ones, the eye will of its own accord turn away from the white, which hurts it, to look at the blue, which reinforces it. In this way it will recognize that in all things moderation is good and pleasing.

The eye will also recognize of its own accord that this is why we are commanded to place blue at the corners of our garments. For garments are always an allegorical representation of ethical acquisitions, as in the verse, *Let your clothes be always white* (Eccles. 9:8).[33] Ethical qualities, *middot,* are even linked etymologically with clothing, as in the verse, *The priest shall put on* middo, *his linen garment* (Lev. 6:3). This means that the priest descends in an ethical sense. It indicates that moderation in all human actions is desirable and pleasing, just as this color is the most moderate of all the colors.

Furthermore, just as the blue thread has one dimension, the form of a line which cannot be divided, so the mean of various things is a single point, which can be abandoned in several directions. Many depart from the straight line, and only a few hold fast to it.[34]

When these three matters are considered together—the thread, its color, and its resemblance to the firmament and the throne of glory—we may derive from them a wonderful truth, which surpasses Aristotle's definition of the mean as described. This is that the divine definition and measure of all actions is the true one on which to rely, not the judgment of human reason. We find this in the verse, *Humans see only what is visible, the Lord sees into the*

33. The interpretation of "garments" as a code word for ethical acquisitions was a commonplace in medieval Christian and Jewish exegesis; see Harry Caplan, *Of Eloquence,* pp. 65, 89–90, 94, for the same interpretation of Eccles. 9:8. Arama (in *ʿAqedat Yiṣḥaq,* chap. 51) noted that both garments and customary behavior are called in the vernacular by the same name, *hábitos* ("habits"). In the following sentences of the present sermon, note the allegorical interpretation of a legal passage, Lev. 6:3; cf. Saperstein, *Decoding,* p. 43.

34. Compare Aristotle's *Ethics* 2.5.1106b: "There are many different ways of going wrong . . . but only one possible way of going right."

heart (1 Sam. 16:7). The measures and definitions of the divine Torah, expressed in all its commandments, are the basis of human life, nothing else.

Since this great principle applies to all commandments involving action and all human acts given to measurement, the sages have said, "*You shall see it and recall all the commandments of the Lord* (Num. 15:39): the verse tells us that observing the commandment of the fringes is tantamount to observing all the commandments, and failing to observe the commandment of the fringes is tantamount to failing to observe all the commandments."[35] For certainly a person who observes this important mode of measurement and definition will thereby observe all the other commanded actions as well, whereas if one departs from this mode of measurement, the other commandments will not be fully observed.

This entire passage has been taken from *ʿAqedat Yiṣḥaq* because it fits so beautifully and sheds such radiant light upon the interpretation to be offered of this marvelous rabbinic statement cited. Indeed, taken as a whole, it contains nothing more than what Arama and the Jew in the *Kuzari* have said.

I have seen fit to include here a passage from *Reʾshit Daʿat*[36] (1:2:2) on the verse, *Delight in the Lord, and He shall grant you the desires of your heart* (Ps. 37:4). The author wrote:

> We know from the second book of Aristotle's *Ethics* that one must follow the path of the mean in all actions and avoid extremes [of excess and deficiency]. However, especially with regard to the ideal of temperance, one should always grasp the extreme of deficiency [i.e., self-denial], because the human proclivity toward self-indulgence is so powerful. Aristotle warns about this in that passage.
>
> However, I say that this may be all right according to the capacity of the human being, but it does not apply to us, the sacred congregation of Israel. For it is God who directs us in our actions. This is what the sages meant when they said, "Let all your actions be for the sake of heaven":[37] this is the perfect mean, which brings all our actions to perfection, as we shall explain, with God's help, in book 3. Consequently, even when we act immoderately and experience pleasures, so long as it is for the sake of heaven, the action will be perfect, not deficient, as Aristotle maintained.

35. Sifre, Num. 115 (on Num. 15:38).

36. A homiletic ethical work by Moses Albelda (1478–1560), published at Venice in 1583. The Aristotelian reference at the beginning of the quotation is from the *Nicomachean Ethics* 2.6.1106a–b and 2.8.1109a. The citation from this book (p. 24a) provides a terminus a quo (1583) for the sermon.

37. Abot 2:12.

This is the meaning of the verse, *Delight in the Lord*: even though the action falls into the category of pleasure and delight, which is the extreme of an excess, this does not make it imperfect, for God will perfect every action performed for His sake. On the verse, *In all your ways, know Him* (Prov. 3:6), the sages have commented, "even with regard to transgression,"[38] as will be explained, with God's help. This is what the rabbis meant when they said that when one makes the Sabbath a delight, even though this departs from the ideal of temperance, it is nevertheless a perfect action, and therefore *He shall grant you the desires of your heart.*[39] For in addition to the perfection of the act, God will bestow a reward.

All of this can be applied to the esoteric meaning of *tekelet,* "blue," as we mentioned, especially to the rabbinic statement that the blue is like the sea, the sea is like the firmament, and the firmament is like the throne of glory.

Now see how the words of the rabbinic statement become clear on the basis of what we have said! "We were traveling in a ship" refers to the voyage of human beings in the ships of this world, which is called "sea." "We saw a chest [set with precious stones and pearls]": this is the ultimate good, desired by all, upon which human felicity and bliss depend. Such bliss is called "chest" because it is sealed up and hidden away as if it had been placed in a box, so that it cannot be seen. "It was surrounded by a species of fish called *birśa*" refers to the appetitive faculty, with its various components.[40] This is the "tortuous serpent" which prevents the contemplative and active attainment of the goal through the pursuit of its base desires, for people are overwhelmed by their impulses every day.

"A diver went down [to retrieve the chest]": this is the philosophical intellect of the human being, which roams afar to know the nature of each kind of created thing and to discover a rational way to moderate actions properly, as indicated above. This image is consistent with a passage in the *Guide* [1:34]: "Just as one who knows how to swim may retrieve pearls from the sea bed, while one who does not know how to swim will drown."[41] "The fish noticed him and tried to wrench his thigh" refers to the power of the oppressor to distract one from attaining the goal. It *wrenches the hip socket* (Gen. 32:33) in order to cast one down to the earth.

"He poured out a bottle of vinegar, and it fled" refers to the power of

38. B. Ber 63a.

39. B. Shab 118b.

40. On the components of the appetitive faculty, see the author's *Qol Yehudah,* on *Kuzari* 1:33 and 3:5, and the report of a discourse by one of Joseph Karo's students in *Masʿot Ereṣ Yiśraʾel,* ed. Abraham Yaari (Tel Aviv, 1976), p. 202.

41. The passage continues, "Therefore only such persons as have had proper instruction should expose themselves to the risk [of studying metaphysics]."

asceticism, through which one may prevail over this evil impulse, subduing it, weakening it, reining it in, molding it fittingly and moderately into fine ethical qualities conducive to beneficial intellectual activity. This was the way of the philosophers, as we have said. "A heavenly voice was heard saying, 'What business do you have [with the chest of the wife of R. Ḥanina ben Dosa, who is to store away blue in it for the righteous in the world to come]?" In other words, "You toil in vain, you humans who work so hard to define appropriate moderate actions through which one can live in accordance with God's will. The key to this is given over to God alone, who knows how to sustain the weary by defining proper ethical attributes and qualities," as in the statements from the *Kuzari* and *ʿAqedat Yiṣḥaq*.

This felicity alluded to in the "chest" is given only to the "wife of R. Ḥanina ben Dosa," referring to the soul of the Jew, which conducts itself according to the measurement given by God, not according to sophistical intellectual speculation. This is the "blue stored away for the world to come," referring to the defining of true thought and right conduct, upon which supreme and eternal bliss depends, as we have indicated through the Arama passage. The wife of R. Ḥanina ben Dosa was taken as a type of the Jewish soul because of her widely known piety and the miracles which she experienced with him, as the sages recorded in the tractate Taʿanit.[42]

Now you may ask, why did the sages speak of ethical and philosophical matters by way of allegories and enigmas, as we have seen in the aggadic statement from the first day [of the holiday], and in both statements incorporated into this sermon? After all, the contents of their teachings are not one of the secret doctrines of the Torah, which we are commanded to conceal. On the contrary, the aggadah includes important principles that should be engraved on the tablets of our hearts. Why then did they not teach them explicitly?

I will answer after noting that the rabbis themselves addressed this issue in several ways. One was, "When they became weary of technical legal study, they engaged in words of jest";[43] another explanation was that this was a way

42. B. Taʿan 24b–25a. This concludes the allegorical exegesis of the aggadah; the preacher now continues to raise and answer a fundamental question about this method of interpretation.

43. This quotation is attributed to the rabbis by Maimonides in chap. 5 of his "Eight Chapters" and by Simeon ben Ṣemaḥ Duran in his *Magen Abot* on Abot 2:16 (Jerusalem, 1961, p. 83), but it is not actually known in this form in the rabbinic literature (cf. B. Shab 30b). For the conception of aggadah as recreation from halakic study, see also Abraham ibn Ezra's introduction to his *Torah Commentary* and to his *Commentary on Lamentations*; for aggadah as jest, see Hillel of Verona, *Tagmule ha-Nefesh* (Lyck, 1874), pp. 25a, 26a. The phrase *to sharpen the mind* is used in the Talmud to explain the motivation for questionable statements, but only in a halakic context (B. Taʿan 7a, ʿErub 13a, Naz 59b, Zeb 13a, Ned 45a). Cf. Maimonides, "Eight Chapters," chap. 5, where he uses this with regard to external disciplines.

of sharpening their minds. However, I will also say my own piece in answer to this question. The sages, recognizing the extreme value and importance of the matters to which they alluded, wanted to make a powerful impression. Now it is clear that people hold in greatest esteem that which they must expend their effort to attain. Proof of this is to be found in children. What is highly esteemed will always be remembered. Furthermore, the effort itself causes the subject to be remembered, as the sages have said, "The wisdom I acquired in anger [has remained with me]."[44]

This is why the sages decided to incorporate these precious teachings, so beneficial to others, in statements that are obscure in their language, knowing that these teachings would remain in the shadows until the true wisdom of their words was discovered by the wisest luminaries among the people. As they plumb the full depth of the sages' teachings, after the effort and toil of their investigation, they will love and esteem what they have discovered. These doctrines will be fully impressed upon their thought, and they will benefit, even if this was not their original intent. Others, too, who hear these statements explained by those who have uncovered their true meaning, will derive benefit from the joy and pleasure which they feel in finally understanding after having been entangled in the realm of allegory and enigma.[45]

In summary, we have found that disciplines other than the divine Torah cannot adequately measure or define that which pertains either to the intellect or to the realm of action. God's Torah, which is perfect, can do both. These are the wings that enable us to ascend to the heights of heaven and find shelter under the wings of the One who is to be blessed, praised, and glorified for His bounteous love and goodness. Let us sing to Him in joy, *How precious is Your lovingkindness, O God! Human beings take refuge in the shadow of Your wings.*

44. See Maimonides, *Code,* I,iii (*Talmud Torah*), 3:12 (interpreting Eccles. 2:9).

45. The preacher thus justifies this technique of instruction through esoteric interpretation of the rabbinic aggadah in terms of its impact on listeners.

Saul ha-Levi Morteira

Saul ha-Levi Morteira was born ca. 1596 in Venice, where one of his teachers was the colorful and versatile rabbi Juddah Aryeh (Leon) Modena. Circumstance brought Morteira to Amsterdam in 1616, and he decided to remain there, holding positions of rabbinic leadership, until his death in 1660. He wrote apologetic tracts in Spanish and in Hebrew dealing with issues hotly disputed in his time: the eternity of the world and the eternity of punishment for the unrepentant sinner, divine providence, and the merits of Judaism as against Christianity.[1] As a leading rabbi of the Sephardic community, he was a member of the rabbinical courts that excommunicated the unorthodox former Marrano intellectual Juan de Prado and the independent philosopher who may once have been his student, Baruch Spinoza.

Morteira's most important contribution to Hebrew literature was his sermons. He had a distinctive style: his sermons are relatively short, carefully structured, lucid investigations of a clearly defined subject.[2] Each is built upon a single verse (the *nośe*) from the weekly Torah lesson, which is connected at some point with an aggadic passage from rabbinic literature (the *ma'amar*). During his first year in Amsterdam, he preached on the first verse of each lesson, then the following year on the second verse, and so on, progressing systematically verse after verse.

Gibʿat Sha'ul, published in Amsterdam in 1645, contains an outline of five hundred sermons and fifty printed in full.[3] Morteira's disciples, who

1. On these aspects of Morteira's writings and thought, see Alexander Altmann, "Eternality of Punishment," *PAAJR* 40 (1973):1–40; Henry Mechoulan, "Spinoza et Morteira au carrefour du socianisme," *REJ* 135 (1976):51–65; Yosef Kaplan, "R. Sha'ul ha-Levi Morteira we-Ḥibburo Ṭeʿanot we-Hassagot neged ha-Dat ha-Noṣerit," *Meḥqarim ʿal Toledot Yahadut Holand* 1 (1975):9–31; Ralph Melnick, *From Polemics to Apologetics* (Assen, 1981), pp. 29–32, 66–69.

2. See Saperstein, "Art Form."

3. The book was reprinted in Warsaw (1902), without the outline of the unpublished sermons, and without the sermons on *Wa-'Etḥanan* and *Niṣṣabim,* the two sermons that speak most directly about Christianity (eliminated, according to the publisher, "for reasons beyond our control" [read: censorship]). That these sermons could be printed in mid-seventeenth-century Amsterdam but not in early twentieth-century Warsaw illustrates something about the atmosphere of "the Dutch Jerusalem." For a discussion of the Warsaw publication, see Ḥayim Liberman, "Sefer *Gibʿat Sha'ul,*" *Sinai* 37 (1973):389–93.

collected the material for this book, wrote in their introduction that the total number of his sermons was fourteen hundred, an average of fifty per year from his arrival in Amsterdam until the book was published. Such a prodigious output indicates that he devoted a considerable proportion of his time and energy to preparation for preaching.[4]

Few of the extant sermons contain as much explicit discussion of contemporary social issues as does the one presented here. Most of them deal with standard problems of medieval Jewish thought, albeit often from a new perspective or with a novel twist. If not entirely typical in its content, however, the present sermon is representative in its form. After the introduction, it is divided into three sections, in which the theme-verse from the Torah lesson and the aggadic statement are explained, and it concludes with a coda and summary. It is quite likely that those in the congregation would have left the synagogue with the major points and the manner in which they were derived from the Torah verse vividly etched in their minds.

The central thesis—that arrogant behavior, ostentatious apparel, and high living by Jews angers both God and their Gentile neighbors—is well known in the ethical literature of Spanish Jewry. Jewish communities in many different periods and geographical locations endeavored to regulate such behavior through the enactment of sumptuary laws. In Amsterdam, the problem was intensified by the conflict between two very different kinds of ethos. As S. W. Baron puts it, "The contrast between the luxury-loving Portuguese and Spaniards, who had brought with them from their home countries an inordinate appetite for costly garments and conveyances, and the sturdy Calvinist Dutchmen was striking."[5] It is this problem that Morteira addresses in such a powerful manner.

4. At first Morteira preached every week. After the merger of the three Sephardic congregations in 1638, he was responsible for preaching three times each month (and teaching Talmud to advanced students). For this he was paid an annual salary of 600 guilders and 100 baskets of peat. See Herbert I. Bloom, *The Economic Activities of the Jews of Amsterdam* (Port Washington, N.Y., 1969), p. 69.

5. Baron, *SRHJ* 15:52. Simon Schama's elegant and erudite study of seventeenth-century Dutch culture, *The Embarrassment of Riches* (New York, 1987), which appeared too late for me to use in annotating Morteira's sermon, requires a refinement of Baron's statement: at stake may have been not so much the conflict between the Iberian and the Dutch Calvinist ethos, but rather a tension within Dutch culture itself. Schama shows that Dutch Calvinist preachers denounced the fruits of economic abundance in their own society—homes adorned with lavish furnishings, ostentatious apparel and jewelry, and sumptuous banquets—in terms quite similar to those used by Morteira. Like Morteira, the Dutch *predikants* were certain that such behavior would arouse God's wrathful punishment. It is therefore Morteira's emphasis on the nature of exile and the jealousy of Christian neighbors, rather than the particular conduct being condemned, that give the sermon its specifically Jewish character. Morteira clearly drew from a tradition of self-criticism in earlier Sephardic literature—the influence of Solomon ibn Verga's *Shebeṭ Yehudah* is especially apparent—but his message would have been reinforced by similar denunciations delivered from Calvinist pulpits. Cf. n. 16 to the sermon, below.

The art of the sermon is expressed in the way the preacher derives his thesis from the traditional sources. In this case, Morteira argues that his contemporaries were courting disaster by making precisely the same mistake their ancestors had made in Egypt. This is sustained through a rather impressive (although not entirely convincing) reinterpretation of key terms in Exodus 1:7, which actually reads the biblical text in light of contemporary realities: *yishreṣu* means "expand" or "spread out" (into larger living quarters), *yirbu* means "become great" (in their own estimation, as manifested by ostentatious clothing), *yaʿaṣmu* means "become corpulent" (by indulging in sumptuous delicacies).

The last interpretation enables Morteira to incorporate the aggadic passage. When the congregation first heard this passage quoted at the beginning of the sermon, there would have been no apparent connection with the Torah verse. By demonstrating a relationship where none was foreseen, the preacher not only provided a certain aesthetic pleasure, but undergirded the contention that his thesis is rooted in the tradition.

Despite the extensive use of biblical and rabbinic material, this is not a sermon intended primarily to elucidate the classical sources for their own sake. Here we see a preacher marshalling the ancient texts in order to address what he considers to be a pressing problem of his time.

The People's Envy
Sermon on *Shemot*
(Ca. 1622, Amsterdam)

The Israelites were fertile, wa-yishreṣu wa-yirbu wa-yaʿaṣmu *very greatly, so that the land was full with them* (Exod. 1:7).[1]

"R. Isaac said, Whoever takes pleasure in an optional banquet will eventually be exiled, for the Bible states, *Who feast on lambs from the flock,* and soon after *Now they shall head the column of exiles* (Amos 6:4, 7).

"Our rabbis taught, Whoever feasts excessively anywhere will eventually destroy his household, make his wife a widow and his fledglings orphans, and forget what he has learned. He will be the center of many conflicts, and his words will not be heeded. He profanes the Name of Heaven and the

1. NJV: *The Israelites were fertile and prolific; they multiplied and increased very greatly, so that the land was filled with them.* The key words in the verse have been left untranslated here, as the proper interpretation will emerge from the preacher's discussion.

names of his father and his teacher; he gives a bad name to himself, his children, and his children's children to the end of time.

"Abbaye said, They call him 'oven heater.'

"Raba said, 'tavern dancer.'

"R. Papa said, 'dish licker.'

"R. Shemaiah said, 'one who folds and lies down' (B. Pes 49a)."[2]

It is clear that the Egyptian exile was called an *iron blast furnace* (Deut. 4:20) because it affected us the way a blast furnace works upon silver or gold placed within it. These are refined by the removal of all dross, prepared to withstand fire, strengthened for the testing stone and the blows of the hammer. So the calamities of Egypt taught Israel to endure as slaves, thereby preparing her to endure the calamities of later exiles.

At the redemption from Egypt, God was called *I will be as I will be* (Exod. 3:14). This means, as the rabbis interpreted it, I will be with them in this agony, as I will be with them in subsequent agony.[3] But it was not only the quality of patient endurance that they learned from that exile; they also learned the quality of confident trust. Later, in periods of great anguish, they would envision the agony and degradation of their ancestors in Egypt, and God's unanticipated act of redemption that removed them from the house of bondage to be kings and princes; this would give them the assurance that God would do the same in the present exile, suddenly, when He so desires. In this way the blast furnace refined us, producing patience and trust.

This was the essence of the experience in Egyptian exile: patient endurance leading to confident trust. But God used that exile to teach us even more. If we would only open our eyes, we could learn lessons of great import, extremely beneficial to us in this current exile. These lessons might even alleviate the misfortunes that weight upon us. For everything God did to our ancestors was intended to help us learn, so that we might behave properly.[4]

This is the point. The first generation of our ancestors who left the land of Canaan knew that they were resident aliens, who had departed from their

2. Note that the aggadic *ma'amar* has no apparent connection with the theme-verse. At first hearing, the theme-verse conveys the impression that the sermon will be an optimistic treatment of Jewish prosperity and success. The aggadic passage immediately undermines that expectation by introducing the motif of exile, which is indeed central to the sermon. The first words following the *ma'amar* are connected with it semantically through the word *exile*. They return to the context of the theme-verse, although not to the verse itself, which speaks of growth and prosperity. Yet the motif of suffering in exile is itself transformed by the reference to the "refining" and "strengthening" effects of that experience.

3. Cf. Rashi, based on B. Ber 9b and Exod. Rabbah 3:6.

4. Compare the technique used by Naḥmanides in his treatment of the patriarchal narratives—"The deeds of the forefathers are a sign for their descendants." See the sermon of Joshua ibn Shueib, above, n. 9.

own land and come to a land not theirs. They continued to think of themselves as aliens, and they did not overreach. The Egyptians loved them and bore them no envy. But after their death, the following generation thought of Egypt as the land of their birth. They grew arrogant and became so provocative in their behavior that they aroused the envy of the Egyptians, who decreed harsh laws against them and enslaved them.

This has frequently been the cause of massacres and expulsions during our own exile. Expelled from certain countries, we have arrived in others totally destitute, and God has graciously enabled us to acquire new wealth and possessions. Those who knew at first hand the circumstances of their arrival lived in peace. But after their deaths, others became arrogant, indulging in empty vanities, until the indigenous population eventually expelled them.

God showed us all this in Egypt, so that we might learn from the past and not repeat the same foolish mistake, but it has been to no avail. Precisely how this behavior caused the oppressive enslavement in Egypt, how God decrees with true justice that this pattern will continue so long as such behavior remains unchanged, how the matter can be remedied: this will be the subject of our sermon today, which we begin with the help of the One who brought us out of the Egyptian blast furnace.[5]

Many of our biblical commentators focus upon the simple meaning of the text. They are not interested in penetrating more deeply into subjects to which the prophets direct our attention, but only in explicating the surface level of what is said. Finding repetition in a verse, such commentators often write, "The same content is repeated in different words."[6] This may indeed be true, according to the simple meaning. For the prophets, desiring to embellish their language with rhetoric—*The Lord God has given me a skilled tongue* (Isa. 50:4)—did repeat certain points in order to make a stronger impression upon the listeners.[7] Some have found other, deeper reasons for this

5. The introduction, which ends here, is characteristic of Morteira's sermons, concluding with a concise statement of the topic to be discussed and an invocation of divine help in beginning the sermon proper. What follows often begins from a new point of departure, as Morteira does here by raising the issue of repetition in biblical language.

6. This phrase is generally associated with the thirteenth-century commentator David Kimḥi (RaDaK). See Louis Finkelstein, *The Commentary of David Kimḥi on Isaiah* (New York, 1926), pp. xxiv–xxv; Frank Talmage, *David Kimḥi: The Man and His Commentaries* (Cambridge, Mass., 1975), p. 105; Ezra Zion Melamed, *Mefareshe ha-Miqra,* 2 vols. (Jerusalem, 1975) 2:833.

7. On the use of rhetoric by the prophets, see Judah Messer Leon's *Nofet Ṣufim,* where the verse from Isaiah quoted by Morteira is explained: "The Lord gave him the language of the most expert practitioners of the rhetorical art" (*The Book of the Honeycomb's Flow,* ed. and trans. Isaac Rabinowitz [Ithaca, N.Y., and London, 1983], pp. 22–23). Morteira differentiates between prophetic writings, where repetition may have a merely rhetorical purpose, and the

technique. However, this is not the proper way to interpret the words of the Torah. Nothing in the Torah is mere rhetoric; everything is of substantial and fundamental significance. There is no repetition without a special purpose.

This being so, there is a serious problem in our theme-verse: *The Israelites were fertile,* wa-yishreṣu wa-yirbu wa-yaᶜaṣmu *very greatly, so that the land was full of them* (Exod. 1:7). All of these phrases seem repetitious; the strongest expression would have sufficed.[8] Nor is it proper to say simply, "The same content is repeated in different words." No, each phrase refers to an essential matter. We therefore maintain that God has taught us from the first exile how to act in all future exiles. It would be well for us if only we paid attention.

We know how upsetting it is for a king who punishes one of his servants if the servant does not even notice the punishment; such behavior reflects contempt for the king's justice. That is why Moses pleaded and prayed at such length, even though it had already been decreed that he would not enter the land. He wanted to show how harsh and painful the punishment seemed to him. Now when the Israelites in Egypt recognized their alien status and behaved like foreigners in exile, they lived in peace and tranquility. But when they forgot their original situation and aspired to be princes and nobles, God made them feel the full weight of the yoke, and many disasters befell them, for they had forgotten the meaning of exile.[9] This has been the cause of all the misfortunes of Israel in all exiles through the ages.

The present passage from the Torah testifies to this fact. It says, *Joseph died, and all his brothers, and all that generation* (Exod. 1:6). This means that the first generation of our ancestors who left the land of Canaan, who knew that they were aliens and behaved moderately, at an appropriate social level, died in peace. Then a new generation arose after them who did not know their place of origin. They began to behave in a domineering and arrogant manner, bringing the evil that eventually occurred upon themselves. The Egyptians grew envious of them and devised nefarious plots, ultimately oppressing them with a heavy yoke. All this was in accordance with God's will, so that they would remember that they were in exile.

Torah, where each word is significant and teaches something new. This approach should be contrasted with that of Joseph Garçon, who wrote a book called *Meᶜarat ha-Makpelah* to show that all apparent redundancies in the prophetic literature had significance. See Garçon, in Benayahu, pp. 52, 161–62, 182.

8. Cf. the discussion of this verse by Neḥama Leibowitz, *Studies in Shemot* (Jerusalem, 1976) 1:13 and 20–21.

9. Cf. Ephraim Luntshitz, *Keli Yaqar,* end of *Wa-Yiggash* and beginning of *Wa-Yeḥi,* on Gen. 47:27. For the much more common contrary view that the Egyptian exile was not caused by sin, see Abraham Bibago, *Derek Emunah* (Constantinople, 1521), p. 23b (ed. Hava Fraenkel-Goldschmidt [Jerusalem, 1978], p. 144). The following sentence hints to the listener that the preacher will make the application to his own generation.

Then the Torah says, *The Israelites were fertile,* after the death of their parents. Then, having reproduced abundantly, they were no longer content to live in their original space. They refused to endure crowded conditions and to remain content with little, so as to avoid the hostile glares of their enemies. Rather, *wa-yishreṣu,* meaning that they spread out. (The verb *sharaṣ* comes from *raṣ,* "run," as does *ereṣ,* "earth," which the sages explained, "It ran to do the will of its Maker.")[10] After they were fecund, they expanded; becoming numerous, they wanted wider spaces.

This is inappropriate for those who live in exile. They should be prepared to endure hardship; happy are those who have what they need and no more. But such a contented disposition is not what we see today. A man who is alone with his wife, or even a single man, lives in a large house with unnecessarily spacious rooms. Such people waste their money, which they may well need some day, by giving it to the Gentiles and receiving nothing of value in return. This is not befitting a people living outside its land, in the land of its enemies.[11]

Even in the land of Israel, the prophet berated an Israelite king for his large houses, and for considering these houses to be a source of security rather than directing his thought to the service of God. The Prophet spoke of one *who thinks, "I will build me a vast palace with spacious chambers, provided with windows, paneled in cedar and painted with vermilion"* (Jer. 22:14). Such unnecessary adornments are nothing but arrogance.

And if such splendid houses are inherently superfluous, examined in light of our own time of exile they become all the more shameful. At a time when God's ark was within the proper curtains, King David still said, *Surely I will not enter the tent of my house, I will not go up upon the bed spread out for me . . . until I find a place for the Lord* (Ps. 132:3, 5). Now, living in exile, when God's ark no longer exists and His house is destroyed, how dare we dwell in spacious chambers, devising all kinds of haughty schemes to glorify ourselves with nonessentials?

This is precisely God's complaint against Israel through His prophet Haggai, who said, *Is it a time for you yourselves to dwell in your paneled homes, while this House is lying in ruins?* (Hag. 1:4). He meant, at a time when the temple lies in ruins, burned together with the other great houses of Jerusalem, it is

10. Gen. Rabbah 5:8. Modern commentators generally understand the midrash as deriving *ereṣ* from *raṣah* ("to desire"): the earth desired to do God's will. However, the form *raṣetah* as third-person feminine singular past of *ruṣ* is attested in rabbinic sources (e.g., B. Taʿan 22a), and *Bereʾshit Rabbati* also links *ereṣ* with *ruṣ* (ed. Ḥanokh Albeck [Jerusalem, 1940], p. 14). For the derivation of *shereṣ* from *ruṣ,* see Eliezer ben Yehudah, *Millon* 15:7469.

11. Cf. Solomon Alami's critique of Spanish Jewry in the early fifteenth century: "Because we have built here in exile, upon the ruins of our holy temple, luxurious houses and beautiful and spacious chambers, we have been banished from our homes to the field and the dung gate" ("Iggeret Musar," quoted by Baer, *HJCS* 2:241).

not fitting for you to have large, paneled, ornamented homes. Your insensitivity to this is astonishing: is it a time for you yourselves to dwell in your paneled homes, while this House lies waste? God will punish Israel severely for this offense, for nothing could show more clearly that the destruction has been forgotten.

Therefore, Scripture said through this same prophet, *You have been expecting much and getting little, and when you brought it home, I would blow on it. Why? says the Lord of Hosts. Because of My House, which lies in ruins, while you all hurry to your own homes* (Hag. 1:9). This means, when these men began in their business affairs, they envisioned great achievements and thought of large profits, but in the end it came to very little. And even this little, brought into their homes, was destroyed by God through theft or fire or other misfortunes.

For when they accumulated wealth, it was not in order to preserve it for their children and to serve God in accordance with their means, but in order to enlarge their homes. One who at first lived in a single room became wealthy, began to think that even five rooms would not suffice, and spent his money for this foolish purpose; that is why God diminished it. This is as the prophet said, *Why? says the Lord of Hosts. Because of My House, which lies in ruins, while you all hurry to your own homes.* This means, each one runs to the house he thinks befits his status, not his real need. They choose houses not according to the number of their children, but according to their social class. All this is repugnant to God in a period of exile, while His House lies in ruins.

In order to teach Israel this lesson, God commanded Jeremiah to offer the Rechabites wine to drink. The Bible tells us that he placed glasses of wine before them in God's House and said, "Drink the wine." But they replied, *We will not drink wine, for our ancestor Jonadab son of Rechab commanded us: "You shall never drink wine, either you or your children. Nor shall you build houses, or sow fields, or plant vineyards, nor shall you own such things; but you shall live in tents all your days so that you may long live on the land where you sojourn"* (Jer. 35:6). There is a problem here. Since Jeremiah told them to drink wine, a sufficient response would have been "Jonadab son of Rechab commanded us not to drink wine." Why the need to recount to him the other commands: that they not dwell in a house nor plant vineyards, and so forth?[12]

God wanted Israel in Jeremiah's time to learn from the example of wine, for they still did not drink wine because an ancestor had enjoined them, while Israel refused to heed God's own prophet. He therefore said, *The commands of Jonadab son of Rechab have been fulfilled: he charged his children not to*

12. Isaac Abravanel raises precisely the same question about the response of the Rechabites in his commentary on the Latter Prophets (Jer. 35: the fourth question). He gives an exegetical solution, not a homiletical one, as we have here.

drink wine, and to this day they have not drunk, in obedience to the charge of their ancestor. But I have spoken to you persistently, and you did not listen to Me (Jer. 35:14). The wine alludes to all physical pleasures.

But God also wanted Israel to learn from the Rechabites a lesson for the future.[13] The subsequent commands were intended to teach Israel what to do in their exile. God wanted them to learn from the injunctions of Jonadab not to build houses or plant vineyards. And indeed, all Jews living in exile should refrain from purchasing houses or vineyards. These make Jews forget God, and they are a troublesome burden in time of expulsion. They isolate Jews from their fellow Jews and cause them to mix in among the Gentiles. Moreover, these possessions are readily seen by all, arousing great envy.[14]

Jews should rather live "in tents," meaning "in the manner of a tent dweller," as one who tarries for the night, not in large houses with expensive ornaments. For in this manner they will "long live on the land where they sojourn," and their enemies will not envy them. The Philistine envy of Isaac was because his territorial holdings were expanding. The Torah says, *The Philistines envied him, and they stopped up all the wells which his father's servants had dug in the days of his father Abraham, filling them with earth* (Gen. 26:14–15). They were jealous because of his many wells. And this was the sin of our ancestors in Egypt, as the Torah says, *The Israelites were fertile* wa-yishreṣu, meaning that they ran to spread out in their fields and houses. When a new king arose over Egypt, this was why he said what he did to his people. It is justly called an iron blast furnace. It can refine us, if we know how to learn from it.

Then the verse says, *wa-yirbu*. It was not only that they expanded in their houses quantitatively, but also qualitatively *they became great* and magnificent

13. For a similar use of the Rechabites as a model in a passage excoriating contemporaries for their excessively luxurious lifestyle inappropriate to exile, see *Sefer ha-Qanah* (Paritsk, 1786), p. 122c–d.

14. Compare the following account, written by a French traveler toward the end of the seventeenth century: "There are Jews in Amsterdam more wealthy than some of our European princes. One of them had a house built in which gold, silver, azure, and marble sparkle on every side. It has a large room inlaid with silver ducatons. He wanted to set bars or gratings of silver in the ground floor apartment facing the street, while all others in the city are made of iron. But the magistrate, both wise and politically astute, knowing that the Jews in general were not beloved by the Christians and that the populace might use this mark of vanity as a pretext for ransacking the house and the houses of the other Jews, prohibited him from doing this. Instead of silver bars, he covered his windows with a grating of gilt iron" (Claude Jordan, *Voyages historiques de l'Europe,* 6 vols. [Paris, 1692–97]. 5:201–02; cf. Werner Sombart, *The Jews and Modern Capitalism* [London, 1913], p. 184). Manasseh ben Israel maintained that the Jews of Amsterdam owned about three hundred houses.

Note the twofold explanation of the sin: theologically, it is conduct inappropriate in exile, arousing God's anger; sociologically, it arouses the hostility of Gentile neighbors in the host country. This double perspective continues throughout the sermon.

(as in the phrase *moshiʿa wa-rab,* "a great deliverer" [Isa. 19:20]).[15] This refers to their manner of dress and to other externals. They began to have expensive clothes and horses and chariots with men running before them, all of which is inappropriate for aliens and exiles in a land not theirs. In addition to increasing envy, it prolongs the exile.[16]

It is like the story of a king whose son had become repugnant to him and was banished to a distant land. After a while, the king began to feel sorry for his son. Thinking of his suffering and anguish in a foreign country, the king said, "How much must he be suffering right now; how much pain must he be enduring. He must be thirsty and hungry; he must be going around without proper clothing. I will be compassionate toward him and have him brought back." But when he investigated the boy's condition, he discovered that his son had forgotten the father's house. There in the land where he was living, he dressed like one of the local princes, or even better. Then the king's mercy vanished, and he said, "This is not a proper punishment, for he has forgotten his father's house. His toil must become more onerous. Then, when he cries out to me, I will respond with compassion."

Such was the case in Egypt. God cast them there, but while sojourning in that land they increasingly took on the trappings of power and honor. Seeing this, God made their enemies' yoke weigh heavily upon them, until they cried out from their toil. He heard their sighs when they were enslaved, not when they were prosperous. Had they not first "become great" through the affectations of power, their exile would have ended with no change in

15. *Moshiʿa wa-rab*: Morteira follows the interpretation of this phrase given by David Kimḥi, and applies it to the verb *wa-yirbu* in Exod. 1:7. Instead of "they became numerous," he understands it to mean "they became great" or "they became grandees."

16. See n. 14, end. Ostentatious dress was a subject of both communal regulation and social criticism in most European countries. For an overview, see Baron, *Community,* 2:301–07. For the Spanish tradition see the statutes passed by the synod at Valladolid in 1432 (Baer, *HJCS* 2:269), and Solomon ibn Verga, *Shebeṭ Yehudah* (Jerusalem, 1947), p. 47. Extravagance of attire was also a constant theme in Christian preaching of social criticism from the twelfth to the seventeenth century; see Chandos, p. 62, n. 1; Smith, p. 125. Indeed, one Dutch Calvinist preacher, Jacob Trigland (1583–1654), berated his congregants on this score by arguing that their Jewish neighbors saw in the lavish dress a betrayal of the religious ideals of the Reformation: "And these days our people display such opulence in attire that even our enemies, who surpass almost all people in expensive adornments and ostentatious display (I am speaking here about the Portuguese Jews), are able to talk about us [as follows]: 'Previously they were [living] in lowliness and humility, especially at the beginning of the Reformation. Then they were not so proud; then they were not so festooned and bedecked, then they did not wear such costly clothes. . . . See how they have changed now! How haughty and puffed up they have become!' and more such mockery." This extraordinary passage, virtually a mirror image of Morteira's argument, was published in *Godgeleerde Bijdragen* (Theological contributions) (1865), p. 783, and cited in *De Navorscher* (1868):6; I am grateful to Ineke and John Carman for their translation from the Dutch.

their mode of life, and they could have been saved without having been afflicted with sorrows.

All this happened to us in the Egyptian exile so that we might learn a lesson for the other exiles. But we have gone astray like a flock of sheep, repeating the same mistake wherever we have been exiled, by dressing more ostentatiously than the nobles of the land. We have caused our own destruction during the period of the exile. And our enemies have responded with general expulsions both out of envy and as a punishment.[17]

Indeed, the agent in these matters deserves severe punishment, for several reasons. First, we well know how many hedges God has placed in His Torah to keep us from destroying our own world and being banished from it in humiliation. We see that He requires death for the rebellious son not because of what the son has actually done, but because he is preparing to do evil. For when that son behaves this way, he will eventually seek his accustomed pleasures, and failing to find them, he will attack and rob.[18] The Torah mandated capital punishment so that he would not become used to such behavior, but be satisfied with little and behave properly.

Similarly, our sages were strict in prohibiting wine touched by idolaters, so that Jews would not go to drink with them. For when wine enters, deliberation departs, and the Jew could end up involved in idolatrous worship, God forbid![19] How much more should Israel in exile be required not to go about in these grandiose and splendid raiments, for those who begin will eventually seek their accustomed pleasures, and failing to find them, they will steal and worship false gods and turns their backs on the God of Israel.

Second, these expenditures are in the category of major transgressions called "communal sins" (cf. Lev. 4:21), a criminal offense that also leads others to transgress. We cannot assume that the righteous who fear God's word will arrange their affairs properly and remain uncontaminated by the perversion of their neighbors. This is nearly impossible. Since only those who dress ostentatiously are honored, and garments are a prime source of prestige, those who refrain from such dress will be called misers. No one will think highly of them. They will be hated and scorned. This would not happen if the entire people were to comport themselves in a clean and thrifty manner.

R. Nehorai may have had this in mind when he said, "One should always

17. See n. 14, end.

18. The reference is to the laws relating to the "wayward and defiant son" (Deut. 21:18–21, Mishnah and Gemara of tractate Sanhedrin, chap. 8). The Mishnah states that such a son is condemned because of what he will eventually do (Sanh 8:5), and Morteira understands this law as a "hedge" intended to keep one from sin.

19. The prohibition of wine touched by an idolater because of the fear of social intercourse eventually resulting in idolatrous acts is stated in B. AZ 36b. "When wine enters . . ." (B. ʿErub 65a).

teach his child a clean and easy occupation,"[20] meaning that a person should live purely and cleanly, but also with ease, without great expense. Then all will behave properly. Otherwise, even good people will be unable to act differently. Along these lines the sages have said, "When you come to a place, follow its customs: when angels descended to the earth, they ate, and when Moses ascended to heaven, he did not eat."[21] This offense must be corrected in a general manner, or else one sin will lead to another and harm us all.

Third, because of this the yoke of our exile will always be heavy. For when our comportment shows that we fail to remember our exiled state, justice requires that God do something that will compel us to remember, heaven forbid! Look at Joseph. In exile from his father's house, while a slave, his master left all his possessions in his care, paying no further attention to them (Gen. 39:6). Ruling over his master's house, he forgot his status of servitude and plaited his hair. The rabbis commented that the verse *Joseph was well built and handsome* is immediately followed by *his master's wife cast her eyes upon Joseph* (Gen. 39:6, 7), and from this followed *they hurt his foot with fetters* (Ps. 105:18).[22] It matters not that he went from prison to a position of authority. If he had not behaved that way in his master's house, he doubtless would have gone directly to rule over all Egypt.[23]

So it is with the Jewish people. If they would willingly accept their exile, behaving moderately—rather than arrogantly overshadowing the inhabitants of the lands where they dwell—they would pass through their exile in fair condition, without suffering, until God favors the remnant of Joseph. For the Bible says, *I will leave within you a poor, humble folk, and they shall find refuge in the name of the Lord* (Zeph. 3:12). That is why sorrows afflict them: so they will remember that they are slaves and exiles, as the Bible says, *remove the turban, and lift off the crown* (Ezek. 21:31).

Fourth is what I have previously explained in connection with the verse, *They have afflicted the women in Zion, the maidens in the cities of Judah* (Lam. 5:11). This means that the women in Zion used to think day and night about various styles of jewelry and clothing, to the point where no woman would be respected unless she had an original wardrobe. Finally the prophet railed against them, reiterating the innumerable modes of new clothes and jewels they used to invent day after day.

20. B. Qid 82b.

21. Compare Gen. Rabbah 48:14: Morteira uses the proverb cited by the rabbis as an expression of the social pressures that prevent good people from exercising moderation in their dress.

22. Compare Gen. Rabbah 87:3: "Said the Holy One, blessed be He: Your father is in mourning, and yet you curl your hair! I shall incite the bear [i.e., Potiphar's wife] against you."

23. Morteira is maintaining that it was not part of the providential plan that Joseph spend time in prison. This was the result of his preoccupation with his appearance.

In addition to ruining their own husbands with their huge expenditures, these women also impelled other women to steal from *their* husbands so that they might deck themselves out like the rest. This was like the sin of stealing from a stranger. They were also responsible for causing many maidens to be afflicted because they remained unmarried, in their fathers' houses. For no man would accept the fixed dowry, knowing the enormous expenses required to enable a woman to go about in style. In this sense were the women afflicted in their fathers' houses; this is the meaning of the verse. And God punished them for this: *instead of perfume, there shall be rot* (Isa. 3:24). All this is implied by the verse about the Israelites in Egypt, *The Israelites were fertile,* wa-yishreṣu wa-yirbu: they *became great* in magnificence and grandeur. Then Pharaoh afflicted them with servitude.[24]

After this, the verse says, wa-yaʿaṣmu *very greatly.* This refers to the fact that their arrogance was manifest in yet another way over and above the spaciousness of their homes and the costliness of their clothing, namely, in sumptuous foods and magnificent furniture. The word *yaʿaṣmu* is derived from *ʿeṣem,* "bone" or "substance"; it means that they grew larger in body and more ruddy than rubies with their fine food and drink. It is improper for anyone to act immoderately in this respect, especially those in exile, for they should consider it a great kindness if they have enough to sustain themselves, without anything extra.

The prophet Amos denounced such behavior when he said, *They lie on ivory beds, stretched upon their couches* (Amos 6:4),[25] reproaching them for their splendid beds, costing fortunes. *Stretched upon their couches* refers to the large cloths that overhang the couch on every side, serving absolutely no function except in their appearance, not to mention the other costly accoutrements of the bed.

Then he said, *Feasting on lambs from the flock, and on calves from the stall* (Amos 6:4). Here he was referring to the various kinds of food with which they contrive to fill their bellies. *They drink from the wine bowls* (Amos 6:6), calling out to each other until they empty the barrels, hurting both those who provide the wine and their own health. *And anoint themselves with the choicest oils,* etc.

While all of this is bad in itself, it is doubly bad when *they are not concerned about the ruin of Joseph* (Amos 6:6), meaning that they forget they are in exile, forget that some of their brothers have no bread at all for themselves or their children. It would be better for them to spend their money inviting the poor and providing them with food and other necessities. But they curse the poor

24. According to this view, the Israelites did not have to suffer real slavery. It became necessary because they failed to learn the proper lesson from their experience of forced labor under taskmasters, a lesser degree of servitude.

25. The verse from Amos prepares for the aggadic *maʾamar,* which uses it as a proof text.

and spend their money on trivial luxuries that can do them no good, giving money again and again to men who mock them as soon as they leave their homes. They do no good to themselves, and they do great harm to their children.

As parents discipline their children, so did the sages not hesitate to give all manner of ethical instruction that would discipline us, for our own benefit. They touched upon this subject directly in the passage cited at the beginning of the sermon, as is clear to all who understand their words.[26] First, they prohibited all feasts and banquets unconnected with the performance of a commandment, saying, "Whoever takes pleasure in an optional banquet will eventually be exiled, for the Bible states, *Who feast on lambs from the flocks,* and soon after, *Now they shall head the column of exiles* (Amos 6:7)." A religious banquet is one for a circumcision, a wedding, completion of study of a talmudic tractate, Rejoicing in the Law (Simḥat Torah), redemption of the first-born son, Purim, Hanukkah, and other ordained festivals. All others are optional banquets.

Even with regard to a religious banquet, they went on to say: "Whoever feasts excessively anywhere." It would not be necessary to say "anywhere" to refer to an optional banquet; this is intended to include the religious banquet. Whoever indulges excessively and unnecessarily in any one of these is destined to "destroy his household." For these are linked together. If he makes a great feast with many delicacies, he will need a comparable style of clothing and furniture, as well as clothing for his wife and children, and in this way he will ruin his household. Afterward "he will make his wife a widow," abandoning her and fleeing to another land, and she will have to wait for him as a widow with her husband still alive.

Further, "he will make his fledglings orphans." Note how they called his children fledglings, implying that he leaves them as orphans with respect to the father's obligation to provide food for his children, as birds do for their young. They are like orphans; the money needed for their food he spends on delicacies and other unnecessary things. He is like a raven that abandons its children, who call out to others and are sometimes answered and sometimes not. "He will forget what he has learned," for this often requires one to forget God by going to a land of idolatry. This causes the fear of God he had learned to be forgotten.

"He will be the center of many controversies": the end of it all is strife and controversy. "And his words are not heeded": a wealthy man who has tried his utmost to preserve his wealth but has become impoverished, not because he has spent too much on luxuries, but because of chance misfortune,

26. Thus the aggadah, which has no apparent connection with the theme-verse, is linked with the interpretation of *wa-ya-ʿaṣmu*. The aggadah is now explicated phrase by phrase.

retains a position of respect. People have compassion upon him and heed his words. But one who becomes impoverished for the other reason is not heeded or thought of at all, for it is said that he has brought about his own downfall. This evil is like a sickness. People see examples of it every day, and they recognize the cause, yet they do not change.

Someone in this situation "profanes the name of his father, his teacher, . . . his children, and his children's children to the end of time," for the very same people who ate in his house, whom he considered his friends, who accepted gifts from him, will quickly forget all, scorning and mocking him in his poverty. They will become estranged from him and call him glutton, drunkard, fool.

The sages referred to this in the phrase "oven heater," meaning one who cares only about eating and drinking; "tavern dancer"—one of those offensive people who dance in taverns; "dish licker"—one who burns after pleasures; "one who folds and lies down"—a drunkard who sleeps in the marketplace.[27] This is the final reward from his friends. Above all, it is a great sin for those who *are not concerned for the ruin of Joseph* (Amos 6:6) and have not remembered that they are in exile, and that it is wrong for exiles to do such things.

In addition to this personal disaster that befalls them, the exile is made more onerous. For God despises this, and He makes the Gentiles among whom they are exiled despise them, as was the case with the Egyptians. The verse says, wa-yaᶜaṣmu *very greatly,* and then, *the land was full of them.* This means that the land and its inhabitants were fed up with them and their deeds. When a person cannot stand another, we say that he is fed up with him. Then *a new king arose* (Exod. 1:8), and sorrows increased. What was even worse, *the more they afflicted them, the grander they became* (Exod. 1:12). This means that, in the midst of their affliction, they remained arrogant. Such is our way today. All of us complain and weep about hard times, but when we get something, we spend a fortune on banquets with wine. The same is true of all the other unnecessary things.

So it was with them, until God burdened them with sorrow upon sorrow. The Egyptians were disgusted with the Israelites, and they threw their sons into the Nile, may God protect us! And He took away from them their spacious houses, and their expensive clothes, and their tasty delicacies.[28] Their spacious houses, as we see in the verse, *I have also seen how the Egyptians crowd you together* (Exod. 3:9); their expensive clothing, for they were covered with mud and clay; their tasty delicacies, for they mentioned fish and onions and

27. The final phrase is understood, following Rashi, as referring to someone so drunk he cannot make his way home, but who folds up an article of his clothing and uses it to sleep on.

28. Note how, in this recapitulating coda, the theme-verse as interpreted by the preacher is totally inverted.

garlic as a great thing (Num. 11:5), and we therefore say [in the Passover Haggadah], "This is the bread of impoverishment, which our ancestors ate [in the land of Egypt]." Unwilling to behave properly as a matter of choice, they descended to a level of greater abasement against their will.

This is how fools are instructed, as the Bible says, *and a rod for the back of fools* (Prov. 26:3). There is no foolishness greater than that of a person who has fields and vineyards for the support of his household but sells them to buy expensive clothing for himself and ornaments for his house, so that when the time of the harvest comes, he is hungry, with no field to reap. So it is with those of us who spend money on jewels and expensive clothing. We have no fields except for our money, and we must use it to serve God and to provide food for our household. Is it not utter foolishness to diminish it for no good purpose, so that when harvest comes, there will be no source of food?

I know full well that this has been the pattern from of old, that it is difficult even to begin to correct it, and that the full remedy is even harder. Other warnings, while not heeded by everyone, will at least benefit certain individuals. But in this matter, unless the entire community reform, the individual will be powerless, for a wise man among fools is thought to be a fool. And reform of an entire community is extremely difficult. But this communal reform is what we need for our own continual welfare of body and soul. We must remember our exile before God. May it be His will to send us our righteous Messiah, soon and in our days.[29] Amen.

29. The conclusion is quite striking, and the one-sentence expression of messianic hope seems almost pro forma. Few sermons in the entire literature have such a pessimistic ending. The frustration of the preacher in the face of the powerful social pressures working against him must have made a considerable impression on his listeners.

Israel ben Benjamin of Bełżyce

Although Israel ben Benjamin of Bełżyce has been a neglected figure in modern scholarship, his two major works are a rich source for understanding the intellectual world of Polish Jewry during a critical stage in its history. Their importance for the history of Jewish preaching will, it is hoped, be soon established.

The first book, *Yalquṭ Ḥadash,* published at Lublin in 1648, was reprinted at least three times in the seventeenth century and frequently thereafter. For reasons not entirely clear, it was published anonymously, and although it was sometimes called *Yalquṭ Yiśre'eli,* the identity of the author was not finally established until the end of the nineteenth century.[1] Following the pattern of the *Yalquṭ Shimʿoni,* the author merely collected quotations from earlier literature without adding much of his own. Yet the book is distinctive both in structure and in scope. It is organized not according to verses from the Bible, but according to broad subjects, arranged alphabetically. These include prominent figures from the Bible (Adam, Noah, Abraham, Isaac, Jacob, Moses, Aaron, Joshua, David), themes in Jewish thought (Creation, Israel, nations, exile, redemption, Messiah, repentance, souls), and institutions of Jewish life (Sabbath, holy days, synagogue, Torah, commandments, circumcision). There are many cross-references from one subject to another.

Under each category as many as three hundred statements are recorded. These are taken from classical Jewish literature (Talmud and Midrashim, *Yalquṭ Shimʿoni,* the Zohar and *Zohar Ḥadash, Sefer Ḥasidim*) as well as later works (for example, *Galya Raza,* Galante's commentary on Lamentations, Shapira's *Megalleh ʿAmuqqot,* Menaḥem Azariah of Fano's *ʿAśarah Ma'amarot,* Ḥayyim Vital's *Sefer ha-Kawwanot*). Each citation is identified with a precise page reference to the book from which it is taken. There can be little doubt that this work was intended specifically as an aid for preachers, similar to a host of Christian texts of this nature.

The sermons written by Israel but never printed have been preserved in a unique manuscript entitled "Tif'eret Yiśra'el."[2] It is organized according to the Torah lessons, with several sermons, delivered in different years, for each

1. See Adolf Neubauer, "R. Yiśra'el Baʿal *Yalquṭ Ḥadash,*" *Ha-Maggid* 14 (1870):397.
2. Oxford Bodleian MS Opp. 37 (Neubauer 989).

lesson. This mode of organization shows that the book was put together by the preacher near the end of his career from individual sermons he had delivered. Apparently he intended that it should be published. That he actually composed the work from his written records can be seen in a chance remark indicating an exception to his general procedure: "The Sabbath before the Day of Atonement, 5340 [1639], in the congregation of Chęciny. This sermon was stolen from me, and this is the little I could remember" (fol. 383r).

Each sermon is identified by year and place of delivery, information that makes a reconstruction of the preacher's career possible. The years range from 1632 to the Sabbath before the Day of Atonement, 1653, and the places include Chęciny, Bełżyce (where he arrived in summer 1644), Lvov, Lublin, Tarczyn, and Ostróg. Frequently the occasion for the sermon is noted. Many are eulogies, with the name of the deceased, his position, and the date of death. Several apply to the preacher's own family: a eulogy for his father in 1637 and another for his first wife in the fall of 1648. One sermon was delivered upon his remarriage, on Lag Be-ʿOmer, 5409 [1649]. Other occasions are noted as well: "on the Feast of Weeks, when the Psalm Society gave a Torah scroll to the synagogue"; "when I made a banquet to celebrate the completion of Tractate Qiddushin, the fifteenth day of Shebat, 5406 [1646]"; "upon the dedication of the synagogue [in Chęciny], on the first day of Adar, 5399 [1639]"; "a eulogy . . . in Chęciny, 5403 [1643]; there was a circumcision then, yet it was a time of sorrow, for many children had died because of an epidemic, and many were sick."

The most dramatic setting is that of the sermon translated here, which was preached during the summer of 1648 at a Sabbath service soon after the Cossack massacres. Contemporary sources indicate that preaching became very important both immediately before and immediately after these traumatic events. Samson of Ostropole "preached frequently in the synagogue and exhorted the people to repent so that the evil would not come to pass."[3] Jeḥiel Michael of Nemirov "preached on the Sabbath before the catastrophe and admonished his people that if the enemy should come (God forbid), they should not abandon their faith, but rather be martyred for the Sanctification of His Name."[4]

Eliezer of Tulczyn "preached on the Ten Commandments; he eulogized the martyrs of Nemirov. . . , then he rebuked the members of his own congregation, instructing them to act justly and ethically, so that they would not

3. Nathan Hanover, *Abyss of Despair,* trans. Abraham Mesch (New York, 1950), pp. 63–64; on Ostropole, see Yehudah Liebes, "Mysticism and Reality: Towards a Portrait of the Martyr and Kabbalist, R. Samson Ostropoler," *Jewish Thought in the Seventeenth Century,* ed. Isadore Twersky and Bernard Septimus (Cambridge, Mass., 1987), pp. 221–55.

4. Hanover, *Abyss of Despair,* pp. 51–52.

suffer persecution," finally calling upon them not to apostatize if the enemy came upon them.[5] Another contemporary, Abraham ben Israel ha-Kohen Rapoport, describes the verses he used for at least three different sermons of eulogy delivered during 1648.[6] Yet as far as I can tell, the sermon translated below is the only sermon actually preserved from this period. It is therefore a valuable historical source, more immediate than the chronicles, demonstrating how effectively traditional sources could be mobilized to assimilate and explain events that might have seemed to shatter the mold.

These traditional sources include, of course, Bible, Talmud, and Midrashim, but the most important influence is the kabbalistic tradition and popularization of Lurianic Kabbalah in the generation of the Cossack massacres. The emphasis on the *qelippah* or "shell" *Nogah* as a point of contact between the realms of good and of evil, especially sensitive to the deeds of the Jewish people, and the image of sparks of light imprisoned by the evil shells as a symbolic representation of Jewish souls, show the impact of the Lurianic worldview. The link between *Nogah* and Greece, originally established in the *Zohar Ḥadash,* takes on an entirely new meaning in an environment where *Greeks* refers not to a people of antiquity but to the Eastern Orthodox Ukrainian neighbors. And the preacher's introduction of the martyrdom motif, which becomes increasingly important as the sermon progresses, places all the kabbalistic material in a poignantly immediate context.

For all the ingenuity of the preacher's explanation, it must be noted that the sermon reflects an interesting tension between the kabbalistic theology employed and the emotion burdening both the preacher and his listeners. The theological framework leads to certain inescapable conclusions. What happened in the Jewish communities of Poland was merely a concrete manifestation of cosmic events caused by the behavior of the Jews. The Eastern Orthodox Cossacks, the embodiment of the shell *Nogah,* were merely acting out a role dictated by forces they could not begin to understand. God does not actively and willfully intervene in the affairs of the world, but responds, almost mechanically, to stimuli from below.

In stark contrast are the beginning and the end of the sermon, with their epithets of opprobrium for the Cossacks ("cursed and wanton Greeks," "wicked Greeks who murder in blind madness"), and the fervent appeals to God to avenge the innocent blood of the slaughtered. These are inconsistent with Lurianic theology. Their language is drawn from the biblical tradition, and they are most plausibly explained as arising from the psychology of the oppressed.

As for the structure of the sermon, it can perhaps best be appreciated by

5. Abraham ben Samuel Ashkenazi, *Ṣaʿar Bat Rabbim,* in Jonas Gurland, *Le-Qorot ha-Gezerot le-Yiśraʾel,* 6 pts. (Przemysl, Cracow, and Odessa, 1887–92), 2:14.

6. Rapoport, pp. 55b, 58d, 61c.

contrast with the technique employed in the sermons of Israel's contemporary, Saul ha-Levi Morteira. While beginning similarly, with a verse from the Torah lesson and a statement of rabbinic aggadah, there is no careful division into three or four component parts, as we find in most of Morteira's work. The structure is based on a chain of exegetical problems, the solution to one providing the key to the next. There is a problem with statement A, for which we need statement B, but the problem in B requires statement C, which can be elucidated on the basis of statements D and E.

This technique, which would become increasingly influential in Jewish preaching of the late seventeenth and the eighteenth century, places great demands upon the listener, and it is clearly open to abuse. However, a careful reading of this particular sermon shows that hardly a sentence is superfluous, that each of the building blocks is employed by the preacher to construct an edifice of thought and emotion that has been carefully planned in advance. The artistry of this construction is of a very different kind from that of Morteira, but at its best, it can produce results no less impressive.[7]

Sermon on *Balaq*
(Summer 1648)

What I preached in the holy congregation of Bełżyce, hurriedly, in mourning over the wrath that burst upon the Lord's community in the year 1648, a year of messianic birthpangs.[1] Men, women, and children were killed, slaughtered, drowned, made to suffer the most vicious forms of death, and many of the greatest scholars, the defenders of the land, were killed for the sanc-

7. I am grateful to Dr. R. A. May, Senior Assistant Librarian of the Bodleian Library, Oxford, for sending me his readings of a number of passages from this sermon too faint to decipher from the microfilm and, at a later date, for allowing me access to the manuscript itself.

1. The Hebrew words *ḥeble mashiaḥ,* "birthpangs of the Messiah," have the numerical equivalent of 408, which corresponds in the Hebrew calendar to the year 1648. A different calculation, originally found in *Midrash ha-Neʿelam* (Zohar 1:139b), made 1648 a year of messianic expectation and ultimately of crushing disappointment; see Gershom Scholem, "ʿAl Debar Maʾamar ha-Zohar ha-Mezuyyaf," *Kiryat Sefer* 7 (1930):149–51; 8 (1931):262–65, and *Sabbatai Ṣevi* (Princeton, 1973), pp. 88–92. The earliest recorded reference in a sermon to 1648 as a messianic year is by Joseph Garçon (Benayahu, p. 57).

tification of God's Name by the cursed and wanton Greeks.[2] May God see and judge and avenge the blood that has been spilt!

From the lesson *Balaq: Lo, it is a people* [hen ʿam] *that dwells alone; among the nations it shall not be reckoned. Who can count the dust of Jacob, or number the stock* [robaʿ] *of Israel?* (Num. 23:9–10).

[We read] in the Midrash: "*Hen ʿam: hen* in the Greek tongue is *one*; they are not reckoned together with any other nation, etc."[3]

> [This is no time] to preach [?],[4]
> For He has filled me with bitterness, sated me with wormwood and gall.
> The flesh of the pious has been left as food for the birds of heaven; they are drunk with their blood as with sweet wine.
> O Lord, God of vengeance, do not hold back or keep silence,
> O earth, cover not their blood, until it is sought out on High![5]

We must try to discover why, according to this midrash, the verse expressed the praise of Israel in the Greek tongue. We shall precede this with a mishnah from the first chapter of [the tractate] Megillah, which also appears at the beginning of the Midrash [Rabbah] on Deuteronomy:

> Halakah: Is it permissible for a Jew to write for himself a Torah scroll in any language? This is what the sages have taught: The only difference between [sacred] books, phylacteries, and *mezuzot* is that [sacred] books may be written in any language. Rabban Gamaliel says, The permission regarding [sacred] books applies only to Greek. What is Rabban Gam-

2. *Greeks* was the term used throughout contemporary Jewish literature to characterize the Ukrainian Cossacks, who followed the Greek Orthodox religion. See, for example, Hanover, *Abyss of Despair,* p. 23. Similarly, Bogdan Chmielnicki referred to the faith of his people as the "ancient Greek religion" (Baron, *SRHJ* 16:299). The use of this terms facilitates the preacher's explanation of the contemporary massacres on the basis of traditional sources.

3. The source is Midrash Yelammedenu on this verse; see *ʿAruk ha-Shalem,* s.v. "*hen.*"

4. The middle of this line, with space for several letters between a *lamed* and the word *li-drosh,* is too faint to read with certainty from the manuscript. My translation is based on the reconstruction *lo ʿet li-drosh* (cf. Gen. 29:7 and Hos. 10:12); according to this rendering, the preacher is following a homiletical convention of saying "I am not going to give a real sermon" as an introduction to the sermon he has planned.

5. The passage in the original is in rhymed Hebrew prose, the lines ending with *li-drosh, we-rosh, we-tirosh, we-taḥarosh.* This elevated introduction, a pastiche of biblical phrases, indicates by its style a special occasion for the sermon, while its content addresses the mood of the congregation. The rhymed prose would of course have been read in Hebrew, like the opening verse and the midrash, even if the rest of the sermon were delivered in the vernacular. See above, "The Preaching Situation," at n. 46.

aliel's reason for permitting the writing of a Torah scroll in Greek? This is what our rabbis have taught: Bar Kappara said, the Torah verse *God enlarge Japheth, and he will dwell in the tents of Shem* (Gen. 9:27) means that the words of Shem will be said in the language of Japheth. This is why they permitted the writing [of sacred books] in Greek.

The Holy One, blessed be He, said: See how beloved is the language of the Torah, which heals the tongue. How do we know this? From the verse, *A healing of the tongue is the tree of life* (Prov. 15:4). The language of the Torah also frees the tongue. Know that in the time to come, God will raise from the Garden of Eden excellent trees, their excellence consisting of their capacity to heal the tongue, in accordance with the verse, *And by the river, there shall grow upon its bank . . . {every tree for food}* (Ezek. 47:12). How do we know that it heals the tongue? From the continuation of that verse: *Its fruit shall serve for food, and its foliage for healing* [*li-terufah*]." R. Joḥanan and R. Joshua ben Levi disputed the meaning of this last word. One said: *li-terafyon*; the other said: Whoever is tongue-tied and eats voraciously from it will have his tongue healed.[6]

This midrash is strange, for its first and second parts seem to be inconsistent.[7] In order to explain it, we must precede it with a passage from the Book of *Tiqqunim,* explained at length in the little tract *Ziz Sadai,*[8] on the statement in the Talmud that four entered the *pardes: Aḥer* became a heretic, Ben Azzai gazed and died, Ben Zoma gazed and went insane, R. ʿAqiba entered in peace and left in peace (B. Ḥag 14b). The *Tiqqunim* applies to this the verse, *Three years it shall be forbidden . . . and the fourth year all its fruit shall be holy, for giving praise to the Lord* (Lev. 19:23–24).

All this means that on high, surrounding holiness, there are four shells, to which Ezekiel alluded when he said, *A stormy wind, a huge cloud, a flashing fire, and* Nogah, *radiance, surrounding it* (Ezek. 1:4). This last is the fourth

6. The text is actually taken from Deut. Rabbah 1:1; cf. Meg 1:8. The rabbi who suggested *li-terafyon* as the meaning of *li-terufah* was probably asserting that it came from the Greek *therapeia* ("cure"), but the preacher will explain this word differently.

7. Thus the midrash cited as the key to the riddle of the opening midrash is itself problematic, and a new source is necessary to enable the preacher to explain the connection between the two assertions: that the Torah may be translated into Greek, and that the tongue or language of the Torah heals the tongue. The "*midrash tamuah*" was one of the fundamental elements of Polish preaching; see Ben-Sasson, *Hagut,* pp. 40–44.

8. Scholem describes this pamphlet, written by Judah Leib ben Moses of Kamienec, as "the first genuinely Lurianic work written and published in Poland" (*Sabbatai Ṣevi,* p. 79, n. 118). This extremely rare and quite interesting tract, published at Lublin in 1634, was recently republished by Abraham Bombeck as part of *Sefer Niṣoṣe Shimshon* (Bene Beraq, 1981). For the passage from the *Tiqqunim,* see *Zohar Ḥadash* (Jerusalem, 1978), p. 107c; it is cited on p. 6 of *Ziz Sadai.*

shell, as close to holiness as the [innermost] shell of the nut that is eaten with the fruit. The first three shells have no contact with holiness, but the shell *Nogah* does. Its disposition is determined by the deeds of Israel. If they do well and their merits prevail, then this shell adheres to holiness.

Because of our sins and those of our ancestors, light has been immersed in the impurity of the other three shells. The innermost shell attracts this light and raises these sparks to the level of holiness. But if, God forbid, sin predominates, then the shell *Nogah* robs the holy light and radiates it into the three surrounding shells, so that it becomes attached to impurity and is itself called impure.[9]

The Zohar states in the section *Mishpaṭim* (2:95b) that the world is governed by the Tree of the Knowledge of Good and Evil. "Good" refers to the scales of justice; their constant desire is to take the sparks of holiness that have been overpowered and fallen into the realm of impurity and to restore them to holiness. "Evil" refers to the scales of deceit, the impure side. Their constant desire is to rob and overpower the sparks of holiness.

The shell *Nogah* is the tongue of the balance. When Israel is worthy in its deeds, then the shell *Nogah,* which is the tongue, inclines toward the scale of justice, which raises the light into the realm of holiness so that it is no longer immersed in impurity. If, God forbid, Israel sins, it inclines toward the side of evil. Then the shells overpower the souls in the scale of justice.[10] (This explains the statement in the *Tiqqunim* that the stormy wind is worse than the cloud, and the cloud worse than the fire, and the fire worse than *Nogah,* radiance.)[11]

Elisha [ben Abuya], *Aḥer,* did not have much insight; his vision was blocked by the four barriers that divide Israel from their Heavenly Father, and that is why he went astray. Ben Azzai was able to break through the first shell, and he gazed through three; this is why he did not go astray, although he died. Ben Zoma broke through two shells and gazed through two barriers; he did not die but went insane. R. ʿAqiba broke through all three shells; the

9. See *Ziz Sadai* (Henceforth ZS) p. 7. The preacher omits the more technical material, including the actual reference to Lurianic works, but the entire paragraph is taken almost verbatim from the pamphlet. On the shell *Nogah* as a "kind of bridge between the two systems" of good and evil in Lurianic Kabbalah, see Isaiah Tishby, *Torat ha-Raʿ we-ha-Qelippah be-Kabbalat ha-ʾAri* (Jerusalem, 1960), pp. 70–71.

10. ZS, p. 8. The original passage in the Zohar is concerned with apostasy and proselytism, and contains no mention of *Nogah.* ZS makes *Nogah* into the "tongue of the balance" (for the phrase in English, see the *Oxford English Dictionary* (1926) s.v. "tongue," 14b), an association obviously important to the preacher for his explanation of midrashic passages about the "Greek tongue" and "the language [lit., "tongue"] of the Torah [that] heals the tongue." The Zoharic phrase "overpowers the souls of Israel" takes on a different significance against the background of the Cossack massacres.

11. ZS, p. 9.

only barrier before him was this thin shell, the "fourth year," that we can redeem from the power of the shells and bring near to the holy. That is why he "entered in peace and went out in peace."[12] The passage [in the *Tiqqunim*] concludes that this is the esoteric meaning of the *pardes in the midst of the garden* (cf. Gen. 2:9) and it asserts that the Torah is also called "garden," as in the verse *a garden locked up* (Song 4:12). That is the end of the passage.

In the Zohar, *Bereʾshit,* column 133 [we read]: *A river goes forth from Eden to water the garden, and from there it separates and becomes four heads* (Gen. 2:10): these are the four who entered the *pardes* . . ." You may verify this.[13] There is also in *Ziz Sadai* a passage applying to this shell the verse *He shall be like a tree planted {by streams of water}, which yields its fruit in season; its foliage does not fade* (Ps. 1:3). Unlike the other three, its fruit can be eaten, and it does not fade.[14]

It also explains that the three other shells are "forbidden," "impure," "disqualified," but this shell can be "permitted," "pure," ["valid"], for it is from the side of holiness.[15] There is another interpretation of the verse *He shall be like a tree planted*; it refers to the student who always wants to discover a novel interpretation yet flounders in expressing himself, indicating that even his teaching is not useless.[16] You can verify it yourselves.

We now come to the explanation of the midrash. But first we must cite a passage from the *Zohar Ḥadash*: "*A stormy wind* is Babylon, *a huge cloud* is Medea, *a flashing fire* is Edom, *and* Nogah, *radiance surrounding it,* this is Greece."[17] Look it up. Thus the shell *Nogah* is the shell of Greece. If Israel is worthy, we can derive great benefit through this shell, for it can restore to Israel sparks of holiness, and keep them from being absorbed among the nations.

We now see that Rabban Gamaliel was correct in saying that the sages gave permission to write the Torah scroll in the Greek tongue, for by means of the Torah scroll, if Israel is worthy, this shell can become pure and adhere

12. Ibid.; the preacher condenses the passage drastically. In the original, the four levels of Torah interpretation, the initial letters of which yield the word *pardes,* are associated with the four barriers and the four who "entered the *pardes.*"

13. The reference given is to the Lublin 1623 edition of the Zohar. It is 1:26b in the standard editions. On this passage cf. Scholem, *On the Kabbalah and Its Symbolism* (New York, 1965), p. 58.

14. ZS, p. 10; this will be used for the preacher's discussion of the statement about the trees from Eden in the midrash.

15. Ibid., p. 21; this will be used for his interpretation of "frees the tongue."

16. Ibid., p. 14; this will be used for the explication of the end of the midrash.

17. *Zohar Ḥadash* (Jerusalem, 1978), *Yitro,* p. 38b; cf. the author's *Yalquṭ Ḥadash,* s.v. "*galut,*" 18. This is crucial in establishing the connection between *Nogah* and the Greeks/Cossacks. (On the original significance of this passage, see Moshe Idel, "Ha-Massaʿ le-Gan ʿEden," *Meḥqere Folqlor Yehudi* 2 [1982]:12–15.) All the material needed for the interpretation of the long midrash has now been provided.

to holiness. This is in accordance with the verse *God enlarge Japheth* (Gen. 9:27). The Holy One said, "See the language of the Torah"—see how great is the power of the Torah if Israel is worthy through it—"it heals the tongue," meaning that the shell of the Greeks, the tongue of the balance, can be healed so as to adhere to holiness.[18] "And the language of the Torah frees the tongue," which can become freely permitted because of its contact with holiness. The other shells are quite different, always bound in prohibition, but *on the fourth year all its fruit {shall be holy}* (Lev. 19:24). This one can become freely permitted.[19]

The Midrash goes on to explain, "Know that in the time to come the Holy One, blessed be he, will raise from the Garden of Eden excellent trees." This refers to the four who entered the *pardes* that is in the midst of the garden. "What constitutes their excellence? Their capacity to heal the tongue, in accordance with the verse, *And by the river. . .* (Ezek. 47:12)." This is the same as the river going out from Eden that became four heads, mentioned above.[20]

How do we know that it heals the tongue? From the continuation of that verse: *Its fruit shall serve for food, and its foliage for healing* (*li-terufah*). One says: "*li-terafyon,* meaning "food," for he interprets the verse *He shall be like a tree planted; it shall yield its fruit in season, and its foliage shall not fade* (Ps. 1:3) with regard to this shell, the fruit of which can become food through the redeeming power of good deeds.[21] The other interprets this same verse as applying to the student who stammers. He therefore said, "Whoever is tongue-tied and eats voraciously from it will be healed so as to speak at once elegant words of Torah." This means that whoever stutters and stammers and is unable to explain a matter well is healed by means of the Torah.[22] "How do we know? From Moses. . . ." This midrash is now fully explicated.

We may similarly explain another statement in the Midrash and the Talmud: "*Dread, dark and great, falls* (Gen. 15:12): *dread* is Babylon . . . , *dark* is Greece, that darkened the eyes of Israel with its decrees. It said to Israel, Write upon the horn of an ox that you have no portion in the God of Israel."[23] This is surprising: why just on the horn of an ox? Our approach will explain it.

But first we need a passage from the Midrash [Rabbah] on [the lesson]

18. In this way the preacher solves the problem of the connection between the two parts of the midrash: both deal with the same theme, the potential for holiness in *Nogah* (= Greeks = Cossacks).

19. See n. 15.

20. See n. 13.

21. See n. 14. The interpretation of *terafyon* as food understands the word as linked with *ṭeref*; see the traditional commentators (*Mattenot Kehunah, Perush MaHaRaZaW*).

22. See n. 16.

23. Compare Lev. Rabbah 13:5, Gen. Rabbah 44:17. The only version of the interpretation of Gen. 15:12 completely consistent with the preacher is in Mid. Tehillim 52:8.

Noaḥ bearing on the subject: "*God enlarge Japheth; he shall dwell in the tents of Shem*: even though God will enlarge Japheth, nevertheless He will dwell in the tents of Shem. Bar Kappara says, Words of Torah will be said in the tongue of Japheth in the tents of Shem."[24] Thus the only authorization for intimate contact with holiness that Noah gave to Japheth (that is, Greece, the descendants of Japheth) was bound up with the Torah scroll, which would be written in the Greek tongue. The descendants of Shem have a higher status, for they have intimate contact with the Holy One, as the Torah says, *Blessed be {the Lord} the God of Shem* (Gen. 9:26). Thus *He {God} shall dwell in the tents of Shem.*

With this our question can be answered, if we will first note the passage in the Midrash of *Yalquṭ Mishle*: "The sole reason why the martyrs were given over to royal authority was the selling of Joseph. R. Abin said, He was speaking about ten in every generation, and that sin is still pending."[25] If so, all those killed by Gentile governments have been killed because of the selling of Joseph, to this very day. Now the blessing of Joseph is well known: *His firstling bullock, majesty is his, and his horns are the horns of the wild ox* (Deut. 33:17). We must also cite the words of the book *ʿAśarah Maʾamarot* that Joseph was a "wise son," {his very face} like a book that helped Jacob remember {what he had learned, thereby serving} in place of a Torah scroll. We mentioned this work above,[26] in a sermon on {the lesson} *Emor* (Lev. 21–24).

Now since the only authorization for intimate contact with holiness given to the Greeks is bound up with the Torah scroll, and since the selling of Joseph was analogous to the defiling of a Torah scroll, the Greeks said, "Write *ʿal qeren ha-shor* {lit., "upon the horn of the ox"} meaning, by the authority of Joseph, who was called "ox," and whose blessing was to gore the peoples;[27] write that you have no portion {in the God of Israel}. Since you have defiled our portion, the sanctity of the Torah scroll, we defile your portion, and you shall have no portion in the God of Israel.

24. Gen. Rabbah 36:8; cf. the passage from Deut. Rabbah quoted at the beginning.

25. *Yalquṭ Shimʿoni* 929 on Prov. 1:13, cited also in the preacher's *Yalquṭ Ḥadash,* s.v. "*ʿAśarah haruge malkut,*" 15. This introduces the theme of martyrdom into the exegetical fabric of the sermon.

26. The Hebrew text gives only the letters *ʿayin* and *mem,* but the full name of the book must have been stated in the oral delivery. The reference is to Menaḥem Azariah of Fano, *ʿAśarah Maʾamarot* (Venice, 1597), 1:1:23 (p. 9c–d). The statement cited here provides the basis for the preacher's assertion that the selling of Joseph, the reason for Jewish martyrdom according to *Yalquṭ Mishle,* was like the defiling of a Torah scroll. This insulted the Greeks by removing their access to sanctity, and they responded with anti-Jewish measures. (For another use of Fano's work by the preacher, see his sermon on *Emor,* fol. 316r, citing the interpretation of the willow twigs in *ʿAśarah Maʾamarot* 1:2:24–25 [p. 22c–d].)

27. The literal meaning of *ʿal qeren ha-shor* is rejected here. The "ox" refers to Joseph; the "horn" is merely the emblem of the ox's power. Cf. *Yalguṭ Ḥadash,* s.v. "*Babel,*" 37.

In this way the verse can be explained.[28] But first we shall cite a passage from the Midrash Rabbah: "*Who can count the dust of Jacob?* (Num. 23:10): who can count the commandments that are fulfilled in the dust?" It goes on to specify them, concluding with, *Three years it shall be for you forbidden* (Lev. 19:23). Thus the commandment of three years' forbidden fruit is one of the commandments fulfilled in the dust.

In this sense it says, *Lo* [hen], *it is a people that dwells alone* (Num. 23:9), meaning, Know, o Israel, that you shall be worthy in your deeds, and then *hen,* by means of the Greek tongue, which is *Nogah,* the tongue of the balance, you shall succeed in being a people that dwells alone, not reckoned among the nations, for your souls will not be intermingled among the shells.[29] And it explains: You shall see this from the commandments fulfilled in the dust, one of which is, *Three years . . . forbidden. Or number the robaᶜ of Israel* refers to the fourth [shell] (*rebiᶜit*), which is dependent upon the deeds of Israel. If they are worthy, they will cling to holiness, but if they are not, then the Greek tongue changes and becomes cruel toward them, overpowering Jewish souls.[30]

Or we might proceed on the basis of a passage from the Talmud, [tractate] Baba Batra 10b: "No creature can attain to the place [in heaven] assigned to the martyrs of the [Roman] government. Who are these? Shall we say R. ʿAqiba and his colleagues? Had they no other merit than being martyrs of the government? Rather it refers to the martyrs of Lod." Rashi explained this as Julianus and Pappus, who were killed by the wicked Tinneius Rufus in Laodicea. He wrote in tractate Taᶜanit (18b) that a devastating anti-Jewish decree was passed because the daughter of a king was found killed, and the Jews were suspected. These brothers went up and said, "Why do you attack the Jewish people [as a whole]? We are the ones who killed her."[31]

We shall also cite a passage from the Midrash in *Yalquṭ Tehillim,* applying to the persecuted generation the verse *Of David: To you, O Lord,* eśśa nafshi, *I lend my soul* (Ps. 25:1). David said this because they had been mortgaged for the sanctification of God's Name, in accordance with the verse *When you lend your neighbor any kind of loan* (Deut. 24:10). In the Talmud, Baba Meṣiᶜa

28. That is, all that is needed for the explanation of the theme-verse has been set forth, with the sole exception of the following passage, from Num. Rabbah 20:19.

29. The question raised at the beginning about the midrash—why the verse praises Israel in the Greek tongue—is thus answered. The Greek tongue, *Nogah,* is decisive in keeping the sparks of holiness (Jews) unique and separate from entrapment by the powers of evil (the nations).

30. By means of the midrash cited in the previous paragraph, the second part of the theme-verse is also linked with the Lurianic conceptual framework constructed in the first part of the sermon.

31. Compare *Yalquṭ Ḥadash,* s.v. "*ʿAśarah haruge malkut,*" 13; Moses Gaster, *The Exempla of the Rabbis* (London, 1924), no. 21.

68a and 108b, the rabbis have said, "What is a *mashkon,* mortgage? *Ba-shekunah gabeh,* something that abides with the mortgagee." You can refer to this yourself.[32]

We have already established that Greece is more likely than any other nation to wreak destruction upon Israel and to murder Jews. This is why the verse says, *it is a people that dwells* (yishkon) *alone,* from the word *mashkon,* mortgage. The meaning is as follows: this people, whose lives were mortgaged by the murderous decree of Greece (hinted at in the word *hen*), namely, those killed for the sanctification of God's Name, will dwell alone, for no creature can attain to the place [in heaven] assigned to them. Lest you think this refers only to R. ʿAqiba and his colleagues, which can be challenged with the response, "Had they no other merit than being martyrs of the government?" the verse hints that the martyrs of whom it speaks are the martyrs of Lod. The hint lies in the fact that the word *le-badad* ["alone"] is equivalent numerically to the word *Lod.*[33]

Among the nations it shall not be reckoned. They said in the Midrash *Yalquṭ*: "In this world, lest the spirit of Israel become too dejected, God allowed the Jewish people to eat with all the nations. When the future redemption comes, they shall eat by themselves, as it is said, *Lo, it is a people that dwells alone.* Said Israel, 'Will what we consumed with the nations in the past be reckoned [as a debit on our account]?' God replied, '*Among the nations it shall not be reckoned.*' "[34]

Following our approach, this can be linked with our subject. We said that the kingdoms mortgage Israel for the sanctification of God's Name, and this is why the verse says *yishkon,* meaning that Israel is a *mashkon,* or mortgage, in their hands. Now you know the rabbinic midrash that Israel in this world is as a daughter living among sons.[35] Therefore, what Jews consume in the lands where they live is, from a legal point of view, like that which is consumed by an orphaned daughter living with the sons: she is to be maintained by her brothers.

But the rabbis in the tractate Ketubbot [43a] were in dispute over the

32. *Yalquṭ Shimʿoni,* 701, on Ps. 25:1. The interplay of Ps. 25:1 and Deut. 24:10, establishing the connection between mortgage and martyrdom, is explained in *Yalquṭ Ḥadash,* s.v. "*Dawid,*" 161: *Eśśa* (in Ps. 25:1, lit., "I will lift") is understood to refer to giving a loan, as in *ki tasheh be-reʿaka mashat* (Deut. 24:10); also s.v. "*ʿAśarah haruge malkut,*" 14. The verb *mashken* is used in the mishnaic formulation of the law based on the Deuteronomy verse (BM 9:13), while the midrash on Exod. 22:24, which similarly deals with loans, speaks of God's mortgaging His temple to the idolaters because of Israel's sins (Exod. Rabbah 31:10).

33. Through the motif of the mortgage, the preacher has now established the link between the theme-verse from the Torah lesson and martyrdom. Both *le-badad* and *Lod* are numerically equivalent to 40.

34. *Yalquṭ Shimʿoni,* Num. 768.

35. Song Rabbah 1:5.

question whether the handiwork she produced and the things she might find belonged to her brothers. They concluded that they do not, because of the verse, *You shall make them* [Canaanite bondmen] *an inheritance for your children after you* (Lev. 25:46). They understood this to exclude by implication making your daughters an inheritence for your sons. Thus one's daughters do not become the property of his sons.[36]

Furthermore, at several places in the Talmud, including the tractate Pesaḥim [31a–b], we find that if a Jew gave his leaven to another Jew as a pledge [before Passover and the creditor uses the leaven] after Passover, he transgresses. But if a Gentile gave his leaven to a Jew as a pledge, there is a dispute between R. Meir and the sages over whether the Jew transgresses or not [if he uses the leaven after Passover because the debt was not paid].

The Talmud explains this as a dispute over the dictum of R. Isaac, who maintained that a creditor acquires title to the pledge, because the verse says, *{You shall surely restore to him the pledge when the sun sets . . .} and it shall be righteousness to you* (Deut. 24:13). If the creditor has no title to the pledge, there is no special righteousness in returning it. The first tanna [scholar] applied this dictum to the situation where a Jew holds a pledge from another Jew, but not where the pledge comes from a Gentile. R. Meir held that if the pledge comes from a Gentile, it is all the more obvious that the Jew has acquired title. Nevertheless, all agreed that a Gentile does not acquire title to a pledge taken from a Jew.[37]

Therefore God said: Since I have asserted that Israel is mortgaged in the hands of the nations, and I actually call them a pledge, and the Torah states that a creditor acquires title to the pledge, one might conclude that Gentiles do indeed acquire Israel as their property. Thus no exclusion is to be derived from Leviticus 25:46. This verse might have served also as the basis for the rule that the Gentile does not acquire the Jew as property, but in this case, they are in the legal status of a pledge, and the creditor acquires title to a pledge. Therefore the Gentiles would seem to be able to acquire title [to the

36. Since the daughter does not inherit with the sons, she may be entitled to support until her marriage at the expense of her brothers, who did inherit (this arrangement may have been an explicit stipulation in the mother's marriage contract). The conclusion would appear to be that while nations are obligated to sustain the Jews in their midst, they do not have an absolute right of title to that which the Jews produce.

37. The issue of title to the pledge of leaven is crucial in determining whether a Jew has transgressed the prohibition in Exod. 13:7. If the Jewish creditor holds title to the pledge during Passover, he has transgressed, and he may not derive any benefit from it even after Passover. According to the Talmud, all agree that a Jew retains title to the leaven that he has given as a pledge to a Gentile creditor. But why should this be, given R. Isaac's dictum that a creditor acquires title to a pledge? In the following paragraph, the preacher derives the exception to Isaac's rule from the second part of the theme-verse, *among the nations it shall not be reckoned*.

Jews in their midst]. And since this is true, and exclusion is not derived from Leviticus 25:46, we might conclude that no exclusion at all is to be made from this verse, and that whatever the Jews produce should belong to the "brothers" in return for the food they eat. If so, there would be a deduction from their share in the world to come, which is what they produce. That is why God said, *among the nations it shall not be reckoned,* indicating that the Gentile does not acquire title to the pledge, as the Talmud says.

All we have said has led to the conclusion that the shell Greece, or *Nogah,* which is close to holiness, can be transformed through the actions of Israel. This is why it is permitted to write a Torah scroll in the Greek tongue. When Jews sin, it becomes cruel, and is called impure, and overpowers Jewish souls. We have also said that Greece is the one that darkens Israel through its decrees and takes Jewish lives.[38]

Look then, and see how our sins must have prevailed so that the evil Greeks could have brought such destruction upon our people! They were not satisfied with the ten martyrs that are due in each generation. No, because of our sins, the number of dead has risen to thousands and tens of thousands. Indeed, they are beyond counting. Moreover, the very glory of Greece, the Torah scroll in all its grandeur, they vilified worse even than did the wicked Titus. He took one Torah scroll and defiled it, while these men, accursed and impure, destroyed several hundred Torah scrolls and made them into shoes for their feet. That which Wisdom made into a crown for its head, these evil men made into sandals for their soles! Woe to us that we have so sinned. May God see it and judge![39]

Yet the very defiling of the Torah scrolls may be the source of healing for our wounds, according to the words of the Zohar of *Aḥare Mot,* column 127:[40] "R. Ḥiyya said, I wonder if anyone besides us knows how to inform the dead. R. Abba replied, The Torah informs them of human suffering when there is no one who knows how to do this. They take out the Torah scroll and bring it near the cemetery, and the dead are curious to know why the Torah has been exiled to such a place. Then someone, for example, Dumah, informs them. At that point they all cry out because the Torah has been dishonored in being exiled to such a place. If the living human beings repent and weep

38. Note the paragraph recapitulating the main theoretical points established, before the explicit application to the contemporary context.

39. Thus, while the Greeks may have been justified in past persecutions of Jews, punishing them for the selling of Joseph—a Jewish insult to the Torah, which provides their access to holiness (see n. 26)—they could never be justified in their destruction of Torah scrolls. For another contemporary source on this action by the Cossacks, see Shabbethai Katz, "Megillah ʿAfah," in *Seder Seliḥot ke-Minhag Qehillot Qedoshot di-Medinot Liṭa* (Amsterdam, 1766), p. 94b.

40. Thus in the Lublin 1623 edition; in the standard editions it is 3:71a. The passage is cited in the original Aramaic. For a discussion of the permissibility of this practice of taking the Torah to the cemetery, see Ezekiel Landau, *Nodaʿ bi-Yhudah* 2, *Oraḥ Ḥayyim,* 109.

wholeheartedly and return to God, then the dead all gather to seek mercy, and they inform those who sleep in Hebron. But if the living human beings do not repent wholeheartedly as they seek to weep over their suffering, woe to them, for they have assembled for nothing; someone has caused the Torah to go into exile without repentance. Therefore they should not go in this manner {to the cemetery} without repentance and fasting. R. Abba said, Without three fasts." Examine the passage; it cites several incidents that occurred in this manner.

Now if the dead are aroused to inform the sleepers of Hebron to pray on our behalf because of the exile of a Torah scroll, how much more will they be aroused by this humiliating disgrace to which our Torah scrolls were subjected, and by the spilling of innocent blood, and by the human corpses left as food for the birds and the beasts, when we had no opportunity for burial!

Wake up, wake up, O sleepers of Hebron,
Arise, Moses and Aaron,
Raise your voice like a shofar, cry aloud,
Pray before the Lord our God, the First and the Last,
That he might put an end to His wrath
And avenge the innocent blood, by smiting the wicked Greeks who murder in blind madness.[41]

And you, our brothers, take this catastrophe to heart, this unprecedented disaster, the result of our great sinfulness, in which tens of thousands of Jews were slaughtered and killed, our synagogue put to the torch, our Torah scrolls trampled underfoot. Our own lives still hang in the balance! Therefore, let all touched by the fear of God set their affairs in order and impose upon themselves acts of self-mortification and repentance and charity. Perhaps God will look and see from the heavens, and avenge the blood of His servants, spilled like water, permitting us to see wondrous acts, as in the days of our Exodus from Egypt. May this come speedily and in our days. Amen, be this His will.

41. The passage in rhymed prose, with lines ending in *Ḥebron, Aharon, be-garon, we-ha-aḥaron, we-ḥaron, u-be-iwwaron, ha-shibbaron,* coming just before the end, as the other passage came near the beginning, frames the sermon symmetrically. Given the powerful emotion in this passage, the absence of any expression of contempt for Christianity is striking. But it is consistent with other contemporary sources: see Jacob Katz, "Ben Tatnu (1096) le-Taḥ we-Taṭ (1648–49)," *Sefer ha-Yobel le-Yiṣḥaq Baer* (Jerusalem, 1961), pp. 319–20. This sermon manuscript confirms Katz's rejection of Ettinger's claim that Jews removed such expressions from printed literature because of their fear of the censors (p. 310, n. 8a).

Elijah ha-Kohen of Izmir

Elijah ben Abraham Solomon ha-Kohen was born and educated in Izmir, Turkey, and served for many years as rabbi and preacher during a most turbulent period in that city's history. Among the many authorities whose interpretations he cited in his works are his grandfather, his uncle, and his father. The influence of his father's scholarship, communal leadership, and personal model is particularly noticeable, as can be seen from the sermon translated below. Abraham Solomon ha-Kohen, who appears in lists of the most important rabbis and judges of Izmir, died in 1659, when Elijah could not have been much younger than thirteen or fourteen. As he himself lived until 1729, his date of birth was probably about 1645.[1]

Elijah ha-Kohen reached maturity at the peak of the messianic excitement generated by the movement of Shabbetai Ẓevi and the spiritual turmoil engendered by Ẓevi's apostasy. Questions about exile and redemption and the figure of the Messiah loom large in Elijah's writings, and Gershom Scholem's analysis of several of his works led him to conclude that they "prove beyond any doubt that the famous preacher was profoundly and clearly influenced in his conception of messianism by Sabbatian writings and teachings." Elijah was among the more moderate Sabbatians, and he may have distanced himself from the movement in his later years, but he never repudiated those doctrines in his writings that reflect Sabbatian influence.[2]

No suspicion of heresy, however, marred his reputation as one of the most popular and powerful preachers of his age. In an introduction to a book completed in the 1690s, he wrote that he had been preaching each Sabbath for some thirty-four years.[3] He was an extremely prolific writer, author of more than thirty different works.[4] Some of these, such as commentaries on various biblical books (Psalms, Song of Songs, Ruth, Esther, Lamentations), bear no direct literary relationship to his sermons. Others, including *Midrash*

1. I follow here the chronology of Gershom Scholem, "R. Eliyyahu ha-Kohen ha-ʾIttamari we-ha-Shabbetaʾut," *Sefer ha-Yobel li-Kebod Alexander Marx* (New York, 1950), pp. 453–54.

2. Ibid., pp. 455, 470.

3. *Semukim la-ʿAd,* cited by Samuel Werses, "Rabbi Eliyyahu ha-Kohen me-Izmir," *Yabneh* 2 (1940):159, n. 26.

4. See the bibliographical studies listed in ibid., p. 156, n. 1.

ha-ʾIttamari and *Midrash Eliyyahu,* from which the sermon below is taken, contain records of sermons identified by their occasion of delivery.

Midrash Talpiyyot, a collection of source material from some three hundred books organized by subject, was written by Elijah in a burst of sustained energy following a period of incapacitating depression after the sudden death of his son.[5] It was probably intended as an aid for preachers, like Israel of Belżyce's *Yalquṭ Ḥadash.*

Elijah's best-known book was *Shebeṭ Musar,* one of the most influential works in Hebrew ethical literature, frequently reprinted, and translated into Yiddish, Ladino, and Arabic. The book, which is clearly the work of a preacher, refers to sermons actually delivered (chap. 42) and is written in a vivid popular style. Its division into fifty-two chapters may be a link with the Torah lessons, although this is neither made explicit nor always readily discerned.[6] Like his sermons, *Shebet Musar* is a rich source for popular Jewish beliefs relating to punishments for sinners after death, the nature of hell, and reincarnation, as well as for dramatic stories and exempla.

The sermon translated below is unique among those included in this anthology in its extensive use of popular materials. Identified as a eulogy occasioned by the death of Jacob Ḥagiz, it is divided into two parts clearly delineated in the written text: the *derush,* or theoretical investigation of a conceptual problem (in this case, the transmigration of souls), and the *tokeḥat musar* ("ethical rebuke"), containing the practical lessons for conduct to be drawn from the *derush.*

The *derush* begins without a biblical verse, citing a passage of rabbinic aggadah. Two exegetical problems are immediately raised and then left temporarily unresolved. Instead, the preacher starts to lay the conceptual groundwork for his discussion of transmigration, beginning with the thesis about the possibility of movement from one level of being to another. This is exemplified by some rather startling narrative material and is then applied to a series of exegetical insights, culminating in an extensive discussion of Job 33. The section concludes by solving the exegetical problems raised at the beginning, the theoretical content of the *derush* now facilitating the solution.

While the second section is called "ethical rebuke," it actually continues the discussion of transmigration, abandoning the homiletical and exegetical approach for a long section in which the preacher appears as storyteller. The transition to social and religious criticism is made in the statement that "when a person feels a special temptation that does not allow him to observe one particular commandment, that is the commandment he was reincarnated to perform, because he did not perform it in his first incarnation." This

5. Ibid., pp. 162–63.

6. See Dan, *Sifrut,* pp. 243–45. For an example of its influence, see Tishby, *Netibe,* pp. 163–67.

allows the preacher to discuss shortcomings in the behavior of his listeners. His narrative art is mobilized here as well, and the sermon ends with a hair-raising evocation of the perils of death and burial. The brief concluding prayer ("May God save us from all this!") would have done little to mitigate the listeners' sense of terror at the sermon's end, an effect not frequently associated with the mainstream of Jewish preaching.

Restoring the Soul: Eulogy for Jacob Ḥagiz (1674)

(The sermon I preached at the passing of the great, pious, and humble R. Jacob Ḥagiz, author of *ʿEṣ Ḥayyim.*[1] It is called "Restoring the Soul."[2] It discusses the transmigration of souls in this world after death, and what occurs to them. Delivered in the sacred Portuguese Congregation, before *many people, the splendor of the King of kings of kings* (cf. Prov. 14:28), the Holy One, blessed be He.)

Tractate Berakot, chapter I [17a]: "When R. Joḥanan finished the Book of Job, he said, The end of the human being is to die, the end of the beast is the slaughter; thus all are doomed to die. Blessed are those who grow up in Torah and labor at Torah."

Many before me have raised their voices about this statement. As for me, before I begin to speak, I will open with two problems. Then, at the end of the sermon, with God's help, I will return to discuss them, for this is my

1. On Jacob Ḥagiz, head of an academy in Jerusalem, teacher of Nathan of Gaza, and one of the Jerusalem rabbis who excommunicated Shabbetai Ẓevi, see Meir Benayahu, "Le-Toledot Batte ha-Midrash Bi-Yrushalayim ba-Meʾah ha-Shebaʿ ʿEśreh," *HUCA* 21 (1948):1–8, and Scholem, *Sabbatai Ṣevi* (Princeton, 1973), pp. 181, 199–202, 246–48. There is nothing personal about Ḥagiz in this sermon. The report of his death was used by the preacher as an occasion for discussing death, the fate of the soul, and the lessons to be drawn by the living. If Elijah indeed harbored Sabbatian sympathies, as Scholem has argued (see nn. 1 and 2 supra), it seems incongruous that he would preach at the death of a man known for his persecution of the "prophet." Perhaps the sermon was intended as a public demonstration of respect, while the failure to utter a word of praise implies a certain coolness.

2. The title of the sermon, "Meshibat Nafesh," taken from Ps. 19:8, is used to refer (through a play on words) to the central subject of the sermon, explained in the following sentence. Cf. *Midrash ha-ʾIttamari,* sermon 12 (Warsaw, 1901, p. 67a).

pattern.[3] The first: how is the ending of the Book of Job relevant to Joḥanan's statement? It would have been more appropriate for him to say this at the end of the Book of Ecclesiastes, for Kohelet, who reigned in realms above and below,[4] still considered everything vanity, as he said: *Vanity of vanities . . . all is vanity* (Eccles. 1:2). There it would be pertinent to say that the end of the human being is to die, remembering that even Solomon ultimately died, despite his glorious stature. The second problem: he should have said, "the end of the human being and the beast is to die." Why did he extend the statement by saying, "the end of the human being is to die, and the end of the beast is the slaughter"?

In order for you to understand this, I must set forth a splendid introductory thesis, set upon foundations of gold, adorned by statements of our holy sages and by biblical verses and other subjects pertaining to this matter and supporting it. It is widely known that of all the character traits, humility and self-abasement are supremely praiseworthy, as they encompass all perfections. This is explained in many rabbinic statements, and in the ethical literature it is dwelt upon at length, especially by the pious author of *Reʾshit Ḥokmah.*[5] Abasement leads in all things to exaltation, for by means of abasement everything in the world rises level after level to reach its perfection.

The four realms of being are the inanimate, the vegetative, the nonrational living creature, and the rational.[6] All of these rise from level to level by means of abasement, after their destruction. From the realm of the inanimate, the earth, there is ascent to the level of vegetation, after the soil is plowed. From the vegetative realm, there is ascent to the realm of nonrational living creatures, for the beasts eat the plants that grow in the field. In this way the vegetative is transformed into the higher level of living creature by means of abasement, for it must first be destroyed and descend to an even lower level.

Then the nonrational animal is destroyed and abased by being slaughtered, but this enables it to ascend to the level of the rational creature, when it is eaten by a Jew after ritual slaughter with the appropriate blessing. This does not occur when it is eaten by Gentiles, *whose flesh is the flesh of donkeys* (Ezek. 23:20).

3. The preacher uses the traditional Sephardic technique of raising questions about the passage to be discussed, but he delays his solution to these problems until the conceptual groundwork is in place.

4. B. Sanh 20b.

5. *Reʾshit Ḥokmah,* by Elijah di Vidas, was one of the most important works of kabbalistic ethical literature; see Mordechai Pachter, "Sefer Reʾshit Ḥokmah le-Rabbi Eliyyahu di Vidas we-Qiṣṣuraw," *Kiryat Sefer* 47 (1972):686–710, and Dan, *Sifrut,* pp. 223–24. It contains a long section on humility called "Shaʿar ha-ʿAnawah," which does not, however, appear to be the source for the specific point discussed here.

6. These four realms (called *domem, ṣomeaḥ, ḥai, medabber*) were commonplaces of medieval Jewish thought. Movement between them was not so common a theme.

This is especially so because of the souls reincarnated into beasts in order to attain spiritual perfection, each according to its own punishment, which determines whether it is reincarnated into a domestic beast or a wild animal or a bird. Look into the books *ʿEmeq ha-Melek, Nishmat Ḥayyim,* [the works of Menaḥem] Recanati, and the writings of Isaac Abravanel: you will find accounts of things that happened in their time, bearing eloquent witness about the souls of wicked people reincarnated into beasts.[7] At the end of this sermon, in the ethical section, I will tell you something I myself saw: a spirit reincarnated into the body of a woman.[8] The purpose of this is to enable the soul to correct some flaw. We must therefore eat everything with a blessing and proper intention.

I heard from the pious sage R. Ḥayyim Alfasi, of blessed memory,[9] that a person who finds a piece of fruit thrown onto a garbage dump and covered with dirt should wash it and clean it and say a blessing over it, for it may contain the spark of some soul which can be restored only by eating the fruit with a blessing.

See now what the pious author of *Sefer Ḥaredim* wrote in chapter 7, page 42a:[10] "It happened in Castile. A bull was prepared by the Gentiles for their sport (their custom is to beat it and torment it). The night before, a certain Jew had a dream in which his father appeared and said, 'Know, my son, that because of my many sins they made me be reincarnated into a bull—the very bull that is prepared to undergo tomorrow the baiting and tormenting that is part of the popular sport. Therefore, my son, redeem me

7. *ʿEmeq ha-Melek,* by Naphtali ben Jacob Bacharach, published in 1648, was an important text in the spreading of Lurianic Kabbalah; see Gershom Scholem, *Kabbalah* (Jerusalem, 1974), pp. 394–95. Manasseh ben Israel's *Nishmat Ḥayyim,* published in 1652, serves as a valuable compendium of doctrines relating to the soul. The preacher cited Menaḥem Recanati's *Torah Commentary* on transmigration from Manasseh's *Nishmat Ḥayyim* (4:13) at the end of chap. 14 of *Shebeṭ Musar.* Abravanel's discussion of transmigration (into human beings, not into animals) is in his commentary on Deut. 25:5.

8. The preacher promises something that will come later in the sermon, arousing anticipation and suspense in the listeners. For the fulfillment of the promise, see the penultimate paragraph of the sermon text below.

9. Elijah cites the teachings of Ḥayyim Alfasi elsewhere in his work, e.g. *Shebeṭ Musar,* chap. 26. The present statement recalls the ancient Manichean doctrine that the best fortune to befall a soul was to be reincarnated into vegetables or fruits and to be eaten by a Manichean saint. See the sources noted by R. J. Z. Werblowsky, *Joseph Karo: Lawyer and Mystic* (Philadelphia, 1977), p. 235, including the reference to St. Augustine's sardonic critique of this doctrine. Cf. also Rachel Elior, "Torat ha-Gilgul be-*Sefer Galya Raza,*" *Meḥqere Yerushalayim be-Maḥashebet Yiśra'el* 3 (1983–84):231.

10. *Sefer Ḥaredim,* by the sixteenth-century Safed kabbalist Eliezer Azikri, was a popular spiritual ascetic manual first published in 1601. This story was obviously a favorite of the preacher, as he repeated it in his *Midrash Talpiyyot,* beginning of "ʿAnaf ha-Gilgul," and in *Shebeṭ Musar,* chap. 18. Cf. Micha Yosef Bin Gorion (Berdichevski), *Mimekor Yisrael,* 3 vols. (Philadelphia, 1976), no. 236, 2:791–92.

and save me when I escape through such and such a place, lest they kill me and tear me apart. You must pay to redeem me—no matter how much it may cost—and have the bull ritually slaughtered, and let me be eaten by impoverished Torah students. For they have informed me from heaven and permitted me to tell you that in this way you can restore my soul from the level of a beast to the level of a human being, so that I may be worthy of serving God, with His help.' "

In the book *Maʾamar Yayin Meshummar* by R. Nathan Shapira, there is something written by R. Zalman son of R. Judah the Pious.[11] I quote: "When I studied in Speyer before R. Jedidiah, I found in his academy a manuscript written by R. Zalman, and this is what it said":

> My father the Ḥasid told me that in his time the following occurred. There was a wealthy man in Speyer who cut his beard with scissors. My father protested to him about this, but he paid no attention, for he claimed to be of feeble health and unable to tolerate the beard.
>
> My father replied, "I want you to know that your end will be bitter indeed, for after your death, demons appearing like cows will come and trample the corner of your beard; this is the punishment for those who destroy the corner of their beards. It is actually hinted in the Torah in the verse, *lo taqqifu peʾat roʾshkem we-lo tashḥit: You shall not mar the corners of your beard nor destroy* (Lev. 19:27): the initial letters of the last four words form the word *parot* [prwt], cows."[12]
>
> When the wealthy man died, the most important dignitaries of Speyer were sitting in his house, my father included. He wrote a certain Name and tossed it on the body of the deceased. Immediately, it stood up. All who were seated there fled in terror. The dead man began to tear out the hair from his head. My father asked him what he was doing. He replied, "Woe to me that I did not listen to you." My father asked him to tell what had happened to his soul. He said, "When my soul departed, a demon appearing like a large cow came carrying a certain implement filled with tar and sulfur and salt; he took my soul and placed it inside, so that it could not escape.

11. On Shapira, see Scholem, *Sabbatai Ṣevi,* pp. 72–74; on this passage, see Meir Benayahu, *Toledot ha-ʾAri* (Jerusalem, 1967), p. 114. Shapira's source was *Sefer ha-Gan* by Isaac ben Eliezer, first published at Venice in 1606 (Lemberg, 1864), pp. 5a–6b). The entire passage was cited by the preacher in *Shebeṭ Musar,* chap. 18; cf. *Mimekor Yisrael,* no. 215, pp. 767–68. On Zalman, son of Judah the Ḥasid, see Y. A. Kamelhar, *Ḥasidim ha-Riʾshonim* (Vacs, 1917), pp. 54–55, n. 18, and Ephraim Urbach, ed., *ʿArugat ha-Bośem,* 4 vols. (Jerusalem, 1939), 1:206, n. 6.

12. Cf. Benayahu, *Toledot ha-ʾAri,* p. 233, on R. Isaac Luria's use of an acronym from this verse to form the word *par* ("bull"). The reason why the passage was cited after the preceding story from *Sefer Ḥaredim* may have been to show why the father had been reincarnated into a bull.

"An angel came from the Heavenly Court, took the implement containing my soul from the demon, and carried it up to the Great Court of the Creator of souls. A voice came from the Court: 'Have you studied Torah?' I replied that I had. It commanded that a Pentateuch be brought and told me to read in it. As soon as I opened the book, I found the verse, *You shall not mar the corners of your beard* (Lev. 19:27). I did not know what to say. Then I heard a voice proclaiming: 'Place this soul in the lowest level of Hell.' While they were lifting my soul to take it to the lowest level, another voice said, 'Wait, my son Judah needs to ask a question of this one, and he has just now prayed for mercy on this soul, so that he might speak with it. Therefore, do not let it descend to Hell.'"

There are many similar stories, too numerous to be written. Thus you see that many souls of the wicked are reincarnated into beasts, or birds, and they are restored to their proper level by being eaten after proper ritual slaughter and blessing.

With this in mind, I have found an explanation of the verse about our father Jacob: *He slept there that night, and he took what came into his hand as a gift for his brother Esau* (Gen. 32:14). If you look at my Torah commentary, you will find that I explained the meaning of the phrase *min ha-ba be-yado,* literally, *what came into his hand.*[13] But now, following our thesis that the souls of the wicked are reincarnated into beasts, I maintain that Jacob thought, "How can I send one of these animals to Esau, an idolater? He might sacrifice it in an idolatrous manner, yet it might contain the reincarnation of a soul from previous generations which has come to be restored." What did he do? He left the choice to the animals, allowing them to come by themselves, knowing that any animal in which there was some aspect of a human soul would certainly not approach him.

From my teacher, the crown of my head, I heard a fine interpretation, fitting our thesis, of the rabbinic statement, "The commandments were given to Israel only in order to refine creatures."[14] This means that through the commandments, Jews can refine and restore all the creatures in the world. Vegetation ascends to the nonrational animals, and from there to the rational ones, in whom it reaches its perfection through the blessing and the com-

13. Elijah's Torah commentary was *Ḥuṭ shel Ḥesed* (Izmir, 1865). On the verse, see the sermon of ibn Shueib, above, at n. 46.

14. Gen. Rabbah 44:1, ordinarily understood "to refine those creatures to whom they were given." Elijah's teacher was probably R. Benjamin Melammed (see the first sermon in *Midrash Eliyyahu,* and Samuel Werses, "Rabbi Eliyyahu ha-Kohen me-Izmir," *Yabneh* 2 (1940):158. Note how the introductory thesis about transmigration is now being used in a chain of exegetical comments moving from one verse or rabbinical statement to another.

mandment. Thus, through the commandment and the blessing said over various things, all creatures in the world can be refined.

This yields an interpretation of the verse, *You have given us like sheep to be eaten, You have scattered us among the nations* (Ps. 44:12). Israel was complaining about having been given like sheep to be eaten. Now you might argue: on the contrary, this is good, for sheep ascend in level when eaten by rational creatures. The reply is, *You have scattered us among the nations,* meaning that the ascent in level occurs when they are eaten by Jews after a proper ritual slaughter, with the appropriate blessing. But *You have scattered us among the nations,* and that is the reason we are lost.

Now I shall follow in my teacher's footsteps. Based on his interpretation just cited, we may interpret the verse, *who devour My people as they devour bread, and do not invoke the Lord* (Ps. 14:4). The prophet was complaining when he said that the Gentiles *devour My people as they devour bread.* Now the eating of bread raises it from the level of vegetation to that of a rational creature, and this is said to be how they are consuming Israel. You might argue: on the contrary, this is good, for they will ascend to a higher level. The reply is, *they do not invoke the Lord,* for an ascent in level occurs only by means of a blessing, and they do not call upon the Lord.

(This can also be interpreted in a different way. The prophet complained that it really should be the opposite, that they should fall into our power so that they could ascend in level, not that we should be in their power. That is the significance of his asking as a rhetorical question, "is the Gentiles' devouring of My people like the devouring of bread," which raises its level? How can it be if *they do not invoke the Lord*?" On the contrary, it should be the opposite, that we consume them, so that they might be refined with us by means of the Torah and the commandments.)

With this, we can understand yet another verse: *For Your sake we are slain all day, we are regarded as sheep for the slaughter* (Ps. 44:23). This means, because we are slain all day for Your sake, it is considered as if we were like sheep for the slaughter. Just as sheep ascend considerably by means of ritual slaughter, rising from the nonrational realm to the rational, so as a result of our being slain all day for the sanctification of Your name, we ascend to a level that other creatures cannot reach. We know this from the rabbinic statement, "No creature can attain to the place [in heaven] assigned to the martyrs slain by the government."[15]

Thus every living beast and fowl ascends in level by means of observant Jews who say blessings and thereby restore them. They do not ascend by means of the Gentiles, nor by means of those Jews who eat without blessing, thereby harming and destroying the fruit in their mouths. Of them it is said

15. B. BB 10b.

(Eccles. 3:19), *the preeminence of man,* meaning that the lowly being who is "man" in name alone, *is nothing.* The only source of preeminence is the pure soul that raises human beings by means of the commandments, and those devoid of commandments are considered like a beast, because of the deficiency of their soul. To the contrary, one who slaughters a beast improperly destroys it and makes it impure, because it has been slaughtered by another beast just like it, like a lion and its prey. The slaughterer, being devoid of a pure soul, is considered a beast, as we said: *The preeminence of man above the beast is nothing,* except for the pure soul.

Based on this we can understand the verse, *Who slaughters an ox, slays a human being* (Isa. 66:3). But on the way I shall explicate from the beginning of the section. . . .[16]

Let us return to our subject: that God makes the soul, separated from the body, return to this world in an animal, bird, or human being in order to restore and cleanse it. This is the doctrine with which Elihu rebuked Job, telling him that he should see the kindness God does for the human soul by making it return three times into this world: *Truly, God does all these things two or three times to a person* (Job 33:29).[17]

Now at first I refrained from writing and speaking publicly about matters concerning transmigration, basing my decision on the words of the author of the *ʿIqqarim,*[18] who repudiated this. Later, however, I saw the discussion in *ʿEmeq ha-Melek,* which states in the name of R. Isaac Abravanel that it is permissible to preach publicly about matters concerning transmigration, contrary to the view of others.[19] For transmigration is not a subject that must be concealed, like the esoteric mysteries of the Torah. If transmigration were one of these mysteries, how could God have revealed it to Pythagoras, who was a Gentile?

When I read these words, sweeter than honey, I myself decided that it would be meritorious to communicate this to all and to implant it in the hearts of the people. For this doctrine helps solve many enormous problems that turn people away from God. For example, the problem of the righteous who suffer, and other such puzzles as well, can be solved through the doctrine of transmigration. If you are wise, you will see this.

16. Omitted are three-and-a-half columns of text that give an exegesis of Isa. 66:1–6.

17. This verse from Job was a favorite peg for kabbalists discussing the doctrine of transmigration. See Gershom Scholem, "Le-Ḥeqer Torat ha-Gilgul ba-Qabbalah ba-Meʾah ha-Shelosh ʿEśreh." *Tarbiẓ* 16 (1945):143, and "Seelenwanderung und Sympathie der Seelen in der jüdischen Mystik," *Eranos Jahrbuch* 24 (1955):69, 73–74, 83, 91; also Werblowsky, *Joseph Karo,* p. 239.

18. Interpreting the Hebrew letters as an abbreviation for *Ha-Rab Baʿal ha-ʿIqqarim.* See Joseph Albo, *Sefer ha-ʿIqqarim,* 4:29 (ed. Husik, vol. 4, pt. 2, pp. 287–88).

19. See Bacharach's *ʿEmeq ha-Melek* (Amsterdam, 1648; Bene Beraq, 1973), intro., p. 7c–d.

I have heard an interpretation of the verses, *I am innocent; I do not know my soul: I despise my life; it is one* [aḥat hi] *therefore I would say that He destroys the innocent and the wicked* (Job 9:21–22). The meaning as follows. Job was asserting the truth of the doctrine of transmigration—that the human soul returns to this world several times. That is why he said, *I am innocent,* yet *I do not know my soul*: I do not know whether in another incarnation it was the soul of a wicked man. Therefore *I despise my life.* I do not speak heretically about the suffering He has brought upon me, for I say that my soul has caused it for me. However, *aḥat hi*: if I were to maintain that the soul *is one,* coming into the world only once, then *I would say that He destroys the innocent and the wicked.* For I am innocent; why would He have brought suffering upon me?[20]

Let us return to our subject: that Elihu rebuked Job by appealing to the doctrine of transmigration and the other acts of kindness God does for human beings so that they will not be destroyed. He set before Job, in order, seven acts of kindness God performs, feeling impelled to speak when he heard that Job had spoken improperly.[21]

Elihu said, *Please* [na] *Job, listen to my words, give ear to all that I say. Now* [na] after I have heard several things that you said, *I open my lips* to respond; *my tongue forms words in my mouth. My words bespeak the uprightness of my heart,* for I do not speak just to chide you; *my lips utter insight honestly* (Job 33:1–3). Or we could say that the first *na* means "now." That is, do not feel aversion for me because now I am the speaker, for I am not like your friends who spoke to you so verbosely. It is like *Now* [na] *I open my lips* afresh. Make your ear like a hopper, for this is something new.

If you think that I say whatever pops out of my mouth without arranging my thoughts, this is not true, for first *My tongue forms words in my mouth,* every single thought before it is uttered aloud. And Job, if you should be thinking, "Why should I believe that what you say is right; you don't say what you really think," know that this is not so. Rather, *my words bespeak the uprightness of my heart,* expressing precisely what I am thinking. The proof that *my lips utter insight honestly* is how clearly and articulately I speak, for this is evidence that I am sincere about what I say. This follows the statement about R. Ḥanina ben Dosa, who used to pray on behalf of the sick and said "If may prayer is fluent, I know that it is accepted."[22] Here too, the clarity and fluency of my speech is a fine indication of the honesty in my heart.

20. Cf. the passage from Solomon Alkabeẓ's *Shoresh Yishai* cited by Werblowsky in *Joseph Karo,* p. 242.

21. This section of the sermon is a homily on the thirty-third chapter of Job, interpreting it as a treatise on God's kindness toward human beings even in death. The subject is obviously appropriate for the occasion of the sermon.

22. Ber 5:5.

He then began to say, *The spirit of God formed me* (Job 33:4). Know this before I make my case against you: I acknowledge that God has made me and created me. That is why he said, *The spirit of God formed me, the breath of Shaddai sustains me. If you can, answer me, argue against me, take your stand* (Job 33:4–5). This means, your intent, Job, is to argue with God and to ask God to respond to your contentions, for you said, *If only God would speak* (Job 11:15). You also said, *A wind passed before my face that made the hair of my flesh stand up* (Job 4:15), which the sages interpreted to mean, "perhaps a stormy wind passed before You, and You mixed up *Iyyob* and *Oyeb*."[23]

Therefore I say to you: whatever you have to ask God, ask me, and I will answer all your questions. *I am as you requested, instead of God* (Job 33:6), I am in His place to answer you, and my mouth is like His to address you. Lest Job think him a heretic in comparing himself to God, he continued, *I too was nipped from clay* (ibid.), made from turbid matter, just like you.

You are not overwhelmed by fear of me. You might say, my whole quarrel is with God, why do you want to answer me in His place? My response is, *You are not overwhelmed by fear of me.* If God should reply to you, you could still claim that you might have answered back but you were terrified. However, *You are not overwhelmed by fear of me; my pressure does not weigh heavily on you* (Job 33:7). If I answer your question, you have no more grounds for complaint. If you have a response, you would not refrain from saying it because you were afraid of me.

I say what I do, as I stand with you before the bench, because *You have stated in my hearing, I heard these words spoken: "I am guiltless, free from transgression; I am innocent, without iniquity, but He finds reasons to oppose me, considers me His enemy"* (Job 33:8–10), for He mixed up *Iyyob* and *Oyeb*. *He puts my feet in stocks, watches all my ways* (Job 33:11) unjustly (heaven forbid!). All these heresies I have heard you utter when you said that you are innocent and that God has brought judgment against you without cause.

Know that *in this* your claim, *you are not right*. For *I will answer you that God is greater than any man* (Job 33:12). I will tell you the great acts of kindness God does for human beings to save their souls from death. Therefore, *why do you complain against Him that He does not reply to any of man's charges?* (Job 33:13). Then Elihu began to tell Job, in order, the seven great and renowned acts of kindness God does for human beings to keep them from destruction.

The first act of kindness. When a person sins during the day, that same night, *in a dream, a night vision, when deep sleep falls on men while they slumber in their beds, He opens men's understanding* (Job 33:15–16a) concerning the sins

23. B. BB 16a; *ʾIyyob* is the Hebrew name of Job. *ʾOyeb* (with the Hebrew letters *yod* and *waw* transposed) means "enemy."

they have committed, so that the nightmare may lead them to repent. The sages have said, "David never had a good dream in his life, and this was in order to impel him to improve."[24] God does all this, communicating through dreams, in order *to turn the person away from the evil done* (Job 33:17) during the day.

Although discipline might have come immediately after the commission of the sin and sealed the decree right away (cf. Job 33:16b), God's only concern is *to turn the person away from the evil done.* Furthermore, He *suppresses the pride of man* (Job 33:17). Even though pride is an abomination of God, who says, "I cannot abide it in the same place with me,"[25] nevertheless, in His mercy, *He suppresses the pride of man,* concealing it from the sight of the prosecutors. Thus we see the first great act of kindness God does for human beings. Why should there be quarrels against Him?

I will tell you the second act of kindness. Sometimes God sees that dreams have not worked to bring about repentance. This was the case with Korah and his faction. Moses said to them, *Come morning, God will make known what is His* (Num. 16:5). The reason why Moses put it off until the morning is that he thought a dream might lead Korah back to the right path. But when he saw that they did not refer to such a dream, he realized that their doom was determined from heaven. That is why he put them off until the morning. (See my Torah commentary for other explanations.) They were not vouchsafed a dream because they had publicly denied the divine origin of the Torah, not only sinning but leading others to sin.[26] For other sins, however, dreams are vouchsafed.

If the sinner does not repent, thinking that dreams have no real significance, or that they speak falsely,[27] then God brings physical suffering upon the sinner. That is why Elihu said, *He is reproved by pains on his bed, and the trembling in his bones is constant* (Job 33:19). It means that God puts intense pain in the person's bones in order to cleanse the sins. If the sinner repents because of this, it is good; if not, God increases the burden with something that, according to the sages, is worse than physical suffering.[28]

This is the third kindness God does for us: poverty. This breaks a person's spirit and impels him to return to God in full sincerity. Therefore Elihu said, *He detests food; fine food {is repulsive} to him* (Job 33:20), for God brings the person to the point where there is no one to break him a crust of bread, and his body is weakened so that *his flesh wastes away until it cannot be seen, his*

24. B. Ber 55b.
25. B. Soṭ 5a.
26. Cf. Num. Rabbah 18:3.
27. B. Giṭ 52a, Zech. 10:2.
28. Cf. B. BB 116a.

bones are rubbed away till they are invisible (Job 33:21). If such severe poverty moves him to repent, it is good.

If not, God performs a fourth act of kindness for him, bringing about his death, for some repent as they are about to die. That is why Elihu said, *He comes close to the Pit, his life verges on death* (Job 33:22). If even death does not move the person to repentance, God sends him to hell. Yet despite it all, God does not utterly destroy the sinner. As he is being led to hell, if there is *one advocate against a thousand who will speak on his behalf and declare his uprightness* (Job 33:23), as expressed through a single commandment the man has performed, God immediately has compassion upon him and keeps him from entering hell.[29] *Then God has mercy upon him and decrees, "Redeem him from descending to the Pit, for I have obtained his ransom"* (Job 33:24). The one good quality that remains with him saves him from hell.

Then God performs a fifth act of kindness for the soul, making it return once more into this world, so that it may collect a greater measure of commandments. That is why Elihu said, *I have obtained his ransom: Let his flesh be healthier than in his youth, let him return to his younger days* (Job 33:25). This means that the ransom is to make him return into this world as in the past, to be young once again, so that he may correct what he has done wrong.

Know further the sixth act of kindness. Even though God has taken the trouble to send the person back into this world, and he has gone back and spoiled things again, God still does not trample him to destruction. As soon as he says *I have sinned,* his prayer is immediately received. Therefore Elihu continues, *He looks upon men, he says, "I have sinned,"* etc. (Job 33:27). This means, after He brings them back into this world and they sin once again, He still observes them. As soon as He sees that they say, *I have sinned, I have perverted what was right, and I have not deserved* all the acts of kindness God has done for me, as soon as He sees that they confess, He immediately *redeems the soul from passing into the Pit, and it sees the light* (Job 33:28) of the King's countenance, having become worthy of beholding the divine presence.

There is another way of explaining the statement *He looks upon men, he says "I have sinned,"* we-yashar heᶜeweti (NJV: *I have perverted what was right* [Job 33:27]). The meaning is that God observes those who have returned to this world and sinned again, and sees that they are confessing and saying *I have sinned,* but this confession is only about an inadvertent offense, while they have actually committed many serious sins and should have confessed about these. That is the meaning of *we-yashar heᶜeweti*: "the right thing [*yashar*] would have been to say *heᶜeweti,* 'I have done perversely.'" Nevertheless, God overlooks this and says, *lo shawah li,* "it is not worthwhile to Me to be a stickler with him for this, for I am merciful."

29. This recalls the story told near the beginning of the sermon, in which the sinner was saved from hell through the intercession of Judah the Pious.

Know this further, Job, and heed my words as I tell of the seventh act of kindness, the most important of all. Even if the person should die this second time in a state of evil and corruption, God still does not destroy him, but the entire process of returning to this world is repeated yet again, until he can perfect his soul to the point where it will not be banished from God's presence. Therefore Elihu said, *Truly God does all these things two or three times to a person* (Job 33:29), *all these things* referring to the process of transmigration, which is repeated two or three times. His purpose in all of this is *to bring the soul back from the Pit that it may bask in the light of Life* (Job 33:30).

Therefore, *pay heed, Job, and hear me; be still, and I will speak* (Job 33:31) about the acts of kindness God does for human beings. How can you say *I am guiltless, free from transgression . . . but He finds reasons to oppose me, considers me His enemy* (Job 33:9–10)? You meant by this that He brought this suffering upon you without any reason—Heaven forbid that God should do such evil! Therefore, go ahead, Job, *if you have what to say, answer me; speak, for I am eager to vindicate you* in these words of rebuke, *but if not, listen to me; be still, and I will teach you wisdom* (Job 33:32–33).

Incidentally, this seems a good time to explicate the verse I mentioned above, *the preeminence of man over the beast is* ayin, *nothing* (Eccles. 3:19), except for the soul. Yet there are other differences between human beings and beasts. We might say that the letters of the word *ayin* (*alef, yod, nun*) stand for the words *amirah,* "speaking," *yediʿah,* "knowing," and *neḥamah,* "relief from the compulsion to revenge."[30] The verse means that human beings, unlike beasts, have, in addition to the pure and blameless soul, the power of speech, intellectual knowledge, and the capacity to be comforted without taking revenge.

As for man's erect posture, as contrasted with the beasts that walk on all fours, we can find a hint of this in the word *ayin,* for its numerical significance in *mispar qatan* is sixteen, like that of the word *qomah,* meaning "stature" or "height."[31] Thus the preeminence of the human being over the beasts is that the human being is erect, like the ministering angels, and unlike the beasts. Again, this is in addition to the difference in the soul.

Now although there are several such differences between man and beast—speech, erect posture, knowledge—all of this redounds to man's benefit only when his soul is pure, for then his speech is true speech, and his knowledge true knowledge. This is not true when his soul is blemished, for then his speech is not distinctively human. Some birds can be taught to speak, but

30. This is the hermeneutical device called *notariqon* (cf. B. Shab 105a).

31. The gematria, somewhat forced, is as follows: *alef,* 1, + *yod,* 10, + *nun,* 5(0), = *ʾayin,* 16; *qof,* 1(00), + *waw,* 6, + *mem,* 4(0), + *heh,* 5, = *qomah,* 16. Therefore *qomah* ("height") can be substituted for *ʾayin* ("nothing"). Cf. above, sermon by Solomon Levi, n. 38.

this does not raise them to the level of human beings. Therefore a person should see to it that all his conversation be about matters of Torah, which raise one to the level of a true human being. Nothing is so painful to God as those who speak about trivial matters, even if such talk is not coarse and vulgar. This is obviously a fault that can be corrected only with the greatest difficulty.

Let us return to our subject: that the human soul is reincarnated several times in this world, and sometimes a father is reincarnated in his son, as occurs in the story I will tell you in the ethical section at the end of the sermon. Based on this, my relative R. Abraham Apumado[32] interpreted the verse in the lesson *Be-Ḥuqqotai* (Lev. 26:3–27:34): *Those that are left of you will pine away in their sins in the lands of your enemies; even in the sins of their fathers they shall pine away with them* (Lev. 26:39). There is a problem here: it should have said simply *in the sins of their fathers they will pine away.* Why the word *ittam, with them,* which seems superfluous?

But this is intended to hint that the fathers are reincarnated into the bodies of their children, so that their sins and the sins of their fathers can both be purged. The thrust of the verse is this: "even in the sins of their fathers, who will be with them in the bodies of their children, and there they will pine away."

Basing himself on this doctrine, R. Y. F.[33] explained the verse *My spirit was consumed, my days were extinct, the graves are ready for me* (Job 17:1). Since Job was a reincarnation of Terah, as the kabbalists have written,[34] he said, *My spirit was consumed, my days were extinct* in Terah, whose soul was reincarnated in me, and I therefore have two graves, one for the first incarnation, when I was in Terah, and one now, when that soul has been reincarnated in me."

The Talmud contains an allusion to transmigration in the statement, "Laban, Balaam, and Cushan Rishathaim are the same," and similarly, "Jannai and Joḥanan are the same."[35] The meaning is not merely that "just as this one was wicked, so was the other one." For they also said, "the serpent, Satan, and the Angel of Death are all the same," and in this case it is clear that all are actually identical. Therefore when they said "Laban and Balaam are the same," the meaning is that Laban was reincarnated into Balaam. This is hinted in the Passover Haggadah. That is why Laban tried to uproot

32. Elijah quotes R. Abraham Apumado frequently in his sermons; see Werses, "R. Eliyyahu ha-Kohen me-Izmir," p. 159. On the Apumado family and its relationship to the preacher, see Meir Benayahu, *Sefer Toledot ha-ʾAri,* pp. 209–11.

33. There are many seventeenth-century rabbis with the initials *yod-peh,* and it is not clear to whom the preacher is referring.

34. See *ʿEmeq ha-Melek,* p. 107c.

35. B. Ber 29a, B. Sanh 105a; with the following quotation, cf. B. BB 16a, "Satan, the evil impulse, and the Angel of Death are the same."

everything, *and he went down to Egypt* (Deut. 26:5), meaning that Laban went down to Egypt reincarnated as Balaam, one of Pharaoh's advisors, who gave the advice to destroy the Hebrews.[36] All this was the interpretation of my relative, R. Abraham Apumado. The hint he found is correct. I have seen something similar in the *Shoresh,*[37] based on the way souls are reincarnated into human beings, as we said about Terah and Job.

With this we may solve the two problems that I raised at the beginning of the sermon. Why did R. Joḥanan say that "the end of the human being is to die" when he finished the Book of Job, and not when he finished the Book of Ecclesiastes? Second, why did he say that "the end of the human being is to die, and the end of the beast is the slaughter"?

We have established that the souls of evil human beings are reincarnated into humans or beasts so that they may be restored through ritual slaughter and blessing. Sometimes they are not restored in this way, for the person in whom the soul is reincarnated may also sin, or the beast may not be slaughtered properly. That is why R. Joḥanan wept upon finishing the Book of Job, who was the reincarnation of Terah, and said that "the end [*sof*] of the human being is to die," and in addition to this end there is another: to come into a beast who will be slaughtered, so that proper ritual slaughter and blessing will restore the soul.

Yet such restoration is only a possibility, not a certainty, for sometimes all ends in death, whether there has been reincarnation into a human being, with the concomitant suffering, or into a beast that has not been slaughtered properly, so that the person dies again. If this occurs, "all are doomed to die," facing death without any restoration. The basis for such restoration, returning to this world so as to accumulate more commandments, becomes a source of greater corruption, for they actually accumulate more transgressions.

Alluding to all this, he spoke "at the conclusion of Job," who had been reincarnated, and said, "the end of the beast is the slaughter," meaning, after the end of a human being there is another end: to enter a beast that will be ritually slaughtered. That is why he did not say, "the *taklit* of the human being is to die," for the word *taklit* means the "final end" or "ultimate purpose" of something, which has nothing beyond it. This is not true for

36. See B. Soṭ 11a. This is used to interpret the passage in the Haggadah, "An Aramean [Laban] would have destroyed my father, and he [Laban!] went down to Egypt" (*The Passover Haggadah,* ed. Nahum Glatzer [New York, 1969], pp. 32–33).

37. On Solomon Alkabeẓ's commentary on Ruth, *Shoresh Yishai,* and its reference to transmigration, see Werblowsky, *Joseph Karo,* pp. 241–42. Elijah apparently called his own commentary on Ruth by the same name (although the published text is called *Beśoret Eliyyahu.* Cf. the end of the first section of the sermon (omitted from this translation; see following note).

the word *sof*, which can mean an end to something that has another end in a different context. The death of a human being is not the ultimate end: never returning to this world again. This is why he did not say, "the *taklit* of the human being is to die. . . ."[38]

(The ethical rebuke, which emerges from the sermon, and speaks about the transmigration of the human soul and what happens to it after death.)

Know that there are instances of transmigration in which, on occasion, the soul of the father enters his child because of a particular sin, punished by his having to suffer once again the pain of death.[39] I will give you an example of this.

It happened in the days of the great rabbi David ibn Zimra.[40] He had three disciples: R. Isaac Ashkenazi [Luria, the Ari],[41] R. Isaac Apumado, and R. Isaac Fasi (May the memories of the righteous be a blessing). They were then about seventeen years old.[42]

One day, R. Isaac Ashkenazi came before his teacher and said, "There are three here whose name is Isaac." The teacher was astonished at this apparently trivial remark, and said, "My son, what do you mean by this? Everyone knows that there are three here whose name is Isaac." He replied, "Rabbi, I meant to say that there are three Isaac-reputations here; that is, three Issacs, each one of whom will be distinguished in a different realm. My reputation will be known throughout the world in Kabbalah, my friend Isaac Apumado will be known throughout the world in the realm of Talmud study,[43] and my friend Isaac Fasi will be known for asking advice, disagreeing with the advice he receives, and doing the opposite."

Indeed, his words came true. All of us have seen for ourselves how great was the wisdom of the Ari in Kabbalah. As for what he said about Isaac Apumado in the realm of Talmud study, this is what happened.

38. Omitted are a column and a half of text giving five other interpretations of the aggadah, and an index (clearly not original but added to the published version, possibly by the editor) giving page references to the verses and rabbinic statements discussed.

39. In Elijah's *Midrash Talpiyyot* (Chernovtsy, 1860), p. 105b, this idea is attributed to R. Isaac Luria, the Ari.

40. On this sixteenth-century rabbinic scholar ("RaDBAZ," ca. 1479–1573), see H. J. Zimmels, *Rabbi David ibn Abi Simra* (Breslau, 1932); Israel Goldman, *The Life and Times of Rabbi David ibn Abi Zimra* (New York, 1970). On the form of the name used by the preacher, "ibn Zimra," see Goldman, p. 199, n. 17.

41. "R. Isaac Ashkenazi" was the name used by Luria's contemporaries in Safed; see Gershom Scholem, *Kabbalah*, p. 420.

42. Not much is known about the other two students. See the material in Benayahu, *Toledot ha-ʾAri*, pp. 209–11.

43. *ʿIyyun*; for this word as a technical term for a mode of intensive Talmud study based on a set of rules, see Chaim Dimitrovsky, "Bet Midrasho shel Rabbi Yaʿaqob Berab bi-Ṣefat," *Sefunot* 7 (1963):77–81.

In the days of R. Samuel de Medina,[44] they used to write from Salonika to the sages of the land of Israel using the title "perfect sages," and letters from the land of Israel would honor the sages of Salonika by using the title "distinguished rabbis." Once it happened that a letter came to R. David ibn Zimra from the sages of Salonika without all the titles of respect that he used when he wrote to them. Angered by this affront to the sages of the land of Israel, he said to his student Isaac Apumado, who was then about eighteen years old, "Go and test them in Talmud study."[45] Apumado took with him about a thousand gold dinars, for he was extremely rich, having been raised in Egypt by a wealthy widow who had no children of her own. Setting out on the journey, he eventually arrived in Salonika.

At that time there was great consternation among the rabbis of Salonika because of a young woman who had been betrothed by three different men, and she did not know which one had been the first. Each of the men brought witnesses for his act of betrothal. All were writing in confusion about the matter. People called her *ʿeglah tilta,* "a third of a calf," because three had betrothed her.[46]

On the day he arrived, Apumado entered the first academy he chanced upon and quickly demonstrated his intellectual acumen in Talmud study, excelling all the others. Seeing this, they said, "We have a learned elder, the head of a certain academy, who is a great master. Go there tomorrow." Then they hurried to warn him that the study should proceed on the highest level, for a "lion" had come from the land of Israel. The rabbi in turn warned all the students in the academy to prepare with the utmost diligence, for he realized that the stranger had come to test them.

The next morning, Apumado went to that academy. Sitting down in the first empty place, he asked his neighbor what they were studying that day. When he was told, he began intense study of the passage. Soon all the students gathered around. He asked his neighbor in a whisper about a technical legal point, and then went out to relieve himself. Now it was his habit to take a long time in the bathroom. When they saw him leave, they waited

44. R. Samuel de Medina ("MaHaRaSHDaM," 1506–89) was perhaps the leading rabbinic scholar of Salonika. See M. S. Goodblatt, *Jewish Life in Turkey in the XVIth Century, As Reflected in the Legal Writings of Samuel de Medina* (New York, 1952).

45. According to Benayahu (pp. 212–13), the historical kernel behind this largely legendary account may have been Medina's rebuke to the rabbis of Safed (including Joseph Karo) for intervening in what he considered to be the internal affairs of Salonika (*Responsa, Yoreh Deʿah,* 86; cf. Goodblatt, pp. 34–35). This occurred in 1560 (when Luria was twenty-six, not seventeen), and RaDBAZ was not directly involved. Medina did write a responsum on a decision of RaDBAZ involving an R. Joseph Apumado (Benayahu, p. 213).

46. Compare B. ʿErub 63a, B. Sanh 65b. This phrase is used to characterize the woman's dilemma in Medina's responsum. See the discussion of the issue and the positions taken by the various rabbis in Benayahu, p. 213.

for an hour. As he did not return, they said, "Apparently he saw that the passage was difficult and went away." Then the one who was sitting next to Apumado got up and asked his question without mentioning the stranger's name, thinking that he had gone. All the scholars of the academy were in a turmoil because the question was so difficult. At this point, Isaac Apumado returned.

The head of the academy said to him, "Look at the problem raised by one of our least advanced students." Apumado, astonished to hear his own question, responded in a clever way that led them to understand that he was the one who had raised it, saying, "He who asked the question will now answer it." He solved the problem easily, and the scholars of the academy were amazed.

Seeing what had happened, the head of the academy then posed seven enormous problems relating to that law. Isaac Apumado turned to the child who recites the halakah[47] and said, "My child, why don't you answer your rabbi when he wants to test you?" The scholars were astonished at this and said to him, "Are these questions not good ones in your opinion?" Isaac Apumado showed them how the difficulties flowed from a textual error, so that they were not reading the talmudic passage correctly, and they admitted that he was right.

Then he raised problems of his own, which they found too difficult. They said, "We will study this tomorrow," but he replied, "These are not really problems that deserve being left until the next day, for this is the solution. But if you need something to study tomorrow, here are some others," and he raised other problems. Amazed at his wisdom, they apologized for not being able to study properly because of the burden of taxes, especially the "fabrics for the royal army."[48] He replied, "If that is true, and you already recognize your own shortcoming, why do you insult the sages of the land of Israel by not writing to them with proper respect as they write to you?" He swore to them that he was one of the least distinguished students of R. David ibn Zimra, and told them about the greatest students. And they undertook to write with the utmost respect, now that they knew the level of learning.

That Sabbath Isaac Apumado was called to the Torah, and he pledged three hundred gold dinars to charity, above and beyond some other charitable works he had done. They were amazed at his generosity, and when he went the following day to the academy of R. Samuel de Medina, they were awed at

47. The Talmudic academies contained students at different levels. This apparently referred to a youngster capable of reciting halakic material by rote but not capable of intensive study by *ʿiyyun*.

48. *Bigde ha-Melek.* On this obligation of the Salonika Jewish community and the increasing difficulty of its fulfillment, see, most recently, S. W. Baron, *SRHJ* 18:229–30, 553, nn. 61–62.

his learning. The rabbi had him sit at his side, and he hugged and kissed him.

That was the day the legal problem of the young woman betrothed by three men came before de Medina in the academy. One of the men had died, so the dispute was between the other two. One brought witnesses that he had betrothed her first. The other hired two scoundrels to testify that the first witnesses should be disqualified because they had seen them in Chios eating all kinds of forbidden food.[49] That is what they testified before R. Samuel de Medina. He cross-examined them, and was almost afraid that the second man would marry her.

At that point, Isaac Apumado stood up before the rabbi and said, "Sir, where there is danger of public scandal, we overlook the niceties of respect for a rabbi.[50] Permit me to judge this case." For Apumado realized that the second witnesses were ignorant men. The rabbi gave him permission. He summoned one witness alone and asked, "That 'forbidden food' these men were eating—was it made of beef or of lamb?" The witness was dumbfounded at the question, for he was really so ignorant that he did not even know what "forbidden foods" were; they had simply coached him to use that phrase.

Seeing that he could not reply, he revealed the whole disgraceful matter to all. Casting off his disguise, he explained that he and his colleague were weavers, whom that contemptible man had hired for five dinars each and taught what to say. When R. Samuel de Medina saw this, he hugged and kissed Apumado, saying "Blessed are you for having prevented me from incurring bloodguilt."[51] Everyone recognized Apumado's intellectual power and learning, and they treated him with utmost respect in Salonika until he left to return to his own land. Thus the words of Isaac Ashkenazi were fulfilled, when he prophesied that Isaac Apumado's reputation for Talmud study would be widely known.

I will now tell you about R. Isaac Fasi, and you will see how Ashkenazi's prophecy about him was fulfilled. When Isaac Fasi was a young man, they brought him a virgin with a dowry of five hundred dinars and a widow with a dowry of a thousand. Uncertain of what to do, he went to seek advice from his friend Isaac Ashkenazi, who advised him to choose the virgin, despite the fact that the widow's dowry was greater. He went and did the opposite, betrothing the widow. Leaving the academy, he sat down in a shop, and was suddenly overcome by fierce passion for his betrothed. He wanted to visit her

49. *Sheqaṣim u-remaśim,* a stereotyped talmudic phrase (e.g., Sanh 8:2). Public eating of forbidden foods would disqualify a man from serving as a witness in a Jewish court.

50. B. Ber 19b.

51. If he had allowed the second man to marry her when the betrothal from the first was actually valid, he would be responsible for making the children from the second marriage *mamzerim,* the products of an adulterous union.

in her home,[52] and he discussed this with intermediaries, who spoke to the widow's brothers, two men distinguished for their learning and their wealth. They made a banquet, to which he was invited.

Now the widow's name was Malkah. At the banquet, he asked her for a cup of water. But when she brought it to him, he suddenly raised his hand and struck her on the face. Then he stood up and actually tried to kill her. The banquet was thrown into turmoil, the joy transformed into grief. He was taken outside. The young woman was asked if she had said something unpleasant to him; she swore that he struck her suddenly, without any provocation.

Once outside, Fasi felt deep remorse over his behavior. Again the passion of love for her burned within him. Less than three days later, he sought a reconciliation. Again they made a banquet, and again he did what he had done the first time.

In short, whenever he was away from her, he was all but consumed with passion for her, but as soon as he saw her he became so incensed that he wanted to strike her. When the townspeople saw what was happening, they tried to settle the matter by advancing the wedding, thinking that perhaps when they were married they would behave like normal people. On the wedding night, he tried to kill her. The guests at the wedding banquet had to break down the door to bring them out of their room.

The woman's brothers saw what had occurred and decided that he should divorce her. He agreed, but first he went to seek advice from his friend R. Isaac Ashkenazi, who advised him against the divorce. Nevertheless, he went and did the opposite. Once he had divorced her, he fell ill because of love for her. Again he went to seek advice from his friend Isaac Ashkenazi, for he wanted to remarry the woman. Ashkenazi advised him not to do this. But he did not follow this advice; rather, he went and appointed intermediaries. The woman's brothers pretended to agree so that they could get him into their courtyard and have him beaten up, and that is what happened.

He returned, beaten, to Isaac Ashkenazi, and said, "I won't budge from here until you tell me the real meaning of these events, from beginning to end." Ashkenazi replied, "At first I told you not to choose the widow but the virgin, for a true covenant exists only between a woman and the man who 'makes her a vessel.'[53] You did not follow this instruction, but married the widow, because of your greed.

"After you married her, I told you not to divorce her, because I knew that the conflict between you would be limited to a period of about six months, until the six-year-old son of the widow Malkah would die. That son was the

52. There was controversy over the propriety of visiting one's betrothed before the wedding; see Baron, *SRHJ* 18:66.

53. B. Sanh 22b, referring to the man with whom she first has sexual intercourse.

soul of his father.[54] The father, a great and pious man, had committed only one sin, and they decreed that he should return to this world to experience once more the pain of death. When he died, he had left his wife pregnant, and the soul of the father was made to enter his son.

"This was the cause of the conflict between you. Whenever you entered the house, the spirit in her son, which was the soul of her first husband, would come out and quarrel with the spirit in you. The child's spirit would say, 'Will he even force Malkah with me in the house?'[55] Your spirit would claim that he was an ignoramus, that the woman had been married according to the law of the Torah, which permits widows to remarry except to the high priest. Thus the strife between you.[56] The child was destined to die soon, and there would have been peace in your home. But you did not follow my advice; you did the opposite, divorcing her. Then I told you not to go back to her, for it was obvious that they were playing a trick, agreeing to this proposal in order to beat you."

The pious author of *{Shene} Luḥot ha-Berit* wrote about this very subject in the lesson *Ki Teṣe* (Deut. 21:10–25:19), page 382a: "You must know that every man leaves a spirit in his wife, for through his wife seven forms are completed. That spirit remains in his wife after his death, especially during the first twelve months, as the Zohar explains at length regarding the Old Man in the section on the lesson *Mishpaṭim* (Exod. 21–24). This spirit fights against the second husband who marries the widow, for he also leaves a spirit in her. These spirits quarrel; sometimes one wins, sometimes the other."[57]

Let us return to our subject. Thus Ashkenazi's prophecy was fulfilled about Isaac Fasi, for he said that Fasi would plead for advice and then disagree in every respect. We see from this story that fathers return in their children, as I indicated earlier in the sermon regarding the verse, *Those that are left of you . . .* (Lev. 26:39). Therefore,[58] every intelligent person should look and be struck with terror, contemplating the agony of transmigration endured by the soul forced to return to this lowly world, with responsibility for wealth

54. Here we see that this story fulfills the promise made at the beginning of the second section.

55. Cf. Esther 7:8: *Will he* [Haman] *even force the queen* [ha-malkah] *with me* [Ahasuerus] *in the house?* There is a play on the widow's name, Malkah.

56. Translated into modern psychological terms, this rather perceptively expresses the jealousy of the new husband who is reminded by the young son's presence of the first husband "who made her a vessel" (above, n. 53).

57. *Shene Luḥot ha-Berit,* by Isaiah Horowitz (first published in 1648) was perhaps the most important work of kabbalistic ethical literature. For the discussion in the Zohar, see especially 2:102a–b. Again, the material may be viewed as an objectification of the wife's inner conflict, pitting the new husband against the memory of the deceased.

58. Having finished his story, the preacher now turns to the rebuke and exhortation.

that can be lost. For a person can become a great sinner, and the soul that has come to rectify a single offense can incur guilt for many more.

Know well that when a person feels throughout his life a special temptation that does not let him observe one particular commandment, this is the commandment he was reincarnated in this world to perform, because he did not perform it in his first incarnation. Temptation therefore aggressively tries to prevent him from observing it, so that he may be driven from this world. A person of intelligence should know this, and understand that whenever a commandment is particularly difficult for him, he should devote all his strength to performing it, for that is the purpose of his coming into this world.

This is especially true for the commandment of *pe'ah,* the corners of the hair and beard, which Jews throughout most of the world find especially difficult to observe.[59] I have heard wicked men claim that they are embarrassed before the Gentiles because this commandment is so readily noticeable, and that is why they do not want to observe it. Woe to them, woe upon their souls! Is this what they will respond to the Lord of souls when He asks them why they did not observe that splendid commandment of *pe'ah*? King David warned about this long ago when he said, *I shall speak of Your testimonies before kings; I will not be ashamed* (Ps. 119:46). We must perform the commandment even if we do feel ashamed. Indeed, if observing a commandment led to worldly honors, it would hardly be meritorious to do so. We must try to observe the commandment even though it may make us the object of scorn and contempt.[60]

I recall that my pious father, of blessed memory,[61] used to make a special effort throughout his life with regard to the redemption of captives. He endured many insults and humiliations in order to collect ransom money on their behalf from hard men who trusted only in their wealth. Another aspect of his effort to perform this commandment was that each Friday he tried to get all those in the prison released [for the Sabbath]. If they had no money, he frequently paid for them himself. Several times it occurred that the prisoner would leave the jail and flee, and my father had to pay [the bail money] for him.

I remember that one day there was a poor man in jail, and my father had no money to pay to have him released. What did he do? He had him released and he took his place in the prison. When the townspeople heard this, they

59. The discussion of *pe'ah* builds upon the story about Judah the Pious told near the beginning of the sermon.

60. This was an important theme of the medieval movement of German Pietism; see *Sefer Ḥasidim,* ed. Jehuda Wistinetzki, no. 976 (Frankfurt, 1924), p. 241; Scholem, *Major Trends in Jewish Mysticism* (New York, 1946), pp. 92–93.

61. On the preacher's father, Abraham Solomon ha-Kohen Ittamari, see Werses, p. 157.

rushed to have my father released, paying what was necessary. In this way the poor man was saved, enabled to return home in joy. Now my father received many insults from empty-headed people who wagged their tongues and said, "What in the world is he doing?" But he appeased them and did not become angry, even though he had the power to destroy them. There are other stories, too many to tell, showing that we must perform a commandment even though we may receive many insults, for this produces a double reward from Heaven.

Furthermore, there are transgressions that people may commit thinking that they have done nothing wrong at all. These are the things for which a person is honored by others. For example, there are those who tell jokes in taverns so that people will laugh at what they say, while the listeners applaud and encourage them to continue with their filthy stories. How angry God becomes at those who laugh when some talk about the shame of others! The ones who talk this way certainly have no share in the world to come, and neither do those who laugh at them, encouraging them in their perversity.

Keep far away from such ugliness! Do not be seduced by those wicked people who say that this is what it means to be a man, who claim that a man worthy of the name must know how to dance in taverns and tell jokes. They boast among themselves when they see others approving of their evil conduct. They think that this is what it means to be a man, this is true wisdom. When they see Torah scholars who act so differently, they call them simple fools who know nothing about the ways of the world.

And when they hear wise words from the scholars' mouths, they are dumbfounded—like those who gasp in amazement upon seeing a talking bird—and they think that the Torah scholars do not understand what they are doing. They fail to realize that Torah scholars know every kind of evil in the world and are familiar with how it is done, but distance themselves from it because of their love for God, who commanded us to refrain from such things. Yet they think that Torah scholars don't act this way because they don't know how!

The following happened to me. One Sabbath I was preaching about some improper behavior that violates the Torah. People had made an agreement not to give charity to the poor each week, but only once a month, because of the heavy burden of their taxes. I spoke at length to them, arguing that this was a violation of the Torah, pointing out that the sages had said, "If people see that their income is limited, let them distribute their money to charity," for "the salt [preservative] of money is diminution."[62]

Later, a scoundrel (may his name be obliterated!) stood up to oppose me, made his mouth gape like a camel's, and cursed all Torah scholars. He said

62. B. Giṭ 7a (from memory, imprecisely); B. Ket 66b.

that all their words are fabricated from their own minds, that they preach whatever they feel like saying, and other things that would be forbidden to recount. In the middle of his diatribe, he asked, "Do Torah scholars even know how to speak properly?" All the others stood there as if transfixed; no one protested at anything he said, because he was wealthy. Woe to them, woe upon their souls! If they are ashamed before [the product of] a fetid drop, what will they do on the Day of Judgment, when God will mete out just recompense for all they have done?

I myself did not actually hear these things, but reliable witnesses testified about him. As God lives, I would have beaten him to death, for my heart is like a lion's when it comes to avenging an insult to the honor of the Torah and those who study it. I would have done this not for my own honor, which I am prepared to renounce before anyone, but because of the insult to the Torah. Those wicked men, accursed and banished by God Himself, think that because He has given them wealth, He must be pleased with *their* conduct rather than with the conduct of those who study His Torah.

My father, of blessed memory, once sought vengeance against a wicked man upon hearing that this man had insulted a Torah scholar, and no one had protested. He stood up to him and excommunicated him. The depraved man said, "What do these Torah scholars ever do for us?" My father then went and gathered all the sages of the city together and admonished them that no scholar should go to perform a wedding service for that family, or give them a bill of divorce, or circumcise their sons, or bury their dead, or give them any legal ruling concerning pure or impure, so that they might know exactly what the rabbis do for them. Not a day passed before they needed something, and they came around shamefacedly. In this way the banner of Torah was exalted. May his merit protect us! Amen.

Therefore, those who fear God's word and desire to serve Him must not fear the transgressors of the Torah. They must stand up to them, ready to smash the teeth of the wicked, and God, the Lord of all creatures, will help them. Woe to those whose courage comes from wealth, for this is not how civilized people should behave. True heroism is to stand up and speak out on behalf of those who love God and study His Torah, even though you may have no wealth at all. Do those who speak in honor of the wealthy think that God needs money for some purpose? Let your heart be like a lion's, saying whatever you understand to be for the glory of God, and no harm will befall you, for the Almighty will help you. . . .

Those who are about to die will see that all their accomplishments and their powers are contemptible. They may chew their own flesh,[63] but they

63. If this is more than a merely figurative expression, it may be compared to the belief among seventeenth-century Christians that cadavers devoured parts of their shrouds. See Philippe Ariès, *The Hour of Our Death* (New York, 1982), pp. 357, 477.

will not be able to turn back the clock, for all their deeds are written in a book,[64] and they will have to render account according to what is recorded. What good will their vaunted powers be then, when all the demons they created during their lives from the impurity of improper seminal emissions gather around them?[65]

This is why the circular processions [around the coffin] were ordained, and the custom developed of throwing all kinds of metal in every direction at each circle, in order to keep harmful spirits away from the deceased.[66] It is also why the burial must take place immediately after the procession, without a moment's pause. Otherwise the demons may return and become intertwined with the corpse, taking it wherever they want and leaving a demon in its place, so that people will think they are burying the deceased when he is not really there.

It once happened in the days of the rabbi[67] that a certain man was not buried immediately after the circular procession. Harmful demons overpowered him, and took him where they wanted, and did what they wanted to him. Later, when the rabbi went with his disciples on a two- or three-hour walk, they found his body strewn in a dump on one of the mountains, cut into pieces. The rabbi said to them, "This is the man you buried; the demons have overcome him and brought him here." When they returned to the grave and examined it, they realized that the one they had buried was a demon temporarily disguised to take his place.

Similar to this is a story told by another spirit who entered a woman. He said that while they were carrying him to be buried, demons burned him seven times on the way. They made his soul enter his body and burned him soul and body together. The spirit was asked, if it is true that demons took him to be burned, how was it that the pallbearers were unaware that they were carrying nothing, and that the burden was unusually light? He replied that a demon had entered the coffin in this place.

May God save us from all this! May He inspire us to return to Him with all our heart and all our soul, to serve Him faithfully, to gaze upon His splendor, to visit His palace, the palace of souls bound up in the bundle of Life. Amen, be this His will.

64. Cf. Abot 2:1.

65. This conception that improper emissions of sperm produced demons goes back to the Zohar (e.g. 1:54b). Later Kabbalah developed the idea that such demons, a man's illegitimate children, assemble at the time of his burial to complain about their fate. See Scholem, *Kabbalah,* pp. 322–23; idem, *On the Kabbalah and Its Symbolism* (New York, 1965), p. 155.

66. On this custom, see (in addition to the two references to Scholem in the previous note) the discussion by R. Ḥayyim Joseph David Azulai, *Ḥayyim Sha'al,* responsum 25 (he confesses his inability to discover who initiated the custom), and the comparative material in Theodore Gaster, *The Holy and the Profane* (New York, 1955), p. 173. I have not found other reference to the casting of pieces of metal during the circular processions.

67. It is not clear to me to whom the preacher is referring.

Jonathan Eybeschuetz

An aura of tragic drama pervades the biography of Jonathan Eybeschuetz. Blessed with a brilliant mind and a powerful personality, he was lionized by thousands throughout Europe. Yet through much of his life he was the object of bitter controversy. He was hounded by distinguished rabbis and denied the respect and honor to which he felt entitled.

Born in Poland around the year 1690, he acquired an outstanding education in both traditional talmudic learning and in Kabbalah, studying in several of the finest centers of Jewish learning in eastern and central Europe. In 1714 he settled in Prague, where he was appointed preacher. Controversy first exploded in 1724. A manuscript entitled "Wa-ʾAbo ha-Yom el ha-ʿAyin," containing extreme Sabbatian theological doctrines, was being circulated among Sabbatian cells.[1] The Sabbatians claimed that the author was Eybeschuetz, and anti-Sabbatian rabbis launched an attack.

Eybeschuetz denied authorship of the work, but even his signature on a ban excommunicating the Sabbatian sect, read in the synagogues of Prague on the Day of Atonement, failed to allay all suspicion. Although he had assisted the chief rabbi, David Oppenheim, in various functions, upon Oppenheim's death in 1736 the office of chief rabbi was held empty, and Eybeschuetz was appointed to the lesser post of president of the rabbinical court and head of the yeshivah.

In 1742 he left Prague to become rabbi of the French community of Metz. Here many of his greatest sermons were delivered. Eight years later, he accepted a prestigious position as chief rabbi of the "Three Communities" of Altona, Hamburg, and Wandsbek. Not long after, at the beginning of February 1751, the noted halakist Jacob Emden publicly accused Eybeschuetz of having written Sabbatian formulae in amulets that were in circulation. Thus began a virulent controversy that continued long after Eybeschuetz's death.[2]

1. On this work and the similarly controversial *Shem ʿOlam,* see M. A. Perlmutter, *R. Yehonatan Eybeschuetz we-Yaḥaso la-Shabbetaʾut* (Jerusalem, 1947).

2. There is a large scholarly literature on this controversy; see the bibliographical references listed by Gershom Scholem, *Kabbalah* (New York, 1974), p. 408 (= *EJ* 6:1076), and, most recently, Sid Leiman, "R. Ezekiel Landau's Attitude toward R. Jonathan Eybeschuetz," paper submitted to the Conference on Eighteenth-Century Jewish Thought, Harvard, 1984.

This fierce onslaught, which was led by many of the greatest rabbinic figures of the age (Emden, Joshua Falk, Aryeh Loeb Loewenstamm), would certainly have destroyed a man of lesser stature. Eybeschuetz defended himself vigorously against all charges of improper behavior or belief, but his opponents were never convinced. Some years later, his son Wolf was also accused of being a Sabbatian. In 1762, Jonathan decided to resign from his position and return to Prague, but at the instigation of the chief rabbi, Ezekiel Landau, his official request for permission to settle in Austrian territory was denied. The news of his death at Altona in 1764 reverberated throughout central Europe. While Landau was ambivalent in his eulogy, others, like his former student Zerah Eidlitz, sang a paean of praises: "If the Jews of the Diaspora had wanted to choose 'one father for them all' (cf. Mal. 2:10), undoubtedly he would have been chosen."[3]

Eybeschuetz's reputation was based primarily on his talmudic lectures and his sermons. Although only one of his legal works was published during his life (*Kereti u-Feleti* [Altona, 1763], on *Shulḥan Aruk, Yoreh Deᶜah*), reports of his novellae were widely available all over Europe through notes taken by his students. A master of the pilpulistic technique, he was universally recognized as one of the finest halakic minds of his age.

If anything, his reputation as a preacher was even greater. His archenemy, Jacob Emden, had to concede that few could match Eybeschuetz in homiletical talent: his eloquence and wit enabled him to hold an audience spellbound for hours at a time. Ezekiel Landau, in his eulogy, called him a "great preacher, beyond peer; . . . no one can deny the greatness of his message; his sermons of ethical rebuke would inspire many to repentance and tears."[4]

Only one of his sermons was publishing during his lifetime. Delivered on a Sabbath afternoon in the late winter of 1751, soon after Emden's public accusation, it is a passionate defense, skillfully weaving traditional material (primarily taken from psalms about David's career) around his personal situation.[5] Many manuscript copies of his sermons were in circulation, however, and Eybeschuetz expressed concern that opponents might insert a heretical phrase to make him look bad. By the time his halakic work was published in 1763, a collection of his sermons was already prepared for publication under the title *Yaᶜarot Debash,* but Eybeschuetz never saw this work in print. His nephew claimed to have prepared the two volumes for the printer from faded, moth-eaten manuscripts that had belonged to his uncle. They were published in Karlsruhe in 1779 and 1782.[6]

These two volumes contain the records of his inaugural sermon in Prague,

3. Landau, *Derushe,* pp. 46c–47b; Eidlitz, p. 12d.

4. Jacob Emden, *Sefer Hitᵓabbequt* (Lvov, 1877), p. 4a–b; Landau, *Derushe,* p. 46d. For an example of Eybeschuetz's wit, see the passage cited by Bettan, p. 366, n. 196.

5. *Luḥot ᶜEdut* (Altona, 1755), pp. 72b–78b.

6. Intro. to *Luḥot Edut,* par. 19; intro. to *Kereti u-Feleti*; intro. to *Yaᶜarot Debash,* vol. 1.

ten undated sermons delivered in the "Three Communities," and twenty-four delivered in Metz between 1743 and 1749. In many ways they exemplify the strengths and weaknesses of eighteenth-century Jewish preaching.[7] Constructed in what I have called the catenary form (see "Structural Options," above), they are long, rambling, and amorphous. The listener would rarely have any conception of where the preacher was leading, or whether the sermon was approaching its end or was still near the beginning. At the same time, they are filled with eloquent passages, original ideas, piquant parables, incisive critiques, and passionate appeals for improvement of conduct. Though certainly not sanguine about the efficacy of his preaching, Eybeschuetz accepted the frustrations of his medium and even confessed that he found no other task so rewarding.[8]

The sermon translated is one of the shorter ones in *Yaᶜarot Debash*. Nevertheless, I have omitted nearly half of it from considerations of space. Deletions are indicated in the notes, and what remains is unaffected by the abridgment. The sermon has some unity because of the recurrences, with different interpretations, of the theme-verse (Hos. 6:1–2), although the technique is not nearly so disciplined and formal as we have seen in Almosnino. What we have is a series of brilliant flashes, not a solid structure. The average listener would have remembered not the sermon as a whole, but rather a few isolated points and—beyond doubt—the preacher himself.[9]

Sermon of Ethical Rebuke Preached . . . during the Penitential Period Preceding the New Year's Day, 5505 [1744], to the Congregation of Metz

The prophet Hosea cried out: *Come, let us turn back to the Lord; He attacked, and He can heal us; He wounded, and He can bind us up. In two days He will make us whole again; on the third day He will raise us up* (Hos. 6:1–2).

7. Cf. the treatment by Bettan, pp. 317–68.

8. *Yaᶜarot Debash* 1:66c, 90a. For indications of his frustration in failing to bring about the changes for which he pleaded in his sermons, see *Yaᶜarot Debash* 1:42d, 63a, 68a, 66a.

9. A few months after completing my translation and annotation of this sermon, I succeeded in obtaining a copy of the new edition of *Yaᶜarot Debash,* published by Or ha-Sefer (Jerusalem, 1984). While not a critical edition of the sermons, this handsome two-volume work is far superior to any previous edition. Identifications of rabbinic citations are incorporation into the text, and there are indices to biblical verses, rabbinic and some medieval quotations, subjects, and names. Although the biographical introduction is somewhat disappointing in its failure to assess Eybeschuetz's significance as a preacher, the publication of these volumes is an important achievement. They will undoubtedly serve as the standard text for future citations of *Yaᶜarot Debash*.

The rabbis have used this last verse to show that the Holy One does not allow the righteous to remain in distress more than three days.[1] But the relevance of this to the preceding verse needs to be explained.

Whether death and suffering can occur independently of sin and transgression, caused merely by the arrows of fortune or the configuration of the stars, is the subject of a well-known dispute.[2] The truth is that this view has led its adherents to the sick and heretical belief that sin never produces punishment in this world. Those who harbor such a belief fail to place their trust in God. And since the eternity of the world to come transcends sense perception, it makes no impact upon the soul that is foolishly immersed in the carnal vanities of this world.

This was the problem with Esau, as I have [elsewhere] explained.[3] Asking "Why these lentils?" he was told that the old man [Abraham] had died. He responded, "If evil has befallen even Abraham, there can be no justice and no Judge."[4] To understand this, we must recall that the rabbis have given two reasons for the custom of eating lentils in connection with mourning: first, their roundness reminds us that death comes in an inexorable cycle to all; and second, their absence of a "mouth" represents the mourner who sits in silence. If we accept the second reason, then we may also prepare eggs for the mourner.[5]

Now according to the view that "there is no death without sin," the first reason—that the round lentil represents the natural cycle of death—does not apply, for the righteous would escape this. Their death would not result from natural causes. This was Esau's opinion at first. He therefore thought the reason for the use of lentils in mourning was that they had no "mouth," and he asked "Why these lentils?" rather than eggs. Jacob's response was to inform him that Abraham had died. Since Abraham was sinless, the conclusion had to be that death occurs independent of sin, and the lentils were to be eaten because [unlike eggs] they are round. When Esau heard that death can come as an accident to the good and the evil alike, he became a heretic.

This explains why the Holy One does not allow a righteous person to remain in distress for more than three days. . . .[6] In order to demonstrate that He watches over every event that pertains to His people, overpowering planetary configurations so that their fate is not governed by the stars, God

1. Gen. Rabbah 91:7.
2. B. Shab 55a–b.
3. See the preacher's *Tif'eret Yonatan* (Lvov, 1866), pp. 29d–30a.
4. Cf. Gen. Rabbah 63:11.
5. B. BB 16b.
6. Omitted is almost a full column devoted to Abraham ibn Ezra's thesis (expressed in comments on Gen. 34:25, Lev. 12:2, and Lev. 22:27) that because of the moon's phases, the third and fourth days of an illness naturally bring the greatest pain.

does not allow the righteous to remain in distress on the third day, which by natural causes should be the most painful. Instead, He fashions a cure to ease the pain. In this way, all peoples can see that God is responsible, not the natural order. All may acknowledge that afflictions occurring to Israel derive not from the stars but from God, who both injures and heals.

This is why the messengers came to heal Abraham on the third day following his circumcision, in the heat of the day, when his pain would naturally be most severe. Yet he was able to run toward them with ease (Gen. 18:1–2). And Isaiah was instructed to tell Hezekiah, *On the third day you will go up to the house of the Lord* (2 Kings 20:5). This was a public miracle.

Likewise, Jacob's sons were in doubt about the men of Shechem, all of whom had entered the covenant through circumcision. They were uncertain whether sincere motivation had made these men acceptable in God's sight, or whether they had been circumcised while remaining inwardly perverse merely out of lust for Jacob's female progeny. Because of this doubt, Jacob's sons were unwilling to harm them until the third day, when they saw these men suffering pain in the natural manner. Had they been sincerely devoted to God, they would not have remained in distress for three days, as we explained. They therefore determined that God's protection had departed from the men of Shechem because of their inner wickedness. That is why they slaughtered them without mercy.

This is what the verse [from Hosea] admonishes. If the people will desist from evil, their afflictions and pain will be suspended, for their suffering is the work of the Almighty. The prophet said, *Come, let us turn back to the Lord; He attacked, and He can heal us, He wounded, and He can bind us up.* All comes from Him, not from the stars. The proof is that *In two days He will make us whole again; on the third day He will raise us up,* for He does not allow one to remain in distress for three full days.[7] This shows that it is not by the stars or by natural causes but by God that we have been stricken, in accordance with our sins. If we would repent, we must return to God, the source of help and deliverance.

This message applies also to us. We too must return in repentance. This season especially should impel us to do so, for these are days of judgment, when the sound of the shofar is heard and our effort at repentance should be great. The most important thing is this: our welfare does not depend upon the kind of "repentance" most people think of, namely, prolonged recitation of liturgical poems and penitential prayers, or even psalms, or fasting, while

7. This answers the question raised at the beginning concerning the relationship between the rabbinic statement and the prophetic verse. Three additional interpretations of the verses from Hosea will be introduced in the course of the sermon. One of them, that the "third day" refers to the Day of Atonement, was also used by Ezekiel Landau, *Derushe,* end of sermon 28, p. 44b.

the basic iniquity remains unchanged.[8] This is not what God wants; this is not the repentance He desires. Such is the essence of my sermon today. It is a message of truth and peace, for lying and deceitful speech enhance the power and prosperity of Esau and the "other side."[9]

According to the rabbis, this season is divided into three parts: "On the day before the New Year, He cancels one third [of Israel's sins], on the New Year's Day another third, and similarly on the Day of Atonement."[10] This statement speaks about three types of sin.

Repentance before the New Year applies to the sins of desire for unnecessary things, for people love to pursue their base passions. This may be diminished by fasting before Rosh Hashanah. Desire for temporal things is generally suppressed as people see the awesome Day of Judgment approaching, knowing that God will review their conduct. How can one fail to cast away such desires?

On the New Year's Day itself, hearing the sound of the shofar, people feel remorse for their sins [in the ritual realm]. Can the shofar be blown, proclaiming God's sovereignty, without instilling dread? What kind of hollow man would not be moved to sincere remorse and firm resolve to act according to the just laws of the Torah?

Yet there remain the transgressions in interpersonal relations: rancor and strife, unwarranted hatred, the falsehoods people say to each other while secretly planning attack, robbery and exploitation, and so forth. These remain buried inside us, sinners that we are, until the arrival of the special fast day. For ten days people examine their conduct; as the Day of Atonement approaches, they try to appease their neighbors by words and by payment, to extirpate their jealous rivalry, their contentiousness, and all such sinful behavior affecting others.

For the Day of Atonement reminds us of the day of death. This is why we wear white. All aspects of its observance are reminders of death.[11] That is its goal. The final third is forgiven on the Day of Atonement. Even at the end of the day, in the liturgy of the closing service, we pray "that we may cease from the exploitation for which we are responsible."[12] All this is hinted

8. For the customs of reciting psalms and fasting during the month of Elul before New Year's Day, see S. Y. Agnon, *Days of Awe* (New York, 1965), pp. 19–20.

9. In the universal typological and exegetical tradition of the Jews, Esau represents the Christians. The "other side" is the kabbalistic term for the system of evil forces in the world.

10. Tanḥuma, *Emor,* 22. Eybeschuetz may have taken this from *Ṭur Oraḥ Ḥayyim,* no. 581 (the introduction to the discussion of Rosh Hashanah); cf. Landau, *Derushe,* p. 42b and d.

11. For the Day of Atonement as a reminder of death, expressed through the wearing of a white robe (*kittel*), see Mordecai Jaffe, *Lebush ha-Tekelet* 610:4. Cf. Jack Riemer, ed., *Jewish Reflections on Death* (New York, 1976), pp. 9–10.

12. From "Attah Noten Yad"; see *The Authorized Daily Prayerbook,* ed. Joseph Hertz (New York, 1963), p. 930; *Maḥzor la-Yamim ha-Nora'im,* ed. Daniel Goldschmidt, 2 vols. (Je-

in the prophet's words: *In two days He will make us whole again* refers to the two days [of Rosh Hashanah], but *on the third day,* which is the Day of Atonement, the ultimate goal, *He will raise us up to live in His presence,* for this is the essence of repentance.[13]

That us why they said in the Midrash: The community of Israel said, "Master of the universe, repentance is Yours." The Holy One responded, "No, repentance is yours.[14] The meaning relates to what I have just said: a person easily feels remorse for sins against God and is quite ready to repent, but transgressions in interpersonal relations involving financial matters are difficult to renounce, especially where envy and hatred are aroused, as I have frequently explained.

If a man comes to ask an expert on Jewish law about some questionable meat in his home, or about leaven on Passover, and he is told to throw it in the river, he will obey without protesting, even though it involve a substantial loss. But if the same judge should render a decision in a civil dispute, giving the man's adversary ten gold pieces, he will go to a [secular] court and lodge a complaint against the judge, and his enmity toward that judge will be long-lasting.[15] It is not the loss of the money that he cares about—he is willing to bless the Giver of Torah—but the fact that the money goes to his opponent. His envy is so powerful that it pains him to heed the judge's decision.

This is always the pattern. Regarding sins against God, Jews become sanctified through their remorse. Especially during these days of repentance, the time of God's favor, they will repent of their transgressions against Him. But not of transgressions in interpersonal relations, for these are not considered significant. Even if a quarrel subsides during this period, and the opponents speak to each other, they are secretly planning the next attack, waiting a bit until the Days of Awe are ended to decide what to do. They certainly do not give back the money they have robbed or extorted or taken as interest. This truly hinders repentance, as I have said.

So when the community of Israel says "Repentance is Yours," what is meant is this: "Repentance basically applies to the worship of false gods and trangression of commandments pertaining to You," for most Jews define repentance in this way. But the Holy One responds, "Repentance is yours,"

---

rusalem, 1970), 2:727. Compare Eybeschuetz's denunciation of preachers who speak about ritual practices yet refrain from criticizing the evils that disrupt interpersonal relations (*Ya^carot Debash* 2:14c, cited in Bettan, p. 329).

13. See above, n. 7.

14. Lam. Rabbah on Lam. 5:21. Cf. the use of this aggadah by Zarfati, p. 275a.

15. On Jews' turning to Gentile courts during this period, see Shochat, pp. 72–88; Solomon Posener, "The Social Life of the Jewish Communities in France in the 18th Century," *JSS* 7 (1945):216.

meaning that it applies to that which affects you, the conduct of interpersonal relations. This is the ultimate test of repentance that God desires. Because of human nature, God is more concerned about rebellion in this realm than about transgressions that pertain directly to Him, for God wants ethical behavior.

This then is the essence of repentance: we must exert the utmost care that we not sin against our neighbors. What guard us from such sins are the standards of truth and peace. People must not harbor hatred for each other inside while outwardly speaking like brothers. Is there any lie greater than this? The quality of truth leads to peace.

Furthermore, the standard of truth repudiates all kinds of deceitful speech. This includes saying a prayer in which the words do not reflect what is in the heart. That too is in the category of falsehood. . . .[16] Yes, much is covered by *lying lips and a deceitful tongue* (Ps. 120:2). It encompasses prayer, which falls in this category unless it is accompanied by inner devotion.

It also encompasses support of Torah and Torah scholars. Our sinfulness has become a source of great pain, causing the Torah to be forgotten by Israel. Gone are the heroes who devote themselves totally to Torah. The precious vessels are lost, for no one supports those who study! Indeed, even knowledgeable Jews do not allow their daughters to marry scholars.

The rabbis said, "We have found a remedy for the untutored," referring to those who allow their daughters to marry scholars.[17] Now this does not apply to the totally ignorant, such as those in the talmudic period, for scholars were prohibited from arranging marriages with such families. The verse *Cursed is one who lies {with any beast}* (Deut. 27:21) was applied to their daughters.[18] No, it applies to those who themselves are not scholars but who could improve their position by having their daughters marry scholars. This would increase the glory of Torah, for one good deed would lead to another. A wealthy man who gives his daughter in marriage to a scholar enhances the Torah in the minds of other Jews, for youngsters become envious and think, "I too will study and thereby become worthy of a good marriage." In this way knowledge increases.

But through our sinfulness the opposite has occurred, and love of Torah has diminished. The stalls are empty; the princes of Torah are like harts that find no pasture; no one grasps the staff of learning. See what an orphaned generation this is! The Torah is all that is left to us in our exile. How dare we pray, "Enlighten our eyes through Your Torah," and similar supplications in the liturgy of Sabbath and festival, such as "Let our portion be in your

16. Omitted are almost two full columns that discuss a "midrash" about a peddler who offers "life" and then quotes Ps. 34:13–14 (cf. B. AZ 19b).

17. B. Ket 111b.

18. B. Pes 49b.

Torah"?[19] How can God give you a portion in the Torah? This is to be given to its students and its supporters, while you turn your back on it.

How can we say, as we will on this New Year's Day, "And all the people see the voices, Moses speaks and God answers him with a voice"?[20] Would the people hear the voice of God and not do what it says? I too say: the voice of the Lord calls out in the wilderness, and every day its echo comes forth from Mt. Horeb proclaiming, "Woe to all creatures because of the affront to the Torah."[21] Is there any affront greater than this, that the masters of Torah upon whom we all depend are deemed inappropriate for marriage? It is as if there were no God present to sustain and support His people!

I have heard the verse *In vain have I stricken your children* (Jer. 2:30) used in this context. In previous times, if a wealthy and powerful man had a disfigured daughter, he would have her marry a scholar, confident that her husband would not hate her because of her defect. That is why it was said that the Torah cures every blemish.[22] Therefore, when God wanted a scholar to have leisure to study Torah and prosper, He arranged for a wealthy man to have a disfigured daughter, thereby serving as the source both of injury and of healing for the scholar.[23] In this regard, the prophet said, *He has wounded, and He can heal us* (cf. Hos. 6:1).[24]

But now, though she may have ever so many imperfections, sons of untutored men are all over her. Fathers give their children for harlots, while the youth who toils in Torah languishes distraught. Hear me, that you may live: cleave to the Torah, for this is the foundation of our life in this world! Without the Torah, full repentance is impossible.

Woe unto those who desire the day of the Lord . . . that day is darkness (cf. Amos 5:18). Many also do not discern the true nature of the New Year's Day. They look forward to it because they enjoy the sound of the singer, who chants melodious hymns with his beautiful voice. Woe to those who do not know what occurs on the day of reckoning: *that day is darkness*! You know that fire is pitch dark, giving forth no light. Though the elemental fire is near the sphere of the moon, it bestows no light upon the world. And hell is all fire; it is darkness and gloom. Its light is derived from an admixture

19. *The Authorized Daily Prayerbook,* pp. 114–15, 380–81.

20. Exod. 20:15, 19:19; cf. *The Authorized Daily Prayerbook,* pp. 884–85, *Maḥzor la-Yamim ha-Nora᾽im* 1:153.

21. Abot 6:2.

22. Cf. Baḥya ben Asher on Exod. 28:17: "The Torah is a cure for the entire body" (based on B. ᶜErub 54a).

23. On this passage, see Shochat, p. 111, citing a story told by Jacob Emden on how R. Ezekiel Katzenellenbogen married the homely daughter of a wealthy man who could find no other suitor. On the unwillingness of fathers to allow their daughters to marry rabbinic scholars, cf. Landau, *Derushe,* p. 16a.

24. See above, n. 7.

of water, but the fire itself is pitch dark. That is why the Bible says of hell, *the wicked shall be silenced in darkness* (1 Sam. 2:9).[25]

Now on the New Year's Day, before the sounding of the shofar, all above is fire—myriad acres of fire—*for God judges by fire* (Isa. 66:16), and it is pitch black. That is why the liturgy for the morning of the New Year's Day contains the liturgical poem, "The *ḥayyot* ("creatures") appear like flaming embers."[26] All is fire, and there is universal shuddering and trembling—until the Jews sound the shofar. Then living water descends from the supernal fount. As at the creation of the world, when God said, *Let there be light* (Gen. 1:3), so light is made above with the sounding of the shofar, and there is rejoicing in all the worlds.

How indeed is the shofar able to bring down the supernal water? Through weeping, when tears flow down like a river. Only through weeping can the power of judgment be broken. This is why they said, "Supernal waters wept."[27] So it is with weeping caused by strong emotion: the water descends from on high. This is how it is above: the water mixes with the fire but does not extinguish it for the ten days [of penitence], until the Day of Atonement, when the fire is quelled.

Therefore I implore you now, take all these things to heart, and do not go about defiantly, performing your religious obligations in a superficial and mechanical way, following the pattern of your parents. When it comes to your worldly behavior, you do not act as your parents did. Your parents never drank coffee or tea or such things.[28] Nor did they use the tobacco plant, for no one knew of its beneficial properties. Yet now that its medicinal quality has been ascertained, rich and poor alike use it, never thinking about whether

25. Compare Eybeschuetz's depiction of hell in a different sermon: "The soul of a man sinks into thousands of miles of molten fire. It is not bright, like our fire; rather, there is overpowering darkness, like the darkness of Egypt. And as for the rest of the punishments, tens of thousands of demons work their destruction like every species of wild animal in the world, and fiery serpents pull and bite without mercy . . ." (*Y.D.* 1:18d). Jewish preachers of the late seventeenth and early eighteenth centuries resorted to graphic descriptions of infernal punishments more often than did preachers in earlier times (see especially the work of Elijah ha-Kohen of Izmir, e.g., *Midrash Eliyyahu,* sermon 7, p. 48c).

26. *Maḥzor la-Yamim ha-Nora'im* 1:122; cf. Ezek. 1:13.

27. Cf. Gen. Rabbah 5:4; Midrash ha-Gadol, *Genesis,* ed. Mordecai Margaliot (Jerusalem, 1947), p. 27; *Rashi ʿal ha-Torah,* ed. Abraham Berliner (reprint ed., Jerusalem, 1962), p. 426. In these sources, however, it is the lower waters that weep.

28. Compare *Y.D.* 2:26a, where "chocolate" is included. Coffee and tea were both relatively novel for German Jews at this time. The first coffee reached northern Europe in the middle of the seventeenth century, but it was not until the middle of the eighteenth that it became a popular drink. European tea consumption began to grow considerably in the 1730s with the start of direct trade between Europe and China. See Fernand Braudel, *Capitalism and Material Life, 1400–1800* (New York, 1975), pp. 179–88.

their parents did so or not.[29] I tell you that fear and service of God is medicine for the soul: why will you not improve upon the pattern of your parents in this realm? Why will you not act appropriately for the time?

Now evening approaches the world, the sun is about to set. Are we not obliged to seize the opportunity for repentance? Toward the end of the Day of Atonement, when the day is almost spent and the sun ready to sink out of sight, we make a final exertion in our prayer. Now too, more than ever, we need a commitment to serve God and repent. Because of our sinfulness, many occasions when we looked forward to the messianic redemption have passed with our hopes disappointed. This is solely because of the absence of repentance. From our heads to the tips of our toes there is not a single sound limb. We are especially guilty of unwarranted hatred, deceitful speech, and scorn for the Torah.

Such unwarranted hatred is what destroyed the Temple, as the rabbis noted,[30] and the prophet cried out, *But they mocked the messengers of God* (2 Chron. 36:16). So it is now, as I said. The prophet cries out, *In vain have I stricken your children* (Jer. 2:30), for despite disfiguring blemishes, fathers will not allow their daughters to marry Torah scholars. This is an area where we need tremendous effort.

Similarly with regard to deceitful speech, in which the Gentiles are extremely careful, thereby causing Satan's vehement prosecution of Israel. I have frequently said that any commandment carefully observed by the Gentiles arouses special wrath against Israel when, in our sinfulness, we fail to pay it sufficient heed. That is why when they asked, "To what point does honoring parents extend?" the sages replied, "Ask Dama ben Netina." He was a Gentile who honored his father beyond what is technically required.[31]

This helps us understand the verses, *Blow the horn on the new moon, on the full moon for our feast day, for it is a law for Israel, a ruling of the God of Jacob. He imposed it as a decree upon Joseph when He went forth from the land of Egypt* (Ps. 81:4–6). These verses clarify an enigma: why the true significance of the New Year's Day is concealed in the Torah, which says only, *You shall observe it as a day when the horn is sounded* (Num. 29:1). The Torah does not

29. The supposed medicinal qualities of tobacco were probably the chief reason for its early use in Europe following its discovery by Columbus in 1492. See Braudel, *Capitalism,* p. 189. For Jewish use at this time, see the passage cited by Shochat, p. 37, and *Y.D.* 2:60b.

30. B. Yoma 9b.

31. B. AZ 23b. The argument that Gentile neighbors were superior to Jews in certain realms of ethical behavior, assumed by the *maśkilim,* was not infrequently used by earlier preachers of rebuke. Cf. Joseph Jabeẓ, *Ḥasde ha-Shem* (Brooklyn, 1934), p. 56: "You will see [the Gentiles] observing the rational commandments, doing justice and loving mercy, better than we do. . . ," and Morteira, *Gibʿat Shaʾul,* p. 129a (end of *Debarim*). For a comprehensive discussion of this argument in the rhetoric of self-criticism, see my "Jews and Christians: Some Positive Images," *HTR* 79 (1986):236–46.

explain that God sits in judgment, as it explains the significance of the Day of Atonement and the other festivals.[32] The answer is that this act of concealment was for Israel's benefit.

You know why Jonah fled and sought to suppress his mission of prophecy to Nineveh. It was, as the rabbis said, because the Gentiles are readily disposed to repent, and their example would have aroused greater anger against Israel, which is so stubbornly reluctant to change its ways. Therefore Jonah was prepared to sacrifice his life out of love for Israel.[33] In the same way, if the Gentiles were as aware as we are that the New Year's Day is a day of judgment and reckoning for the entire year, they would vigorously repent, marvelously reforming all aspects of their conduct. This would provide Satan with a powerful charge against Israel, arousing divine wrath.

God therefore concealed this judgment day from the Gentiles, lest they make Israel appear more guilty. If it had been written in the Torah, it would be widely known, for most of the Gentile nations believe in the written Torah and acknowledge that it is divinely revealed. This is why God concealed its nature as a day of judgment, incorporating this theme into the oral law, which the Gentiles dismiss, as you know. It was for our own good.

David said: *He issued His commands to Jacob, His statutes and rulings to Israel; He did not do so for any other nation, of such rulings they know nothing* (Ps. 147:20–21). This means that He concealed from them the day set aside for legal judgments and rulings. Therefore the psalm concludes, *Hallelujah*: it is our duty to praise God for this act, in which His abundant love for us is revealed. . . .[34]

Yet in our sinfulness we refuse to return to God. We go about defiantly, thinking that the essence of the New Year's Day is for foolish cantors to sing their feeble tunes, though Satan himself comes to be present in their midst. They have raised their voices against Me, therefore I hate them (cf. Jer. 12:8). At a time when even the ministering angels are not singing, how can we sing and raise our voices in such foolish and inane melody? It is like that terrible practice during the period of the First Temple, when people would bring their children to be burned in the valley of the son of Hinnom and sing loud songs accompanied by instruments.[35]

So it is now: above there is supernatural fire, a fire before which even the sacred *ḥayyot* tremble with terror, and below the cantors are singing in their

32. Cf. RaMBaN 1:214, Joshua ibn Sheuib, p. 89c–d, and Luntshitz, *ʿOlelot,* chap. 33, par. 221, on this same question.

33. Mekilta *Pisḥa* 1, ed. Lauterbach (Philadelphia, 1949), 1:7–8; *Pirqe de-Rabbi Eliezer,* chap. 10.

34. Omitted is almost a full column discussing the interpretation of Pharaoh's dreams by the Egyptian magicians and Joseph.

35. See Lam. Rabbah 1:9:36.

grievous style, crying out with the voice of fools, concealing beneath their song a sick heart. . . .[36]

I am ashamed because of you, pure-hearted, devoted ones: how can you not feel the need for reverence on this Day of Awe? It would be better for you to sleep all day long than to get up to hear the voice of these fools who sing with evil heart, devoid of inner devotion or genuine religious feeling. They want only to make the sound of their singing as sweet as the chirping of impure birds. They project their voice, and He calls back "Impure, impure."

This song confronts you as a witness that because of our sinfulness, vision and wisdom have long since departed. No place is given to proper prayer, which calls out to God from the depths. We do not choose a suitable leader for worship, one who knows to Whom he prays, who is worthy of admiration in every respect.[37] I implore you, my brothers, do not act perversely in this matter. Serve God with reverence, fear His judgment, make every effort to walk in His ways. He makes peace on high, as it is said, "for He mixes fire with water."[38] So should you have peace in every way.

Now we must try to understand the significance of the phrase, *Who makes peace on high* (Job 25:2). After all, even down here, every physical body is composed of four elements.[39] Water may drip from the flint in the wall, and when you strike it sparks of fire are produced, for it is composed of all four. All chemists will confirm this experimentally. So that even below, this peace exists.

36. I have omitted two lines, more rhetoric than substance, which I cannot confidently render in intelligible English.

37. This diatribe against cantors, stylistically a pastiche of biblical phrases and on a high rhetorical level, is part of an old tradition. See Baḥya ibn Paquda, *Ḥobot ha-Lebabot, Shaʿar Yiḥud ha-Maʿaśeh,* chap. 5, ed. Moses Hyamson (New York, 1925–47; reprint ed., 2 vols., Jerusalem, 1962), 2:42–43, and the sources listed by Haim Schwartzbaum, "International Folklore Motifs in Joseph ibn Zabara's 'Sepher Shaʿshuʿim,'" *Studies in Aggadah and Jewish Folklore* 7 (Jerusalem, 1983): 76, n. 51. The attacks seem to crescendo from the mid-seventeenth century through the eighteenth. For other representative examples, see Luntshitz, *ʿAmmude,* pp. 22a, 24b, 63b; Berechiah Berak, *Zeraʿ Berak* (Amsterdam, 1730), intro. to pt. 2; Enoch Ḥenek of Solkova, "Tokeḥah Megullah," in *Reʾshit Bikkurim* (Frankfurt, 1708), p. 29a–b; Joseph Samuel Pinso, "Qolot Nishbarim," ed. Shlomo Simonsohn, *Mikaʾel* 7 (1982):313; Samuel ben Eliezer, *Darke Noʿam* Königsberg, 1763), p. 9b (cited by Piekarz, p. 311); Eidlitz, p. 79b–d; Fleckeles, 1:5a–6a; Judah Leib Margolioth, *Ṭal Orot* (Pressburg, 1843), p. 38c. It piques the imagination to picture the actual situation in which Eybeschuetz spoke these harsh words. Was the cantor actually present? If so, did the preacher look him straight in the eye, or direct his gaze in a different direction?

38. Cf. Num. Rabbah 12:8, Deut. Rabbah 5:12.

39. Cf. Maimonides, *Code,* I,i (*Yesode ha-Torah*), 4:2. The theory of the four elements remained current in the early eighteenth century among both Christians and Jews. For Eybeschuetz's use of "scientific" material for homiletical points, see Bettan, p. 353; for his general level of scientific knowledge, see Shochat, pp. 210–20.

The true meaning of *making peace* is not merely making opposites like fire and water coexist in one body. This exists below, and this is our kind of peace. Two enemies may enter the same group, yet inwardly they will be far apart, one intending to destroy and the other to build, as fire tends to burn and water to extinguish. But the *peace on high* is that fire actually takes on the nature of water.

The nature of fire is to ascend, never to descend like water. Yet it is written of this realm, *I saw . . .* nehar dinur (which is a river of fire) *issuing forth* (Dan. 7:10). In other words, from a high place, the realm of the *ḥayyot,* it was descending lower and lower until, as the rabbis said, it reached the depths of Sheol, the heads of the wicked.[40] And the supernal water remains on high without descending, actually rising ever higher, this being the nature of fire. Such is the ultimate peace: that one person change his nature because of the other, and take on the nature of the other so they can be at one. This is also the ultimate unity and truth, for truth is the sign of unity, as the Talmud says, "Truth is the seal of God, showing that He is one."[41]

Now one should truly be diligent with regard to repentance. The essence of repentance is not self-affliction, but rather the imposing of restrictions. That this is the essence can be seen in the rabbinic statement, "Be as careful with a minor commandment as with a major one."[42] What David said, as explained in the Midrash, was truly beautiful: "I do not fear the most serious transgressions, precisely because they are serious; I fear the minor transgressions because they appear to be minor."[43]

This means that a man does not lightly have an affair with a married woman, God forbid! The thought never occurs to him. Rather, at first it occurs to him to gaze upon her beauty. Even though this is forbidden, it seems trivial to him, for he thinks, "What is the great prohibition in this? It is not that I really desire her." In this way he goes on to speak to her in an insipid and flirtatious way. Even though this is forbidden, he thinks, "What is so important about mere words?" On the contrary, he muses, this will enable him to become close to a wealthy lady, and to provide for his old age, while acquiring a reputation as a do-gooder. Such is the prattle of the evil impulse, which eventually leads to a sexual approach, and ultimately to a sexual sin.[44]

This is the meaning of the statement "I fear the minor transgressions," because they will lead me to serious ones. "I do not fear the serious sins in

40. B. Ḥag 13b.
41. B. Shab 55a.
42. Abot 2:1.
43. Tanḥuma, *ʿEqeb,* 1.
44. Eybeschuetz frequently complains in his sermons about the laxity in sexual mores. See *Y.D.* 1:15d, 17b, 22d–23a, 53c, 72c; 2:2a; Shochat, pp. 162–73.

themselves," because their gravity makes one loath to transgress them, but the evil impulse easily seduces one to minor infractions, and they lead to serious offenses. That is why I fear them.

This is also related to the rabbinic interpretation of the verse, *For Heshbon was the city of Sihon the king of the Amorites, who had fought the king of Moab first, and taken all his land from him, as far as the Arnon. Therefore* ha-moshelim [lit., "those who speak in parables"] *would say, "Come to Heshbon* [boʾu Ḥeshbon]" (Num. 21:26–27). The rabbis paraphrased homiletically: "Therefore *ha-moshelim be-yiṣram,* those who rule over their impulse, say, *Boʾu u-neḥasheb,* Come, let us calculate the reward for fulfilling the commandment against the loss incurred by its fulfillment, and the gain acquired by a transgression against the loss it involves."[45]

Now this is puzzling. How is it connected to the previous verse, which says that Heshbon was the city of Sihon? How is this related to their interpretation of *therefore* ha-moshelim *would say*? The answer, apparently, is that *Heshbon the city of Sihon* exemplifies the lesson drawn by the rabbis. It teaches that a person should not say, "What is so important about these minor commandments? They are only a fence [around the law], and by ignoring them there may be opportunities for several other commandments." This is the "loss incurred by fulfilling a commandment calculated against its reward."

The illustration for this is Heshbon, which was a Moabite border city. If the king of Moab had paid proper attention to it, Sihon would never have been able to conquer it. But since it was not particularly large, the Moabite king did not think it important to muster all his armed forces. Yet when Sihon had conquered Heshbon, the way was paved for the conquest of the entire kingdom. This is the meaning of the verse, *For Heshbon was the city of Sihon . . . who had fought against the king of Moab first* (Num. 21:26), that is, in Heshbon, when the Moabite king did not consider it important. Then he conquered and *took all his land from him.* The meaning of this illustration is that when one allows the "old and foolish king" [the evil impulse] to conquer just a bit, he will eventually conquer all and rule over it tyranically. That is why it says, *Therefore those who rule* [over their impulse] *would say.*

Now understand that it is the pattern of the evil impulse to proceed slowly, one day at a time. At first it comes appearing to have the highest motives, acting for the sake of religion. It makes you feel obliged to enter a controversy and act with zeal on God's behalf, thereby bringing the fires of strife within it. Later it appears like the waters of arrogance, angrily overpowering (as the rabbis said, "It is like a torrent of water").[46] This is why so much care is

45. B. BB 78b.
46. B. Sanh 7a.

needed. True, we should act zealously against wrongdoers, but this must be done without creating new strife. It is said, "From the day when the violent prevailed, it has not been possible to maintain intact all the requirements of the law."[47] Therefore the pious should weigh their actions carefully before entering a quarrel, even if it has religious significance, lest it eventually become like a torrent of water, God forbid.[48]

In this connection David said: *Therefore let every pious man pray, that the rushing mighty waters not overtake him* (Ps. 32:6). For the pious should be zealous to do battle with the wicked, but they should also pray that it not become like a torrent of water. The sages said, "Which is a conflict for the sake of God? That between Hillel and Shammai."[49] It must be totally bound up with the Torah, otherwise it should not be called "for the sake of God," for even if there are religious issues involved, the "other side" also has a part in it, and evil will come in the end. It is the technique of the evil impulse to say that something is for the sake of God; that is how it deceives people in all they do.

This is what the prophet meant: *God said, "What do you see?" I responded, "I see a seething pot,* u-fanaw mi-pene ṣafonah [lit., "its face is from the north"]." *God responded, "Evil begins* mi-ṣafon [lit., "from the north"]" (Jer. 1:13–14). This is based on the following parable.[50] Good and Evil used to travel throughout the earth. Good wore fine clothes, reflecting his own essential goodness, while Evil wore foul and soiled clothes, reflecting his own essential evil. Wherever Evil went, people fled from him, for the power of his evil was recognized. No one would stay near him or even engage him in conversation. By contrast, Good was widely welcomed, and those who clung to him were honored and respected.

This disturbed Evil deeply, and he devised an evil scheme. Knowing that Good always acted benevolently toward others and never refused their requests, he approached Good walking by the way and asked that he lend him his fine clothes for an hour or two, and that Good temporarily put on the soiled ones. Good, being good, could not refuse this request, and he did

47. Cf. Maimonides, *Code,* XIV,i (*Sanhedrin*), 21:5, and the interpretation of this cited in *Bayit Ḥadash* on *Ṭur Ḥoshen ha-Mishpaṭ* 17:5: "Since we are scattered among the Gentiles, we must remove conflict from our midst so that we can survive peacefully in their midst." This fits the preacher's context. The quotation used by Eybeschuetz is attributed in the printed text of *Y.D.* to *resh-mem-alef,* ordinarily R. Moses Isserles.

48. Conceivably Eybeschuetz is alluding here to the first public controversy over Sabbatianism, in which he figured so prominently (see the introduction to the sermon).

49. Abot 5:17.

50. The entire story and the exegetical context from which it emerges appear in a sermon on repentance for the Sabbath preceding the New Year's Day by Leon Modena (see *Midbar Yehudah,* p. 15a, and the discussion by Rosenzweig, pp. 79–81). Modena says that he "heard" the parable and does not give a Jewish source. It probably has a Christian or pagan origin.

what he was asked. But Evil, who was essentially lies and deceit, did not return the fine clothing to Good.

From that point on, Evil has walked about in the fine clothes that belong to Good, and Good in the foul clothes that belong to Evil. As a result, when Evil comes to town, everyone honors him and holds him in esteem, seeing the good clothes and failing to see the evil within, and he causes them great ill. As for Good, when they see that he is wearing foul clothes, they set him at a distance, so that much good is lost.

So it is with the evil impulse. If it were to proclaim its evil nature publicly, no one would pay it any heed. But it comes dressed in fine clothing, and it speaks of God and religion, while inside it is evil. This is the sickness that deceives people. And this is the meaning of the dialogue in which God asks, *What do you see?* and the prophet replies, *A seething pot,* referring to the evil impulse, turbulent and seething inside with hot air.

He then continues, *u-fanaw mi-pene ṣafonah,* meaning that its inner being, entirely evil and deadly as the venom of a poisonous snake, is hidden and concealed, so that people do not recognize it.[51] Then God says, *You have seen well, for evil begins* mi-ṣafon. If people knew at the outset that it was evil, they would certainly never approach it. But it is *ṣafun,* hidden, while its clothing is attractive, as in the parable. That is why God says *begins,* for this is how evil starts. But once people have been seduced by it, even if they later discover that it is evil, their attraction and commitment to it are very strong.

We must therefore be extremely careful of the evil impulse and its beguiling speech, especially if its seductiveness produces greed for wealth. While the evil may prosper, their wealth will eventually harm them. Because of our sins, there are some whose children are falling into bad ways. This is because these children are pampered and raised in the lap of luxury, and when they grow up they are unable to find the accustomed pleasures that they seek. It also leads them to mix with the Gentiles and learn their patterns of behavior. In many other ways, too, wealth leads to loss and destruction, both in this world and the next.[52]

You can learn this from Sihon. If he had not conquered Heshbon from Moab, the Israelites would never have passed through his land, for the path of their journey was by Heshbon and its surrounding villages. He would not have had a war with Israel, and he and his people would not have suffered defeat. But he succeeded in conquering Heshbon and its surrounding villages from Moab. Proud of his accomplishment, he thought his star was in the ascendant. This led him to refuse the Israelites permission to pass there,

51. The preacher interprets *fanaw* and *pene* (both forms of *panim,* "face") to mean "inner being" (*penimit*), and *ṣafonah* (lit., "north") to mean "hidden" (*ṣefunah*).

52. Cf. Shochat, pp. 29–35, on the rising standard of living of German Jews at this time, and the reaction of preachers to the diversions of wealth.

resulting in the war that brought destruction upon him and his people. Thus his success led eventually to misfortune and devastation. We should learn from this example.

The rabbinic comment on the verse *For Heshbon was the city of Sihon* was "Therefore, *ha-moshelim be-yiṣram,* those who rule over their impulse, say *bo'u u-neḥasheb,* come, let us calculate the loss incurred by fulfilling a commandment, etc." This means, "Do not be seduced if the transgression brings some benefit, for it will eventually bring misfortune, destruction, and downfall, as occurred with Heshbon and Sihon. Learn a lesson from this parable (*mashal*). The Bible says quite nicely, *those who spoke in parables* [ha-moshelim] *therefore would say* (Num. 21:26–27).

In short, we should all exercise discretion so that we may guard against the trap set by the evil impulse. This can be done through the study of Torah. Most important, every person, whether a scholar or not, whether man or woman, should study a page of ethical literature each day, according to the level or need of the individual, whether *Shene Luḥot ha-Berit* or the other ethical works. This study can be done in Yiddish, for there are many books in Yiddish with significant ethical content.[53] Happy are those who ponder them. This discipline will provide a strong wall that cannot easily be breached by the "old and foolish king," despite his many ploys. . . .[54]

When people repent in their youth, while they are physically strong, their repentance is worthy of being deemed perfect. Such people walk "after the divine presence." But when people repent in old age, when they are physically weak and their evil impulse has abated, then their repentance is not so powerful and efficacious as to enable them to walk "after the divine presence," but only before it, without gazing upon it directly.

You know that there are three major divisions of life: youth, middle age, and old age. This is connected with the meaning of the verse, *Come, let us turn back to the Lord . . . in two days He will make us whole again,* referring to the first two stages of youth and middle age, when repentance is fully efficacious, but *on the third day,* namely, old age, when it is not fully efficacious, He will only *raise us up that we may live before Him* (Hos. 6:1–2).[55] Note that it says one will walk *before* the divine presence, not after it so as to gaze with pleasure upon it.

53. On the recommendation to study ethical literature, including that available in Yiddish, see *Re'shit Bikkurim,* p. 27a; *Binat Yiśśakar,* p. 12d; Landau, *Derushe,* p. 13a; and *Y.D.* 1:71a, 73b; 2:2c, 74b.

54. The "old and foolish king" is a commonplace epithet for the evil impulse; see Eccles. 4:13 and Eccles. Rabbah. This looks like a climactic point that should come quite near the end of the sermon. In fact, a full third remains, and the preacher immediately launches into an entirely new point relating to the evil impulse. I have incorporated only a few passages from the remainder.

55. See above, n. 7.

We must therefore rouse ourselves to repent now, rather than waiting until old age, for who knows if we will then have the opportunity? Every moment that passes is lost forever. These days are especially appropriate for repentance. In a different context, I have explained that the Balak-Balaam affair occurred during this period. The wars of Sihon and Og occurred during the month of Elul, as is clear from the Midrash.[56] Thus it happened that Balaam thought God would be reminded during this period of Adam's sin and the like, and that this would make God angry, so that his curses would take effect.

But God subverted his plan, and He did not grow angry during the entire period, because of the shofar, through which anger was transformed into compassion. It became established that the Holy One does not grow angry during this period. That is why these days are especially appropriate for repentance. This is the meaning of Balaam's cry, *How can I curse them? . . . None has beheld iniquity in Jacob . . . and the King's blasting is in its midst* (Num. 23:8, 21). By means of the blasting [of the shofar], wrath is transformed into compassion.

But at present, in our sinfulness, Balaam's counsel to Balak has been fulfilled: *Let me advise you what this people shall do to your people in the end of days* (Num. 24:14), namely, at the end of the Holy Day period, on the holiday Rejoicing in the Law [Simḥat Torah]. This is a time when Satan holds sway, and Balaam's prediction has virtually come true. On that day men mix with women. The youth of both sexes dance like rams and goats and foxes. Immorality bursts forth, negating all the good achieved through the Days of Awe.[57] Woe! This is Balaam's prediction of what will be done at the end of the days.

I find such behavior bitterly painful at the conclusion of [our reading of] the Torah. Indeed, the Torah wears sackcloth in mourning for this. Thank God it is true that such immorality does not occur here in our congregation! But I am pained at what I have heard about other places where they behave in such a foolish manner, negating the good they have attained through the Days of Awe. These days are truly appropriate for repentance, but the utmost care must be taken not to relapse to the previous state, God forbid. For then all God's blessings bestowed upon Israel will be reversed as well, becoming

56. See the preacher's *Tifʾeret Yonatan,* p. 105c; Ginzberg, *Legends,* 3:343 and 6:117, n. 660.

57. On the carnival atmosphere that prevailed during some Simḥat Torah celebrations, see Todd Endelman, *The Jews of Georgian England,* p. 218, and the essay by Cecil Roth in *The Sukkot and Simhat Torah Anthology,* ed. Philip Goodman (Philadelphia, 1973), pp. 138–40, including the famous quotation from the diary of Samuel Pepys, Oct. 14, 1663: "To see the disorder, laughing, sporting and no attention but confusion in all their service, more like brutes than people knowing the true God, would make a man forswear ever seeing them more." On the problem of mixed dancing during festivals, see the responsum of Joseph Steinhardt, trans. Solomon Freehof, *A Treasury of Responsa* (New York, 1973), pp. 206–10.

just as Balaam intended them. If Israel turns away from its repentance, so will the blessings turn away. . . .

During these days, the period of God's favor, we are required to pray and return to God from the depths of our hearts. Then will God respond to our voice, inscribing us in the Book of Good Life. Our youthful vigor will be restored like the eagle, and a redeemer will come to Zion. May he come speedily and in our days! Amen.

Hirschel Levin

Hirschel Levin (Hart Lyon) was a member of one of the great rabbinic families of eighteenth-century Europe. His maternal grandfather was the renowned halakist Ḥakam Ṣebi Ashkenazi. He was the nephew of Jacob Emden, whom he supported in the bitter controversy against Eybeschuetz, although not quite so vigorously as Emden would have liked. His father, Aryeh Loeb Loewenstamm, served as rabbi of Amsterdam until his death in 1755; his brother, Saul, author of *Binyan Ari'el,* succeeded their father in this prestigious post.

Hirschel's career was no less impressive than the careers of his relatives. In 1756, turning down an offer from Dubno, where his brother had served, he accepted a position as rabbi of the Great Synagogue of the Ashkenazic community in London. He remained there during the turbulent period of the Seven Years' War.[1] Apparently dissatisfied with the intellectual level of Jewish life in London, he later accepted offers of rabbinic posts in the most important communities of Germany: Halberstadt in 1764, Mannheim in 1770, and Berlin in 1773, where he remained chief rabbi until his death in 1800. In his later years, he would occasionally indulge in caustic reminiscences about his career: "In London I had money but no Jews, in Mannheim Jews but no money, in Berlin no money and no Jews."[2]

Even before arriving in Berlin, he had established a friendly relationship with Moses Mendelssohn, and his interest in secular literature generated sympathy for the thrust of Mendelssohn's work. He wrote an approbation for the German translation of the Torah and collaborated with Mendelssohn in producing *Ritualgesetze der Juden* (Berlin, 1778), a tract requested by the Prussian government to enable Christian judges to adjudicate appeals from the Berlin rabbinic court. However, the publication of Naphtali Herz Wessely's *Dibre Shalom we-'Emet* drove a wedge between the two, with Levin being urged by Polish rabbinic colleagues to suppress Wessely's work and Mendelssohn rushing to the support of his embattled friend.[3]

1. On this period, see Charles Duschinsky, *The Rabbinate of the Great Synagogue, London* (London, 1921), pp. 7–28.

2. *Ṣebi la-Ṣaddiq* (Pietrokov, 1904), p. 143; cf. Baron, *Community,* 2:82.

3. For the approbation, see Altmann, pp. 379–80; on *Ritualgesetze,* Altmann, p. 470; on the conflict over Wessely, Altmann, pp. 381, 483–84, and the annotation to the Landau sermon translated below.

Later Levin was again involved in controversy over the book *Beśamim Rosh* published by his son Saul Berlin in 1793. It purported to be a newly discovered collection of responsa by the medieval halakic authority Asher ben Jeḥiel, but it was actually a forgery expressing Berlin's maskilic and reformist tendencies. Along with Ezekiel Landau, Levin had written an introductory approbation for the work, and he continued to defend his son under attack.[4]

Although his rabbinic contracts required sermons only two or three times a year, Levin was known as an able and effective preacher. "Ṣebi la-Ṣaddiq," edited by Levin's grandson, contains sermons for the Sabbaths preceding the Day of Atonement and Passover, delivered in Germany. They are rather complex discussions of exegetical problems, primarily halakic in nature, that show little concern with contemporary events, social criticism, or the cultivation of homiletical art.

The same book, however, contains a report by someone who heard Levin tell "in a sermon in Berlin" that he had met a certain person on three occasions, in three different places, and each time the person was acting differently. The first time, he was sitting, angry and depressed; the second time he was running around from place to place, so busy that he hardly had time to respond to a greeting; the third time he was sitting contentedly over a glass of wine in a gaming house. When the rabbi asked him about the changes in his demeanor, the man explained that he was *yeṣer ha-ra*ᶜ (the evil impulse). The first time they met was in Halberstadt, a community of God-fearing Jews who paid him no heed. The second time was in London, where he found a fertile field that kept him busy day and night. The third time was in Berlin, where he had nothing to do because everyone was already acting according to his wishes.[5] Such a passage indicates that Levin was capable of a wit and humor not generally evident in the written versions of his sermons.

More important is the manuscript of sermons delivered by Levin during his tenure in London.[6] Of the twenty-three sermons in the manuscript, most are for Sabbaths preceding the Day of Atonement and Passover, from the years 1758 through 1763. There are several for the New Year's Day (1758, 1759), and two eulogies, each mentioning several rabbis who had died during the previous year.[7] The four that remain were sermons for special occasions "ordered by the king," days of national prayer or thanksgiving connected

4. On this episode, see most recently the discussion by Louis Jacobs, *Theology in the Responsa* (London, 1975), pp. 347–52, and the references on p. 347.

5. *Ṣebi la-Ṣaddiq,* pp. 142–43.

6. MS Adler 1248; (JTS MS R 79). On the history of this manuscript, see "Ṣebi la-Ṣaddiq," p. 167; Duschinsky, p. 8, n. 3.

7. A full list of the rabbis eulogized is provided by Duschinsky, pp. 19–21.

with events of the Seven Years' War. These sermons are a significant source for Jewish perceptions of contemporary historical events that affected them as subjects of a nation-state. The issues of war and peace, addressed in a context devoid of any messianic speculation or fervor, represent a new emphasis in Jewish preaching.

Unlike the sermons in "Ṣebi la-Ṣaddiq," the London sermons contain not only exegetical material but a substantial component of social and religious criticism. Some of the sermons contain a section identified explicitly as *ʿinyene musar,* "ethical content." These texts convey important information about the social and religious history of British Jewry in the middle of the eighteenth century.[8]

The sermon translated may have been the first delivered by Levin in London. In any case, it is the earliest of his sermons preserved. In structure it is quite different from his complex sermons in the catenary style, and it certainly does not bear out Cecil Roth's characterization of the London sermons as an hour-and-a-half talmudic discourse followed by an hour-and-a-half homily.[9]

Beginning with a verse from the Torah lesson and a rabbinic aggadah in the classic Sephardic style, Levin in the first section speaks to the occasion, praising the wisdom of the British king in ordering a day of national prayer "to beseech God's favor" in the war effort. The preacher discusses the obligation of the Jews to obey their kings and argues that the supreme contribution of the Jews to the country where they live is not through military service but through prayer. Toward the end of this section, he conveys rather vividly the economic and political disruption engendered by the war.

Speaking of the need for prayer leads naturally to the subject of repentance, the central motif at the heart of the sermon. After a general treatment of the need for repentance to accompany prayer—highlighted by an important analogy between the waging of war among nations and the ethical life as a battle against the evil impulse—the preacher proceeds to enumerate the offenses of the community in need of reform. The final section, devoted to exegesis of the verse from the Torah lesson and the aggadah, builds on the analogy between external and internal war established in the middle of the sermon. Both statements, speaking of war, are applied to the ethical life. The sermon concludes with a prayer for the king and the armed forces of the nation, and a messianic aspiration for universal peace.

8. For other relevant sources on this subject, see Todd Endelman, *The Jews of Georgian England, 1714–1830* (Philadelphia, 1979).

9. Cecil Roth, *History of the Great Synagogue, London, 1690–1940* (London, 1940), p. 110.

Sermon on *Be-Haᶜaloteka* (1757 or 1758, London)

When you are at war in your own land against an aggressor who attacks you, you shall sound short blasts on the trumpets, that you may be remembered before the Lord your God and be delivered from your enemies (Num. 10:9).

Mishnah Rosh Hashanah [3:8], p. 29[a]: "*Then, whenever Moses held up his hand, Israel prevailed, but whenever he let down his land, Amalek prevailed* (Exod. 17:11). Did the hands of Moses actually wage war or hinder the battle? No, the meaning is this: when Israel looked heavenward and subdued their hearts toward their Heavenly Father, they prevailed, and when they did not, they fell."

In Proverbs, chapter 21, we read, *Like channeled water is the mind of the king in the Lord's hand; He directs it to whatever He wishes* (v. 1).[1] From this verse we learn that when a king is inspired to do something worthwhile and propitious, that inspiration comes from God. He is the one who has placed the thought in the king's mind to act as he does. When we see a king commanding his subjects to beseech and cry out to God, each group in accordance with its own traditions, we realize that that king fully acknowledges the First Cause and His providence. He knows that the power of horses cannot guarantee either victory or escape, but that victory is in the power of God alone, the sole source of true success.

That is why our lord His Majesty the king has wisely decided to command the subjects under his dominion to proclaim a convocation today to beseech God's favor.[2] We further see that this is not an idle gesture, but inspiration from above. God wants to serve as his support, and He therefore placed these thoughts in the king's mind. It is like the verse, *He gives wisdom to the wise* (Dan. 2:21). Thus it is obvious that every person throughout the king's realms is obliged to carry out his command.

This is all the more true for us, the people of Israel, for we are under oath to God never to disobey the order of the king under whose protection we

1. Compare Isaac Nieto, p. 15. At the beginning of his "Prayer for the King," Nieto says that the king's "actions are but the index of Thy will" and cites the same verse from Proverbs.

2. For the tradition of national fast days accompanied by preaching, see Hugh Trevor-Roper, *Religion, the Reformation and Social Change* (London, 1984), pp. 294–344 ("The Fast Sermon").

live.[3] The sages spoke of this in tractate Ketubbot, page 111[a], deriving it from the verse *I adjure you {maidens of Jerusalem}* (Song 2:7). Our obligation is especially strong, since according to this talmudic passage, God made the nations swear that they would not subjugate Israel excessively. They are fulfilling their oath not to press the yoke excessively upon our necks, particularly in this kingdom, where their benevolence toward us in every respect arouses wonder.

This appears to me to be the meaning of the verse from Ecclesiastes, chapter 8: *I; obey the king's orders, and in view of your oath to God* (Eccles. 8:2). According to Rashi's commentary, these words apply to the community of Israel. Their statement *I; obey the king's orders* means "I, more than any other nation, am prepared to obey the king's orders, because of the oath that God made us swear in this regard."

Now it is obvious that we are always obliged to pray for the welfare and prosperity of our kings. Even if we are not specifically commanded by the king to do this, we should take the initiative ourselves. For how else can we serve the king under whose protection we live? If we were to suggest that we serve him by fighting in his armies, "what are we, how significant is our power?"[4]

3. The question of the Jews' capacity to live as obedient subjects of the king had been forcefully raised during the controversy over the "Jew-Bill" of 1753, on which see Thomas Perry, *Public Opinion, Propaganda and Politics in Eighteenth-Century England* (Cambridge, 1962), and Todd Endelman, *The Jews of Georgian England.* Anti-Jewish tracts like "A Modest Apology for the Citizens and Merchants of London" and William Romaine's "An Answer to a Pamphlet," fusing religious and political arguments, accused Jews of high treason because of their continued justification of the Crucifixion. What the argument hinged on can be seen in a quotation from the latter tract: "While Christ is the Head of the State, and the King acts as his deputy, and the subjects obey their king under that character, how can we . . . admit the Jews into our Christian state, who deny all the fundamental maxims of our civil and religious Establishment?" "Philo-Patriae," in response, insisted that Jews considered it a religious obligation to obey the laws of the state.

The issue addressed by the preacher was therefore a vital one. The passage from B. Ket 111a to which the preacher refers would continue to play an important role in the debate over Emancipation in Europe. Cf. Moses Mendelssohn, "Remarks Concerning Michaelis' Response to Dohm," in *The Jew in the Modern World,* ed. Paul Mendes-Flohr and Yehuda Reinharz (Oxford, 1980), p. 43.

4. The phrase is from the liturgy (see *The Authorized Daily Prayerbook,* ed. Joseph Hertz (New York, 1963), pp. 26–27. The question of serving in the king's army had special resonance at the time. William Pitt's Militia Bill (whose goal was to replace the Hessian and Hanoverian mercenaries with a permanent body of soldiers for defense of the homeland), by which all would be liable for service and the quota filled by ballot, became law in June 1757, although attempts to enforce it resulted in riots. See O. A. Sherrard, *Lord Chatham: Pitt and the Seven Years' War* (London, 1955), pp. 95–97, 177, 226; Robert Spector, *English Literary Periodicals and the Climate of Opinion during the Seven Years' War* (Paris, 1966), pp. 35–42. Whether Jews should be subject to conscription would be another fiercely debated problem of the Emancipation.

It was to teach this lesson that the Prophets compared us to a vine, as King David did in Psalm 80:9: *You plucked up a vine out of Egypt*. Ezekiel dwelt at length on this image in chapter 15: *The word of the Lord came to me: O mortal, how is the wood of the grapevine better than the wood of any branch to be found among the trees of the forest? Can wood be taken from it for use in any work? Can one take a peg from it to hang any vessel on? Now suppose it was thrown into the fire as fuel and the fire consumed its two ends and its middle was charred—is it good for any use? Even when it was whole it could not be used for anything; how much less when fire has consumed it and it is charred! Can it be used for anything at all?* (vv. 1–5).

The author of the *ʿAqedah* gave a fine explanation of this in chapter 84.[5] In comparing Israel to the wood of the vine, God chose something that in itself, judged by the material it is made of, has no value for any kind of work. Its only value is in its fruit, which *brings joy to God and human beings* (Judg. 9:13). If that fruit should go bad, if the vine produces sour grapes instead of sweet ones, then it is the most worthless and contemptible of all trees, easily destroyed when it falls into the fire. So it is with this people. Even when they were in their own land, at their best, their constitution was not sufficient to ensure their survival, for it was *not by their sword that they took possession of the land* (Ps. 44:4). How clear it is that they would be unable to survive once punishment began to weaken them in numbers and in strength! This is the end of the passage in the *ʿAqedah*.

Similarly, the prophet Isaiah compared them to a vine in chapter 5, saying, *Now I shall tell you what I will do to My vineyard: I will remove its hedge that it may be ravaged, I will break down its wall that it may be trampled* (v. 5). By this he meant that the other trees, tall and strong, will not necessarily be destroyed by wild beasts, and certainly not by domestic animals, even if their wall is broken or their hedge removed. This is not true of the vine. Its branches are low, trained to hang upon pieces of wood like a *sukkah*. When its fence is broken down, it can be trampled and dragged away even by lambs. So with this people: when God breaks down its wall—a metaphor for the removal of His providence from them—they are liable to punishment, and *the baby lambs will drag them away* (Jer. 49:20).

How then indeed shall we serve our king? Our only strength is in our speech. The sages expressed this in commenting upon Isaiah 41:14, "*Fear not, O worm Jacob*: just as the worm's power lies only in its mouth, so the power of Israel is only in its prayer."[6] It is incumbent upon us to pray for

5. The reference is to Isaac Arama's *ʿAqedat Yiṣḥaq,* one of the most frequently cited and influential homiletical works in Jewish literature (cf. Moscato's sermon, above, at n. 30). For the passage cited, see the Warsaw 1883 ed., Numbers, p. 177.

6. Mekilta *Be-Shallaḥ* on Exod. 14:10 (ed. Lauterbach, 1:207). The idea is that the worm can eat through the mighty cedar tree by the power of its mouth. So the greatest contribution Jews can make to the war effort is by the power of their prayers.

the welfare of the sovereign under whose protection we live, and for the welfare of the land in which we reside, for our own welfare is bound up with theirs.

Indeed, we have an even greater stake than most. We see the waters sweeping over us (Ps. 124:5), and something like a fire shut up in our bones (Jer. 20:9), for the high prices are a calamity. Because of our sins, the verse of the prophet Haggai has been fulfilled in us: *You have sowed much and brought in little, you eat without being satisfied.* Commerce progressively deteriorates in every country, *and the wage-earner earns for a purse full of holes* (Hag. 1:6).[7]

I look at the earth, it is waste and empty, at the heavens, but their light is gone; I look at the mountains, they are quaking, and all the hills are reeling (Jer. 4:23–24). This means that the *earth*—referring to the miserable poor, their spirits bowed low in the dust, clinging to the ground—are wiped out, for they have no means of support. They lift their gaze to the heavens, namely, the rich, who are called *heavens* because they bestow their bounty upon the earth, *but their light is gone,* referring to the bounty that reaches heaven itself. This too is not as it once was. The result is that everyone says, "It is enough to take care of my own needs."

I thought to myself, how could such misfortune occur to all human beings? *I look at the mountains, they are quaking.* The *mountains* are royal rulers, as Rashi and RaDaK [David Kimḥi] explained on Isaiah 41:15.[8] *And the hills* are the ministers, as explained there in their comments. Thus it is said that kings tremble with the tumult of fierce, full-scale wars. *And the hills,* the ministers, those who wield authority without a crown, lower than the kings, are reeling even more, for the sword threatens their lives, and the burden of war all but destroys them.[9]

Therefore, my brothers, pay careful attention to your conduct. *All of you are standing today in the presence of the Lord your God* (Deut. 29:9), for you have gathered in this house to pray to God. You must know that prayer without repentance not only does no good; to the contrary, it is harmful. The rabbis

7. The beginning of the Seven Years' War brought both a crisis in national morale and severe economic hardship to the British population. The period from March 1757 through June 1758 was one of the chief periods of hunger in the eighteenth century. Between 1755 and 1756 the price of a bushel of wheat and a loaf of bread jumped by 50 percent. See T. S. Ashton, *Economic Fluctuations in England, 1700–1800* (Oxford, 1959), pp. 36, 181; Spector, *English Literary Periodicals,* pp. 77–83.

8. This interpretation is given by David Kimḥi (RaDaK), but not by Rashi, on Isa. 41:15.

9. The phrase *malkuta be-la taga* is talmudic (B. Sanh 99b, 105a). Listeners may well have thought of the fall of the Newcastle government and the execution of Admiral John Byng for his failure to assist the British garrison on Minorca, under siege by the French, at the beginning of the war.

said, "Three things bring a person's sins to mind." One of them is "devotion in prayer," referring to the desire that one's supplication be accepted.[10]

I will give you a parable. There once was a king, a kind man who sustained all his subjects generously, filling all their needs, and watching carefully to protect them from all trouble. Yet some of his subjects were extremely perverse, disobeying all that the king commanded them and ignoring his laws. One day enemies came upon them and plundered all that they owned.

Now the behavior of the king's ministers was also known. They had been deprived of all sustenance, even that which they once received from the royal table, for the king had commanded that whoever disobeyed his commands be deprived of all favors. The king had heard about their base behavior and the extent to which they disobeyed his commands. He had heard that his ministers had scorned him and that his advisors still did not believe in him or in his power to save. Nevertheless, the king did not want to have them put to death, for he was kind. Instead, he removed his protection from them, so that various misfortunes could occur.

Now they come and cry out to the king, "Where is your kindness, our king? Look, your subjects are beaten and scourged, while you have neglected us and failed to come to our defense." Surely the king will not refrain from responding in anger, "Know that for some time you have been guilty of a capital offense. You are not satisfied with my kindness and patience, expressed in my sparing of your lives. You have the audacity to seek favors and ask me to save you!" Then the king will have them ushered out of his presence in disgrace, and their story will be told with mockery throughout the land.

The application of this parable need not be spelled out. Each of you should understand it by yourself and recognize your sickness and your sores. You should say to yourself: If the king told me to do something important, would I not do it to honor him, especially if the act were for his benefit and the good of the entire realm? How much more when the King of kings of kings says, *Bathe and be pure of your sins* (2 Kings 5:13)?

However, this repentance must be totally sincere, with pure heart concerning the past and with clean hands concerning any recurrence of the evil deed in the future. Since you have taken me and appointed me as a watchman to admonish the people, I am compelled to inform the people and warn them about all the evil being done, so that we may wage war against the rabble within: the appetitive soul that is constantly fighting the rational soul and seeking to overthrow it. Truly, however much peace is loved in the world, it

10. B. Ber 55a, B. RH 16b; see Rashi and Tosafot RH 16b, *we-ʿiyyun.* The idea is that those who pray with fervent devotion assume that their request will be fulfilled. If it is not, they begin to think about their past sins and repent.

is loved even more when it prevails within the body and the soul, which are bound so intimately together.[11]

Indeed, the ways of the macrocosm should teach us about the microcosm. Aristotle wrote in his *Ethics* that war is utterly hateful because of its essential nature, killing many people. But if it is waged for the sake of a peace for which all citizens hope, then it may be praiseworthy.[12] This should be clear to every rational person. All who have eyes can see the misfortunes wars bring to a land and its inhabitants: how many people are killed, how many nobles fall, how many kingdoms are destroyed, how much wealth is consumed in flames.

Nevertheless, there are occasions when the king must resort to it. When he foresees the misfortune that will eventually be brought upon his people by foreigners who would devour it, he is compelled to dress in his armor and lead his forces against the enemies, so that the people of his realm will eventually be able to live in peace. When war is waged for such a great goal, not only should it not be condemned; on the contrary, *the discerning will draw it out* (Prov. 20:5), and *the wise will ultimately praise it* (Prov. 29:11).[13]

That is why we see that sometimes kings quarrel with each other over matters that seem trivial, and eventually go to war for a reason no rational person could believe to be the actual cause of the fighting. The real reason, however, is known by the kings, about whom the wise king Solomon testified, *The mind of kings is unfathomable* (Prov. 25:3). They can foresee what will eventually develop from this trivial matter, and they therefore anticipate and go to war to prevent evil times.

Precisely the same is true of the microcosm. Concerning the verse, *If you pamper your servant from youth, you will eventually see him turn into a master* (Prov. 29:21), the sages said: if a person is allowed the most minor offense at first, he will certainly deviate in the most serious matters.[14] We see this ourselves with regard to the shaving of the beard.[15]

11. The second part of the sermon shifts to the realm of religious and ethical rebuke. The analogy between the external war and the inner conflict between impulses toward good and evil in the soul is a commonplace in Jewish ethical literature. See Baḥya ibn Paquda, *Ḥobot ha-Lebabot, Yiḥud ha-Maʿaśeh,* chap. 5, ed. Hyamson, 2:22–23; Anatoli, p. 31a.

12. The reference is not to the *Ethics* but to the *Politics, 7:14 (1331a35); Benjamin Jowett, The Politics of Aristotle* (Oxford, 1885), p. 235.

13. In the second verse, *yeshabbeḥennah* is apparently understood in the common meaning "praise," rather than the meaning "suppress" or "silence" usually applied in this context.

14. Cf. Gen. Rabbah 22:6. The idea that it is better to resist at the beginning than to allow potential danger to grow is common in Jewish ethical literature (cf. the last section of Eybeschuetz's sermon, above. It is the analogy in the political realm that is more significant here.

15. On the shaving of beards, see Endelman, pp. 122–23; Eybeschuetz, *Y.D.* 1:86b, 64d; 2:28a, 66c; Shochat, pp. 55–58.

The same is true of sexual relations with an unmarried woman. By its nature, this involves intercourse with a woman in a state of menstrual impurity, a sin punishable by excision from the community (Lev. 20:18). Eventually all is thought to be permissible, the couple living together as husband and wife, as a matter of public knowledge, despite her menstrual impurity.[16] Can God be expected to exercise restraint when such things occur? Not only this. I see from some with whom I have discussed this matter that they consider it to be fairly insignificant! They fail to remember that with all the evils we did when we were in our land, God characterized our behavior as being *like the impurity of a menstruous woman.*[17]

There is also the profaning of the Sabbath by having a Gentile woman light a fire to heat water for tea or coffee.[18] They do two forbidden things, and *we endure fire and water* (Ps. 66:12). As for eating hot Sabbath food stored away in a stove, we read in tractate Shabbat 119[a]: Caesar said to R. Joshua ben Hananiah, "Why does the Sabbath food have such a fragrant aroma?" He replied, "We have a certain spice called *shabbat*. . . ." The emperor said, "Give me some." R. Joshua replied, "It is beneficial to all who observe the Sabbath, but it has no effect upon those who do not observe it."

Also there in the Talmud is the statement, "Fire breaks out only in a place where the Sabbath is profaned, as we see in the verse, *But if you do not obey My command to hallow the Sabbath day and to carry no burden through the gates of Jerusalem on the Sabbath day, then I will set fire to its gates; it shall consume the fortresses of Jerusalem* (Jer. 17:27)." Now we see ourselves how Jews carry burdens even outside the City, where it is totally impermissible.[19] More than this, they sin with fire itself. What can we do when God exacts punishment? How can we respond when He arises? *For with fire will the Lord contend* (Isa. 66:16).[20]

(Also regarding menstrual impurity: that they do not bother to wait, but lie with her before she has immersed herself.)[21]

16. On the question of changing sexual mores, see Endelman, pp. 129–31 and 224–25; Jacob Katz, "Niśśu'im we-Ḥayye Ishut be-Moṣa'e Yeme ha-Benayim," *Zion* 10 (1944–45):21–54; Shochat, pp. 166–70; Eyebeschuetz's sermon, above, n. 44.

17. See the concluding phrase of Ezek. 36:17.

18. On tea and coffee, see Eybeschuetz's sermon above, n. 28. On the casual observance of the laws of Sabbath rest, see Endelman, pp. 134–35, and Charles Duschinsky (intro., n. 1), p. 14.

19. The word *City* appears in Hebrew characters in the text. The passage seems to imply that there was an *ʿerub* (a marker noting that private and public domains had been "blended" in order to permit movement from one to the other within the city limits on the Sabbath) in London; see Duschinsky, p. 10, n. 7, and cf. Jacob Sasportas, *Ohel Yaʿaqob* (Amsterdam, 1734), no. 46, denying the existence of such an *ʿerub* in London in 1672. On Jewish peddlers, see Endelman, pp. 179–85.

20. This passage would make most sense if it were referring to a serious fire that had occurred in London not too long before the sermon was delivered.

21. This sentence clearly does not belong here, but rather in the discussion of sexual

As for the sin of water, look and see what happened in Portsmouth.[22] Without a doubt, God is repaying measure for measure, *for this people has spurned the gently flowing waters of Shiloah* (Isa. 8:6). If perhaps those who drowned did not sin, "all Israel are sureties for each other."[23] Look at this great disaster. Upon them was fulfilled the rabbinic statement on the verse, *Your wives shall be widows* (Exod. 22:23),[24] which was a punishment for the oppression of widows and orphans (Exod. 22:21). And we must rectify still other matters in which people stumble unwittingly, for we have the power to do so. Therefore, *Pick from each of your tribes men who are wise, discerning, and experienced* (Deut. 1:13), one from each, and let them share with me the burden of this people by looking into the affairs of this community.

After all I have said, the emergent truth—that we must fight against the tyrant, the evil impulse that rules over our bodies—is precisely the message of the verse I recited at the very beginning: *When you are at war in your own land against an aggressor who attacks you* (Num. 10:9). There appears to be superfluous language here, for you would certainly not be at war against a friend, but only against an enemy. Moreover, at the beginning of the verse he is called *ṣar,* "aggressor," and at the end *oyeb,* "enemy."

This can be understood when we raise for ourselves the question of the Talmud: "Did the hands of Moses actually wage war?" We can apply this to the trumpets mentioned in the verse: do they actually remind God, or save you? The answer is precisely the same as the answer given by the sages. It

---

behavior above. The text may have been prepared in advance, and the writer, temporarily forgetting a point he wanted to make, wrote it down when he remembered it, intending to incorporate it at the proper time during delivery. Or it could have been written after the sermon was delivered, with the aberrant sentence indicating a temporary lapse of memory on the author's part about what he had actually said. The translation reflects the ambiguity and problematic syntax of the Hebrew.

22. This passage has been understood to refer to the tragedy in which eleven Portsmouth Jews drowned when the sailing boat they had hired to take them to the man-of-war *Lancaster* capsized. The date was Friday, February 10, 1758 (second day of Adar 1, 5518). On this episode, see Cecil Roth, "The Portsmouth Community and Its Historical Background," *Transactions of the Jewish Historical Society of England* 13 (1932–35):164–65, and the quotation from *The Gentleman's Magazine,* 1758, p. 91, cited by Maurice Myers in *Transactions* 5 (1902–05):224. *The Daily Advertiser* for February 10 and February 17, 1758, corroborates the presence of the *Lancaster* in Portsmouth, but does not mention the mishap. The problem is that this event occurred eight months after the sermon is supposed to have been delivered. Duschinsky identifies the reference (pp. 10–11) without noting the obvious problem for his dating of the sermon in June of 1757 (p. 8).

23. B. Sheb 29a. Thus some Jews can be held accountable for sins that other Jews commit.

24. The rabbis considered the simple meaning of Exod. 22:23 superfluous after Exod. 22:22, and they therefore interpreted it to mean that the wives would be left in limbo, unable to remarry, because the death of the husbands could not be legally established through an eyewitness. This could occur when the body of a presumed drowning victim was washed out to sea and never recovered, as was the case with five of the victims of the Portsmouth tragedy.

is well known that the sound of the blasting of horns is intended to rouse the heart to repentance,[25] to serve as admonition, reminding the people, so that evil times will not come upon them. The word *teruʿah,* "blast," is etymologically linked with the word *teroʿem, you shall smash them with an iron mace* (Ps. 2:9), as we explained in our discussion of the New Year's Day.[26]

The verse says, *when you are at war in your land* (meaning, when those who hate you come against your land). Know well that it is because of the evil impulse, which impels you to sin. We know that this is the cause. This is the meaning of *against an aggressor who attacks you,* for the aggressor, *ṣar,* is the *yeṣer ha-raʿ,* the evil impulse. So we have found in our country, for they are attacking you, and this is why the evil comes upon you. How should you act? *You shall sound short blasts on the trumpets,* warning the people, reminding them of repentance, and thereby *you may be remembered before the Lord your God and be delivered from your enemies.* For when they subdue their hearts toward their Heavenly Father, they will be victorious,[27] as we have already explained.

Our only support is our Heavenly Father. Let us lift up our hearts to Him, together with our hands, and pray with all sincerity that He may be merciful toward us, and compassionately protect our lord His Majesty the king, his royal line, his ministers, and his state. May God make His voice resound before their army; may He give them respite from their enemies on all sides, and grant peace in their land, peace within all their borders. May He lead the navy upon still waters. And our lord His Majesty the king and his line—may God allow them to possess a glorious throne, and exalt them as in the past.

In their days and in ours, may God rebuild Zion, and make all people pure of speech, so that all may call upon the Name of the Lord. *Let nation not lift up sword against nation* (Isa. 2:4) in order to extend their borders. *Let us no longer need to teach one another and say "Heed the Lord," for all, from the least to the greatest, shall heed the Lord* (Jer. 31:34). Blessed is the Lord, the God of Israel from eternity to eternity. Amen.[28]

25. This view, classically formulated by Maimonides in *Code,* I,v (*Teshubah*), 3:4, became conventional in subsequent Jewish literature.

26. This seems to imply that Levin was in London and preached there on the previous Rosh Hashanah. See Duschinsky, p. 7, n. 1, for the dating of the beginning of Levin's tenure in London.

27. Here the preacher returns to the language of the aggadah cited at the beginning. The integration of verse and aggadah is complete.

28. The concluding prayers are primarily for the welfare of the state and for universal peace, making this different from the traditional sermon conclusion, which generally refers more explicitly to the coming of the Messiah. Compare the similarly patriotic and universalist conclusion of Isaac Nieto, pp. 17–18. The sentence about the rebuilding of Zion indicates that patriotic loyalty to the country of residence was not thought to be inconsistent with traditional messianic aspirations. Cf. Raphael Mahler, "Yahadut Ameriqah we-Raʿyon Shibat Ṣiyyon bi-Tequfat ha-Mahpekah ha-ʾAmeriqanit," *Zion* 15 (1950):106–34.

Ezekiel Landau

The career of Ezekiel Landau as a scholar, halakic authority, and rabbinic leader progressed steadily to the very pinnacle in his age.[1] He was born in 1713 in the eastern Polish town of Opatów, where his unusual talents were soon recognized. After completing his traditional education, he served for ten years as judge in the noted Ukrainian center of Brody, and was then, at age thirty, selected as rabbi of Yampol in Volhynia. There he exercised the skills that spread his fame: as preacher, as teacher in traditional Polish talmudic study, and as author of his first legal responsa.

In 1752 he intervened in the conflict between two of the greatest rabbis of the generation, Jacob Emden and Jonathan Eybeschuetz, which was rending the fabric of European Jewry. His letters, addressed to the principals and to other leading rabbis, called for an end to the venomous attacks upon Eybeschuetz, but insisted that Eybeschütz refrain from writing the controversial amulets and publicly condemn the allegedly Sabbatian tracts that were circulating under his name.[2]

This mediating position, promoting a compromise intended not to antagonize either party (although it actually won him the enduring enmity of Emden), made it possible for Landau to be offered in 1754 one of the most prestigious rabbinical posts in Europe, the chief rabbinate of Prague, a position that had remained vacant since the death of David Oppenheim in 1736. He held this position, recognized by the Austrian government as the supreme rabbinical authority in Bohemia, until his death in 1793.

Landau's most famous and influential work, containing some 860 erudite legal responsa, was called *Noda*ᶜ *bi-Yhudah*; indeed, this is the name by which Landau himself is often referred to in rabbinic literature. He was also esteemed for his novellae on several tractates of the Talmud, called *Ṣiyyun le-Nefesh Ḥayyah (Ṣelaḥ)*.

As a preacher, Landau may have been overshadowed by other luminaries

1. On Landau, see the studies by A. L. Gelman, *Ha-Noda*ᶜ *bi-Yhudah u-Mishnato* (Jerusalem, 1962) and Solomon Wind, *Rabbi Yeḥezqel Landau: Toledot Ḥayyaw u-Fe*ᶜ*ulato* (Jerusalem, 1961).

2. A trenchant reappraisal of this entire episode was given by Sid Leiman in "R. Ezekiel Landau's Attitude toward R. Jonathan Eybeschuetz," paper submitted to the Conference on Eighteenth-Century Jewish History, Harvard, 1984.

in Prague, but his writings reveal considerable homiletical talent. *Doresh le-Ṣiyyon* contains thirteen discourses delivered in Yampol between 1745 and 1752 on the Sabbaths preceding the Day of Atonement and Passover. They are lengthy technical discussions of legal issues, structured according to an associative chain in which the solution of one exegetical problem leads to the examination of another.

The sermons delivered in Prague, shorter and in a less intellectually demanding style, were obviously intended for a much more general audience. *Derushe ha-Ṣelaḥ* contains forty-five sermons, thirty of them intended for delivery during the forty-day period of penitence ending with the Day of Atonement: the first day of the month of Elul, inaugurating the penitential period, the first or second day of Rosh Hashanah, the Fast of Gedaliah, the Sabbath preceding the Day of Atonement, or just before the beginning of the evening service for the Day of Atonement. Many of them contain powerful social and religious criticism as well as homiletical and exegetical insights. The other sermons are associated with the Sabbath preceding Passover or Passover itself, the Sabbath during Hanukkah, and the Feast of Weeks. There is also a record of the eulogy Landau delivered at the death of Jonathan Eybeschuetz. *Ahabat Ṣiyyon* contains sermons for the beginning of the period of penitence, two sermons honoring the Gemilut Ḥasidim Society, and part of a poignant eulogy for his wife.

Two occasional sermons, published during Landau's lifetime soon after they were delivered, were not included in any of the collections. One was a eulogy for the empress Maria Theresa in 1780.[3] The empress had been responsible for the expulsion of the Jews from Prague a generation before, and her anti-Jewish sentiments were widely known, but Landau, as he held an official position, had to speak well of the deceased, and even managed to do so convincingly. The second, a thanksgiving sermon occasioned by news of the Austrian victory over the Turkish forces at Belgrade in 1789, reflects the development of patriotism among European Jews in this generation.[4]

Contemporaries praised not only the content of Landau's sermons but the manner of his delivery. One young member of his congregation reported many years later that he had never forgotten the gripping and soul-stirring voice with which Landau uttered the words "*I am asleep but my heart is awake* (Song 5:2): I am asleep in exile, but my heart is awake to the redemption" at the beginning of a funeral eulogy, "bringing tears to the eyes of all."[5]

The sermon delivered on the Sabbath preceding Passover, 1782, reveals

3. *Derush Hesped . . . ʿal Mitat ha-Qesarit Maria Theresa* (Prague, 1780). See "Sermons and History," above, n. 20.

4. *Shebaḥ we-Hodaʾah ʿal Haṣlaḥat Adonenu ha-Qesar Yosef ha-Sheni be-Lokdo ʿIr ha-Beṣurah Belgrade* (Prague, 1789).

5. Guttmann Klemperer, "The Rabbis of Prague," *Historia Judaica* 13 (1951):58, n. 10.

the preacher facing the pressures of powerful forces that were just beginning to transform European Jewish society. Several months before, the Austrian emperor Joseph II had issued the Edict of Toleration, which seemed to presage a new conception of the relationship between the Jews, their Gentile neighbors, and the state. Naphtali Herz Wessely, champion of the Berlin Enlightenment, had written a passionate defense of this edict that challenged the foundations of the traditional paideia. Sabbatian heresies continued to seethe underground. From the east came reports of the new movement we know as Hasidism. Alert to the enormous responsibilities of his position at this critical moment, Landau sought to define a stance that would defend tradition without appearing to be critical of what the emperor had done.

The sermon's structure is not at all obvious, but it may be divided into two major sections. The first begins with exegetical and conceptual problems emerging from a statement in the Passover Haggadah and moves to a defense of the Edict of Toleration and an attack upon Wessely. The second begins by enshrining faith, paradigmatically expressed in the sacrificial cult, as the foundation of Judaism, and defends the tradition against the innovations of contemporary sects, eventually returning to exegesis of a talmudic passage connected with Passover. Polemic is framed by exegesis in a traditional homiletical mode, grounding the message in the liturgy of the holiday about to be celebrated.

Sermon for the Sabbath Preceding Passover (1782, Prague)

We were slaves to Pharaoh in Egypt.

A careful reading might suggest that the Passover Haggadah should have said only "We were slaves in Egypt," for what difference did it make whether we were slaves to Pharaoh or to someone else? The essence of the miracle was that we emerged from slavery to freedom. Furthermore, all this commotion in celebrating the holiday of Passover at the present time may seem strange. Now, too, we are in exile, outside our land. Why then such great joy at the Exodus from Egypt?[1]

1. The sermon begins with two questions drawn from the occasion: (a) an exegetical problem, the apparently superfluous word in the passage from the Haggadah (see *The Passover Haggadah,* ed. Nahum Glatzer, New York, 1969, pp. 22–23), and (b) a conceptual problem concerning the relevance of the Passover observance in exile. On this latter question, cf. Abravanel, *Zebaḥ Pesaḥ,* in J. D. Eisenstein, ed., *Oṣar ha-Perushim ʿal Haggadah shel Pesaḥ* (New York, 1920; reprint ed., Tel Aviv, 1969), p. 76.

However, the one to whom you are enslaved does indeed make a difference. We find that Ezra said, *For bondsmen are we, though even in our bondage God has not forsaken us, but has disposed the king of Persia favorably toward us, to furnish us with sustenance* (Ezra 9:9). The tax paid to such a king is fair. He is the lord of the land, and it is fitting and proper that all who enjoy his protection should pay a tax. The gracious king does not make the burden of taxes too heavy. What he takes is collected legally and fairly for his own welfare. When a person leases out a room in his house, the rent he demands is not intended to cause grief to the tenant; it is a proper return for the room. In fact, if the landlord sees the tenant prospering in his quarters, he is happy.[2]

Pharaoh, by contrast, was by nature an evil king, a cruel man filled with hate for those who found refuge in his realm. His intention in subjugating the children of Israel was not to improve his own lot but rather to degrade the Israelites, to cause them sorrow, and to embitter their lives. This is what the Bible says: the Egyptians *embittered their lives . . . with all the work that they ruthlessly imposed upon them* (Exod. 1:14). In addition to the taxes and the forced labor, the Israelites were debased and humiliated in Egyptian eyes. Even the servants of the Egyptians lorded it over Israel. This is what Rashi wrote on the verse, *to the firstborn of the slave girl* (Exod. 11:5): "Why were the slave girls stricken? Because even they made Israel subservient."

That bitter Egyptian exile was unlike the experience in Persia. Although we were in exile there, we were considered important and respected. Cyrus and Darius were compassionate and merciful toward us. This is also the case in our own time, when our lord His Majesty the emperor has decided to help us and to raise us from our degradation.[3] May God reward him for his good deed and raise his glory ever higher! How abundant is his gracious beneficence!

We Jews should not for this reason become insolent and begin to behave with haughtiness and arrogance. We should act respectfully toward the inhabitants of this kingdom. It is their own land, while we are only guests. A sense of submissiveness is good when it comes from within.[4] It is enough

2. This justification of the legitimacy of the taxes exacted from the Jews by their rulers has a long tradition in Jewish thought; see B. BB 55a; Maimonides, *Code,* XI,iii (*Gezelah*), 5:11; *EJ* 15:844.

3. The reference is to the Austrian emperor Joseph II and the famous Edict of Toleration, promulgated on January 2, 1782, several months before this sermon. Although this was not Landau's first response to the edict (see below), discussion of its provisions is an important part of his message. On the edict, see Jacob Katz, *Out of the Ghetto* (Cambridge, Mass., 1973), pp. 161–66, and Ruth Kestenberg-Gladstein, *Neuere Geschichte der Juden in den böhmischen Ländern* (Tübingen, 1969), pp. 34–66. A convenient though abridged text is in *The Jew in the Modern World,* ed. Paul Mendes-Flohr and Yehuda Reinharz (Oxford, 1980), pp. 34–36.

4. The Hebrew is *ṭobah mardut be-libbo shel adam mi-ṣad ʿaṣmo*; cf. B. Ber 7a and Rashi, s.v. "*mardut.*" Although this submissiveness should not be imposed upon Jews by others,

that His Majesty the emperor has extended his protection over us, so that no one will use force to harm or degrade us. That is what Ezra said: "We *consider ourselves* to be bondsmen; even though God has not forsaken us in our bondage and has disposed the king of Persia favorably toward us," nevertheless, we consider ourselves to be bondmen.

This may have been intended by the author of the Haggadah in the passage beginning, "This is like the bread of affliction." That passage ends, "Now we are here, next year may we be in the land of Israel. Now we are slaves, next year may we be free." The apparent redundance is noteworthy. An explanation for this is given in the book *Binyan Ari'el* "in the name of my grandfather, the *ga'on* rabbi Heshel, of blessed memory."[5] We, however, may interpret it in accordance with our thesis, thereby explaining the order of this passage followed by "Why is this night different?" and then "We were slaves."

The author of the Haggadah was warning us not to become insolent and arrogant. Even if there should be a gracious and compassionate king who abundantly helps us, we should inwardly know that we are in a land not our own, and that we should remain submissive to the peoples of that land. Therefore he said: "Even if you know that the year of redemption is definitely near, even if you are certain that this will be your last year here and that in future years you will be in the land of Israel, still you should not become arrogant, for now you are still slaves, and you should continue to behave submissively.[6] Only next year, when you are in the land of Israel, our own ancestral estate, will you be truly free."

Landau maintains that it must be retained despite the new spirit of tolerance. Compare the argument in the sermon of Morteira, above (which, however, gives a totally different presentation of the nature of Egyptian slavery). A century later, the German anti-Semitic preacher Adolf Stöcker would argue that the Jews had misunderstood the act of emancipation and begun to think of themselves as citizens, when they should have behaved as "tolerated strangers" (Jacob Katz, *From Prejudice to Destruction* [Cambridge, Mass., 1980], p. 262).

5. Saul Loewenstamm, *Binyan Ari'el* (Amsterdam, 1778), 1:1, p. 32c–d. The interpretation there relates the two sentences to the rabbinic dispute over whether the redemption would occur in Nisan or in Tishri. Loewenstamm was the brother of Hirschel Levin, author of the preceding sermon. The grandfather mentioned is Ṣebi Hirsch Ashkenazi (Ḥakam Ṣebi), father of Jacob Emden and of Loewenstamm's mother.

6. This emphasis on the obligation of Jewish political submissiveness even in the context of incipient messianic redemption should be seen against the background of one of the arguments against Emancipation: that Jews could not be loyal to the countries where they lived because of their hope for the ingathering of the exiles; see, e.g., Johann David Michaelis in *The Jew in the Modern World,* p. 37. A generation later, Abraham Lowenstamm would argue in his *Ṣeror ha-Ḥayyim* that Jews would be obliged to maintain their posture of political quietism and submissiveness even after the Messiah arrived. See the discussion by Barukh Mevorakh, "Ha-'Emunah ba-Mashiaḥ be-Fulmose ha-Reformah ha-Ri'shonim," *Zion* 34 (1969):215.

This is therefore followed by a question: since it is so that we are still slaves, why is this night of Egyptian exile different from all the other nights of exile under other kingdoms? Why all this commotion on the night when we went out from Egypt, if we are still slaves?[7] The answer is that there is a great difference, for then in Egypt we were slaves to Pharaoh, a cruel king, a king who made us suffer without benefit to himself, solely in order to humiliate us. But now there is a gracious and compassionate king. Even though we are slaves, he has removed from us the stigma of bondage, removed all externally recognizable signs of servitude. If we inwardly take it upon ourselves to be submissive, this is as it should be.[8]

Therefore, my brothers and friends, be careful to avoid an arrogant disposition. If a Jew hears himself being insulted, he should remain silent, for *starting a quarrel is like opening a sluice* (Prov. 17:14). Our father Abraham was considered extremely important by both God and men, yet he prostrated himself before the people of the land, the children of Heth, and spoke submissively: *I am a resident alien among you* (Gen. 23:4).

Three times each day we ask in prayer, "May my soul be like dust to all."[9] How then can we possibly be arrogant? But because of our many sins, our prayer has become mere empty words, unaccompanied by a contrite and humble heart. And then we ask, "Open my heart to Your Torah, and let my soul pursue Your commandments," while there is no true desire for Torah or commandments.[10]

In my opinion, these two requests are linked together because at times there is some good in feeling pride. An example is the envy leading to emulation of the great leaders of Israel who excel in Torah learning and in good deeds. Although this is not ultimately a worthy motive—for the ul-

7. The second question raised at the beginning, concerning the relevance of Passover in exile, is now addressed through a play on the beginning of the "four questions" (*The Passover Haggadah,* pp. 20–21). The "night different from all other nights" is not the night of the Seder service, but the night of the Egyptian enslavement, fundamentally different from all other experiences of exile.

8. Quite similar is the statement of Gershom Mendes Seixas, preaching in New York in 1789: "Though we are, through divine goodness, made equal partakers of the benefits of government by the constitution of these states, with the rest of the inhabitants, still we cannot but view ourselves as captives in comparison to what we were formerly, and what we expect to be hereafter, when the outcasts of Israel shall be gathered together" ("A Religious Discourse: Thanksgiving Day Sermon, November 26, 1789," reprinted by the Jewish Historical Society of New York, 1977, p. 12).

9. For the texts cited in this paragraph, see *The Authorized Daily Prayerbook,* pp. 156–57. Here the preacher maintains that the two requests are not exemplified by the actual conduct of his people. In the following two paragraphs, he will show the logical connection between the two requests.

10. The observations on the texts from the liturgy are commonplaces in Jewish ethical and religious literature.

timate motive must be only to act purely out of love, leading to communion with God—nevertheless, such communion is not achieved at the beginning. This is why the rabbis said, "One should always engage in Torah and commandments, even for impure reasons, for what begins with impure motivation may end with pure motivation."[11] In any case, there is some need for envy and pride, for it may lead to the service of God.

But all this applies only to the religious realm. Envy of worldly things, such as the wealth of a rich man, or arrogance because of them, is reprehensible. Nothing good results from it. The sages have said, "*Do not compete with the wicked*—to be like them; *do not envy the evil-doers*—to be like them."[12] The Bible also says, *Do not envy sinners in your heart, but only the God-fearing, at all times* (Prov. 23:17). This means that we should envy those who fear the Lord. Yet we pray, "May my soul be like dust to all." Lest the fulfillment of this request prevent one from being worthy of Torah and commandments by keeping him from proper envy of those who fear God and study His Torah, the prayer continues, "Open my heart to Your Torah, and let my soul pursue Your commandments."

But now, because of our many sins, I have seen everything overturned. How can one envy the study of Torah, when an evil man has arisen from our own people and brazenly asserted that the Torah is not at all important, that an animal carcass is worth more than talmudic scholars, that etiquette is more vital than the Torah? This man is certainly blind to his own faults. *He* is worse than an animal carcass, and in the end his corpse will lie like dung upon the field![13]

Now as to the substance of the matter—the value of etiquette and of

11. B. Pes 50b.

12. B. Ber 7b on Ps. 37:1.

13. It would have been obvious to all listeners that the preacher was referring to Naphtali Herz Wessely. Landau had enthusiastically endorsed the publication of Wessely's commentary on Abot, *Yen Lebanon,* in 1775, but the tract *Dibre Shalom we-ʾEmet,* published at Berlin in 1782 to marshal support for the Edict of Toleration, unleashed a storm of fierce protest among the traditionalists. Much of the opprobrium focused on a single rhetorical flourish. Wessely used a rabbinic hyperbole, "As for a scholar who lacks sense (*deʿah*), a carcass is better than he" (Lev. Rabbah 1:15), to support his claim that a rabbinic scholar bereft of social grace is of no benefit to anyone. This lies behind Landau's retort that he, Wessely, is worse than an animal carcass.

Compare the diatribe against Wessely delivered on the same Sabbath by David Tevele ben Nathan of Lissa, part of which is published in translation in *The Jew in the Modern World,* pp. 67–69. Tevele Schiff, who received a copy of that sermon, described it as being "in very pure language, full of pious and wise words, careful not to offend the majesty of the emperor" (Charles Duschinsky, *The Rabbinate of the Great Synagogue, London,* pp. 177, 249). On Wessely's tract and the reactions it provoked, see Altmann, pp. 478–89, and Mordecai Eliav, *Ha-Ḥinnuk ha-Yehudi be-Germanyah bi-Yme ha-Haśkalah we-ha-Emanṣipaṣyah* (Jerusalem, 1961), pp. 39–51.

grammatical knowledge of the languages spoken by our neighbors—I too esteem these things. The government has done a great favor in deciding to teach our children to speak correctly.[14] Even in the Bible we were criticized for not knowing how to speak the various languages. Do not think that you know how to speak the German language. No one can be said to know a language unless he can speak it grammatically.

This is what Maimonides wrote in the second chapter of *Hilkot Qeri᾿at Shema*ᶜ, halakah 10 [*Code*, II,i,2:10]: "A person may recite the Shemaᶜ in any language that he understands. If one recites the Shemaᶜ in a secular language, he must take care to avoid errors in that language, and be as scrupulous in saying the Shemaᶜ correctly in that language as he would be if he were reading it in the sacred tongue." Nehemiah said: *A good number of their children spoke the language of Ashdod, and did not know how to speak Judean or the language of those various peoples* (Neh. 13:24). Thus he criticized them for not knowing how to speak various languages.

Therefore, His Majesty the emperor has done us a great favor in commanding us to learn the language grammatically so that we can speak it properly, as I stated in a sermon last winter.[15] Even in the time of the last prophets, the king commanded that Daniel, Hananiah, Mishael and Azariah be taught the literature and language of the Chaldeans, and they distinguished themselves both in this area and in their knowledge of Torah and their performance of good deeds.

Those who fear the Lord have eyes to see, and they will be able to master both, making Torah the basis, yet also learning to speak correctly and behave according to the patterns that guide a person on the right path. "Torah unaccompanied by labor will eventually come to naught," but most of our labor is in the area of trade and commerce, which requires the ability to write and to speak the language of the country.[16] Likewise, the members of

14. Having first praised the emperor and his edict, and then attacked the best-known public supporter of that edict, Landau must now define his middle ground, defending the edict yet opposing the movement of the Berlin Enlightenment that centered around Mendelssohn. The edict provided that "the tolerated Jews may send their children to the Christian primary and secondary schools so that they have at least the opportunity to learn reading, writing [of the German language], and counting." Landau goes on to justify from traditional sources the goal of learning correctly the language of the Christian environment.

15. Landau must have preached about the edict almost immediately after it was promulgated. Perhaps the ensuing controversy and the large congregation expected for the Sabbath preceding Passover impelled him to return to the subject. By the summer, however, Tevele Schiff could write of a report that "the rabbi of Prague [Landau] at first preached against [Wessely's tract] at Prague; now, however, he is obliged to remain quiet in public and he is working secretively to arouse rabbis of other famous congregations" (Duschinsky, pp. 177–78, 249–50).

16. Abot 2:2. The edict stated, "Considering the numerous openings in trades and man-

the Sanhedrin, the pillars of the Torah faith, were required to understand the languages of other peoples.[17]

Indeed, how good God has been to us; His counsel will endure. It was God who impelled the exalted government to think well of His people. All this has come about because of God's great mercy, not because of our own goodness. Our behavior is poor, and we are very lax in Torah, prayer, and the observance of the commandments, yet God has been merciful to us because of the merit of our ancestors, the patriarchs, Abraham, Isaac, and Jacob. The covenant with the patriarchs has not come to an end!

When we see all the good God has done for us, we should carefully examine our behavior and ask how we have deserved such kindness. When God announced to our father Abraham that his descendants would inherit the land, he said, *O Lord God, how shall I know that I am to possess it?* (Gen. 15:8). Rashi interpreted this to mean, "through what merit will these things be established?" God answered, *Bring Me a three-year-old heifer* (Gen. 15:9): "through the merit of the sacrifices."

Now we might well ask, why through the merit of the sacrifices? After all, there is study of Torah and performance of commandments, which apply to us everywhere. I would say in response that of all the commandments of the Torah, nothing is as remote from human reason as the sacrifices. For eating, drinking, perception of aroma, and other such human qualities cannot be applied to God. Therefore there is no rational explanation of the sacrifices at all. They are based entirely on faith: God said, and it was; He commanded, and it was established, though the reason be hidden from us.

In this there is a warning that we should not delve too deeply into investigating matters pertaining to faith. All such inquiries, whether emanating from our own people or any other, are nothing but futility when applied to that which human reason cannot comprehend. The basis of all is faith, not reason or philosophical inquiry.[18]

Our father Abraham was beyond peer in philosophical inquiry; this is what brought him to his faith. Yet he did not question God's command. Indeed,

---

ifold contacts with Christians resulting therefrom, the care for maintaining common confidence requires that the Hebrew and the so-called Jewish language and writing of Hebrew intermixed with German . . . shall be abolished." Landau focuses not on the "abolition" of Yiddish but on the need for learning German. On this passage, Eliav writes, "It is difficult to know to what extent these words reflect his true opinion, and to what extent they were influenced by the delicate situation of a public sermon by the chief rabbi of Prague, a subject of the emperor, whose reform had been praised by Wessely, while the censor was certainly listening carefully" (*Ha-Ḥinnuk ha-Yehudi be-Germanyah,* p. 44).

17. B. Sanh 17a.

18. Having defended the edict, Landau moves to an attack against the Berlin Enlightenment by emphasizing the centrality of faith in Judaism. The sacrifices are the paradigm of faith, as no rational justification for them can be given.

"God helps those who want to become pure."[19] Abraham's mind led him to scorn the idols worshiped in his time, and he began to investigate with his reason. Then God appeared to him and helped him to prevail through his reason even in spheres that human reason cannot naturally comprehend. But after Abraham, successful inquiry was again impossible. Whatever is written about such matters is ephemeral, for one tears down what the other builds. If one problem is solved through philosophical inquiry, other new ones arise.[20]

The basis of all is faith. So we see that the Bible says of Abraham, *Because he believed in the Lord, He reckoned it to his merit* (Gen. 15:6). Of our ancestors in Egypt it is said, *The people believed* (Exod. 4:31). The root of our Torah is faith; we are not to investigate the traditions received from our ancestors. Of such rational inquiries I say *deep from hell* (Job 11:8), meaning that through them, people descend to the bottom level of hell, never to be worthy of beholding God's tenderness, neither in their lives nor after their deaths.[21]

Therefore, my brothers and friends, hear me, that you may live. To each and every one of you present I say, *Fear the Lord, my son, and the king, and do not mix with the unstable, for disaster comes from them suddenly, the doom of them both who can foreknow?* (Prov. 24:21–22). I admonish you to *Fear the Lord and the king,* to do the will of His Majesty our king, while remaining very careful to fear the Lord. For as you become accustomed to the language, you will also want to read books that are not aids in learning the language but philosophical inquiries pertaining to matters of Torah and faith, which may lead you to harbor doubts about the faith, God forbid![22] For whoever speaks

19. B. Shab 104a, B. Yoma 38b. Abraham is presented in this paragraph as a philosopher, who discovered God first through his own reason (see Maimonides, *Code,* I,iv (*ʿAKU"M*), 1:2, and the rabbinic sources on which it is based), then through God's help. But he is a unique figure, not a model for emulation.

20. Compare ibn Ḥazm's statement, "Every demonstration in support of a thesis of dogma is offset by another demonstration against it" (cited by Americo Castro, *The Spaniards* [Berkeley, 1971], p. 505), and Solomon ibn Adret, *Teshubot* (Bene Beraq, 1958), 1:5a, no. 9, on Plato and Aristotle.

21. The preacher plays on the phrase *ʿamuqqah mi-sheʾol,* rejecting the simple meaning ("deeper than Sheol") for the meaning "deep from hell."

22. The tightrope upon which the preacher is walking is apparent in this passage. On the one hand, he supports the learning of proper German; on the other, he is keenly aware of the danger that those who know German will read the works of German philosophers, whose speculation will lead them far from traditional Jewish belief. Landau's central criticism of Mendelssohn's translation of the Torah was his belief that it would attract Jews to study German language and literature (see Altmann, pp. 486–87, 381–83, 396–98). Indeed, Gutmann Klemperer, who drew some of his material about Landau from eyewitnesses, reported that "in a sermon on Sabbath Hagadol [Landau] pronounced a curse on Mendelssohn's translation of the Pentateuch and worked himself into such a state of excitement that his sable cap nearly fell from his head" ("The Rabbis of Prague," *Historia Judaica* 13 [1951]:62). Such a curse is not recorded in the extant texts of Landau's sermons. Cf., however, the attack by Eliezer Fleckeles in Fleckeles 2, sermon 1 (discussed by Altmann, p. 487).

and writes about matters of faith on the basis of reason cannot help but diminish that faith, which is the root of everything. It is the legacy of our sainted ancestors, from Abraham, peerless among the faithful. More than this, it is based upon the Torah of Moses, from the mouth of God, which should be as a high wall in your hearts.

Do not mix with those who are "unstable"—those who follow arbitrary whims, who cogitate and ponder with their confused intellects, darkening the religion of the Torah, whether they be Jews or from any other people, those who deny individual providence over the affairs of men, who deny the revelation of the Torah and supernatural miracles, who say that religion was not given by the Creator. Now because of our many sins, various strange sects have multiplied among our people, each different from the other—except in their common proclivity to undermine the perfect faith. It was about such sects that Solomon warned: *Do not mix with the unstable, for disaster comes from them suddenly, the doom of them both who can foreknow?* (Prov. 24:21–22). He was alluding to those sects that are alike in their capacity for evil.

But we, God's people, are obliged to sacrifice our lives for our sacred Torah, both the written Torah and the oral one. Whatever we are admonished in the Talmud must be equivalent in our minds to what is written in the Ten Commandments. What do we care if these sects mock us? We shall walk in the name of the Lord, in the path trodden by Alfasi and Maimonides and Rabbenu Asher and the Tosafists, who found bright light as they walked in the path of the Talmud, who had no interest in esoteric doctrines, yet were deemed worthy of eternal life. The foundation of all is faith![23]

In his wonderful epistle admonishing Jews to be prepared for martyrdom, our great teacher Maimonides wrote an interpretation of the verse, *No weapon formed against you shall succeed, every tongue that contends with you at law you shall defeat. This is the heritage of the Lord's servants* (Isa. 54:17). His interpretation was that many adventurers have attempted to drive us away from our religion. At first evil men reigned, and they arose against the Torah with weapons of war, putting to death those who observed it. Examples in this category are Nebuchadnezzar and his cohorts, and Haman. Many tragedies befell us in those early generations, but we endured them all, never repudiating the faith of our forefathers.

23. Isaac Alfasi (1013–1103), Asher ben Jeḥiel (1250–1327), and the Tosafists (French and German scholars of the twelfth and thirteenth centuries) were all outstanding authorities on the Talmud. In this powerful exhortation, it is quite striking that Landau includes Maimonides, preeminent both as a rabbinic scholar and as a philosopher, in the great Torah tradition worthy of emulation. The listener might well have perked up at this name, and the preacher now continues by citing Maimonides' "Epistle to Yemen"; cf. Abraham Halkin and David Hartman, eds., *Crisis and Leadership: Epistles of Maimonides* (Philadelphia, 1985), p. 97. Landau's criticism of Maimonides is kept for later.

Later there were good kings and rulers, who graciously allowed us to observe our Torah, but such philosophers as Aristotle and his colleagues wrote polemical books that heaped scorn upon the Torah and denied the miracles. Despite it all, we clung to our faith. This is the meaning of the verse. *No weapon formed against you shall succeed* refers to the first group that arose against the Torah with weapons. *Every tongue that contends with you at law* refers to the philosophers who contended with you, attempting by argument to refute whatever was inconsistent with nature. All will be pronounced guilty, and you will remain standing through the faith of the Torah, a tower of strength, a secret refuge from all harm.

The verse (Isa. 54:17) then indicates the source of power by which we prevail over these challenges. *This* refers to the Torah as in *This is the Torah which Moses set* (Deut. 4:44). *The heritage of the Lord's servants* informs us that this faith is indeed a heritage and a legacy from our forefathers. It is not derived from philosophical inquiry, which can be refuted and made to look foolish by a subsequent inquiry. No, it is our unending heritage, *the heritage of the Lord's servants. And their just reward,* which we have seen for the select few who fully understand this, such as our ancestor Abraham and the like, *is from Me, says the Lord* (Isa. 54:17), for the Holy One opens for them the gate of illumination, enabling them to know what natural reason cannot comprehend.

When our ancestors went forth from Egypt and received the Torah, they saw supernatural occurrences as miraculous signs: the dividing of the Reed Sea into two, the signs accompanying the manna and Mt. Sinai. Comprehending what they did, they could say, *This is my God, I will glorify Him*: truly my God. And we can say, *the God of my father, I will exalt Him* (Exod. 15:2), declare Him exalted above any blessing or praise.[24]

The basis of all is belief in the Creator: belief that He created everything according to His will, watches over it providentially at all times, rewards those who do His bidding, and punishes those who transgress it; that all that happens is part of His providence, that He gave us the Torah publicly in the sight of all Israel, and commanded Moses orally; that this was handed down by Moses until it reached the sages of the Mishnah and the Gemara, so that every word of the Talmud is to be considered as if it came from the Great Sanhedrin in the Chamber of Hewn Stone, and whoever doubts a single law of the Torah as fixed by the Talmud denies the Torah of Moses, which says *in accordance with the law which they shall teach you* (Deut. 17:11). All this must be constantly before your eyes and upon your hearts, for through

24. As with Abraham, Landau distinguishes between those who experienced God through miracles directly and those, including all of us, who must rely on tradition. He then goes on to specify the doctrines that he considers to be under attack, which for him make up the content of Jewish belief. Compare his sermon in *Derushe,* p. 40a.

this we shall be worthy of beholding God's tenderness, even if we never learn any esoteric teachings. Would that we might be worthy of understanding what has been revealed, and observing the commandments according to their simple meaning!

Of us in this generation, I say that "man is the tree of the field" and we are implements of wood: if they are flat, they are pure, but if they are hollow they are impure, for the intention makes them abhorrent.[25] Because of our many sins, we have among us the sect of Shabbetai Ẓevi, who transgress explicit statements of the Torah. They are like yeast with a high level of acidity, which makes one liable to excision from the community. There is also the sect of those who make every day into a holiday, constantly stuffing their bellies with all kinds of delicacies. They are like honey, sweet to the palate. Of the two groups, I say: *You must not turn into smoke any leaven or any honey as an offering by fire to the Lord* (Lev. 2:11).[26]

The root of all is faith in the Torah, the knowledge that even though we are ignorant of the reason for the commandments, we are not permitted to search for such reasons. We must be as careful with regard to a "minor" commandment as with the most serious, for we cannot comprehend how important such a "minor" commandment may be in the supernal realm.[27] The entire Torah, and all the commandments, are of supreme importance.

This is especially true with the study of Torah: every single utterance has its impact on high. You may say, "Are not the words we speak of a physical nature? How can they affect that which is purely spiritual?" Yet since this is what God commanded, it is His will that they have an effect on high. Therefore *life and death are in the power of the tongue* (Prov. 18:21). The same is true of the other commandments. Even though they are performed through physical instruments, the human limbs, all have an effect on high.

The proof of this is the sacrifices, as we have said above. Our great teacher Maimonides was too clever about this in the *Guide for the Perplexed*. His

25. A dense cluster of wordplays on traditional phrases that must have delighted the more learned in the audience. The rhetorical question in Deut. 20:19—*is the tree of a field a man?*—becomes a proposition (cf. B. Taʿan 7a; Moscato, *Nefuṣot Yehudah*, sermon 15; Pardo 1, fols. 74v and 76r; Elijah ha-Kohen of Izmir, *Shebeṭ Musar*, chap. 22). The law relating to the ritual purity of wooden implements is found in Kelim 2:1, but the phrase *peshuṭehen ṭehorim u-mequbbalehen ṭemeʾim*, which in the talmudic context refers to the shape of the implement, can also be translated, "their simple meanings are pure [see the end of the previous paragraph], but their kabbalists are impure." The final phrase, *be-maḥashebet piggul*, is taken from B. Zeb 109a.

26. Another rhetorical flourish, in which humor is used for a polemical end. The second group apparently refers to the Hasidim of the Baal Shem Tov; the phrases used by Landau were common in the early anti-Hasidic writings. On this passage, see Piekarz, p. 337. In an earlier sermon, Landau speaks of the "Sabbatians" and the "philosophers" as the two most dangerous groups (*Derushe*, p. 40a).

27. Cf. Abot 2:1.

explanation of the reason for the sacrifices was as follows: since the Israelites in Egypt participated enthusiastically in idolatrous worship and were accustomed to sacrificing to idols, they would never have accepted the Torah had God in His revelation prohibited sacrifices entirely. They simply assumed that sacrifices bring man closer to God. Therefore, in order to prevent the people from sacrificing to goats, God ordained that sacrifices be made to Him.

Naḥmanides, however, wrote a decisive refutation of this. How could Maimonides explain the ox sacrificed by Adam on the day of his creation, which was willingly accepted by God, as the Bible says, *That will please the Lord more than an ox* (Ps. 69:32)? Or the offering of Abel, which the Holy One received respectfully (Gen. 4:4)? These sacrifices were certainly in themselves of supreme importance.[28]

Now since human intellect cannot comprehend the effect of this on high, you might say, "How can I perform an action with my limbs, which are all physical, and expect that this will have an effect on the spiritual realm?" Yet the action itself is not fundamental, but rather the will and the desire and the heart's joy in the performance of a commandment. It is this joy in performing the will of our Heavenly Father that is spiritual.

We may find an allusion to this in the mnemonic given near the end of the tractate Megillah [31a] for the scriptural readings on this sacred festival: *Meshok tora, qaddesh be-kaspa, pesol be-midbara, shelaḥ bukra.*[29] *Meshok* refers to the first commandment given us by God in Egypt, *Pick out* [mishku] *and take yourselves lambs* (Exod. 12:21). You must not say that this is not of supreme importance but is intended only to attract you away from idolatry, as Maimonides maintained. It is not so. Rather, even though you have already observed the commandment to draw your hand away from idolatry, and you no longer participate enthusiastically in idolatrous worship, you must still *take yourselves lambs for the Passover offering,* for the sacrifices are in themselves of supreme importance. The proof of this is in the *tora,* the "ox" sacrificed by Adam, following the argument of Naḥmanides.

Lest you say, "How can physical actions have an effect on the spiritual realm on high?" it is said, *qaddesh be-kaspa,* "sanctify through desire," as in the verse *niksefah . . . nafshi, I long, I yearn for the courts of the Lord* (Ps. 84:3). For through arduous desire one may sanctify oneself below and become sanctified on high, where *my heart and my flesh* are equivalent, for the heart burns with a flaming desire, and then *they sing for joy [to the living God]* (Ps. 84:3).

28. See Maimonides, *Guide* 3:46, and Naḥmanides' commentary on Gen. 4:3 and Lev. 1:9. (For the "ox sacrificed by Adam," see B. Shab 28b.) Compare Landau's sermon for the first day of the penitential period in 1761 (*Ahabat Ṣiyyon,* p. 3b).

29. As he nears the end of his sermon, Landau returns to the occasion. The mnemonic consists of key words (in pairs with a Hebrew imperative and an Aramaic noun) from Exod. 12:21, Lev. 22:27, Exod. 13:2, Exod. 22:24, Exod. 34:1, Num. 9:1, Exod. 13:17, and Deut. 15:19, but the preacher reinterprets them in accordance with his message.

Pesol be-midbara refers to the tablets on which were written the Ten Utterances, containing hints of the entire written and oral Torah. This is why there were two, standing for the written and the oral. Thus the word *pesol,* "hew" which refers to the tablets, was also *be-midbara,* "with speech," namely, the oral Torah given through speech from God to Moses on Sinai. Now in our times there are many Jews who reject the words of the sages and set out intentionally to keep their children from the oral Torah. I warn you, children: do not consent to hear of such a thing from anyone.

I do not suspect that the *Normallehrer* would do such an evil thing and utter such falsehoods, God forbid![30] This would be against the desire of the exalted government, which established the position solely for the purpose of teaching children language, writing, mathematics, ethical behavior, and etiquette, and not to speak calumnies against our religion. If in any town or city such a teacher should be found transgressing in this matter and acting with duplicity, pay him no heed whatsoever.

Hear me, my fine children: take what is good from them, but if you should discover in them something not good, do not follow in their path. *Shelaḥ bukra,* "send away the firstborn," namely, the evil impulse, which is the firstborn, present in each person in varying degrees from birth, while the good impulse arrives only at the age of bar mitzvah.[31] Send away the firstborn, and bring near that impoverished child, the impulse toward good.

I now return to the commandment of the day. On this festival, we went forth to freedom of body and soul, and God sanctified us through His commandments. This Sabbath, called "the Great Sabbath," is a reminder of the Sabbath of creation, and a reminder of the redemption to come, which will truly be a Great Sabbath, a day that is entirely Sabbath and rest, if we too will sanctify ourselves through Torah and commandments. It can happen today, if we would but hearken to His voice.[32] May we soon be worthy of the full redemption, when we shall eat of the sacrifices and the Passover offerings, and a redeemer will have come to Zion. Amen.

30. *Normallehrer* refers to the teachers in the schools the Jews were to establish at government order to provide Jewish children with a German civic education. See Kestenberg-Gladstein, *Neuere Geschichte,* pp. 39–45.

31. *ARN* 16 (=YJS 10:83).

32. Cf. B. Sanh 98a and its use of Ps. 95:7.

Sources for the History and Theory of
Jewish Preaching

1. *The Chronicle of Ahimaaz*[1] (Mid-eleventh century, Italy)

By the grace of God, who formed the earth with His power, who forgives iniquity and sin, I will mention the incident that occurred at Venosa.[2] A man had come from the land of Israel, profoundly learned in God's Torah, a master of wisdom. He remained there for some time. Every Sabbath he would give instruction and expound the Torah before the community of God's people. The master would discourse on the lesson from the Torah, and R. Silano would then elucidate.[3] Then one day, men came in wagons from the villages to the city. They began to quarrel among themselves. Some women came out of their houses, carrying long staves charred by the fire, used for raking the oven. With these the men and women beat one another.

R. Silano, in a mistaken spirit of levity, resolved to make use of the incident, and committed a great wrong. He took the homily on the scriptural lesson that the scholar was to expound on that Sabbath, erased two lines of what was written, and wrote the story told above in their place. This is what

1. The Chronicle of Ahimaaz records the local history of a family of Jewish scholars, liturgical poets, and statesmen who flourished in southern Italy. It was written in rhymed Hebrew prose in the middle of the eleventh century. The event described here can be dated in the ninth century. See Benjamin Klar, *Megillat Aḥimaʿaṣ* (Jerusalem, 1974), and *The Chronicle of Ahimaaz,* trans. and ed. Marcus Salzman (New York, 1966). (My translation of the passage is based on Salzman's but modifies it at several key points.) On the work as a whole see *The Dark Ages,* ed. Cecil Roth (New Brunswick, N.J., 1966), pp. 102–08, 250–53; Baron, *SRHJ* 6:216–17; and the bibliography listed by Robert Bonfil, "Tra due mondi," *Italia Judaica* (Rome, 1983), p. 137, n. 5.

2. On this passage, see Baron, *SRHJ* 6:156, 400; Bonfil, "Tra due mondi," p. 139, and n. 14. Bonfil suggests that the joke of introducing alien material into a text to be read in public was a medieval literary topos. For example, it is reported that once, as a practical joke, the emperor Henry II deleted the first two letters of the words *famulis* and *famulabus* in the missal used by Bishop Meinwerk of Paderborn, so that the bishop read *mulis* and *mulabus,* not "grant forgiveness of sins to Your servants," but "grant forgiveness of sins to Your mules" (*Vita Meinwerci Episcopi Patherbrunnensis,* ed. Franz Tenckhoff [Hanover, 1921], pp. 106–07); cf. James Thompson, *The Literacy of the Laity in the Middle Ages* (New York, 1960), p. 84.

3. The master would *doresh,* and R. Silano would *mefaresh.* Goitein understands this to mean that a sermon would be given in Hebrew and then translated by the local rabbi; he notes that no evidence of such a practice has been found in the Genizah documents (*Ḥinnuk,* p. 131; cf. *EJ* 14:1532, which goes on to misrepresent the episode). However, Silano could not have been merely translating into a language that the people could understand, for his joke would have been pointless unless the people could understand the text as read by the guest scholar. The guest from the land of Israel was apparently using a written text that he considered authoritative; hence his reluctance to depart from it. He was probably reporting midrashic traditions, in which the Palestinian sages were expert, and Silano's role was to explain this material (possibly in the vernacular) and perhaps to develop it into a sermon. The discovery of a midrashic passage that might have been modified into the words surreptitiously inserted would elucidate Silano's wit.

R. Silano inserted: "The men came [to the city] in wagons. The women came from their houses and beat the men with staves."

On the Sabbath, as the scholar came upon these words, he stopped reading and all speech failed him. He looked at the letters and scrutinized, examined, pondered, and went over them several times. Finally, in his naiveté, he read them, using the words he found written as part of his instruction. Then R. Silano, in mocking laughter, said to the assembled congregation, "Listen to the master's discourse on the quarrel that occurred among you yesterday, when the women beat the men, striking them with oven staves and driving them off all around."

When the master realized what had been done, he became very pallid and faint. He hurried to his colleagues, who were in the schoolhouse engaged in study, and told them of the dreadful experience he had just undergone. They were all deeply pained and distressed, and they placed the clever R. Silano under the ban.

2. Moses ben Maimon (Maimonides) (End of twelfth century, Egypt)

a. *Question*:[1] What would our master Moses, eminent rabbi in Israel, son of R. Maimon . . . say in the following matter? On the Sabbath of [the lesson] *Wa-Yera* (Gen. 18–22), the head of the congregation[2] came to the august sanctuary built for the remnant of Israel in the city of Cairo. The judge Abū al-Ḥakam and many scholars . . . were present at this ceremonial gathering. When the cantor had finished the Eighteen Benedictions, before the sacred Torah was taken out, the head of the congregation, God protect him, gave a discourse of religious content to the congregation, as he is accustomed to do.[3] He began with the fundamentals of the faith, supporting the points made concerning the weekly lesson with other verses from the sacred Torah and with quotations from the prophets and the sages, adducing proofs for his ideas in the manner of the exegetes and the preachers.[4]

1. *Teshubot ha-RaMBaM*, ed. Joshua Blau (Jerusalem, 1957), pp. 189–91.

2. "Head of the congregation" follows Blau's translation of the Arabic *al-ra'īs*; Goitein understands this to refer to the judge (*dayyan*) of Cairo (*Ḥinnuk*, p. 132; cf. *A Mediterranean Society*, vol. 2, *The Community* [Berkeley and Los Angeles, 1971], pp. 27–34).

3. On the sermon preceding the reading of the Torah, see the discussion above in "The Preaching Situation." This text would fit the theory propounded by Joseph Heinemann ("The Proem in the Aggadic Midrashim: A Form-Critical Study," *Studies in Aggadah and Folk Literature* [Scripta Hierosolymitana 22] [Jerusalem, 1971], pp. 100–22) that the sermon was an introduction to the reading of the Torah lesson.

4. "In the manner of . . . preachers" indicates the prevalence of preaching and the existence of a common homiletical tradition at this time, despite the absence of sermon texts. Note also Maimonides' answer, referring to "things that preachers routinely say."

Then, while the head of the congregation was discussing fundamentals of the faith, Master Solomon, known by the name al-Jabalī, said to him in front of everyone, "How long will this delirium last? All you have said is nonsense; it should not be heard, it cannot be understood!" He referred to the words of God as nonsense! The others were in an uproar over this, saying, "We have never heard or seen anyone act in such a reprehensible manner," for it was a public insult to our sacred faith. Attached to this question is the text of what the head of the congregation said, just as it was,[5] so that you may examine it and determine whether such a reaction was required, and whether one who said such things is required by law to be punished or excommunicated, and what his culpability is regarding the officer whom he publicly insulted. Your heavenly reward will be double.

Answer: In all that has been told there is no indication that the sermon contained anything worthy of reproach. These are things that preachers routinely say. If there is nothing more than what has been noted, the critic has very grievously transgressed by humiliating another person in public without cause. If this critic were not himself a scholar, we would say some very unpleasant things about him and specify his liability.

However, since he is known for his piety and wisdom, it is improper to speak about him until he himself is heard, for the sacred Torah requires us to honor scholars and give them the benefit of the doubt and to overlook the errors and mistakes that they may make, as is well known to the pious and the wise. Therefore I advise that if the aggrieved party consents, you overlook the punishment requested in this query. If not, he should go to trial with his opponent and be judged in a court of law, so that the response of the accused may be heard, if he so desires. This is what Moses has written.

b. The worst offenders are preachers who preach and expound to the masses what they themselves do not understand. Would that they kept silent about what they do not know, as the Biblical verse indicates: *If only they would be utterly silent, it would be accounted to them as wisdom* (Job 13:5). Or they might at least say, "We do not understand what our sages intended in this statement, and we do not know how to explain it." But they believe they do understand, and they vigorously expound to the people what they think rather than what the sages really said. They therefore give lectures to the people on the tractate Berakot and on the present chapter ["Ḥeleq" of tractate Sanhedrin] and other texts, expounding them word for word according to their literal meanings.[6]

5. The "text" sent to Maimonides is not known to be extant. It was apparently prepared before the sermon rather than written afterward, since its value as evidence would have been suspect if it had been written from memory at the end of the Sabbath.

6. Compare Isadore Twersky, *A Maimonides Reader* (New York, 1972), p. 408. The passage is significant in confirming the widespread practice of preaching, pointing to the aggadah

c. Twenty-four things hinder repentance. . . . Among these there are five offenses that close the paths of repentance to those who commit them. . . . Fifth is the offense of those who hate rebuke, since they do not leave themselves a path to repentance, for it is rebuke that brings about repentance. When people are told of their faults and thereby put to shame, they repent. We see this from what is written in the Torah: *Remember, never forget . . . you have continued defiant* (Deut. 9:7); *The Lord has not given you a mind to understand* (Deut. 29:3); *O dull and witless people!* (Deut. 32:6).

Thus too Isaiah rebuked Israel and said, *Ah, sinful nation! . . .* (Isa. 1:4); *The ox knows its owner. . .* (Isa. 1:3); *Because I know how stubborn you are* (Isa. 48:4). And indeed God commanded him to rebuke sinners, as it is said, *Cry aloud, without restraint* (Isa. 58:1). Similarly, all the prophets rebuked Israel until they repented. Hence it is necessary to appoint in every community a great scholar, advanced in years, God-fearing from his youth, and beloved by the people, to rebuke the multitude and cause them to repent.[7] But those who hate rebukes will not go to the exhorter nor hear his words, and they will therefore persist in their sins, which seem good to them.

3. Sources from the Conflict over the Study of Philosophy[1] (1302–05, southern France and Aragon)

a. The heresy has reached such a point that one of those preachers misled by the intellect loudly proclaimed that anyone who believes that the sun stood

as an important component of its content, and identifying the literal interpretation of aggadah in sermons as leading to contempt for the sages. Note that the sources in section 3, below, agree on the first and second points, but identify the problem as the opposite of what is criticized here: not literal interpretation, but far-fetched allegorical interpretation, of the aggadah.

7. This prescriptive conclusion, affirming an obligation on the part of each community to appoint a preacher of rebuke and outlining a job description, is not identified by the standard commentaries as based on any rabbinic statement. It appears to flow from the inner logic of the passage, including the assumption of continuity between the critical orations of the prophets and the ethical and religious rebukes of contemporary preachers. It may also have reflected the long-standing practice of the Jewish communities (see Dinur, p. 133, n. 12). The passage was cited by subsequent writers; see, e.g., Pukhovitser, below.

1. On the history of this conflict, see Baer, *HJCS* 1:289–305; Joseph Sarachek, *Faith and Reason* (Williamsport, Pa., 1935), pp. 73–127; Abraham Halkin, "Yedaiah Bedershi's Apology," *Jewish Medieval and Renaissance Studies,* ed. Alexander Altmann (Cambridge, Mass., 1967), pp. 165–84; Charles Touati, "La Controverse de 1303–1306 autour des études philosophiques et scientifiques," *REJ* 127 (1968):21–37; Joseph Shatzmiller, "Ben Abba Mari le-Rashba," *Meḥqarim be-Toledot ʿAm Yiśraʾel we-ʾEreṣ Yiśraʾel* 3 (1974):121–37. In the literature of this controversy, there are many accusations about preachers and sermons based on hearsay; I have included here sources that purport to be based on firsthand evidence.

still for Joshua is simply wrong, a fool who believes in what is impossible. Concerning the voice heard at Sinai, such slander was uttered that all who hear it would have to rend their garments, and all who repeat it would need to make atonement.[2] We have heard many such things about these pernicious men who have all but stripped the Torah of its simple meaning, leaving it naked and bare.

b. It was written and sealed with the seal of the congregational leaders to silence the preachers and to keep them from speaking a word, because some of them perverted the meaning of the Torah, addressing prayer to false gods. However, the other group here in Montpellier did not agree at that time with our position. . . .[3]

Then one day, at the wedding of one of the leading families in the city, an important notable gave a speech containing things painful to hear.[4] He said that Abraham and Sarah in the Bible were form and matter.[5] Upon the section from Abraham's leaving of Haran to *He favored Abraham for her sake* (Gen. 12:4–16) he built a silvery tower, which we considered pernicious. He linked this with the aggadah of R. Bena'ah (B. BB 58a), which he explained at length, interpreting the entire episode in a philosophical manner.[6] Now all was in an uproar over this speaker. . . .

2. The miracle of the sun "standing still" in Josh. 10 was particularly troubling for the Jewish philosophers, since it implied an interference in the perpetual motion of the heavenly bodies. Apparently this preacher's position was similar to that later defended by Gersonides in his commentary on Josh. 10:12 (possibly justified by an ambiguous passage in Maimonides' *Guide* 2:25). As for the voice heard at Sinai, the "heretical" view may have been similar to the one attested (but not endorsed) by Maimonides in his letter to Ḥasdai ha-Levi: that the voice used by God to communicate with Moses was inaudible and present only in the mind of Moses.

3. The attempt to control the pulpit and restrict the incorporation into sermons of unsuitable doctrines was an important theme in this controversy; see sects. e, f, and g, below. Compare the experience of Jacob Anatoli, forced to abandon his weekly preaching because of opposition within the congregation.

4. The preacher is identified as an important and influential Jew but not as a rabbi or a distinguished scholar. For weddings as occasions for preaching, see above, "The Preaching Occasion"; cf. sect. f, below.

5. On the allegorical interpretation of man and woman as form and matter, see *Guide* 1:17 and Saperstein, *Decoding,* pp. 60–62.

6. The aggadah states that R. Bena'ah came to the burial cave of the patriarchs and was told by Abraham's servant, Eliezer, that Abraham was sleeping in the arms of Sarah, who was looking fondly at his head. To the Jewish philosophers committed to traditional literature, this passage obviously needed an allegorical interpretation to replace the plain meaning of the words. The critical question is whether the same allegorical interpretation, applied to Gen. 12:4–16, was intended to replace the plain meaning—thereby undermining the historicity of the patriarchal narratives—or merely to supplement it with a deeper level. The defenders of philosophy insisted that no one rejected the plain meaning of Abraham's exploits as recounted

Had I not seen it, I would not have believed it, but I was there, sitting next to him on the platform as he said these things. When he finished speaking, I waxed angry. . . . Yet our complaint was not about the figurative treatment of the aggadah—this was not so important—but rather about the figurative treatment of a verse from the Torah, which should not have been spoken even privately, certainly not before an entire congregation.

c. I inform you about one of the leading men of our city. We were in the synagogue on the Sabbath of [the lesson] of *Balaq* (Num. 22:2–25:9). The cantor read the verse *u-qesamim be-yadam* (22:7), and I explained that these were instruments of divination, such as the astrolabe, and other such instruments used for astrological and astronomical purposes.[7] He was astonished at this and said that my words were most surprising—as if I had said something forbidden in linking the astrolabe with the *kele qesem*—and that the astrolabe was an instrument used by our sages in determining the new moon. I responded. . . .

d. Many of the congregation, from the family of R. Jacob [Anatoli], gathered on the Sabbath of [the lesson] *Parah* (Num. 19:1–22:1), before the afternoon service, and read from the *Malmad*. . . .[8]

e. In addition, you should ban whoever removes the stories of the Torah or the commandments from their simple meaning, whether in their sermons or in written works undermining the tradition of the sages, from this day on. If certain leaders of your community should not agree to this, do it through your rabbinical court in order to set the Torah right, and send us a sealed document signed by your communal leaders. We will then try to do as you have done.

f. You should add to your ordinance that even those who are wise and mature must not preach using material from physics or metaphysics at a wedding celebration, nor speak about such matters before the masses at all, lest they praise what is a worthless coin. Let them speak of it only in the presence of those who are expert in Torah.

---

in the Bible: see Yedaiah ha-Penini in Adret's *She'elot u-Teshubot* 1, no. 418 (Bene Beraq, 1958):159a–60a; Halkin, "Yedaiah Bedershi's Apology," pp. 166–67.

7. On the astrolabe, see Solomon Gandz, "The Astrolabe in Jewish Literature," *Studies in Hebrew Astronomy and Mathematics* (New York, 1970), pp. 245–62. It is not clear whether Abba Mari's remarks were a formal sermon or merely an explication of the Torah lesson, but they clearly followed the Torah reading.

8. Note the evidence that chapters from Anatoli's *Malmad ha-Talmidim* were occasionally read in public in place of an original sermon. On the use of the hour before the Sabbath afternoon service for homiletical purposes, see above, "The Preaching Situation."

g. We consider it disgraceful that ignorant men, with no expertise either in Bible or in the rabbinic tradition, are always getting up to preach publicly, teaching things improper, interpreting simple biblical verses in far-fetched figurative ways. But these ordinances of ours [banning the study of philosophy by anyone under twenty-five] do not help us at all. For the preachers do not preach from Aristotle's *Physics,* or *De caelo,* or *De meteoris,* or *De generatione et corruptione,* or *De sensu et sensibile,* or *De anima,* or the *Metaphysics.*[9] Indeed, some of them do not know even a single page of these books. They know only what they have read in [Maimonides'] *Guide,* or in [Anatoli's] *Malmad,* or in [Samuel ibn Tibbon's] commentary on Ecclesiastes or his treatise *Yiqqawu ha-Mayim,* and other such works. They find there some figurative interpretations and do their work with them. . . .

This is the ever-present perversion, an evil renewed for thousands every day. These preachers now constitute a sect; they sing their song and go their way. But we have seized upon a problem that does not exist, the danger of which is far-fetched. The real danger is not addressed by our ordinance, despite the need for a great effort.[10] I would not repudiate these preachers completely. Rather, I would give them permission to interpret figuratively to their hearts' content verses from Job, Proverbs, Song of Songs, Ecclesiastes, and the rabbinic homilies related to their content, and certain Psalms relevant to the physical sciences. But they must not touch upon the "three chariots" (Isa. 6, Ezek. 1 and 8) or the work of Creation (Gen. 1), or any of the secrets of the Torah, or prophecy, or esoteric doctrines, or any of the aggadot pertaining to these matters.

4. Solomon Alami, *Iggeret Musar*[1] (Early fifteenth century, Spain)

Look what happens when a congregation gathers to hear words of Torah from a rabbinical scholar. Slumber weighs upon the eyes of the officers; others

9. These Aristotelian works had all been translated into Hebrew during the second half of the thirteenth century and were therefore available to Jewish intellectuals unable to read Arabic. Menaḥem Meiri's argument here confirms that the preachers at issue, unlike Anatoli or the Christian Scholastic preachers, were not competent in technical philosophy. Infatuated with the philosophical weltanschauung, they derived their approach to the Bible and rabbinic aggadot from popular Jewish texts and extended it further. (For a similar type, see Saperstein, *Decoding,* pp. 89, 210.) The mid-fifteenth-century text of ibn Mūsā (translated below) provides a striking contrast.

10. Note Meiri's reference to a class of peripatetic preachers lacking deep roots in Jewish society. He agrees about the need for control over what is said from the pulpit, but differs from his opponents on the method.

1. Compare Nahum Glatzer, *Faith and Knowledge* (Boston, 1963), pp. 121–27. On Alami and his work, see Baer, *HJCS* 2:239–42. On talking and sleeping during sermons, see above,

converse about trivial affairs. The preacher is dumbfounded by the talking of men and the chattering of women standing behind the synagogue. If he should reproach them because of their behavior, they continue to sin, behaving corruptly, abominably. This is the opposite of the Christians. When their men and women gather to hear a preacher, they stand together in absolute silence, marveling at his rebuke. Not one of them dozes as he pours out his words upon them. They await him as they do the rain, eager for the waters of his counsel. We have not learned properly from those around us.

5. Ḥayyim ibn Mūsā, "Letter to His Son"[1] (Mid-fifteenth century, Spain)

Letter sent to his firstborn son, the sage R. Judah, responding to a preacher who preached that R. Hillel said in tractate Sanhedrin, "There is no Messiah for Israel" [99a], without explaining R. Hillel's true meaning.[2]

My son . . . , I have heard from many the disturbing report concerning the preacher who spoke in your city about the aforementioned view of R. Hillel, and who noted also that R. Hillel continued, "[the Jewish people] already enjoyed [the messianic age] at the time of Hezekiah." As the preacher did not explain the meaning of this statement, many in the congregation were perplexed, and there was strife among the people.

Our complaint is against the preachers—may God sustain those who are inwardly upright and good. But as for those who turn onto crooked paths, who consider themselves wise and clever, but are evil speakers of perversion, philosophizers who have long led Israel astray—may God lead them into the power of the inimical angels of Samael.

Once in my youth I heard a preacher speak, using the technique of philosophical investigation, about the unity of God. Several times he said, "If God is not one, then such and such must necessarily follow [leading to a reductio ad absurdum]. Finally one of the leaders of the synagogue, a deeply religious man, rose and said, "They seized all of my property in the massacres

"Preachers and Congregations." A similarly positive view of contemporary Christian preaching is expressed by Joseph ibn Shem Ṭob and Isaac Arama in the texts translated below. Pointing to Christian neighbors as a positive model worthy of Jewish emulation was not unusual in Jewish ethical and homiletical literature; cf. the sermon by Jonathan Eybeschuetz, above, n. 31.

1. Cf. Baer, *HJCS* 2:253–54, where the passage is erroneously identified as coming from ibn Mūsā's polemical work *Magen wa-Romaḥ*.

2. The statement of R. Hillel was a classical crux for medieval Jewish thinkers; cf. Saperstein, *Decoding*, p. 110. Here the problem is not one of allegorical interpretation but of failure to interpret what requires explanation. Cf. Maimonides' attack (above, sect. 2b) on preachers who expound passages from chapter *Ḥeleq* of Sanhedrin according to their simple meaning.

of Seville [in 1391]; they beat me and covered me with wounds until they left me for dead. All this I endured through my faith in *Hear, O Israel, the Lord our God, the Lord is One* (Deut. 6:4). Now you come upon the tradition of our ancestors with your philosophical investigation, saying, 'If God is not One, such and such must follow!' I believe more in the tradition of our ancestors, and I have no desire to hear this sermon." With that, he walked out of the synagogue, and most of the congregation followed.[3] Even though Maimonides engaged in this kind of analysis, his purpose was to argue against the Gentiles, not to preach it to the congregation.

I have also seen one of the preachers—renowned as one of the most learned in the realm—who homiletically interpreted the entire lesson beginning *You shall be holy* (Lev. 19:2) in a figurative manner. In the middle of his sermon he said, "*Et shabbetotai tishmoru* [lit., "You shall keep My Sabbaths"] (Lev. 19:3) means 'My insignificant things,' *las mis cosas baldías,*" heaven help us! I had some words with him, and I criticized all that he said, especially this interpretation. He replied that Rashi had said the same thing on the first verse of the lesson *ʿEqeb* (Deut. 7:12): "the lesser commandments that people trample underfoot." I said, "There is no comparison. That homiletical interpretation is appropriate there, but it is heretical here." We argued at great length.[4]

I have also seen students disputing each other in their sermons, speaking about matters alien to our tradition. This occurred in the presence of the esteemed rabbi Don Abraham Benveniste, may he be remembered for life in the world to come.[5] Two young talmudic scholars preached this way, using figurative interpretations so provocative that the rabbi arose and castigated their dispute, quoting, *I am peace, but when I speak they are for war* (Ps. 120:7). He then said to the congregation, "My brothers, children of Abraham, believe that when the Bible says *In the beginning God created* (Gen. 1:1) or *Jacob left Beersheba* (Gen. 26:10), it is to be understood in its simple meaning. Believe

3. On the 1391 massacres in Seville, see Baer, *HJCS* 2:94–97. This preacher, who must have been active around the year 1400, is criticized not for the content of his message (the unity of God) but for using in his sermon philosophical argumentation to demonstrate a fundamental principle of Jewish belief. Cf. the "reincarnation" of this story in a Hasidic context, recounted by Hillel Halkin, *Letters to an American Jewish Friend* (Philadelphia, 1977), p. 109.

4. The Spanish citation in the middle of the Hebrew text is apparently an attempt to report precisely what was said, and is evidence for vernacular preaching; see "The Preaching Situation," above. As in the preceding episode, the problem is not the substance but the method, in this case, the interpretation of the word *shabbetotai* in Lev. 19:3. Presumably, the distinction drawn by the author would have been that Rashi's interpretation of Deut. 7:12 was occasioned by the unusual use of *ʿeqeb,* while there is no problem with the plain meaning of *shabbetotai.*

5. Benveniste was a courtier and scholar who held the government position of "Rab de la Corte" under King John II of Castile; see Baer, *HJCS* 2:250, 259–70.

also in all that is written in the Torah, and what the rabbis explained in accordance with their tradition. Do not believe those who provocatively speak of alien matters."

Truly, my son, even worse sinners than these are the ones who preach about aggadot that were not intended for public discussion, whether the hyperboles, such as the account of Og, who uprooted a mountain three parasangs high [B. Ber 54b], or the tales of Rabbah bar bar Ḥana [B. BB 73a–74b], or statements of esoteric truth. They quote such statements according to their simple meaning, thereby engendering contempt for the sages among the idlers.[6]

Now there is a new type of preacher. They rise to the lectern to preach before the reading of the Torah, and most of their sermons consist of syllogistic arguments and quotations from the philosophers.[7] They mention by name Aristotle, Alexander, Themistius, Plato, Averroës, and Ptolemy,[8] while Abbaye and Raba are concealed in their mouths. The Torah waits upon the reading stand like a dejected woman who had prepared herself properly by ritual immersion and awaited her husband; then, returning from the house of his mistress, he glanced at her and left without paying her further heed.

We should say the mourner's prayer over this entire situation. . . . Happy is the one who shuts his eyes and does not see them, who stops up his ears and does not hear their evil words. It should be enough for them to begin with a biblical verse or a rabbinic dictum, to incorporate the obvious meaning of biblical verses and rabbinic statements into words of ethical import, and

6. This is similar to Maimonides' complaint (above, sect. 2b). The rabbinic account of the mountain hurled by Og, ridiculed by Petrus Alfonsi in *Dialogi* (*PL* 157:565–66), was interpreted by various commentators, including Solomon Adret, *Ḥiddushe ha-Rashba ʿal Aggadot ha-Shas* (Jerusalem, 1966), pp. 58–61, and Shem Ṭob ibn Shapruṭ, *Pardes Rimmonim* (Sabionetta, 1554; reprint ed., Jerusalem, 1968), p. 42b. The stories of Rabbah bar bar Ḥana inspired the ingenuity of generations of exegetes and preachers; see Saperstein, *Decoding*, p. 231, n. 33, and the sermon by Moscato, above.

7. On preaching before the reading of the Torah, cf. the question addressed to Maimonides, above, sect. 2, n. 3. For examples of the use of syllogisms in sermons (from the end of the fifteenth century), see Israel, "Dober Mesharim," fol. 191; Aboab, p. 23a; Joel ibn Shueib, p. 105a–b. On Christian preaching "secundum formam sillogisticam," see Owst, *Preaching*, p. 327; Rouse, *Preachers*, pp. 191–94.

8. These philosophers were apparently cited from Hebrew translations of their works. Aristotle's *Ethics* was quoted in fifteenth-century Spanish Jewish preaching (Zerahiah ha-Levi, p. 100; Joel ibn Shueib, p. 105a–b; Shem Ṭob, pp. 5d, 15a, 21c, 59d, 74c, 82a, and elsewhere). Joseph ibn Shem Ṭob cited Aristotle's *De anima*, *Physics*, *Metaphysics*, and *De sensu et sensibile* (*Derashot*, fols. 189v–190r). Perhaps the most striking example is Aboab, p. 32d, citing Aquinas' discussion of Averroës on Aristotle's *Metaphysics*, apparently drawn from Abraham ibn Naḥmias' translation into Hebrew of Aquinas' *Commentary* on the *Metaphysics*. (That a Spanish Jewish preacher would cite Averroës from Aquinas shows that much had changed since the fourteenth century!)

to speak of the laws relating to the Sabbath and the festivals.[9] If they proudly bring appropriate principles from the sciences, provided they are not harmful and do not corrupt faith or divert the heart of a single member of the congregation into thinking improper thoughts, this is all right.

6. Joseph ibn Shem Ṭob, "ʿEn ha-Qore"[1] (Mid-fifteenth century, Spain)

a. The fourth part explains the meaning of the simile *like a shofar raise your voice* (Isa. 58:1).[2] Do not think that this refers to projecting the voice loudly; that is already implied in the first part of the verse, "Cry aloud," so that such a meaning here would be redundant and superfluous. I think, rather, that there are three aspects of this comparison: first, the purpose of the sound of the shofar; second, its time; and third, the different kinds of sounds. A sermon is related to all three.

First, the purpose in the sounding of the shofar is to make the hearts of sinners quake. The prophet said, *When a shofar is sounded in the town, do the people not take alarm?* (Amos 3:6), showing clearly that its effect is to instill fear. In tractate Rosh Hashanah [16b], the rabbis said, "Why do they blow when the people are sitting, and then blow again while they are standing? In order to confuse the prosecutor [*śaṭan*]." So the sermon should be such that it instills fear and awakens the hearts of sinners, so that they will return to God and be forgiven.

Second, the sounding of the shofar is appropriate at one particular time: on the New Year's Day and on the Day of Atonement. Similarly, the sermon must conform with the occasion and its theme. In this way it will be appropriate, and its benefit will be received. The sages said, "On a holiday, one should preach about the theme of the holiday"; in tractate Megillah they said, "We choose a prophetic reading related to the theme of the Torah lesson."[3]

9. On the fluidity of form in mid-fifteenth-century Spanish Jewish preaching, see "Structural Options," above.

1. On the author, see the introduction to his sermon, above. Note the comment of Isaac Rabinowitz on *ʿEn ha-Qore*: "That this theoretical and perceptual treatise . . . remains to be critically edited and published speaks eloquently of modern scholarly neglect of the department of rhetoric more practised by Jewish speakers and writers than any other, namely homiletics and preaching" (Rabinowitz, p. 140).

2. Isa. 58:1 became a favorite topos of Jewish preachers, enabling them to assert a continuity between their task and that of the prophets. See, below, Ephraim Luntshitz (sect. 11d), Zerah Eidlitz (sect. 16) and, for a more general treatment, Saperstein, "Shofar." Much of Abravanel's comment on this verse is taken directly (without attribution) from this passage by his teacher. Cf. also the sermon on repentance by the author's son, Shem Ṭob ibn Shem Ṭob, p. 87b–c.

3. Cf. B. Meg 4a, 23a, and 31a.

Most of the preachers of our generation err in this respect, for I have not seen them preach sermons related either to the theme of the day or to the audience.[4] In my judgment, it is proper that on every Sabbath throughout the year the sermon be related to the theme of the Torah and prophetic reading, and on the festivals it should be about the theme of the festival. On the ten days between the New Year's Day and the Day of Atonement, sermons should always relate to the nature of this period, namely, sin and the healing of souls. I praise this approach, unless there is a reason against it, such as a newly arising matter which requires a novel sermon outside the framework of the biblical chapters. . . .

One of the most desirable qualities in a preacher is the ability to observe the kind of audience before him and to speak for a length of time that will not cause them to grow weary of the sermon, for if they do, the desired benefit will not accrue. We are indeed guilty in this matter. The sentences issuing from our mouths are sweet to our palate, and we are therefore not conscious of whether the sermon is long or short, or if the air is cold or hot, nor are we hungry or thirsty. We think that the same is true for those in the congregation who hear us! We therefore become a burden upon the community, and we are led to other errors as well. This often happens to preachers of this generation. It should be corrected in our sermons. For we do not preach to ourselves but to others, and we should therefore always think of the purpose of the sermon insofar as possible.[5]

Third, there are two primary sounds of the shofar: a simple, straightforward sound, and one that is very wavering and staccato. The first is called *teqiʿah,* the second *teruʿah*; these terms are derived from biblical language. Then there is another intermediate sound, a composite of the other two, called by the talmudic sages *sheber*. . . . Similarly, the preacher should look up and see who is in the congregation, and bearing these three sounds in mind, begin to speak and arrange his sermon intelligently.

The congregation may consist of wise and learned people, or it may consist of ordinary people, or possibly even of a mixture of both categories. Now the preacher must speak in such a way that his message will be understood, gearing the content to his audience.[6] If the congregation consists of ordinary Jews, he should speak about simple matters, so that the audience will under-

4. This complaint is significant: although most *collections* before the sixteenth century are organized according to the weekly Torah lesson and closely linked with it, we cannot automatically assume that most *sermons* followed this practice. In choosing sermons for a book, preachers naturally tend to select ones cast in a more traditional form.

5. A similar point is made in Anonymous, "Disciple of R. Asher," fol. 66v. It may have been a topos in Jewish as well as in Christian homiletics.

6. Another topos in the homiletical writings of both traditions. Cf. Joel ibn Shueib, and Modena, below.

stand and the desired benefit will be obtained. This is similar to the *teqiʿah,* a simple sound. If there are learned and knowledgeable people present, he should speak of profound and original matters, not straightforward truths that are known to all. This is like the *teruʿah,* a complex sound.

If both categories are present together, his speech should be composed of both kinds of material, like the *sheber,* intermediate between *teqiʿah* and *teruʿah.* He may divide his sermon into separate parts appropriate for each group, or he may give one sermon appropriate for all. But if he divides it into parts, while he is delivering the section intended for the learned, the masses will be there to no avail, and while he delivers the part intended for the masses, there will be no purpose in the presence of the wise. The ideal is to have the entire speech encompass both groups, so that the wise will find something new, and the masses will understand. If this is indeed possible, it is preferable to the other way.

Now it has been explained elsewhere that there are five categories of speech, which are the same as the five well known arts of reasoning: logical demonstration, sophistry, dialectic, rhetoric, and poetry.[7] It is worth investigating which of these arts is the most appropriate for use in preaching. We say that the art of logical demonstration is difficult to use for two reasons. First, the subjects of most homiletical statements, whether affirmative or negative, are not known through logical demonstration, for we have few logical axioms that apply to such matters. For the most part, they are investigations of Torah problems, the truth of which cannot be established by demonstration.

The second reason is that the art of logical demonstration is extremely exalted. There are few preachers who can use this mode of argumentation having fully mastered all its subtleties, and it is extremely unusual or even impossible to find an appropriate audience. This is apparent to any expert in logic. Obviously this category of speech cannot encompass an audience containing both the learned and the masses.

The art of sophistry should be repudiated by every preacher, for the purpose of the sophist is to expound upon something untrue. Not only does this fail to remove the sickness from the souls of the listeners; it actually exacerbates that sickness.

As for the art of dialectic, the purpose of the debater is to convince the people of his view—whether it be true or not. His sole concern is that his argument be compelling. But the purpose of the preacher is to convince the people only of what is true. He should therefore repudiate this art as well, insofar as possible, using it only when it is necessary to resort to the dis-

7. On the five categories of speech, see Maimonides, *Commentary on Abot* 1:17 (*A Maimonides Reader,* pp. 390–92); on the Aristotelian arts of reasoning, see Maimonides, *Millot ha-Higgayon,* chap. 8; Israel Efros, ed., *Maimonides' Treatise on Logic* (New York, 1938), pp. 48–49. The link between these two groups of five is not known to me from another source.

tinctive premises of its syllogisms: namely, premises that are generally accepted opinions. In such circumstances it may be permissible for the homiletical art. The difference between these three disciplines—logical demonstration, sophistical reasoning, and dialectic—has been explained in the third book of the *Metaphysics*.[8] You may look there.

The art of poetry is inappropriate for preaching because it is remote from the nature of the masses. The ancients also condemned those who spoke of theoretical matters in this way, as Aristotle said, condemning Plato in the *Poetics*.[9] It is abundantly clear that whoever indulges in this art is dealing with something totally alien to the nature of homiletics.

This leaves only the art of rhetoric, which attempts to beautify even the most profound ideas and to express them through vivid analogies, so that the masses can attain an accurate image of them and the intellectuals can see them in a new light. This is especially true for the content of Torah investigations, the material suitable for the homiletical art, for the expression of esoteric matter through analogy, parable, or allegory attracts the attention of people, so that they will listen, and accept or spurn as appropriate.

Thus the best of the arts for preaching is the art of rhetoric. The more the preacher masters this art, and the more at home he is in the techniques of speech and argumentation that will persuade the listeners to accept what he says, the greater will be his stature in homiletics. Indeed, the art of preaching is included in the category of rhetoric. The ancients actually called the art of rhetoric *homiletics,* and they called its modes of argumentation *homiletical argument*. . . .

Most of the preachers in our time fail in this regard. Some preach about midrashim and rabbinic statements according to their simple meaning in a manner that benefits neither the masses nor the wise. Some speak about false doctrines in the fashion of debaters or sophists, using these two arts—dialectics and sophistical arguments; or they somehow use the art of poetry, citing the profound words of the sages and ascribing deep meanings to the aggadot; or they speak confusingly with syllogistic arguments, benefiting no one. They think that they excel in syllogistic proofs, but for the most part they preach about things that neither they nor their listeners understand, hoping that they will be esteemed as intellectuals because they preach about the mysteries of creation and of the Torah.

I once heard people tell of a man who thought much of his own intellectual

8. See *Metaphysics,* G.2.1004b. It is striking that the author directs his reader to an Aristotelian text rather than to Maimonides' treatise on logic.

9. This does not appear in the text of the *Poetics* as it exists today. Compare the aphorism attributed to Aristotle in the Middle Ages by Muslims and Jews, "the best of poetry is a lie" (see Jefim [Ḥayyim] Schirmann, *Ha-Shirah ha-ʿIbrit bi-Sefarad u-bi-Provans,* 4 vols. [Jerusalem, 1961], "General Introduction," 1:37).

abilities. He began a sermon delivered to the leaders of the community by saying that his sermon would be divided into three parts: the first part would be comprehensible to him and to them, the second part comprehensible to him but not to them, and the third part neither to him nor to them.[10] Indeed, I would think that many sermons of our time are of this third category.

What has happened to the art of preaching is the same as what happened to medicine, which wise men have described as a courtyard without gates, meaning that so many people have access to it. Whoever wants to take a fee and kill people for their money may come and take a fee, and the expert cannot be distinguished from the nonexpert. . . .[11] This is especially true for the Jewish people, for we all think of ourselves as wise and understanding. This matter should be corrected. . . .

The fifth part explains the meaning of the phrase, *Declare to My people their transgression* (Isa. 58:1). This teaches about the purpose of the sermon: to recall the sins, offenses, and transgressions committed by the elders and leaders of the people. It teaches that the preacher must be neither ashamed nor afraid of them, for God will be with him in his conflict. This is the meaning of *My people.* He said *their transgression* because the sin is essentially related to the sinner himself and the one for whom the sin is committed. I have already explained this in my sermons, where it is made clear that the greater the status of the sinner, the greater will be considered the sin. . . .

From this it becomes clear that the master of this art must be strong in God's sight, not a meek and self-effacing personality. He must have the heart of a lion and be prepared to reproach kings and nobles for their sins, so that they will emerge truly chastened. . . . Most of the preachers of our generation are too obsequious, especially to the powerful. They tell such men that they are righteous because they depend upon those men for their livelihood.[12]

The harm that comes from such sycophancy is readily discernible; indeed, this was the reason for the destruction of Solomon's Temple. You can see in the Book of Kings that the false prophets, those of evil counsel, were always telling the kings, "You are a good man, you are doing what God wants." The true prophets vigorously protested. *If a ruler listens to falsehood, all who serve him are evil* (Prov. 29:12); the sages understood this verse to apply to what I have said. They also stated, "From the day when sycophancy prevailed, the decree was sealed against us for our sins."[13]

10. This story, based on hearsay, sounds apocryphal.

11. This attack upon physicians has a long tradition in medieval Hebrew literature; cf. Kalonymos ben Kalonymos, *Eben Boḥan,* in Schirmann, *Ha-Shirah ha-ʿIbrit* 4:510–14.

12. This theme was taken up by many Eastern European moralists in the seventeenth and eighteenth centuries; see sources 11c and 16 translated below.

13. B. Ḥul 4b; B. Soṭ 41b.

This frequently occurs with our nation, more so than with others, from what I have observed of these matters. A Gentile may preach against kings and nobles, proclaiming their sins for all to hear.[14] But in our own nation no one will raise his tongue against any Jew whatsoever, and certainly not if the man is wealthy or a potential benefactor. Now since the cause of this harmful situation is the fact that the preachers of rebuke are poor and destitute, it is desirable that such men, who stand before the God of Israel, should not be devoid of material wealth. Solomon noted long ago that *the poor man's wisdom is despised, and his words are unheard* (Eccles. 9:16).

Therefore, the qualities either necessary or desirable in the preacher include wisdom . . . , admirable ethical traits . . . , inner courage . . . , and the wealth necessary to provide for his sustenance. Note that I said "necessary"; superfluous wealth is an obstacle to his success, as the philosopher noted in the tenth book of his *Ethics*. . . .[15] The most important of these qualities is strength of character, not of body. For even if the king or the noble should wax angry at his sermons, it is on God's behalf that he preaches. . . . This is why R. ʿAqiba was killed: because he had the people gather in congregations and he preached publicly, despite the wrath of the evil king. . . .[16]

7. Isaac Arama, Introduction to *ʿAqedat Yiṣḥaq*[1] (End of fifteenth century, Spain)

These Jews among whom I lived [in Tarragona] loved God's Torah deeply. They desired nothing so much as to listen to its words with exegetical and homiletical commentary, to understand interpretations both ancient and new, to search for reasonable explanations of problematic passages. This is what they looked forward to day and night, on each festival and Sabbath.

I set myself to satisfy this desire from the works of the great masters of the past, who have illumined our path with their interpretations. But I was unable to fill the needs of the people as expressed to me by their questions. For our Jews are an intellectual people [*ʿam binot*], and they dwell in the midst of another people with profound and articulate speakers everywhere: the refined people of Edom [i.e., the Christians]. In every city, their scholars master all branches of knowledge, their priests and princes stand at the fore in philosophy, integrating it with their theological doctrine. They have writ-

14. Compare n. 1 to the text by Solomon Alami, above.

15. *Nicomachean Ethics* 10.8.1178b–1179a.

16. Note the interpretation of ʿAqiba's martyrdom as a consequence of his public preaching, where the talmudic source (B. Ber 61b) speaks only of his "engaging in Torah" (i.e., studying and teaching a limited circle of students).

1. On Arama, see Bettan, pp. 130–91, and Heller-Wilensky.

ten many books, on the basis of which biblical texts are expounded before large congregations. Each day their preachers give important insights into their religion and faith, thereby sustaining it.[2]

For some time now, calls have gone out far and wide, summoning the people to hear their learned discourses. They have fulfilled their promise. Among those who came were Jews. They heard the preachers and found them impressive; their appetites were whetted for similar fare. This is what they say: "The Christian scholars and sages raise questions and seek answers in their academies and churches,[3] thereby adding to the glory of the Torah and the prophets, as do the sages of every people. Why should the divine Torah with all its narratives and pronouncements be as a veiled maiden beside the flocks of her friends[4] and her students?

"The Gentiles search enthusiastically for religious and ethical content, using all appropriate hermeneutical techniques, even the thirteen rules for interpreting the Torah, including the argument a fortiori and the verbal analogy. But our Torah commentators do not employ this method that everyone admires. Their purpose is only to explain the grammatical forms of words and the simple meaning of the stories and commandments. They have not attempted to fill our need or to exalt the image of our Torah to our own people by regaling them with gems from its narratives and laws."

8. Joel ibn Shueib, Introduction to *ᶜOlat Shabbat*[1] (End of fifteenth century, Spain)

The author of a book, especially one intended for a large audience encompassing both those who are intellectually superior and those who are more

2. Note the high regard for Spanish Christian culture in general and preaching in particular; cf. n. 1 to the Alami text, above. Arama goes on to speak of a cultural competition between Jews and Christians, with Jewish preachers challenged to rise to the standard set by their Christian counterparts.

3. The technique of formulating a series of problems that arise out of a particular passage, and then answering those problems as part of the commentary, was common in Scholastic literature. Arama, who used this pattern in his own work, may be pointing here to the Christian origin of the form and justifying its use in Jewish writing. Cf. "Structural Options," above, at n. 28.

4. This image, based on Song 1:7, may also draw upon the personification of Torah as a concealed maiden awaiting her beloved in Zohar 2:99a–b.

1. On Joel ibn Shueib as preacher, note the following characterization by Basnage (based on Bartolucci): "This preacher was prolix and diffuse, the common Vice of those who harangue the People; because they have more complaisance for themselves than their Auditories; but yet he was much esteemed because he was a Learned Man, and good Judges have thought his Explication of some Chapters of the Pentateuch very solid" (Jacques Basnage, *History of the Jews* [London, 1708]), 7:692.

ordinary, should be concerned not only with the necessary and good but also with the beautiful and pleasing. We would say in general that whoever wants to write a book, particularly if it deals with matters of Torah, should perfect his presentation both in content and in style.

As for the content, he should pay careful attention to two things. First, that the listeners benefit from all that he says. Though the subject be profound, he should explain it so that it will be comprehensible to the masses, insofar as it is suitable for them to understand. And though the subject be of general interest and not at all profound, he should discuss it in such a way that the intellectuals will benefit. This all comes under the rubric of the greatest good.

Second, he should speak of matters pertaining to all the listeners: for the intellectuals, matters of philosophy and faith, and for the ordinary people, simple and generally known topics appropriate to their intellectual ability and relevant to their conduct.[2] This is what the Talmud indicated in reporting that R. Meir divided his discourse into three parts, one third devoted to Torah, one third to halakah, and one third to parables {B. Sanh 38b}.[3] He did not speak exclusively about profound matters, for this would have repelled the masses, who are the majority. Nor did he do the opposite, for then there would have been nothing for those of superior ability.

This is corroborated by the statement in the Midrash: "R. Abbahu and R. Ḥiyya came to a certain place. R. Ḥiyya bar Abba preached about {legal} traditions, R. Abbahu preached aggadah. Everyone left R. Hiyya and went to hear R. Abbahu. R. Ḥiyya became dejected, but R. Abbahu said to him, 'I will give you an analogy: if there are two men, one selling trinkets and the other precious stones, which one will everyone jump all over? The one selling trinkets'" {B. Soṭ 40a}.

Therefore the author should divide his message so that everyone will find something of interest. It does not matter whether you are preaching to listeners or writing a book; as Maimonides wrote, the author of a book is like a preacher to a congregation of many people.[4] All this comes under the rubric of the necessary, for once it is established that a book is being written both for the elite and the multitude, both groups should be able to benefit from it.

Now as for style, the author must be concerned about three things. First, the quantity: there must not be excessive or superfluous and irrelevant material, for the listeners or the readers will become disgusted and fail to understand the main point. . . . Rather, it should be moderate, the length

2. Compare Joseph ibn Shem Ṭob, above, at n. 6.

3. Compare the extensive discussion of this passage on preaching by Pukhovitser, sects. 13a and b, below.

4. Maimonides, *Guide* (ed. Michael Friedländer), intro., p. 8.

of the message fitting the material and the audience, so that they may understand it. Second, the order: the message must be connected, not amorphous and digressive. Third, the aesthetic dimension: the expression should be in literate and beautiful language that gives pleasure to the audience.

9. Israel, Author of "Dober Mesharim"[1] (Late fifteenth or early sixteenth century, Spanish origin)

a. The lesson *Attem Niṣṣabim* (Deut. 29:9–30:20), when it was read before New Year's Day, separate from the lesson *Wa-Yelek* (Deut. 31:1–30). . . . *God is willing to pardon him. God is not willing to pardon him.*[2]

"Bluria the proselyte put this question to Rabban Gamaliel: It is written in your Torah, *Who does not show favor* (Deut. 10:17), and it is also written, *The Lord shall bestow his favor upon you* (Num. 6:26). R. Jose the priest joined the conversation and said to her, I will give you a parable that will illustrate the matter. A man lent his neighbor a certain amount and fixed a time for payment in the presence of the king, and the borrower swore by the life of the king to repay him. When the time arrived, he did not repay him, and he went to excuse himself to the king. The king, however, said to him, 'The wrong done to me I excuse you, but go and obtain forgiveness from your neighbor.' So here: one text speaks of offenses committed by a human being against God, the other of offenses committed by one human being against another" (B. RH 17b).

The words of my theme-verse clearly show that this discourse will be constructed upon a debate over antithetical propositions. But before I begin it, I shall briefly discuss the question, whether it is permissible for a preacher to deliver this kind of discourse in the presence of the Torah. For whoever does so is required in some way to give support for the proposition antithetical to the truth, and this may sometimes cause problems for the masses.[3]

1. To my knowledge, this author and his manuscript of sermons have not been previously discussed, although his importance for the history of Jewish preaching is considerable.

2. Compare Deut. 29:19. On this technique of dividing and repeating the theme-verse from the Torah lesson, see "Structural Options."

3. The preacher is saying that he will use the structure of the Scholastic "disputed question," in which two antithetical positions are asserted, with arguments given to support each one, before the conflict is resolved either by refuting the arguments on one side or by introducing a distinction that will allow both positions to be maintained. This structure, which can be traced back in Jewish preaching at least to Ḥasdai Crescas (see Ravitsky, "Ketab," and "Zehuto"), must have remained controversial, as the present preacher feels compelled to justify its use by citing Jewish precedents. Cf. the warning in an anonymous late fifteenth-century Christian tract that the preacher should never frivolously put a belief to the test, and when bringing up disputed questions, should not end his sermon without settling the point clearly (Caplan, pp. 72–73; cf. Douglass, pp. 33–34).

Yet I can truly cite precedent and support for this enterprise from a number of sources. For example, toward the end of his life, Joshua spoke to the people about the service of the true God, and he did so with antithetical propositions. So did Elijah when confronting the prophets of Baal on Mount Carmel.[4] And Maimonides, of blessed memory, discussed in his *Guide* many fundamental principles of the Torah in this manner, as did Gersonides in his *Wars of the Lord,* as well as many others.

So as not to be overlong, I will cite only one source, from the sages in tractate Baba Meṣiᶜa [33a]: "Our rabbis taught, Those who occupy themselves [exclusively] with Bible are of indifferent merit, with Mishnah are indeed meritorious and are rewarded for it, with Gemara—there can be no greater merit." Why did they consider Talmud study to be on the highest level? Because in the Talmud every detail is isolated, analyzed, and justified by those who debate it. One person is always challenging another and raising problems with the other's position. This is not in order to undermine the truth; rather, it is because the truth emerges from this kind of debate.[5] Thus we have explained that there is justification for doing this.

But it remains for me to explain what compels *me* to do so. An explanation is required because of my inner consternation. In light of all the scholars who have preached adequately concerning repentance, I should really have remained silent on this matter.[6] On the other hand, there are two considerations that impel me to speak. The first is that we are now at the time especially appropriate for repentance, namely, two days before the New Year's Day. . . .[7] And second, the subject of repentance is central to this Torah lesson, and is therefore a fitting subject for discussion. In the midst of my confusion, something inside me said, "Get up, go ahead, why do you stumble? I shall counsel you how to preach about repentance without [merely] preaching about rabbinic statements. . . ."

4. See Josh. 24:14 (*Serve the Lord*) and 24:19 (*You will not be able to serve the Lord, for He is a holy God, He is a jealous God, He will not forgive your transgressions and your sins*). On the latter verse, Abravanel commented, "He said this because the Israelites knew that both reasons are the opposite of the truth." For Elijah, see 1 Kings 18:27: *Shout louder! After all, he is a god, but he may be in conversation*—a statement antithetical to the truth, from which the truth emerges.

5. Compare Isaac Canpanton, *Darke ha-Gemara* (Vilna, 1901), p. 14.

6. This is a convention in fifteenth-century Jewish preaching: in the introduction to the formal occasional sermon, the preacher states why it would have been preferable for him to remain silent, and then goes on to explain the "reasons" that impel him to overcome this temptation and to preach. Cf. "Structural Options," above, at nn. 32 and 33, and the sermon of Joseph Garçon.

7. This detail, indicating that Rosh Hashanah began the following Sunday night, as well as the introductory characterization informing us that the sermon was delivered in a year when the lesson *Haʾazinu* was read separately from *Wa-Yelek,* identify this text as a record of a sermon actually preached rather than as a model for future use (cf. n. 10 below).

Now I shall begin to speak about the actual subject of my discourse, using the antithetical facets[8] of my theme-verse. Although I began with the affirmative in order to begin with the truth that is my primary intention, nevertheless in investigating the antithetical facets of the verse I will discuss the negative first. . . .

I therefore assert that the Holy One does not pardon the sinner, nor does He want him.[9] I will prove this in three ways, first from God's own exaltedness, second from this Torah lesson, and third from empirical evidence. (I actually explained first the proof from the lesson and then from God's exaltedness and then from empirical evidence, so that in refuting these arguments I could begin immediately with the lesson). . . .[10]

Now I shall speak on the affirmative side, namely, that God does want to pardon the sinner. This can be established in three other ways. I shall not cite too many proofs, lest our opponent claim that we wore him down with endless arguments;[11] instead, I shall follow in his footsteps. The three ways of argument are: from God's own exaltedness, from the lesson, and from empirical evidence. . . .

Now it remains for us to discuss the arguments of our opponent and to refute his claims. . . .[12]

Thus the arguments of the challenger are refuted. And we may now affirm the words with which we began, that "God is willing to pardon him." But it remains for us now to explain the other two antithetical facets of the theme-verse. We have resolved the first two, which were read as questions, but what about the others, which were read as affirmations? First we said that God is willing to pardon him, and then we went back and said that God is not willing to pardon him.[13]

This may be explained by means of the rabbinic statement with which we began. The simple meaning of this statement indicates that there are some sins, namely those between human beings and God, that God will forbear

8. For this term (*ḥelqe ha-soter*), see the sermon by Joseph Garçon, n. 46.

9. Philosophical arguments against God's acceptance of repentance were apparently common in this period; cf. Aboab, p. 25a; Zarfati, p. 275c.

10. This parenthetical remark in the manuscript may indicate that the preacher had a written version of his sermon before delivery but decided to rearrange the oral presentation for greater effectiveness.

11. The reference to "our opponent" is a rhetorical flourish. The preacher is arguing both sides of the question in a kind of dramatic dialogue.

12. After the threefold argument has been given on both sides, the argument on the fallacious side must be refuted, in accordance with the rules governing the form.

13. The beginning of the text in the manuscript gives no indication of this double reading of the "antithetical facets" of the theme-verse. Here we see that at the very beginning of the sermon, the preacher read the two phrases first as questions, indicating that a choice had to be made between them, and then as affirmations, indicating that both were indeed correct. This is maintained through a distinction based on the opening rabbinic statement.

and pardon, but that there are others, namely those between human beings, that God will not forbear and pardon. Thus we must be extremely careful regarding sins that affect our neighbors, whether through words or through thoughts. . . .

b. Now if someone should say that whoever did not enter the synagogue did not hear a word of what the preacher said, it may be deduced from this that they did not understand anything, for if they did not hear it, how could they understand? But if he should say the opposite, namely, whoever did not enter [the synagogue did not understand], it may not be deduced from this that they did not hear. That may not be true. It is possible that someone may hear all that the preacher says from the entrance to the synagogue, or from the [women's] chamber, without understanding it.[14]

10. Leib ben Bezalel (MaHaRaL) of Prague[1] (End of sixteenth century)

[We read] in the Talmud [B. ʿArak 16b]: "R. Eleazar said, I would be surprised if there is anyone in this generation who accepts rebuke, for if one says to him, 'Remove the chip from between your teeth,' he answers, 'Remove the beam from between your eyes!' R. ʿAqiba said, I would be surprised if there is one in this generation who knows how to rebuke. R. Joḥanan said, I call heaven and earth to witness for myself that ʿAqiba ben Joseph was punished because I used to complain about him to Rabban Gamaliel, yet all the more did he shower love upon me, in order to fulfill the verse, *Do not rebuke a scoffer, for he will hate you; rebuke a wise man, and he will love you* (Prov. 9:8)."

The phrase used here, "Remove the chip from between your teeth," means, you are sinning and you do not see the sin. It is like a chip caught between

14. This passage has been included for two reasons. First, it is an interesting example of a preacher giving a logic lesson to his congregation; second, it tells us something of the *Sitz im Leben*: that the women's chamber was so far removed from the preaching stand that it was often difficult for women to make out what the preacher was saying. That this, rather than linguistic difficulty, is given as the reason for a failure to understand, may be taken as a further argument for the vernacular delivery of the sermons.

1. English treatments of this towering figure of sixteenth-century intellectual history include Byron Sherwin, *Mystical Theology and Social Dissent* (London and Toronto, 1982); Aaron Mauskopf, *The Religious Philosophy of the Maharal of Prague* (New York, 1966); Ben Zion Bokser, *From the World of the Cabbalah* (New York, 1954); Friedrich Thieberger, *The Great Rabbi Löw of Prague* (London, 1955). On the author's major ethical work, *Netibot ʿOlam,* from which the passage is taken, see Marvin Fox, "The Moral Philosophy of MaHaRaL," *Jewish Thought in the Sixteenth Century,* ed. Bernard Cooperman (Cambridge, Mass., 1983), pp. 167–85.

a person's teeth, that he does not see. The response, "Remove the beam from between your eyes," means, it is *you* who are sinning, and your sin is like a beam between the eyes, so close to you that you should see it, but you do not. Yet you see the chip hidden between my teeth! This meaning is quite different from the implication of Rashi's comment. He wrote, "[The listener] can say, 'Remove the beam from between your eyes,'" indicating that he is actually justified in saying this. That does not seem to me to be the point. Rather, it is as we said, that the generation does not accept ethical rebuke at all, and the people respond this way even though what they say is untrue.[2]

Therefore R. ʿAqiba answered, "I would be surprised if there is one in this generation who knows how to rebuke." This means that preachers do not know how to deliver a rebuke in such a way that those being criticized will accept the criticism. Much depends on whether the rebuke is accepted, and this requires wisdom and artifice on the part of the preacher. R. ʿAqiba's statement is extremely profound: there must be great wisdom in the sermon of rebuke if the preacher's message is to be accepted by the congregation. Sinners have already turned to sin; to turn them away from what they have done requires the wisdom to speak words so pleasant and reasonable that they will penetrate to the heart.[3] The preacher who rebukes people, [urging them] not to behave improperly, must say things tasteful and true, penetrating and breaking down the defenses of even the hardest heart.

Certainly, his message must not contain anything that diverges from the truth, anything that listeners will recognize as devoid of basis or foundation. Yet this is the practice of many who now preach publicly in these regions.[4] They interpret biblical verses and rabbinic statements to mean something never intended, something which never occurred to those who said them. They claim to be explaining the meaning of these statements, but the result is harmful. If they would just leave the words of the sages as they are, these statements, understood simply, would display great wisdom. But they transform sweet into bitter, with destructive intent.

How could this not be the case? The simple meaning of the rabbinic statements reflects profound wisdom. Even the casual conversation of the rabbis should be studied, for it is as close to pure reason as the leaf is close to the fruit, . . . and if this is true of their casual conversation, how much

2. According to Rashi's exegesis, the preacher was just as bad as those he was criticizing (cf. the selection from Luntshitz, below, sect. 11c). MaHaRaL understands the complaint as a baseless excuse, making the problem not the religious stature of the preachers but the technique of criticism.

3. The paradox inherent in the sermon of rebuke, that those most in need are the least likely to respond, was noted by many Polish preachers and moralists.

4. Here MaHaRaL moves beyond the exegesis of a talmudic passage and applies his thesis to the contemporary preaching context. The problem is the use of far-fetched interpretations of ancient texts not as philosophical allegory but as ethical homilies.

more is it true of their actual teachings! All are profound wisdom, which must be studied with deep concentration to be understood. The more irrational these statements seem, the more we know that they conceal profound wisdom, requiring thorough and probing investigation.[5] But this is not what these preachers do. They say things they know to be dishonest. It would be better for them to preach in public about matters that have nothing to do with Torah than to preach the way they do!

This way of treating the words of the perfect Torah must be vigorously protested, for a great religious duty is turned into fraud when such interpretations are incorporated into public sermons. These preachers want only to show off to people who do not know any better, by pretending to discover novelties in the Torah. They may reply, "If we do not do this, we say nothing new, only what others already know." But how can they think that those whom they come to rebuke will accept their message? They know that the point has no basis in the rabbinic statement the preachers have cited, the only reason they tie their message to a novel interpretation of a talmudic statement being their assumption that otherwise they will have done nothing original—for everyone knows the simple meaning of the statement—and that therefore their sermon will be worthless, and they might as well remain silent.[6]

Will anyone accept these totally groundless lies? People will say rather that the sermons contain not wisdom but merely one individual's fabrication. It would be better if they would speak their piece without any talmudic statement at all, for people would then say, "These are the words of a preacher of ethical rebuke."[7] Although this is not entirely proper, for the words of the sages are certainly worthy of being taught and used to rebuke the congregation, it would still be better to eliminate them entirely. But now that they take someone else's thoughts and peg them onto rabbinic statements that everyone knows have nothing at all to do with the subject being discussed and provide no true basis for their point, how can they think their sermons are beneficial? They actually neglect the great religious duty of the Sabbath sermon: allowing many to hear words of Torah. . . .

In his commentary on the Talmud [B. Shab 115a], Rashi explained that the sages used to preach about nonlegal subjects [aggadah], but within the

5. Compare the discussion by Jacob Elbaum, "Rabbi Judah Löw of Prague and His Attitude to the Aggadah," *Scripta Hierosolymitana* 22 (1971):28–47.

6. A systematic defense of the use of far-fetched interpretations in sermons of an ethical character was given by David Darshan in his *Ketab Hitnaṣṣelut le-Darshanim* (Darshan, pp. 121–70). For the accusation that the interpretations were a kind of intellectual exhibitionism, see also the selection by Luntshitz, below, sect. 11c.

7. MaHaRaL's proposal, that ethical and religious rebuke should be given without linking it with traditional texts, raises the problem of the authority of the preacher (cf. the discussion in "Preachers and Congregations," above).

body of their sermons they would teach the people what was permitted and what was forbidden. It was inconceivable not to include such halakic material within the aggadah, and it was wise to preach on a halakic subject in the context of aggadah.[8] For it is through aggadah that people become enamored of Torah. When, in the middle of an aggadic sermon, the preacher admonishes the congregation with words of Torah, the message penetrates to the listeners' hearts. They accept it, and it remains with them, affecting their future behavior. It is about this kind of sermon that the Midrash said [*Yalquṭ Mishle* 951, discussed earlier in the passage] that people who are gathered to hear a sermon make the Holy One king. It was not about the kind of sermon for which both the preacher and the congregation bear the preacher's guilt. . . .

If R. ʿAqiba said, "I would be surprised if one is able to rebuke," what would be said in *our* generation? And R. Eleazar's statement, "I would be surprised if there is in this generation one who accepts rebuke," also applies to our own time. Worse than this, in our generation, there is absolutely no one who can rebuke, for we see enormous sins being committed publicly by the entire people, and no one holds the fort or stands in the breach. For example, the prohibition of wine touched by Gentiles is transgressed throughout this country as if it had become permitted. . . .[9] Furthermore, we find today that if someone comes from afar to rebuke others for behavior scandalous in any Jew, behavior that profanes God's Name, the members of the community say, "Are not all of us holy, are not God and His Torah in our midst? We will not heed or accept ethical instruction from another."[10] This is why there is no one who can rebuke and give ethical criticism.

11. Ephraim Luntshitz[1] (Late sixteenth-century Poland, Prague)

a. When I grew older, the most pious implored me, and many others did as well, saying "Arise, speak your piece for all to hear in the sacred congregations of Poland, especially on the day of the annual fair in Lublin, where

8. Note the endorsement of a mixture of legal and nonlegal material in the same sermon, with the edifying and the hortatory complementing each other.

9. For the controversy over Gentile wine in MaHaRaL's time see the discussion in Sherwin, *Mystical Theology and Social Dissent*, pp. 94–102.

10. The quotation is based on Num. 16:3, where it presents the claim of Korah and his band of rebels. For resistance to the rebuke of outsiders, see the selection from Eidlitz, sect. 16, below.

1. On Luntshitz, see Bettan, pp. 273–316; H. H. Ben-Sasson, "Osher we-ʿOni be-Mishnato shel ha-Mokiaḥ R. Ephrayim Ish Luntshitz," *Zion* 19 (1954):142–66; Ḥayyim Rabinovitz, "Rabbi Shelomoh Efrayim Luntshitz: Ha-Mokiaḥ ba-Shaʿar," *Sinai* 30 (1966):174–84.

virtually all the scholars of the land gather with the craftsmen and smiths."[2] It was my practice there to speak before kings—for "Who are kings? the rabbis"[3]—reaching the entire community, including the powerful and distinguished. I did not turn back for anyone, even though it resulted in my being persecuted. I did not hide from the scourge of the masses' prattle.

Indeed, I was responsible for many becoming my persecutors and enemies. It would have been better for me to have refrained from speech, for then I would have had some respite from the persecutors and their hordes, the tumultuous masses. It is their manner to invent fictions about the preachers of rebuke, saying "Remove the beam [from between your eyes]" [B. ʿArak 16b].[4] Some of them say, "Who set you up as such a model? Are you better than the fine people of this region?" Others cast aspersions upon the preacher out of envy. All these travails befell me, and I knew full well that I was the cause of the people's envious calumnies. Perhaps I should have been more concerned with my own reputation, but I set my own will aside before God's will.

b. It should also be ordained in every community that preachers should speak on the Sabbath about ethical matters and Torah laws, not about the meaning of the rabbinic homilies, for the masses of Jews have no need of this. This was the practice of our ancestors: all their sermons were intended to inform about the laws of the Torah and ethical matters, in order to awaken those asleep in the midst of their lives, so engrossed in their passions that they forget their final end.[5]

c. The second quality [of leadership] is found in the phrase *who shall go out before them* (Num. 27:17). This refers to those who rebuke their contemporaries in order to lead them away from the transgressions they commit; it teaches that the one who rebukes must first *go out before them* and himself depart from that crooked path. It is as the sages said, "Correct yourself, then correct others" [B. Sanh 18a]. So Moses said *who shall go out before them,* meaning that he must first remove any iniquity from himself. It is similar to the verse, *If there be iniquity in your hand, put it far away, and let not unrighteousness dwell in your tents* (Job 11:14); rather, first make it depart from

2. On the Lublin Fair, see Baron, *SRHJ* 16:236, 428.

3. Cf. B. Giṭ 62a.

4. Cf. MaHaRaL of Prague, above, at n. 2.

5. Cf. Maimonides, above, sect. 2c; the motif of awakening those who are asleep in the midst of their lives is drawn from Maimonides' discussion of the shofar in *Code* I,v (*Teshubah*) 3:4, with the link between the role of the shofar and that of the preacher established through Isa. 58:1 (below, sect. 11d).

your tents before you speak to others, lest they say, "Remove the beam [from between your eyes]" [B. ʿArak 16b].[6]

This is why I have noticed that people pay little heed to the preachers who rebuke them. When they see the preacher diverging from the proper path even a hair's breadth, they stop listening to his message of rebuke and say, "Yesterday he himself did such and so, and today he is rebuking us!" They also claim that he is preaching only for his own glory.

Indeed it is true that most of the preachers I have seen do preach for their own glory.[7] When they take a passage of aggadah and remove it from its simple meaning, interpreting it in a novel manner and discovering in it some fine rhetorical flourish, then all the listeners, laughing, praise him: *How he knows what lies in the darkness, truly the light dwells with him!* (Dan. 2:22). All day long they whisper about him: "How clever is this man who knows how to change one form into another," for he strips off the simple clothing of a rabbinic statement and dresses it in other garments. Yes, the people are pleased. They do not care whether there is any ethical content in the message or not. Nor does the preacher care about anything—except whether they give him flattery and praise.

I have wanted no part of this pattern, so prevalent in our age. I have seized upon the simple meaning of rabbinic statements, focusing upon their ethical content and their relevance for our behavior, hoping that the people would pay heed.

d. The form and shape of the shofar is intended to apply to the sermon of rebuke, providing guidance for those who deliver it. We learn this from the words of Isaiah, *Like a shofar raise your voice, and declare to My people their transgression* (Isa. 58:1); thus the sound of his ethical instruction is compared to the shofar.[8] At the end he said, *Refrain from trampling the Sabbath* (Isa. 58:13). By this he taught that one should speak on the Sabbath day, when

6. See above, at n. 4. Here the criticism of preachers' characters is conceded to have elements of truth, although there is also some hypocrisy in the congregation that seizes on the most minute deviation from the norm by the preacher as a justification for refusing to heed his message.

7. This charge, pertaining not to the external conduct but to the inner motivation of contemporary preachers, is admitted by the author. Accusations of intellectual exhibitionism later became common in Eastern European ethical literature. This paragraph should be compared with the source cited in "Preachers and Congregations," above, at n. 31, in which early sixteenth-century preachers were denounced for their *lack* of originality.

8. Compare Joseph ibn Shem Ṭob's *ʿEn ha-Qore,* above. Here the analogy between the shofar and the sermon of rebuke is developed even further through the use not only of Isa. 58:1 but of the halakic regulations governing the use of the shofar on Rosh Hashanah.

the shofar is not sounded, and the voice should take the place of the shofar. This will be explained in section 219.[9]

Since the preacher of rebuke must first correct himself, the prophet says *A day of horn blasts and alarms* (Zeph. 1:16), and then *Gather together, gather* (Zeph. 2:1). From this verse the sages derived the principle that one must first correct himself. Only then may he correct others.[10]

Just as the shofar must be bent, so one who rebukes others must speak with a heart that is bent, broken, and contrite. He must not be one of the deceitful, who speak high-sounding words and preach for their own glory—borne aloft by their own hot air—ambitious for power. They want to augment their reputations as fine preachers who know what is concealed in obscurity and can alter the meaning of every simple statement, changing its appearance by making it don new garb. This technique has already spread among the preachers; their ultimate purpose is as I said.

The shofar also contains a reminder that the preacher be strong enough to prevail over the high-handed, in accordance with the verse, *Gird your loins now like a man . . . , see the proud and humble them* (Job 40:7, 12). This means that he must not fear anyone, nor be obsequious toward the wicked, no matter how powerful they may be. For this reason, the shofar may not be decorated with different colors, for this would symbolize a hypocritical sycophant. The sages said, "When one is dependent upon others, his face turns many different shades, as we see in the verse, *The* kerum *is reviled by human beings* (Ps. 12:9)."[11] This is a wonderful allusion to the person dependent upon others, who has to act obsequiously toward the next person: his face will undoubtedly turn many different shades. He appears to someone now to be laughing, but behind the person's back he may be furious. There is no consistency in his speech. This is inherent in the nature of sycophancy, as is well known.

In most such cases, people are obsequious toward the wealthy, because of the pleasure money can bring. That is why preachers of rebuke tell the wicked that they are righteous. Therefore the sages said that when a shofar is plated with gold, if its sound changes it is disqualified from use.[12] So with the preacher: because they plate him with gold, his voice changes, and he tells

9. The exegetical problem is why, at the end of the section (Isa. 58) beginning with the mention of the shofar and continuing with the most general of sins, the Sabbath is singled out for special emphasis. The author's solution ties the entire passage together: "refrain from trampling the Sabbath" refers to the custom of not sounding the shofar when New Year's Day falls on Saturday; the prophet therefore indicates the obligation to preach on the Sabbath and to articulate through the sermon the call to repentance that would have been heard in the shofar's sounds.

10. B. Sanh 18a (cf. sect. 11c, above).

11. B. Ber 6b; the Talmud understands the word *kerum* as referring to "a bird that changes color when the sun shines on it."

12. B. RH 27b; Maimonides, *Code* III,vi (*Shofar*) 1:6.

the wicked that they are righteous. Their faces turn many different shades, as we said.

Just as the shofar takes in [air] at one end and emits [it] at the other, so many words of ethical instruction go in one ear and out the other. More than this: a little goes in and a lot goes out, like the shofar, into which sound enters through a small hole and exits through a large one. This is the opposite of the sages' advice: "Make your ear like a hopper,"[13] that is, an implement through which material is poured into the wide end, exiting by the narrow one.

If fragments of different shofars are glued together [to make a whole one] so that it may be sounded, it is disqualified from use.[14] This teaches us about the preacher who does not cite the source for the material he uses, wrapping himself in someone else's prayer shawl. All that he says is stolen, fragments broken off from various compositions, a little from here and a little from there, as if this made a complete discourse. I have heard it said that this is the simple meaning of the verse, *Turn my heart to Your decrees and not to love of gain* (Ps. 119:36). In other words, make me broad-minded, so that I can explore the realm of ideas, but not for love of gain, so that I would steal from other books.

12. Judah Aryeh (Leon) Modena[1] (Late sixteenth and early seventeenth centuries, Italy)

a. I studied with Rabbi Hezekiah Finzi for eight months.[2] It was his practice to have the students studying Alfasi compose an original sermon on the lesson each Sabbath. On the Sabbath day, a *minyan* [ten males older than thirteen] would be gathered in the schoolhouse, and a youngster would preach before them. When it was my turn, the lesson was *Terumah* (Exod. 25:1–27:19). I took as a *nośe Gold and silver and bronze* (Ezod. 25:3), and as a *ma'amar,* "Rabban Simeon ben Gamaliel said, The world stands on three things, on

13. B. Ḥag 3b.

14. B. RH 27a.

1. Modena (1571–1648) was one of the most versatile and talented Jews of his age, and an extremely gifted preacher. His preaching is discussed by Ellis Rivkin, "The Sermons of Leon of Modena," *HUCA* 23/2 (1950–51):295–317, and Israel Rosenzweig, *Hogeh Yehudi Mi-Qeṣ ha-Renesans* (Tel Aviv, 1972), esp. chap. 4.

2. The event described in this passage occurred early in 1581, when Modena was about ten years old. He had been sent by his father to Ferrara to live with a relative and study with important teachers, including Finzi. For the importance of homiletical training (both listening to and delivering sermons) in the curriculum of Italian Jews, see Assaf, *Meqorot* 2:119, 149, 157, 177, 191 (the passage itself is cited by Assaf on p. 124). For homiletical training from a young age outside of Italy, see Hacker, "Ha-Derashah," pp. 114–15.

Torah, on worship, and on deeds of lovingkindness."[3] My message was that the first three alluded to the latter three, and that this is what God desired, the means through which the divine presence came to dwell among Israel.[4]

When I concluded, Rabbi Hezekiah said to two of the elders who were present, "I am certain that this youngster will deliver sermons to the Jewish people, for his manner shows that his preaching will bear fruit." Later, in the years 5365–67 [1604–07], when I preached each Sabbath in the Great Synagogue at the congregation's behest, he would always come to my sermons. When people praised what I had said, he replied, "Twenty-five years ago I predicted that he would be an effective preacher."

b. The first time I preached in the Great Synagogue was on the Sabbath following the Ninth of Ab.[5] There were so many people, including scholars, that the synagogue could not hold them all. It was printed in my book of sermons, *Midbar Yehudah.* God helped me make a favorable impression upon all who heard me. In the month of Iyar, 5354 [1594], the wealthy gentleman Kalonymos Belgrado established an academy in his gardens.[6] I was the main preacher, and I have continued so for twenty-five years to this day, establishing a reputation throughout the land for my preaching, as is well known.

For more than twenty years I have taught Bible and rabbinic literature each weekday evening and morning, and preached on the Sabbath in three or four different places, yet this congregation has never grown weary of hearing my sermons. Indeed, each time the listeners find them totally new. Friars and priests,[7] nobles and dignitaries also come to hear me, and through God's grace, they extol me and give me praise—may it be to His glory and the glory of Judaism, not my own.

c. To my distress, the truth is that I do not know a single book from that discipline which today they call "Kabbalah" and "true wisdom."[8] Neverthe-

3. On *nośe* and *ma'amar,* see "Structural Options," above. The *ma'amar* chosen by Modena is from the first chapter of Abot, although it substitutes the statement of Simeon the Righteous at the beginning of that chapter for the statement of Simeon ben Gamaliel at the end.

4. The boy preacher took a phrase pertaining to the tabernacle and devoid of any direct relevance to contemporary reality and made it into a key to the religious life, applying both to ancient times and to the present.

5. A portion of the introduction to this sermon is translated below as sect. 12f.

6. Compare Bonfil, *Rabbanut,* p. 19, n. 13. The sermon at the dedication of this academy was recorded in *Midbar Yehudah,* pp. 55b–58b.

7. This reference to Christian clergy coming to hear his sermons indicates that the sermons were originally delivered in Italian. See the discussion at the end of "The Preaching Situation," above.

8. Modena was in fact an implacable adversary of Kabbalah and wrote a trenchant critique of it entitled *Ari Nohem.*

less, I was able to appear publicly in my sermons as if I too knew a little of it. This was like those preachers who need to preach about the talmudic tractate ʿErubin in order to placate the confused minds of their listeners.[9] However, as the wise man said, "Teach me wisdom so that through it I may grow up with the wise, not so that I may preen myself with it before the ignorant."[10]

It can be extremely destructive to reveal such matters to the multitude, for they stir up minds that are at rest and confuse people of limited intellectual ability. The danger is even greater while we live among the nations, who either denounce us for kabbalistic teachings that oppose their beliefs or twist the doctrines in their own way.[11] This can be seen in what is told about this scholar who wanted to preach that Adam's sin caused a blemish in *Yesod,* etc.[12]

I call heaven and earth to witness that for thirty-three years I have been engaged in the sacred task of preaching Torah in this great city where I dwell, in other sacred communities of Italy, and elsewhere, and I have not spoken at all about the esoteric mysteries of the Godhead, except to touch in passing upon some simple and elementary teaching, for I was aware of the harm that could come from delving too deeply into such matters in public. In short, concerning that place where the four entered, if this scholar has possession of the chariot used by Absalom in fleeing, let him be content with that in his public sermons. As for the chariot used by Pharaoh when he entered the midst of the sea, let him leave that aside, for a day without light, and heavy, thick clouds [cf. Zech. 14:6].[13] Those things that are concealed in this world will be revealed in the world to come. . . .

9. This appears to refer to a popular demand for technical halakic discussions in sermons, a demand for which Modena had little sympathy. Compare Modena's justification of a limited use of Kabbalah in his preaching in *Ari Nohem, Leqeṭ Ketabim,* ed. Pnina Nave (Jerusalem, 1968), p. 206.

10. Cf. Judah Alḥarizi's Sefer *Taḥkemoni,* chap. 44: "Learn Wisdom *not* to lord it over the wise and not to deceive the ignorant" (cited in Davidson, p. 119).

11. A reference to the development of Christian Kabbalah, spearheaded by Pico della Mirandola. Cf. *Ari Nohem,* in Nave, pp. 208 and 243.

12. The original question sent to Modena, in which the preacher's sermon was apparently described in detail, has not survived. The idea that the sin of Adam caused a flaw in the entire realm of creation was not unusual in Kabbalah, but this formulation is more extreme, in that the flaw occurs in the realm of the Godhead, the *sefirah Yesod.* Cf. Gershom Scholem, *Kabbalah* (Jerusalem, 1974), p. 154; Judah Rosenthal, *Meḥqarim u-Meqorot,* 2 vols. (Jerusalem, 1974), 1:436–37, n. 12; Daniel Matt, *Zohar: The Book of Enlightenment* (New York, 1983), pp. 215–16.

13. "That place where the four entered" refers to the *pardes* mentioned in B. Ḥag 14b; see Gershom Scholem, *Jewish Gnosticism, Merkabah Mysticism, and the Talmudic Tradition* (New York, 1965), pp. 14–19. In the Middle Ages it was taken to represent a realm of esoteric knowledge. Although the thrust of the sentence is clear, the contrast between the chariots of Absalom and of Pharaoh is obscure.

d. To an Amsterdam scholar who wanted to punish one who preached that the world was eternal. . . .[14]

The man did not act properly by probing deeply such a sermon topic. Look at the learned [Azariah] de' Rossi, of blessed memory, the author of *Meʾor ʿEnayim.*[15] After devoting a chapter to this investigation, the forty-fourth chapter in the section called "Imre Binah," and weighing all the arguments, he came to the general conclusion that in all such profound and esoteric matters, it is certainly better not to delve too deeply.

How much more is it true that in speaking publicly before a congregation, where there are bound to be both learned and ordinary listeners, one should not set forth all the arguments on both sides of such an issue. This would encourage all to say their piece and express their views, whether good or bad, and to decide for themselves. It is better to refrain from preaching publicly on such matters. Our Torah is *broader than the sea* (Job 11:9), and there is no lack of acceptable Torah subjects that are more pleasant and more beneficial to the listeners than this.

e. When they Preach, they use the Language of the Country, that all the Congregation may understand them. They quote the Texts of Scripture and the Rabbins in Hebrew, and then interpret it in the Vulgar Tongue.[16]

Their manner of Preaching is: When all the Congregation are silent in the Synagogue, he that is to preach (which is easily granted to any one that desires it) either with his *Taled* [*ṭallit,* or prayer shawl] or without it, stands against the little wooden Table spoken of before, and begins with a Verse taken out of the Lesson which is read that week, which they call a *Nose,* a text, which he seconds with a Sentence out of the Rabbins, called a *Maamar.*[17] Then he makes a Preamble or Preface, and proposes a Subject pertinent to the Lesson whence he took his Text: he discourses upon it, and quotes Texts of Scripture and the Rabbins; every Man according to his own Stile, which is very different, among the several Countries.

This is done mostly upon Sabbath Days, and the chief Festivals; except there be a Funeral Oration for some Person of Note (which is done upon any Day, tho' it be no Festival) or some other extraordinary Occasion.

f. For a painter who loves to draw forms correctly, there is a straightforward

14. At issue here is not the Aristotelian doctrine denying creation, but the more controversial doctrine (defended by Maimonides) that the world would endure forever.

15. Azariah de' Rossi (ca. 1511–ca. 1578) was perhaps the outstanding Jewish intellectual of sixteenth-century Italy; his work relating to ancient Jewish history and chronology aroused a storm of controversy. See S. W. Baron, "Azariah de' Rossi's Attitude to Life," *Israel Abrahams Memorial Volume* (New York, 1927), pp. 12–53.

16. This is one of the clearest pieces of evidence for the vernacular delivery of sermons.

17. Cf. n. 3, above.

path. Any defect he notices can be repaired while he is still working. With brush in hand, he makes his strokes to the right and left, up and down, changing the lines, altering the hues, rearranging things until the blemish disappears.[18] By contrast, consider the sculptor who chisels a statue in stone. If he makes an error, rendering the nose too flat or protracted, once that blemish has been sculpted the statue is defective. It can never be corrected. The sculptor might as well throw the stone away, for his work upon it can no longer succeed. Only God works perfectly in both realms. . . . There is no artist like Him, whether in painting or in sculpture, no artist whose work is without fault, never in need of correction.[19]

It has often occurred to me that this essential difference between the painter and the sculptor in stone applies also to the relationship between writer and speaker.[20] In the course of writing, one may notice while the pen is still in hand that an error has been made: the sentence may be too concise or too verbose, or ambiguous, or there may be some other flaw. The writer may then use that same pen to add something or correct what is there so that no error remains. But if a speaker allows something improper to escape from his lips—and this is very likely, for errors are unavoidable when one speaks at length—there is no taking it back. This would be true even if the speaker were the Prince of the Universe [Metatron], with all his power. For the more one tries to correct what has been said, the more the error is compounded. . . .

Now since we have concluded that sculptor and speaker are superior to painter and writer, we may go further.[21] Suppose such a sculptor, working diligently in stone, should make a statue of a beautiful model. Suppose further that he is not content with the pleasure he could derive from gazing upon it alone, or even together with his patron or friend. He would then set it up along a public thoroughfare in the sight of all who passed by.

Yet this would in fact be looking for trouble, for the masses are like a body

18. The Hebrew text (*meshanneh ha-qawwim u-maḥalif et ha-gewanim u-mesadder et ha-maṣṣabim*) is a witty and daring parody of the first blessing after the call to worship in the evening service, where these actions are attributed to God as sustainer of the natural order. It is likely that this was actually said in Hebrew in the oral sermon, since the force of the parody is far clearer when heard than when read.

19. For the topos of God as painter, see E. R. Curtius, *European Literature and the Latin Middle Ages* (Princeton, 1953), p. 562.

20. The analogy of painting and poetry (or rhetoric) was common in antiquity; see George Kennedy, *Greek Rhetoric under Christian Emperors* (Princeton, 1983), pp. 171–72. For the analogy between preachers and artists in fifteenth-century Italian preaching, see O'Malley, p. 65, and cf. Bayley, pp. 51, 60, 88.

21. On this issue, cf. Robert Clements, *Michelangelo's Theory of Art* (New York, 1961), p. 301: "A Renaissance dogma held sculpture the major art, since God had practiced it to form man."

with many wagging tongues. If the sculpture is tall, some will find its height repulsive and condemn it. If it is short, it will fail to please the great. If the edge of the stone or the metal is sharp, some who see it will not be satisfied. If its bones and veins and sinews are not at rest, but protrude, as they should, some will say that the work is not authentic. And if by chance everything should be absolutely perfect, he will still be devoured by swordlike tongues. They will say, "Why did he place this monument here in our midst? It could only be to vaunt his prodigious talent and ability. See how he seeks after power." In the end they will curse by their king all who lift a hammer to do such work. . . .

Such has been, is, and will continue to be the fate of the work of every intellectual who puts forth the buds and blossoms of new ideas. Impelled by the spiritual power of his thought, he is not content to remain in his own private realm or to limit his discussion to close friends, and he therefore goes to speak his piece in public. Such a person can expect immediate trouble, while his reward is distant.[22] If he soars like an eagle and speaks of the great and profound mysteries of wisdom, his proud speech will not sit well with the "badgers," who are weak[23] in the deeper meaning of the Torah. They will say, "What is this?" for they will not know what he is talking about. But if he should speak at a low level, simply and plainly, the learned who hear him will turn their backs and say, "What does he think he is teaching us?"

If he speaks softly, and fails to reach the very pinnacle of rhetoric and eloquence, they grow tired of hearing him. And if the veins and sinews of his discourse—the biblical verses and rabbinic statements—are not given brilliant and elegant interpretations, they will open their mouths wide against him, saying that a fool who remains silent is better than he. Even if he never falters at a single step, people will still complain: "Why does he speak in such a grand manner? It must be to make his reputation for learning widely known, so that he will be called 'Rabbi.'"[24] Thus whoever preaches in public is looking for trouble, kindling contention. He should say several times, "Let my thoughts never pass through my mouth."

g. When God came down upon Mt. Sinai to give the Torah to His people, He made thunderous sounds; the earth trembled and quaked; there was a piercing blast of the shofar. For *the Righteous One knows the soul of His beast* (Prov. 12:10). God knew the way of the children of Israel, knew that some of them doze off and slumber as soon as they hear the voice of someone

22. This complaint that it is impossible to please everyone is a commonplace among Jewish preachers, although it is rarely expressed in such an original context.

23. Phrase based on Prov. 30:26.

24. Compare Luntshitz, sect. 11c above, at n. 7.

speaking words of Torah, as is the case to this very day among those who listen to sermons. He therefore caused this awesome tremor so that they would awaken from their sleep and hear the words He spoke to them.

Unfortunately, I cannot produce the sound of many earthquakes or thunder or the blast of the horn for you to hear, my lords, to awaken the slumbering while my lips utter praise through God's Torah. I can only beseech and implore every single one to cast the bonds of sleep from your eyes. Then I believe that you will listen to me.[25]

h. To my teacher, R. Samuel Archivolti:[26]

[Necessity], which is neither to be praised nor censured, has compelled me to publish in print a first selection of the sermons I preached as a young man here in the holy congregation of Venice.[27] It was not my own desire to publish them. I selected some eighteen or twenty sermons delivered on Sabbaths and holidays, at weddings and circumcisions, and as eulogies for distinguished scholars. They are but a few, in a small work, perhaps thirty full sheets. Had it not been for the pressures of time—each day as I wrote them down on paper,[28] they would print them—I would certainly have agreed to submit them to your critical review, which I greatly esteem. I could not do this, for time did not permit. . . .[29]

The name I have chosen for the book is *Midbar Yehudah*.[30] The sermons blaze a truly new path, for I have made them a blending of the Christian sermon and the traditional Jewish homily.[31] After the verse from the Torah

25. On the problem of sleeping during sermons, see "Preachers and Congregations."

26. In addition to his work as rabbi and halakic authority, Samuel Archivolti (1515–1611) was known as a poet and grammarian, the author of *'Arugat ha-Bośem* (Venice, 1602), an influential work of Hebrew prosody and grammar.

27. Modena was driven by financial need to publish this selection of early sermons. He was disappointed by the sales of the book.

28. Elsewhere, Modena indicates that the sermons in *Midbar Yehudah* were reconstructed from the "outline notes (*rimze rashe peraqim*)" that he had written at the time of delivery; see "The Nature of the Sources," n. 43.

29. Here Modena requests a poem from Archivolti, to be printed as the epigraph to the book.

30. A pun on the Biblical "Wilderness of Judah," here meaning "Speech of Judah." Modena's Hebrew name was Yehudah Aryeh.

31. *Ha-deras* (lit., "trampling") *we-ha-derash*. Boksenboim, the editor of the letter, notes that the word *deras* or *derasah* is used by Modena's grandson Isaac min ha-Lewiyyim in referring to a Christian sermon: *Medabber Tahpukot*, ed. Daniel Carpi (Tel Aviv, 1985), p. 80. This fits the present context and underlies my translation. However, the same word is used by Isaac to refer to the preaching of a Jew (ibid., p. 53), so that the word does not seem to have the clearly negative connotation that its Hebrew etymology would imply. Modena's interest in Christian homiletics can be documented, from a later period in his life, by the books in his library, which included a volume of Savonarola's sermons and a manual on preaching (Adelman, p. 327).

lesson [*nośe*] and the rabbinic statement [*ma'amar*][32] comes a brief introduction, which the Christians call *prologhino.* Then comes the first part of the sermon, and then the second part, followed by an explanation of the *nośe* and the *ma'amar.* At the end there is a recapitulation of the entire sermon called an *epiloghino,* and finally a petitionary prayer, in the accustomed manner. This is the structure of every sermon.[33]

There is no section without some biblical verse or rabbinic statement. The sermon is amplified through associations made in accordance with the art of rhetoric. I have not seen any printed sermons that follow this path. The language also is intermediate between the language of [Judah] Moscato, of blessed memory, which is so highly polished and stylized that many do not like it, and the language of most of the Levantine and Ashkenazic rabbis, which is much simpler.[34]

13. Judah Leib Pukhovitser[1] (Second half of seventeenth century, Poland)

a. I was able to immerse myself fully in study and contemplation for several years in the great academies. I was then accepted by communities well known for their piety: the sacred congregation of Slutsk, where I served as master of the academy, and later the sacred congregation of Pinsk, where I was born. It was our pattern to preach words of ethical rebuke each day, thereby fostering humility.[2] Every Sabbath I would preach novel interpretations of the Torah pertaining to the weekly lesson, based primarily upon the novellae in the works of Alsheikh[3] and those in *Sefer ha-Gilgulim* attributed to the Ari [Isaac

32. On these terms, see "Structural Options," above.

33. Among the sermons included in this book, the structure outlined by Modena is most clearly exemplified by the sermon of his disciple Saul Morteira of Amsterdam.

34. Cf. Joseph Zarfati's statement about literary language in sermon collections, quoted in "The Nature of the Sources," above, at n. 44.

1. On Pukhovitser, see *EJ* 13:1380–81; Isaiah Tishby, *Netibe Emunah u-Minut* (Jerusalem, 1982), pp. 111–42; Piekarz, passim.

2. Note the reference to daily preaching, in addition to the weekly Sabbath sermon based on the lesson in an Ashkenazic context. See the discussion in "The Preaching Situation," above.

3. Moses Alsheikh, one of the greatest scholars of sixteenth-century Safed, was known as a preacher, although his sermons were recast in the form of biblical commentaries. See Shimon Shalem, *Rabbi Mosheh Alsheikh* (Jerusalem, 1966), and Pachter, "Sifrut," pp. 260–93. *Sefer ha-Gilgulim,* which treats the doctrine of the transmigration of souls, was written by Ḥayyim Vital, the disciple of Isaac Luria (the "Ari").

Luria]. (The soul of R. Samuel bar Naḥmani was attached to the soul of R. Moses [Alsheikh]; that is why he became a great preacher. . . .)[4]

This was followed by ethical content from the Zohar and other ethical writings, especially from the works of Alsheikh, for the ethical content of his books is convincingly expressed and clearly related to biblical verses, and it penetrates to the inmost recesses of the heart. . . . It was also our pattern to admonish about some of the laws that are neglected, in accordance with the talmudic statement, "When R. Meir preached publicly, he preached one third *shemateta,* one third *aggadeta,* and one third *mitle*" [B. Sanh 38b].[5] Although I was later in many communities, I followed this pattern daily, and every Sabbath. I therefore thought it would be desirable to write my words in a book. . . .

It is necessary to appoint in every Jewish community a great scholar, advanced in years, one who has feared God from his youth, to reproach the masses and point the way back through repentance, as Maimonides wrote [*Code* I,v (*Teshubah*) 4:2]. . . . That scholar must also exert himself to know the sins of those in his community, even if they are not apparent, as it says in the Zohar on Ruth, p. 7.[6]

Even more, we find that the leaders are obliged to travel through the villages under their charge and to teach people the proper way to conduct themselves. . . . It may well have been an ancient custom that the leading rabbis would travel every year or two through their settlements to teach the isolated Jews and tax farmers the laws and behavior required by our sacred faith. For example: the observance of the Sabbath as it pertains to the sale of beverages and the moving of things from one realm to another, the laws of Passover pertaining to the sale of leavened food and the making of unleavened bread, the laws of prayer, and many others that are neglected, which we have arranged in part 2. This is not the case now. Most of those who travel through the provinces and settlements do so merely for the income it provides, intending to fill their satchels with money and food.[7] They do not

4. Samuel bar Naḥmani was a Palestinian *amora* of the late third and early fourth century, renowned for his mastery of aggadah. For Alsheikh as his reincarnation, cf. Meir Benayahu, *Sefer Toledot ha-ʾAri* (Jerusalem, 1967), p. 170, n. 9.

5. See the following selection for Pukhovitser's understanding of these terms.

6. The full passage to which the author is referring states: "The judge must actively seek to know the behavior of those in his community, for he is held responsible for their sins. The judge should not say, 'My role is to adjudicate civil cases [that are brought before me] and nothing more.' No, all the deeds of the community hang upon his neck. If he closes his eyes to the behavior of his neighbors, he is held responsible for their sins." The author apparently used the *Zohar Ḥadash* on Ruth published separately in Cracow (1593) under the title *Tappuḥe Zahab,* where the passage begins at the bottom of p. 7. For the Maimonides reference in the previous sentence, see above, sect. 2c.

7. This complaint became increasingly frequent among Eastern European writers. See the Polish sources below, and "Preachers and Congregations."

teach at all. . . . It is not a source of honor to the Torah to be like one who goes begging from place to place.

When a community accepts a rabbi, its leaders should clearly stipulate that he must watch over all that is done in the city and preach words of ethical rebuke every day, or at least each Sabbath.[8] If he does not, they should appoint another in his place. . . . I have long been pained, and I am still astonished, to see how trivial this is considered by the scholars and the lay leaders of our generation, who do not see fit to set their contemporaries straight themselves or to fulfill what Maimonides wrote. . . . This is especially important in our generation, which because of our sinfulness has suffered economically and physically. Indeed, blood has been spilled, and we are a few remaining out of many.[9]

b. In tractate Sanhedrin, chapter "Ḥeleq" [sic; text on 38b], we read, "When R. Meir preached publicly, he preached one third *shemateta,* one third *aggadeta,* and one third *mitle.*" *Shemateta* means "laws," *aggadeta* means interpretations of the simple meaning of biblical verses and rabbinic statements, *mitle* are the patterns of ethical behavior, as is explained in *Qeneh Ḥokmah,* p. 9c, in the name of the SheLaH.[10] Yet further explanation is needed. First, why did he preach in this order, first discussing legal material, then giving exegetical interpretations and ethical guidance? Second, it is a clear and obvious responsibility of the leaders in each age to teach the people laws and give words of ethical rebuke, as I explained in *Qeneh Ḥokmah* on page 8b and c, based upon the Talmud and Midrash. But whence this impulse to include exegetical interpretations in the same sermon between these parts?

This may be explained in accordance with the Mishnah [Abot 1:17]: "The essence is not study but conduct." The commentators have explained that we must not make the essence of our sermons novel interpretations of the Torah intended to demonstrate our wisdom, but rather "conduct"; we should preach about what pertains to conduct, admonishing the people to turn from their evil way and teaching them how to improve.[11] Now it is clear that since the Mishnah says [the *essence* is] to teach what pertains to conduct, one may

8. See n.2, above.

9. Pukhovitser lived through the Cossack massacres of 1648 (see the sermon by Israel of Bełżyce, above), and he was an eyewitness to a massacre of Jews by Muscovite soldiers at Bykhov in 1659, during which one of his daughters was killed.

10. Discussed in *Shene Luḥot ha-Berit* ("SheLaH") by Isaiah ben Abraham Horowitz (ca. 1565–1630), one of the most influential of Polish kabbalistic-ethical writings, this rabbinic statement was frequently used in subsequent works. See Piekarz, p. 135, n. 122.

11. See Samuel Uceda, *Midrash Shemu'el,* on Abot 1:17 (Warsaw, 1875; reprint ed., Jerusalem, 1960), p. 18a–b.

include in the same sermon novel interpretations of Torah.[12] R. Meir understood this mishnaic statement as these commentators did, and therefore when he preached about laws and ethical matters, he included interpretations as well.

But you may say that there is a contradiction here. If material pertaining to conduct is the essence, then the entire sermon should be devoted to practical matters. And second, the commentators said that we must not make the essence of our sermons novel interpretations of the Torah intended to demonstrate our wisdom. But if this is a preacher's intention, his motives are obviously impure, bound up with personal arrogance, and this should disqualify such content even if it is not the major portion of the sermon. . . .

The answer is derived from the verse in Hosea, *Yet* [ak] *let no man quarrel, nor let any man rebuke* (4:4). The book *Marʾot ha-Ṣobeʾot* interprets this on the basis of the rabbinic statement that the words *ak* and *raq* always have the function of limiting.[13] Thus it is the limited man who is precluded from quarreling with or rebuking the majority, for they will say, *Who made you a man {to rule over us and judge us?}* (Exod. 2:14).[14] Now since the Mishnah indicates that it is necessary to rebuke the people, it also implies that it is necessary to give novel interpretations of the Torah, so that the preacher may demonstrate that he is a "man."[15] The phrase "the essence is not study" means, even though it is permissible to preach novel interpretations of the Torah publicly in order to demonstrate wisdom, for the reason stated, we must never make this the essence. The essence must be that which pertains to conduct, and the novel interpretations must remain of secondary importance.

R. Meir followed the mishnaic statement in his sermons, first speaking about *shemateta,* or laws, for the simple meaning of "conduct" is behavior according to the commandments. It is explained there in the name of the SheLaH[16] that the preacher must inform those with limited education of the

12. The author infers two things from this statement: (1) novel interpretations of Torah verses ("study") must not be the most important part of the sermon, and (2) such interpretations are permissible in a secondary role. On this second point, contrast the position taken by Luntshitz in sect. 11b, above.

13. The rabbinical principle of interpreting the words *ak* and *raq* is found in P. Ber IX, 14b. *Marʾot ha-Ṣobeʾot* was the commentary on the prophets written by Moses Alsheikh (see above, n. 3); the interpretation cited is found in the comment on Hos. 4:4.

14. This verse, expressing an early challenge to the leadership of Moses, was frequently used in attacks on preachers, reflecting the problematic nature of their claim to authority. See "Preachers and Congregations."

15. I.e., the novel, ingenious interpretations may be used to establish the preacher's intellectual credentials and validate his chastisement of the congregation—provided that such interpretations do not become the essence of the sermon.

16. See above, n. 10.

laws they need to know. Since this is the essence, he preached about them first, never preceding them with exegetical interpretations. Then, before he preached *mitle,* the ethical rebuke that is also obligatory (as I have explained at length), he preached *aggadeta,* interpretations, to show that he was a "man." What I have said is a clear condemnation of most preachers in our generation, who do not include words of ethical rebuke. Even if they occasionally do so, this material is so minimal that it seems to be of minor importance.

14. Abraham ben Eliezer ha-Kohen, *Ori we-Yishʿi*[1] (Late seventeenth century, Poland)

a. Once, as I was castigating the people in an ethical discourse, I looked out at the congregation and noticed some who scoff at God's spokesmen, refusing to hear the divine message of rebuke. The majority, however, did want to listen carefully to what I had to say; they wanted me to provide criticism and guidance. I therefore put a muzzle on the mockers. This is what I said:

What did the sages of sacred memory mean when they said, "Those who are insulted but do not insult [*ʿolebin*], hear their reproach without answering, of them Scripture says, *Those who love him are as the sun rising in might* (Judg. 5:31)"?[2] There are problems in this statement that need to be resolved. First is their use of the form *ʿolebin,* an intransitive verb, where we would expect the form *maʿalibin,* a transitive verb, clearly meaning "to insult others." Second, why did they add the phrase, "who hear their reproach without answering," which appears to be redundant? Both our esteemed and revered rabbi and teacher, the author of *Shene Luḥot ha-Berit,* and the versatile Rabbi Joseph Pinto have written that this phrase refers to those who hear the person who attacked them being reproached by others who say that he has this strange quality of attacking others.[3] You may consult what they said. Nevertheless, there is room for me to make my own point.

My explanation is as follows. It should be obvious to all Jews that when a preacher stands at his post, rebuking the humble impartially, with honesty and integrity, the holy people must remain silent. The sages said that silence is becoming to the wise, for a wise man endures his infirmity in silence; how much more is it becoming to fools.[4] Humorists have noted that a fool is

1. On Abraham ben Eliezer and his work *Ori we-Yishʿi,* see Piekarz, pp. 101–04 and passim; S. Z. Rubashow, "Derashot R. Yehudah he-Ḥasid," *Zion* 6 (1941):213–14.

2. B. Shab 88b, B. Yoma 23a, B. Giṭ 36b.

3. On *Shene Luḥot ha-Berit,* see sect. 13, n. 10. Cf. the commentary of Josiah ben Joseph Pinto on *ʿEn Yaʿaqob* (B. Shab 88b and B. Giṭ 36b).

4. Cf. B. Pes 99a.

worse than a *mamzer* [offspring of an adulterous or incestuous union] conceived by a woman in a state of ritual impurity.[5] Why? They tell that once a *mamzer* and a fool decided to go on a journey together. Said the *mamzer* to the fool, "For mercy's sake, refrain from speaking nonsense and do not reveal that I am a *mamzer*. I, in turn, will not reveal that you are a fool." The fool answered that this would be fine.

When they arrived at an inn, the *mamzer* said, "I will enter first, and say that a learned man is following me; we will then be greatly honored." The fool replied, "Yes, I hope it works out this way." The *mamzer* did as he had said, and the fool then followed with his walking stick. But the walking stick got stuck in the doorway, and the fool was unable to enter. Soon everyone began to laugh at him. The fool then said, "Obviously that *mamzer* told you that I am a fool." From this we see that a fool is worse than a *mamzer*.

Even when the preacher speaks of their corrupt and disgraceful behavior, shooting his verbal arrows at the heart of each listener, so that all cover their faces in shame, not a single one of them so much as whispers. There is absolute silence. Although beyond doubt there are guilty ones in their midst, no individual is humiliated, for it is not publicly known to whom the preacher is referring in his rebuke. He speaks in general terms, and those to whom his words apply feel ashamed.[6] In this way the arrogance of the congregation as a whole is subdued, and people think, "Yes, what God's servant has said is true."

But occasionally someone will rise to subvert the speaker's faithful message. An evil scoundrel will stand up in the midst of the congregation, face the preacher of rebuke, open his mouth, and say, "*Who made you chief and ruler over us?* (Exod. 2:14). Do you want to kill me with your words? Insult yourself in your preaching—don't insult me. Let a true priest perform the divine service, not a puny pauper like you. Have you ever seen such a man? You're a phony and a fraud! My walking stick will communicate with you if you don't shut up!"[7]

To this reprobate, the preacher of rebuke should reply, "Why are you the one who feels compelled to shout? Why does it pain you more than the others? It can only be your insolence, your bad conscience, your own wickedness telling you that you are as good as dead. Did I speak to you alone? Did I not speak to the others as well? Why are they silent, while your mouth

5. Davidson, *Oṣar*, p. 112, gives this passage as the only source for the quotation.

6. The technique of restricting criticisms to general statements was one solution to the problem of preaching rebuke. It was endorsed by others (e.g., *Binat Yiśśakar*, p. 5a), and vehemently attacked as cowardly by Zerah Eidlitz; see the discussion in "Preachers and Congregations."

7. Compare the discussion of the motifs in this passage in "Preachers and Congregations," at n. 36.

gapes open like a camel's? It must be that the sickness has spread through your heart, impelling you to defy God's majestic glance." Then all the others will say, "Cursed is such a man! He has acted abominably, speaking perversely against God and falsely against God's anointed. No one may attack a preacher with impunity."

Then the preacher can stun his opponent by saying, "Because of what you have done, I shall reveal to all what I have concealed until now. Such and such is what you have done, and this is the fruit of your sins, you who are uncircumcised and unclean." In this way, a perverse man like the one I described testifies against himself, for *Where there is much talking there is no lack of transgression* (Prov. 10:19). Had he remained silent, he would not have been harmed as he sat in the midst of the congregation during the sermon of rebuke. He might have fulfilled the verse, *Happy is the one whose transgression is overlooked, whose sin is covered over* (Ps. 32:1).

This provides the explanation for the statement of the rabbis. When they said, "Those who are insulted but do not insult," they referred to that group of people who are insulted by others but do not feel it as an insult. . . .[8] Of this group it is said, "they hear their reproach," meaning that together with the rest of the congregation they hear their own reproach from the preacher of rebuke, yet they do not reply to the preacher; rather, they think of themselves as part of the community as a whole. The rebuke is therefore not considered a personal insult, for no one knows to which members of the congregation the preacher is referring. Each individual can say, "I am guiltless; he was criticizing someone else, not me." Even though his conscience may secretly torment him with the knowledge that God is aware of his failings, he may still clear himself in the sight of others. Therefore he will not mock the message of a learned man, but rather listen attentively to the words of the living God.

The talmudic statement concludes, "of them Scripture says, *[Those who love him] as the sun rising in might* (Judg. 5:31)," meaning those who love the preacher, who is as the sun rising in might. For just as the sun rising over the earth does not direct its light to any particular individual but to the entire earth, while all who want to protect themselves may withdraw from the sun and make a shelter for their heads, so the person who remains silent is covered and remains hidden from shame. "I have not found anything better for a person than silence" [Abot 1:17]. The sages may have alluded to this in the Talmud, Tractate Berakot [34b] when they said, "I consider impertinent a person who openly recounts [his sins]," meaning, it is considered an act of impertinence when someone from the congregation rises to argue

8. The new interpretation of *ʿolebin* distinguishes it from the transitive *hifʿil* form *maʿalibin* by rendering it not "insult (others)" but "feel the insult."

with a preacher who is rebuking him when he could remain silent, for then it would not be known to whom the preacher was referring.

With these words I confuted the troublemaker. It was as if he had been struck dumb; he could not open his mouth.

b. How sweet to my palate are the words of the great preacher of rebuke, the saintly Rabbi Jacob Ratner, of blessed memory.[9] In one of his ethical sermons, he used an analogy to make the point that the preacher must rebuke the people in his accustomed manner even if he brings healing to no more than one or two individuals. His analogy was with a king who goes out to the field with his nobles to hunt, hoping to catch a wolf or other such prey. All day long he wearies himself and his attendants on horseback, like one who hunts a partridge in the hills, chasing from tree to tree and from branch to branch, on rocky cliffs and in the woods.

When evening comes, he may have caught only a single hare, weighing but a few pounds. Many traps were shot full of arrows, many horses galloped far, and all he has is one tiny creature. Yet the king rejoices in his success as a valiant hunter, finding comfort in the thought that some day soon he will also catch a lion, or a wolf, or a splendid buck.

This is what the preacher of rebuke to a congregation should think. The first time he may help one person, the second time another, until eventually his power will increase to the point where he will help many, including some who are more important than these. The sages referred to this when they said, "Whoever saves a single soul of Israel, it is as if he had saved the entire world" [B. Sanh 37a]. They said "soul," not "person," thereby alluding to the evil soul that the preacher saves from the pit of destruction. By keeping this one from tipping the scales of his own personal fate, and of the entire world, in the direction of guilt, the preacher who saves an evil soul saves the entire world.

15. Ezekiel Landau, *Ahabat Ṣiyyon*[1] (1757, Prague)

One who rebukes another will eventually find favor (Prov. 28:23). This verse may be explained on the basis of the challenge that can be raised to the very concept of preaching words of rebuke, namely the claim that "it is better that they sin out of ignorance than out of rebelliousness" [B. Shab 148b]. Indeed, if, God forbid, the wicked cling to their evil and do not accept the rebuke, then the rebuke will retroactively work to their detriment by in-

9. On Ratner, see Glicksberg, p. 260; Piekarz, p. 104, n. 27.
1. See the introduction to Landau's sermon, above.

creasing the severity of their sin. It would thus have been better if the preacher had not rebuked them.[2]

However, the preacher is not a prophet. He is obligated to do his part in fulfilling the commandment, *Rebuke your neighbor* (Lev. 19:17). In tractate Shabbat {55a}, it says that Strict Justice accused the elders of Jerusalem with the argument, "Master of the Universe, if it was clearly known to You that {the wicked} would not accept rebuke, was it clearly known to {the elders}?" Therefore do not say that if the wicked fail to accept the rebuke, God forbid, the preacher will be punished for rebuking them and thereby increasing their guilt.

Scripture testifies in the Book of Ezekiel (33:7–9), *Now, O mortal, I have appointed you a watchman for the house of Israel, and whenever you hear a message from My mouth, you must transmit My warning to them. When I say to the wicked, "O wicked, you shall die," but you have not spoken to warn the wicked about their ways, the wicked shall die for their sins, but I will demand a reckoning for their blood from you. But if you have warned the wicked to turn back from their ways and they do not, they shall die for their own sins, but you will have saved your life.*

This proves that if the preacher has carried out his responsibility of rebuking, he saves his own soul, even if the rebuke is of no avail, the wicked remain evil, and they die in sin. Although the preacher is fulfilling his obligation, the wicked will undoubtedly hate him passionately, for there is no denying the evil they have done. If the wicked do not change their ways, it is obvious that they will not like the preacher, but if they do change, then in retrospect they may love the preacher for having saved them from death for eternal life and restored to them their lost soul.

Now the preacher cannot know whether his rebuke will be accepted, but this is certainly known to God, as Strict Justice said. Thus when he stands up to deliver his rebuke, the preacher himself does not know how he will marshal his words, with regard either to the content or to the manner of speech.[3] All depends upon the divine inspiration that comes to him, not upon his own merit. Even though he may be personally unworthy, the merit of the congregation thirsting to hear his words of rebuke may lead God to inspire him with power and eloquence so that his words will have an impact upon his listeners. It is as the prophet Isaiah said, *The Lord has given me a skilled tongue* (Isa. 50:4). This is truly a gift from God. It occurs when it is clear to God that the words of the preacher will bear fruit, and the people

2. This passage reveals a consciousness of the frequent failure to effect real change through sermons, and of the paradox that preaching may actually increase the sinfulness of unrepentant sinners. See the discussion in "Preachers and Congregations."

3. This implies a mode of preaching without a fully prepared text and a theory unusual among Jewish writers in its reliance upon the category of divine inspiration.

will accept his rebuke and return in penitence; then God adds to his strength, for God prefers lovingkindness and wants the evil to repent.

But when it is clear to God that the evil are not prepared to repent, then although the preacher must do his part, he is left to his own meager resources. Why should God inspire him and make his message more eloquent? There is no question that when the preacher is an amateur like myself, it is only because of the merit of the congregation that God helps him and keeps him from stumbling in his speech. But this assumes that the message of rebuke will benefit the congregation. If, God forbid, they do not accept it, then the rebuke is not to their benefit, and the merit of the congregation is of no avail to the preacher who is himself unworthy.

I would say that even if the preacher were worthy, God would still not help him, for the greater the power and the eloquence of the preacher's words, the greater would be the sin of the wicked who fail to accept the rebuke. If, however, the preacher is inarticulate and speaks briefly—and even that in a bumbling manner that could not be expected to influence anyone—then the punishment for not accepting the rebuke is not so great. Part of the fault is the preacher's own inadequacy. Since it is clear to God that the rebuke will not be accepted, why should He help the preacher by making him more eloquent? This would only increase the punishment due to the wicked, God forbid, and the Holy One does not want the death of the wicked.

This would appear to be the meaning of the verse, *Human beings arrange their thoughts; what is said depends on the Lord* (Prov. 16:1). It means that when *human beings arrange their thoughts,* that is, when those in the congregation prepare their hearts to heed the preacher's message so that his rebuke may have its effect upon them, then *what is said* by the preacher *depends on the Lord.* But if, God forbid, they do not accept the rebuke, then God makes the preacher stumble in his speech, so that he will shorten his message of rebuke.[4]

16. Zerah Eidlitz,[1] *Or la-Yesharim* (1766, Prague)

To explain the verse with which we started,[2] we will set forth another thesis. It is a custom in Israel—and custom has the status of Torah—for preachers

4. The thrust of the passage is to shift the blame for poor preaching (as well as the credit for good preaching) from the preacher to the congregation.

1. A loyal disciple of Jonathan Eybeschuetz, Eidlitz was one of the great preachers in Prague during the third quarter of the eighteenth century. His book of sermons, *Or la-Yesharim,* is worthy of intensive study.

2. The verse is Isa. 58:1; its use in the context of preaching goes back at least to Joseph ibn Shem Ṭob (see *ʿEn ha-Qore,* sect. 6, above).

to travel from city to city to rebuke the people. Many of the ignorant masses err by not heeding their message because these preachers accept money for their sermons. The fools say that the preachers' rebuke is only a means of enriching themselves, and that their motives are therefore impure.[3]

I once heard a parable about this from Rabbi Joel the Preacher, may the memory of the righteous be for a blessing.[4] In one city of Poland, there were no houses made of hewn stone. All were made of wood from the forest, and the roofs were covered with straw, like the village houses in our country. A man and a woman lived there in a garret under the roof. Once the woman went to bed at night while her husband was still awake, and he had a lighted candle. Before it was extinguished, he too went to bed, leaving the candle burning. His wife berated him: "What are you doing! Don't you know that we sleep under the roof, and the house is made entirely of wood, and the roof is covered with straw, and everything is dry as clippings? A single flying spark could burn down the entire city, God forbid!"

While she was speaking, the night watchman came and, following the universal practice, proclaimed the time. He then made an announcement, warning the people to be careful about their candles and telling them why they should not go to sleep leaving a candle still lit. But the man replied, "This is nonsense. Do you think that the watchman is making this announcement in sincerity? I happen to know that he has no money at all, no estate to bequeath, not even a single stick anywhere. What does he care if there is a fire or not? He makes the announcement only because the town pays him to do so. If they paid him to proclaim that people should burn down their houses, he would do that as well. Since this man does not speak sincerely, I won't pay any attention to what he said. I'm going to sleep, and I'll leave the candle burning."

Just what the woman had predicted actually happened. Soon after the man lay down and fell asleep, the candle fell over on the table, the house started to burn, and there was a great conflagration, destroying most of the city. He and his wife barely escaped alive, having lost all their possessions.

Now think about this fool. Unwilling to heed the words of the watchman because he did not speak sincerely, the man let his house burn down. The same is true of the itinerant preacher, who admonishes the people to abandon

3. Compare the witticism attributed to the Baal Shem Tov, cited in Samuel Dresner, *The Zaddik* (New York, 1960), p. 224. Issachar Baer Bloch argued that preachers should not accept any payment, so that they would not provide the masses with an excuse to ignore their words (*Binat Yiśśakar,* p. 5a).

4. Joel Mokiaḥ, who did not leave any written works, was apparently an itinerant preacher who used this parable to establish his own credibility. A similar parable, though lacking the domestic setting of this one, was used by Elijah ben Moses Gerson in the introduction to his *Hadrat Eliyyahu* (Prague, 1785), p. 4a; cf. Piekarz, p. 120.

their evil deeds, lest they fall into hell, where their bodies will be burned (for the Bible says, *Lo! that day comes, burning like an oven* [Mal. 3:19]; compare the verse *Can a person stir up fire in his breast without burning his clothes?* [Prov. 6:27]).[5] Yet the fools, saying that the preacher rebukes us not for pure reasons but because he is paid, heed him not, until the fire comes upon them. There can be no foolishness greater than this. This is the end of the quotation from Rabbi Joel, may the memory of the righteous be for blessing.

Now we would say that a preacher who criticizes the people for religious reasons is indeed preferable to one who does so because of the money he earns, for "Words emanating from the heart penetrate to the heart."[6] When the preacher speaks solely for the sake of the money, his words do not emanate from the heart, and they therefore do not have as great an impact. Although it is extremely foolish not to heed the watchman according to the above parable, this may not apply to a substandard preacher. Even worse, sometimes a preacher will come to a town, and the officers will say to him, "You just need the money; take the money and go your way without rebuking us." When the preacher refrains from speaking critically for this reason, he has certainly not done right.[7]

It appears that the Talmud alluded to this in speaking about the shofar.[8] The rabbis said, "A shofar plated with gold in the place where the mouth is set is unfit. If plated on the inside, it is unfit; if on the outside, it is unfit if its sound is changed from what it was, but if its sound is unchanged, it is fit" [B. RH 27b]. Now we find that the Bible compares the preacher to a shofar, saying *Like a shofar raise your voice* (Isa. 58:1). Thus a shofar "plated in the place where the mouth is set" refers to a preacher who sets his mouth because they give him money. Such a man is unfit to preach a sermon of rebuke.

Similarly, "plated on the inside" refers to a preacher who inwardly cares only about the money and has no religious concerns. He too is unfit. "Plated on the outside" refers to one who is inwardly pure, unconcerned about money, but who accepts money for another reason—because he has no other source of sustenance and is like an itinerant pauper. Of such a person it says, "If its sound is changed from what it was," namely, that because of this he refrains from rebuking those who pay him lest they become angry at him, he too is unfit, for he should trust in the Lord and cast his burden upon

5. This literal invocation of hell was not at all uncommon in eighteenth-century Jewish preaching; cf. the sermon of Eybeschuetz at n. 25.

6. Although not an attested rabbinic statement, this was frequently cited in later Jewish literature (e.g., Moses ibn Ezra, *Sefer ha-ʿIyyunim we-ha-Diyyunim* [Jerusalem, 1975], p. 219.

7. Compare the sources cited by Hacker, "Ha-Derashah," p. 113.

8. Note the homiletical interpretation of halakic material pertaining to the shofar. Cf. Luntshitz, above, sect. 11d, at n. 12.

God, who will provide for his need. But "if his sound does not change," he is fit.

And so, my brothers and friends, when a preacher comes here and accepts money, you may have something of an excuse. Even though the preacher acts for religious reasons, without any special interest, rebuking even the communal leaders, nevertheless you may say that deep within he does have an ulterior motive, and his words are not sincere. This is sheer nonsense, for the message is a true one, as we already explained in the parable. What difference does it make to you what his inner motivation may be? Nevertheless, there is a bit of an argument and an excuse for the evil impulse, that words not emanating from the heart do not penetrate to the heart. But if you pay no heed to *me,* what excuse or rationalization can you have?[9]

17. Mordecai ben Samuel, *Shaʿar ha-Melek*[1] (Eighteenth century, Poland)

Let us return to this period we are discussing: the twenty-one intermediate days between the Seventeenth of Tammuz and the Ninth of Ab, analogous to the intermediate days between the New Year's Day and the Day of Atonement. During this period, it is particularly appropriate to distribute charity to the poor and the needy. Moreover, it is well for pure-hearted Jews to hearken to preachers of rebuke during this period, especially to those who travel from town to town.

Would that these preachers were given an ample reward! A year never ends without their being on the road, uprooted from their home in body and spirit, taking exile upon themselves with a sigh that could break the heart. They are called "the encampment of the *shekinah,*" for they are, as it were, partners with the *shekinah.*[2] Just as she wanders from her home (so to speak), so do these preachers of rebuke wander from their homes, saying, "It is enough for a servant to be like his master" [B. Ber 58b].

They are truly the emissaries of the Compassionate One. God sent his servants the prophets to go from place to place, from rampart to rampart. It

9. Thus, after a defense of itinerant preachers, Eidlitz ends by distancing himself from them and making a claim for the superior status of a local rabbi.

1. On this author, see Piekarz, pp. 75–78 and 153–56. This passage is one of the most eloquent and impressive defenses of itinerant preachers in the literature.

2. The phrase "encampment of the *shekinah* [the divine presence]" is used in Sifre Numbers 1 to identify the sacred area of the tabernacle; cf. also B. Pes 68a. In kabbalistic literature, the concept was considerably extended; see, e.g., R. J. Z. Werblowsky, *Joseph Karo: Lawyer and Mystic* (Philadelphia, 1977), p. 59.

is said in Jeremiah, *Go and proclaim to Jerusalem . . .* (Jer. 2:2); in their days they traveled because of instructions they heard directly from God, thus performing His mission. Later, there was resort to the heavenly voice, the *bat qol*. But now, because of our sins, there is no voice, and no one to respond. God's emissaries go forth because they are sent by the Heavenly Court, which has afflicted them with economic hardship; this is what impels them to travel.[3]

Therefore, let no one say that these emissaries go forth to speak only because of the coins they will be given. Certainly not! They take to the road in order *to pass among the numbered ranks of the Lord* (Exod. 30:13). Therefore, God arranges things so that they will be economically afflicted. It is as the verse says, *He is wounded because of our sins, crushed because of our iniquities* (Isa. 53:5). God crushes them so that they will go forth in their need and serve as the world's oars, bringing people toward the good.[4]

This is like a king with a faithful servant, to whom he spoke directly about all that concerned him. Later, the servant lost his power of speech. Yet he still listened, and when he heard the king inform him of his command, he went out to perform the royal mission, using the inarticulate sounds he could make. Later, the servant became deaf. Not only was he unable to speak, he was now unable to hear. He would then go in to the king and receive his communication through signals, for his intelligence remained, and he could comprehend the signals communicated by the king. Finally the servant lost his wit, and he could no longer understand the signals. He would then be taken and pointed in the direction he was to follow.[5]

The meaning is this. In the first generations, there were prophets, faithful servants of the universal King, who spoke to them directly. Later, prophecy ceased, and we were made dumb, but the *bat qol* was used; if there was no articulate speech, the sound of the voice was still heard, and we performed the King's command based on that sound. Later, the *bat qol* ceased, and we became deaf, like one who can neither hear nor speak. Yet wisdom was not lost, for there were rabbis who went about their business based on signals, interpreting the Torah through its allusions and recondite meanings, wisely expounding at every point innumerable laws.

But now wisdom has been lost, and we are become fools; wisdom has been

3. Note the doctrine that economic reverses are caused by God precisely in order to require preachers to travel and spread their message.

4. This link of the itinerant preachers with the "suffering servant" of Isa. 53 does not imply a doctrine of vicarious atonement. The sinfulness of the people requires the message of rebuke as a cure, and God therefore causes those who can deliver this message to suffer economic hardship, which forces them to take to the road.

5. This version of the parable, probably not original with our author, is earlier than the Hasidic version told by S. Y. Agnon and used by Scholem at the conclusion of *Major Trends in Jewish Mysticism* (pp. 349–50).

banished without permission to return. God has, as it were, banished the *shekinah* from His home, and she does not return, for people do not repent. Then God brings affliction upon us, especially upon the good men of each generation, crushing them with poverty, and God points the way with His finger, so that they will take to the road in their need, to rebuke the world and to lead it back to the good.

Therefore, listen to the preachers of rebuke who travel from town to town to awaken the people, concentrating especially on the wicked. As they enter each city, they ask who is doing evil, and then they speak heartfelt words to inspire them and awaken them from their sleep. Be sure to honor these preachers, for whoever oppresses them is as one who oppresses the *shekinah*. They should be sustained and supported and fed in their hour of need. Your benevolence should anticipate them on the day they preach; you should fill their pockets. No one should say that they come only for money. If money brings someone out, it also brings something in: namely, the fear and love of God that the preacher instills in the human heart.

Think of the analogy with a physician, who does what he can to cure the sick, not knowing whether the medicine will be effective or not. Yet he takes his fee from the head of the family, who gives it graciously. If the medicine works to heal the patient, the physician is given every possible honor, together with a handsome fee.[6] This principle should pertain all the more to the preacher of rebuke, who comes to cure the soul and enable it to attain eternal life. He is obviously doing something good, if only we would not refuse to listen. Those who do listen will certainly be inspired. . . . Why then should the preacher not receive his fee? To the contrary, it should be given him graciously. . . .

But this is not done in our generation, when God's Torah and God's preachers are despised. . . . Communal leaders sit outdoors and keep watch over the crossroads, so that they will see an important personage coming while he is still in the carriage. But the idle loafers say to each other, "This is only a preacher, we can tell by the look on his face." Seeing him at a distance, they plot how best to express the contempt they feel for God's Torah. They say to one another, "Come, let us beguile him with flowery words, and then cast him into one of the nearby pits; we shall not give him a single penny."[7]

The preacher might even say, "Listen to me, my sons; I will teach you fear of God. Just as you come for nothing, so will I: I won't take a fee for the sermon I have come to deliver in the hope it will lead you far from your

6. The analogy with the physician is one of the most familiar in Jewish ethical literature, but it is used here in a somewhat novel way.

7. This paragraph and the next are based on verbal echoes of the biblical account of Joseph's persecution by his brothers. See Piekarz, p. 156.

Instead, they ask, "Why should we listen to his dreams?" Thus *they continue to hate him even more because of his dreams, and because of his words* (Gen. 37:8). Woe to us at the Day of Judgment! Woe to us because of the preacher's rebuke that we have dismissed with contempt!

18. Joseph ben Dov Baer[1] (End of eighteenth century, Poland)

A further word: Because Koheleth was a sage, he continued to instruct the people. He listened to and tested the soundness of many parables (Eccles. 12:9).

Public preaching may follow various techniques. There is the preacher who first arranges for himself the words he will say, and then preaches them to others, instructing them.[2] Then there is another on a higher level. God has made such a person so worthy that in the midst of his sermon, while he is preaching, the wells of wisdom are opened to him, and he perceives patterns of association that link verses of the Torah with the Prophets, and Prophets with the Writings, and the Writings with rabbinic homilies, all convincingly and with total fluency, producing wonderfully wise new insights into the meaning of the Torah. All this comes as new to him while he is actually preaching. Beforehand, these associations never occurred to him at all.

As for King Solomon, the wisest of all the sages, not only were the fountains of wisdom opened to him while he was instructing the people in his ethical sermons, [revealing] wonderful thoughts that had not occurred to him before; he also had an additional quality. At the very moment when the fountain of wisdom was opened to him while instructing the people, he would produce a beautiful, complete parable, which enabled the people to comprehend the ethical message. This marvelous quality made him superior to all other sages, for it usually takes quiet reflection to create a proper parable.[3] But to Solomon it came immediately flowing like the waters of a spring. This is the meaning of the verse. . . .

Now it may occur to you to ask, should not one who instructs the people say precisely what he means, teaching ethical standards and admonishing the people straightforwardly to do what the Torah says to do and refrain from

1. The work quoted from here is a commentary on the five Scrolls; on the author and the passage, see Piekarz, pp. 64, 127–28. For other interpretations of this verse in the context of preaching, see Moscato, sermon 31; Judah Eidel, *Afiqe Yehudah*, 2 vols. (Lemberg, 1912) 1:7a–b.

2. Note that preaching from a fully prepared text is considered to be the lowest level of the art. The ideal of spontaneity and improvisation is clearly higher.

3. The spontaneous creation of an apt parable was the hallmark also of great contemporary preaching, as can be seen in the stories told about the Maggid of Dubno (Heinemann, *Maggid*, pp. 260–68).

doing what it prohibits? This is the desired goal: to instruct the people to observe all the commandments. Why the parable and the rhetorical figure, which are merely words for enjoyment and pleasure?[4]

The answer is that if the preacher were to quote verses of the Torah simply and straightforwardly as they are written, telling the people what to do and what not to do, his words would have no effect on the listeners. On the contrary, they would laugh at him and say, "Why is he telling us something written simply and directly in the Torah? We know all this without his sermon."[5] However, when the preacher says things that the masses of people enjoy—namely, rhetorical figures like parables—it is like the sweet foods we give to a child so he will want to go to school and learn.[6] In this way, fine parables are enjoyable, so sweet to hear that everyone loves them. After the parable, they will also hear its meaning, which is the essence of ethical instruction and piety.

That is why the words of the sages, which teach the people ethical standards and piety, are compared to the cow's goad, the yoke of the plow (Eccles. 12:11).[7] Without this goad, the cow would not walk in the furrows at all; it would go wherever it wanted. The goad makes it walk and plow in the furrows, keeping it in the path intended by the person plowing. The same is true when a scholar instructs people in the proper moral path. Without the parable, the thoughts of those standing around him would wander, and they would think of other things. His fine words would never be heard, for their minds would be occupied elsewhere. But through the parable, he captures the attention, so that people will hear what he says. This way they also hear the essence of his ethical message, the meaning of the parable. . . .[8]

Therefore do not let the stories in the parables seem trivial to you, for they exemplify what was commanded in the Torah of Moses. . . . Because of the collections of those who tell parables, in which they bring together many such stories, they are called *baʿale asuppot* (Eccles. 12:11).[9] They will receive a reward from God because of the parable, even if it seems trivial.

4. For resistance to the parable, see the discussion in "Sermons and Literature."

5. On the demand for originality by the congregation compare the passage by MaHaRaL of Prague, sect. 10 above, at n. 6 (where it is used to justify ingenious interpretations of biblical verses, rather than parables).

6. Cf. Maimonides, *Commentary on the Mishnah,* intro. to Sanhedrin, chap. 10 (in *A Maimonides Reader,* ed. Twersky, pp. 404–05).

7. B. Ḥag 2a–b.

8. Compare the other defenses of the parable discussed in "Sermons and Literature."

9. I.e., "masters of collected [parables]."

Abbreviations of Works Cited

MANUSCRIPTS

Alkabeẓ. Solomon Alkabeẓ, "Derashot." British Library MS Or. 6361.

Anatoli MS. Jacob Anatoli, "Malmad ha-Talmidim." British Library Add. MS 26,898.

Anonymous. Jewish Theological Seminary MS L978/1.

Anonymous "Bibago." Sassoon MS 702.

Anonymous "Disciple of R. Asher." British Library Add. MS 27,292.

Anonymous "1425." Cambridge University Add. MS 1022/3.

Ayllon. Solomon ben Jacob Ayllon, "Derashot." Amsterdam, Ets Haim MS 47D33.

Balbo. Michael ben Shabbetai ha-Kohen Balbo, "Derashot" and other writings. Vatican Hebrew MS 105.

Cantarini. Isaac Cantarini, Italian sermons. Budapest, Kaufmann MSS 314–19.

Dato. Mordecai Dato, "Derashot." British Library Add. MS 27,050.

Ephraim ha-Darshan. Ephraim ben Gerson of Veroia, "Ṣinṣenet Ha-Man." British Library MS Or. 1307.

Garmizan. Samuel Garmizan, "Imre Noʿam" (vol. 2). Jerusalem, Benayahu Collection.

Ḥayyim ben David. Ḥayyim ben David, "Maʾamarim be-Qabbalah." Jerusalem, Musaioff MS 64/14.

Ibn Basa. Samuel ibn Basa, "Tenaʾe Darshan." Columbia University MS X 893 T 15 Q.

Isaac Śar Shalom. Isaac Śar Shalom, "Maṭṭeh ʿOz." Oxford Bodleian MS 1001.

Israel, "Dober Mesharim." Oxford Christ Church MS 197 (Neubauer 2447).

Israel of Bełżyce. Israel ben Benjamin of Bełżyce, "Tifʾeret Yiśraʾel." Oxford Bodleian Opp. MS 37 (Neubauer 989).

Jacob ben Hananel. Jacob ben Hananel of Sicily (ha-Siqili), "Torat ha-Minḥah." Vienna MS 37.

Joseph ibn Shem Ṭob. Joseph ibn Shem Ṭob, "ʿEn ha-Qore" and "Derashot." London, Montefiore MS 61.

Joseph ibn Shem Ṭob, "Derashot." Harvard University Hebrew MS 61.

Joseph of Benevento. Joseph ben Ḥayyim of Benevento, "Derashot." Parma, Hebrew MS 2627 (De' Rossi 1398).

Joshua ibn Shueib, MS. Joshua ibn Shueib, "Derashot ʿal ha-Torah." Vatican Hebrew MS 237.

Karo. Isaac ben Joseph Karo, "Ḥasde David." Oxford Bodleian Opp. MS 238 (Neubauer 987).

Levin. Hirschel Levin, "Derashot." Jewish Theological Seminary MS R 79 (Adler 1248).

Moses ben Joab. Moses ben Joab, "Derashot." London, Montefiore MS 17.

Pardo. Josiah ben David Pardo, "Mizbaḥ ha-Zahab." Amsterdam, Ets Haim MS 51 (2 vols.).

Portaleone. Samuel ben Elisha Portaleone, "Derashot." British Library Add. MS 27,123.

Shem Ṭob, MS. Shem Ṭob ben Joseph ibn Shem Ṭob, "Derashot." Cambridge University MS Dd.10.46/6.

Yizhari. Mattathias Yizhari, "Parashiyyot." Parma, Hebrew MS 2365 (De' Rossi 1417).

Printed Primary Sources

Aboab. Isaac Aboab, *Nehar Pishon.* Żolkiew, 1806.

Adret. *She'elot u-Teshubot* [Responsa] *ha-RaSHBA.* 5 vols. Bene Beraq, 1958.

Alba. Jacob di Alba, *Toledot Ya'aqob.* Venice, 1609.

Albelda. Moses Albelda, *Darash Mosheh.* Venice, 1603.

Alfalas. Moses Alfalas, *Wa-Yaqhel Mosheh.* Venice, 1597.

Almosnino. Moses Almosnino, *Me'ammeṣ Koaḥ.* Venice, 1588.

Anatoli. Jacob Anatoli, *Malmad ha-Talmidim.* Lyck, 1866.

Arama. Isaac Arama, *'Aqedat Yiṣḥaq.* Warsaw, 1883.

Assaf. Simḥah Assaf, *Meqorot le-Toledot ha-Ḥinnuk be-Yiśra'el.* 4 vols. Tel-Aviv, 1930–54.

Ashkenazi. Naphtali ben Joseph Ashkenazi, *Imre Shefer.* Venice, 1601.

Azulai. Ḥayyim Joseph David Azulai, *Ma'gal Ṭob.* Jerusalem, 1934.

Baḥya, *Kad ha-Qemaḥ.* Baḥya ben Asher, *Kad ha-Qemaḥ,* in *Kitbe Rabbenu Baḥya,* ed. C. B. Chavel. Jersualem, 1970.

Baḥya, *Encyclopedia.* Baḥya ben Asher, *Encyclopedia of Torah Thoughts,* trans. and ed. C. B. Chavel. New York, 1980.

Bibago. Abraham Bibago, "Zeh Yenaḥamennu." Salonika, 1522?

Binat Yiśśakar. Issachar Baer Bloch, *Binat Yiśśakar.* Prague, 1785.

David ha-Nagid. *Midrash David ha-Nagid, Genesis,* ed. Abraham Katsh. Jerusalem, 1964.

Derashot. Derashot u-Ferushe Rabbenu Yonah Gerondi 'al ha-Torah, ed. Samuel Yerushalmi. Jerusalem, 1980.

Derashot ha-RaN. Nissim ben Reuben Gerondi, *Shenem 'Aśar Derashot,* ed. Leon Feldman. Jerusalem, 1974.

Dibre Shelomoh. Solomon Levi (Shelomoh le-Bet ha-Lewi), *Dibre Shelomoh.* Venice, 1596.

Eidlitz. Zerah Eidlitz, *Or la-Yesharim.* Prague, 1785.

Eisenstein. Judah Eisenstein, *Oṣar Derashot.* New York, 1919.

Elijah, *Shebeṭ Musar.* Elijah ha-Kohen of Izmir, *Shebeṭ Musar.* Vilna, 1819.

En Duran. *Ḥoshen Mishpaṭ,* ed. David Kaufmann. *Tif'eret Śebah (Zunz Jubelschrift).* Berlin, 1884. Pp. 142–74.

Eybeschuetz. Jonathan Eybeschuetz, *Ya'arot Debash.* Jerusalem, 1968.

Figo. Azariah Figo, *Binah le-ʿIttim.* Warsaw, 1866.
Fleckeles 1. Eliezer Fleckeles, *ʿOlat Ḥodesh.* Prague, 1785.
Fleckeles 2. Eliezer Fleckeles, *ʿOlat Ḥodesh Sheni.* Munkács, 1907.
Garçon, in Benayahu. Meir Benayahu, "Derushaw she-le-Rabbi Yosef ben Meir Garçon." *Mikaʾel* 7 (1982):42–205.
Ḥayyim ben Isaac. *Pisqe Halakah shel R. Ḥayyim Or Zaruʿa (Derashot MaHaRaḤ),* ed. Isaak S. Lange. Jerusalem, 1972.
Ibn Mūsā. "Miktab ha-Rab Ḥayyim ibn Mūsā," ed. David Kaufmann. In *Bet ha-Talmud* 2 (1882):110–25.
Isaac Nieto. Isaac Nieto, *A Sermon Preached in the Jews' Synagogue on Friday, February 6, 1756, Being the Day Appointed by Authority for a General Fast.* London, 1756.
Jaffe. Meir Benayahu, "Hespedo shel Rabbi Shemuʾel Yafeh Ashkenazi ʿal Abiw Rabbi Yiṣḥaq Yafeh," *Qobeṣ ʿal Yad* 8 (18) (1976):435–49.
Joel ibn Shueib. Joel ibn Shueib, *ʿOlat Shabbat.* Venice, 1577.
Joseph ben David. Joseph ben David of Saragossa, *Perush ʿal ha-Torah,* ed. Leon Feldman. Jerusalem, 1973.
Joshua ibn Shueib. Joshua ibn Shueib, *Derashot ʿal ha-Torah.* Cracow, 1573. Reprint ed., with an introduction by Shraga Abramson. Jerusalem, 1969.
Katzenellenbogen. Samuel Judah Katzenellenbogen, *Shenem ʿAśar Derashot.* Venice, 1594.
Landau, *Ahabat.* Ezekiel Landau, *Ahabat Ṣiyyon.* Jerusalem, 1966.
Landau, *Derushe.* Ezekiel Landau, *Derushe ha-Ṣelaḥ.* Warsaw, 1899. Repint ed. Jerusalem, 1966.
Landau, *Doresh.* Ezekiel Landau, *Doresh le-Ṣiyyon.* Warsaw, 1880.
Landau, *Hesped.* Ezekiel Landau, *Derush Hesped la-Qesarit Maria Theresa.* Prague, 1780.
Luntshitz, *ʿAmmude.* Ephraim Luntshitz, *ʿAmmude Shesh.* Warsaw, 1875.
Luntshitz, *ʿIr.* Ephraim Luntshitz, *ʿIr Gibborim.* Amsterdam, 1769.
Luntshitz, *ʿOlelot.* Ephraim Luntshitz, *ʿOlelot Efrayim.* Tel Aviv, 1975.
Luzzatto. Moses Ḥayyim Luzzatto, "Maʾamar ʿal ha-Derashah." In *Sefer ha-Meliṣah,* ed. Abraham Habermann. Jerusalem, 1950.
MaHaRIL. Jacob Moellin, *Sefer MaHaRIL.* Shklov, 1796.
Margolioth. Judah Leib Margolioth, *ʿAṣe ʿEden.* Frankfurt an der Oder, 1802.
Maṭṭeh Mosheh. Moses ben Abraham, *Maṭṭeh Mosheh.* Warsaw, 1875.
Medabber Tahpukot. Isaac min-ha-Lewiyyim, *Medabber Tahpukot,* ed. Daniel Carpi. Tel Aviv, 1985.
Minḥat Qenaʾot. Abba Mari of Lunel, *Minḥat Qenaʾot.* Pressburg, 1838.
Modena, *Midbar.* Leon Modena, *Midbar Yehudah.* Venice, 1602.
Morteira (1645). Saul ha-Levi Morteira, *Gibʿat Shaʾul.* Amsterdam, 1645.
Morteira. Saul ha-Levi Morteira, *Gibʿat Shaʾul.* Warsaw, 1902.
Moscato. Judah Moscato. *Nefuṣot Yehudah.* Warsaw, 1871.
Nave. Pnina Nave, *Yehudah Aryeh mi-Modena: Leqeṭ Ketabim.* Jerusalem, 1968.
Ori we-Yishʿi. Abraham ben Eliezer ha-Kohen, *Ori we-Yishʿi.* Berlin, 1714.
Pinqas Liṭa. Pinqas ha-Medina (Liṭa), ed. Simon Dubnow. Berlin, 1925.
Pinqas Waʿad. Pinqas Waʾad Arbaʿ Araṣot, ed. Israel Halpern. Jerusalem, 1945.

RaBaD, R. H. Abraham ben David of Posquières, *Derashah le-Rosh ha-Shanah,* ed. Abraham Halevi. London, 1955.

RaMBaN. Kitbe Rabbenu Mosheh ben Naḥman, ed. C. B. Chavel. 2 vols. Jerusalem, 1963.

Rapoport. Abraham ben Israel ha-Kohen Rapoport, *Quntres Aḥaron.* In *Etan ha-Ezraḥi.* Ostróg, 1796.

Reʾshit Bikkurim. Enoch ben Abraham, *Reʾshit Bikkurim.* Frankfurt, 1708.

Ṣebi la-Ṣaddiq. Hirschel Levin, *Ṣebi la-Ṣaddiq.* Piotrków, 1903.

Sermoẽs. Sermoẽs que pregaraõ os Doctos Ingenios do K. K. de Talmud Torah desta Cidade de Amsterdam. . . . Amsterdam, 1675.

Shem Ṭob. Shem Ṭob ibn Shem Ṭob, *Derashot.* Salonika, 1525.

Stadthagen. Joseph Stadthagen, *Dibre Zikkaron.* Amsterdam, 1705.

Taqqanot Mehrin. Taqqanot Medinat Mehrin, ed. Israel Halpern. Jerusalem, 1952.

Ṭodros ha-Levi. Ṭodros ben Joseph Ha-Levi Abulafia, "Derashah" (Toledo, 1281). In Judah ben Asher, *Zikron Yehudah.* Berlin, 1846. Pp. 43a–45b.

Tosafot . . . Liṭa. Tosafot u-Milluʾim le-Finqas Medinat Liṭa, ed. Israel Halpern. Jerusalem, 1935.

Travelers. Jewish Travelers, ed. Elkan Adler. New York, 1931.

Vega. Judah ben Moses Vega, *Malke Yehudah.* Lublin, 1616.

Yaari, *Iggerot.* Abraham Yaari, *Iggerot me-ʾEreṣ Yiśraʾel.* Jerusalem, 1940.

Zahalon. *A Guide for Preachers on Composing and Delivering Sermons: The* Or ha-Darshanim *of Jacob Zahalon,* ed. Henry Sosland. New York, 1987.

Zarfati. Joseph ben Hayyim Zarfati, *Yad Yosef.* Amsterdam, 1700.

Zeraḥiah ha-Levi. "Derush R. Zeraḥiah ha-Levi." *He-Ḥaluṣ* 7 (1865):96–101.

Secondary Works on Jewish Preaching

Adelman. Howard Adelman, "Success and Failure in the Seventeenth-Century Ghetto of Venice: The Life and Thought of Leon Modena, 1571–1648." Ph.D. diss., Brandeis University, 1985.

Altmann. Alexander Altman, *Moses Mendelssohn.* Tuscaloosa, Ala., 1975.

Altmann, "Ars Rhetorica." Alexander Altmann, "Ars Rhetorica as Reflected in Some Jewish Figures of the Italian Renaissance." In *Jewish Thought in the Sixteenth Century,* ed. Bernard Cooperman. Cambridge, Mass., 1983.

Baer, *HJCS.* Yitzhak (Fritz) Baer, *A History of the Jews in Christian Spain.* 2 vols. Philadelphia, 1961, 1966.

Baron, *Community.* Salo Wittmayer Baron, *The Jewish Community.* 3 vols. Philadelphia, 1942.

Baron, *SRHJ.* Salo Wittmayer Baron, *A Social and Religious History of the Jews.* 18 vols. Philadelphia and New York, 1952–1983.

Benayahu. Meir Benayahu, "Derushaw she-le Rabbi Yosef ben Meir Garçon." *Mikaʾel* 7 (1982):42–205.

Ben-Sasson. *Ḥaim Hillel Ben-Sasson, Hagut we-Hanhagah.* Jerusalem, 1959.

Bettan. Israel Bettan. *Studies in Jewish Preaching: Middle Ages.* Cincinnati, 1939.

Bonfil, "Dato." Robert (Reuven) Bonfil, "Aḥat mi-Derashotaw shel R. Mordekai Dato." *Italia* 1 (1976):1–32.

Bonfil, *Rabbanut.* Robert (Reuven) Bonfil, *Ha-Rabbanut be-ʾItalyah bi-Tequfat ha-Renesans.* Jerusalem, 1979.

Cassuto, *Ha-Yehudim.* Umberto Cassuto, *Ha-Yehudim be-Firenṣe bi-Tequfat ha-Renesans.* Jerusalem, 1967.

Cassuto, "Rabbino." Umberto Cassuto, "Un rabbino fiorentino del secolo XV." *Rivista Israelitica* 3 (1906):116–28, 224–28; 4 (1907):33–37, 156–61, 225–29.

Chazan. Robert Chazan, "Confrontation in the Synagogue of Narbonne: A Christian Sermon and a Jewish Reply." *Harvard Theological Review* 67 (1974):437–57.

Dan, "ʿIyyun." Joseph Dan, "ʿIyyun be-Sifrut ha-Derush ha-ʿIbrit bi-Tequfat ha-Renasans be-ʾItalyah." *Proceedings of the Sixth World Congress of Jewish Studies.* Jerusalem, 1977. Division 3:105–10.

Dan, *Sifrut.* Joseph Dan, *Sifrut ha-Musar we-ha-Derush.* Jerusalem, 1975.

Dan, "Tefillah we-Dimʿah." Joseph Dan, "Derush 'Tefillah we-Dimʿah' le-R. Yehudah Moscato." *Sinai* 76 (1975):210–32.

Davidson, *Oṣar.* Israel Davidson, *Oṣar ha-Meshalim we-ha-Pitgamim.* Jerusalem, 1939.

Dinur. Ben-Zion Dinur, "Reshitah shel ha-Ḥasidut wi-Ysodoteha ha-Soṣiyaliyyim we-ha-Meshiḥiyyim." In *Be-Mifneh ha-Dorot.* Jerusalem, 1955.

Dresner. Samuel Dresner, *The Zaddik.* New York, 1974.

Elbaum, "Aspects." Jacob Elbaum, "Aspects of Hebrew Ethical Literature in Sixteenth-Century Poland." In *Jewish Thought in the Sixteenth Century,* ed. Bernard Cooperman. Cambridge, Mass., 1983.

Elbaum, "Derashot Ashkenaziyyot." Jacob Elbaum, "Shalosh Derashot Ashkenaziyyot Qedumot." *Kiryat Sefer* 48 (1973):340–47.

Elbaum, "Zeramim." Jacob Elbaum, "Zeramim u-Megamot be-Sifrut ha-Maḥashabah we-ha-Musar be-Ashkenaz u-be-Polin ba-Meʾah ha-Ṭet-Zayin." Ph.D. diss., Hebrew University, 1977.

Funkenstein, "Parshanuto." Amos Funkenstein, "Parshanuto ha-Ṭippologit shel ha-RaMBaN." *Zion* 45 (1979–80):35–49.

Funkenstein, "Symbolical Reading." Amos Funkenstein, "Naḥmanides' Symbolical Reading of History." In *Studies in Jewish Mysticism,* ed. Joseph Dan and Frank Talmage. Cambridge, Mass., 1982, pp. 129–50.

Ginzberg, *Legends.* Louis Ginzberg, *Legends of the Jews.* 7 vols. Philadelphia, 1912.

Glicksberg. Simon Glicksberg, *Ha-Derashah be-Yiśraʾel.* Tel Aviv, 1940.

Goitein, *Community.* S. D. Goitein, *A Mediterranean Society.* Vol. 2: *The Community.* Berkeley, 1971.

Goitein, *Ḥinnuk.* S. D. Goitein, *Sidre Ḥinnuk.* Jerusalem, 1962.

Hacker, "Ha-Derashah." Joseph Hacker, "Ha-Derashah ha-'Sefaradit' ba-Meʾah ha-Ṭet-Zayin." *Peʿamim* 26 (1986):108–27.

Hacker, "Ha-Peʿilut." Joseph Hacker, "Ha-Peʿilut ha-Inṭeleqtuʾalit be-Qereb Yehude ha-Imperyah ha-Otmanit." *Tarbiẓ* 53 (1984):569–603.

Hacker, "Li-Demutam." Joseph Hacker, "Li-Demutam ha-Ruḥanit shel Yehude Sefarad be-Sof ha-Meʾah ha-Ḥamesh-ʿEśreh." *Sefunot* 2 (17) (1983):21–95.

Hacker, "Ha-Yeʾush." Joseph Hacker, "Ha-Yeʾush min ha-Geʾulah we-ha-Tiqwah ha-Meshiḥit be-Kitbe R. Shelomoh le-Bet ha-Lewi mi-Saloniqah." *Tarbiẓ* 39 (1969–70):195–213.

Heinemann, *Maggid.* Benno Heinemann, *The Maggid of Dubno and His Parables.* New York, 1967.

Heller-Wilensky. Sarah Heller-Wilensky, *R. Yiṣḥaq Arama u-Mishnato ha-Pilosofit.* Jerusalem, 1956.

Horowitz, "Shuʿeib." Carmi Horowitz, "R. Joshua ibn Shuʿeib: A Literary and Historical Analysis of his Sermons." Ph.D. diss., Harvard University, 1980.

Horowitz, "Unpublished Sermon." Carmi Horowitz, "An Unpublished Sermon of R. Joshua ibn Shuʿeib." In *Studies in Medieval Jewish History and Literature,* ed. Isadore Twersky. Cambridge, Mass., 1979. Pp. 261–82.

Hurvitz, "Śeridim." Eleazar Hurvitz, "Śeridim mi-Derashat ha-Pesaḥ le-ha-RaBaD." *Ha-Darom* 35 (1972):34–42.

Jacobson. Yoram Jacobson, "Torat ha-Geʾulah shel R. Mordekai Dato." Ph.D. diss., Hebrew University, 1982.

Jellinek, *Bibliographie.* Adolf Jellinek, *Bibliographie hebräischer Trauer- und Gedächtnisreden.* Vienna, 1884.

Kaufmann, "Dispute." David Kaufmann, "The Dispute about the Sermons of David del Bene of Mantua." *JQR* 8 (1895–96):513–34.

Marx, "Gimpses." Alexander Marx, "Glimpses of the Life of an Italian Rabbi of the First Half of the Sixteenth Century." *HUCA* 1 (1924):605–16.

Nigal, "Katzenellenbogen." Gedaliah Nigal, "Derashotaw shel R. Shemuel Yehudah Katzenellenbogen." *Sinai* 36 (1971–72):79–85.

Pachter, "Curiel." Mordechai Pachter, "Yeṣirato ha-Darshanit shel R. Yiśraʾel di Curiel." *Kiryat Sefer* 55 (1980):802–16.

Pachter, "Demuto." Mordechai Pachter, "Demuto shel ha-ʾAri be-Hesped she-Hispido R. Shemuʾel Uceda." *Zion* 37 (1972):22–40.

Pachter, "Sifrut." Mordechai Pachter, "Sifrut ha-Derush we-ha-Musar shel Ḥakme Ṣefat ba-Meʾah ha-Ṭet-Zayin u-Maʿareket Raʿyonoteha ha-ʿIqariyyim." Ph.D. diss., Hebrew University, 1976.

Piekarz. Mendel Piekarz, *Bi-Yme Ṣemiḥat ha-Ḥasidut.* Jerusalem, 1978.

Pollack. Herman Pollack, *Jewish Folkways in Germanic Lands, (1648–1806).* Cambridge, Mass., 1971.

Rabinovitz. H. R. Rabinovitz, *Deyoqnaʾot shel Darshanim.* Jerusalem, 1967.

Rapoport-Albert. Ada Rapoport-Albert, "The Problem of Succession in the Hasidic Leadership, with Special Reference to the Circle of R. Nachman of Braslav." Ph.D. diss., University of London, 1974.

Rabinowitz. Isaac Rabinowitz, "Pre-Modern Jewish Study of Rhetoric: An Introductory Bibliography." *Rhetoric* 3 (1985):137–44.

Ravitsky, "Ketab." Aviezer Ravitsky, "Ketab Nishkaḥ le-R. Ḥasdai Crescas." *Kiryat Sefer* 51 (1976):705–11.

Ravitsky, "Zehuto." Aviezer Ravitsky, "Zehuto we-Gilgulaw shel Ḥibbur Pilosofi she-Yuḥas le-R. Mikaʾel ben Shabbetai Balbo." *Kiryat Sefer* 56 (1981):153–63.

Regev. Shaul Regev, "Teʾologyah u-Mistiṣizm Raṣyonalisṭi be-Kitbe R. Yosef ibn Shem Ṭob." Ph.D. diss., Hebrew University, 1983.

Rosenzweig. Israel Rosenzweig, *Hogeh Yehudi mi-Qeṣ ha-Renesans.* Tel Aviv, 1972.

Roth, *Renaissance.* Cecil Roth, *The Jews in the Renaissance.* Philadelphia, 1959.

Ruderman, "Exemplary Sermon." David Ruderman, "An Exemplary Sermon from the Classroom of a Jewish Teacher in Renaissance Italy." *Italia* 1 (1978):7–38.
Saperstein, "Art Form." Marc Saperstein, "The Sermon as Art Form: Structure in Morteira's *Gib*ʿ*at Sha*ʾ*ul.*" *Prooftexts* 3 (1983):243–61.
Saperstein, *Decoding.* Marc Saperstein, *Decoding the Rabbis.* Cambridge, Mass., 1980.
Saperstein, "Empress." Marc Saperstein, "In Praise of an Anti-Jewish Empress." *Shofar* 6 (1987):20–25.
Saperstein, "Pesach." Marc Saperstein, "Preaching for Pesach." *Journal of Reform Judaism* 34 (1987):25–34.
Saperstain. "Shofar." Marc Saperstein, "Your Voice Like a Shofar." *Conservative Judaism* 38 (1985):83–90.
Saperstein, "Stories." Marc Saperstein, "Stories in Jewish Sermons (The 15th–16th Centuries)." *Proceedings of the Ninth World Congress of Jewish Studies,* Jerusalem, 1986. Division C. Pp. 101–08.
Shochat. Azriel Shochat, *ʿIm Ḥillufe Tequfot.* Jerusalem, 1960.
Spitzer, "Derashot." Solomon Spitzer, "Derashot we-Dinim be-Hilkot Pesaḥ le-Rabbenu Yaʿaqob Weil." *Moriah* 11 (1982):21–30.
Spitzer, "Dinim." Solomon Spitzer, "Dinim u-Derashot le-Rabbenu Yaʿaqob Weil." *Moriah* 10 (1980–81):5–13.
Spitzer, *Hilkot.* Solomon Spitzer, *Hilkot u-Minhage Rabbenu Shalom mi-Neustadt.* Jerusalem, 1977.
Tishby, "Genizah." Isaiah Tishby, "Dappe Genizah me-Ḥibbur Meshiḥi-Misṭi ʿal Gerush Sefarad u-Fortugal." *Zion* 48 (1983):55–102.
Tishby, *Netibe.* Isaiah Tishby, *Netibe Emunah u-Minut.* Jerusalem, 1982.
Twersky. Isadore Twersky, *Rabad of Posquières.* Philadelphia, 1980.
Wachstein, *Bibliographie.* Bernhard Wachstein, *Zur Bibliographie der Gedächtnis- und Trauervorträge in der hebräischen Literatur.* 4 vols. Vienna, 1922–1932.
Wachstein, *Randbemerkungen.* Bernhard Wachstein, *Randbemerkungen zu meinen Inschriften des alten Judenfriedhofes in Wien.* Vienna, 1934.
Wieder. Naphtali Wieder, "Shalosh Derashot le-Taʿanit Geshamim min ha-Genizah, Shetayim ba-ʾAramit Galilit." *Tarbiẓ* 54 (1984–85):21–60.
Yaari, *Sheluḥe.* Abraham Yaari, *Sheluḥe Ereṣ Yiśraʾel le-Dorotehem.* Jerusalem, 1951.
Zunz. Leopold Zunz, *Ha-Derashot be-Yiśraʾel.* Ed. Ḥanokh Albeck. Jerusalem, 1974.

Secondary Works on Christian Preaching

Baldwin. John W. Baldwin, *Masters, Princes and Merchants.* 2 vols. Princeton, 1970.
Bataillon. Louis-Jacques Bataillon, "Approaches to the Study of Medieval Sermons." *Leeds Studies in English* 11 (1980):19–31.
Bayley. Peter Bayley, *French Pulpit Oratory, 1598–1650.* Cambridge, 1980.
Blakney. *Meister Eckhardt: A Modern Translation.* Trans. Raymond B. Blakney. New York, 1941.
Bremond. Claude Bremond et al., *L'"Exemplum."* Turnhout, 1982.
Caplan. Harry Caplan, *Of Eloquence: Studies in Ancient and Mediaeval Rhetoric.* Ithaca, 1970.

Catédra. Pedro M. Catédra, *Dos estudios sobre el sermon en la España medieval*. Barcelona, 1981.

Chamberlin. John S. Chamberlin, *Increase and Multiply: Arts of Discourse Procedure in the Preaching of John Donne*. Chapel Hill, 1976.

Chandos. John Chandos. *In God's Name: Examples of Preaching in England, 1534–1662*. Indianapolis, 1971.

Charland. Th.-M. Charland, *Artes Praedicandi*. Publications de l'Institut d'Etudes Médiévales d'Ottawa 7. 1936.

Crane. T. F. Crane, *The Exempla (or Illustrative Stories from the* Sermones Vulgares*) of Jacques de Vitry.* London, 1890.

D'Avray. D. L. D'Avray, *The Preaching of the Friars: Sermons Diffused from Paris before 1300*. Oxford, 1985.

Deferrari. Roy J. Deferrari, "St. Augustine's Method of Composing and Delivering Sermons." *American Journal of Philology* 43 (1922):97–123, 193–219.

Deyermond. Alan Deyermond, "The Sermon and Its Uses in Medieval Castilian Literature." *La Corónica* 8 (1980):127–45.

Douglass. E. Jane Dempsey Douglass, *Justification in Late Medieval Preaching: A Study of John Geiler of Keiserberg*. Leiden, 1966.

Downey. James Downey, *The Eighteenth Century Pulpit*. Oxford, 1969.

Erb. Peter C. Erb, "Vernacular Material for Preaching in MS Cambridge University Library I. III. 8." *Mediaeval Studies* 33 (1971):65–84.

Gilman. Sander L. Gilman, *The Parodic Sermon in European Perspective*. Wiesbaden, 1974.

Grasso. Domenico Grasso, *Proclaiming God's Message*. Notre Dame, 1965.

Jones and Jones. Phyllis M. Jones and Nicholas R. Jones, *Salvation in New England: Selections from the Sermons of the First Preachers*. Austin, 1977.

Kennedy. George Kennedy, *Greek Rhetoric under Christian Emperors*. Princeton, 1983.

Lecoy de la Marche. Albert Lecoy de la Marche, *La chaire française au Moyen Âge*. Paris, 1886.

Longère. Jean Longère, *La Prédication médiévale*. Paris, 1983.

MacLure. Millar MacLure, *St. Paul's Cross Sermons, 1534–1642*. Toronto, 1958.

Mitchell. W. Fraser Mitchell, *English Pulpit Oratory from Andrewes to Tillotson*. London, 1932.

Molho. Maurice Molho, "Les Homélies d'Organya." *Bulletin Hispanique* 63 (1961):186–210.

Moser-Rath. Elfriede Moser-Rath, *Predigtmärlein der Barockzeit*. Berlin, 1964.

Neale. John Mason Neale. *Mediaeval Preachers and Mediaeval Preaching*. London, 1856.

O'Malley. John W. O'Malley, *Praise and Blame in Renaissance Rome*. Durham, N.C., 1979.

Owst, *Literature*. G. R. Owst, *Literature and Pulpit in Medieval England*. New York, 1961.

Owst, *Preaching*. G. R. Owst, *Preaching in Medieval England*. New York, 1965.

Petry, Roy C. Petry, *No Uncertain Sound: Sermons that Shaped the Pulpit Tradition*. Philadelphia, 1948.

Powell and Fletcher. Susan Powell and Alan J. Fletcher, " 'In Die Sepulture seu

Trigintali': The Late Medieval Funeral and Memorial Sermon." *Leeds Studies in English* 12 (1981):195–228.

Roberts. Phyllis Roberts, *Studies in the Sermons of Stephen Langton*. Toronto, 1968.

Rouse and Rouse, *Preachers*. Richard H. and Mary A. Rouse, *Preachers, Florilegia and Sermons*. Toronto, 1979.

Rouse and Rouse, "Statim." Richard H. and Mary A. Rouse, "Statim Invenire: Schools, Preachers, and New Attitudes to the Page." In *Renaissance and Renewal in the Twelfth Century*, ed. Robert Benson and Giles Constable. Cambridge, Mass., 1982. Pp. 201–25.

Seaver. Paul S. Seaver, *The Puritan Lectureships*. Stanford, 1970.

Simpson. Evelyn Simpson, ed., *John Donne's Sermons on the Psalms and Gospels*. Berkeley and Los Angeles, 1963.

Smalley. Beryl Smalley, *English Friars and Antiquity in the Early Fourteenth Century*. Oxford, 1960.

Smith. Hilary Dansey Smith, *Preaching in the Spanish Golden Age*. Oxford, 1978.

Smyth. Charles Smyth, *The Art of Preaching*. London, 1940.

Spencer. Helen Spencer, "Vernacular and Latin Versions of a Sermon for Lent: A Lost Penitential Homily Found." *Mediaeval Studies* 44 (1982):271–305.

Tubach. Frederic C. Tubach, *Index Exemplorum*. FF [Folklore Fellows] Communications 204. Helsinki, 1969.

Tugwell. Simon Tugwell, *Early Dominicans: Selected Writings*. New York, 1982.

Tugwell, *Way*. Simon Tugwell, *The Way of the Preacher*. London, 1979.

Welter. J.-Th. Welter, *L'Exemplum dans la littérature religieuse et didactique du Moyen Âge*. Paris, 1927.

Zink. Michel Zink. *La Prédication en langue romane avant 1300*. Paris, 1976.

Texts Translated

Sermons

1. Jacob Anatoli, *Malmad ha-Talmidim* (Lyck, 1866), pp. 49a–51b.
2. Anonymous, *Derashot u-Ferushe Rabbenu Yonah Gerondi,* ed. Samuel Yerushalmi (Jerusalem, 1980), pp. 69–73.
3. Joshua ibn Shueib, *Derashot ʿal ha-Torah* (Cracow, 1573; reprint ed., Jerusalem, 1969), pp. 13a–15b.
4. Mattathias Yizhari, "Parashiyyot," Parma Hebrew MS 2365 (De Rossi 1417), fols. 35v–39r.
5. Joseph ibn Shem Ṭob, Montefiore MS 61, fols. 112r, 118r–22r.
6. Shem Ṭob ben Joseph ibn Shem Ṭob, *Derashot R. Shem Ṭob ibn Shem Ṭob* (Salonika, 1525), pp. 21a–22b; Cambridge University MS Dd. 10.46/6, fols. 53v–54r, 54v–55r.
7. Joseph Garçon, in Meir Benayahu, "Derushaw she-le-Rabbi Yosef ben Meir Garçon," *Mikaʾel* 7 (1982):134–41.
8. Moses Almosnino, *Meʾammeṣ Koaḥ* (Venice, 1588), pp. 3a–15b.
9. Solomon ben Isaac Levi, *Dibre Shelomoh* (Venice, 1596), pp. 230d–31d.
10. Judah Moscato, *Nefuṣot Yehudah* (Warsaw, 1871), sermon 13, pp. 36b–38b.
11. Saul ha-Levi Morteira, *Gibʿat Shaʾul* (Warsaw, 1902), pp. 109–14.
12. Israel of Bełżyce, "Tifʾeret Yiśraʿel," Oxford Bodleian MS Opp. 37 (Neubauer 989), fols. 342r–44r.
13. Elijah ha-Kohen of Izmir, *Midrash Eliyyahu* (Izmir, 1759), sermon 3, pp. 9d–14a.
14. Jonathan Eybeschuetz, *Yaʿarot Debash* (Jerusalem, 1968), 1:36c–41b.
15. Hirschel Levin, Jewish Theological Seminary MS R 79 (Adler 1248), fol. 2.
16. Ezekiel Landau, *Derushe ha-Ṣelaḥ* (Warsaw, 1899; reprint ed., Jerusalem, 1966), pp. 53a–54a.

Sources for the History and Theory of Jewish Preaching

1. *The Chronicle of Ahimaaz,* ed. Marcus Salzman (New York, 1966), pp. 5–6, 67–68.
2. Moses ben Maimon
   a. *Teshubot ha-RaMBaM,* ed. Joshua Blau (Jerusalem, 1957), pp. 189–91.
   b. *Mishnah ʿim Perush ha-RaMBaM: Neziqin,* ed. Joseph Kafiḥ (Jerusalem, 1964), p. 201.
   c. *Code* I.v (*Teshubah*), 4:1–2.

3. Sources from the Conflict over the Study of Philosophy
   a. Abba Mari of Lunel, *Minḥat Qena'ot* (Pressburg, 1838), p. 59.
   b. En Duran, *Ḥoshen Mishpaṭ,* ed. David Kaufmann, *Tif'eret Śebah (Zunz Jubelschrift)* (Berlin, 1884), p. 147.
   c. *Minḥat Qena'ot,* p. 106.
   d. Ibid., p. 139.
   e. Ibid., p. 69.
   f. Ibid., p. 134.
   g. Menaḥem Meiri, in *Ḥoshen Mishpaṭ,* pp. 166–67.
4. Solomon Alami, *Iggeret Musar* (St. Petersburg, 1912; reprint ed., Jerusalem, 1965), p. 27.
5. Ḥayyim ibn Mūsā, in David Kaufmann, "Miktab ha-Rab Ḥayyim ibn Mūsā," *Bet ha-Talmud* 2 (1882):117–18.
6. Joseph ibn Shem Ṭob, "ʿEn ha-Qore," Oxford Bodleian MS Mich. 350 (Neubauer 2052), fols. 113r–17v; British Library MS Or. 10550, fols. 14v–20r.
7. Isaac Arama, *ʿAqedat Yiṣḥaq* (Warsaw, 1883), p. 8a.
8. Joel ibn Shueib, *ʿOlat Shabbat* (Venice, 1577), p. 1a–b.
9. Israel, "Dober Mesharim," Oxford Christ Church MS 197 (Neubauer 2447).
   a. fols. 175r–82v.
   b. fol. 123v.
10. Leib ben Bezalel (MaHaRaL) of Prague, *Netibot ʿOlam,* "Netib ha-Tokeḥah," chap. 3, in *Sifre MaHaRaL mi-Perag,* 12 vols. (New York, 1969), 8:195–98.
11. Ephraim Luntshitz
   a. *ʿAmmude Shesh* (Warsaw, 1875), intro., p. 2a–b.
   b. Ibid., p. 63d.
   c. *ʿIr Gibborim* (Amsterdam, 1869), "Pinḥas," p. 10b.
   d. *ʿOlelot Efrayim* (Tel Aviv, 1975), pt. 2, sect. 31, pars. 210–11.
12. Judah Aryeh (Leon) Modena
   a. Ḥayye Yehudah, ed. Daniel Carpi (Tel Aviv, 1985), pp. 40–41.
   b. Ibid., pp. 49–50.
   c. *Ziqne Yehudah,* ed. Shlomo Simonsohn (Jerusalem, 1956), responsum 55, p. 168.
   d. Ibid., responsum 16, p. 77.
   e. *The History of the Present Jews (Riti Ebraici),* trans. Simon Ockley (London, 1707), pp. 67–68.
   f. *Midbar Yehudah* (Venice, 1602), sermon 1, pp. 5a–6b.
   g. Ibid., sermon 9, p. 48a.
   h. *Iggerot R. Yehudah Aryeh Modena,* ed. Yacob Boksenboim (Tel Aviv, 1984), letter 40, pp. 83–84.
13. Judah Leib Pukhovitser
   a. *Qeneh Ḥokmah* (Frankfurt an der Oder, 1681), intro., pp. 8b–c, 9a.
   b. *Derek Ḥokmah* (Frankfurt an der Oder, 1681), intro., pp. 1b–2a.
14. Abraham ben Eliezer ha-Kohen, *Ori we-Yishʿi* (Berlin, 1714).
   a. "Teshubah," chap. 10, p. 18b–d.
   b. "Teshubah," chap. 11, p. 19d.

15. Ezekiel Landau, *Ahabat Ṣiyyon* (Jerusalem, 1966), sermon for the first day of the penitential period, 1757, p. 2a.
16. Zerah Eidlitz, *Or la-Yesharim* (Prague, 1785), p. 7a–c.
17. Mordecai ben Samuel, *Shaʿar ha-Melek* (Horodno, 1816), pt. 2, chap. 3, sect. 5, pp. 95c–96a.
18. Joseph ben Dov Baer, *Toledot Yosef* (Shklov, 1797), comment on Eccles. 12:9, p. 30b.

Passages Cited

Bible

Genesis

General Index